WHAT TO EXPECT®
THE
FIRST YEAR

3RD EDITION

Also Available from What to Expect®

What to Expect® the Second Year

What to Expect® When You're Expecting

Eating Well When You're Expecting

What to Expect® Before You're Expecting

*The What to Expect® When You're Expecting
Pregnancy Journal & Organizer*

*Qué puedes esperar® cuando estás esperando
(What to Expect® When You're Expecting—Spanish Edition)*

*Qué puedes esperar® en el primero año
(What to Expect® the First Year—Spanish Edition)*

The What to Expect® Baby-Sitter's Handbook

WHAT TO EXPECT®
THE
FIRST YEAR

3RD EDITION

By Heidi Murkoff
and Sharon Mazel

Foreword by Mark D. Widome, M.D., M.P.H., Professor of Pediatrics,
Penn State Hershey Children's Hospital, Hershey, Pennsylvania

Workman Publishing • New York

Library of Congress Cataloging-in-Publishing Data available upon request.
ISBN: 978-0-7611-8150-7

Workman books are available at special discount when purchased in bulk for premiums
and sales promotions as well as for fund-raising or educational use. Special editions or book
excerpts can also be created to specification. For details, contact the Special Sales Director
at the address below or send an email to specialmarkets@workman.com.

Workman Publishing Co., Inc.
225 Varick Street
New York, NY 10014-4381

Printed in the United States of America
First printing September 2014
10 9 8 7 6 5

Note: All children are unique, and this book is not intended to substitute for the advice
of your pediatrician or other physician who should be consulted on infant matters,
especially when a baby shows any sign of illness or unusual behavior.

Dedication

To Erik, my everything

To Emma, Wyatt, and Russell, my greatest expectations

*To Lennox, beautiful baby of the beautiful baby who started it all
(my sweet full circle!)*

To Arlene, with so much love always and forever

To my What to Expect family—moms, dads, and babies everywhere

Even More Thanks (and Hugs)

So, you'd think that by now—after all these years of writing and rewriting What to Expect books—I'd be able to do it by myself, in my sleep, and (hey, why not?) with two hands tied behind my back. Well, the sleep part—I've probably done at least once or twice on deadlines, but I've always needed two hands (it's a typing thing) and I've always needed lots of help. I couldn't do what I do by myself—and I wouldn't want to try.

I owe so much to so many, but let's start with thanks to:

Erik, not only the man who planted the seed for What to Expect (literally, since he's the father of Emma, the baby who started it all), but the man who's helped me grow, nurture, nourish, and protect it—really, co-parent it. You know how they say that the more things change, the more they stay the same? Plenty has changed about my life and my life's work since the day I delivered Emma and a proposal for *What to*

Expect When You're Expecting within just hours of each other, but there is one thing that, lucky me, stays the same (only consistently better): the man I work with, live with, and love with. And the babies we made together, Emma and Wyatt, who long ago passed me in height and shoe size—and, I like to joke, in age—but who will always be my bundles of joy (and adding to the joy, son-in-law Russell). And of course, to Lennox, for making me a grandmother, and the happiest imaginable one at that—but also for his contributions to *First Year* (chief among them, being in his first year while I was writing it). And for being the cutest cover baby ever, and that's not just the grandma talking.

Always, Arlene Eisenberg, my first partner in What to Expect and always my most valued. Your legacy of caring and compassion continues to shape, inform, inspire, and, of course, live on through the next generation of What to Expect and beyond. You will always be loved and never be forgotten. All my family, epecially Sandee Hathaway, Howard Eisenberg, Abby and Norman Murkoff, and Victor Shargai.

Sharon Mazel, for taking up the What to Expect mission without hesitation, joining me on the third edition of *What to Expect When You're Expecting* . . . and, thankfully, never leaving me, even as the hours (and the indexes) got longer. Great minds may think alike, but few have probably thought alike as much as we have—and that always makes me smile, and always makes me grateful. Thanks to you, and to Jay, Daniella, Arianne, Kira, and Sophia, for sharing the amazing woman who is your wife and mom.

Suzanne Rafer, friend and editor, one of the very few who've been with me since conception—at least of What to Expect. I don't know if that makes you a glutton for punishment, but I do know it makes you an exceptionally important person in my life. I've lost count of editions and passes, but not of the contributions you've made to our babies.

Peter Workman—a publishing giant who outgrew many office spaces since the day I first met him, but never outgrew his small publishing roots and values. And everyone else at Workman who has helped so much along the way: Suzie Bolotin, Lisa Hollander, Beth Levy, Barbara Peragine, Jenny Mandel, and Emily Krasner, and all the many in sales and marketing busy selling what I'm writing.

Matt Beard, our favorite photographer (and one of our favorite people ever), for perfectly capturing that Lennox essence for our cover. Lynn Parmentier, for her quilting genius and Karen Kuchar, for babies so beautiful you could practically scratch and sniff their sweetness.

Dr. Mark Widome, professor, pediatrician, and fellow grandparent—not only for knowing it all, but for being able to dispense that knowledge with equal doses of common sense, care, compassion, wisdom, and good humor. I'm more grateful than I can say for vetting our latest baby—my only beef being that you practice too far away to be Lennox's pediatrician. Happily, that role is filled by LA's finest, Dr. Lauren Crosby, who has helped Lennox (and his parents) through feeding struggles, sepsis, slow growth, reflux, and more with endless energy and empathy.

The AAP and pediatricians, pediatric nurses, nurse practicioners, and physician assistants everywhere, for caring so much about the health and well-being of our little ones. The passionate doctors, scientists, and public health advocates at the CDC—for absolutely everything you do, and do with such passion and tireless dedication. The greater good is so much better off because of you. And 1,000 Days—for our shared vision (together, we'll make it happen!): healthy moms, healthy babies, and a healthy future that begins before the beginning.

All of my passionate, purple-wearing friends at WhatToExpect.com, (especially Michael Rose and Diane Otter, Ben Wolin and Scott Wolf, the awesome edit and product team) for making my online and mobile home feel, well, like home. I love working with you, because it never feels like work. My beautiful, sweet, nurturing publicist and friend, Heidi Schaeffer. And the other men in my life: my agent, Alan Nevins, and my attorney, Marc Chamlin.

The amazing USO, for partnering with the What to Expect Foundation to create Special Delivery—and give me the opportunity to hug so many military mamas and babies.

And most of all, to the mamas and daddies who sacrifice sleep, showers, and sit-down meals to nurture the babies we all get to love on. You inspire me every moment of every day. So much love, especially, to my WhatToExpect .com family of families, as well as my Twitter and Facebook families (keep those baby fixes coming!).

Big hugs,

heidi

Contents

Double Up on Diaper Stations • Gear for Outings • Seal of Approval • Car Seat Accessories to Skip • The LATCH System • A Place for Baby • Supervised Seating • Buying for Baby's Future • No Walkers Are Safe Walkers

The Second Month 238

The Third Month 262

============== CHAPTER 9 ==============

The Fourth Month 302

============== CHAPTER 10 ==============

The Fifth Month 317

=============== CHAPTER 13 ===============

The Eighth Month 410

=============== CHAPTER 14 ===============

The Ninth Month 428

=============== CHAPTER 15 ===============

The Tenth Month 446

========================== CHAPTER 16 ==========================

The Eleventh Month..468

Feeding Your Baby: Weaning from the Bottle 468

What You May Be Wondering About.................................... 472

========================== CHAPTER 17 ==========================

The Twelfth Month 490

Feeding Your Baby: Weaning from the Breast......................... 490

What You May Be Wondering About.................................... 496

A New Baby Bible

The first year of life is like no other—and it's arguably the year that most impacts all the years that follow: how healthy they are, how happy they are, even how many of them there are. Clearly, the first is a very big year for those so little.

Take growth, with a typical doubling of birth weight in the first 20 weeks and a tripling of birth weight by the first birthday. Length (or height, by the time your child is standing at a year) has increased by perhaps 50 percent, and brain growth (as roughly measured by head circumference) has increased by 30 percent.

One-year-olds are already 40 percent of their adult height, and their brains are nearly 80 percent of adult size. Who else but an infant grows 10 inches in a year? But physical growth is not the most remarkable change. Within minutes and hours of birth, a baby's physiology remarkably transforms from one that is suited only for intrauterine life to one that can survive *unattached*. Before birth, oxygen comes not from the air but from the mother's blood circulating to the placenta. Unborn babies get nutrition by that same route, bypassing their unused digestive tracts. Likewise, for eliminating most of the products of metabolism.

But, as the umbilical cord is cut, blood flow dramatically shifts from placenta to lungs, and breathing is established to exchange oxygen and carbon dioxide. Not long after, as the newborn baby is put to breast or bottle, the digestive tract is also recruited to do its new job.

Fortunately, parents do not need to do much to make all this happen. The transitions at birth mostly occur automatically, flawlessly, and on schedule. Without minimizing the challenges of pregnancy, labor, and delivery, mothers (and fathers, too) soon realize that greater challenges lie ahead. Namely, nurturing a newborn's development.

* * *

Most of the behavioral repertoire of newborns is—to use a popular, but imperfect term—*hardwired*. A newborn's brain and nervous system are preprogrammed to do what babies need to do to survive and to thrive—at least initially. Babies are programmed to cry, to suck. They are programmed to startle and to be soothed. Without thinking, they provide eye contact to their parents. And, gratefully, they are programmed to smile. Babies do not need to be taught to enjoy their parents' voices and songs, and they have built-in clocks to eventually accommodate their parents' daily rhythms of wake and sleep—though this accommodation may not happen right away, as many of you will soon learn.

But, returning to the machine metaphor of a baby's brain being "wired," for development over the early months, it is important to know that there is an early and ongoing process of *rewiring*. This is because the neural pathways in babies' brains are highly plastic. Rewiring (think: fine-tuning) of the brains of infants and toddlers has been an important and central insight of modern neuroscience research. Learning language and motor skills, developing social skills, being able to process new information by exploring the world with all of the senses, and particularly listening to the human voice, all help rewire the infant's brain. Listening to stories being read and playing with parents on the living room floor are examples of neuroscience in action. Parenthood is largely about reshaping and fine-tuning these neural pathways. For brain development, the first 3 years are most important, but the first 12 months are critical. Parents have tremendous influence over how well this happens—by providing for their infant's physical and emotional needs, by keeping their child safe and healthy, and by facilitating early learning.

This all sounds like a huge responsibility—not only like a job for a grown-up, but a job for a professional. And, if this is your first baby, you will not be alone in feeling, at times, underprepared for the job . . . and overwhelmed by it. And yet how could it be that the responsibility for overseeing this most important year in a child's life is given to the parents with the least experience—new parents?

But, fortunately, just as newborns are endowed with some essential survival tools, so are parents. Parental instinct may not kick in as swiftly and automatically as a newborn's—but that's okay. Between the nurturing parents received themselves as newborns and the nurturing (and support, and advice) they'll turn to friends, family, online communities, and professionals for, it's remarkable how quickly that gap is filled. And it clicks.

The more you know about the job ahead, the faster it clicks. Twenty-five years ago, when the first edition of *What to Expect the First Year* was introduced, it quickly became the "bible" of baby care—much as my 2,500-page pediatric textbook served as my pediatrics "bible." And today, even with access to information about all things parenting at the fingertips of anyone with a smartphone, I'm confident that this brand new third edition will step in to hold the hands of a new generation of new parents in a way no other resource can.

Not every parent has the time—or inclination—to read a book like this cover-to-cover, and happily, you don't have to. You can glean what you need to know, when you need to know it through a uniquely intuitive format that allows parents to take that first year one step (and month) at a time. Each age-relevant chapter begins with an "At a Glance" section reviewing sleep, eating, and playing: three areas intended to provide a mental scaffold for *what you might expect*. Parents can then read for a more detailed discussion of "Feeding Your Baby," "What You May Be Wondering About" (the familiar equivalent of FAQ). And throughout, there is discussion relevant to the lives and needs of *parents*—how they fit into this necessarily baby-focused year. This latter section helpfully covers topics such as postpartum depression, carving out couple time, deciding whether to go back to work, and helping siblings cope. While this volume includes lots of practical detail, particularly around breast- and bottle-feeding, treatment on injuries and first aid, choosing a doctor, and sleep patterns and problems, it is a book that implicitly recognizes that parents will use multiple sources of information as they raise their children in the second decade of the 21st century. Parents will, of course, supplement their learning with electronic resources such as websites, chat rooms, medical portals, and social media—and they should. But a particular word comes to mind in this electronic era that is, I believe, descriptive of what Heidi has skillfully accomplished in this book. That word is *curate*. Heidi has become the curator of a vast amount of information on parenting and child health, not all of which is of equal quality and validity. She has picked, chosen, and organized the best of it (what is most relevant, useful, and interesting) into something you can hold in your lap, keep on your shelf, or leave open on the kitchen table. It is reliable for concise information, guidance, and often reassurance. Every chapter informs, instructs, or explains. What do I need to keep in the medicine cabinet? (See Chapter 2.) Tell me about storing breast milk. (See Chapter 6.) What do I look for in shoes for the non-walker and for the walker? (See Chapters 11 and 16, respectively.) Should I learn/teach signing? (See Chapter 13.) Why is my baby biting me? (See Chapter 15.) I'm worried about the safety of vaccines. (See Chapter 19, where reassurance awaits.)

Parents will benefit from the considerable experience Heidi brings to this book. She is at once an expert on parenting, a parent, a grandparent, and a practiced communicator in tune with the needs of today's moms and dads and how they prefer to read. The user-friendly format relies heavily on boxes that highlight especially important content, as well as the friendly, familiar question-and-answer format. The strong index makes finding whatever you're looking for as quick and efficient as any search engine could (with far more uniformly reliable results). Importantly, this book is written to complement, rather than replace, advice and information from other sources: relatives, friends, physicians, and—for better or worse—the vast, *uncurated* Internet.

It is remarkable to consider what Heidi has accomplished—not only with this book, but when considered together with its companion volumes between which it is sandwiched: *What to Expect When You're Expecting* and *What to Expect the Second Year*. (As a new grandparent, I have come to appreciate the virtues of reliability and continuity.) *First Year* owes much of its success to its reliability over time—but as much or more to its ability to adapt and evolve over time. Parents' trust has been fully earned, and re-earned. Whether you are new to parenting or a seasoned veteran, you will find this updated volume to be a companion you can always count on.

Mark D. Widome, M.D., M.P.H.
Professor of Pediatrics
Penn State Hershey Children's Hospital
Hershey, Pennsylvania

A Very Different First Year

You know all that stuff they say about becoming a grandmother? How amazing it is . . . how much you'll love it . . . how it's all the best parts of being a parent—without the sleep deprivation?

Well, they don't tell you the half it. Becoming a grandmother, as I did on February 12, 2013, when Lennox entered the world, and minutes later, my welcoming arms, was life-changing, mind-blowing, heart-swelling . . . thrilling to the core. The heavens opened up. The earth moved. The love that washed over me as I held that sweet bundle for the first time was instantaneous, it was intense, it was unabashed . . . it hit me like a ton of bricks, and practically knocked me off my feet. I was smitten.

And I knew just how to hold him.

Rewind 29 years earlier, and the picture was a little different. Babies, as they say, don't come with instructions (and P.S. . . . I hadn't written the instructions yet either, so I couldn't very well follow them). Clueless? That would be giving me far too much crib cred. I was hopelessly clueless. Didn't know

how to hold Emma. Didn't know how to feed her. To diaper her. To rock her or burp her or calm her or even talk to her. I knew that I loved her, but I was pretty sure this squalling red stranger sniffing at my breast didn't feel the same about me. And who could blame her? Yes, I'd carried her and nurtured her before delivery with ease—even the delivery had been pretty much a piece of cake (if you didn't count those 3½ hours of pushing). But now what? I fumbled as I tried to support her wobbly head, jam floppy arms through the sleeves of her t-shirt, guide my nipple into her unwilling mouth. Maternal instincts, I prayed, don't fail me now(they did).

My crumbling of confidence followed me home. Stop me if you've heard this one: Two new parents walk into an apartment with a crying baby . . . and suddenly realize that not only is this crying baby theirs—but that she's their full-time responsibility. Cue . . . my crying. Fortunately, Erik's instincts kicked in quicker than mine did, and between his cool head and uncanny natural ability and my frantic flipping through my mother's tattered copy of Dr. Spock, we managed to find our way, one diaper blowout, one botched bath, one sleepless night, one colicky afternoon at a time.

So what did I do next? I did what any young, naive and clueless mom would do—motherhood being the mother of invention, I decided to write a book. A book that would help other parents steer through that first year with more confidence, more knowledge, more joy, less stress: *What to Expect the First Year* (though first, of course, I wrote a book on pregnancy, *What to Expect When You're Expecting,* that did the same for parents-to-be). I didn't write about my experience—which, let's be real, wasn't anything to write home about, never mind publish— but I wrote with experience. I'd been there, I'd done that, and I'd lived to write about it—that is, after I learned, through research and more research, everything that there was to know about it. And when it came to the first year the second time around (in the form of a baby boy named Wyatt), I had a book to turn to, and also—some mom cred to fall back on. Knowledge and know-how—a powerful parenting punch.

The moral of the story? While today's parents definitely have the information edge when it comes to what to expect the first year of their baby's life (there's not only a book now, but a website and an app for that, and Emma was lucky to have access to all three), tiny babies still bring huge challenges, especially for newbie moms and dads. And even with an ever-expanding array of resources, new parents still do much of their learning on the job, in the trenches . . . much as Erik and I did three decades ago.

Still, the more you know, well, the less you have to learn. Which is where this third edition of *What to Expect the First Year* comes in—a brand new baby-care guide for a brand new generation of new parents.

What's new in the new *First Year?* It's easier to use, making flipping to need-to-know info (yes, even frantic flipping) faster than ever. It's just as empathetic and reassuring as ever (because we all need a hand to hold, a shoulder to cry on, a parental pep talk when the going gets tough), but even more fun to read (because we all need a good laugh, too). It covers both the timeless baby basics (diaper changing 101) and the baby trends (all-in-one cloth diapers). There's much more on making breastfeeding work (including how to take it back to work), baby classes and technology (iBaby?), and buying for baby (so you can navigate that dizzying selection of nursery products vying for your consideration . . . and your credit card). There's a whole new developmental timeline to keep track of baby's milestones, practical new tips for new parents (including stay-at-home dads), and an expanded chapter for parents of preemies (with a glossary of medical terms and acronyms you'll hear tossed around the NICU). A monthly at-a-glance look at feeding, sleeping, and playing. New strategies for feeding your baby well and getting your baby to sleep, as well as boosting baby's brain power (without ever cracking a curriculum). And of course, the most up-to-date information available on your baby's health (from the latest on vaccines and vitamins to the lowdown on baby CAM therapies, probiotics, and homeopathics) and safety (choosing and using the safest products, first aid for every emergency).

I wrote the first edition of *What to Expect the First Year* with Emma's first year just barely finished—the experience still so fresh I could easily summon up that sweet new-baby smell (not to mention a whole lot of other new-baby smells, not so sweet). I wrote the third edition during Lennox's first year—with his sweet smell just five minutes away, inspiring me, refreshing my memories, and providing not only a mountain of new material (from feeding struggles to GERD to an umbilical site infection that landed him in the hospital) but a plethora of new perspectives.

All that, and a new cover, too, thanks to Lennox, our new cover baby. He's the baby of the baby who started it all—and one of my proudest joys yet.

And, I know just how to hold him.

heidi

WHAT TO
EXPECT®
THE
FIRST YEAR

CHAPTER 1

Get Ready, Get Set

....

Y ou've watched (the ultrasound screen) and waited for 9 months, counting kicks and punches, playing Name That Bump, and dreaming of your baby-to-be. And now there's finally a light at the end of the tunnel . . . maybe even effacement and dilation at the end of the cervix. But with just weeks to go before D-day, have you come to terms with your baby coming to term? Will you be ready when that big moment—and that little bundle—arrives?

Though being 100 percent prepared for your baby's arrival probably isn't possible (there are bound to be surprises, especially if you're a first-time parent), there are steps you can take and decisions you can make now—before baby makes three (or more)—to help make the transition a smoother one. From selecting the right baby name to selecting the right doctor. Deciding

between breast and bottle—or opting to go combo. Choosing to circumcise (or not) or hire a postpartum doula or baby nurse (or not).

Feeling a little overwhelmed by the flurry of prepping? First, think of it as good training for what you're prepping for: your hectic new life with a new baby. Second, read on to get ready, get set, and get going.

Choosing Breast or Formula, or Both

T here's no question you'll be feeding your baby (a lot), but maybe you're still questioning how. Will it be all breast, all the time? A breast start to the first year, and a formula finish?

Formula from day one? Or a creative combo that lets you give your baby the breast . . . and yourself some flexibility? Still questioning those questions and more? Not to worry. The best way to bring that fuzzy baby-feeding picture into focus is to explore the facts and factor in your feelings.

First, the facts:

Breastfeeding

What's the best food—and food delivery system—for babies? There's no question about that: Breast is best by far. Here are just some of the reasons why:

- It's custom-made. Tailored to the needs of human infants, breast milk contains at least 100 ingredients that aren't found in cow's milk and that can't be synthesized in the laboratory. And unlike formula, the composition of breast milk changes constantly to meet a baby's ever-changing needs: It's different in the morning than it is in the late afternoon, different at the beginning of a feeding than at the end, different the first month than the seventh, different for a preemie than for a full-term newborn. It even tastes different, depending on what you've been snacking on (just like your amniotic fluid does when you're pregnant). A one-of-a-kind food for your one-of-a-kind baby.

- It goes down easily. Breast milk is designed for a new baby's brand new digestive system. The protein and fat in breast milk are easier to digest than those in cow's milk formula, and its important micronutrients are more easily absorbed. The bottom line for newborn nursers: better nourishment.

- It's a tummy soother. Breast milk is not only easier going down, it's easier staying down . . . and easier going out. Breastfed babies are less likely to have tummy troubles (including excessive gas or spitting up) and almost never become constipated (formula

can sometimes clog up the works). And although their poops are normally quite soft, nursers rarely have diarrhea. In fact, breast milk appears to reduce the risk of digestive upset both by keeping harmful microorganisms in check and by encouraging the growth of beneficial ones. You know the much-touted pre- and probiotics that are added to some formulas? They're naturally occurring in breast milk.

- It's naturally safe. You can be sure that the milk served up from your breasts is always perfectly prepared—and never spoiled, contaminated, expired, or recalled.

- It's virtually allergy-proof. Babies are almost never truly allergic to breast milk (though occasionally an infant may be sensitive to something mom has eaten). The formula flip side? About 2 to 3 percent of babies turn out to have an allergy to cow's milk formula. And there's more good news on the allergy front: evidence that breastfed babies may be less likely to develop asthma and eczema than babies fed formula.

- It doesn't make a stink. Breastfed babies fill their diapers with sweeter-smelling stool—at least until solids are spooned up.

- It's a diaper rash eradicator. That sweeter-smelling poop is also less likely to trigger diaper rash—for a sweeter (and softer) bottom line.

- It's an infection fighter. With each and every feeding, nursers get a healthy dose of antibodies to boost their immunity to bugs of all varieties (some pediatricians like to refer to breastfeeding as a baby's first immunization). In general, breastfed babies will come down with fewer

When You Can't or Shouldn't Breastfeed

For some moms, the benefits of breastfeeding are beside the point. These moms don't have the option of nursing their new babies, either because of their own health (kidney disease, for instance, or a disease that requires medication harmful during lactation), their baby's health (a metabolic disorder, such as PKU or severe lactose intolerance, that makes even human milk impossible for baby to digest, or a cleft lip and/or cleft palate that interferes with suckling), or because of inadequate glandular tissue in the breasts (which, by the way, has nothing to do with breast size), damage to the nerve supply to the nipple (as from injury or surgery), or a hormonal imbalance.

Sometimes there are ways around a full-on ban on breastfeeding. For instance, a baby with a malformed lip or palate can be fitted with a special mouth appliance and/or can be fed pumped milk. Medications mom has to take can be adjusted. A mom who isn't able to produce all of her baby's milk because of a hormonal imbalance or because of past breast surgery (a breast reduction is more likely than breast augmentation to cause supply problems) may be able to produce enough to make breastfeeding worthwhile, even if supplementary formula is needed. But if you can't or shouldn't breastfeed (or don't want to), not to worry, not to feel guilty, not to stress, not to regret. The right formula can nourish your baby well—as will the love you offer with that bottle.

Another option: supplementing with breast milk from a milk bank. See page 93 for more.

colds, ear infections, lower respiratory tract infections, urinary tract infections, and other illnesses than bottle-fed infants, and when they do get sick, they'll usually recover more quickly and with fewer complications. Breastfeeding may improve the immune response to immunizations for some diseases. Plus, it may offer some protection against Sudden Infant Death Syndrome (SIDS).

- It's a fat flattener. Breastfed infants are less likely to be too chubby. That is, in part, because breastfeeding lets baby's appetite call the shots—and the ounces. A breastfed baby is likely to stop feeding when full, while a bottle-fed infant may be urged to keep feeding until the bottle's emptied. What's more, breast milk is actually ingeniously calorie controlled. The lower-calorie foremilk (served up at the start of a feed) is designed as a thirst quencher. The higher calorie hindmilk (served up at the end of a feed) is a filler-upper, signaling to a nurser that it's quitting time. And research suggests that the fat-defeating benefits of breastfeeding follow a baby out of the nursery—and into high school. Studies show that former breastfeeders are less likely to battle weight as teens—and the longer they were breastfed, the lower their risk of becoming overweight. Another potential health plus for nursers once they've graduated to adulthood: Breastfeeding is linked to lower cholesterol levels and lower blood pressure later in life.

- It's a brain booster. Breastfeeding appears to slightly increase a child's IQ, at least through age 15, and possibly beyond. This may be related not only to the brain-building fatty acids

(DHA) in breast milk, but also to the closeness and mother–baby interaction that is built into breastfeeding, which is believed to nurture a newborn's intellectual development. (Bottle-feeding parents can tap into this benefit, too, by keeping close during feeds, even doing skin-to-skin feeds).

- It's made for suckers. It takes longer to drain a breast than a bottle, giving newborns more of the comforting sucking satisfaction they crave. Plus, a breastfed baby can continue to comfort-suck on a nearly empty breast—something an empty bottle doesn't allow.

- It builds stronger mouths. Mama's nipples and baby's mouth are made for each other—a naturally perfect pair. Even the most scientifically designed bottle nipple can't match a breast nipple, which gives a baby's jaws, gums, and palate a good workout—a workout that ensures optimum oral development and some perks for baby's future teeth. Babies who are breastfed may also be less likely to get cavities later on in childhood.

There are also breastfeeding benefits for mom (and dad):

- Convenience. Breast milk is the ultimate convenience food—always in stock, ready to serve, and consistently dispensed at the perfect temperature. It's fast food, too: no formula to run out of, shop for, or lug around, no bottles to clean or refill, no powders to mix, no meals to warm (say, when you're on a conference call and baby's wailing in the background). Wherever you are—in bed, on the road, at the mall, on the beach—all the nourishment your baby needs is always on tap, no muss (or mess), no fuss.

- Free feedings, free delivery. The best things in life are free, and that includes breast milk and breast milk delivery. On the other hand, bottle-feeding (once you factor in formula, bottles, nipples, and cleaning supplies) can be a pretty pricey proposition. There's no waste with breastfeeding, either— what baby doesn't end up drinking at one feed will stay fresh for the next.

- Speedier postpartum recovery. It's only natural that breastfeeding is best for newly delivered moms, too—after all, it's the natural conclusion to pregnancy and childbirth. It'll help your uterus shrink back to prepregnancy size more quickly, which in turn will

The Breast Team

It takes two to breastfeed, but it can take more to make breastfeeding a success. A lactation consultant (LC) can be an indispensable member of your breastfeeding team and will be especially helpful if you encounter some bumps on the breastfeeding road. Consider getting a head start on enlisting one by calling the hospital you'll be delivering in to find out if it has LCs on staff and whether you'll automatically be hooked up with one at birth. Also tell your prenatal practitioner and the pediatrician that you'd like good lactation support as soon after delivery as is practical, and ask whether they have any LC recommendations. Check, too, with friends and online resources for recommended lactation consultants. Having a doula attend the birth? She will likely be able to help you get off to a successful breastfeeding start, too. For more on lactation consultants, see page 62.

Breastfeeding Myths

Myth: You can't breastfeed if you have small breasts or flat nipples.

Reality: Breasts and nipples of all shapes, sizes, and configurations can satisfy a hungry baby.

Myth: Breastfeeding is a lot of trouble.

Reality: Once you get the hang of it, this is as easy as feeding a child gets, and will ever get. Breasts, unlike bottles and formula, are ready when baby is. You don't have to remember to take them with you when you're planning a day at the beach, lug them in a diaper bag, or worry about the milk inside them spoiling in the hot sun. Open shirt, pull out breast, feed baby, repeat as needed.

Myth: Breastfeeding ties you down.

Reality: It's true that nursing a baby requires that the two of you be in the same place at the same time. But it's also true that pumping milk for bottle-feeds or supplementing with formula can free you up as needed or wanted—whether you need to work or go to school, or you want time off for a movie with friends or a dinner date with your partner. And when it comes to stepping out with baby, breastfeeding puts you in the driver's seat (or on the hiking trail, or on an airplane) without a thought of where that next feed is going to come from.

Myth: Breastfeeding will ruin your breasts.

Reality: Afraid breastfeeding will leave you . . . deflated? It's actually not nursing that ultimately changes the shape or size of your breasts or the color or size of your areolas, but pregnancy itself. During pregnancy, your breasts prep for lactation, even if you don't end up breastfeeding—and these changes are sometimes permanent. Extra weight gain during pregnancy, hereditary factors (thanks again, Mom), age, or lack of support (going braless) can also take your breasts down, at least somewhat, during pregnancy and beyond. Breastfeeding doesn't get the blame.

Myth: Breastfeeding didn't work the first time, so it won't work again.

Reality: Even if you had trouble navigating nursing with your first newborn, research shows that you'll likely produce more milk and have an easier time breastfeeding the second time around. In other words, if at first you didn't succeed, try, try breastfeeding again. Just make sure you enlist all the help and support you need this time around to get the breastfeeding ball rolling.

Myth: Dad won't bond with baby because he can't breastfeed.

Reality: Breastfeeding isn't open to dads, but every single other area of newborn care is. From bathing and diapering, to holding, baby-wearing, rocking, and playing, to bottle-feeding expressed milk or supplemental formula and eventually spooning up those solids, there will be plenty of opportunities for dad to get in on the baby-bonding action.

Myth: I have to toughen up my nipples so breastfeeding won't hurt.

Reality: Female nipples are designed for nursing. And, with very few exceptions, they come to the job fully qualified, without the need for any (yes, any) preparation.

reduce your flow of lochia (the post-partum discharge), decreasing blood loss. And by burning upward of 500 extra calories a day, breastfeeding your little one can help you shed those leftover pregnancy pounds faster. Some of those pounds were laid down as fat reserves earmarked specifically for milk production—now's your chance to use them.

- *Some* protection against pregnancy. It's not a sure bet, but since ovulation is often suppressed in nursing moms for several months or more, exclusively breastfeeding your baby may offer some family planning perks, as well as a reprieve from periods. Is this a bet you should take without a birth control backup? Definitely not, unless back-to-back pregnancies are your objective. Since ovulation can quietly precede your first postpartum period, you won't necessarily know when the contraceptive protection offered by breastfeeding will stop—leaving you unprotected against pregnancy.

- Health benefits. Plenty of perks here: Women who breastfeed have a slightly lower risk of developing uterine cancer, ovarian cancer, and premenopausal breast cancer. They're also less likely to develop rheumatoid arthritis than women who don't breastfeed. Plus, women who nurse have a lower risk of developing osteoporosis later in life than women who have never breastfed.

- Rest stops. A nursing newborn spends a whole lot of time feeding—which means a nursing mom spends a whole lot of time sitting or lying down. The upshot? You'll have frequent breaks during those exhausting early weeks, when you'll be forced to get off your feet and take a rest, whether you feel you have time to or not.

- Nighttime feeds that are a (relative) breeze. Have a hungry baby at 2 a.m.? You will. And when you do, you'll appreciate how fast you'll be able to fill that baby's tummy if you're breastfeeding. No stumbling to the kitchen to prepare a bottle in the dark. Just pop a warm breast into that warm little mouth.

- Eventually, easy multitasking. Sure, nursing your newborn will take two arms and a lot of focus. But once you and baby become nursing pros, you'll be able to do just about anything else at the same time—from eating dinner to playing with your toddler.

- Built-in bonding. The benefit of breastfeeding you're likely to appreciate most is the bond it nurtures between you and your little one. There's skin-to-skin and eye-to-eye contact, and the opportunity to cuddle, baby-babble, and coo built right into every feed. True, bottle-feeding mamas (and daddies) can get just as close to their babies—but it takes a more conscious effort.

Formula Feeding

While the facts heavily favor breast-feeding, there are also a few practical perks for those who opt for formula, at least some of the time:

- Less frequent feeds. Infant formula made from cow's milk is digested more slowly than breast milk, and the larger curds it forms stay in the tummy longer, helping a baby feel fuller longer—and extending the time between feeds to three or four hours even early on. Such long feed-free stretches are but a pipe dream for breastfeeding moms, who can count on feeding far more frequently (breast milk is digested faster and more easily, leaving baby hungry sooner). These frequent feeds serve a practical purpose—they stimulate the production of milk and improve mom's supply—but they can definitely be time-consuming and exhausting, especially when those feeds come at the expense of z's.

- Easy-to-track intake. Bottles come with calibrations to measure baby's intake, breasts do not. A formula-feeding parent can tell at a glance how many ounces have been consumed, a breastfeeding parent can gauge a baby's intake only from output (counting dirty and wet diapers) and weight gain. The upside of easy-to-track intake: less stress over whether a baby's taking too little or too much at feeds. The potential downside: Parents may push those last ounces in the bottle, even after baby's had enough.

- More freedom. To breastfeed, mom and baby must be in the same place at the same time—not so when feeds come from a bottle. A formula-feeding mom can work for the day, meet friends in the afternoon, take a business trip, or grab a weekend getaway without worrying about where baby's next meal will come from. Of course, the same holds true for a breastfeeding mom who chooses to pump or opts to supplement with formula.

- More rest for the weary. New moms are tired moms . . . make that, exhausted moms. While bottle-feeding mamas can buy themselves a nap or a good night's sleep by handing off some feeds to daddy or another secure set of warm arms, breastfeeding moms can't. And although breastfeeding is far more convenient than formula feeding, especially at 3 a.m., it's also more physically draining.

- More daddy time. Dads of nursing newborns clearly don't have what it takes to feed their little ones—that is, unless they're giving supplementary bottles of formula or breast milk. Bottle-fed babies, on the other hand, will happily let their fathers do the feeding.

- No fashion don'ts. Breastfeeding moms learn early to put function (easy, discreet access to breasts) over form (read: no one-piece dresses that don't button down the front). When you're bottle-feeding, anything in your closet that fits is fair game.

- More contraception options. For formula-feeders, most types of hormonal birth control are usable—not so for breastfeeders. Still open to breastfeeders: the progestin-only "mini-pill."

- More menu options. Eating well while breastfeeding definitely comes with fewer restrictions than eating well during pregnancy (the sushi bar is open once again, and hamburgers no longer have to be served up gray), but a formula-feeder still has more freedom of eats (and drinks). She can say yes to that second round or that third coffee, eat garlic with abandon (some, though definitely not all, breastfed babies object to certain pungent flavors in mom's milk), and never worry about whether the meds she takes will be shared with her baby. She can also fast-track her weight loss—within the scope of what's sensible for a tired new mom—while a breastfeeding mom should take it somewhat slower (but may end up losing weight more easily, since milk production burns so many calories).

- Fewer awkward moments for modest mamas. While public breastfeeding is protected by law in more and more states, it isn't always protected by public opinion—which means, unfortunately, that a mom nursing her baby still can attract some uncomfortable stares or even glares, especially when she chooses not to feed under cover (as is increasingly her right). Bottle-feeders, on the other hand, can be buttoned up about feeding—literally. No unfastening, untucking, or redressing required—and no worries about baby kicking off that napkin midmeal. Of course, hang-ups about public breastfeeding usually get hung up pretty quickly—as they should be. After all, there's never anything inappropriate about feeding a hungry baby . . . ever. And nursing cover-ups have come a long way, baby.

- Potentially, more fun in bed. Breastfeeding hormones can keep your vagina dry and sore, making postpartum sex a pain (plenty of foreplay and even more Astroglide can ease reentry). Bottle-feeding may speed a return to lovemaking as usual—that is, if you can rise above the spit-up stained sheets and crying-baby-interruptus.

Your Feelings

Maybe you're convinced by the facts, but nagging doubts are still keeping you on the breastfeeding fence. Here's how to work through a few common negative feelings about breastfeeding:

The feeling that it's impractical. So you'd like to give breastfeeding a shot, but you're afraid it won't fit a demanding work schedule? As many moms have discovered, even an early return to work doesn't rule out breastfeeding. So consider giving it a try. Whether you end up fitting nursing into your work schedule for just a few weeks or for a year or more, offer breast milk exclusively or in combination with formula—any amount of breastfeeding is beneficial for you and baby. And with a little extra dedication and planning (okay, maybe a lot of extra dedication and planning), you may find that mixing business with breastfeeding is a lot easier than you thought (see page 262).

The feeling that you won't enjoy it. Having a hard time picturing yourself with a baby at your breast—or maybe you're just not that into the idea of breastfeeding? Before you write off breastfeeding entirely, here's a suggestion: Try it, you may like it. You might even love it. And if you're still not feeling the breastfeeding love after 3 to 6 weeks of best breast efforts (that's about how long it takes for moms and babies to sync up into a good nursing rhythm), you can quit, knowing you've given your baby a head start on a healthy life. No harm done, lots of benefits gained, especially in the form of antibodies that will boost your little one's immune system, and particularly if you've given breastfeeding a full 6 weeks. Every feed counts, no matter how many or how few baby ends up racking up.

The feeling that your partner's not on board. Studies show that when dads are supportive of breastfeeding, moms are far more likely to stick with it. So what do you do if your partner's not on board with breastfeeding—either because he's turned off by it, unsettled by it, or feels threatened at the thought of sharing you in such a physical way? Try to win him over with the facts—after all, they're pretty compelling stuff. Talking to other dads whose partners have breastfed their babies will also help him feel more comfortable, and hopefully more amenable. Or suggest a trial of breastfeeding—chances are you'll be able to turn his feelings around quickly, and if not, you'll still be giving your baby and yourself the best health benefits possible, something he's bound to appreciate.

If you choose to give breastfeeding a try—no matter what facts, feelings, or circumstances bring you to that decision, and no matter how long you end up staying with it—chances are you'll find it a rewarding experience. Emotional and health benefits aside, you're also likely to find it the easiest and most convenient way to feed your baby, hands down (and eventually, hands free) . . . at least, once you've worked out early kinks.

But if you choose not to breastfeed, or you can't breastfeed, or you can or choose to breastfeed only for the briefest of times, there's no need for second-guessing, regret, or guilt. Almost nothing you do for your baby is right if it doesn't end up feeling right for you—and that includes breastfeeding. You can offer your baby as much nurturing and share as much intimacy during bottle-feeds as you could with breast-feeding—and in fact, a bottle offered lovingly is better for your little one than a breast offered with reservations, or a side of stress.

Choosing to Circumcise or Not

Circumcision is probably the oldest medical procedure still performed. Though the most widely known record of the practice is in the Old Testament, when Abraham was said to have circumcised Isaac, its origins probably date back before the use of metal tools. Practiced by Muslims and Jews throughout most of history as a sign of their covenant with God, circumcision became widespread in the United States in the late 19th century, when it was theorized that removing the foreskin would make the penis less sensitive (it definitely doesn't), thus making masturbation a less tempting pursuit (it definitely didn't). In the years that followed, many other medical indications for routine circumcision have been proposed—including preventing or curing epilepsy, syphilis, asthma, lunacy, and tuberculosis. None of them have panned out.

So are there any proven medical benefits to circumcision? It does reduce the risk of infection of the penis (but cleaning under the foreskin once it is retractable—usually around the second birthday—does just as well). It also eliminates the risk of phimosis, a condition in which the foreskin remains tight as a child grows and can't be retracted as it normally can in older boys (between 5 and 10 percent of uncircumcised males have to undergo circumcision sometime after infancy because of infection, phimosis, or other problems). And studies show that the risk of developing a urinary tract infection (UTI) in the first year of life is higher for baby boys who are uncircumcised (though the actual risk of an uncircumcised boy developing a UTI is very low—about 1 percent). The rates of penile cancer and STDs, including HIV, may also be slightly lower for circumcised males.

Wondering where the experts come down on circumcision? Actually, most don't—and that includes the American Academy of Pediatrics (AAP), which maintains that while the health benefits

Diaper Decisions

Cloth or disposable? While you don't have to decide which type of diaper you'll use for your baby's bottom until there's a bottom that needs covering (and you can always change your mind once you start changing diapers), thinking about your options now makes sense. For a heads-up on all the bottom-covering options and features out there, see page 34.

of circumcision outweigh the risks of the procedure, it's still a decision best left to the parents. They recommend that parents be advised of the risks and benefits of circumcision and then make the unpressured choice that's right for their baby and their family—factoring in what matters most to them (whether that's having their son match up with dad, following a religious or cultural tradition, or just the belief that baby boys should be left intact).

Just over half of all boys in the United States are circumcised—the rate having dropped considerably in recent years. The most common reasons parents give for opting for circumcision, in addition to just "feeling it should be done," include:

- Religious observance. The religious laws of both Islam and Judaism require that newborn boys be circumcised.

- Cleanliness. Since it's easier to keep a circumcised penis clean, cleanliness is next to godliness as a reason for circumcision in the United States.

- The locker-room syndrome. Parents who don't want their sons to feel different from their friends or from their father or brothers often choose circumcision. Of course, as the

percentage of circumcised babies steadily declines, this becomes less of a consideration.

- Appearance. Some maintain that a foreskin-free penis is more attractive.

- Health. Some parents just don't want to take even the slightest added risk when it comes to their newborn's health.

The reasons why parents decide against circumcision include:

- The lack of medical necessity. Many question the sense of removing a part of an infant's body without a really good reason.

- Fear of bleeding, infection, and worse. Though complications are rare when the procedure is performed by an experienced physician or medically trained ritual circumciser, they do happen—and that's enough reason for some parents to be understandably apprehensive about circumcising their newborn.

- Concern about pain. Evidence shows that newborns circumcised without pain relief experience pain and stress measured by changes in heart rate, blood pressure, and cortisol levels. The AAP recommends that circumcision be done with effective pain relief (such as topical EMLA cream, dorsal penile nerve block, or the subcutaneous ring block).

- The locker-room syndrome. Some parents choose not to circumcise a newborn so he will look like his uncircumcised dad or like other boys in a community where circumcision isn't widely practiced.

- A belief in a newborn's rights. Some parents prefer to leave this important life decision up to their son—when he becomes old enough to make it.

- Less risk of diaper irritation. It's been suggested that the intact foreskin may protect against diaper rash on the penis.

If you remain undecided about circumcision as delivery day approaches, read about circumcision care on page 222 and discuss the issue with the doctor you have chosen for your baby—and possibly with relatives, friends, or social media buddies who have gone either route (keeping in mind that the debate between pro and con camps can get pretty heated).

Choosing a Name

So, maybe you've been settled on your munchkin's moniker since you were a munchkin yourself. Maybe you devoted notebooks to baby names in high school—or later, cocktail napkins. Maybe your baby's name became as clear as a 4-D ultrasound the first moment you learned "it's a boy" or "it's a girl." Or maybe, if you're like a lot of other parents approaching delivery day, you're still playing the name game . . . late in the game.

Whether you're looking for something classic, something meaningful, something quirky, something trendy, or something completely different, whether you're sure you'll know the right name when you hear it or wondering if you'll ever know it, deciding what to name your baby can be a pretty daunting challenge. After all, a name is not just a name—it's an integral part of your child's identity. And, it tends to stick for life—from the cradle to the playground to the homeroom to the workplace and beyond. Add to that awesome responsibility the drama and debate, which can get pretty heated between some couples (and among other opinionated family members): The name your spouse is set on may be the name you're set against. Your cousin delivered first and took your favorite name with her. Both grandmas are lobbying for different family names. A coworker burst out laughing when you told him the name you had in mind. And the name you love best is the one you're afraid no teacher will ever be able to pronounce. Or spell.

So get ready to run through the alphabet (and your share of baby-name apps, websites, and books) at least a few dozen times. Try before you buy—toss around as many possibilities as you can before your baby's due—and don't be too quick to reject new entries (you never know which names might grow on you). It also pays to start paying attention to what parents in your orbit are calling their little ones. You may be inspired or discover that a name you were considering doesn't have that ring after all—especially after you say it out loud a few dozen times.

Here are some more tips on choosing a name for your baby:

Make it meaningful. Have an all-time favorite actor or character from a book or film? A beloved family member or ancestor? A sports or music legend you'd love to honor? Or maybe you'd prefer to find your inspiration from the Bible or another spiritual source. Or from the location of your little one's conception. A meaningful name can mean more than a random one—and attaches a special background story and historical context to a brand new life.

Consider the less common. It's never easy to be one of many same-named in the class, so if you're looking to make your little one stand out in a crowd, opt for a baby name that didn't make last year's top-ten list.

But maybe not the unheard-of. Thinking of making a name up, celebrity-style? One-of-a-kind names can make a child feel unique—or like the odd kid out (especially if your little one won't be running in a celebrity crowd). Remember, a name is forever (or at least until your baby's old enough to legally change it)—and what sounds cute now may not look so cute on a college or job application. Think twice, too, before you go with an extremely creative spelling of a more common name (can you spell annoying?).

Avoid the trendy. Considering naming your little darling after the film, TV, or music industry's latest darling? Before you hitch your baby to any star, consider that they often fade quickly—or can end up making entertainment news for all the wrong reasons.

Mean what you name, and name what you mean. Learning the meaning of a name can definitely influence your decision. You might be ambivalent about Annabella until you find out it means "grace and beauty" or iffy about Ian until you see that it translates to "God is gracious." On the other hand, Cameron may be a contender until you discover that you're naming your baby "bent nose"—or you may decide the meaning has no meaning to you after all.

Go back to your roots. Trace your ancestry or ethnicity and you may just come across the name you've been searching for. Shake the family tree,

---

For Parents: Preparing an Older Child

Wondering how to tell your still very young firstborn that a new baby is on the way? Or how to ease the transition from only child to big brother or sister? Check out *What to Expect the Second Year* for the tips you'll need to help prepare your older little one for that big new role.

---

scout the homeland, revisit your religious roots if you're so inclined—you're bound to discover a baby-name bounty.

Consider gender generalizing. Yes, you know that your Morgan's all boy and your Jordan's all girl—but will others be clued in, or thrown off, by the name you choose? Does it cross (or blur) gender lines—and if so, does that matter to you? Many parents decide that it doesn't.

Sound it out. When choosing a baby name (middle included) consider the cadence (Michaela Mackenzie Morton-Mills is quite a mouthful) and be careful about combinations that could turn your child's name into a joke (Justin Case, Paige Turner . . . and worse). As a general rule, a short last name goes well with a long first name (Isabella Bloom) and vice versa (Drew Huntington), while two-syllable first names usually complement two-syllable last names (Aiden Carter).

Don't forget to initial. Considering naming your little girl Abigail Sasha Smith? You want to think through those initials before you make an Abigail Sasha Smith out of her and yourself.

Keep it under wraps. Share your chosen name with others only if you dare to open it up to debate. If, on the other hand, you'd rather spare yourself a lot of unsolicited advice and comments (or hopeful hints from Great Uncle Horace), keep the name under wraps until it's wrapped around your little bundle.

Stay flexible. Before you engrave that chosen name in stone—or stencil it over your baby's crib—make sure it fits. Once you meet your sweet Samantha, you may be surprised to find out she's really more of a Miranda . . . or maybe (it's happened) more of a Sam.

Choosing Help

Newborn babies are helpless . . . newly delivered parents definitely shouldn't be. In fact, you'll need all the help you can get after you've brought baby home, not just to do all the things babies can't do for themselves (changing diapers, giving baths, comforting, feeding, burping), but to do all the things you won't have time to do or will be too exhausted to do yourself (say, shopping, cooking, cleaning, and those piles of laundry).

Help wanted? First, you'll need to figure out what kind of help you want, what help will be available to you, and, if you're thinking of paying for help (at least part-time), what kind of help you can afford—and feel comfortable with. Which set of hands (or sets of hands) do you envision giving you a hand in those challenging first weeks and months? Will it be a grandma (or two)? A friend? A baby nurse? A doula? Or someone to care for the house while you're busy caring for yourself and your baby?

Baby Nurse

The care (and, if baby's not nursing, the feeding) of newborns is their specialty—though some baby nurses will also tackle light housework and cooking. If you've determined there's enough money in your budget for a baby nurse (they don't come cheap), you'll probably want to consider several other factors before deciding whether or not to hire one. Here are some reasons why you might opt for professional help from a baby nurse:

- To get some hands-on training in baby care. A good baby nurse will be able to show you the ropes when it comes to the basics—bathing, burping, diapering, and maybe even breastfeeding. If this is your reason for hiring a nurse, however, be sure that the one you hire is as interested in teaching as you are in learning. Taking charge is one thing—taking over is another. Letting you get some rest is great—not letting you get near your baby isn't. Ditto constant critiquing of your baby-care techniques, which can wear on your nerves, and your confidence.

- To avoid getting up in the middle of the night for feedings. If you're formula feeding and would rather sleep through the night, at least in the early weeks of postpartum fatigue, a baby nurse or doula, on duty 24 hours a day or hired just for nights, can take over or share baby feeding duty with you and your spouse. Or, if you're breastfeeding, bring baby to you for nursings as needed.

Help Wanted

Looking to hire a baby nurse or post-partum doula, but not sure where to find the right one? As always, your best resource will be recommendations from other parents—so put the word out to friends, colleagues, and neighbors who've used (and been happy with) a baby nurse or doula. Agencies are another good place to start—even better if you've been referred by a satisfied parent customer and/or if objective online reviews seem promising. Just keep in mind that agencies can charge a hefty fee—sometimes a yearly or monthly membership, sometimes a surcharge on each service, sometimes both.

Consider the job description before you begin considering candidates. Are you looking for baby care only—or a side of housework, errand running (with or without a car of her own), and cooking? Full- or part-time? Live in or out? For night duty or day, or some of each? For a

week or two postpartum, or a month or two—or longer? Will you hope to learn some baby-care basics from the care provider, or just cash in on the extra rest? And if price is an object, how much will you be able to budget for?

There's no substitute for a face-to-face interview, since you can't judge personality or your comfort level on paper (or on the phone, or via an email exchange). Check out references fully, too, and if you're hiring through an agency, make sure the candidates you're culling from are licensed and bonded. Any care provider should also be up-to-date on immunizations (including a Tdap booster and a yearly flu vaccine) and screened for TB. She should also be trained (and recertified within the last 3 to 5 years) in CPR and first aid and safety, as well as up-to-date on baby-care practices (back-to-sleep and other safe sleep recommendations, for instance).

- To spend more time with an older child. Want to squeeze in some extra time with the newly big sib (or sibs)? A baby nurse can be hired to work just a few hours a day so you can lavish baby-free attention on an older little one.

- To give yourself a chance to recuperate after a cesarean or difficult vaginal birth. If you're scheduled for a C-section, it may be smart to schedule that extra postpartum help, too, if you can. But even if you're not sure how easy—or difficult—your baby's birth (and your recovery from it) will be, it's not a bad idea to do some scouting around in advance for nurses, just in case. That way, you'll be able to call up that much-needed reserve help before you've even arrived back home from the hospital.

A baby nurse may not be the best postpartum medicine if:

- You're breastfeeding. Since a nurse can't nurse your baby, she may not prove to be all that helpful initially. In that case, household help—someone to cook, clean, and do laundry—is probably a better investment, unless you can find a nurse who's willing to pitch in around the house, too.

- You'd prefer to go nuclear (family). Unless you have a separate space for a nurse to stay in, live-in means live with—and that may feel intrusive. If sharing your kitchen, your bathroom, your sofa with a stranger (even a really sweet and accommodating one) sounds more like a crowd than a convenience, you might be better off with part-time help.

For Parents: Prepping the Family Pet

Already have a baby in the house—the kind with four legs and a tail? Then you're probably wondering how your dog or cat will react when you bring home a baby of a different kind (the human kind)—a tiny, noisy, and intrusive intruder who will soon be sharing a place in your heart and on your lap, and possibly taking your pet's place in your bed or bedroom. Though some initial moping—and even some regression in the house-training department—may be inevitable, you'll want to prevent all the fur sibling rivalry you can, especially unexpectedly aggressive reactions. Here's how to prepare your pet:

- Consider basic training. Is your home your pet's castle—and amusement park? It's time for rules to rule your roost, even when it comes to your furry friend (and even if life has so far been a fun-filled free-for-all for Spot or Mittens). Living with consistent expectations will help your pet feel more secure and act more predictably, especially around your predictably unpredictable baby. Even a pet who's always been more frisky than ferocious, who's never threatened or felt threatened by a human, may become uncharacteristically aggressive and dangerously territorial when your home is invaded by a human newborn. Consider enrolling your pet in an obedience training program (yes, cats can be trained, too)—and remember, for your pet to be trained, you have to be, too. Attend classes with your pet, take homework seriously (practice, practice, practice what's learned in class), and continue to be consistent about rules and rewards (key to the success of pet training) even after graduation.

- Schedule a checkup. Visit the veterinarian for an exam, and make sure that all shots are up-to-date. Discuss any concerning behavior issues (like marking) and possible solutions with the veterinarian, too, and evaluate flea and heartworm prevention for safety around your expected human bundle. Just before baby is due to arrive, have your pet's nails trimmed. Consider spaying or neutering, which can make pets calmer and less aggressive.

- Bring in the babes. Try to get your dog or cat acclimated to babies by arranging carefully supervised encounters (with a baby at the park, with your friend's newborn). Invite friends with babies over to your house so your pet can become familiar with human baby smells and their moves. Do some baby holding around your pet, too.

- Play pretend. Using a baby-size doll as a prop will help get your pet used to having a baby around the house (pretend rock, feed, change, play with the doll, strap it into the car seat and stroller). Play audio of a newborn crying, cooing, and making other baby sounds, too—and (if you've already stocked the house with baby paraphernalia) turn on the infant swing, to accustom your pet to the sound and action (with that doll strapped in). And as you close in on the delivery day, start getting your pet used to scents of baby products you'll be using on baby's skin by applying it to yours (baby wipes, baby wash), and allow sniffing of clean diapers. During these desensitizing sessions, reward your pet with treats and cuddles.

- Don't give your pet any ideas. While it might seem smart to let your pet snuggle in your expected baby's bassinet or car seat or play with those piles of new stuffed animals, it isn't. That approach can lead your fur baby to believe that those items are his or hers—and set up territorial disputes (potentially risky ones).

- Taper off on time with your pet. It sounds a little mean, but getting your dog or cat used to less mommy and daddy attention now may prevent sibling rivalry later. If mama is your pet's favorite, start weaning onto more time with daddy.

- Do some belly bonding. Many dogs and cats seem to have an uncanny baby sixth sense, so if yours is clamoring to cuddle up with your bare bump, let the bonding between baby and pet begin. By the way, even a large dog can't harm your well-protected baby by nestling against your belly.

- Get on board with room and board changes. If sleeping arrangements will change (and they probably should if you've been co-sleeping with your pet), change them well before delivery. If your baby will have a separate room, train your pet to stay out of it while you're not there. A gate to block the doorway will help discourage unsolicited visits. Also, train your pet not to go near the baby's crib, no matter what room the crib is in. Another must-do: Move your pet's feeding station somewhere a curious crawler can't get to, since even a mellow mutt or kitty can attack when food is threatened. Two more reasons why babies and pet food don't mix: Kibble and treats are a choking hazard (and a tempting one), and both food and bowls (including water bowls) can become contaminated with dangerous bacteria, like salmonella. Cat litter should also be kept in a baby-free zone, and if that will require a change of place, make the move now. In general, cats and dogs should have a "safe" space (which could be a room or a crate) where they can retreat for a respite from baby.

- Sniff out jealousy. After delivery, but before you introduce your new baby to your fur baby, bring in an unwashed piece of clothing your newborn has worn (baby's nursery beanie, for instance) and encourage sniffing. Bring on the hugs and treats so that the scent becomes a happy association. When you bring baby home, greet your pet first—and then let the meet-and-greet (including sniffing of your well-swaddled, well-protected newborn) begin. Reward that first sniff with praise, a treat, and a pat for your pet. Try to stay calm and avoid scolding.

- Include the furry new big sib. Scratch your cat while you nurse. Take your dog on especially long walks with baby in tow. Reward gentle behavior around the baby with treats.

- Be protective, but not overprotective. Allow supervised visits of baby spaces and supervised sniffing of baby and baby's things—protecting your baby from suddenly snappish behavior but without setting off jealous stress signals that could trigger aggression.

- Don't take any chances. If your pet seems hostile toward the new arrival, keep the two safely separated until those feelings have been worked out.

For more tips on prepping your pet, go to whattoexpect.com/pet-intro.

- You'd rather do it yourselves. If you and your partner want to be the ones giving the first bath, catching sight of the first smile (even if they say it's only gas), and soothing baby through the first bout of crying (even if it's at 2 a.m.), there may not be much left for a baby nurse to do—especially if dad's around full-time while he's enjoying paternity leave. Consider springing for household help (or food delivery or laundry service) instead—or saving your money for that high-end stroller you've been eyeing.

Postpartum Doula

Thought doulas were just for delivery? Though birth doulas specialize in caring for expectant moms and their families during late pregnancy and childbirth, a postpartum doula can offer the support that keeps on giving, all the way through those challenging early weeks with a new baby and beyond. Unlike a baby nurse, whose focus is on newborn care, a postpartum doula cares for the entire newly delivered family, pitching in to help with just about anything you'll need help with—from household chores and cooking to setting up the nursery and caring for older children. The right postpartum doula will be a reassuring resource (on baby care, postpartum care, and breastfeeding), a shoulder to lean on (and even cry on), and your biggest booster—picking up the slack, but also building up your confidence as parents. Think of a doula as a professional nurturer—someone to mother the new mom (or dad) in you.

Another perk of postpartum doulas is flexibility—some will work a few hours a day or night, others will pull the overnight shift, still others will do a full 9 to 5. You can hire a postpartum doula for just a few days or as long as a few months. Of course, since most are paid by the hour instead of the week, costs can rack up fast. For more information on doulas or to locate one in your area, contact Doulas of North America at dona.org or the Childbirth and Postpartum Professional Association at cappa.net.

Grandparents

They're experienced (they raised you, didn't they?), they're enthusiastic, they'll happily work for cuddles—and though some may come with generational baggage (and perhaps old-school baby care strategies), grandparents have at least 101 uses. They can rock a crying baby, cook a real dinner, do the grocery shopping, wash and fold laundry, and best of all, let you get some of the rest you need—all at no cost. Should you take your parents or in-laws up on their volunteer baby care and household help in the first weeks, that is if they're able, willing, and available? That depends on whether you can handle a little (or a lot) of well-meant, (mostly) good-natured interference—and how you would respond if "helping out" morphs into a full-on takeover (it happens in the best of families).

You feel the more generations the merrier? By all means, extend the invite. Suspect that two generations would be cozy company but that three could be a stressful crowd? Don't hesitate to let the soon-to-be-grandparents know that you'd rather spend those early weeks bonding your brand new family unit and becoming comfortable in your brand new roles as parents. Promise a visit once everyone's adjusted—with the reminder that baby will be more responsive, more interesting, more awake, and more fun by then.

For Parents:
Running Grandparent Interference

Have a set (or two) of parents who haven't quite accepted that you're about to become the parents now? That's not surprising—after all, you probably haven't fully grasped that reality yet, either. But it can be a red flag of grandparental interference to come . . . or that's already arrived.

One of your first responsibilities as parents? Letting your parents know it while helping them ease into their brand new (supporting, not starring) role as grandparents.

Say it early (and as often as necessary), say it firmly, and most of all, say it lovingly. Explain to any well-meaning but meddling grandparents that they did a wonderful job of raising you and your spouse, but that it's your turn to wear the parent pants. There will be times when you'll welcome their know-how (especially if grandma has cataloged somewhere in her vast reserves of experience a surefire trick for calming a crying newborn) but other times when you'll want to learn from your pediatrician, books, websites, apps, parent peers, and your

mistakes—much as they probably did. Explain, too, that not only is it important for you to set the rules (as they did when they first became parents), but that many of the rules have changed since they were in the parenting game (babies are no longer put to sleep on their tummies or fed on a schedule), which is why their way of doing things may no longer be recommended. And don't forget to say it with humor. Point out that chances are the changing tables will turn once again when your child becomes a parent—and rejects your parenting strategies as old school.

That said, try to keep two things in mind—especially when you find yourself butting heads with butting-in grandparents. First, they may come across as know-it-alls, but they probably know more than you'd like to give them credit for—and there's always something to learn from their experience, even if it's only what not to do. And second, if parenthood is a responsibility (and it is), grandparenthood is the reward (and it should be).

Choosing a Baby Doctor

Feel like you've practically been living at your ob's office (or on the phone with the ob's office) over the 9 months of pregnancy? Well, that's nothing, baby—at least, nothing compared with the time you'll spend with your baby's doctor (or on the phone or email with your baby's doctor) over the next year. Even the healthiest baby needs a lot of health care—from well-baby checkups

to regular immunizations. Factor in those inevitable first sniffles and tummy aches, and you'll see why your baby's doctor will play such an important role in your little one's first year—and in your first year as a parent.

And beyond . . . potentially, way beyond. After all, the doctor you choose could be seeing baby—and you—through some 18 years of runny noses,

Health Insurance for a Healthy Family

Think health insurance is complicated and expensive? Get ready for
about eight more pounds of complications and expense. If you're already
covered under a family plan, adding
your new bundle is as easy as making a
phone call once baby is born (just don't
forget to make that call, since coverage
for baby doesn't kick in automatically).
If you're covered by a plan but only as
an individual, you'll need to do a little
more legwork to figure out how switching to a family plan might impact your
bottom line—switching from an HMO
(Health Maintenance Organization) to
a POS (Point of Service plan) or PPO
(Preferred Provider Organization),
for instance, will likely increase your
costs—and which type of coverage will
best suit your growing family's needs.

Speak to someone in human
resources where you work, call your
insurance company directly, or check
out your state's health insurance
exchange/marketplace (as mandated by
the Affordable Care Act), where you'll
be able to find, compare, and purchase
the coverage you'll need. Ask what services the plan covers (routine checkups, immunizations, sick visits, speech,
hearing, and vision tests, lab and x-ray
services, prescription meds, speech and
physical therapy), if there are any limits
on the number of well-baby or sick-
baby visits, and what out-of-pocket
expenses you'll have to pay. To find
out more about the Health Insurance
Marketplace in your state, visit
healthcare.gov or call 800-318-2596.

Worried that you won't be able to
afford insurance? Under the Affordable
Care Act, you may be eligible for subsi-
dies or tax breaks. Medicaid programs
cover those with low incomes, and the
Children's Health Insurance Program
(CHIP) provides low-cost health
insurance for children in families who
earn too much income to qualify for
Medicaid, don't have employer health
insurance available, and can't afford
private health insurance. Find out more
from insurekidsnow.gov or by calling
877-KIDS-NOW. There are also local
community health centers that provide
care at low or no cost, depending on
your income. Go to findahealthcenter
.hrsa.gov. The CDC's Vaccines for
Children Program offers vaccines at
no cost for eligible children. Go to cdc
.gov/features/vfcprogram.

---

earaches, sore throats, upset stomachs,
bumps and bruises, and more. You
won't be living with your baby's doctor
during those years (though there will be
times, particularly nights and weekends,
when you'll wish you were), but you'll
still want him or her to be someone you
feel comfortable and compatible with—
someone you'd feel at ease asking questions that aren't easy, someone who's
equally patient with both tiny patients
and their nervous parents.

Still looking for Baby Doctor
Right? Start your search here.

Pediatrician or Family Practitioner?

The first step on your search for Baby
Doctor Right? Deciding what type
of practitioner is right for you. Your
choices:

The pediatrician. Babies, children, and
sometimes adolescents are their business—their only business. And, they're
trained well for it. In addition to 4
years of medical school, pediatricians
have had 3 years of specialty training

in pediatrics. If they are board certified (they should be), they have also passed a tough qualifying exam. The major advantage of selecting a pediatrician for your baby is obvious—since they see only children, and lots of them, they know their stuff when it comes to little ones (including when not to sweat the small stuff). They're more familiar with childhood illnesses, and more experienced in treating them. And they're more likely to have ready answers to the questions parents (like you) ask most—from "Why doesn't she sleep?" to "Why does he cry so much?"—because they've heard them all, many times before.

A good pediatrician will also be tuned in to the whole family picture—and will realize when a change at home (say, a dad's deployment or a mom's return to work) may be the root of a change in a child's behavior, sleeping or eating habits, or even health.

The only downside to choosing a pediatrician? If the entire family comes down with something (strep all around), you may need to call on more than one doctor.

The family practitioner. Like the pediatrician, the family practitioner usually has had 3 years of specialty training following medical school. But an FP residency program is much broader, covering internal medicine, psychiatry, and obstetrics and gynecology, in addition to pediatrics. The advantage of choosing a family practitioner is that it can mean one-stop doctoring—you can use the same doctor for prenatal care, the delivery of your baby, and to care for the whole family. Already using a family practitioner? Adding your new baby to the patient roll means you won't have to transition to a brand new doctor, doctor's office, or doctor protocol—and that you'll (hopefully) already have a comfortable doctor-patient rapport on day one with baby. One potential disadvantage: Because family physicians have had less training and experience in pediatrics than their pediatrician colleagues, they may be less practiced in fielding common new parent questions, and less proficient at spotting (or treating) uncommon problems. This might mean more referrals to other doctors. However, the more babies an FP sees, the more pediatric know-how he or she is likely to have built up, minimizing this potential downside.

What Kind of Practice Is Perfect?

Decisions, decisions—and here's another one on your list: What type of practice will best fit your needs, and your baby's?

The solo practitioner. Like the idea of one doctor, all the time? Then a solo practitioner might be right up your alley. The most obvious perk of a solo practitioner: You and your little one will have the chance to develop a close relationship with one doctor (which can mean fewer tears and fears at checkup time). The flip side of this perk: Solo practitioners aren't likely to be on call around the clock and around the calendar. They'll be around for scheduled appointments (unless called to an emergency), and on call most of the time, but even the most dedicated among them will take vacations and occasional nights and weekends off, leaving a covering physician in charge (a doctor you and your little one may not know, or at least probably won't know very well). The way to cash in on the upside of a solo practitioner while minimizing the downside? Find out who covers for the doctor you're considering and whether your little one's records will be accessible even when the doctor is not.

The partnership. Often, two doctors are better than one. If one isn't on call, the other almost always is. If you see them in rotation, you and your baby will be able to build a relationship and a comfort level with both. The potential downside, which can also be a potential upside? Though partners will probably agree on most major issues and will likely share similar philosophies of practice, they may sometimes offer different opinions—and advice. Having two points of view (say, on a sleep problem or a feeding issue) can be confusing, but it can also be enlightening. One doc's tips didn't cut the colic? Maybe the other's will.

Before you settle on a partnership practice, ask whether or not scheduling checkups with your doctor of choice will be an option. If not, and if you discover you (or your baby) prefer one to the other, you may spend half of the visits with Baby Doctor Not-So-Right. Of course, even if you get your choice for checkups, sick kids are usually seen based on doctor availability.

The group practice. If two are good, will three or more be better? In some ways probably yes—in others, possibly no. A group is more likely to be able to provide 24-hour coverage by doctors in the practice, but less likely to ensure close doctor-patient relationships—again, unless you can schedule the same doctor or two for regular checkups (most practices offer this option). The more physicians a child will be exposed to on well-child and sick-call visits, the longer it may take to feel comfortable with each one, though this will be much less of a problem if all the doctors score high on warmth, caring, and baby charm. Also a factor here: The more doctors, the more opinions and

advice—sometimes a perk, sometimes a potential problem.

A combined practice. Any of the above types of practices may include one or more highly trained and skilled pediatric practitioners who aren't pediatricians. Pediatric nurse practitioners (PNP) are the equivalent of the nurse-midwife in the obstetrician's office—they hold a BSN or RN with additional training (generally at the master's degree level) in pediatrics. Pediatric physician's assistants (PA), who work under the supervision of a physician, spend 2 years training at an accredited program after completing college. A PNP or PA usually handles well-baby checkups and often the treatment of minor illnesses as well, consulting with physician colleagues as needed. Problems beyond the scope of a PNP or a PA are referred to one of the doctors in the office. Like a midwife, a PNP or PA will frequently spend more time on each visit—which means more time for questions and answers (something you'll really appreciate as a new parent). Having them on your baby's health care team will also help keep costs and wait times down. Concerned that you'll have less confidence in the care your baby receives from a PNP or PA? You probably don't have to be. Studies have shown that nurse practitioners and physician's assistants are, on average, at least as successful as, and sometimes more successful than, physicians at diagnosing and treating minor illnesses. Another welcome addition to any pediatric practice if you'll be breastfeeding: a certified lactation consultant on staff.

Finding Dr. Right

Once you've narrowed your field to the right type of practice, it's time to get serious in your search for Baby Doctor Right—and the right doctor

Topics to Discuss

Found Doctor Right? You may not have delivered yet, but you probably have plenty of baby-centric questions swirling around in your head. While you can certainly save a few questions for your first visit with your little bundle (keeping in mind that the bundle may be screaming through that entire first visit), some docs are more than happy to go through a Q&A session before delivery. This can be especially helpful because some of the issues you'll probably want to discuss may come up at or soon after delivery. Here are some topics to consider discussing:

Your obstetrical history and family health history. What impact will these have on your new baby's health?

Hospital procedures. Ask: Any thoughts on cord blood banking and delayed cord clamping? Which tests and immunizations are routine after birth? How will jaundice be handled? How long is the recommended hospital stay? What procedures need to be taken care of if you plan to deliver at home?

Circumcision. What are the pros and cons? Who should perform the procedure and when, if you do opt for it? Will pain relief be given to baby?

Breastfeeding. If, after the first visit's breastfeeding assessment, you're still having difficulty nursing (or just want a reassessment of your technique and progress), can an extra office visit at one or two weeks postpartum be arranged? Is there an LC in office, or one you can be referred to?

Bottle-feeding. Whether you will be formula feeding, supplementing with formula, or expressing milk for bottles, you might want to ask what type of bottles, nipples, and formula the doctor recommends.

Baby supplies and equipment. Get recommendations on health supplies such as acetaminophen, thermometers, and diaper rash ointment, and equipment such as car seats.

---

usually comes with the right recommendations. Here's where to look for those referrals:

Your obstetrician or midwife. Happy with the prenatal care you're getting? Then you'll likely be just as happy with a pediatric practitioner suggested by your ob or midwife. After all, doctors usually refer patients to other doctors with similar styles and philosophies. Not a fan of your prenatal provider? Look elsewhere for a recommendation.

An obstetric or pediatric nurse, a doula, or a lactation consultant. These professionals get an insider's perspective on doctors, so tap into any you know who work with pediatricians, in either an office or a hospital setting. You're likely to get a pretty accurate—and honest—assessment of the care they provide.

Parents. No one can tell you more about a doctor's bedside (or exam table–side) manner than satisfied (or dissatisfied) patients—or, in this case, parents of patients. So ask parents you know—especially those you know who are like-minded when it comes to hot button topics that matter a lot to you, such as breastfeeding, nutrition, alternative therapies, or attachment parenting.

Online medical directories. The American Medical Association website's DoctorFinder.com provides basic professional information, such as credentials, specialty, location, and training, on the majority of licensed physicians in the United States. Medical websites often offer searchable doctor directories, as do most professional associations for medical specialties, such as the American Academy of Pediatrics (healthychildren.org). Just remember that these directories give you only names, not ratings or information on a doctor's quality of care.

Referral services. Some hospitals, medical groups, and entrepreneurs have set up referral services to supply the names of doctors in specific specialties. You probably won't get a good read on personality, practice style, or philosophies on parenting practices from these kinds of services, but they will provide information on where doctors you're considering have hospital privileges, as well as on specialties, training, and board certification. Such services will also be able to tell you whether the doctor you have in mind has been sued for malpractice.

There are also plenty of online lists, referral sites, and user generated ratings for local doctors. Just type your city's name and "pediatrician" in a search engine and you'll get plenty of hits. Or, check out reviewing websites. One caveat when reading reviews on rating websites: You don't know the reviewers (or any potential beef they might have with a particular provider), so it's hard to get a true sense of who the doctor is and what his or her expertise, quality of care, and personality is really like. Plus, many of these sites contain inaccuracies (from where the doctor trained to what types of insurance the office accepts)—so be prepared to confirm details through your own research, too.

La Leche League. If breastfeeding is a priority, your local La Leche chapter (lllusa.org) can supply you with names of pediatricians who can offer you the support and know-how you'll need. Some pediatricians have certified lactation consultants on staff.

Health insurance provider. Your HMO or health insurance provider will likely give you a list of physicians available to you under your insurance plan— which may narrow down the field quite a bit if you're not prepared to go out of network.

Making Sure Baby Dr. Right Is Right for You

So you have a list of names—and now you're ready for the next steps: narrowing it down to an even shorter short list, and scheduling consultation appointments with the finalists, if possible. Some doctors charge for these visits, others don't. Either way, a late-pregnancy meet-and-greet will help you feel confident that you've found that special someone (or group of someones)—the doctor (or doctors) who's right for you and your baby-to-be.

Here are some key factors to consider:

Hospital affiliation. It's a definite plus if the doctor you choose is affiliated with a nearby hospital that has a good reputation for pediatric care. That way, he or she can provide or coordinate care if your little one ever has to be hospitalized or receive emergency treatment. Also a perk: If that doctor has privileges at the hospital where you are planning to deliver, he or she can check your baby out before discharge. But affiliation should definitely not be a deal breaker for an otherwise top-notch candidate. A staff pediatrician can perform the hospital exam and arrange for discharge, and you can take your baby to see the chosen doctor after you've checked out.

Credentials. A must-have for any doctor you're considering for your baby's care: a residency in pediatrics or family medicine and board certification by either the American Board of Pediatrics (ABP) or the American Board of Family Practice (ABFP).

Office location. Lugging a size-42 belly with you everywhere you go may seem like heavy lifting now, but it's traveling light compared with what you'll be toting after delivery. Going the distance will require more planning than just hopping behind the wheel of your car or onto a bus or subway. And the farther you have to go, especially in nasty weather, the more complicated every outing will become, including those trips to the doctor. Factor in an illness or injury, and a nearby office isn't just convenient—it can mean faster care for your little bundle. Your favorite candidate by far isn't the closest one? Baby Doctor Right may be worth the trip.

Office hours. Working 9 to 5? Then you'll probably prefer a doctor who offers some early morning, evening, or weekend hours.

Office atmosphere. You'll get your first impression of a doctor's office before you've even stepped inside. When you called for an appointment, were you treated to a voice that was eager to help or one that can't be bothered? Remember, you'll be on that line often as a new parent—phone friendliness matters, and compassion counts. You'll gain more insight when you step up to the front desk of the doctor's office. Is the front desk staff warm and welcoming, or frosty and brusque? Are

little patients (and their parents) treated patiently? Or with equal parts annoyance and exasperation? Read between those lines—and you'll learn volumes.

Office decor. A baby doctor needs more than a couple of magazines on the table and a few tasteful prints on the wall to make the right design statement in the waiting room. On your consult visit, look for features that will make long waits less painful for both you and your expected: a fish tank, a comfortable play area, a selection of clean, well-maintained toys and books appropriate for a range of ages, low chairs or other sitting space designed for little bodies. Walls painted in bold colors and child-friendly patterns (orange kangaroos and yellow tigers rather than understated earth tones) and bright pictures also score comfort points with the smaller set. A welcome addition in the family doctor's office: separate waiting areas for adults only and adults with children, as well as separate entrances for well visits and sick visits.

Waiting time. A 45-minute wait when you're pacing with a fussy infant or trying to distract a restless toddler with yet another picture book can be a trying experience for everyone. If you're running on a tight schedule yourself, an inconveniently long wait may also be a logistical nightmare. Keep in mind, though, that squirmy babies and sick kids are (and should be) given priority over consults with expectant parents—so don't judge the average waiting time by how long you're kept waiting. Instead poll the parents in the waiting room (and ask how much of the waiting generally goes on in the exam room, too—since that wait can be the hardest of all).

A long average wait can be a sign of an inefficiently run office, of overbooking, or of a doctor's having more patients than he or she can handle.

But it can also mean that the doctor or doctors in the office spend more time with their patients (or answering parent questions) than allotted—something you're likely to appreciate more during the exam than during the wait. It can also mean that it's office policy to squeeze in sick kids (or phone calls with worried parents) even when there's no room in the schedule—something you're sure to value when your child is the one who's sick or you're the parent who's worried.

House calls. Yes, a few pediatricians and family practitioners still make them, though often at a premium cost. Most of the time, however, house calls aren't only unnecessary, they aren't best for baby. At the office, a doctor can use equipment and perform tests that can't be stashed in a little black bag. Still, situations may come up when a house call may be just what the doctor ordered—say, when your preschooler is home from preschool with a bad stomach bug, baby's down with a high fever and a chesty cough, and you're on duty at home alone . . . in a snowstorm.

Call-ins. There will be times (probably more than you'll want to count in that first year) when questions and concerns come up, and you just don't feel comfortable waiting for an answer or some reassurance until baby's next scheduled visit. Enter the phone call—or in more and more practices, email or text. Different offices handle parent calls differently, so be sure to ask about this very important protocol. One approach is the call-in hour: A particular time is set aside each day for the doctor to field calls and/or texts or emails—which means you're pretty much assured of getting the advice you need, if you call at the designated time. Other offices use a call-back system—the doctor (or PA or PNP) will call back

to answer questions when there's a free moment between patients or at the very end of the day (questions are usually screened and prioritized by the staff). This approach may work better than a call-in hour if you suspect you'll be the type of parent who can't confine concerns to between 7 and 8 in the morning or 11 and noon, or can't contemplate waiting until tomorrow's call hour for relief from today's worries. Still other pediatric offices use on-call nurses to answer common questions and dispense advice, passing only urgent or complicated medical issues to the doctor. Nurses can also "triage" the situation, helping a parent decide whether the baby should be brought in for an office visit and how soon. This system usually yields a prompter response (and faster relief for parental stress).

Protocol for emergencies. Emergencies happen—and as a soon-to-be parent you'll want to know how they're handled by a doctor you're considering. Some instruct parents to head to the ER for care in case of an emergency (though your insurance plan may require that you call the doctor first). Others ask you to call their office first and, depending on the nature of the illness or injury, will see your baby in the office or meet you at the ER. Some physicians are available (unless they're out of town) days, nights, and weekends for emergencies. Others use colleagues or partners to cover for them during off-hours, and some may refer you to Urgent Care as appropriate.

Financial matters. Some offices ask that you make any necessary payments or co-payments at the time of a visit, others will issue a bill. Some will bill insurance for you or submit paperwork, others won't. Some offer an optional package deal for first-year care that covers any number of visits. Though the package costs more than the sum of fees for the year's scheduled number of checkups, it's usually a good bet: Two or three sick visits, and you'll likely come out even or ahead (plus you'll stress less about the cost of extra appointments). Insurance reimbursements for sick visits, package deal or no, will be handled according to the terms of your coverage.

Payment schedules are also available in some offices, either routinely or under special circumstances, such as financial hardship. If you think you might need such an arrangement, discuss this with whoever is in charge of billing.

You might also want to ask whether routine lab work is done in the office, which can save time and money.

Practice style—and personality. When you're in the market for a doctor, as when you're shopping for baby furniture, the style that's right will depend on your style. Do you prefer a doctor who's laid-back and casual (maybe even a hugger)? Or one who's buttoned up (and in a dress shirt, at that)? One who's a kidder (even with parents) or

one who's all business? A doctor who likes to call all the shots or one who treats you as a full-fledged partner in your little one's care?

No matter what your style in doctor styles, chances are you'll want to pick a pediatrician or family physician who's a good listener and a clear communicator, who's open to all questions and who's nonjudgmental, who's patient with little patients and their parents, and most of all, seems to really love caring for children . . . which, of course, most baby doctors do.

Philosophy. You won't agree with your baby's doctor on every topic, but it's best to find out up front (and before you make a commitment) whether you're mainly on the same page with major issues. To make sure your baby care philosophies mesh comfortably with those of the doctor who may be caring for your baby, ask about his or her positions on parenting topics or trends you might be interested in, from breastfeeding to circumcision, attachment parenting to co-sleeping, complementary and alternative medicine to immunizations.

CHAPTER 2

Buying for Baby

Y ou've probably been itching to belly up to the nearest baby superstore or online baby registry for months now—maybe even before you had a belly. After all, those too-cute onesies (is that a matching hat and socks?), cuddly stuffed animals, and magical mobiles are hard to resist. But between the slings, swings, and strollers, the cribs and car seats, the burping cloths and blankies, the bibs and booties, buying for baby can get a little overwhelming (make that head-spinning), not to mention credit-card-maxing. So before you start sliding that card (or clicking "register now"), be sure to read up on baby gear must-haves, nice-to-haves, and probably-don't-needs, so you can stock your little one's nursery without cluttering it up—and without cleaning out your bank account.

Buying the Baby Basics

With so many products to buy and register for, you may be tempted just to grab a virtual shopping cart and get started. But before you proceed to checkout, check out these baby buying guidelines:

- Do your homework before you bring products home. Babies tend to bring out the impulse buyer in everyone— but especially in starry-eyed first-time expectant parents (and particularly in hormone-hazy moms-to-be). To avoid buyer's remorse (when you realize that a newborn's bottom is warm

enough without prewarmed wipes or that 41 newborn onesies were probably 31 too many or that you didn't really need Hollywood's favorite jogging stroller when you don't ever plan on jogging in Hollywood—or anywhere), think and link before you buy. Read online reviews, do comparison shopping, and tap into your most in-the-know network, other parents— including those on WhatToExpect .com. They'll tell you like it is, and isn't, when it comes to much-hyped and high-priced products and product features.

■ Shop for the right registry (or registries). Before you narrow down your layette list, narrow down the list of stores where you'll be buying or registering for most of those goodies. Consider return policies (because you may end up with too much of a good thing—or find that some good things aren't so good after all), restocking charges, whether purchases and exchanges can be made both online and in stores, and convenience (is there a brick-and-mortar store close to you and most of your friends and family?). But also ask around—your message board and Facebook buddies who've shopped this way before will be your best registry resources (or even have lists of their own must-haves they've shared—check out the "Love-it Lists" at whattoexpect.com/loveit. Though you may not be able to find one-stop shopping for all your baby needs, try to keep your registries down to a reasonable two or three by looking for sites or stores that carry most of what you're signing up for.

■ Shop for baby in baby steps. Start with newborn needs (that will be plenty). Hold off buying gear you won't need until later in your baby's first year, when you'll better know your needs and your little one's. (Though, consider registering for big ticket items anyway, even if you won't need them right away—especially if you're hoping friends and family will step up to the plate . . . and the high chair.) Decided to play the baby gender guessing game? Some stores will allow you to order your layette and not pick it up or have it delivered until after the baby is born—at which time you can specify the colors and patterns to make a more gender-specific statement, if you're not a fan of neutral shades. But also remember, there's no layette law that says girls can't wear blue overalls and boys pink polos—or that a girl's nursery can't reach for the stars (and planets) and a boy's can't feature bunnies.

■ Be a baby-stuff borrower. You're bringing home your own baby, of course, but that doesn't mean you can't bring home some of your friend's baby stuff. Or your cousin's. Or your sister's. Since babies need so much stuff (or really, parents need so much stuff to care for their babies), it makes sense—and saves dollars—to borrow what you can. All of the gear that really gets used will soon have a lived-in (or grown-out) look anyway, whether you borrow or buy new (that's definitely true of clothes). Just keep in mind that safety regulations change and that you should check out any product for recalls or features that don't meet current standards. A car seat is one item that's definitely safest bought brand new.

A Buyer's Guide

Ready to lay out a bundle for your little bundle's layette and nursery? It's true that your tiny baby—who will arrive in the world equipped with nothing but a birthday suit—will be a whole lot more high-maintenance in the next 12 months than he or she was in the past 9. But before you get overwhelmed by the lists of clothes, supplies, gear, and furniture that follow, remember they're

Wardrobe Wise

The best thing about shopping for baby clothes: They're so cute. The worst thing about shopping for baby clothes: They're so cute. Before you know it, you've bought out the store (and then another store, and another store), and the nursery closet is jam-packed and the dresser drawers won't close. And your baby has outgrown half of those oh-so-precious purchases before you even had a chance to unfold them for the first time. To avoid buy, buy, buying too much for baby, keep these practical pointers in mind as you finalize your layette list and head to the store or enter that portal:

- Babies don't mind wearing hand-me-downs. Fast-forward 7 or 8 years, and hand-me-down clothes may be a much tougher sell—but fashion ignorance is bliss for babies. Even if you're a stickler for style, you'll appreciate having even less-than-styling onesies and rompers standing by for those days when spit-up reigns, diapers leak . . . and the washer's on the blink. Those hand-me-downs are a little worse for wear? That's okay—the same will be true of the new clothes you're shelling out those big bucks for by the second time baby wears them. So before you shoot down all those offers you may be lucky enough to get, consider just saying yes instead. And don't forget to check off items borrowed or handed down before finalizing your list.

- Laundry has a way of piling up. When calculating your needs, consider how many times a week you'll be doing laundry. If you'll be doing loads just about every day, you can buy the smallest suggested number of items on the list—and that goes for cloth diapers, too. If you'll have to lug loads down to the local Suds 'n Spin and can do laundry only weekly, then buy the largest number.

- Convenience and comfort come first, cuteness second (really). Tiny buttons may be way too precious for words, but the struggle to fasten them when baby's squirming up a storm won't be. An organdy party dress may look festive on the hanger, but the party may be over if it rubs baby's delicate skin the wrong way. An imported sailor suit may look dashing—that is, until you try to change your little matey and find there's no access to the poop deck. And baby skinny jeans? Well, enough said.

just meant to guide you. Don't feel compelled to buy (or borrow) everything on these lists, or everything on any registry or layette list—certainly not all at once. Your baby's needs (and yours) will be unique and ever evolving (just like you and your baby).

Baby Clothes

By far the most fun you'll have preparing for baby will be shopping for those itty-bitty, crazy-cute clothes. In fact, it may take considerable reserves of willpower to keep yourself from overfilling your baby's closet with too many adorable outfits. Just keep in mind—less is usually more than enough, especially when it comes to small sizes, since newborns grow fast.

Undershirts, onesies (aka creepers, bodysuits). For your newborn, your best bets are undershirts (short or long sleeved, depending on the weather)

So, resist the irresistible (and impractical, unwashable, and unwearable) and remember that babies are happiest when they're comfiest, and parents are happiest when dressing baby is a dream, not a drag. With this in mind, look for outfits made of soft, easy-care fabrics, with snaps instead of buttons (inconvenient, and should baby manage to chew or pry one off, unsafe), head openings that are roomy (or have snaps at the neck), and bottoms that open conveniently for diaper changing. Feel underneath to make sure seams are smooth, too. Room for growth is another important feature: Adjustable shoulder straps, stretch fabrics, and elasticized waistlines will come in handy. Shop for safety, also—no strings or ribbons longer than 6 inches.

- Shopping up is smart. Since newborns don't stay newborn size very long (some babies have grown out of newborn sizes before they're born), don't stock up on small sizes unless your baby is predicted petite. It's always more practical to roll up sleeves and pants legs for a few weeks while your little one grows into a size 6 months. In general, shop at least one size ahead (most 6-month-old babies wear 9- or 12-month sizes, and some even fill out 18-month sizes), but eyeball before buying, because some styles (particularly imported ones) can run much larger or smaller than average. When in doubt, buy big, keeping this in mind: Children grow and (cotton) clothes shrink.

- Seasons change. If baby is expected on the cusp of a season, buy just a few tiny items for the immediate weather and larger ones for the weather expected in the months ahead. Continue to consider the seasons as baby grows—and do the season math when buying ahead. That adorable August-perfect tank top at half price may seem like a total deal—until you realize that your fall baby will have outgrown it long before spring's thaw.

- No tags, and you're (keeping) it. Of course, you're eager to unpack all that new baby booty into your baby's new dresser. But try to resist. It's actually best to keep most of your newborn's clothes tagged or in their original packages (with all receipts). That way, if baby checks in much larger or much tinier than expected (it happens)—or even a different gender than anticipated (ditto)—you can exchange for bigger or smaller sizes or a different color or pattern.

that open in the front, with snaps on the sides. These are easier to get on that floppy frame in the first few weeks, and until your baby's umbilical stump falls off, it's better not to have tight clothes rubbing against it. Another option: a onesie with a specially designed opening at the navel to expose the stump to air and prevent rubbing. Once the stump does fall off, you can switch to the pullover onesie style, which is smoother and more comfortable for baby. These one-piece bodysuits (also called creepers) have snap openings on the bottom for easy diaper access and don't ride up, keeping tummies covered in cool weather. Look for a wide opening at the neck for easy on, easy off. Once style starts to matter more, you can graduate to bodysuits that look more like shirts (long or short sleeved), made to be worn under pants, skirts, or leggings. For now, consider buying 5 to 10 undershirts (newborn size) and 7 to 10 onesies.

Stretchies with feet. Footed outfits keep tootsies toasty without socks, making them especially practical (as you'll soon find out, socks and booties—cute as they are—rarely stay put for long). Make sure they have snaps or zippers at the crotch for easy access to baby's bottom, which you'll be visiting quite often. Otherwise, you'll be undressing and redressing at every diaper change. You may find that zippers have the edge, since they'll save you the frustration of trying to line up all those little snaps when you're sleep-deprived or in a rush, or baby's crying for a feed. Consider buying around 7 footed stretchies.

Rompers. These are one-piece, short- or long-sleeved outfits with or without legs that typically snap at the crotch and down the legs. Consider buying 3 to 6.

Two-piece outfits. These are smart-looking but not as sensible as one-piece (two pieces are twice as tricky to put on and take off), so try to limit yourself—it will be hard!—to 1 or 2 of them. Look for two-piecers that snap together at the waist so the pants don't slide down and the shirt doesn't ride up.

Nightgowns with elastic bottoms. While stretchies can also stand in as sleepwear, some parents prefer nightgowns for their babies, especially in the early weeks, when the easy-open bottoms make those middle-of-the-night diaper changes a snap (without the snaps). Consider buying 3 to 6 nightgowns—and avoid gowns that close at the bottom with drawstrings (strings over 6 inches are a safety hazard). Sleepwear for children must meet federal standards for flame resistance—a label will tell you whether or not a particular outfit is designated as safe-for-sleep or not.

Blanket sleepers or sleep sacks. These sleepers keep baby cuddly warm without a comforter or blanket (which should be avoided because of the risk of suffocation or SIDS; see page 270). These wearable blankets provide plenty of kicking and arm-waving room and can keep a baby cozy during those nights when a stretchy or nightgown doesn't provide enough warmth. They come in lightweight cotton (for summer nights when the AC is on) and fleece (for winter sleeping—though to avoid overheating be sure not to dress your baby too warmly underneath the sleep sack). Consider buying 2 to 3 seasonally appropriate ones.

Sweaters. One lightweight sweater will do the trick for a warm-weather baby, 1 to 2 heavier ones will be needed if baby's arriving in winter. Look for sweaters (or sweatshirts or hoodies, but without strings) that are washable and dryable as well as easy on, easy off.

Hats. Summer babies need at least 1 lightweight hat with a brim (for sun protection). Winter babies need 1 or more heavier-weight hats to stay warm (a lot of the body's heat escapes through the head, and since a baby's head is disproportionately large, there's a lot of potential for heat loss). Hats should be shaped to cover the ears snugly but not too tightly. Another outdoor accessory to consider for an older baby: good-quality sunglasses (see page 456 for more).

Bunting bag or snowsuit with attached mitts, for a late fall or winter baby living in a four-season climate. A bunting bag is easier on, easier off than a snowsuit (no trying to negotiate feet into leg holes), but it may have to be retired once baby is more active. Some buntings convert into snowsuits. Any bunting you use should have a slot on the bottom for a car seat strap, to make buckling up easier and more secure.

Booties or socks. As you'll soon find out, these are often kicked off within moments after they're put on (something you probably won't notice until you're halfway down the street or on the other side of the mall), so look for styles that promise to stay put. You'll need just 5 to 6 pairs for starters—add more as baby grows.

Bibs. Even before you introduce your sweetie to sweet potatoes, you'll need bibs to protect clothes from spit-up and drool. Consider buying a minimum of 3 bibs—you'll always have at least one in the laundry basket.

Baby's Linens

Soft against baby's skin is a given, but here are some other practical hints for choosing the right linens. You'll notice that bumpers and crib blankets and comforters don't make this list at all—that's because none of them are recommended for use in a baby's crib or other sleeping area.

Fitted sheets for crib, portable crib, bassinet, and/or carriage. Whatever colors and patterns you choose, when it comes to sheets, size matters. For safety's sake, sheets should fit very snugly, so they can't get loose in the crib. You'll need around 3 to 4 of each size—especially if your baby spits up a lot and you're changing the sheets often. You might also consider half sheets that tie or snap on to the crib bars and go on top of the fitted sheet. It's easier to change just the half sheet than to take up the hard to remove fitted sheet. Be sure the half sheets are securely attached. Also for safety's sake, don't use any top sheets or other loose bedding.

Waterproof pads. How many pads you'll need will depend on how many surfaces in your home will need protecting:

think crib (put the pad under the mattress cover), carriage, furniture, laps. At a minimum you'll want 1 to 2.

Quilted mattress pads for crib. Again, the fit should be very snug. And skip the kinds that have plush tops. Two pads should be enough (one to use when the other's in the wash).

Blankets for carriage or stroller. Blankets are fine to use over a baby who's buckled into a car seat or stroller (or a baby who's otherwise being supervised). But don't use any blankets on your baby during sleep (except for that swaddler or sack), since loose bedding of any kind is a SIDS risk factor. It's much safer to rely on sleep sacks or other toasty sleepwear to keep your little one comfortably warm. Buy 1 to 2 blankets and you're covered.

Towels and washcloths. Hooded towels are best, since they keep baby's head warm after a bath (and weren't you eyeing that one with the puppy ears anyway?), and wash mitts are easier to use than standard cloths (plus they're often cuter). Look for soft towels and washcloths, and consider buying 2 or 3 towels and 3 to 5 washcloth mitts.

Burp cloths, for protecting your shoulders when burping baby, for emergency bibs, and much more. A dozen burping cloths are a good start. If you find you're going through many more because your little one has proven to be a big-time spitter, you can always add to your collection.

Receiving/swaddling blankets, swaddlers with velcro, or zip-up pods. Most newborns like being swaddled right from the start, especially during sleep, which is one reason hospitals routinely bundle them in receiving (or swaddling) blankets. See page 169 for tips on how to swaddle your baby safely—and keep in mind there are many easier alternatives to do-it-yourself swaddles, from velcro wraps (some secure baby's arms with swaddle "wings" within the swaddler) to snug zip-up pods (two-way zippers allow you to access the diaper region without unswaddling baby) to hybrid swaddle sacks (swaddle on top, sack on the bottom). Since you may have to do some switching around to see what type works best for you and your baby, don't overbuy. Also remember to check the weight minimums and maximums for a swaddler (a very small baby needs to grow into certain kinds—and a very large baby may outgrow them all in no time). You probably won't need more than 4 swaddlers, total.

Diapers

So, it's a given your baby will need diapers and lots of them—but the question is, which kind? From several subgroups of cloth to a bewildering range of disposables, there are ever-more entries in the diaper derby, but no conclusive winners. How will you choose the diaper that best fits your baby's bottom (and your bottom line)? First, check out the options:

Disposable diapers. They're the first choice of parents by far, and there are plenty of reasons why. Among the perks: Disposables are convenient to reach for and a cinch to change (even for brand new parents), plus they're easy on the go (you can dump dirty diapers in the trash instead of carting them back home for laundry or pickup). What's more, since they're ultra-absorbent and have an inner liner that keeps wetness away from baby's tender skin, they don't have to be changed as often as cloth diapers (a change for the better, some would say). The extra absorbency and snugger fit also makes them less prone to leaks.

Of course, there's a flip side to these favored features. For one thing, a super-absorbent diaper can lead to too-infrequent changes, which can lead to rashes. For another, when fluid is soaked up so efficiently, it's harder to gauge how much your little one is peeing—making it tougher to judge whether he or she is getting enough to eat. (Much) later on, the ultra-absorbency in disposables can make potty training trickier: Because toddlers are less likely to feel wet and uncomfortable, they may not be as quick to say bye-bye to diapers. Having to shop for and lug the diapers home is also a potential disadvantage, but this drawback can be avoided if you order online.

Another con is price. While cloth diapers come with a greater initial investment, they're way cheaper over the long haul than disposables. (And heads up: It will definitely be a long haul before your tot is out of diapers.) Something else to add to the con list: If you pull too hard, the tabs on some disposables can easily rip (and inevitably it'll happen when you're on the run and you're down to the last diaper). Also on the minus side: Disposable diapers definitely aren't the greenest way to manage your baby's BM—disposables account for 3.4 million tons of landfill waste per year and don't decompose. (There are some disposable insert liners that are flushable and biodegradable. You use them with nondisposable covers, so they're like a hybrid diaper.)

Wondering about going green when it comes to disposable diapers? While there are no conclusive studies to show that any of the chemicals (such as dioxin), chlorine, dyes, and gels that lurk in traditional disposables are harmful, a few babies can have allergic reactions to some of that stuff. Choosing from the (small) array of truly greener disposable varieties can potentially help avoid such allergies and help you feel better about doing your part for the environment. But there are many shades of green, so you'll have to do your homework before settling on one brand. Some diapers that claim to be environmentally friendly actually contain chemical gels, chlorine, or plastic. Others contain corn or wheat, which can be allergenic for some babies. And still others are either not biodegradable at all or are only 60 percent compostable. Better than zero percent, certainly, but important to factor in. You'll also want to try out a few brands until you find one that works for you and your little one's bottom, since some green disposables aren't top notch when it comes to poop control. One last consideration: These "eco-friendly" disposables are typically not wallet-friendly.

Cloth diapers. Available in cotton, terry cloth, or flannel, cloth baby diapers can come either as prefolded pieces of cloth liners or as all-in-ones (diapers and covers that look similar to a disposable diaper). Unless you're using a diaper service (which rents out cloth diapers, washes them, and delivers clean ones to your door), cloth diapers will save you some money compared to disposable diapers for the same amount of time. If you're worried about the dyes and gels used in some disposables, or want to diaper "green," cloth diapers are the way to go. Another consideration: Since cloth diapers are less absorbent than disposables, you'll need to change diapers more often (a con if you consider diaper changing a chore, a pro if you find more frequent changes results in fewer rashes). Another plus: Potty training (when the time comes) may be easier to accomplish, since cloth-bottomed tots are likely to notice wetness sooner—a possible incentive for graduating to underpants.

The downside to cloth diapers, however, is that they can be messy, although some come with disposable liners that make them easier to clean, and they're more cumbersome to change, unless you use the all-in-ones (which are more expensive and take a lot longer to dry). You'll be doing more laundry, too—probably 2 to 3 extra loads per week—and that means higher utility bills. If you use diaper companies to launder the cloths, remember they'll be using plenty of chlorine to disinfect them, so they're not the completely chemical-free option, either. And, unless you're using disposables when you're out, you'll probably have to carry a few poopy (and smelly) diapers back home with you. Something else to keep in mind: Many cloth diapers aren't that absorbent initially, thanks to their natural materials, so it'll take a number of washings in hot water (at least 5 or 6) before they reach optimal absorbency.

Have a fear of diaper commitment? Some parents decide to use cloth diapers for the first few months—a time when a baby usually spends more time at home than on the go—and then graduate to disposables as the logistics of toting cloth become too much like hard work. Others do the diaper combo right from the start—cloth when they're convenient, disposables when they're not (or at bedtime, when greater absorbency can spell a better night's sleep).

Also, prepare to . . . yes . . . go with the flow when it comes to your diaper selection. Some babies end up with a sensitivity or even an allergy to a certain type of disposable diaper, other babies may just be the kind of heavy wetter or messy pooper that's just not easily contained by cloth. It's always possible you'll be ready for a change of diapers after you've logged in a couple of months of diaper changes.

The Bottom Line on Cloth Diapers

Trying to get to the bottom of which cloth diapers will best fit your baby's bottom—and your needs? Here's a little Cloth Diaper 101:

Flats and prefolds. These plain pieces of cotton fabric (similar to the cloth diapers your great-grandparents used on your grandparents) may look simple to use (and they're certainly the cheapest cloth diapers around), but they require some skill: You need to fold the square or rectangular cloth just so to fit your baby's bottom, fasten it with separate snaps or pins (not so easy when you've got a wee wiggler on your hands) or lay baby in a wrap-style cover, then cover it with a waterproof diaper cover (if you're using pins or snaps) to avoid leaks.

Contoured. No folding required with these diapers that have an hourglass shape meant to fit your baby's bum better. Like flats and prefolds, you'll have to fasten them with separate snaps or pins or a wraparound cover and add a waterproof cover to protect against leaks.

Fitted. Fitted cloth diapers look similar to the disposable kind and have built-in snaps, hooks, or velcro to fasten them around your baby's tush. And thanks to the elastic around the waist and legs, these diapers fit more securely than prefolds or contoured cloth diapers—which could mean fewer leaks. You still have to use a separate waterproof cover, though.

All-in-ones. All-in-ones (aka AIOs) have elastic around the waist and legs, have built-in snaps, hooks, or velcro to fasten them, and come in cute colors and designs. Plus, there's no need for a separate cover, because the waterproof material is sewn right over the absorbent cloth lining (that's why they're called all-in-ones). They're a relative breeze to use—no diapers to fold or separate covers to add—and are great at keeping the mess inside (instead of trickling down baby's leg), but convenience comes at a price. Washing and drying them can also be more time-consuming (and expensive) because of their multiple layers.

Pocket diapers. Like all-in-ones, pocket diapers have an inner cloth lining and a waterproof outer lining (so no need for a separate cover), but there's a separate piece of fabric that you insert into the pocket of the diaper's inner lining. The benefit: It's much easier to adjust to your baby's wetting needs (you can add extra liners to increase absorbency).

All-in-twos. These diapers are similar to pocket diapers, except the diaper insert goes directly against your baby's skin (you either snap or lay it in). That way, you can simply change out the insert instead of changing the entire diaper, making diapering a cinch. Another plus: Separating that layer from the rest of the diaper makes for less time in the dryer—and lower energy costs.

Doublers and liners. Cloth doublers are fabric inserts that provide extra protection, no matter which type of cloth diaper you're using (even pocket diapers). Doublers are great overnight and during long naps, but they add bulk and restrict mobility, so you probably won't want to use them when your baby's awake and wriggling. Liners are biodegradable, flushable sheets of fabric or paper that fit any type of cloth diaper. While liners don't provide extra protection, they do make cleanup easier, especially once your baby's eating solids and his or her poop becomes stickier and harder to scrape off the diaper.

If you're using disposable diapers, buy one or two packages of the newborn size and then wait until after baby is born (so you'll know how big your baby is) before stocking up on more. Baby's born smaller than expected? You can quickly order or pick up a stash of preemie size. If you're using cloth diapers and plan to wash them yourself every three or so days, purchase 2 to 3 dozen (more if you'll be doing laundry less often), plus 2 dozen disposable diapers (once you know baby's size) so you can use them for outings and emergencies. If you're planning to use a diaper service, sign up in your eighth month and they will be ready to deliver as soon as you do.

Baby's Grooming Supplies

Babies smell pretty terrific naturally, they stay pretty clean (at least, initially), and as far as their grooming, they're pretty low maintenance. When you look for baby toiletries, less is more in number of products—you need far fewer than manufacturers and retailers would have you believe—and in number of product ingredients:

Baby bath wash, liquid or foam. To freshen up your baby at bath time, look for a gentle formulation baby bath wash. Some do convenient double duty as shampoo and body wash.

No-tears baby shampoo. For young infants, no-tears baby shampoo is best. The foam kind may be easier to control because it stays put.

Baby oil. This can come in handy if you need to gently clean a sticky poop off a sore bottom. It's also often prescribed for cradle cap. But no need to use it routinely or to cover your baby in the stuff—remember, oiled-up babies are slippery babies.

Ointment or cream for diaper rash. Most diaper rash creams or ointments are the barrier kind—meaning they act as a barrier between baby's tender tush and the harsh ingredients in pee and poop. Ointments go on clear, while creams (especially those that contain zinc oxide) usually smear on white. The creams, which are thicker than the ointments, tend to provide better protection against—or even act to prevent—diaper rash. Some brands also contain other soothing ingredients such as aloe or lanolin.

It's always best to try a brand out before you start stocking up—some work better for some babies than others.

Petroleum jelly, such as Vaseline. You can use this to lubricate some rectal thermometers (others require a water-based lubricant, such as K-Y Jelly or Astroglide). It can also be used as a diaper rash preventer, though not as a treatment for rash.

Diaper wipes, for diaper changes, hand washing on the go, cleanups after spit-ups and leaky diaper incidents, and dozens of other uses. There are also reusable cloth diaper wipes if you'd rather go green, or if your baby turns out to be allergic to certain brands. Thinking of buying a diaper-wipe warmer to go with? Though some parents swear by a warm wipe (especially on chilly nights), the bottom line is they're not a must-have. Bottoms are plenty warm without prewarmed wipes. Plus, some warmers dry the wipes out quickly. Another consideration if you're thinking about a warmer: Warm wipes are an easy habit for babies to buy into, and once they do, they may be reluctant to switch to straight-from-the-package.

Cotton balls, for washing baby's eyes and for cleaning that sweet bottom in the first few weeks. Skip the cotton swabs, since they aren't safe to use on a baby.

The Green Scene

Forget pink or blue. The hot color these days is green—at least when it comes to baby-care products. From organic shampoo to all-natural lotion, store shelves (and online shopping portals) are stocked with all things green for your little one. That's because many parents are understandably concerned about lathering up or rubbing their baby's soft and sweet-smelling skin with chemical additives and fragrances. But will you really need to shell out the big bucks for green products for your new bundle?

The good news is that it's easier and increasingly less expensive to keep your baby green or nearly so—especially as increased demand from parents is bringing supply and selection of green baby products up, and costs down. One example of this greening of baby care products: Many manufacturers have removed phthalates (chemicals that have been linked to problems in the endocrine and reproductive systems of infants) from shampoos and lotions. Other manufacturers have removed formaldehyde and 1.4 dioxane—two more ingredients that have come under scrutiny by environmental groups and concerned parents—as well as other possibly harmful chemicals, including parabens, from baby-care products.

Reading labels helps you be more selective about the products that touch your baby's brand new skin, whether you're screening for green or just concerned about ingredients that might be irritating. Choose ones that are alcohol-free (alcohol is drying to a baby's skin) and contain no (or the fewest possible) artificial colors or fragrances, preservatives, and other chemical additives (truly green ones will already have these boxes clearly checked off). And do your research, too, by checking out the Environmental Working Group's database at ewg.org/skindeep, which will tell you about the ingredients in the products you're thinking of using on your little one.

Another thing to keep in mind: It's not just chemicals that you may want to screen for when stocking up on baby-care products. If your baby has a skin condition or is allergic to nuts (perhaps there's a family history of nut allergy or your breastfed baby has had a reaction when you eat nuts), ask the doctor whether it's necessary to go nuts avoiding products that contain nuts (almond oil, for instance). Also be wary of any product that contains essential oils that may not be baby safe—again, the pediatrician will be your best resource in screening for those.

Baby nail scissors or clippers. Sharp adult nail scissors are too risky to wield on a squirmy baby—and those tiny nails grow faster than you'd think. Some clippers come with a built-in magnifier so it's easier to see what you're doing.

Baby brush and comb. Far from all babies have hair to brush or comb, so you may or may not end up needing these items in the first few months.

Baby tub. New babies are slippery when wet—not to mention squirmy. All of which can serve to unnerve even the most confident parents when it comes time for that first bath. To make sure it's fun and safe to rub-a-dub-dub when your infant's in the tub, invest in or borrow a baby tub—most are designed to follow a newborn's contours and offer support while preventing him or her from sliding under the water. They come in myriad styles: plastic, foam cushions, mesh sling, and so on. Some "grow" with your baby and can be used all the way through the toddler years (when placed in a regular bathtub).

When buying a baby tub, look for one that has a nonskid bottom (inside and out) and a smooth rounded edge that will retain its shape when filled with water (and baby), is easy to wash, has quick drainage, a roomy size (large enough for your baby at 4 or 5 months, as well as now), support for baby's head and shoulders, portability, and has a mildew-resistant foam pad (if applicable). Another option to the baby tub, at least initially, is a thick sponge specially designed to cushion the baby in a sink or a tub.

Baby's Medicine Cabinet

Here's one area where less isn't more—and less may actually not be enough. Because you never know when you might need one of the following items (and when you don't have it is when you're most likely to need it, Murphy's Law and all), err on the side of excess. Most important, store all of these items safely out of reach of infants and children:

Acetaminophen, such as Infant Tylenol, which can be used after age 2 months. You can use ibuprofen (Infant Advil, Infant Motrin) once your baby is older than 6 months.

Antibiotic ointment or cream, such as bacitracin or neomycin, for minor cuts and scrapes, if recommended by baby's doctor.

Hydrogen peroxide, for cleaning cuts. A nonstinging, nonaerosol spray that numbs or relieves pain as it cleans can make the job even easier.

Calamine lotion or hydrocortisone cream (0.5 percent), for mosquito bites and itchy rashes.

Electrolyte fluid (such as Pedialyte), for fluid replacement in the case of diarrhea. Use it only if your baby's doctor has specifically advised it he or she will let you know what the right dose is, depending on the age of your little one.

Sunscreen, recommended for babies of all ages (but don't rely on sunscreen to protect your newborn's extra tender skin—keep him or her out of direct sunlight, especially during seasonal peak hours).

Rubbing alcohol, for cleaning thermometers.

Calibrated spoon, dropper, medicine pacifier, and/or oral syringe, for administering medications (but always use the one that comes with a medication, when provided).

Bandages and gauze pads, in a variety of sizes and shapes.

Adhesive tape, for securing gauze pads.

Tweezers, for pulling out splinters.

Nasal aspirator. You'll definitely get to know and love this indispensable product, fondly known in baby-care circles as "the snot sucker." The traditional bulb syringe is inexpensive and works well for clearing a stuffy nose, so you probably won't need to spring for the battery-operated type. There are other kinds of nasal aspirators on the market, including one that gets its suction from you (through a tube you suck on).

Cool mist humidifier. If you choose to buy a humidifier, cool mist is the best (warm mist or steam humidifiers can lead to burns), but keep in mind that they must be cleaned thoroughly and regularly according to the manufacturer's directions to avoid the growth of mold and bacteria.

Thermometer. See page 543 for choosing and using a thermometer.

Heating pad and/or warm-water bottle, for soothing a colicky tummy or other ache—but be careful not to use one that gets hot and always wrap it in a cover or cloth diaper.

Baby Feeding Supplies

If you'll be breastfeeding exclusively, you're already equipped with your two most important supplies. Otherwise, you'll need to stock up on some or all of the following:

Bottles. BPA-free baby bottles and their nipples (all bottles and nipples are required by the Food and Drug Administration to be BPA-free; see page 341) come in a dizzying variety of shapes—from angle-necked bottles to ones with disposable liners, wide bottles to natural flow ones, orthodontic-shaped nipples to breast-shaped nipples, as well as a nipple that rolls as baby's head moves. Choosing the right bottle and nipple for your baby will be based on a combination of trial and error, recommendations from friends (and online reviewers), and your personal preference. Don't worry if the bottle you originally choose for how it looks and feels ends up being the wrong fit for your little one—just switch styles until the right one sticks (a good case for trying before you stock up). Choose from the following bottle styles:

- Standard bottles come with straight or curvy sides and can be made from BPA-free plastic, glass, or even stainless steel. Some bottles come with bottom valves that are supposed to minimize air intake during feeding—theoretically minimizing gas in your little cutie's tummy.

- Wide-neck bottles, which are shorter and fatter than standard bottles, are meant to be used with wider nipples so that they feel more like the breast to babies. There are also some wide-necked bottles that come with nipples that are shaped more like those on a breast. These bottles could be your go-to choice if you're doing the combo (breast and bottle).

- Angle-neck bottles are bent at the neck, making it easier for you to hold but potentially a little more difficult for your little one to hold once he or she starts grabbing at the bottle. The angle allows the breast milk or formula to collect at the nipple, making your baby less likely to swallow air. And though these bottles make it easier to feed your little one in a semi-upright position—especially important if he or she is prone to spitting up, gassiness, or ear infections—they can be more difficult to fill (you'll have to turn them sideways or use a funnel when pouring in liquid).

- Disposable-liner bottles have a rigid outer holder into which you slip disposable plastic liners (or pouches). As your baby drinks from the bottle, the liner collapses, leaving no space for air that might eventually find its way into your little one's tummy. After feeds, just toss the empty liner.

- Natural flow bottles have a straw-like vent in the center of the bottle aimed at eliminating air bubbles that could increase gassiness. The downside is that there is more to clean after feeds—not only do you have to wash the bottle but also the straw mechanism—and that could be a pain (though perhaps not as much pain as you'll be sparing baby's tummy).

Feeding Chairs: As Your Baby Grows

Breast or bottle will deliver all the nutritional goods to your baby for about the first 6 months, which means your bundle will be doing all of his or her eating in your arms at first. But while feeding seats won't be on your must-have list right away (and don't you already have enough on your must-have list?), it'll help to have a peek into your baby's feeding future—and maybe even to register for those future needs now.

High chair. You won't need a high chair until your baby starts opening wide for solids, usually at about 6 months. Even then, those first bites can be spooned up with baby in an infant seat. Still, next to the crib and the car seat, the high chair will probably get more use (and possibly abuse) than any other furnishing you buy for baby. You'll find a staggering number of models to choose from, with a variety of features. Some have adjustable height, others recline (which makes them perfect for feeding babies under 6 months), while still others fold up for storage. Some are made out of plastic or metal, others are made from wood. Some models have storage baskets underneath, others morph into toddler booster seats, and still others have dishwasher safe trays (a feature that you'll find priceless). Many have wheels for easy transport from kitchen to dining room to deck and back.

When choosing a high chair, look for a sturdy, nontip base, a tray that can be easily removed or locked in place with one hand, a seat back high enough to support baby's head, comfortable padding, safety straps that secure your little one across the hips and between the legs (it'll make it nearly impossible for your escape artist to break free), wheels that lock, a secure locking device if the chair folds, and no sharp edges.

Booster seat. Booster seats are a nice-to-have for older babies and toddlers. They come as plastic chairs that strap onto a regular chair at the table (or stand alone on the floor) and hook-on styles that lock directly onto the table. Some can be used for babies as young as 6 months (or younger), others are a better fit for older babies and toddlers (boosters can become especially indispensible when an active little one starts resisting confinement in a high chair or begins coveting a seat at the big people's table). A booster (especially a clip-on type) can also be invaluable when you're visiting friends or family or dining at restaurants that don't provide seating that's appropriate or safe for your baby's size or stage of development. For ultimate portability, choose a clip-on chair that's lightweight and comes with a travel bag. Many boosters have adjustable seat levels and some have attachable trays. If your high chair is a multitasking one, it could transform into a booster seat that can be adjusted for different ages, sizes, stages, and table heights.

Stock up with four 4-ounce bottles and ten to twelve 8-ounce bottles. If you're combining bottle-feeding with breastfeeding, four to six 8-ounce bottles should be plenty. If you're nursing exclusively, one 8-ounce bottle is enough as a just-in-case.

Utensils for formula preparation. Exactly which items you'll need will depend on the type of formula you plan to use, but the shopping list will usually include bottle and nipple brushes, large measuring pitcher and measuring cup if you're using powdered formula, possibly a can opener, a long-handled mixing spoon, and a dishwasher basket to keep nipples and rings (collars) from being tossed around the dishwasher.

A bottle and nipple rack. Even if you're doing most of your bottle washing in the dishwasher, you'll get plenty of use out of a drying rack specifically designed to hold and organize bottles and nipples.

Pumping supplies, if you're breastfeeding but will be expressing milk. This includes a breast pump (see page 173 for information and advice on choosing one of the types of breast pumps available and information on insurance coverage), storage container bags made specifically for storing and freezing breast milk (they are sterile, thicker than regular plastic bags or bottle liners, and lined with nylon to prevent the fat from adhering to the sides) or bottles (plastic or glass) to collect and freeze breast milk, a thermal insulated bag to keep pumped milk fresh during transport, and possibly hot/cold packs for relieving engorgement and encouraging let-down.

A pacifier. It's not technically a feeding supply, but it will satisfy your baby's between-feed sucking needs. Plus, pacifiers are suggested for use during sleep, since they have been shown to reduce the risk of SIDS. There are plenty of styles and sizes to choose from—different babies show a preference for different pacis, so be prepared to switch around to find your little one's favorite. You'll also need to switch to larger sizes as baby grows, for safety's sake.

There are the standard-shaped pacifiers with a straight, elongated nipple, the orthodontic pacifiers, which have a rounded top and a flat bottom, and the "cherry" nipples, which have a trunk that becomes ball shaped toward the end. The nipples themselves can be made of silicone or latex. Some reasons to opt for silicone: It's sturdier, longer-lasting, doesn't retain odors, and is top-rack dishwasher safe. Latex, while softer and more flexible, deteriorates faster, wears out sooner, can be chomped through by baby teeth, and isn't dishwasher safe. Babies (like adults) can also be sensitive to or allergic to latex.

There are some one-piece pacifiers entirely made out of latex, but most pacifiers have plastic shields, usually with ventilation holes on them. The shields can be different colors (or transparent) and differently shaped (butterfly, oval, round, and so on). Some shields curve toward the mouth and others are flat. Some pacifiers have rings on the back, while others have "buttons." Ring handles make the paci easier to retrieve, but button handles may make it easier for your baby to grasp the pacifier. There are pacifiers with handles that glow in the dark so they're easier to find at night.

Some pacifiers have a built-in cover that automatically snaps closed if the pacifier is dropped, others have snap-on caps to help the paci stay clean (though a cap is another thing to keep track of—and you'll need to keep it away from baby because it's a choking hazard). And talking about hazards, remember: No matter how tempting it is to attach the paci to your baby's clothes—especially after the twelfth time it's slipped out of his or her mouth and onto the floor—never attach a cord or ribbon that's more than 6 inches long to a pacifier. Clips and shorter tethers designed for pacis are fine.

Baby's Nursery

A newborn's needs are basic: a pair of loving arms to be cuddled and rocked in, a set of breasts (or a bottle) to feed from, and a safe place to sleep. In fact, many of the products, furnishings, and accessories marketed as nursery must-haves are really un-neccessaries. Still, you'll be doing plenty of buying when it comes to baby's new room—or,

Crib Notes on Crib Safety

Fortunately, when it comes to crib safety, the government's got your back—and your baby's. The U.S. Consumer Product Safety Commission (CPSC) has made crib safety a top priority by setting strict standards for both manufacturers and retailers. These requirements include stronger mattress supports and crib slats, extremely durable crib hardware, and rigorous safety testing. Though you'll still want to take any crib you're considering through the checklist below, the CPSC standards should make crib safety assessment a lot simpler.

Here's how to make sure you're buying (or borrowing) a safe crib:

- The slats and corner posts of a crib should be no more than 2⅜ inches apart (smaller than the diameter of a regular soda can). Wider slats pose an entrapment danger for little heads.

- Corner posts should be flush with the end panels (or no more than $\frac{1}{16}$ inch higher).

- Hardware—bolts, screws, brackets—should be firmly secured, with no sharp edges or rough areas and no spots that can pinch or otherwise injure your baby. The crib's wood should be free of cracks or splits, and there shouldn't be any peeling paint.

- Standard-size mattresses for a full-size crib should be firm and at least 27¼ inches by 51⅜ inches and no more than 6 inches thick. Oval- or round-shaped cribs need a mattress specially designed to fit snugly.

- Make sure the mattress fits snugly against the inside of the crib. If you can fit more than two fingers between the mattress and the crib, the mattress isn't a good fit. (The harder it is for you to make the bed, the safer for your baby.)

- Never put plush toys or soft or loose bedding in the crib with your baby (even the adorable pillow and comforter that may come with the crib bedding set) because they can pose a suffocation hazard. The AAP also strongly advises against using bumper pads (even thin, breathable mesh ones or padded slat covers), since they may increase the risk of SIDS, suffocation, and entrapment.

- Don't use antiques or cribs more than 10 years old. It may be hard to pass up a passed-along, passed-down, or thrift store crib, but do. Older cribs (especially those made before 1973, but also some made from the 1980s through the early 2000s) may be chic, charming, or of great sentimental value (and value, too, if they're inexpensive or free), but they don't meet current safety standards. They might have slats that are too far apart, may have lead paint or cracked or splintered wood, may have been recalled (particularly drop-side cribs), or may pose other risks you might not even notice, such as unsafe corner posts.

if you'll be sharing, baby's corner of your room. Of course you'll want to fill your baby's nursery with an eye toward cuteness (even though the room's chief resident won't care much about whether the wallpaper matches the curtains), but you'll also want to keep both eyes on safety. Which means, among other things, a crib that meets current safety standards (many hand-me-down

Bye-Bye, Bumpers

Nothing makes a crib look cuter and comfier than a plush comforter and coordinated bumpers. But according to guidelines from the AAP (and a ban on sales in Maryland and in Chicago, with bans in other locations being considered), it's time to remake the traditional baby bedding set to include nothing but the fitted sheet. The only place that's safe for a baby under the age of one to sleep, say experts, is a firm surface free of blankets, comforters, pillows, stuffed animals, and yes, those bumpers. That's because bumpers and other bedding increases the risk for sleep-related deaths, including suffocation, entrapment, and SIDS. A young infant's head can all too easily become trapped between a fluffy bumper and a crib slat. Or a baby might roll over onto a blanket or stuffed animal or against a bumper and suffocate. Resourceful older babies and toddlers can also use a bumper as a leg up when trying to scale their crib walls.

Wondering about your little one's risk for injury without that bumper? No worries. A little bump on the head or trapped arm or foot is considered minor when stacked against the potentially life-threatening risks of using a bumper (even mesh "breathable" ones or those that attach individually to crib slats). So bump the bumpers from your baby's crib, along with the comforters and pillows. If they've come in a bedding set, you can use them to cleverly decorate your baby's room (bumpers can be strung along the wall, used as a window valance, or used to trim a hamper or changing table or to pad a sharp-edged table). Your baby will be safer for it.

---

cribs, cradles, and bassinets don't), a changing table that won't take a tumble, and lead-free paint on everything.

Be sure to follow the manufacturer's directions for assembly, use, and maintenance of all items. Also, always send in your product registration card or register online so that you can be notified in case of a recall.

Crib. Style matters, of course, but not as much as safety (see the box on page 43), comfort, practicality, and durability, especially if you're hoping to reuse it for any future siblings—assuming safety standards haven't changed again by then.

There are two basic types of cribs—standard and convertible: Standard cribs can come with a hinged side to make it easier to lift baby out (don't confuse these with drop-side cribs, which were banned by the Consumer Product Safety Commission in 2010) and sometimes will have a drawer on the bottom for storage. A convertible crib, if it's built to last, can take your tiny newborn all the way to strapping teen, converting from a crib (sometimes even a mini-crib) to a toddler bed and then to a daybed or full-size bed. That's a lot of sweet dreams.

You should look for a crib that has a metal mattress support (which will withstand a jumping toddler better than wood will), adjustable mattress height so the mattress can be lowered as your baby grows, and casters (with a wheel lock) for mobility.

While most cribs are classic rectangles, some are oval or round shaped, offering a cocoonlike environment for your little one. Just keep in mind that you will need to buy a mattress, mattress covers, and sheets made to fit—standard sizes won't.

Crib mattress. Because your baby will be sleeping on it a lot (hopefully), you'll want to make sure the crib mattress you select is not only safe and comfortable, but made to go the distance. There are two types of crib mattresses, innerspring and foam:

- An innerspring is the heavier of the two types of mattress, which means it will usually last longer, keep its shape better, and offer superior support. It's also more expensive than foam. A good (though not an absolute) rule of thumb when choosing an innerspring mattress is to look for one with a high number of coils. The higher the count (usually 150 or more), the firmer (and better quality, and safer) the mattress.

- A foam mattress is made of polyester or polyether, weighs less than an innerspring mattress (which means you'll have an easier time lifting it to change those sheets), and is generally less expensive (though it may not last as long). If you're buying foam, look for a mattress with high foam density, which will mean more support and safety for your baby.

The most important criteria in selecting a crib mattress? Safety. Make sure that the mattress is firm and fits snugly in the crib, with no more than two adult-finger widths between mattress and frame.

Bassinet or cradle. You can definitely skip these cozy crib alternatives and start using a crib from day one, but they can come in handy early on. For one thing, they're portable—making it easy to bring your snoozing sweetie with you no matter what room of the house you're in. Some can hit the road, too, folding neatly for travel and then setting up easily for safe sleeping and napping at grandma's or in a hotel room. For another, the snugger sleep space it provides may be more comforting to a newborn than the wide open spaces of a crib. Still another perk of the bassinet or cradle: Its height is usually fairly close to that of your bed, allowing you to reach over and comfort (or lift out) your baby in the middle of the night, without even getting out of your bed. Planning to have your infant room in with you in the early months (as recommended by the AAP for safer sleep; see page 271)? A bassinet or cradle will save space in your bedroom, compared with a crib.

If you're springing for a cradle or bassinet, look for a sturdy model with a wide and stable base. Also, make sure the sides of the bassinet or cradle—from the mattress (which should be firm and fit the interior securely) to the top—are at least 8 inches high. Wheels make it much easier to move from room to room, but they should come with locks—the legs should lock securely, too, if it's a folding model. If there's a hood, it should fold back so you'll be able to transfer your sleeping baby easily from your arms into those cozy confines. And precious though they may be, steer clear of handcrafted or antique bassinets or cradles—they're just not safe. Any model you use should meet current safety standards.

Play yard/portable crib. Play yards (also known as portable or travel cribs) are usually rectangular in shape, with a floor, mesh sides, and rails that lock and unlock for easy (but safe) collapsibility and folding. Most fold into a long rectangle and come with a carrying case for easy transport. Some have wheels, others have removable padded changing stations that fit on top, built-in bassinets for newborns, side storage areas, and even a canopy for shade (useful

Safe Bedside Sleeping

Bedside sleepers have a high padded rim on three sides and one open side that fits flush against your bed mattress at the same height as an adult bed. A bedside sleeper allows for easy access to baby (it's just a reach in the middle of the night for a reassuring pat). But be aware: Many models have been recalled for safety concerns—babies have become trapped between the bedside sleeper and the adult bed. If you're thinking about using a bedside sleeper, be sure it meets the stringent Consumer Product Safety Commission standards that went into effect in July 2014.

if you bring the play yard outdoors). Play yards can also be used as portable cribs when traveling or even as baby's primary digs in the first few months (or beyond) if you opted not to spring for a bassinet (or if you're not planning to get a crib). Do keep in mind that once you stop using the bassinet insert, shorter moms and dads may find it a stretch to lay baby down on the bottom of the play yard. When choosing a play yard, look for one with fine-mesh netting that won't catch fingers or buttons, tough pads that won't tear easily, padded metal hinges, a baby-proof collapse mechanism, quick setup, easy folding, and portability. It should also take removable fitted sheets for easy cleanup.

Changing space. By the time your baby has reached his or her first birthday, chances are you'll have changed nearly 2,500 diapers (and sometimes, it will seem as though you've changed nearly

that many in a single day). With such staggering numbers in mind, you'll want to set up a comfortable place to change those diapers—one that is also convenient, safe, and easy to clean.

The obvious choice is a changing table—and if you choose one, you'll have two options: a stand-alone changing table or a combination dresser/changing table, which has an oversize top or a flip-open top with a pad. With either option, look for one that is sturdy and has solid legs, safety straps, washable padding, diaper storage within your reach, and supply storage out of baby's reach. Also test it out to make sure the height and maneuverability are comfortable for you. There are intuitively designed changing tables that allow you to position baby vertically instead of horizontally, making it easier to access the business end. If using the flip-open type of changing table, do not place baby's weight on the outer edge: That can cause the entire chest to topple. One clear advantage of a combo changing table is the space-saving storage it provides.

While a designated changing table is definitely nice to have, it isn't necessary if you're short on space or money. You can actually turn an ordinary dresser or table into a changing space. If you go that route, you'll need to shop for a thick pad with a safety strap to place on the dresser to keep it protected and to keep baby secure and comfortable. Make sure, too, that the dresser height is comfortable for you (and whoever else will be doing diaper duty) and that the pad doesn't slide off the dresser top when you're diapering a squirmy baby.

Diaper pail. Your baby's bottom is sure to be sweet and adorable. But what comes out of it probably won't be. Luckily, diapers are there to catch it all. But to catch all those dirty diapers, you'll want a diaper pail designed to whisk away and store the evidence (and odor). If you're using disposable diapers, you can choose a fancy diaper pail that tightly seals (or even coils) diapers in an odor-preventing plastic liner. Or look for one that uses ordinary garbage bags (because the special liner refills can get expensive). Whichever type you use, remember to empty the pail often (but hold your nose when you do, because the stench of stored diapers can knock you off your feet). Deodorized pails make sense for obvious reasons.

If you are using cloth diapers, choose a pail that is easy to wash and has a tight-fitting top that a baby or toddler can't pry open. If you're using a diaper service, the service will usually provide you with a deodorized diaper pail and cart away the stinky contents weekly.

Glider. Most parents are off their rockers these days, choosing a glider for the nursery instead. Gliders beat out rockers in comfort and safety, since they don't tip over as easily and they're free of runners, which children (and pets) can get caught under. While a glider isn't technically a nursery necessity, you're bound to get a lot of use out of one—not only for rocking your baby, but for feeding, snuggling, and years of cuddly story times (which you'll want to start from birth; see page 425). Secondhand gliders usually still have lots of life left in them, so if someone you know is looking to unload theirs, you may want to snag it. If you're buying new, let comfort guide you. Test before you buy, preferably using a doll as a prop—the arms of the chair should support your arms well in a feeding position, and the height should be at a level that allows you to get up smoothly while holding baby, without any stumbles that could startle your sleeping bundle. Many gliders come

---

Double Up on Diaper Stations

Say baby's room (and changing table) is upstairs, but your baby spends most of the day downstairs. Because there are bound to be diaper blowups downstairs, too, it'll be especially convenient to have a second diaper changing station close by—and it doesn't have to cost big bucks. All you'll need is an extra diaper caddy filled with diaper supplies (diapers, wipes, and cream) and an extra changing pad that can be easily stashed.

---

with matching gliding ottomans so you can kick up your tired dogs as you glide with your little puppy.

Baby monitor. A baby monitor allows parents to keep tabs on a sleeping infant without standing watch over the crib (though, realistically, you'll be doing plenty of that in the first few weeks, too). It's especially useful when your baby isn't sharing a room with you, or if you're in another part of the house when he or she is sleeping during the night or naps. Even if baby's not within earshot of you, the monitor will alert you when he or she wakes.

There are a few types of monitors. The basic audio monitors transmit sound only. The transmitter is left in your baby's room, and the receiver either goes where you go or stays in the room you'll be in. Some monitors have two receivers so both parents can listen in (or you can keep one receiver in your bedroom and the other in the kitchen, for example). An added feature to the audio monitor is the "sound-and-light" feature. Such a monitor has a special

LED display that enables you to "see" the sound level of your baby. An audio-video model allows you to see and hear your baby on a TV screen using a small camera placed near the baby's crib. Some models have infrared technology so you can see your baby even if it's dark in the nursery, and apps that allow you to peek in on baby's sleep when you're out and the sitter's on duty. There are also movement sensor monitors—a sensor pad is placed under the mattress to detect baby movement. If the baby stops moving suddenly, an alarm sounds. Just keep in mind that research doesn't show any SIDS prevention benefits from using these monitors.

Prefer to keep tabs on baby the old-fashioned way (by listening for crying)? Skip the monitor—after all, it's hard not to hear a crying baby, even down the hall.

Nightlight. As you stumble out of bed for yet another middle-of-the-night feeding, you'll be thankful for a nightlight (or a lamp with a dimmer). Not only will it keep you from tripping over that stuffed giraffe you left in the middle of the floor, but it will also keep you from having to turn on a bright light—guaranteed to disturb the sleepy darkness and make a return to dreamland more elusive. Look for a plug-in model that can safely be left on, and remember to put it in an outlet that baby can't reach. Want a nightlight that does double duty as a soother for baby? Consider a light projector that displays a bright yet soothing, slowly rotating scene on the ceiling—stars, an underwater scene, a rain forest. Some play music—lullabies or peaceful ocean or white noise sounds—and most have a soft nightlight when the projection shuts off so you can find your way when you go in for diaper changes. Just make sure you don't shine a bright light on baby's room during sleep, since that can

mess with natural sleep rhythms. And to protect baby's delicate ears, keep any kind of light projector that plays musical sounds on a low-volume setting and don't place it right next to the crib.

Gear for Outings

Thinking of leaving the house? You'll want to, you'll need to, and you'll have to be prepared to—with, at minimum, a car seat and a stroller. As with other baby stuff you'll be buying, there will be endless styles, colors, finishes, and features to choose from when picking gear for outings—and you'll have to make your choices with safety, comfort, and your budget in mind. Lifestyle should be factored in, as well as ease of use and convenience (a plush stroller may look great on the sidewalk, but not as you're struggling to fold it with one arm while holding a squirming baby in the other).

In general, look for items that meet federal safety standards and have adequate safety straps at the crotch and waist, where appropriate. You should avoid choosing any items that have rough edges, sharp points, small parts that might break loose, exposed hinges or springs, or attached strings, cords, or ribbons. Be sure to follow the manufacturer's directions for use and maintenance of all items. Also, always send in your product registration card or register online so that you can be notified promptly in case of a recall.

Stroller. The right stroller (or strollers) can make your daily life with baby—from that walk in the park to that hike through the mall—much more manageable and much less exhausting. But wading through the dozens of choices (and price tags) in the store can be overwhelming. Because there are so many different types of strollers, carriages, travel systems, joggers, and stroller/ carriage combinations available, you'll need to consider your lifestyle in order to find the one (or ones) right for you. Will you be taking long, leisurely strolls with your baby on quiet suburban streets (or in that park)? Or will you be hitting the jogging trails with Junior? Do you spend a lot of time getting in and out of your car? Or more time climbing in and out of buses or subway stations? Will you be taking mostly short walks to the corner store, or will you also be taking long trips with your baby on airplanes or trains? Do you have a toddler at home who still likes to be in a stroller? Are you (or your spouse or caregiver) very tall or very short? Do you live in a small walk-up apartment, an elevator building, or a house with many steps at the front door? Once you've answered these questions, you're armed with enough information to make your choice. And, depending on your budget, you might consider buying more than one type for more flexibility in your mobility.

The basic strollers and carriages available include:

- Full-size carriage strollers. If you're looking to invest in one stroller that'll wheel your baby right through the toddler years—and even convert into a double stroller when your firstborn gets a travel companion (aka a new sibling), you might consider a full-size stroller. These full-service and high-end strollers come with accessories that not only make baby's ride a joy (toy attachments, bottle holders, plush, fully reclining seats, and in some cases, bassinets or other newborn/infant inserts), but also make your life easier (think large storage baskets and even iPod hookups). Most models fold flat easily, and while they're heavier and more

---

Seal of Approval

Before buying any baby gear, be sure it is JPMA approved. The Juvenile Products Manufacturers Association puts its seal of approval only on products that meet their rigorous safety standards—something you'll be thankful for when it comes to the safety of your little one.

---

cumbersome than lightweight strollers, they are also very durable and will last many years (and through many babies, if you're so inclined). And it's a good thing, too, since they're usually pretty pricey.

The downside to the large strollers is just that—they're large, and sometimes difficult to navigate through crowds, doors, and aisles. Plus their extra weight (up to 35 pounds for some models) makes it a pain to be carried up and down stairs (especially when you add in the weight of your baby).

- Travel system stroller. You already know you'll need both a car seat and a stroller, so why not get an all-in-one stroller that combines both in one convenient package? Travel system strollers are perfect for parents (and babies) on the go, combining a full-size, stand-alone stroller with an infant car seat that clips into the stroller when you're on foot. The beauty is that since most babies drift off on even short car rides, an infant stroller travel system allows you to switch your sleeping beauty from car to stroller without disturbing those sweet dreams. Once your baby outgrows the infant car seat, the stand-alone stroller goes solo for the long haul. Of course, while a travel system can come in handy, there are some downsides. Some are heavy and bulky, making it tough to load into and out of your trunk, or even to fit into your trunk. Plus (another potential minus), you can use only the car seat that comes with the stroller. So if baby will be traveling in more than one car, you may need to buy a second car seat if you don't want to unhook and reattach the one base the stroller comes with. This problem can be avoided if the car seat you buy offers the option of sold-separately bases, so you can leave a base in both your cars.

- **Umbrella (lightweight) stroller.** Umbrella strollers are ultralight (often weighing as little as 6 pounds) and exceptionally easy to fold. When folded, they are extremely compact for convenient carrying and storing. Since most do not recline or offer sufficient padding or support, they aren't appropriate for small babies, but they're ideal for older ones, especially when traveling, using public transportation, or getting in and out of a car often. You may want to hold off on buying an umbrella stroller until your baby's big enough to be toted in it.

- **Jogger stroller.** Looking for a way to get back into shape and bring baby along for the ride? If you're an avid jogger or enjoy long walks in the country or otherwise off the pavement, a jogger stroller might be the right choice for you. These strollers have three large wheels and great suspension, provide a smooth ride for your little passenger on all terrains thanks to shock absorbers, and are easy to maneuver. Many have a braking system and come with wrist straps and a storage pouch or basket. Most aren't designed to tote newborns, so if you're looking to hit the jogging path sooner rather than later, choose one that is designed with younger babies in mind (carefully check and follow the manufacturer's age and weight recommendations). The biggest downside to the jogging stroller is the fixed front wheel, which makes it difficult to turn. Not to mention the large size, which could make it tough to navigate through crowded spaces and be a challenge to fold and store.

- **Double (or triple) stroller.** If you're expecting baby number two and you have a toddler at home, or if you'll be toting twins, you'll need a double stroller (or triple if you're expecting triplets, have a toddler and new twins, or have twin toddlers and a new baby). Double strollers offer the convenience of pushing two children as comfortably (almost) as pushing one. Choose from side-by-side models or front-to-back ones (one seat in front of the other). If you're buying a side-by-side model, look for one that has reclining seats and can fit through doorways and aisles (most do, but some are too wide for narrow passageways). A tandem model is great for a newborn and a toddler but can be heavy to push, and when baby gets bigger or if you have twins, your little ones may fight over who gets the "front seat." These models often accept two car seats to operate as a travel system for as long as your babies fit into their infant car seats, and then serve as a regular stroller after that. Another option if you have an older child: a single seat stroller that has a sitting ledge or standing platform in the front or back so big sib can hitch a ride.

Regardless of which type of stroller you buy, be sure it meets current safety standards. A good brand will also have buckles that are easy for you (but not your crafty baby) to latch and unlatch. Seat belts should fit snugly around your baby's waist and crotch, be adjustable, and be comfortable. A jogging stroller should have a five-point harness (with shoulder straps) for maximum safety—nearly all new models do, but an older one might not. Washable fabric and padding that is removable are a plus, as you'll find out the first time the diaper leaks or the juice spills.

Each type of stroller comes with its own set of bells and whistles. Decide from the many available features what you won't be able to live without, what you'll find useful, and what you probably won't end up needing at all: a large basket or storage area (don't overload handles with bags or other items, since the weight could tip the stroller over and baby with it), adjustable handle height if anyone who will be pushing the stroller is very tall, a rain shield, a mosquito net, a child feeding tray, a cup holder for parents, a sun canopy or umbrella, an adjustable footrest, one-handed fold, one-handed steering. Most important: Before buying any stroller, take it for a test drive in the store to see how easy it is to handle, how comfortable it is, and how it folds and unfolds.

Car seat. Car seats aren't just for your peace of mind and your baby's safety—they're required by law. In fact, most hospitals won't even let you take your baby home unless you have a rear-facing infant car seat securely strapped into your car's backseat. Even if you don't own a car, you'll need a car seat if you ever plan to get into a cab or transportation van, go for a drive in someone else's car, or rent a car. More than any other item on your shopping list, this is the one to have on hand (and installed) before that first contraction hits.

When choosing a car seat, be sure it meets Federal Motor Vehicle Safety Standards (FMVSS). Never borrow an older car seat (besides potentially not meeting current safety requirements, the plastic tends to become brittle and weak—and therefore unsafe—over time) or use one that's already been in even a minor crash (it could have been damaged by the forces of the impact—even if you don't see any obvious damage). Some car seats have "do-not-use-after" dates stamped on the bottom or expiration dates on the model number sticker, so be sure to check for that before borrowing or buying one used. Also be sure to send in the registration card or register online so the manufacturer can notify you if there is a recall on your car seat. See page 156 for information on installing your baby's car seat properly and for more safety tips.

For the first 2 years, your little one will be in a car seat that faces the rear of the car (in the backseat only—never place a car seat up front). That's because a rear-facing child safety seat does a much better job of protecting a young child in a car crash than those that face forward. In a rear-facing car

The five-point harness has five straps: two at the shoulders, two at the hips, and one at the crotch. All new car seats are equipped with a five-point harness—and that's a good thing, since it offers more points of protection.

A rear-facing car seat should be used until age 2—or until the child outgrows the weight limit (usually around 35 pounds). The harness slots should be at or below your baby's shoulders and the harness chest clip should be at the infant's armpit level. Check the instructions to see how the carrying handle should be positioned during travel. Never place a rear-facing infant seat in the front seat of a vehicle.

A convertible seat. Designed for children from birth to around 40 to 60 pounds, this unit faces the rear in a semi-reclining position for infant use, then can be switched to an upright, front-facing position when baby is older (over age 2). When in the front-facing position, the car seat should be in the upright position, and the shoulder straps should be moved to the slots above your child's shoulders. The harness chest clip should be at your child's armpit level. Place this seat (and all children under the age of 13) in the rear seat of the vehicle.

seat, the child's head, neck, and spine are better supported, making the risk of serious injury much less likely. Research shows that children under age 2 are 75 percent less likely to be severely or fatally injured in a crash if they are rear-facing while riding.

You'll have two choices of rear-facing car seats:

■ Infant car seat. Most models have a stay-in-car detachable base that allows you to quickly install the car seat (after baby's safely buckled in, you simply lock the seat into the base) and quickly remove it once you've arrived at your destination. The seat can also be used outside the car (to tote or seat baby wherever you go). The biggest advantage of an infant car seat is that it's designed to fit a little baby, offering a more comfortable ride for a newborn—and potentially, the safest. The downside to the infant car seat? Your infant won't be an infant for long, and once his or her shoulders reach above the highest harness position or your little bruiser reaches the maximum weight for the infant seat (depending on the size of your baby, it could happen at anywhere from 9 to 18 months), it's time

Car Seat Accessories to Skip

When it's cold outside, you'll need to dress your baby in a snow-suit or other heavy coat. Problem is, it's unsafe to strap a bundled up baby into a car seat because the seat's harnesses need to be as close to the baby's body as possible to keep him or her properly secured. Which is why many parents turn to (or are gifted with) thick and cuddly car seat covers that thread through the harness straps and act like a bunting—keeping baby cozy and warm on even the coldest of days. Sounds great—right? Wrong. You're better off skipping these car seat accessories since they don't meet federal safety guidelines (despite what the manufacturers state on the packaging) and they're not safe for your little one. Anything that goes under or behind your baby's body and the harness straps will make the straps too loose and will interfere with the proper—and safe—functioning of the straps, making your baby unsafe and more prone to injury during a car crash. In fact, many car seat manufacturers will void your car seat warranty if you use a car seat cover.

A better option for cold weather? A bunting that baby wears and that has a slot on the bottom to slip the car seat strap through. Another option? A car seat cover that goes around the entire car seat only. Or strap your unbundled (but warmly dressed—hat included) baby into the car seat, then cover baby with a light blanket that gets tucked into the sides of the car seat (but not under baby's body) and top with a warm blanket over the entire car seat. Snug and warm as a bug—and most important, safe and secure.

Ditto for any aftermarket item you purchase for your baby's car seat (head positioners, toy bars, anti-escape clips, and so on). If it doesn't come with the car seat itself, it isn't subject to the same rigorous approval requirements and therefore can actually make your little one less safe—plus, using them will void the manufacturer's warranty.

---

for a new ride for your baby. Since your little one will have to stay rear-facing until he or she is at least age 2, you'll have to switch to a convertible seat (see next bullet). Car seat too big for your small (or preemie) baby? Be sure the car seat is made for small babies (most are designed to accommodate babies starting at 4 or 5 pounds). Some seats come with the option of an insert for preemies or very small babies.

- Convertible car seat. Convertible car seats can be adjusted and converted from a rear-facing position to a forward facing one—but more relevant for the first year, they can accommodate bigger and heavier babies in the rear-facing position than the infant car seats can. They are also long lasting, able to accommodate a child up to 40 to 60 pounds. The only problem: The fit of a convertible seat may be slightly less secure for a newborn, so if you choose this model, make sure your baby fits snugly in it.

If the car seat you choose seems too loose for your newborn, use a padded head bumper or rolled-up blanket to pad *around* his or her body (not under or behind the body, which could affect the security of the harness) to keep your baby from wobbling. Use *only* inserts/positioners that came with the car seat.

The LATCH System

Is your car seat properly LATCHed in? The LATCH safety seat attachment system (for Lower Anchors and Tethers for CHildren) makes correct installation of a car seat much less complicated because you don't need to use seat belts to secure the safety seat.

Vehicles made after model year 2002 have lower anchors located between the vehicle's seat cushion and seat back, which enables a rear-facing or forward-facing car seat to be latched into the anchors for a secure fit. Forward-facing child car seats are also equipped with top tether strap attachments. The adjustable tether strap is a belt that better stabilizes the car seat and reduces the potential for your child's head to be thrown forward in a collision. The tether strap is anchored to the upper back of the child car seat and hooks into the rear shelf area or the floor of your vehicle.

Together, the lower anchors and upper tethers make up the LATCH system. Remember, if you have a car made before model year 2002, you still must use your car's seat belts to secure the car seat.

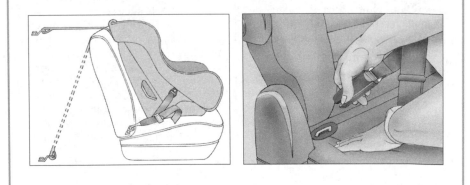

Aftermarket products (items that are made for car seats but are sold separately from the car seat) are not regulated, do not have to pass any crash or safety tests, and might make your baby less safe. What's more, using them will void the car seat's warranty.

Diaper bag. Have baby, will travel. And while you can certainly stuff your extra-large shoulder bag full of all the baby on-the-go supplies you might need, a diaper bag is definitely a nice carryall to have—since you will have to carry all. But with so many bags on the market—high-end designer bags, bags specifically designed for dads, bags that don't look like diaper bags, and those that most certainly do—how do you choose?

First consider size and carrying comfort. You'll probably want one that's large enough to fit most of the supplies you'll need on any given outing, but you may not want one that's heavy and unwieldy before you even fill it up. Next, think about the features you want. If you're doing any bottle-feeding, you'll want a diaper bag that has a separate insulated bottle holding area (later, you can use it to keep baby's food chilled). Multiple roomy compartments—well divided and easy to reach into—will come in handy for keeping diapers, especially dirty ones, separated from bottles, pacifiers, spoons, and food (including snacks for you). A moisture-resistant material will protect against bottle, medicine, or diaper ointment leaks. A changing pad that comes with the bag and folds compactly inside is an added bonus. And if you'd rather the diaper bag do double duty as a handbag, look for one with compartments for your wallet, phone, keys, makeup, and other stuff that normally ends up in your own bag. Finally, decide on the style. Shoulder strap or backpack style? Sleek, sophisticated diaper bag that could pass as an oversize handbag or one that screams "baby"? Remember, too, that you can also adapt any other carrier (such as a gym bag, backpack, or large handbag) for carrying baby gear.

Shopping cart cover. Not a must-have, but certainly a nice-to-have, a shopping cart cover—a fabric seat cover that fits into the sitting area of a shopping cart (as well as a restaurant high chair)—helps protect your cutie from nasty germs while providing him or her with a cozy, comfy, and stylish place to sit. Some models include handy pockets to store pacis and loops to attach toys, so baby's favorites don't get tossed onto the floor of aisle 3 (and 4, and 5). Look for one that folds up for easy toting, has ample padding for optimum comfort, and provides good cart coverage (no exposed metal or plastic), as well as one that has a dual safety-belt system—one strap that keeps baby in place and another to attach the cover to the cart (and be sure to use both every time you shop).

A Place for Baby

While you can certainly hold your baby in your arms all day (and when he or she is first born that's likely all you'll want to do), there'll be times

---

Supervised Seating

Whether your baby's contentedly snoozing in a car seat or infant seat, watching the world go by in a stroller, rocking out in a swing, or bopping in a Boppy, don't forget the most important baby-seating rule of all: supervision. Never leave your baby unsupervised in a seat of any kind, even if he or she is safely buckled in.

---

when you'll need your hands for other things—like cooking dinner, uploading those adorable baby pictures, and even (hey, it could happen!) showering. Which is why you'll want a place where you can safely deposit your little one—whether it's in a sling close to your beating heart, in a fun jumper or stationary entertainer, on a play mat, or in an infant seat or swing all his or her own.

Baby carrier or sling. If you're like most parents, you'll love carriers or slings for the hands-free baby comfort they offer—giving weary arms a break from holding and rocking, plus allowing you to multitask while you're soothing your sweetie. And there's no easier way to go for a stroll with your baby, fold laundry without putting baby down, walk the mall or the market, or hold your little one while you push a big sib on the swings.

But the benefits of "wearing" a baby go way beyond the hands-free convenience and efficiency. Studies show that babies who are worn more cry less (a definite perk during those fussy times of the day or if your baby has colic), not surprising when you consider that being snuggled against your chest approximates the cozy cocoon of the womb. The physical closeness built into baby wearing also builds that parent-infant bond—plus it feels really amazing. Happiness, as you'll soon discover, is a warm baby.

There are as many styles of carriers and slings to choose from as there are reasons for buying or borrowing one. Keep in mind that while reviews and recommendations from other parents can be really helpful, different carriers and slings work for different moms and dads (and that trying before you buy isn't that helpful if you're trying it while you're still expecting—bumps can get in the way). Here are some options to consider:

- Front carriers (as well as mei tais) consist of a fabric compartment supported by two shoulder straps that distribute weight evenly so that your back and shoulders share the load. They are designed so your baby can face either inward (especially useful for when baby is sleeping or for a newborn who doesn't have good head control yet) or outward (so an older baby can enjoy the same sights as you, though there may be some potential downsides to the outward-facing position if you haven't positioned baby properly, see page 382). Most can accommodate an infant up to 30 pounds, though some parents prefer to switch to a backpack once their baby is over 6 months—and, in fact, some front carriers convert to backpacks (and even offer front-in, front-out, side- and back-seating options). When choosing a front carrier, look for one that's easy to get on and take off without help and that won't require you to wake up your baby to slip him or her out. It should have adjustable, padded straps that don't dig into your shoulders, be made from easy washable, breathable fabric (so baby won't overheat), have head and shoulder support for baby, and offer a wide seat that supports bottom and thighs.

- A sling carrier (or ring sling, pouch, or wrap) is a wide swath of fabric that slings across your body, supported by a shoulder strap. Infants are able to lie down comfortably in them or face outward. An older baby can straddle your hip while being supported by the sling. An additional plus for nursing mothers: Slings allow discreet and convenient breastfeeding. When choosing a sling, look for washable, breathable fabric, a well-padded and comfortable strap, and trimness (one that isn't bulky with extra fabric). Just remember that different babies and different parents feel comfortable in different slings, making buying ahead especially tricky. Slings may also require some getting used to.

- A framed carrier is a backpack frame made of metal or plastic with a fabric seat. Unlike front carriers, which distribute baby's weight on your shoulders and neck, a backpack carrier places the weight on your back and waist. This type of carrier is not recommended for babies under 6 months old but can be used for children up to 50 pounds and age 3 (depending on the model). When choosing one, look for models that have a built-in stand—it helps make loading and mounting easier. Other features to look for: moisture resistant and cleanable fabric, adjustability, safety straps or harness to prevent your little one from climbing out, firm and thick shoulder strap padding, lumbar support to help distribute the weight down toward your hips, and storage pockets for baby stuff (so you don't have to lug a separate diaper bag on your shoulder as well).

Infant seat. Bouncer seats, baby rockers, or infant activity seats (designed for newborns to age 8 or 9 months) are a boon for babies and their busy parents. For baby, an infant seat provides cozy seating, a great view, and often, built-in soothing entertainment. For you, it's a secure place to put baby so he or she can safely watch you go about your business—whether it's making the bed, unloading the dishwasher, checking in at work, using the toilet, or taking a shower. And since infant seats are light-weight and take up little room, they can be moved from kitchen to bathroom to bedroom easily as you switch locales.

There are a few basic types of infant seats: The lightweight framed seat (also known as a bouncer seat) has a flexible frame covered with a fabric seat and bounces or rocks back and forth or side to side using your baby's weight and movement. The hard-shelled battery-operated infant seat provides comforting rocking or vibrating motions at the flip of a switch. Both kinds of infant seats usually come with sunshade canopies (useful if you'll be using the seat outdoors) and a removable toy bar that can provide enter-tainment and activities for your baby. Some models have a sounds-and-music feature for extra diversion (which means you might even be able to steal an extra five minutes in the shower—or even dry your hair). There are even multitasking infant seats that double as travel bassi-nets, while still others can grow with your baby and become a toddler seat.

When choosing an infant seat, look for one with a wide, sturdy, stable base, nonskid bottom, safety restraints that go around baby's waist and between his or her legs, comfortable padding, and a removable padded insert so the seat can be used for your newborn and then later for your older infant. Choose one that is lightweight and portable and, if bat-tery operated, has an adjustable speed. For optimum safety, be sure to always keep your baby safely strapped in and

supervised. And even if you're right beside your baby, don't leave him or her in an infant seat on a table or counter or near something (such as a wall) he or she could push off from suddenly. Don't carry the seat with your baby in it, and never use an infant seat as a car seat.

Another option in the infant seat category is the soft infant support pil-low (such as the Boppy). This C-shaped pillow is quite versatile—you can use it during breastfeeding sessions (just tuck it around your waist, lay baby across it, and say bye-bye to neck, back, and arm strain), or to prop up baby dur-ing tummy time (see page 236). And once baby has enough head control, the pillow can be used as a semireclining "seat." For safety's sake, never leave your baby unsupervised when propped up in a Boppy, and never let your baby sleep in one (it's a SIDS risk).

Finally, there are also cushioned baby chairs shaped like feeding booster seats that can be used on the floor as an infant seat. These come with detachable trays that can be used for toys or books or to serve up food. Wait until baby has good head control (around 3 months) before you use this kind of seat.

Baby swing. There's a reason why baby swings are so popular among new par-ents—they're an easy, hands-free way to soothe most fussy babies (a few just don't end up liking the mechanical rocking motion). But a swing is defi-nitely not a "must-have." Before buy-ing or borrowing a swing, check the manufacturer's weight and age recom-mendations and look for good safety features, including secure straps and a sturdy base and frame. Also consider whether you'll want to be packing the swing to go—if so, you'll want to select a lightweight, portable model, so you can bring it along when visiting friends or family.

Buying for Baby's Future

Now that you've bought the truckloads of baby gear you'll need for the first year (and then some), it's time to put some thought into the kind of planning that's not sold in any stores—planning that will protect your baby's future. These are probably the last things you feel like thinking about or discussing as about-to-be parents, but they're steps every parent should take:

Write a will. Nearly three-quarters of all Americans do not have a will. Being without a will is always a financially risky proposition, but it can result in especially unfortunate circumstances should parents of minors pass away, leaving their children unprotected and unprovided for. Even if you don't have many financial assets, you'll need to name at least one guardian (with their knowledge and consent) who will be able and willing to raise your child (or children) if you and your spouse die before your children reach the age of 18. If you don't have a will stating your preferences, the courts will determine who gets custody of your children—and how they will be cared for financially.

Start saving. As much as you think it will cost to raise your child, it will probably cost a lot more. The sooner you start stashing money away for your child's future expenses (especially education), the better, because your initial investment, even if it's small, will have more time to grow. Consider starting now, with your next paycheck—18 years from now, you'll be glad you did.

Buy life insurance for yourself (not baby). But make sure it's the right kind. Financial planners advise that parents buy term life insurance to protect the rest of your family in case you die. Such insurance provides a benefit upon death without any cash accumulation. You should also consider disability insurance for yourself and your spouse, since younger adults are more likely to be disabled (and thus unable to earn sufficient income) than to die prematurely.

Use the swing only when you're in the same room—never use it as a substitute for supervision. And though babies often fall asleep in their swings, it's best for your little one to do most of his or her sleeping in a safe bassinet or crib (the swing sleep habit can be hard to break). Also, limit the amount of time your baby spends in the swing, especially at high speeds, since some babies can get dizzy from a lot of swinging time. Plus, too much swing time, especially as your baby gets older, isn't great for motor development since it limits the time baby spends flexing his or her muscles.

Stationary entertainers (ExerSaucer). These stationary entertainment toys (commonly called ExerSaucer) allow a baby who can hold his or her body up well (around 4 months) to bounce, jump, spin, and play while staying safely in one place.

When choosing, look for one with height adjustment (so it can grow with baby), a padded, washable seat that spins in a full circle, a sturdy stationary base, and a wide selection of attached toys and activities. If you do opt for an ExerSaucer, make sure you do not leave your baby in it for long periods of time (see page 367 for reasons why).

Jumper. Want to add some bounce to your baby's playtime while freeing up your hands? A jumper—either a stationary activity jumper or a doorway jumper—can be just the ticket. There are a couple of options to choose from:

- A stationary activity jumper looks like a mix between an ExerSaucer and a baby swing with a little "boing" added in. A seat is suspended with springs between a supporting frame, letting your active little one bounce up and down each time he or she flexes and pushes off those growing leg muscles. Most come jam-packed with an array of games, activities, and even light and sound toys within easy reach. A few have height adjustments to grow with your baby, and some can be folded for storage or to take on the go.

- A doorway jumper is a suspended seat attached with a bungeelike cord to the top of a door frame. The doorway jumper is considered less safe than the stationary jumper because the jumper's straps or clamps can break (causing a bad fall) and because vigorous bouncers can bump into the sides of the door frame (and little fingers or toes can get a bad bruising as a result).

Before investing in either type of jumper, remember that no amount of jumping will speed your little one's motor development, and too much time spent bouncing in one can actually do the opposite. Also consider that some babies get motion sick from all those ups and downs. If you do decide to buy (or borrow) one, be sure your baby has good head control before letting the bouncing begin—and take the jumper away once baby starts climbing and/or cruising.

Play mat. Baby doesn't always have to be "in" something to be entertained.

No Walkers Are Safe Walkers

Don't buy or borrow a mobile walker (also called an "infant walker"). Not only are they no longer recommended, but because they carry a huge risk of injury and even death, the AAP has called for a ban on the manufacture and sale of walkers. No walker is a safe walker.

Often, the best and most productive playtime comes when your little one has the freedom of movement—even before he or she is able to move around much. Plus, your baby needs plenty of tummy time practice (see page 236), and that's something he or she can't get while perched in your arms or strapped into an infant seat. Enter the play mat (or play gym or tummy mat)—a virtual amusement park of entertainment at your baby's reach.

Play mats come in a variety of shapes (round, square, rectangle) and designs. Most are brightly colored and patterned (and even differently textured), some play sounds and music, and others have mirrors and plush toys either attached with plastic rings or hung from an arched activity bar (great for developing those crucial fine-motor skills). Size definitely matters when it comes to a play mat—you'll want one that's big enough to accommodate your little one's body size (not a problem when baby's a newborn, but when buying one, think ahead and buy one your baby can grow with). Another feature that matters: washability (you'll understand why after the third spit-up and second pee leak). The best perk of the mat? It folds up easily and usually compactly—great for storage or travel.

CHAPTER 3

Breastfeeding Basics

They make it look so easy, those breastfeeding moms you've seen. Without skipping a beat of conversation or a bite of lunch, with one hand and no sweat, they open a button and latch on a baby—as though breastfeeding were the most natural process in the world. But while the source may be natural, nursing know-how—especially for newbie mamas and their babies—often doesn't come naturally at all, particularly at first.

Your early breastfeeding experiences may be the stuff new mom dreams are made of—your just-delivered baby latches on instantly and suckles like a little pro. Or, maybe, not so much. Instead, your breastfeeding debut may seem more like a dud. Baby can't seem to get a hold on your nipple, never mind suckle on it. You're frustrated, baby's fussy, and soon both of you are crying. Your baby's not getting fed, and you're getting fed up.

Whether it's a first-time breeze, something of a struggle, or somewhere in between, every brand new breastfeeding team has a lot to learn. Some seem to have even more to learn than others. Happily, with a little time and a little help (which is what this chapter is here to provide), it won't be long before your baby and your breasts are in perfect sync, and you're making it look completely easy—and completely natural, too.

Getting Started Breastfeeding

Know you'd like to give breastfeeding your best but aren't sure where to begin? There are plenty of steps you can take to give you and your baby an edge in breastfeeding success:

Learn all about it. Reading up can help you get a leg up on breastfeeding. Feel like you need even more training before you hit the starting gate? Consider a breastfeeding class, offered by many hospitals, lactation consultants, or your local La Leche League. Breastfeeding classes teach the basics and beyond—how breastfeeding works, how to help boost your milk supply, how to get a good latch, and how to troubleshoot—and many are geared to both parents (a great way to get dad involved from the get-go).

Get an early start. Early-bird nursers tend to catch on sooner, not to mention latch on sooner. Babies are born ready to breastfeed—and in fact, they show extra eagerness to suck during the first two hours after birth, with the sucking reflex at its most powerful about 30 to 60 minutes following delivery. So plan to breastfeed as soon as you can—right in the birthing room is ideal, after some initial cuddling—assuming both you and your new arrival are up to it. But don't stress if your baby (or you) don't catch on right away, or if one of you needs a little extra care, making first-thing breastfeeding impossible. Just catch up as soon as it's practical.

Got an early start, but still find that you and baby are fumbling at feedings? Not to worry. Just about every breast-feeding team needs practice, prac-tice, practice (and patience, patience, patience) before they perfect their technique.

Get together. Clearly, breastfeeding takes togetherness—and the more time you and baby spend together in the hospital, the easier getting together for feeds will be. So opt for full-time rooming-in if you can—not only will it be more convenient, but you'll also be assured that no one is mistakenly (inad-vertently) offering your baby bottles or a pacifier in the nursery. If you're exhausted from a long labor or don't feel confident enough yet to deal with your baby on a 24-hour basis, partial rooming-in (days, but not nights) can

offer a good compromise. With this sys-tem you can have your baby with you all day for demand feeding, and have a nurse deliver your little bundle for night feeds—so you can catch a few z's in between.

If you'd like to room in with your baby, put in a request in advance if you can. If rooming-in isn't an option for you (some hospitals allow rooming-in only in private rooms or when both patients in a shared room want to keep their newborns with them), or you decide to opt out of it, just ask to have baby brought to you whenever he or she is ready to feed, or at least every 2 to 3 hours.

Work the system—and ban the bot-tle. Since hospital nurseries are busy places—with a whole lot of crying going on at any given time—it's not surprising that staff can be quick to calm a fussy baby with a bottle. Understandable, but if you're trying to get breastfeeding off to the best start, not the best plan. Glucose water or formula can sabotage early breastfeed-ing efforts by satisfying your newborn's tender appetite and urge to suck. And since an artificial nipple yields results with less effort, you may find your baby reluctant to tackle your harder-to-work nipples after a few encounters with a bottle. Worse still, if baby's getting that sucking satisfaction elsewhere, your breasts won't be stimulated to produce enough milk—and a vicious cycle can begin, one that interferes with estab-lishment of a good demand and supply system.

Don't let the hospital system dis-rupt your breastfeeding system. Be bossy when it comes to breastfeeding your baby. Explain your preferences (demand feeding, no supplementary bottles of formula or water unless medi-cally necessary, no pacifiers if you're choosing to forgo the paci at first) to the nursing staff—and if you meet any resistance, ask your practitioner to make your case. You may even want to put a friendly reminder on the baby's bassinet that reads "Breastfeeding only—no bottles, please."

Take requests—but don't wait for one. Feeding babies when they're hungry (on demand) instead of when the clock says to (on a schedule) is ultimately best for breastfeeding success. But since babies aren't born hungry (appetite generally picks up somewhere around the third day), chances are there won't be much demand at first, and that you'll have to initiate (and even push) most of the feedings. So get pushy. Aim for at least 8 to 12 feedings a day, even if the demand isn't up to that level yet. Not only will this keep your baby happy, but it will also stimulate your breasts to increase your milk supply so it can meet the demand as it grows. Going longer than 2 to 3 hours between feeds, on the other hand, can increase engorgement for you and decrease supply for baby.

Baby's more interested in z's than feeds—or can't seem to stay awake for more than a few moments of suckling? See page 139 for tips on waking that sleeping baby.

Know the hunger signs. Ideally, you should feed your baby at the first signs of hunger or interest in sucking, which might include mouthing those tiny hands, rooting around for a nipple, or just being particularly alert. Crying is a late sign of hunger, so try not to wait until frantic crying begins to start feeding. But if crying has already commenced, settle your little one down with some rocking and soothing before you start nursing. Or offer your finger to suck on until baby calms down. After all, it's hard enough

for an inexperienced sucker to find the nipple when calm—when your baby has worked up to a full-fledged frenzy, it may be flat-out impossible.

Practice, practice, practice. Practice makes perfect, but it doesn't make milk—at least not right away. It takes about four days for milk to arrive, and that's actually a good thing. Your supply is tailored to your baby's needs, and in those first few days of life, those needs are minimal—easily filled by the minuscule amounts of colostrum, power-packed premilk (see page 72) that you're producing while you're practicing. So consider those early feeds "dry runs"—a chance to perfect your technique while you pump up the milk supply to come.

Give it time. No successful breastfeeding relationship was built in a day—or even in a really, really long night. Baby, fresh out of the womb, is certainly a nursing newbie—and so are you if this is your first time. You both have a lot to learn on the job, so expect plenty of trial and even more error before supplier (you) and demander (baby) are working in sync. Even if you've successfully nursed another baby before, remember, every baby is different—which means the road to breastfeeding success may take different turns this time around.

Baby's arrival was a long haul, and you're both feeling a little extra groggy? You may need to sleep it off before you get serious about tackling the road ahead—and that's fine, too.

Get support. Your breastfeeding team will definitely benefit from having a coach (or even a team of coaches) to help you get started, offer tips on technique, and cheer you on if you're slumping. Most hospitals and just about all birthing centers provide routine breastfeeding support—and if yours does, you'll be teamed up with a lactation specialist who will join you during at least a couple of your baby's first feedings to provide hands-on instruction and helpful hints. If this service isn't offered to you automatically at delivery, ask for it (preferably ahead of time)—and if it's not available, see if there is a lactation consultant (LC) or a nursing-knowledgeable nurse who can observe your technique and redirect you if you and your baby aren't on target. Or, if it's financially feasible, try to find a local LC willing to make a house call to the hospital. If you leave the hospital or birthing center before getting help (hopefully this won't happen), make sure that someone with breastfeeding expertise—the baby's doctor, a doula, or an outside LC—checks out your technique within a couple of days.

You can also find empathy and advice by contacting your local La Leche League chapter. Volunteers at La Leche are experienced nursing moms who are trained to become accredited leaders. Or enlist the support of friends or relatives who have nursing know-how.

Keep your cool. Feeling a little overwhelmed (or even a smidge stressed out) by the 7 to 8 pounds or so of swaddled responsibilities you've just been

---

Getting the Breast Help

Looking for breastfeeding support? Whether it's ahead-of-time tips or help getting over a glitch once breastfeeding is under way, here are some reliable resources you can call on:

La Leche League International: 877-4-LALECHE; llli.org (International) or lllusa.org (United States)

International Lactation Consultant Association: 919-861-5577; ilca.org

National Women's Health Information Center Breastfeeding Helpline: 800 994 9662; womenshealth.gov/breastfeeding

---

handed? Of course you are. But tension can inhibit the let-down of the milk you make (or will soon be making)—which means you might not be able to dispense it until you relax. If you're feeling on edge just before a feed, try to chill out first with a few relaxation exercises (they should be fresh in your mind just after labor) or some deep breaths. Or just close your eyes and listen to soft music for a few minutes—baby's likely to be relaxed by the vibe, too.

Breastfeeding 101

Knowledge is always power—but it's particularly powerful when it comes to building a successful breastfeeding relationship with your baby. The more you know—about process (how milk is made and how it's dispensed), about technique (how to position your baby properly), about mechanics (how to tell whether your baby's getting milk to swallow, or so much milk that he or she is gulping), and about logistics (knowing when a meal is over or when it's time for another)—the more confident (and empowered) you'll feel as a breastfeeding mom. To raise your breastfeeding IQ before you put your baby to breast, take this mini-course in breastfeeding basics first.

How Lactation Works

Just when you thought your body couldn't do anything more mind-blowing than making a baby, it follows up that amazing act with lactation, which is considered the natural completion of the reproductive cycle—and it's a pretty phenomenal finale. Here's how it works:

- How milk is made. The process of milk production is automatically initiated the instant you push out the placenta (or it's delivered during a C-section). That's your body's signal—after spending 9 months feeding your baby inside you—to gear up for the shifts in hormones that will allow you to feed baby from the outside. The levels of the hormones estrogen and progesterone decline dramatically in the moments after delivery, and the level of the hormone prolactin (one of the hormones responsible for lactation) rises dramatically, activating the milk-producing cells of your breasts. But while hormones trigger the start of lactation, they can't keep milk production going without some help, and the help comes in the form of a tiny mouth—namely your baby's. As that tiny mouth suckles at your breast, your prolactin level increases, stepping up milk production. Just as important, a cycle begins—one that ensures that a steady production of milk will continue: Your baby removes milk from your breasts (creating demand), and your breasts produce milk (creating supply). The greater the demand, the greater the supply. Anything that keeps your baby from removing milk from your breasts will inhibit the supply. Infrequent feeding, feedings that are too brief, or ineffective suckling can all result in diminished milk production. Think of it this way: The more milk your baby takes, the more milk your breasts will make. Even before that first sip, baby's first demands for the premilk colostrum power that production line.

- How it flows. The single most important function that affects the success of breastfeeding is the let-down reflex, which allows the milk to flow. Let-down occurs when your baby suckles, prompting the release of the hormone oxytocin, which in turn stimulates that milk flow. Later on, when your breasts get the hang of let-down, it may occur whenever suckling seems (at least, to your body) imminent—as when your baby's due for a feeding, or even when you're just thinking about your baby.

- How it changes. The milk your baby gets isn't uniform in the way that formula is. Ingeniously, the composition of your milk is, well, fluid—it changes from feeding to feeding and even within the same nursing session. The first milk to flow when your baby starts suckling is the foremilk. This milk has been dubbed the "thirst quencher" because it's diluted and low in fat—it quenches your baby's thirst without satisfying his or her appetite. As the nursing session progresses, your breast produces and dispenses hindmilk—milk that is high in protein, fat, and calories—and that's the filling stuff. Cut a nursing session short—or switch breasts too soon—and your baby will miss out on hindmilk, causing hunger to strike sooner, and even preventing weight gain (a foremilk-only diet is too low-fat and too low in nutrients). To make sure your little one gets his or her fill of nourishment, wait until one breast is well drained (it's never completely empty) before starting the other. How to tell? A breast that is well drained will feel much softer at the end of the feeding than it did at the start—and you'll also notice that the milk flow has decreased to a trickle and that your baby is swallowing less often.

Getting Comfortable

As half of the breastfeeding team, your needs matter during feeds, too. Here's how to get yourself situated for a successful breastfeeding session:

- Seek some peace and quiet. Until breastfeeding becomes second nature to you and baby (and it will!), you'll need to focus as you feed. To do this, get settled in an area that has few distractions and a low noise level. As you become more comfortable with breastfeeding, you can keep a book or magazine, phone or tablet handy to occupy you during long feeding sessions. But don't forget to put it down periodically so you can interact with your little nurser—that's not just part of the fun for you, it's part of the benefit for baby. Talking on the phone can be too distracting in the early weeks, so let any incoming calls go to voice mail. You may also want to avoid watching TV during feedings until you get the hang of breastfeeding.

- Get comfy. Settle into a position that's comfortable for you and your baby. Try sitting on the couch, in an arm chair or glider, or propped up in bed. You can even nurse lying down in bed (now, doesn't that sound pretty good right now?). If you're sitting up, a pillow across your lap (or a specially designed breastfeeding pillow) will help raise your baby to a comfortable height. Plus, if you've had a cesarean, the pillow prevents baby from putting pressure on the incision site. Make sure, too, that your arms are propped up on a pillow or chair arms—trying to hold baby without support can lead to arm cramps and aches. Elevate your legs, too, if you can. Experiment to find the position that works best for you—preferably one you can hold for a long time without feeling strained or stiff.

- Quench your own thirst. Have a drink—of milk, juice, or water—by your side to replenish fluids as you feed. Avoid hot drinks, in case of spilling. And if it's been a while since your last meal, add a healthy snack to keep you energized.

Getting Into Position

There are plenty of positions you and your baby can eventually explore while breastfeeding—you may even end up inventing a few of your own. But the most important one to know is the "basic" position, the one from which most other positions take form. Here's how it goes: Position your baby on his or her side, facing your nipple. Make sure that baby's whole tiny body is facing your breasts—with his or her ear, shoulder, and hip in a straight line (your baby's face will be parallel with the breast he or she will be feeding on, and those little boy or girl parts will be parallel with the other breast). You don't want your baby's head turned to the side—instead it should be straight in line with his or her body. After all, imagine how tricky it would be for you

Crossover hold

Football or clutch hold

to drink and swallow while turning your head to the side—it's the same for baby.

Lactation specialists recommend two nursing positions during the first few weeks: the crossover hold and the football (or clutch) hold. Once you're more comfortable with breastfeeding, you can add the cradle hold and the side-lying position. So get into your starting (basic) position, and try these:

- Crossover hold. Hold your baby's head with the hand opposite to the breast you'll be nursing from (if you're nursing on the right breast, hold your baby's head with your left hand). Your wrist should rest between your baby's shoulder blades, your thumb behind one ear, your other fingers behind the other ear. Using your right hand, cup your right breast, placing your thumb above your nipple and areola at the spot where your baby's nose will touch your breast. Your index finger should be at the spot where your baby's chin will touch the breast. Lightly compress your breast. This will give your breast a shape that more closely matches the shape of your

baby's mouth. You are now ready to have baby latch on.

- Football or clutch hold. This position is especially useful if you've had a cesarean delivery (and you want to avoid putting baby's weight on your incision site), if your breasts are large, if your baby is small or premature, or if you're nursing twins. No previous experience on the gridiron is required. Just tuck your baby under your arm like you would a football: Position your baby at your side in a semi-sitting position facing you, with baby's legs under your arm (your right arm if you are feeding on the right breast). Use pillows to bring the baby up to the level of your nipple. Support your baby's head with your right hand and cup your breast with your left hand as you would for the crossover hold.

- Cradle hold. In this classic breastfeeding position, your baby's head rests in the bend of your elbow and your hand holds your baby's thigh or bottom. Baby's lower arm (if you're nursing from your right breast, it's baby's

Cradle hold

Side-lying position

left arm) is tucked away, under your arm and around your waist. Cup your breast with your left hand (if nursing from the right breast) as in the cross-over hold.

■ Side-lying position. This position is a good choice when you're nursing in the middle of the night or when you need some rest (that is, when you're able to have some—you'll always need some). Lie on your side with a pillow supporting your head. Position your baby on his or her side facing you, tummy to tummy. Make sure his or her mouth is in line with your nipple. Support your breast with your hand as in the other nursing positions. You may want to put a small pillow behind your baby's back to hold him or her close.

Whichever position you choose, be sure you bring baby to the breast—not breast to the baby. Many latching-on problems occur because mom is hunched over baby, trying to shove her breast in her little one's mouth. Instead, keep your back straight and bring your baby to the breast.

Getting the Right Latch

A good position is a great place to start. But for breastfeeding to succeed, a proper latch—making sure that baby and breast hook up just right—is a skill you'll have to master. For some moms and newborns, it's effortless—for others, it takes practice.

■ Know what a good latch looks like. A proper latch encompasses both the nipple and the areola (the dark area surrounding the nipple)—not just the nipple alone. Baby's gums need to compress the areola and the milk ducts located underneath it in order to start the flow. Sucking on just the nipple will not only leave your infant hungry (because the glands that secrete the milk won't be compressed) but will also make your nipples sore and even cracked. Be sure, too, that your baby hasn't completely missed the mark and started eagerly sucking on another part of the breast entirely (newborns, born suckers that they are, often will keep sucking even when they're not getting milk). This can cause a painful

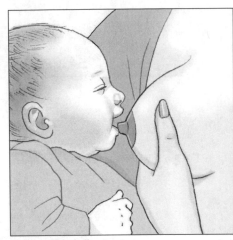

Tickling baby's lip

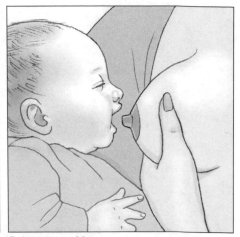

Baby opens wide

bruise on tender breast tissue—and of course, won't get baby fed or supply stimulated.

- Get ready for a good latch. Once you and your baby are in a comfortable position, gently tickle your baby's lips with your nipple until his or her mouth is open very wide—like a yawn. Some lactation specialists suggest aiming your nipple toward your baby's nose and then directing it down to the lower part of your baby's upper lip to get him or her to open the mouth very wide. This prevents the lower lip from getting tucked in during nursing. If your baby isn't opening up, you might try to squeeze some colostrum (and later on, milk) onto his or her lips to encourage latching on.

    If your baby turns away, gently stroke the cheek on the side nearest you. The rooting reflex will make baby turn his or her head toward your breast. (Don't press on both cheeks to open your baby's mouth; that will just cause confusion.) Once baby starts catching on to latching on, just the feel of the breast, and sometimes even

the smell of milk, will cause him or her to turn toward your nipple and open up wide.

- Seal the deal. Once the mouth is open wide, move your baby closer. Do not move your breast toward the baby, and don't push your baby's head into your breast. And be sure not to stuff your nipple into your baby's unwilling mouth—let your baby take the initiative. It might take a couple of attempts before your baby opens wide enough to latch on properly. Remember to keep your hold on your breast until baby has a firm grasp and is suckling well—don't let go of your breast too quickly.

- Check the latch. You'll know your baby is properly latched on when that sweet chin and the tip of that button nose are touching your breast. As your baby suckles, your nipple will be drawn to the rear of his or her throat, and those tiny gums will be compressing your areola. Baby's lips should be flanged outward, like fish lips, rather than tucked in. Also check to be sure your baby isn't sucking his or her own lower lip (newborns will

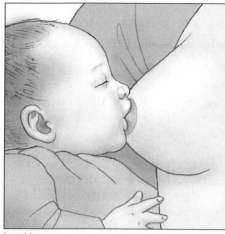

Latching on

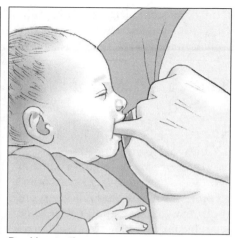

Breaking suction

suck on anything) or tongue (because your nipple is positioned underneath the tongue instead of over it). You can check by pulling baby's lower lip down during nursing. If it does seem to be the tongue that's being sucked, break the suction with your finger, remove your nipple, and make certain

Sucking Versus Suckling

It's a subtle distinction that can make all the difference in the success of breastfeeding. To make sure your baby is suckling (that is, extracting colostrum or milk from your breast), not just sucking (gumming your nipple), watch for a strong, steady, suck-swallow-breath pattern. You'll notice a rhythmic motion in baby's cheek, jaw, and ear. Once your milk comes in, you'll also want to listen for the sound of swallowing (sometimes even gulping) that will let you know that suckling is in progress.

baby's tongue is lowered before you start again. If it's the lip, gently ease it out while baby suckles.

Breastfeeding won't hurt if your baby is latched on properly. If you feel nipple pain while nursing, your baby is probably chewing on your nipple instead of gumming the entire nipple and areola. Take baby off your breast (see below) and latch him or her on again. Your baby is also not latched on properly if you hear clicking noises.

- Give baby some room to breathe. If your breast is blocking your baby's nose once he or she's latched on, lightly depress the breast with your finger. Elevating your baby slightly may also help provide a little breathing room. But as you maneuver, be sure not to loosen that latch you both worked so hard to achieve, or mess with alignment.

- Unlatch with care. If your baby has finished suckling but is still holding on to your breast, pulling it out abruptly can injure your nipple. Instead, break the suction first by putting your clean finger into the corner of baby's mouth (to admit some air) and gently pushing your finger between his or her gums until you feel the release.

Knowing How Long to Feed

Maybe you've heard that the best way to toughen up nipples is to go easy on them at first—starting out with short feeds (5 minutes per breast or so) to prevent soreness and cracking. But the truth is that sore nipples don't come from feeding too long, but from positioning wrong. So instead of setting time limits on feeds, let your sweetie take his or her sweet time at the breast—which initially can be a very long time. Don't be surprised if early feeds end up being marathon sessions—though the average time to complete a feeding is about 20 to 30 minutes, some newborns take up to 45 minutes. Don't pull the plug arbitrarily on the first breast—wait until your baby seems about ready to quit on breast one, and then offer (but don't force) breast two.

Feeding Standard Time

Remember (and wasn't it just yesterday—or even late last night?) when you were timing contractions from the start of one to the start of another? Well, keep that timing technique in mind, because feeds are calculated the exact same way—from the start of one feed to the start of the next. Which means you'll actually have less time between feeds than you might have thought (just like you had less time to rest between contractions).

Ideally, at least one breast should be well drained at each feeding—and that's more important than being sure that baby feeds from both breasts. Then you'll know that your baby gets the hind (or fatty) milk that comes at the end of a feeding, and not just the foremilk (essentially, the skim milk) that comes at the start.

The best way to end a feeding is to wait until your baby lets go of the nipple. If your baby does not let go of the nipple (babies often drift off to sleep on the job), you'll know to end the feeding when the rhythmic suck-swallow pattern slows down to four sucks per one swallow. Often, your baby will fall asleep at the end of the first breast and either awaken to nurse from the second (after a good burp, see page 160) or sleep through until the next feeding. Start the next feeding on the breast that baby didn't nurse on at all last time or didn't drain thoroughly. As a reminder, you can fasten a safety pin to your nursing bra on the side you started with at the previous feeding, or you can tuck a nursing pad or tissue in the bra cup on that side. The pad also will absorb any leakage from the breast you're not nursing on (which will be letting down with anticipation).

Knowing How Often to Feed

At first, you'll need to nurse often—at least 8 to 12 times in 24 hours (sometimes even more if baby demands it), draining at least one breast at each feeding. Break that down, and it means you'll be nursing every 2 to 3 hours (counting from the beginning of each nursing session). But don't let the clock be your guide. Follow your baby's lead (unless your sleepyhead isn't waking up for feedings), keeping in mind that

What Type of Nurser Is Your Baby?

Just as every baby has a unique personality, every baby also has his or her own nursing style. Your baby may fall into one of these categories . . . or, you may find, develop a nursing persona all his or her own.

Barracuda. Your baby's nursing style is barracudalike if he or she latches on to the breast tenaciously and suckles voraciously for 10 to 20 minutes. A barracuda baby doesn't dawdle—he or she is all business at the breast. Sometimes, a barracuda baby's suck is so vigorous that it actually hurts at first—even with perfect positioning. If your nipples fall victim to your barracuda baby's strong suck, don't worry—they'll toughen up quickly as they acclimate to nursing with the sharks. (See tips for soothing sore nipples on page 78.)

Excited Ineffective. If your baby becomes so wound up with excitement when presented with a breast that he or she often loses grasp of it—and then screams and cries in frustration—it's likely you have an excited ineffective on your hands. If so, you'll have to practice extra patience, working to get your baby calm before getting back to work. Usually, excited ineffectives become less excited and more effective as they get the hang of nursing, at which point they'll be able to hold on to the prize without incident.

Procrastinator. Procrastinators do just that—procrastinate. These slowpoke babies show no particular interest or ability in suckling until the fourth or fifth day, when the milk comes in. Forcing a procrastinator to feed before he or she's game will do no good (neither will forcing one to do homework before the last minute, but you'll find that out later on). Instead, waiting it out seems to be the best bet—procrastinators tend to get down to the business of nursing when they're good and ready.

Gourmet. If your baby likes to mouth your nipple, taste a little milk, smack his or her lips, and then slowly savor each mouthful of milk as if composing a review for OpenTable, you're likely serving a gourmet. As far as the gourmet is concerned, breast milk is not fast food. Try to rush these foodie feeders through their meals and they'll become thoroughly furious—far better to let them take their time enjoying the feeding experience.

Rester. Resters like to nurse a few minutes and then rest a few minutes. Some even prefer the nip-and-nap approach: nurse for 15 minutes, fall asleep for 15 minutes, then wake to continue the feeding. Nursing this type of baby will take time and it will take patience, but hurrying a rester through his or her courses, like rushing a gourmet, will get you nowhere.

feeding patterns vary widely from baby to baby. Some newborns will need to nurse more often (every 1½ to 2 hours), others a little less frequently (every 3 hours). If you have a more frequent nipper, you may be going from one feeding to the next with only a little more than an hour in between—not much rest for your weary breasts. But don't worry. This frequency is only temporary, and as your milk supply increases and your baby gets bigger, the breaks between feedings will get longer.

How regularly spaced your baby's feedings are may vary, too, from those of the baby down the block. Some thoughtful babies feed every 1½ hours during the day, but stretch the time between night feedings to 3 or even 4 hours. Consider yourself lucky if your baby falls into that category—just be sure to keep track of your baby's wet diapers to make sure he or she is getting enough milk with all that sleep (see page 182). Other babies might operate like clockwork around the clock—waking every 2½ hours for a feeding whether it's the middle of the morning or the middle of the night. Even these babies will settle down into a more civilized pattern over the next couple of months—as they begin to differentiate between day and night, their grateful parents will welcome the gradually longer stretches between nighttime feedings.

But while the temptation will be great to stretch out the time between feedings early on—especially when you're starting to feel like you're working all the shifts at a 24-hour diner—resist. Milk production is influenced by the frequency, intensity, and duration of suckling, especially in the first weeks of life. Cutting down on that necessarily frequent demand—or cutting nursing sessions short—will quickly sabotage your supply. So will letting baby sleep through feedings when he or she should be eating instead. If it's been 3 hours since your newborn last fed, then it's time for a wake-up call. (See page 139 for techniques to wake your baby.)

What You May Be Wondering About

Colostrum

"I just gave birth a few hours ago—and I'm beat and my daughter's really sleepy. Can we rest up before we try nursing? I don't even have any milk yet."

The sooner you nurse, the sooner you'll have milk to nurse with, since milk supply depends on milk demand. But nursing early and often does more than ensure that you'll be producing milk in the coming days—it also ensures that your newborn will receive her full quota of colostrum, the ideal food for the first few days of life. This thick yellow (or sometimes clear) substance, dubbed "liquid gold" for its potent formula, is rich with antibodies and white blood cells that can defend against harmful bacteria and viruses and even, according to experts, stimulate the production of antibodies in the newborn's own immune system. Colostrum also coats the inside of baby's intestines, effectively preventing harmful bacteria from invading her immature digestive system, and protecting against allergies and digestive upset. And if that's not enough, colostrum stimulates the passing of your baby's first bowel movement (meconium; see page 153) and helps to eliminate bilirubin, reducing any potential jaundice in your newborn (see page 152).

A little colostrum goes a long way—your baby will extract only teaspoons of it. Amazingly, that's all she needs. Since colostrum is easy to digest—it's high in protein, vitamins, and minerals, and low in fat and sugar—tiny amounts will satisfy your sweetie's tender appetite while serving up the perfect appetizer for milk meals to come. Suckling on colostrum

Milk Stages

What are your breasts serving up today? That depends, actually. Each stage of breast milk is designed for your baby's age, making it the perfect food from the first day of suckling, to the fifth day, to the tenth day . . . and beyond:

- Colostrum. First on tap are small amounts of this thick yellow (or sometimes clear) premilk that's packed with so many antibodies and white blood cells that it's dubbed "liquid gold."

- Transitional milk. Next on the tasting menu is transitional milk, which your breasts serve up between colostrum and mature milk. It resembles milk mixed with orange juice (fortunately, it tastes much better than that to new babies) and is the milk that appears when your milk first "comes in." It contains lower levels of immunoglobulins and protein than colostrum does, but it has more lactose, fat, and calories.

- Mature milk. Arriving between the tenth day and second week postpartum, mature milk is thin and white (sometimes appearing slightly bluish). Though it looks like watery skim milk, it's actually power packed with all the fat and other nutrients that growing babies need. Mature milk is divided into two types of milk—the foremilk and the hindmilk. You can read more about that on page 64.

for a few days will get your baby off to the healthiest start in life while stimulating the production of the next course: transitional milk (see box, above, for a menu of milk stages).

So grab a short nap if you both need to—and then grab your breastfeeding buddy and get busy. There's milk to be made!

Engorged Breasts

"Since my milk came in today, my breasts are swollen to three times their normal size, hard, and so painful I can barely stand it. How am I supposed to nurse this way?"

They grew and grew through 9 months of pregnancy—and just when you thought they couldn't get any bigger (at least, not without the help of a plastic surgeon), that's exactly what happens in the first postpartum week. And they hurt—a lot, so much that putting on a bra is agony, never mind latching on a hungry baby. What's worse, they're so hard and so swollen that the nipples may be flat and difficult for your baby to get a grasp on, making breastfeeding not only a major pain, but a serious challenge.

The engorgement that arrives with the first milk delivery comes on suddenly and dramatically, in a matter of a few hours. It most often occurs on the third or fourth day postpartum, though occasionally as early as the second day or as late as the seventh. Though engorgement is a sign that your breasts are beginning to fill up with milk, the pain and swelling are also a result of blood rushing to the site, ensuring that the milk factory is in full swing.

Engorgement is more uncomfortable when nursing gets off to a slow start, is typically more pronounced with first babies, and also occurs later with first babies than with subsequent ones. Some lucky moms (usually ones who nursed before) get their milk without paying the price of engorgement, especially if they're nursing regularly from the start.

Fortunately, even the worst engorgement is temporary. It usually lasts no longer than 24 to 48 hours (occasionally it can linger up to a week), gradually diminishing as a well-coordinated milk supply-and-demand system is established.

Until then, there are some steps you can take to ease those aching breasts so your baby can get a grip on them:

- Use heat briefly to help soften the areola and encourage let-down at the beginning of a nursing session. To do this, place a washcloth dipped in warm, not hot, water on just the areola, or lean into a bowl of warm water (yeah, you'd probably want to try this only at home). Or use microwaveable warm packs designed to be slipped into your bra (these can also be chilled after feeds to relieve soreness). You can also encourage milk flow by gently massaging the breast your baby is suckling.

- Use cool after nursing—you can chill the warm/cool packs and place them in your bra for relief, or use ice packs. And though it may sound a little strange and look even stranger, chilled cabbage leaves may also prove surprisingly soothing. (Use large outer leaves, rinse and pat dry, chill, then make an opening in the center of each for your nipple, and position a leaf over each breast.)

- Wear a well-fitting nursing bra (with wide straps and no plastic lining) round the clock. Pressure against your sore and engorged breasts can be painful, however, so make sure the bra isn't too tight. And wear loose clothing that doesn't rub against your super-sensitive breasts.

- Remember the rules of engorgement: The more frequently you feed, the less engorgement you'll encounter and the faster you'll be able to nurse pain-free. The less frequently you feed, the more engorgement you'll encounter and the longer nursing will be a pain. So don't be tempted (understandable as it is) to skip or skimp on feedings because they hurt. If your baby doesn't nurse vigorously enough to relieve the engorgement in both breasts at each feeding, use a breast pump to do this yourself. But don't pump too much, just enough to relieve the engorgement. Otherwise, your breasts will produce more milk than the baby is taking, leading to an off-balance supply-and-demand system and further engorgement.

- Gently hand-express a bit of milk from each breast before each feed to ease the engorgement. This will get your milk flowing and soften the nipple so that your baby can get a better hold on it. It'll also mean less pain for you during the feed.

- Alter the position of your baby from one feeding to the next (try the football hold at one feeding, the cradle hold at the next; see page 66). This will ensure that all the milk ducts are being emptied and may help lessen the pain of engorgement.

- For severe pain, consider taking acetaminophen (Tylenol), ibuprofen (Advil or Motrin), or another mild pain reliever prescribed by your practitioner (ask if it should be taken just after a feeding).

"I just had my second baby. My breasts are much less engorged than with my first. Does this mean I'm going to have less milk?"

Actually, less engorgement doesn't mean less milk—it means less pain and less difficulty with breastfeeding, and that's definitely a case of less is more. And it's a case that holds true for most second-time breastfeeding moms. Maybe it's because your breasts are more experienced—having been there and done that before, they're better prepared for the incoming milk. Maybe it's because you're more experienced—you know a good latch when you see it, you're a positioning pro, and you were finessing those first feeds in no time, with less fumbling and less stress.

Even first-timers can get off easy in the engorgement department—often because they've gotten off to a good and early start on breastfeeding (not because they're short on milk supply). Very rarely, a lack of engorgement—combined with a lack of let-down—is related to inadequate milk production, but only in first-time moms. But there's no reason to worry that a milk supply might not be up to par unless a baby isn't thriving (see page 182).

Let-Down

"Every time I start to feed my baby, I feel a strange pins-and-needles sensation in my breasts as my milk starts to come out. It's almost painful—Is it normal?"

The feeling you're describing is what's known in the breastfeeding business as "let-down." Not only is it normal, it's also a necessary part of the nursing process—a signal that milk is being released from the ducts that produce it. Let-down can be experienced as a tingling sensation, as pins and needles (sometimes uncomfortably sharp ones), and often as a full or warm feeling. It's usually more intense in the early months of breastfeeding (and at the beginning of a feeding, though several let-downs

---

Pain During Breastfeeding

Pain just before breastfeeding is probably due to let-down. Pain just after a feed is likely a sign that your breasts are gearing up (and filling up) for the next feed. Generally, most of those pains are fleeting and ease up after the first few weeks—and most important, they're normal.

What's not normal is a stinging or burning pain during nursing, which may be related to thrush (a yeast infection passed from baby's mouth to mom's nipples, see page 150). Another common cause of nipple pain during nursing: incorrect latching (see page 67 to get your baby's latch on track).

---

may occur each time you nurse) and may be somewhat less noticeable as your baby gets older. Let-down can also occur in one breast when your baby is suckling on the other, in anticipation of feeding, and at times when feeding's not even on the schedule (see page 77).

Let-down may take as long as a few minutes (from first suckle to first drip) in the early weeks of breastfeeding, but only a few seconds once breast and baby have worked out their kinks. Later, as milk production decreases (when you introduce solids or if you supplement with formula, for instance), let-down may once again take longer.

Stress, anxiety, fatigue, illness, or distraction can inhibit the let-down reflex, as can large amounts of alcohol. So if you're finding your let-down reflex isn't optimal or is taking a long time to get going, try doing some relaxation techniques before putting baby to breast, choosing a quiet locale for feeding sessions, and limiting yourself to

For Parents: It Takes Three

Thought breastfeeding was just between a mom and her baby? Actually, fathers factor in plenty. Research shows that when dads are supportive, moms are far more likely to try breastfeeding—and to stick with it. In other words, while it only takes two to breastfeed, three can make breastfeeding even more successful.

only a single occasional alcoholic drink. Gently stroking your breast before nursing may also stimulate the flow. But don't worry about your let-down. True let-down problems are extremely rare.

A deep, shooting pain in your breasts right after a nursing session is a sign that they're starting to fill up with milk once again—generally those post-feeding pains don't continue past the first few weeks.

Overabundant Milk

"Even though I'm not engorged anymore, I have so much milk that my baby chokes every time she nurses. Could I have too much?"

Sure, it may seem like you have enough milk right now to feed the entire neighborhood—or at least a small daycare center—but soon, you'll have just the right amount to feed one hungry baby: yours.

Like you, many moms find there's too much of a good thing in the first few weeks of nursing. Often so much that their babies have a hard time keeping up with the overflow—gasping, sputtering, and choking as they attempt to swallow all that's gushing out. That overflow can also cause leaking and spraying, which can be uncomfortable and embarrassing (especially when the floodgates happen to open up in public).

It may be that you're producing more milk than the baby needs right now, or it may be that you're just letting it down faster than your still fledgling feeder can drink it. Either way, your supply and delivery system are likely to work out the kinks gradually over the next month or so, becoming more in sync with your baby's demand—at which point overflowing will taper off. Until then, keep a towel handy for drying the spilled milk off of you and baby during feedings, and try these techniques for slowing the flow:

- If your baby gulps frantically and gasps just after you have let-down, try taking her off the breast for a moment as the milk rushes out. Once the flood slows to a steady stream she can handle, put baby back to the breast.

- Nurse from only one breast at a feeding. This way, your breast will be drained more completely and your baby will be inundated with the heavy downpour of milk only once in a feeding, instead of twice.

- Gently apply pressure to the areola while nursing to help stem the flow of milk during let-down.

- Reposition your baby slightly so that she sits up more. She may let the overflow trickle out of her mouth as she feeds (messy, yes, but what isn't these days?).

- Try nursing against gravity by sitting back slightly or even nursing while lying on your back with your baby on top of your chest.

- Pump before each feeding just until the initial heavy flow has slowed.

Then you can put your baby to breast knowing she won't be flooded.

- Don't be tempted to decrease your fluid intake. Drinking less won't decrease your milk supply (any more than increasing fluid intake will increase production).

Some women continue being high-volume milk producers—and if you find that's the case with you, don't worry. As your baby becomes bigger, hungrier, and a more efficient nurser, chances are she'll eventually learn to go with the flow.

Leaking and Spraying

"Am I supposed to be leaking milk all the time?"

There's no contest when it comes to wet t-shirts (and wet sweatshirts, and wet sweaters, and wet nightgowns, wet bras, and even wet sheets and pillows): Newly nursing moms win hands down. The first few weeks of nursing are almost always very damp ones, with milk leaking, dripping, or even spraying frequently and often unexpectedly. The leaks spring anytime, anywhere, and usually without much warning. Suddenly, you'll feel that telltale tingle of let-down, and before you can grab a new nursing pad to stem the flow or a towel or sweater to cover it up, you'll look down to see yet another wet circle on one or both breasts.

Because let-down is a physical process that has a powerful mind connection, you're most likely to leak when you're thinking about your baby, talking about your baby, or hearing your baby cry. A warm shower may sometimes stimulate the drip, too. But you may also find yourself springing spontaneous leaks at seemingly random times—times when baby's the last thing

on your mind (like when you're sleeping or making the car payment) and times that couldn't be more public or less convenient (like when you're about to give a presentation at work or you're in the middle of making love). Milk may drip when you're late for a feeding or in anticipation of it (especially if baby has settled into a somewhat regular feeding schedule), or it may leak from one breast while you nurse from the other.

Living with leaky breasts definitely isn't fun, and it can be uncomfortable, unpleasant, and endlessly embarrassing, too. But this common side effect of breastfeeding is completely normal, particularly early on. Over time, as the demand for milk starts meeting the supply, and as breastfeeding becomes better regulated, breasts begin to leak considerably less. While you're waiting for that dryer day to dawn, try these tips:

- Keep a stash of nursing pads. These can be a lifesaver (or at least a shirt saver) for leakers. Put a supply of nursing pads in the diaper bag, in your purse, and next to your bed, and change them whenever they become wet, which may be as often as you nurse, sometimes even more often. Don't use pads that have a plastic or waterproof liner. These trap moisture, rather than absorbing it, and can lead to nipple irritation. Experiment to find the variety that works for you— some women favor disposables, while others prefer the feel of washable cotton pads.

- Don't wet the bed. If you find you leak a lot at night, line your bra with extra nursing pads before going to bed, or place a large towel under you while you sleep (or a waterproof pad or mattress cover). The last thing you'll want to be doing now is changing your sheets every day—or worse, shopping for a new mattress.

- Opt for prints, especially dark ones. You'll soon figure out that these clothes camouflage the milk stains best. And as if you're looking for another reason to wear washable clothes when there's a newborn around, leaking should seal it.

- Don't pump to prevent leaking. Not only will extra pumping not contain the leak—it'll encourage more of the same. After all, the more your breasts are stimulated, the more milk they produce.

- Apply pressure. When nursing is well established and your milk production has leveled off (but not before), you can try to stem an impending leak by pressing on your nipples (probably not a good idea in public) or folding your arms tightly against your breasts. Don't do this often in the first few weeks, however, because it may inhibit milk let-down and can lead to a clogged milk duct.

Not leaking at all—or leaking just a little? That can be just as normal. In fact, if you're a second-time mom, you might notice that your breasts leak less than they did the first time. Just chalk it up to breast experience.

Cluster Feedings

"My 2-week-old baby had been nursing pretty regularly—every 2 to 3 hours. But all of a sudden, he's demanding to be fed every hour. Does that mean he's not getting enough?"

Sounds like you have a hungry boy on your hands—and at your breast. He might be going through a growth spurt (most common at 3 weeks and again at 6), or he might just need more milk to keep him satisfied. Either way, what he's doing to make sure he gets that milk is called "cluster feeding." His instincts tell him that nursing for 20 minutes every hour is a more efficient way of coaxing your breasts to produce the extra milk he needs than nursing for 30 minutes every 2 or 3 hours. And so he treats you like a snack bar rather than a restaurant. No sooner does he happily finish a meal than he's rooting around again, looking for something to eat. Put him to the breast again, and he'll do another feed.

These marathon sessions are definitely draining for you—not only literally, but physically and emotionally. Fortunately, cluster feeds usually last only a day or two. Once your milk supply catches up with your growing baby's demand, he's likely to return to a more consistent—and civilized—pattern. In the meantime, bring on the feed as often as your little bottomless pit seems to want it.

Sore Nipples

"Breastfeeding my baby is something I always wanted to do. But my nipples have become so painfully sore—I'm not sure I can continue nursing her."

Ready for breastfeeding to become the pleasure you always thought it would be instead of the pain you never expected? Of course you are—so are your poor, sore nipples. Fortunately, most moms find their nipples toughen up quickly, usually within the first couple of weeks of nursing. Some, however (especially those who have a "barracuda" baby—one who has a very vigorous suck), suffer longer or harder—and if that's what you're up against, the soreness, cracking, and even bleeding may have you dreading feeds instead of looking forward to them.

To find some relief while your nipples adjust to the demands of nursing life (and they will!), try these tips:

- Be sure your baby is correctly positioned, facing your breast with the areola (not just the nipple) in her mouth when nursing. Not only will her sucking on the nipple alone leave you sore, but it will also leave her frustrated, since she won't get much milk. If engorgement makes it difficult for her to grasp the areola, express a little milk manually or with a breast pump before nursing to reduce the engorgement and make it easier for her to get a good grip.

- Vary your nursing position so a different part of the nipple will be compressed at each feeding, but always keep baby facing your breasts.

- Try not to favor one breast because it's less sore or because the nipple isn't cracked. Try to use both breasts at every feeding, but nurse from the less sore one first, since baby will suck more vigorously when she's hungry. If both nipples are equally sore (or not sore at all), start off the feeding with the breast you used last and didn't drain thoroughly.

- Expose sore or cracked nipples to the air briefly after each feeding. Protect them from clothing and other irritations, and change nursing pads often if leaking milk keeps them wet. Also, make sure the nursing pads don't have a plastic liner, which will only trap moisture and increase irritation. If your nipples are extremely sore, consider surrounding them with a cushion of air by wearing breast shells (not shields).

- A little dry heat will help if you live in a humid climate—wave a blow dryer, set on warm, across your breast

Inverted Nipples

If you have inverted nipples (your nipples retract into the breast tissue instead of sticking out when you're cold or when you compress your breast with your fingers at the edge of the areola), don't worry. Once breastfeeding is initiated, most inverted nipples do their job as well as the standard issue variety. You can help draw out your nipples before a feeding by pumping just a little (don't pump too much—the idea isn't to get milk, but rather to draw out the nipples). If that doesn't work, you can try using breast shells—plastic shells that gradually draw out flat or inverted nipples by exerting painless pressure on the breasts. On the downside, breast shells can be embarrassingly conspicuous through clothing and may also cause sweating and rashes.

(about 6 to 8 inches away) for no more than 2 or 3 minutes. In a dry climate, moisture from your own milk will be more helpful—so after feedings, leave any residue to dry on your nipples. Or express a few drops of milk (often the best medicine) at the end of a feeding and rub it on your nipples—just make sure they're dry before putting your bra back on.

- Wash your nipples only with water, whether they're sore or not. Never use soap, alcohol, or hand sanitizer. Your baby is already protected from your germs—and the milk itself is clean.

- Apply natural lanolin, such as Lanisoh, on your nipples as needed after nursing to prevent and/or heal cracking. You'll probably need to do this only when you're feeling sore,

Bumps on the Road to Success?

Chances are you had breastfeeding support in the hospital or birthing center just after delivery, helping you through that first feed or two. Maybe you were even lucky enough to have a lactation consultant on call during your whole stay—just a call button away. Only problem is, most breastfeeding problems don't crop up until a week or two postpartum, long after mom's checked out, leaving that call button and that support behind.

There are lots of unexpected bumps new moms can encounter on the road to breastfeeding success—from seriously sore nipples to latching-on issues—but most of them can be smoothed out in no time with a little professional help. So before breastfeeding problems have you wondering whether it's the end of the nursing road for you and baby, call for help. And don't wait, either, for a little problem (say, with positioning) to develop into a big one (like baby not getting enough to eat). Whether it's a session with a La Leche League volunteer by phone, an in-home visit or two from a lactation consultant, or advice from a breastfeeding specialist at the pediatrician's office, it's likely to level those bumps and get you and your baby back on track quickly.

---

since nipples are naturally protected and lubricated by sweat glands and skin oils. Avoid petroleum-based products and petroleum jelly itself (Vaseline) and other oily products.

- Wet regular tea bags with cool water and place them on your sore nipples. The properties in the tea will help to soothe and heal them.

- Relax for 15 minutes or so before feedings. Relaxation will enhance the let-down of milk (which will mean that baby won't have to suck as hard—and you'll have less pain), while stress may suppress it.

- If the pain is severe, ask your practitioner about taking an over-the-counter pain medication to relieve it.

Sometimes germs can enter a milk duct through a crack in the nipple—so if your nipples are cracked, be especially alert to signs of breast infection. Nipple pain can also be the result of a yeast infection. See pages 86, 87, and 150 for information on clogged ducts, mastitis, and thrush (yeast infection).

Time Spent Breastfeeding

"I really feel like the baby is attached to my breasts these days—and as much as I'm starting to like breastfeeding him, I'm also feeling like there's no time to do anything else."

Breastfeeding a newborn can feel like a full-time job—make that a full-time job with double overtime. Immensely satisfying, once you've gotten the hang of it, but all-consuming (as in, your baby is consuming all you've got, all the time).

Will you and your breasts ever catch a break? Absolutely. As your baby becomes more efficient at his job of feeding, you'll be able to spend less time at your job of feeding him. The number of feeds, and the length of each feed, will become more manageable—and you'll stop feeling like you're serving milk 24/7. By the time your baby's sleeping through the night, you'll probably be down to five or six feedings, taking a reasonable total of only 3 or 4 hours out of your day.

Meanwhile, since you can't catch much of a break, use those many hours of breastfeeding to catch some rest and relaxation—and your breath—while capturing some of the most special time you'll ever spend with your little one. Chances are, when your baby's nursing days are over, you'll look back and think about how much you miss those many hours of breastfeeding (and how easy it was compared with feeding a picky toddler).

Mom Falling Asleep While Nursing

"I'm so tired these days, and sometimes I just can't keep my eyes open anymore when feeding my baby. Is it okay for me to fall asleep while nursing?"

Breastfeeding babies are sleepy babies—but guess what, so are breastfeeding mommies. That's because the same hormones that relax your baby during a nursing session—oxytocin and prolactin—relax you, too. That feel-good hormone-induced stupor, especially when combined with the physical and emotional challenges and demands of being a new mom, topped off with the inevitable life-with-a-new-baby sleep deprivation, can definitely lead you to nod off midnursing. Being cozily cuddled by a warm little bundle of sweet-smelling baby can have a lulling effect, too. And if you're nursing lying down, well, it's a pretty sure bet you'll doze off at least some of the time.

Here's the good news. It's okay to nap while nursing. Just make sure you don't start out breastfeeding sessions in precarious positions (you should both be comfortably supported) or while holding a hot beverage (something you shouldn't do with baby in your lap anyway). Keep in mind, too,

Breast Milk: It's Not Just for Breakfast Anymore

Clearly, breast milk is nature's wonder food—but did you know, it can also be the best medicine? Sure, each mama's milk is tailor-made for her baby's nutritional needs, but there are plenty of other much touted (if not clinically proven) off-label uses for breast milk. You've already learned that it can help heal sore nipples, but there may be plenty more healing magic in that milk of yours. Baby's got a clogged tear duct? Drip some drops of breast milk into the corner of baby's eye to possibly help speed healing. Baby's got cradle cap? Rub some of that super fluid onto his scalp. Your cutie's face is filled with pimples? Breast milk can help with that, too (consider it baby's first zit cream). Thanks to breast milk's antimicrobial properties, mama's milk can also help with nasal congestion (squeeze a few drops into baby's nose to loosen congestion), diaper rash, eczema and other rashes, and mosquito bites, to name a few more. Best of all, breast milk is free and always on hand (no rummaging through medicine cabinets at 3 a.m. or mad dashes to the drugstore).

that you'll likely wake as easily as you nod off—since new moms tend to sleep very lightly next to their little ones— probably nature's way of keeping your mommy radar on high alert. Chances are that as your baby becomes more alert at the breast, so will you.

What to Wear

"When I was pregnant, I couldn't wait to get back into my regular clothes. But I didn't realize how much breastfeeding my daughter would limit what I can wear."

Dressing for breastfeeding success probably isn't as tricky as dressing when you're expecting (at least once you've settled back into jeans you can actually zip up), but it still presents some unique challenges—say, how to feed your baby in public without stripping from the waist up, or how to keep a last-minute leak under wraps when you're about to walk into a job interview.

Sure, you'll have to make some fashion concessions in the name of easy breast access and other practical considerations, but with a few adjustments, you'll be able to satisfy your baby's appetite for milk and your appetite for style with the very same outfits.

The right bra. Not surprisingly, the most important item in your breastfeeding wardrobe is the one very few will ever see: a good nursing bra, or more likely, several. Ideally, you should purchase at least one nursing bra before your baby is born so that you'll be able to use it right away in the hospital. But some moms find breast size expands so much once their milk comes in that stocking up ahead isn't cost effective (though some clever designs are expandable).

There are many different styles of nursing bras available—with or without underwire, no-nonsense and no-frills or lacy, with cups that unsnap, unzip, or unhook on the shoulders or in the center of the bra, or those that just pull to the side—as well as bras designed for hands-free pumping. Try on a variety, making your decision with comfort and convenience as top priorities—and keeping in mind that you'll be unhooking the bra with one hand while holding a crying, hungry baby in the other. Whichever style you choose, make sure the bra is made of strong, breathable cotton and that it has room to grow as your breasts do (for the clearest indication, try on bras when your breasts are full, not recently drained). A too-tight bra can cause clogged ducts, not to mention discomfort when breasts are engorged and nipples are sore. Another option: Turn any bra that fits well into a nursing bra (you can find how-to's online or have alterations done for you).

Two-piece outfits. Two-piece is the fashion statement to make when you're breastfeeding—especially when you can pull up the top of the outfit for nursing access. Shirts or dresses that button or zip down the front can also work (though you may be exposing more than you'd like in public if you need to unzip from the top for baby to reach his target, so unfastening from the bottom is usually a better bet). You might also want to look for nursing dresses and tops that are designed with hidden flaps to facilitate discreet nursing and easy access for pumping. Such nursing wear is also designed to fit a nursing mom's larger bust size, a big plus.

Stay away from solids if you're a leaker. Solid colors, whites, and anything sheer will spill your milky secrets more obviously than dark patterns, which will not only provide better cover for your leaks but also the lumpiness of your breast pads.

Wear washables. Between leaking milk and baby spit-up, your local dry cleaner will be as happy as you are that there's a new baby in your house—unless you wear clothes you can toss in the washer and dryer. And after a few incidents involving your good silk blouses, chances are that washables will be all you'll be wearing.

Pad your bra. A breastfeeding mom's most important accessory is the nursing pad. No matter what else you're wearing, always tuck one or two inside your bra.

Nursing in Public

"I'm planning to breastfeed my baby for at least 6 months, and I know I can't stay in my house all the time. But I'm not so sure about nursing in public."

Breasts are celebrated on screen, magazine covers, billboards, and beaches—but, ironically, they can still be a tough sell when they're being used to feed a baby in public. While public nursing is becoming more accepted—and increasingly protected by law, too—it still seems to attract a lot more attention than bottle-feeding. And unfortunately (and unfairly), not always the "awww, so sweet" kind of attention.

Chances are you'll quickly hang up any hang-ups you might have about feeding your baby in public—especially once you realize that hungry babies wait for no mom, at least not happily. Plus, with a little practice (and you'll probably have a lot of practice pretty fast), you'll learn how to breastfeed so discreetly in a crowd that only you and your little diner will know she's having lunch. In the meantime, here are some tips to make public breastfeeding more private:

- Dress the part. With the right outfit (see previous question), you can breastfeed your baby without exposing even an inch of skin. Unbutton your blouse from the bottom, or lift your shirt up slightly. Your baby's head will cover any part of your breast that may be exposed.

- Try this at home first. Practice in front of a mirror, and you'll see how a little strategic positioning can provide a lot of coverage. Or enlist your spouse (or a friend) to watch you as you feed the baby the first few times in public to alert you to any wardrobe malfunctions.

- Drape a blanket, shawl, or nursing cover (aka Hooter Hider) over your shoulder (see illustration below) to tent your baby. To make sure she has room for easy feeding and also easy breathing (and doesn't get overheated), be sure her tent is well ventilated. When you and baby are eating out together, a large napkin can provide cover.

- Wear your baby to lunch. Or to the movies. Or the mall. Or for a stroll through the park. A sling makes breastfeeding in public extremely

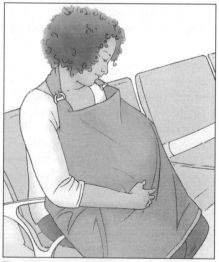

Breastfeeding in public

discreet (people will think she's just snoozing in her sling)—and incredibly convenient.

■ **Create your own privacy zone.** Find a bench under a tree, pick a corner with a roomy chair in a bookstore, or sit in a booth in a restaurant. Turn away from people while your baby is latching on, and turn back once your baby is well positioned at your breast.

■ **Look for special accommodations.** Many large stores, shopping malls, airports, and even amusement parks have rooms set aside for nursing mothers, complete with comfortable chairs and changing tables. Or, seek out a bathroom with a separate lounge area for your baby's dining pleasure. If none of these are options where you'll be going, and you prefer to nurse without a crowd, feed baby in your parked car before heading out to your destination, temperature permitting.

■ **Feed before the frenzy.** Don't wait until your baby becomes frantic with hunger to start nursing her. A screaming, flailing baby only attracts the attention you probably aren't looking for when you're nursing in public. Instead, watch for your baby's hunger cues, and whenever possible, preempt crying with a meal.

■ **Know your rights—and feel good about exercising them.** Legislation in most states gives women the right to breastfeed in public, stating that exposing a breast to nurse is not indecent and is not a criminal offense. In 1999, a federal law was enacted to ensure a woman's right to nurse anywhere on federal property. Even if you're in a state that doesn't have such legislation yet, you still have every right to feed your baby when she is hungry—breastfeeding is not illegal anywhere (except in a moving car, where even a hungry baby must be secured in a child safety seat). For more information about the laws that protect you if you'll be breastfeeding at work, see page 265.

■ **Do what comes naturally.** If feeding your baby in public feels right, go ahead and do it. If it doesn't, even after some practice, opt for privacy whenever you can.

Tandem Nursing

"I've been nursing my toddler throughout my entire pregnancy and am not ready to wean him yet. Can I continue to nurse him once my baby girl is born and I start nursing her? Will I have enough milk for both?"

Tandem nursing, as it's known in breastfeeding speak, is a way for a mom who has breastfed throughout her pregnancy to continue meeting the needs of her older nursing child while also meeting the demands of a newborn breastfeeder. It's not always easy for mama—especially during the early weeks when challenges abound (such as figuring out how to juggle two hungry babies with their own nursing needs and styles)—but once you get the hang of it (with a lot of dedication on your end and support and encouragement from those around you), it can be—and usually is—extremely enjoyable and fulfilling for the threesome (mom, newborn, and tot). An added bonus: Most moms who tandem nurse find it brings the new siblings closer together, allowing the older child to feel more connected to the new baby without feeling pushed aside by mom.

But what about the practical stuff? First, there's no need to stress about whether or not you'll have enough milk to go around. Research shows that nursing moms can produce enough milk to nurse more than one child at a time

I'll Have What He's Having

Is your older child curious about (and maybe a little jealous of) how the nursing half eats? Then don't be surprised if your long-weaned toddler suddenly asks for a turn at baby's feeding station, too—older (but still young) sibs often do. Weirded out? Don't be—it's really no different from asking to have a turn being rocked like the baby, and it's definitely fueled by the same impulse ("I want what he's having").

Game to offer a quick nip, with the hopes of nipping curiosity in the bud? Go ahead. Chances are that's all it will take for your older child to realize that the grass isn't really greener on baby sib's side—and that the milk (if your retired nurser can even manage to extract any) doesn't taste nearly as good, either. Don't feel comfortable honoring the request? Distract your tot with a just-for-big-kids snack or activity.

If your toddler continues to show an interest in nursing, or if he or she objects to baby's indulging, it's probably not breast milk he's craving, but a breast (and a mommy) to snuggle up against—along with an extra serving of that extra attention baby is always served up with meals.

To give your older child what he or she is really hungry for, make breastfeeding more inclusive. Take the quiet opportunity offered by feedings to read a story, help with a puzzle, or listen to music together. Do some simultaneous snuggling, too. And be sure that your firstborn also gets plenty of hugs and cuddles when you're not feeding the baby.

(just ask nursing moms of twins!), and when it comes to tandem nursing, many moms find their problem is one of overabundance of milk, not diminished supply. In fact, your breasts will do a wonderful job of adapting to the needs of both your newborn and your tot (who, don't forget, will be nursing a lot less frequently than your newborn). Do be sure, however, to feed your newborn first—especially during the early postpartum days when your body is producing colostrum. After all, your newborn needs all those antibodies and white blood cells found in colostrum to help stimulate the production of antibodies in her own immune system. Once your milk is back up and running (and bountiful), your baby doesn't always have to get first dibs. You might even find it easiest to nurse your two at the same time—though you'll have to experiment with a few different positions until you find one that works for both your baby and your older child (a double cradle, for instance, where your newborn's legs rest on your toddler, or a double football hold with your newborn propped on a pillow and your tot sitting next to you with knees pointing away). Always latch baby on first, then toddler second (or let your older child arrange himself comfortably in his favorite nursing position)—and try to give baby your fuller breast (keeping in mind that your little one depends on your milk for all her nutrition, while your older child is getting most of his nutrition from solid food and other drinks). And remember to hang in there. Tandem nursing can be tough (and doubly draining) for sure, but you'll find your reward when you have two pairs of eyes gazing up at you in pure bliss as you nurse your bundles of joy together. Of course, if double-mommy duty is taking its toll on you and weaning your older baby feels like the only option, don't feel guilty about it (see page 490 for tips on weaning).

A Breast Lump

"I've suddenly discovered a lump in my breast. It's tender and a little red—and I'm a little worried."

As any woman who's ever discovered one knows, it's impossible to feel a lump in your breast without feeling one in your throat. And even if you know it's probably nothing to worry about, that probably won't keep you from worrying anyway. Happily, the lump you describe is likely just a milk duct that has become clogged, causing milk to back up. The clogged area usually appears as a lump that is red and tender. Although a clogged duct itself isn't serious, it can lead to a breast infection, so it shouldn't be ignored. The best treatment is to keep milk flowing:

- Warm it up. Put warm compresses or a warm pack on the clogged duct before each feeding. Gently massage the duct before and during the feeding.

- Drain, baby, drain. Make sure the affected breast is thoroughly drained at each feed. Offer it first (assuming baby feeds from both breasts at each meal), and encourage baby to take as much milk as possible. If there still seems to be a significant amount of milk left after nursing (if you can express a stream, rather than just a few drops), express the remaining milk by hand or with a breast pump.

- Keep the pressure off. Be sure your bra isn't too tight and your clothes aren't too constricting on the clogged duct. Rotate your nursing positions to put pressure on different ducts at each nursing.

- Enlist baby for a massage. Positioning your baby's chin so that it massages the clogged duct during suckling will help clear it. Or give yourself a massage while baby's busy nursing.

- Dangle feed. Try breastfeeding while leaning over baby (put baby on the bed and lean over your little one). It might not be the most comfortable position, but the gravity could help in dislodging the plug.

- Sometimes milk that's left on the nipple after a nursing session can dry and crust, causing the outlet of the duct to become clogged. If milk can't flow out the duct because it's plugged up with dried milk, the duct itself can become clogged, causing a red lump. Washing the nipple with warm water can often help clear the crust and the outlet clog.

- Don't stop nursing. Since it's all about draining the clogged duct, now is definitely not the time to wean your baby or to cut back on nursing—which will only make the problem worse.

Occasionally, in spite of best efforts, an infection can develop. If the tender area becomes increasingly painful, hard, and red, and/or if you develop a fever, call your doctor (see next question). If you want more reassurance that the lump isn't something more than a clogged duct, have it checked out by your gynecologist.

Mastitis

"My little guy is a bit of a chomper, but even with my nipples being so cracked and sore, breastfeeding was going pretty well. Until now—one of my breasts is all of a sudden so tender and so sore, worse than when my milk first came in. And I have chills."

Sounds like mama has mastitis, a breast infection that can happen anytime during lactation but is most common between the second and sixth postpartum weeks. And though he definitely didn't mean any harm, chances are your baby barracuda's aggressive feeding habits may be at least partly responsible for this painful inflammation.

Mastitis usually starts when germs (often from a baby's mouth) enter a milk duct through a crack in the skin of the nipple. Since cracked nipples are more common among first-time breastfeeding moms—not surprisingly, since their nipples are tender newbies, too—so is mastitis.

The symptoms of mastitis include severe soreness, hardness, redness, heat, and swelling over the affected duct, with generalized chills and usually fever of about 101°F to 102°F—though occasionally the only symptoms are fever and fatigue. Since it's important to get prompt medical attention for mastitis, call your practitioner right away if you notice these symptoms, even if you're not sure what the cause is. You'll probably be prescribed lactation-safe antibiotics, bed rest, pain relievers (especially for before feeds), and heat applications. It's always wise to take probiotics during a course of antibiotic treatment to prevent a yeast infection from developing (though don't take the probiotics within two hours of the antibiotics).

Nursing from the infected breast can be extremely painful, but not only is it safe for your baby to feed from it (those were probably his germs to begin with), keeping that milk flowing will prevent clogging and further problems. If your baby doesn't do a thorough job draining the breast at each feeding, empty it by hand or with a pump.

Delay in treating mastitis could lead to the development of a breast abscess, the symptoms of which are excruciating, throbbing pain; swelling, tenderness, and heat in the area of the abscess; and temperature swings between 100°F and 103°F. Treatment generally includes antibiotics and, frequently, surgical drainage under local anesthesia. If you develop an abscess, feeding on that side will have to stop temporarily, though you should continue to empty it with a pump until healing is complete and nursing can resume. In the meantime, baby can continue feeds on the unaffected breast.

Favoring One Breast

"My baby hardly ever wants to feed on my right breast—she only seems to want the left one for some reason. And now my breasts look totally lopsided."

Some babies play favorites. It could be that your baby's more comfortable cradled in the arm you're more comfortable cradling her in, so she developed a taste for the breast on that side. Or that you got into an early habit of starting her on the left side so that your right hand was free to eat, text, or make another to-do list (or the reverse, if you're left-handed). Either way, a breast that's skimped on can soon become skimpier in size and production—which means there's less in it for baby, who then skimps on it even more. And it sounds like that's the cycle your breasts and baby are caught in.

Whatever the reason, if your baby plays favorites, one of your breasts is bound to come up short—which means you're bound to end up looking pretty lopsided. Though you might try to increase production on the less favored side by pumping daily and/or starting every feeding with it, it's not likely that your breast or your baby will take the bait—typically, once a favorite, always a favorite. The lopsidedness between your breasts will even out after weaning, though a slightly bigger-than-normal difference may always continue.

Breastfeeding When You're Sick

"I think I'm coming down with a bug. Can I still breastfeed my baby without her getting sick?"

Not only can't your baby catch a bug through your breast milk—she's actually less likely to catch one because of it. Breast milk doesn't carry germs, but it is packed with powerful antibodies that help your little one defend her brand new immune system from bugs of all varieties.

The rest of you, however, is a different story. You can pass germs along to your baby through other contact with her, a good reason to be even more hyper about hygiene when you're sick. Wash your hands before you touch your baby or her stuff, as well as before feeds—and don't forget to cover sneezes and coughs with a tissue (not

Birth Control and the Breastfeeding Mom

Women who are breastfeeding have plenty of birth control options—from the "mini-pill" (a progestin-only version of the Pill) to progestin injections to the IUD to barrier methods. Discuss this with your practitioner, and for more on birth control postpartum and while breastfeeding, go to WhatTo Expect.com.

your hand). And keep the kisses away from her sweet mouth—and the tiny hands that will find their way into it. If she ends up getting sick despite your best efforts, see the treatment tips starting on page 554.

To speed your own recovery as well as keep up your milk supply and your strength while you're down with a cold or other bug, drink extra fluids, continue taking your prenatal vitamin, eat as well as you're able, and take any opportunity you can to get some rest. Check with your doctor before you take any medication, even your standard over-the-counter or herbal remedies.

Breastfeeding and Your Period

"I just got my first postpartum period, even though I had my son only 3 months ago. Will getting my period so early have any effect on my milk or my supply?"

Many breastfeeding moms do get a much longer period reprieve—sometimes a year or longer. But almost a third get a break as brief as 3 months before their cycles reset, and that's just as normal.

The start of your periods doesn't mean the end of breastfeeding, or even the beginning of the end. You can expect breastfeeding business pretty much as usual, even while you have your period. Though you may notice a temporary drop in production during your period, continuing to nurse your baby frequently, particularly during the beginning of your cycle, may help give your supply the boost it needs. If not, your supply will return to normal as soon as your hormone levels do.

Some extra-picky babies aren't fans of the slight change in the taste breast milk can pick up when mom has her

Time to Stock Up on Tampons?

While there's no telling for sure when your menstruation vacation will end, there are some averages to consider. The earliest an exclusively breastfeeding mom might expect her period is 6 weeks postpartum, though such an early reset is rare. Up to 30 percent will get their first period within 3 months after delivery, just over 50 percent by the 6-month mark (and moms who aren't exclusively breastfeeding may see a return even earlier). Still others won't be shopping for tampons until closer to the end of the first year, and a few who continue breastfeeding will be period-free well into the second year.

On average, women who don't breastfeed will find themselves back on schedule sooner. The first period may occur as early as 4 weeks after delivery (though again, this is less common); 40 percent will resume their cycle by 6 weeks postpartum, 65 percent by 12 weeks, and 90 percent by 24 weeks.

Though some moms have a sterile first cycle (without an egg being released), the longer that first period is delayed, the more likely it will be a fertile one (a good case for using reliable birth control if you're not yet ready for another baby).

period, and may be slightly off their feed for a few days. They may nurse less often or less enthusiastically, reject one breast or both, or just be a little more fussy than usual, but that's nothing to stress about. Other babies don't miss a breastfeeding beat during mom's cycle. Another way your cycle may affect breastfeeding: You may find your nipples are more tender during ovulation, during the days before your period, or at both times.

Exercise and Nursing

"Now that my baby is 6 weeks old, I'd like to go back to my old workout. But I've heard exercise will make my milk taste sour."

What you've heard is old news. The new, improved news? Moderate to high-intensity exercise (such as an aerobic routine four or five times a week) doesn't turn milk sour. What's more, a reasonable amount of working out doesn't affect the composition of milk or the production of it.

So by all means, hit the running trail (or the step climber, or the pool). Just be careful not to overdo it, since exercising to the point of exhaustion might increase lactic acid levels enough to sour your milk. To play it extra safe, try to schedule your workout for immediately after a feeding, so that in the very unlikely event that lactic acid levels reach milk-souring heights, they won't affect baby's next meal. Another advantage to exercising right after a feeding: Your breasts won't be as uncomfortably full. If for some reason you can't fit in a feed before an exercise session, try to pump and store your milk ahead of time, and then feed the preexercise milk in a bottle when your baby is ready. And since salty milk doesn't taste any better than sour milk, if you're breastfeeding after a workout, hit the showers first (or, at least, wash the remnants of salty sweat off your breasts).

Keep in mind that if you exercise excessively on a regular basis, you might have trouble maintaining your milk supply. This may have more to do with persistent motion of the breasts and excessive friction of clothes against the nipples than the actual exertion of the exercise. So be sure to wear a firm sports bra made of cotton any time you work out. Also, since strenuous arm exercises can cause clogged milk ducts in some women, pump iron with caution.

Finally, remember to drink a glass of water (or other liquid) before and after a workout to replace any fluid lost while exercising, especially during hot weather.

Combining Breast and Bottle

"I know all about the benefits of breastfeeding, but I'm not sure I want to breastfeed my daughter exclusively. Is it possible to combine breastfeeding and formula feeding?"

Full-time breast may be best for baby, but it isn't always realistic—or even possible—for mama. Sometimes it's the logistics (a busy work schedule, frequent business trips, or other time-consuming obligations) that make exclusive breastfeeding too much of a challenge. Sometimes it's physical—either for mom (maybe multiple breast infections, chronically cracked nipples, or supply issues have taken their toll) or for baby (maybe she's not thriving, despite mom's best efforts, and the doctor has prescribed supplementary formula). And sometimes, full-time breastfeeding just isn't a commitment that a mom feels comfortable taking on.

Either way, there's good news. Breastfeeding isn't an all-or-nothing proposition, as many moms assume—which means a mom who wants to breastfeed her baby (but can't or doesn't want to breastfeed her exclusively) can . . . by doing the combo. Combining breast milk and formula isn't only possible, for some moms and their babies it provides the best of both feeding methods—and is definitely better by far than giving up on breastfeeding altogether.

There are important things to remember, however, if you're going to "do the combo":

Put off the bottle. Try to delay giving your baby a formula bottle until breastfeeding is established—at least 2 to 3 weeks. This way, your milk supply will be built up and your baby will be used to breastfeeding (which takes more effort) before the bottle (which takes less effort) is introduced. The exception: If baby is not thriving and supplementing with formula is medically necessary, putting off the bottle is not wise.

Go slow. Don't switch to the combo abruptly—instead, make the transition slowly. Introduce the first formula bottle an hour or two after a breastfeeding session (when baby's hungry

Combo Amounts

Wondering how much formula and breast milk to feed your cutie if you're doing the combo? Adapt the basic guidelines in each month's chapter, taking into account how much breastfeeding or formula feeding you're doing. You can also ask your baby's doctor for advice on amounts.

Nipple Confusion Got You Confused?

Maybe you'd like to try the "combo" of breast and bottle. Or maybe you'd just like to introduce a bottle so you have the option of falling back on one every now and then. But you've heard that bringing on the bottle too soon or in the wrong way can cause "nipple confusion," and now you're confused about how to proceed. Though some lactation consultants warn that starting a bottle before breastfeeding has been mastered may sabotage nursing, others believe that there's no such risk—and no such thing as nipple confusion. And in fact, the majority of infants seem to agree, switching effortlessly between breast and bottle if the combo is started at the right time.

Timing is key in introducing the bottle. Bring it on too soon, and baby may get hooked on the bottle's easy-feed features and decide to reject the harder-to-work breast. Bring the bottle on too late in the game, and baby may already be too attached to mom's nipples to consider sampling the factory-made variety. Personality plays a part, too, in whether a baby will go for both breast and bottle—some babies are more flexible when it comes to feeding (as long as they get fed), others are intractable creatures of habit. Most important, however, is perseverance. While your breastfeeding baby may well be puzzled by this unfamiliar milk dispenser at first—and may even reject it repeatedly—chances are he or she will eventually take the bottle bait. For more on introducing a bottle, see page 238.

but not starving). Gradually build up to more frequent bottles and decrease nursing sessions, preferably allowing a few days in between each new bottle addition, until you are offering a bottle instead of a breast every other feeding (or as often as you choose). Taking the slow approach to eliminating a breastfeeding session may help prevent the development of a clogged duct or a breast infection.

Keep an eye on the supply. When you do begin supplementing, the decrease in demand for your breast milk may quickly result in a diminished supply. You'll need to make sure that you fit in enough breastfeedings so that your milk supply doesn't drop too much. (For most women, 6 thorough breastfeeds in a 24-hour period is enough to maintain adequate milk production for

a newborn.) You might also need to pump occasionally to keep your milk supply up. If your baby doesn't nurse enough (or if you're not pumping to make up those missed nursings), you may find you don't have enough milk to continue breastfeeding—and the combo can backfire.

Choose the right nipple. You've got the right nipples for breastfeeding—now choose the right one for the bottle. Pick a nipple that resembles those made by nature, one with a wide base and a slow flow. The shape of such a nipple enables your baby to form a tight seal around the base, rather than just sucking the tip. And the slow flow ensures that your baby has to work for the milk, much as she has to when breastfeeding. Keep in mind that some babies are pretty picky about their

When Formula Is Necessary

You're committed to exclusive breastfeeding but something's not working out as planned (your milk won't come in because of a hormonal imbalance, for instance, or baby's not able to suckle effectively) and now the doctor is telling you that formula is medically necessary to adequately nourish your little baby. But you're reluctant. After all, you've heard over and over that breast is best—and of course, you want to give your baby the best. That breastfeeding isn't always easy and takes time to work out all the kinks—so of course, you want to give it more time. And that supplementing with formula sabotages the chances of breastfeeding success—and of course, you want breastfeeding to succeed.

Completely understandable—you're feeling the way you feel for all the right reasons. And yet, there are sometimes reasons to rethink a breast-only approach (either temporarily or long term) or to rethink breastfeeding entirely. The truth is, breast-only is best only when breast alone can nourish your baby the optimum way (and in the way a newborn needs). When it isn't, supplemental or exclusive formula may be needed so your baby can thrive (and in some extreme cases, even survive).

If your baby's doctor (or the hospital staff) has told you that supplementation is necessary to protect your baby's well-being, ask why—and whether there are alternatives (such as pumping to pump up your supply or getting intensive help from a lactation consultant). In some cases, routine policy might be at the root of the recommendation. For instance, formula may be prescribed when a baby has hypoglycemia (low blood sugar), even though many experts agree that breastfeeding can help baby regulate blood sugar just as well (except when the condition is severe). If that seems to be the case with your baby, consider asking for a second opinion.

But if supplementing or switching to formula turns out to be necessary, don't hesitate—and definitely don't wait to follow the doctor's orders. Refusing formula that's needed for medical reasons can put your baby at risk.

Do keep in mind that just because you're giving your newborn formula that's medically necessary, it doesn't mean you'll have to give up completely on breastfeeding. It's very possible you'll still be able to make it work—with the combo (see page 90) or by relactating (see facing page). Also remember that there's nothing more important than your baby's health and well-being, no matter where his or her first nourishment comes from.

---

nipples, so you may have to experiment to find one that she'll happily accept.

Choose the right formula. Ask the pediatrician which formula you should supplement with. There are many different kinds (see page 126), including one designed specifically for supplementing. It contains lutein, an important nutrient found in breast milk, as well as more prebiotics than other formulas to help keep your baby's stool soft and seedy—like a breastfeeding baby's poop.

Relactation/ Pumping Up Supply

"I've been feeding my 10-day-old baby both formula and breast milk since birth, but now I want to breastfeed him exclusively. Is this possible?"

It won't be easy—even this short stretch of supplementing has cut down on your supply—but it's definitely doable. The key to weaning your baby off formula will be to produce enough milk to make up the difference. Here's how you can pump up your milk supply, and make a successful transition to exclusive breastfeeding:

- Go for empty. Because frequent draining of your breasts is critical to milk production (the more you use, the more you'll make), you'll need to drain your breasts (either by nursing or pumping) at least every 2½ hours during the day and every 3 to 4 hours at night, or more if your baby demands it.

- Top off with the pump. Finish each nursing session with 5 to 10 minutes of pumping to ensure that your breasts are thoroughly drained, stimulating even further milk production. Either freeze the pumped milk for later use (see page 178) or feed it to your baby along with any supplemental formula (you can mix the two).

- Ease off the formula. Don't wean off formula cold turkey. Until full milk production has been established, your baby will need supplemental feedings, but offer the bottle only after breastfeeding sessions. As your milk supply increases, gradually feed less formula in each bottle. If you keep track you should see a slow decrease in the amount of formula baby takes daily as your milk supply increases.

Banking on Milk Banks

You're determined to give your new bundle nature's best—your own breast milk. But what happens if you can't, for whatever reason? Would someone else's breast milk be next best?

It might be. Research shows that donated breast milk can nourish babies just as well as mother's own milk can. Just as safely—well, that depends. Though you can obtain milk through private donations (from friends or family) or through online milk share collectives, studies show that it may be unsafe for your baby—in some cases carrying infectious disease or containing harmful bacteria due to unregulated collection, storage, and shipping practices. Accredited, nationally recognized milk banks screen all donors and pasteurize milk before freezing and sending on to hospitals and families, ensuring its safety.

There are a growing number of milk banks in the U.S. that operate under the strict guidelines set up by the Human Milk Banking Association of North America (HMBANA), an organization of pediatricians and other health care workers. You can search for one at hmbana.org/milk-bank-locations.

- Consider a supplementer. Using a supplemental nursing system (SNS), such as the Medela Supplemental Nursing System or the Lact-Aid Nursing Trainer System, may make your transition from breast and bottle to breast alone a lot smoother. While it doesn't work for every mom-baby team (and it may take a lot of practice before you and baby feel comfortable

Breastfeeding an Adopted Baby

Once a baby's born, there's just about nothing that a biological mother can do that an adoptive mother can't. And that even goes, to some extent, for breastfeeding. Though most adoptive moms don't end up lactating enough to breastfeed their babies exclusively, a few moms do manage to breastfeed at least partially.

Breastfeeding will be possible only if the baby you are adopting is a newborn and not yet attached to bottle-feeding, and if you have no medical condition (such as a history of breast surgery) that might prevent you from producing milk. Even with all those boxes ticked, however, it's important to also consider this: Establishing lactation will be extremely challenging, and even if you're serious about facing those challenges—and giving your effort to breastfeed everything you've got and then some—you may not manage to reach your goal.

Keep reality in mind, but if you're determined to do whatever it takes to try breastfeeding your baby, you should definitely consider going for it. Following these steps will increase your chances of success:

- Read up. This chapter will tell you everything you need to know about breastfeeding.

- Visit the doctor. See your gynecologist to discuss your plan and to be sure that you don't have any condition (or take any medication) that will make breastfeeding especially difficult or even impossible. Ask for advice on logistics, too. If your doctor isn't familiar with lactation induction, ask for a referral to one who is. Also loop in the pediatrician you've chosen for your baby.

- Start popping. A prenatal vitamin or supplement designed for lactation can help boost your nutritional status and get your body geared up for baby feeding.

- Get help. Contact the La Leche League for advice and to recommend a local LC who can join your support team. You also may want to consider enlisting an acupuncturist or other CAM practitioner who has experience with breastfeeding issues.

- Get a head start. If you know approximately when your baby will be arriving, begin priming your breasts for that momentous day. About a month or so in advance, start stimulating lactation with a breast pump, preferably a powerful double electric one. Try to pump every 2 to 3 hours during the day and twice at night (if you don't mind interrupted sleep even before your baby arrives). If you successfully produce milk before your baby arrives, bag it and freeze it for future use. See page 171 for information about expressing milk.

with it), an SNS is designed to help you feed your baby formula while he sucks at the breast (see page 184). This way, your breasts get the stimulation they need and your baby gets all the food he needs. If possible, try to enlist an LC to help you get started on the SNS.

- Do diaper counts. Remember to keep track of your baby's wet diapers and bowel movements to make sure he's getting enough to eat (see page 182). Also, keep in touch with the pediatrician to make sure baby's getting enough to eat during the transition.

- Feed frequently. Once baby arrives, you'll want to nurse often, depending on the age of baby (at least every 2½ hours during the day and every 3 to 4 hours at night for a newborn), being sure to supplement with formula so your new arrival gets the nutrition he or she needs.

- Stimulate while you feed. A supplemental nursing system (SNS, see page 184) will allow your baby to stimulate your supply by suckling, and at the same time, get the feed he or she needs from supplementary formula. Even if baby arrives unexpectedly—and you didn't have a chance to get a head start on milk production by pumping—an SNS may help you catch up, without shorting your little one on nutrients. And if you don't end up making enough milk to meet your baby's needs completely, you can keep supplementing with the SNS (if your baby cooperates with SNS feeding—not all will) as long as you breastfeed.

- Encourage let-down. If you're having trouble with milk let-down (that is, there's milk in your breasts, but it needs hormonal help making its way out), ask your doctor whether a prescription for oxytocin nasal spray might be useful. Just keep in mind that so far the use of oxytocin for boosting let-down is a little controversial—studies show that it isn't always effective, and some experts believe more research should be done before it can be safely recommended.

- Relax. Get plenty of rest, relaxation, and sleep. Even a woman who has just given birth can't produce enough milk if she's super stressed and super exhausted. Stress can also interfere with let-down, so try to do some serious relaxing before each nursing or breast stimulation session.

- Don't give up too soon. A pregnant woman's body usually has 9 months to prepare for lactation—give yours at least 2 or 3 months to get it going.

You'll know your body is making milk if you feel the sensation of let-down in your breasts. But the only way to know if you're making enough milk is if your baby shows signs of adequate intake (such as contentment after feeding, wet diapers, frequent bowel movements). If it doesn't seem like you're meeting all your little one's needs, continue to use the SNS.

If, in spite of all your hard work, you don't succeed at producing milk, or don't produce enough to make you the sole supplier of your baby's nourishment (some biological mothers don't, either), you can quit knowing you and your baby have already shared some of the important benefits of breastfeeding. Or you can continue nursing for all the nonnutritive perks and pleasures it offers. Just supplement your baby's intake of breast milk, if any, with formula, either through the SNS, with a bottle, or a combination.

- Possibly, try medication. There are herbal options (some lactation consultants recommend fenugreek in small amounts to stimulate milk production or herbal tea combos like "Mother's Milk Tea"), and even a medication called Reglan that may help stimulate milk production (though it's not approved by the FDA for the purposes of stimulating milk production, and there are side effects for mother and baby). But, as with all herbs and medications, don't take anything to stimulate your milk production without the advice of your practitioner, your baby's pediatrician, and/or a certified LC familiar with your situation.

- Consider CAM. Complementary and alternative therapies, such as acupuncture, may help pump up supply. Ask your LC or pediatrician for a referral to a CAM practitioner who has experience in treating moms with milk supply issues.

- Be patient, and be supported. Relactation is a time-consuming process, and you'll need all the patience you can muster—and all the help, too. Enlist family and friends to help out with household chores and other obligations so you can focus your time and energy on your relactation campaign. An LC or advice from a La Leche League volunteer can also provide the support you'll need.

Relactating will take round-the-clock effort on your part for at least a few days and as long as a few weeks, but chances are your hard work will pay off. Once in a while, however, even with best efforts, relactating doesn't take and you won't be able to produce enough milk to breastfeed exclusively. If that does end up being the case with you, and you end up having to bottle-feed either partially or completely, don't feel guilty. Your efforts to nurse should make you proud. And remember, any breastfeeding—even for a short time—benefits your baby greatly.

ALL ABOUT:
Keeping Your Milk Healthy and Safe

Tired of watching your diet like an expectant hawk? Then you'll be happy to hear that compared with pregnancy, breastfeeding actually makes pretty minimal demands on your diet—and your menu choices (a good reason to celebrate if you've been craving cold cuts, starving for sushi, or pining for an oaky Chardonnay). Still, as long as you're breastfeeding, you'll need to pay a certain amount of attention to what goes into you—so you can be sure that everything that goes into your baby is healthy and safe.

What You Eat

You may be what you eat—but your breast milk, not so much. In fact, the basic fat-protein-carbohydrate composition of human milk isn't directly dependent on what a mom eats at all—even women who aren't well fed can feed their babies well. That's because if a mother doesn't consume enough nutrients to produce milk, her body will tap its own stores to fuel milk production—that is, until those stores are depleted.

But just because you can make milk on a less-than-adequate diet doesn't mean you should. Clearly, no matter how many nutrients your body may have stockpiled, the goal when you're nursing should never be to deplete those stores—that's too risky a proposition for your own health, short and long term. Taking nutritional shortcuts will also shortchange you on energy you'll need to keep up with the demands of new mommyhood. Flip side: You'll have more pep in your step if you have higher octane fuel in your tank (lean protein, low-fat dairy, fresh fruits and

Bone Up for Breastfeeding

Breastfeeding can be a drain—especially when it comes to your bones. Studies show that nursing moms can lose up to 3 to 5 percent of their bone mass during breastfeeding, thanks to milk production, which draws the calcium a growing baby needs from mom's reserves. Sounds like a pretty good deal for baby but a pretty bum deal for your bones. The good news is that bone lost during breastfeeding is usually recovered within 6 months postweaning—and that you can give your bones a leg up by boosting your intake of calcium. Experts recommend that nursing moms get a minimum of 1,000 mg of calcium daily as part of a balanced breastfeeding diet. But since that's a minimum, it's smart to aim higher—as high as 1,500 mg per day, the equivalent of 5 servings of calcium foods (that's up 1 serving from your pregnancy requirement of 4). Whether your calcium comes from milk and other dairy products, fortified juices, other nondairy sources (fortified soy milk or almond milk, tofu, almonds, green vegetables, canned salmon with the bones), and/or from a supplement, you'll be giving your baby's bones the best start in life—while keeping your bones healthier for the rest of your life. For better bone building, also bone up on vitamin D and magnesium.

And while you're thinking about your balanced breastfeeding diet, don't forget that it should include plenty of DHA-rich foods to promote baby's brain growth. You can find this fabulous fat in walnuts, flaxseed oil, and omega 3-enriched eggs, but experts recommend that breastfeeding moms go fish, too—eating a minimum of 8 ounces per week (see page 103 for a list of fish and seafood that's low in mercury). Not a fish fan? You can also score those fats in a supplement designed for pregnancy or breastfeeding.

Speaking of supplements, keep taking your prenatal vitamin or one for lactation. Counting calories? Breastfeeding burns plenty—500 or more calories a day. Just keep in mind that you may need to increase your caloric intake as your baby grow bigger and hungrier, or decrease it if you supplement nursing with formula and/or solids, or if you have considerable fat reserves you would like to burn.

---

veggies, whole grains, nuts and seeds—after 9 months of pregnancy, you know the drill). So be sure to eat—no matter how eager you are to shed weight—and to eat well.

Here's another reason to keep reaching for nutritious nibbles: Your taste in food now may affect your baby's tastes in food later. What you eat actually "seasons" your breast milk (as it did your amniotic fluid during pregnancy), affecting its flavor and smell, and acclimating your little one to whatever's on your menu—which means that the carrots you crunch on today may have your baby reaching for carrots tomorrow. And that goes, too, for the curry you crave, the salsa you savor, the Thai you try—a good case for picking a wider variety of foods when you're breastfeeding, expanding your little one's culinary horizons well before his or her first bite of solids, and maybe even minimizing the potential for pickiness. Sounds far-fetched? Plenty of research backs up the booster seat benefits of a mom's varied diet while she's breastfeeding.

Can Foods Make Milk?

Every breastfeeding mom has heard about at least one food, drink, or herbal potion with the supposed power to increase milk production. They make up a rather unusual menu—from milk to beer, from blends of so-called Mother's Milk teas (made from herbs such as fennel, blessed thistle, fenugreek, anise, coriander, caraway, nettle, and alfalfa) to chicken broth brewed with ginger, from brewer's yeast to licorice, from garbanzo beans to potatoes, olives, carrots, and turnips. Though some breastfeeding moms, lactation consultants, and alternative practitioners report milk-boosting benefits from these home remedies, research has yet to back up the claims. Most experts continue to maintain that the effects of such "milk-makers" are largely psychological. If a mother believes that what she eats or drinks will make milk, she'll be relaxed. If she's relaxed, she'll have a good let-down. If her let-down reflex is good, she'll interpret it to mean she has more milk and that the potion worked its magic. In most cases, the remedies cause no harm (and in the case of such nutritionally charged foods as carrots and other root vegetables, they can do any newly delivered body a lot of good). But the bottom breastfeeding line is: The best way to increase your milk supply is to breastfeed more often.

Do strong flavors always work in your baby's favor? That depends on your baby. While most babies will slurp up breast milk no matter what it has been peppered with (including hot peppers), and some will even relish mom's milk more if she's been hitting the pesto and scampi, there are a few whose palates are picky right from the start. They'll detect and reject even the smallest hint of garlic or strong spices. You'll quickly tell which category fits your baby, and you'll be able to modify your menu accordingly.

And while it's also not common (and actually hasn't been backed up by scientific study), some moms maintain that certain foods they eat (especially gas-producing foods like cabbage, broccoli, onions, cauliflower, or Brussels sprouts) unsettle their little ones' tummies. Other breastfeeding moms find that their diet is connected to colic in their babies—and that cutting out dairy products, caffeine, onions, cabbage, or beans from mom's menu minimizes baby's fussiness. A maternal diet heavy in melons, peaches, and other fruits may cause diarrhea in some sensitive breastfed babies, and red pepper can cause a rash in others. And a very few babies are actually allergic to foods in their mother's diets, with the most common offenders being cow's milk, eggs, citrus fruits, nuts, and wheat (see page 198 for more on allergies in breastfed babies). Don't assume, though, that your baby will have a reaction to what you eat— and keep in mind that what seems like a reaction (fussiness, gassiness) is much more likely to be newborn baby business as usual—gas happens a lot in those first few months, and so does fussiness.

Sometimes what you eat can change the color of your milk, and even the color of your baby's pee—and those changes can be shockers. Sip orange soda and you might find your breast milk a pink-orange hue, your baby's urine a bright pink, and yourself in a momentary panic. Pop seaweed in tablet form, kelp, or certain other supplements, and you may be seeing green breast milk (fine for St. Patrick's Day, but probably not something you'd want to see on a regular basis).

It takes between 2 and 6 hours from the time you eat a certain food until it affects the taste and aroma of your milk. So, if you find your baby is gassy, spits up more, rejects the breast, or is fussy a few hours after you eat a certain food, try eliminating that food from your diet for a few days and see if your baby's symptoms or reluctance to nurse disappear. If not, there's no reason not to add the food right back to your diet.

What You Drink

How much more do you have to drink to make sure your baby gets enough to drink? Actually, no more at all—the same eight daily glasses of fluid recommended for adults in general are recommended for breastfeeding ones as well. In fact, too much fluid can actually decrease the amount of milk you make.

That said, many adults don't do a very good job of filling their fluid requirement every day, and breastfeeding moms are no exception. How can you tell if your fluid intake measures up without measuring every ounce you drink? As a general rule, waiting until you're thirsty to drink means you've waited too long, so make a habit of drinking up before thirst kicks in. Another good way to make sure you're keeping your fluids flowing? Drink when baby drinks—a cup for every nursing session, and (at least in the early weeks, when you'll be nursing at least 8 times a day) you'll be filling your quota easily. Keep in mind that your milk supply won't tell you if your fluid intake

is low (it'll decrease only if you're seriously dehydrated—yet another example of how a mom's body puts her baby's needs first), but your urine will (it'll become darker and scanter when you're not drinking enough).

Getting enough fluids, whether you're breastfeeding or not, is particularly important when you're recovering from your baby's birth (you lose a lot of fluids very quickly during childbirth). Not drinking enough can also set you up for a variety of health issues you definitely don't want to be dealing with as a new mom—including urinary tract infections (UTIs) and constipation. And being even mildly dehydrated can increase fatigue. (Do you really need another reason to feel tired right now?)

There are some drinks you should limit when you're breastfeeding. See page 101 for more.

What Medication You Take

Most medications—both over-the-counter and prescription—don't affect the quantity of milk a breastfeeding mom makes or the well-being of her baby. While it's true that what goes into your body usually does make its way into your milk supply, the amount that ultimately ends up in your baby's meals is generally a tiny fraction of what ends up in you. Most drugs, in typical doses, appear to have no effect on a nursing baby at all, others a mild, temporary effect, and a very few can be significantly harmful. But since not enough is known about the long-term effects of medications on breastfeeding babies, it's best to play it safe when you're considering taking over-the-counter or prescription drugs while you're breastfeeding.

Back on the Menu

Have you been sad without your sushi? Steamed after 9 months of steamed turkey sandwiches? Are you way over those overdone burgers? Ready to kiss your queso cheese, you've missed it so much? Well, you're in luck. The food rules are far more relaxed during breastfeeding than they were when you were expecting—which means you can once again order up:

- Sushi, sashimi, crudo, ceviche, oysters on the half shell and the rest of that raw bar you've been resisting, along with rare salmon and barely seared scallops. Just choose fish selectively, since guidelines on mercury still apply (see page 103).

- Unpasteurized soft cheese (feta, queso blanco, queso fresco, brie, camembert cheeses, blue-veined cheeses, panela).

- Cold cuts that are actually cold. No more soggy steamed turkey sandwiches or any other heated cold-cut baloney. Cold deli meats are back on the menu, as are cold smoked fish and meat.

- Pink, or even red, meat. Not a fan of the color gray, at least not when it comes to steak and burgers? It's your time to have it your way again—even if that's the bloody rare way (or even the steak tartare way).

- An occasional alcoholic drink. Cheers! See facing page for more.

How can you tell whether the medication you're about to pop is safe for your breastfeeding baby? Just about all over-the-counter and prescription medications and supplements carry a warning (on the label, package, or both) to consult a doctor before using them if you're breastfeeding—but many of them are actually considered safe to take occasionally as needed, and others are believed to be safe to take as prescribed. To sort out drug safety during lactation, your best source of information will be your baby's pediatrician or your prenatal practitioner, who can give you the short list of common medications that are breastfeeding compatible (and that you can take as needed without getting clearance each time) as well as advise you on whether medications or supplements you've been prescribed or take regularly (say, for a chronic condition) may need to be adjusted until you

wean your little one. You can also check out the National Library of Medicine's Drug and Lactation database at toxnet .nlm.nih.gov (click on LactMed). Or Motherisk at motherisk.org (click on Breastfeeding and Drugs). Do be sure that any doctor, dentist, or other health-care provider who prescribes a medication for you knows that you're breastfeeding.

The most recent research indicates that most medications (including acetaminophen, ibuprofen, most sedatives, antihistamines, decongestants, some antibiotics, antihypertensives, antithyroid drugs, and some antidepressants) can be used safely during breastfeeding—but, again, check with the pediatrician for the most up-to-date info. Some medications, however, including anticancer drugs, lithium, and ergot (drugs used to treat migraines) are clearly harmful, and the research jury is still out on others, making them suspect. In some cases, a less-safe medication can safely be discontinued while a mom is breastfeeding, and in others, it's possible to find a safer substitute. When medication that isn't compatible with breastfeeding is needed short term, nursing can be stopped temporarily (with breasts pumped and milk tossed—aka "pump and dump"). Or dosing can be timed for just after nursing or before baby's longest sleep period. As always, take medicines—and that includes herbals and supplements—only with your practitioner's approval.

What You Should Avoid

Ready to pop a cork, add an extra shot to your latte, or order your burger rare after 9 months of a job (and meat) well done? Go ahead—you earned it. Just remember that while breastfeeding moms definitely have more wiggle room when it comes to diet and lifestyle, there are still some substances that are smart to avoid or cut back on while you're nursing your little one. Fortunately, many are the same ones you probably already weaned yourself off of in preparation for or during pregnancy—so you're not likely to have new habits to kick or curtail.

Nicotine. Many of the toxic substances in tobacco enter the bloodstream and eventually your milk. Heavy smoking (more than a pack a day) decreases milk production and can cause vomiting, diarrhea, rapid heart rate, and restlessness in babies. Though the long-term effects of these toxic substances on your baby aren't known for sure, it's safe to speculate that they aren't positive. On top of that, it is known that secondhand smoke from parental smoking

can cause a variety of health problems in offspring, including colic, respiratory infections, and an increase in the risk of SIDS (see page 270). So talk to your doctor about getting the help you need to quit. If you can't manage to stop smoking, your baby is still better off being breastfed than being formula-fed. However, do try cutting back on the number of cigarettes you smoke each day, and don't smoke just before breastfeeding.

Alcohol. Alcohol does find its way into your breast milk, though the amount your baby gets is considerably less than the amount you drink. While it's probably fine to have a few drinks a week (though no more than one in a single day), it's smart to limit your consumption of alcoholic drinks in general while nursing.

Heavy drinking comes with some serious risks when you're breastfeeding. In large doses, alcohol can make baby sleepy, sluggish, unresponsive, and unable to suck well. In very large doses, it can interfere with breathing. Too many drinks can also impair your own functioning (whether you're nursing or not), making you less able to care for, protect, and nourish your baby, and can make you more susceptible to depression, fatigue, and lapses in judgment. Also, excesses in alcohol can weaken your let-down reflex.

If you do choose to have an occasional drink, sip it right after you nurse, rather than before, to allow a couple of hours for the alcohol to metabolize. If you're not sure if your body has metabolized the alcohol by the time you're ready for a next feeding, you can test your breast milk using Milkscreen: Just dip the plastic strip that comes with the kit into expressed milk, wait 2 minutes, and check to see if the test pad on the end of the strip turns colors. If it has, it means there's still alcohol present (and that means you should reach into the freezer for some stored breast milk instead).

Caffeine. One or two cups of caffeinated coffee, tea, or cola a day won't affect your baby or you—and during those early sleep-deprived postpartum weeks, a little jolt from your local coffee bar may be just what you need to keep going. More caffeine probably isn't a good idea because too many cups could make one or both of you jittery, irritable, and sleepless (enough said?). Caffeine has also been linked to reflux and colic in some babies. Keep in mind that since babies can't get rid of caffeine as efficiently as adults, it can build up in their systems. So limit your caffeine while you're breastfeeding, or switch to or supplement with caffeine-free drinks.

Herbal medications. Although herbs are natural, they aren't always safe. They can be just as powerful—and in some cases, just as toxic—as some drugs. And as with drugs, chemical ingredients from herbs do get into breast milk. The problem is, few studies have been done looking at the safety of herbs, so little is known about how they affect a nursing baby. To add to the confusion, there are no rules for the distribution of herbs, and the FDA doesn't regulate them. Even herbs like fenugreek (which has been used for centuries to increase a nursing mother's milk supply and is sometimes recommended in small amounts by lactation consultants) can have side effects. So to play it safe (always a good policy when nursing your little one) ask your doctor before taking any herbal remedy. Think twice before drinking herbal tea or breastfeeding brews, too, which the FDA has urged caution on until more is known (ask the pediatrician if you're not sure). For now, stick to reliable brands of herbal teas that are thought to be safe during lactation (these include chamomile, orange spice, peppermint, raspberry, red bush, and rose hip, among others), read labels carefully to make sure other herbs haven't been added to the brew, and drink them only in moderation.

Chemicals in your diet. Nobody goes out of their way to add more chemicals to their diet—and really, you don't have to go far too far to find them (additives, preservatives, artificial colors and flavors, pesticides and other residues on produce; hormones in poultry, meat, and dairy . . . it's a chemical jungle out there). Happily, it's easier than ever to stay away from chemical additives and chemical residues, because manufacturers are offering more and more products that are mostly or completely free of them. Since chemicals added to your diet are added to your breastfed baby's, it makes sense to steer clear from as many as possible, something you can do by practicing a little prudence—and a lot of label reading. As a general rule, try to avoid processed foods that contain long lists of additives, and try the following tips for safer eating:

- Sweeten safely. If you're looking to save calories without sparing sweetness, you have more options than ever. Stevia, Nectresse, Sunett, Splenda, and Equal/Nutrasweet are all considered safe during lactation (though it's best to use Equal in moderation, and avoid it entirely if you have PKU or your baby does). Agave can be used during lactation but in small amounts. Whey-Low, a refined sugar substitute (it's a blend of sucrose, fructose, and lactose but with many fewer calories than regular sugar), is safe during lactation (and it's not thought to be a problem for the lactose intolerant, either). The one sweetener that's not sweet when you're breastfeeding: Sweet 'n Low (aka saccharine).

- Go organic. Certified organic fruits and vegetables are now widely available in supermarkets, as are organic dairy products and organic poultry, meat, and eggs, and products made with organic grains (like cereal and bread). Choose them whenever you have the choice (and can afford the usually steeper price), and you'll be minimizing the number of chemicals your baby is exposed to through your breast milk. But also realize that a certain amount of pesticides and other questionable chemicals will most likely end up in your diet, and thus your baby's, despite best efforts— and that small amounts are nothing to stress about. In other words, it isn't necessary to drive yourself crazy (or drive yourself all over town, or drive your marketing budget into uncomfortable territory) in order to fill your grocery cart with organic-only products. When organic isn't available, or if you just can't afford the extra cost, peel or scrub fruits and vegetable skins well (use produce wash for extra protection). Keep in mind that local produce usually contains lower levels of pesticides and preservatives than produce that must travel long distances—a good reason to visit a farmers market, or even to grow your own.

- Stay low-fat. As it was during pregnancy, it's smart to choose low-fat dairy products, as well as lean meats and poultry without the skin, for two reasons. First, a low-fat diet will make it easier to shed your pregnancy weight gain (something you're likely eager to do). Second, the pesticides

and other chemicals ingested by animals are stored in their fat (and in their organs, such as liver, kidneys, and brain, which is why you should eat these meats only rarely while you're breastfeeding). Going lean means you'll be avoiding more of those chemicals. Since organic dairy, poultry, and meat products don't pose the same potential risk, select them when you can, especially when you're reaching for a higher-fat variety.

- Fish selectively. The same EPA guidelines on fish safety that apply to pregnant women apply to breastfeeding ones. So to minimize your (and your baby's) exposure to mercury, avoid eating shark, swordfish, king mackerel, and tilefish, and limit your consumption to 6 ounces per week of tuna (chunk light tuna contains less mercury than tuna steaks and canned albacore) and 12 ounces (total) per week of salmon (wild is best), sea bass, flounder, sole, haddock, halibut, ocean perch, whitefish, pollack, cod, tuna (canned is safer than fresh), butterfish, catfish, crab, mussels, scallops, calamari, and farm-raised trout. Anchovies, clams, tilapia, sardines, and shrimp are low in mercury and can be eaten while breastfeeding as well. Wondering whether going fish-free might be a healthfier option for you and your baby? Actually, guidelines recommend that breastfeeding moms eat a minimum of 8 ounces per week of low mercury fish, since the nutrients found in seafood (especially fatty fish like salmon and sardines) have been shown to boost a baby's brainpower.

  Want some really good fish news? Sashimi, raw oysters, and rare salmon can be ordered up again.

The First Year at a Glance

P renatal development (from microscopic egg to cuddly newborn) may be a tough act to follow—but the first 12 months of your baby's developmental life (taking your little one from tiny blob to buzzing, busy toddler) will be pretty impressive, too. Make that mind-blowing—hard to believe, and amazing to watch. Your little one's large motor skills will progress at an astonishing pace—first head control and then progressive body control (rolling over! sitting! cruising!). Sensory and thinking skills (baby brain power) will soar—at first your newborn will turn toward a sound or to watch someone's face, but by year's end baby will be copying sounds and actions. Coos will evolve to babble and then to real words. Small motor skills will be finessed—holding a rattle at first with a full fist, then neatly snatching up a small piece of food with chubby thumb and tiny index finger.

These developmental milestones follow roughly the same timeline for most babies in the first year, but the pace and pattern of development is far from uniform. Some 5-month-old babies may be sitting pretty (and unsupported) while others haven't even rolled over yet. Some 10-month-olds may be walking up a storm, others talking up a storm, and some are taking their sweet time with both. Some babies may speed ahead early in most departments, while others get a later start, eventually catching up or even zipping past. Some babies are relatively consistent in

their pace of development while others develop in fits and starts. Illness or a major change in baby's life can temporarily throw development off pace altogether. But most of the time, what's normal developmentally is what's normal for your one-of-a-kind baby.

If babies are all over the map developmentally, why bother mapping development at all? Developmental norms are useful for comparing your baby to a broad range of normal infants in order to assess his or her progress and to make sure your baby's development is on target. Or for comparing your baby's

You Know Your Baby Best

Maybe you don't have a degree in child development, but when it comes to your child's development, even the experts agree that you're something of an expert. Unlike a pediatrician, who usually sees your baby only once a month or less—and who sees hundreds of other babies in between— you see your baby every single day. You spend more time interacting with your baby than anyone else. You probably notice nuances in your baby's development that others might miss.

Whenever you have a concern about your child's development—whether it's because some areas are lagging, or because a skill that was mastered seems to have been forgotten, or just because you've got a nagging feeling that something's not quite right—don't keep it to yourself. Child development experts believe that parents not only are their children's best advocates but can also be key in the early diagnosis of developmental disorders, such as autism. Early diagnosis can lead to the kind of early intervention that can make an enormous difference in the long-term developmental future of a child with autism or another developmental disorder.

To help parents better help their children, doctors have pinpointed a number of developmental red flags to look out for as early as 9 months. Your baby's pediatrician will screen for these red flags as well during well-baby checkups. But if you notice your almost 1-year-old doesn't exchange back-and-forth sounds with you, doesn't smile or gesture with you, fails to establish and maintain eye contact with you, doesn't point or use other gestures to get needs met, doesn't enjoy playing social games such as peekaboo or pat-a-cake, fails to respond when you call his or her name, or doesn't look when you point at something, let the doctor know. It could be that nothing at all is wrong. But further assessment, and perhaps referral to a specialist, can help determine whether there is reason for concern.

rate of development one month to the next—to see if he or she is holding steady, lagging a little, or racing ahead. Your doctor will also look for certain milestones at each well-baby visit, to be sure that your baby's development fits within the (very) wide range of normal for his or her age.

Your baby, like every baby, is one of a kind—incomparable, really. Which is why comparing your baby with the baby down the block or an older sibling can be misleading—and sometimes, unnecessarily stressful. So can obsessing over developmental timelines. As long as your baby is reaching the majority of milestones on time, his or her development is on target—which means you can sit back and marvel at those amazing achievements instead of analyzing them. If, on the other hand, you notice that your baby is consistently missing milestones or seems to be suddenly slipping significantly in development—or if you have that gut feeling that something isn't right—check in with the doctor. Most likely there's no problem at all (some babies just move forward on a slower-than-average pace), and you'll get the reassurance you're looking for. If a lag is identified, the right intervention will help your little one maximize his or her developmental potential.

Not interested in seeing where your baby falls out on the developmental timeline? That's perfectly fine. Timelines aren't a must-do—especially if your little one is regularly being assessed at well-baby visits. Let your baby do the developing and leave the screening to the doctor.

For more on developmental milestones, go to WhatToExpect.com.

Developmental Milestones in the First Year

Newborn

Most newborns will probably be able to . . .

- Lift head briefly when on the tummy

- Move arms and legs on both sides of the body equally well

- Focus on objects within 8 to 15 inches (especially your face!)

Newborn to 1 Month

Most babies will probably be able to . . .

- Lift head briefly when on the tummy (tummy time should be supervised)

- Focus on a face

- Bring hands to face

- Suck well

Half of all babies will be able to . . .

- Respond to a loud noise in some way, such as startling, crying, quieting

Some babies will be able to . . .

- Lift head 45 degrees when on tummy

- Vocalize in ways other than crying (such as that adorable cooing)

- Smile in response to a smile (a "social" smile)

A few babies will be able to . . .

- Lift head 90 degrees when on tummy

- Hold head steady when upright

- Bring both hands together

- Smile spontaneously

1 to 2 Months

Most babies will probably be able to . . .

- Smile in response to a smile

- Notice own hands

- Respond to a loud sound in some way, such as startling, crying, quieting

- Grasp and shake hand toys

Half of all babies will be able to . . .

- Vocalize in ways other than crying (cooing, for instance)

- Lift head 45 degrees when on tummy

Some babies will be able to . . .

- Hold head steady when upright

- While on the tummy, raise chest, supported by arms

- Roll over (tummy to back is usually first)

- Pay attention to an object as small as a raisin (but make sure such objects are kept out of baby's reach)

- Reach for a dangling object

A few babies will be able to . . .

- Lift head 90 degrees while on tummy

- Bring both hands together

- Smile spontaneously

- Laugh out loud

- Squeal in delight

- Follow an object held about 6 inches above baby's face and moved 180 degrees (from one side to the other), with baby watching all the way

2 to 3 Months

Most babies will probably be able to . . .

- Lift head 45 degrees when on tummy—assuming baby has been given enough tummy time to practice

- Kick energetically and straighten legs when on back

- Bring hands to mouth

Half of all babies will be able to . . .

- Lift head 90 degrees when on tummy

- Smile spontaneously

- Laugh out loud

- Follow an object held about 6 inches above baby's face and moved 180 degrees (from one side to the other), with baby watching all the way

- Hold head steady when upright

- While on tummy, raise chest, supported by arms

It's Cumulative

Babies gather lots of new skills every month but typically hold on to last month's achievements (and the month before last, and so on). So assume that your baby's skill set will incorporate those "will probably be able to" items from previous months in addition to brand new ones acquired this month.

- Reach for a dangled object

- Pay attention to an object as small as a raisin (but make sure such objects are kept out of baby's reach)

Some babies will be able to . . .

- Roll over (tummy to back is usually first)

- Squeal in delight

- Bring both hands together

- Reach for an object

- Turn in the direction of a voice, particularly mommy's or daddy's

A few babies will be able to . . .

- Bear some weight on legs when held in standing position

- Keep head level with body when pulled to sitting

- Razz (make a wet razzing sound)

- Say "ah-goo" or similar vowel-consonant combination

Preemie Timing

Premature infants generally reach milestones later than other babies of the same birth age, often achieving them closer to their adjusted age (the age they would be if they had been born at term), and sometimes later.

3 to 4 Months

Most babies will probably be able to . . .

- Lift head 90 degrees when on tummy and turn head from side to side—assuming baby has been given enough tummy time to practice

- Lift head when held in your arms at your shoulder

- Anticipate being lifted

- Laugh out loud

- Follow an object in an arc about 6 inches above the face for 180 degrees (from one side to the other), with baby watching all the way

Half of all babies will be able to . . .

- Quiet down at the sound of a soothing voice or when held

- While on the tummy, raise chest, supported by arms

- Keep head level with body when pulled to sitting

- Roll over (tummy to back is usually first)

- Pay attention to an object as small as a raisin (but make sure such objects are kept out of baby's reach)

- Reach for an object

- Squeal in delight

- Turn in the direction of a voice, particularly mommy's or daddy's

Some babies will be able to . . .

- Say "ah-goo" or similar vowel-consonant combinations

- Razz (make a wet razzing sound)

A few babies will be able to . . .

- Bear some weight on legs when held in a standing position

- Sit without support

- Object if you try to take a toy away

4 to 5 Months

Most babies will probably be able to . . .

- Hold head steady when upright

- While on tummy, raise chest, supported by arms

- Keep head level with body when pulled to sitting

- Roll over (tummy to back is usually first). Babies who spend little time on their tummies during playtime may reach this milestone later, and that's not cause for concern.

- Pay attention to an object as small as a raisin (but make sure such objects are kept out of baby's reach)

- Squeal in delight

- Smile spontaneously

- Reach for an object

- See across the room

Half of all babies will be able to . . .

- Bear some weight on legs when held upright

- Say "ah-goo" or similar vowel-consonant combinations

- Razz (make a wet razzing sound)

- Play with toes when on back

Some babies will be able to . . .

- Pass a cube or other object from one hand to the other

A few babies will be able to . . .

- Sit without support

- Pull up to standing position from sitting

- Stand holding on to someone

- Object if you try to take a toy away

- Work to get to a toy out of reach

- Look for a dropped object

- Rake with fingers a tiny object and pick it up in fist (but keep all dangerous objects out of baby's reach)

- Babble, combining vowels and consonants such as ga-ga-ga, ba-ba-ba, ma-ma-ma, da-da-da

5 to 6 Months

Most babies will probably be able to . . .

- Play with toes

- Roll over

- Help hold bottle during feedings

- Say "ah-goo" or similar vowel-consonant combinations

Half of all babies will be able to . . .

- Bear some weight on legs when held in standing position

- Sit without support

- Coo or babble when happy

- Razz (make a wet razzing noise)

Some babies will be able to . . .

- Stand holding on to someone or something

- Object if you try to take a toy away

- Work to get a toy that's out of reach

- Pass a toy or other object from one hand to the other

- Look for a dropped object

- Rake with fingers a tiny object and pick it up in fist (keep all dangerous objects out of baby's reach)

- Babble, combining vowels and consonants such as ga-ga-ga, ba-ba-ba, ma-ma-ma, da-da-da

- Recognize books and the rhymes in those books

A few babies will be able to . . .

- Creep or crawl (more likely if baby has had plenty of tummy time, but crawling is not a "must-do" milestone)

- Pull up to standing position from sitting

- Get into a sitting position from tummy

- Pick up a tiny object with thumb and finger (keep all dangerous objects out of baby's reach)

- Say "mama" or "dada," but without meaning

6 to 7 Months

Most babies will probably be able to . . .

- Sit in a high chair

- Open mouth for a spoon

- Razz (make a wet razzing sound)

- Coo or babble when happy

- Smile often when interacting with you

- Explore by mouthing objects

- Turn in the direction of a voice

- Bear weight on legs (and possibly even bounce) when held in standing position

Half of all babies will be able to . . .

- Sit without support

- Object if you try to take a toy away

- Work to get a toy that's out of reach

- Look for a dropped object

- Rake with fingers an object and pick it up in fist (keep all dangerous objects out of baby's reach)

- Pass a toy or other object from one hand to the other

- Babble, combining vowels and consonants such as ga-ga-ga, ba-ba-ba, ma-ma-ma, da-da-da

- Play along in a game of peekaboo

- Recognize books and the rhymes in those books

Some babies will be able to . . .

- Creep or crawl (though babies who spend little time on their tummies during playtime may reach this milestone later—or skip straight to cruising—and that's not cause for concern)

- Pull up to standing position from sitting

- Get into a sitting position from tummy

- Stand holding on to someone or something

A few babies will be able to . . .

- Clap hands or wave bye-bye

- Pick up a tiny object with thumb and finger (keep all dangerous objects out of baby's reach)

- Feed self a cracker or other finger food

- Walk holding on to furniture (cruise)

- Say "mama" or "dada" without meaning

7 to 8 Months

Most babies will probably be able to . . .

- Bear weight on legs (and even bounce) when held in standing position

- Roll from tummy to back and from back to tummy

- Reach for utensil when being fed

- Feed self a cracker or other finger food

- Find a partially hidden object

- Rake with fingers an object and pick it up in fist (keep all dangerous objects out of baby's reach)

- Look for a dropped object

Half of all babies will be able to . . .

- Stand holding on to someone or something

- Get into a sitting position from tummy

- Pass a cube or other object from one hand to the other

- Object if you try to take a toy away

- Work to get a toy that's out of reach

- Play along in a game of peekaboo

Some babies will be able to . . .

- Creep or crawl (though babies who spend little time on their tummies during playtime may reach this milestone later—or skip straight to cruising—and that's not cause for concern)

- Pull up to standing position from sitting

- Pick up a tiny object with thumb and finger (keep all dangerous objects out of baby's reach)

- Say "mama" or "dada" without meaning

A few babies will be able to . . .

- Clap hands or wave bye-bye

- Walk holding on to furniture (cruise)

- Stand alone momentarily

- Understand "no" (but not always obey it)

8 to 9 Months

Most babies will probably be able to . . .

- Get into a sitting position from tummy

- Work to get a toy that's out of reach

- Respond to own name

- Smile at self in mirror (though not knowing that image is their own)

- Follow your gaze when you look away

Half of all babies will be able to . . .

- Pull up to standing position from sitting

- Creep or crawl (though babies who spend little time on their tummies during playtime may reach this milestone later—or skip straight to cruising—and that's not cause for concern)

- Stand holding on to someone or something

- Object if you try to take a toy away

- Pick up a tiny object with thumb and finger (keep all dangerous objects out of baby's reach)

- Say "mama" or "dada" without meaning

- Play peekaboo

Some babies will be able to . . .

- Walk holding on to furniture (cruise)

- Stand alone momentarily

- Clap hands or wave bye-bye

- Understand "no" (but not always obey it)

A few babies will be able to . . .

- Stand alone well

- Play ball (roll ball back to you)

- Drink from a cup independently

- Say "dada" or "mama" with meaning

- Say one word other than "mama" or "dada"

- Respond to a one-step command with gestures ("Give that to me," said with hand out)

9 to 10 Months

Most babies will probably be able to . . .

- Stand holding on to someone or something

- Pull up to standing position from sitting

- Object if you try to take a toy away

- Say "mama" or "dada" without meaning

- Play along in a game of peekaboo and other anticipation games

- Exchange back-and-forth gestures and sounds with you

Half of all babies will be able to . . .

- Walk holding on to furniture

- Clap hands or wave bye-bye

- Pick up a tiny object with thumb and finger (keep all dangerous objects out of baby's reach)

- Understand "no" (but not always obey it)

Some babies will be able to . . .

- Stand alone momentarily

- Stand alone well

- Say "dada" or "mama" with meaning

- Say one word other than "mama" or "dada"

- Point to something to get needs met

A few babies will be able to . . .

- Indicate wants in ways other than crying

- Drink from a cup independently

- Play ball (roll ball back to you)

- Pick up a tiny object neatly with tips of thumb and forefinger (keep all dangerous objects out of baby's reach)

- Use immature jargoning (gibberish that sounds as if baby is talking in a made-up foreign language)

- Respond to a one-step command with gestures ("Give that to me," said with hand out)

- Walk well

10 to 11 Months

Most babies will probably be able to . . .

- Pick up a tiny object with thumb and finger (as always, make sure dangerous objects stay out of baby's reach)

- Understand "no" (but not always obey it)

- Look at what you're pointing at and then look back at you with a reaction

Half of all babies will be able to . . .

- Walk holding on to furniture (cruise)

- Point or gesture to something to get needs met

- Clap hands or wave bye-bye

- Drink from a cup independently

Some babies will be able to . . .

- Stand alone momentarily

- Say "dada" or "mama" with meaning

- Say one word other than "mama" or "dada"

- Respond to a one-step command without gestures ("Give that to me," said without hand out)

A few babies will be able to . . .

- Stand alone well

- Walk well

- Play ball (roll ball back to you)

- Use immature jargoning (gibberish that sounds as if baby is talking a made-up foreign language)

- Say three or more words other than "mama" or "dada"

11 to 12 Months

Most babies will probably be able to . . .

- Walk holding on to furniture (cruise)

- Use a few gestures to get needs met—pointing, showing, reaching, waving

- Respond to name when called

- Drink from cup with help

- Bang two blocks or other toys together

- Cooperate with dressing by offering a foot or arm

- Raise arms when want to be picked up

Half of all babies will be able to . . .

- Clap hands or wave bye-bye (most children accomplish these feats by 13 months)

- Drink from a cup independently (assuming baby has been given practice)

- Pick up a tiny object neatly with tips of thumb and forefinger (many babies do not accomplish this until nearly 15 months—continue to keep all dangerous objects out of baby's reach)

- Stand alone momentarily (many don't accomplish this until 13 months)

- Say "dada" or "mama" with meaning (most will say at least one of these by 14 months)

- Say one word other than "mama" or "dada" (many won't say their first word until 14 months or later)

- Copy sounds and gestures you make

Some babies will be able to . . .

- Play ball (roll a ball back to you, though many don't accomplish this feat until 16 months)

- Stand alone well (many don't reach this point until 14 months)

- Use immature jargoning—gibberish that sounds like a foreign language (half of all babies don't start jargoning until after their first birthday, and many not until they are 15 months old)

- Walk well (three out of four babies don't walk well until 13½ months, and many not until considerably later. Good crawlers may be slower to walk and when other development is normal, late walking is rarely a cause for concern)

- Respond to music with body motion

A few babies will be able to . . .

- Say three words or more other than "mama" or "dada" (a good half of all babies won't reach this stage until 13 months, and many not until 16 months)

- Respond to a one-step command without gestures ("Give that to me," said without hand out; most children won't reach this stage until after their first birthday, many not until after 16 months)

- Respond to another person's upset by becoming upset (beginnings of empathy)

- Show affection, particularly to mommy and daddy

- Show stranger and/or separation anxiety (some children never will)

Growth Charts

How does your baby's growth measure up? By plotting measurements of length, weight, and head circumference at each well-baby visit, the doctor can see how your baby stacks up percentage-wise against other babies of the same age and gender.

More important, tracking growth allows the doctor to compare your baby against him- or herself and follow your baby's growth trends over time—a more important measure than which particular percentile he or she falls into at a given time. For instance, if your little one has been consistently hovering around the 15th percentile month after month, he or she may be destined to be on the small side (or may be destined to have a dramatic growth spurt later on in childhood). On the other hand, if your baby has been in the 60th percentile for months and then abruptly dips to the 15th percentile, that sudden deviation from the usual growth pattern might raise questions: Is baby sick? Getting enough to eat? Is there some underlying medical reason for the sudden growth slowdown?

Assessing how your baby grows isn't just a simple numbers game. To get a really clear picture of growth, the doctor will also consider the relationship between weight and length. While the percentiles for length and weight don't have to match up precisely, they should be within a 10 to 20 percent range of each other. If length is 85th percentile but weight is 15th percentile, your baby might be underweight. The other way around? Your baby may be overfed. Figuring out whether your little one is overweight, underweight, or more likely, just right becomes easier when you plot your infant's progress on the length/weight charts used by most pediatricians. The charts that follow, which come from the World Health Organization (WHO), are based on the growth of almost 19,000 breastfed babies (in five cities in five different countries who grew up in optimal living conditions). Both the CDC and the AAP recommend that doctors use the WHO charts for babies under age 2.

These days more and more babies are measuring either above or below standard length and weight ranges. In other words, they're "off the charts"— or hovering very closely to its edges. Experts say the number of extra-large babies is due to rising obesity rates (obese or overweight expectant moms are more likely to have babies who are considered overweight), while the number of undersize babies is a result of the increasing number of premature infants who are born tiny and survive. Formula-fed infants are also more likely to be overweight.

You can plot your baby's progress on these charts. Notice that one set of the charts that follow calculates the relationship between weight and length (plus records head circumference), and the other keeps track of weight and length separately. There are also separate charts for boys and girls. That's because even at this age, boys tend to be taller, heavier, and grow faster than girls do.

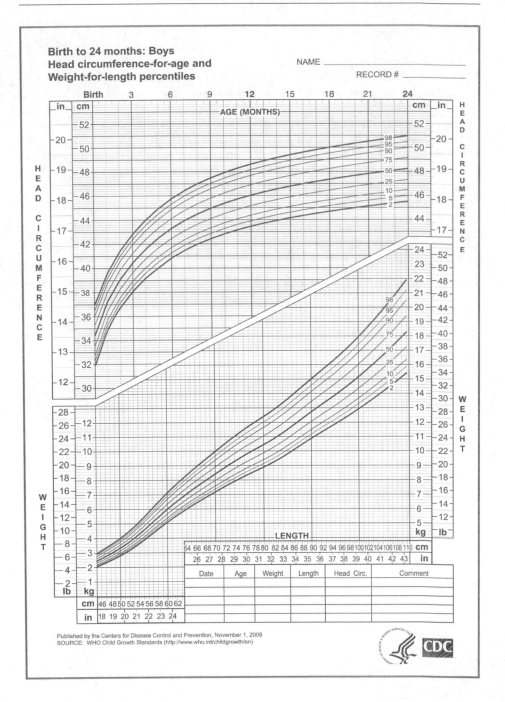

Birth to 24 months: Boys
Head circumference-for-age and
Weight-for-length percentiles

NAME _____

RECORD # _____

Published by the Centers for Disease Control and Prevention, November 1, 2009
SOURCE: WHO Child Growth Standards (http://www.who.int/childgrowth/en)

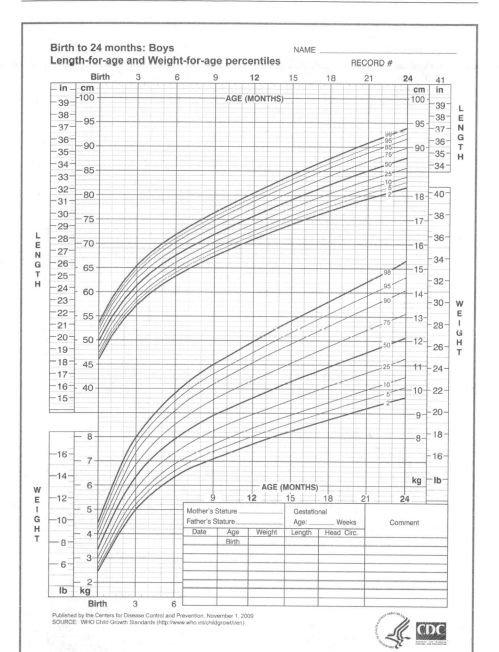

Birth to 24 months: Boys
Length-for-age and Weight-for-age percentiles

NAME _____

RECORD # _____

Published by the Centers for Disease Control and Prevention, November 1, 2009
SOURCE: WHO Child Growth Standards (http://www.who.int/childgrowth/en)

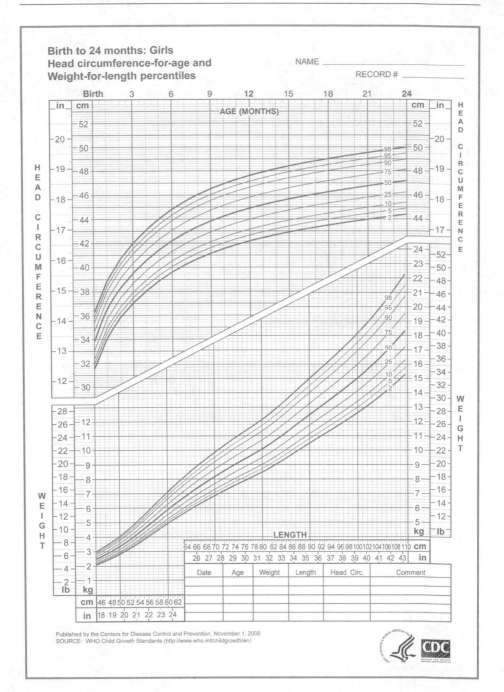

Birth to 24 months: Girls
Head circumference-for-age and
Weight-for-length percentiles

NAME _____

RECORD # _____

Published by the Centers for Disease Control and Prevention, November 1, 2009
SOURCE: WHO Child Growth Standards (http://www.who.int/childgrowth/en)

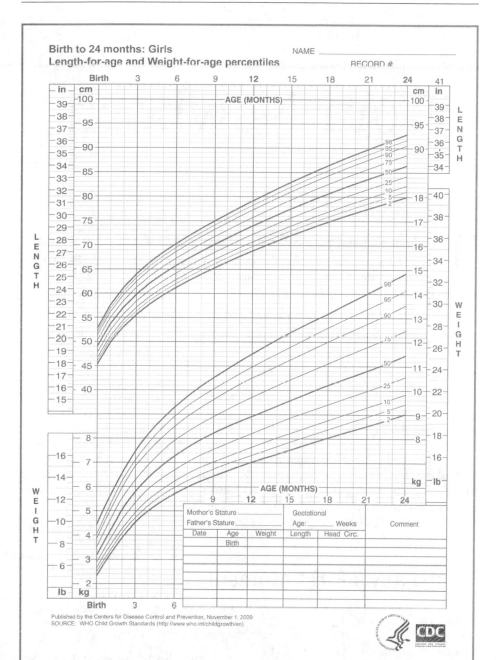

Birth to 24 months: Girls
Length-for-age and Weight-for-age percentiles

NAME _____

RECORD # _____

Published by the Centers for Disease Control and Prevention, November 1, 2009
SOURCE: WHO Child Growth Standards (http://www.who.int/childgrowth/en)

CHAPTER 5

Your Newborn

T he long wait is over. Your baby—the little person you've been eagerly expecting for 9 months—is finally here. As you hold this tiny, warm, sweet-smelling bundle in your arms for the first time, you're bound to be flooded by 1,001 emotions, ranging from over-the-moon thrilled to over-the-top nervous. And, especially if you're a first-time parent, by at least 1,001 questions, ranging from . . . well . . . you name it. Why is her head such a funny shape? Why does he have acne already? Why can't I get her to stay awake long enough to breastfeed? Why won't he stop crying?

As you search around for the operating instructions (don't babies come with them?), here's something you need to know: Yes, you've got a lot to learn (after all, nobody's born knowing how to bathe a slippery baby or massage a clogged tear duct), but give yourself half a chance and you'll be surprised to find how much of this parenting thing actually comes naturally (including the most important operating instruction of all: Love your baby). So find the answers to your questions in the chapters that follow, but as you do, don't forget to tap into your most valuable resource: your own instincts.

Your Baby's First Moments

You've labored and pushed, and you're finally meeting your new bundle of joy face-to-face. Once the initial meet-and-greet is over, baby will need to be checked over. You can expect that a doctor, midwife, or nurse will do some or all of the following:

■ Clear baby's airways by suctioning his or her nose (which may be done as

soon as the head appears or after the rest of baby is delivered).

■ Clamp the umbilical cord in two places and cut between the two clamps—although dad may do the cutting honors. (Antibiotic ointment or an antiseptic may be applied to the cord stump, and the clamp is usually left on for at least 24 hours).

- Assign baby an Apgar score (rating of baby's condition at 1 and 5 minutes after birth, see page 123).

- Administer antibiotic ointment to baby's eyes (see page 135) to prevent infection.

- Weigh baby (average weight is 7½ pounds; 95 percent of full-term babies weigh between 5½ and 9½ pounds).

- Measure baby's length (average length is 20 inches; 95 percent of newborns are between 18 and 22 inches).

- Measure head circumference (average is 13.8 inches; normal range is from 12.9 to 14.7 inches).

- Count fingers and toes, and note if baby's body parts and features appear normal.

- Put baby on your tummy, skin-to-skin (aka kangaroo care; see page 132), for some getting-to-know-your-baby time.

- Before baby leaves the delivery or birthing room, place ID bands on baby, mom, and dad. Baby's footprints and mom's fingerprint may also be obtained for future identification purposes (the ink is washed off your baby's feet, and any residual smudges you may note are only temporary).

The baby's doctor (or a staff pediatrician if your chosen doctor doesn't have privileges at the hospital where you delivered) will perform a more complete examination of the new arrival sometime during the next 24 hours. Try to be on hand for this exam—it's a good time to start asking the many questions you're sure to be collecting. The doctor will check the following:

- Weight (it will probably have dropped since birth and will drop a little more in the next couple of days), head

Delayed Cord Clamping

Cutting the cord is a momentous moment for new parents, but one you're probably best off waiting on—at least for a few more moments. Studies show that the optimal time to clamp (and then cut) the cord is when it stops pulsating—around 1 to 3 minutes after birth—instead of the immediate clamping and cutting that was once done routinely (and still is sometimes done). There seem to be no drawbacks and many potential benefits to delaying cord clamping—a good reason to consider adding this protocol to your birth plan.

Planning to bank baby's cord blood? Cord blood collection can be done after the cord stops pulsating, which means that it doesn't necessarily interfere with delayed clamping. But just to be sure your practitioner's on the same page about this, talk over the plan well before your baby's arrival.

circumference (may be larger than it was at first as any molding of the head begins to round out), and length (which won't actually have changed, but might seem to have because measuring a squirmy baby isn't exactly an exact procedure)

- Heart sounds and respiration

- Internal organs, such as kidneys, liver, and spleen, examined externally by touch

- Newborn reflexes (see page 146)

- Hip rotation

- Hands, feet, arms, legs, genitals

- The umbilical stump

Testing Your Baby

A few drops of blood can go a long way. Those drops, taken routinely from babies' heels before hospital discharge, are used to test for 21 (or more) serious genetic, metabolic, hormonal, and functional disorders, including PKU, hypothyroidism, congenital adrenal hyperplasia, biotinidase deficiency, maple syrup urine disease, galactosemia, homocystinuria, medium-chain acyl-CoA dehydrogenase deficiency, and sickle-cell anemia. Though most of these conditions are very rare, they can be life-threatening if they go undetected and untreated. Testing for these and other metabolic disorders is inexpensive, and in the very unlikely event that your baby tests positive for any of them, your baby's pediatrician can verify the results and begin treatment immediately—which can make a tremendous difference in the prognosis.

Since 2009, all 50 states and the District of Columbia require newborn screening for at least 21 disorders and more than half of all states test newborns for all 29 disorders for which the American College of Medical Genetics (ACMG) recommends testing. Check with your doctor or state health department to find out what tests are done in your state. You can also look up your state's requirements at the National Newborn Screening & Genetics Resource Center (NNSGRC) website: genes-r-us.uthscsa.edu. If your hospital doesn't automatically provide all 29 tests, you can arrange with your doctor to have them done. For more information about newborn screening, contact the March of Dimes at marchofdimes.com.

The CDC also recommends, and some states require, screening tests soon after birth for congenital heart disease (CHD). This condition, which affects 1 in 100 babies, can lead to disability or death if not caught and treated early (happily, early treatment can reduce those risks significantly—and in most cases, completely). Screening for CHD is simple and painless: A sensor is placed on your baby's skin to measure your little one's pulse and the amount of oxygen in his or her blood. If the results of the screening test seem questionable, the doctors will be able to do further testing (echocardiogram—an ultrasound of the heart—for instance) to determine if anything is wrong. If your hospital doesn't routinely perform the test, ask the doctor if it could be given to your baby anyway.

During your baby's hospital stay, the nurses and/or doctors will:

- Record your newborn's first pees and poops to rule out any problems in the elimination department.

- Administer a vitamin K shot, to enhance baby's blood clotting ability.

- Take blood from your infant's heel (with a quick stick), to be screened for phenylketonuria (PKU) and other metabolic disorders (some states mandate tests for only 21 disorders, but you can arrange for a private lab to screen for 30 to 40 metabolic disorders; see box above).

- Possibly (depending on the state and hospital you deliver in) screen for congenital heart disease using pulse oximetry (see box, above).

- Administer the first dose of the hepatitis B vaccine sometime before hospital discharge. (See page 536 for a complete immunization schedule.)

- Conduct a hearing screening (see box, page 124).

Apgar Test

The first test most babies are given—and which most pass with good scores—is the Apgar test. The scores, recorded at 1 minute and again at 5 minutes after birth, reflect the newborn's general condition and are based on observations made in five assessment categories. Babies who score between 7 and 10 are in good to excellent condition and usually require only routine postdelivery care, those scoring between 4 and 6 are in fair condition and may require some resuscitative measures, and those who score under 4 are in poor condition and require immediate attention. While this test can tell a lot about your baby's condition in the few minutes after birth, it doesn't tell you much about anything long term. In fact, even babies whose scores remain low at 5 minutes usually turn out to be completely healthy.

For Babies Born at Home

You'll have more control over the birth, comfortable surroundings, way better food, no limits on the number of friends and family who welcome your little bundle with you, and no bags to pack—but having your baby at home also means you'll have more homework to do later. Some procedures that are routine in hospitals and birthing centers may just be bureaucratic red tape that you and your baby can easily skip. Others, however, are necessary for your baby's health and future well-being, and still others are required by law. Give birth in a hospital, and the following are automatically taken care of, but give birth at home, and you'll need to:

- Give some thought to eye ointment. Some midwives allow the parents of a newborn to give informed consent not to administer antibiotic eye

APGAR TABLE			
SIGN	POINTS		
	0	1	2
Appearance (color)	Pale or blue	Body pink, extremities blue	Pink
Pulse (heartbeat)	Not detectible	Below 100	Over 100
Grimace (reflex irritability)	No response to stimulation	Grimace	Lusty cry
Activity (muscle tone)	Flaccid (weak or no activity)	Some movement of extremities	A lot of activity
Respiration (breathing)	None	Slow, irregular	Good (crying)

Newborn Hearing Screening

Babies learn everything about their environment from their senses—from the sight of daddy's smiling face, to the feel of warm skin as they're cradled in loving arms, to mommy's familiar scent, to the sound of her voice as she matches coo for coo. But for approximately 2 to 4 out of every 1,000 babies born in the United States, the sense of hearing—so integral to the development of speech and language skills—is impaired. Since a hearing deficit can affect so many aspects of a young child's development, early diagnosis and treatment is key. Which is why the AAP endorses universal screening of infants for hearing loss and why nearly three-quarters of all states require that newborns be tested in the hospital for hearing defects. (If your state is not among those that require newborn hearing screening, make sure you ask for it before your baby leaves the hospital.)

Newborn hearing screening tests are highly effective. One test, called otoacoustic emissions (OAE), measures response to sound by using a small probe inserted in the baby's ear canal. In babies with normal hearing, a microphone inside the probe records faint noises coming from the baby's ear in response to a noise produced by the probe. This test can be done while the baby is sleeping, is completed within a few minutes, and causes no pain or discomfort. A second screening method, called auditory brainstem response (ABR), uses electrodes placed on the baby's scalp to detect activity in the brain stem's auditory region in response to "clicks" sounded in the baby's ear. ABR screening requires the baby to be awake and in a quiet state, but it is also quick and painless. If your baby doesn't pass the initial screening, the test will be repeated to avoid false-positive results.

---

ointment (which protects babies from infection) after birth. Though the ointment used is not irritating to baby's eyes, it can blur vision, making that first eye-to-eye contact in mommy's and daddy's arms less clear (see page 135). That said, avoiding the ointment can lead to blindness in a baby if infection is missed, so discuss this with your practitioner before delivery.

■ Plan for routine shots and tests. All babies born in a hospital receive their first dose of hepatitis B vaccine, and all receive a shot of vitamin K (to prevent serious bleeding) shortly after delivery. They're also given a heel stick to screen for PKU, hypothyroidism, and a variety of other conditions (see box, page 122). Speak to your baby's doctor about when these procedures can be performed on your newborn. Also ask the pediatrician about arranging a hearing test (see the box, this page) and congenital heart disease (CHD) screening test, typically administered to newborns before they leave the hospital (see page 122). The test for CHD is most valuable if done in the first day or two of life to pick up conditions that can make a baby very sick by day 3 or 4.

■ Take care of business. The filing of a birth certificate is usually taken care of by hospital staff. If you're planning to give birth at home, you (or

Don't Forget to Cover Your Baby

With insurance, that is. One of the many calls you'll need to make after the birth of your baby will be to your health insurance company, so your new arrival can be added to your policy—something that doesn't happen automatically. (Some insurance carriers require that they be notified within 30 days of the birth of a baby.) Having baby on the policy will ensure that those doctor's visits will be covered right from the start. Don't have insurance? See page 20. Want to change plans? Since having a baby qualifies you for a Special Enrollment Period, you can enroll in or change Marketplace coverage.

your birth attendant) will need to be responsible for the paperwork. Contact your state's Office of Vital Records and Statistics for information on how to file a birth certificate.

- Schedule baby's first doctor appointment, stat. Be sure to contact your pediatrician immediately after the birth to arrange an appointment for your baby as soon as possible.

Feeding Your Baby: Getting Started Formula Feeding

There's not much you need to learn about feeding your baby a bottle—and not much your baby needs to learn, either (newborns have little trouble figuring out how to suck from an artificial nipple). But while breast milk is always on tap and ready to serve, formula must be selected, purchased, sometimes prepared, and often stored—and that means you'll need a lot of know-how before you mix up that first baby bottle. Whether you're formula feeding exclusively or just supplementing, here's what you'll need to know to get started. (See page 40 for tips on choosing nipples and bottles for your formula-fed baby.)

Selecting a Formula

Formula can't replicate nature's recipe for breast milk precisely (for instance, it can't pass along mama's antibodies), but it does come pretty close. Today's formulas are made with types and proportions of proteins, fats, carbohydrates, sodium, vitamins, minerals, water, and other nutrients similar to breast milk's, and must meet standards set by the FDA. So just about any

Need Help at the Breast?

If you're breastfeeding—either exclusively or in combination with the bottle—you'll find everything that you need to know in Chapter 3, beginning on page 60.

Formulas of Formula

With so many types of formula on the market, choosing the right one for your little one can be a confusing proposition, whether you'll be feeding formula exclusively or as part of the breast-bottle combo. Here's a rundown of varieties you'll see on the store shelves or on online shopping portals. If you're considering trying a specialty formula (say, one that's soy-based), ask the doctor before you stock up:

Milk-based formulas. The vast majority of babies do well on standard milk-based formulas—and that even goes for those babies who end up being fussy (most babies are) or have colic. Most of the time, cow's milk formula can't be blamed for those symptoms. Still, some babies with mild tummy troubles seem to do better on cow's milk–based "sensitive" formulas geared to lactose-sensitive infants, in which the milk proteins are easier to digest. Ask the doctor about switching to a sensitive formula if your baby seems to be especially gassy on standard milk-based formula—just keep in mind that the much higher price may be hard for you to swallow (these formulas are more costly).

Soy-based formulas. Formula made with soy proteins are plant-based and don't contain lactose (the sugar found in milk). It's the formula alternative for vegan families, and may also be recommended for some babies who have certain metabolic disorders such as galactosemia or congenital lactase deficiency. If your baby ends up having a true allergy to cow's milk formula, it's unlikely the doctor will recommend a soy-based one, because many babies who are allergic to cow's milk are allergic to soy milk as well. Hydrolysate formulas (see below) will be a better bet.

Protein hydrolysate–based formulas. In these formulas, the protein is broken down into small parts that are easier for your baby to digest (it's why they are often called "predigested" formulas). These hypoallergenic formulas are recommended for babies who have true allergies to milk protein, and possibly for those with skin rashes (like eczema)

iron-containing formula you choose for your baby will be nutritionally sound. Still, the vast selection of formulas on store shelves can be dizzying—and more than a little confusing. Before you contemplate that selection, consider the following formula facts:

- Your baby's doctor knows a thing or two about formula. In your search for the perfect formula for your precious bundle—whether you'll be using it as a supplement to breast milk or as baby's exclusive feed—start with a recommendation from the pediatrician. But for best results, look to your baby as well. Different formulas work

well for different babies at different times. Coupled with the advice of the pediatrician, your baby's reaction to the formula you're feeding will help you assess what's best.

- Cow's milk formula is best for most babies. The majority of formulas are made with cow's milk that has been modified to meet the nutritional and digestive needs of human babies (regular cow's milk is a no-go until the first birthday). Organic formulas made from milk products untouched by growth hormones, antibiotics, and pesticides are readily available, if at a premium price.

or wheezing caused by allergies—but don't change your baby's formula to hydrolysate without the doctor's advice. Preemies may also need a hydrolyzed formula if they have trouble absorbing nutrients (if a specialized preemie formula isn't recommended, that is). These formulas are also more expensive than standard milk formulas. Hydrolysate-based formulas also have a very different taste and smell, which many babies (and their parents) find unpleasant, making a switch difficult for finicky infants (though some babies have no trouble chugging it down).

Lactose-free formulas. If your baby is lactose intolerant, or if he or she has galactosemia or congenital lactase deficiency, the doctor might recommend a lactose-free formula instead of soy-based, sensitive, or hydrolysate ones. These are cow's milk–based formulas that are completely free of lactose.

Reflux formulas. Reflux formulas are prethickened with rice starch and are usually recommended only for babies with reflux who are not gaining weight. Sometimes a doctor will also recommend a reflux formula for a baby whose reflux is causing very uncomfortable symptoms (not just standard spitting up).

Preemie formulas. Babies who were born early and/or at a low birthweight sometimes need more calories, protein, and minerals than a regular formula can provide. The doctor may recommend a special type of preemie formula, many of which also contain a more easily absorbed type of fat called medium-chain triglycerides (MCT), for your tiny baby.

Supplementation formulas. Doing the combo (breastfeeding and supplementing)? There is formula designed specifically for supplementing breastfed babies. It contains lutein, an important nutrient found in breast milk, as well as more prebiotics than other formulas to help keep your baby's stool soft and seedy—like a breastfeeding baby's poop.

There are also other, specially developed formulas for babies with heart disease, malabsorption syndromes, and problems digesting fat or processing certain amino acids.

- Iron-fortified is always best. Formulas come in low-iron formulations, but they aren't considered a healthy option. The AAP and most pediatricians recommend that babies be given iron-fortified formula from birth until 1 year to prevent anemia (see page 365).

- Special formulas are best for some babies. Vegan parents can select soy-based formula for their babies. There are also formulas available for premature babies, babies who have a hard time digesting regular formula, babies who turn out to be allergic to cow's milk and/or soy, babies who are lactose intolerant, and babies with metabolic disorders, such as PKU. For some babies, these formulas are easier to digest than standard formulations, but not surprisingly, they are much more expensive. See box above, for more.

- Follow-ups are not always best. Follow-up formulas are designed for babies older than 4 months who are also eating solid foods. Most doctors don't recommend them, as regular formula plus a healthy diet (once solids are introduced) provides all the nutrients your little one needs until he or she is a year old, when you can

How Much Formula?

How much formula does your baby need? Start your newborn out slowly. For the first week or so, your baby will probably take about 1 or 2 ounces at each feeding (every 3 to 4 hours or on demand). Gradually up the ounces, adding more as the demand becomes greater, but never push baby to take more than he or she wants. After all, pushing can lead to overfeeding, which can eventually lead to overweight. It can also lead to overflow, in the form of excessive spit-up. After all, your baby's tummy is the size of his or her fist (not yours). Put too much in the tummy, and it's bound to come back up. For a guide to how much formula to feed as your baby grows, see each month's chapter and page 302.

switch to cow's milk (no "toddler formula" needed). Check with your baby's doctor before using follow-up formula.

Once you've narrowed your selection down to a general type, you'll need to choose between:

Ready-to-use. Premixed ready-to-go formula comes in 2-, 4-, 6-, and 8-ounce single-serving bottles and is ready for baby with the simple addition of a bottle nipple. It doesn't get easier and more convenient than this—especially because the unopened bottles don't need to be refrigerated—but this is definitely the priciest option.

Ready-to-pour. Available in cans or plastic containers of various sizes, this liquid formula need only be poured into the bottle to be ready for use. It's less expensive than single-serving feedings, but the formula left in the container needs to be stored properly, and used within 48 hours. You'll also pay more for the convenience of ready-to-pours than you would for formulas that need to be mixed.

Concentrated liquid. Less expensive than ready-to-pour but a little more time-consuming to prepare, this concentrated liquid is diluted with equal parts water to make the finished formula.

Powder. The least expensive option, if a bit more time-consuming, powdered formula is reconstituted with a specified amount of water. It's available in cans, plastic containers, or single-serving packets. Besides the low cost, another compelling reason to opt for powder (at least when you're out and about with baby) is that it doesn't need to be refrigerated until it's mixed. Look for bottles that allow you to keep fresh water and formula powder separate until you mix them together.

Bottle-Feeding Safely

For the safest formula prepping and feeding:

- Always check the use-by date on formula, not only when you buy it, but when you prepare it. Don't purchase or use expired formula. And steer clear of dented, leaky, or otherwise damaged cans or other containers.

- Wash your hands thoroughly before preparing formula.

- If necessary, use a clean punch-type opener to open cans of liquid formula, making two openings on opposite sides of the can to make pouring easier. Wash the opener after each use.

Most powdered formula cans come with special pull-open tops, making the use of a can opener unnecessary. If you're using a single-serving bottle, make sure you hear the top "pop" when you open it.

- It isn't necessary to sterilize the water used to mix formula by boiling it. If you're unsure about the safety of your tap water, or if you use well water that hasn't been purified, have your supply tested and, if necessary, purified. Or just use filtered water. Also ask your baby's doctor if fluoride levels in your area's tap water are appropriate for baby.

- Here's another step you can save: Bottles and nipples don't need to be sterilized with special equipment. Dishwashers (or sink washing with detergent and hot water) get them clean enough. If your baby's doctor does recommend sterilizing for any reason, it's easy to do. Just submerge the bottles and nipples in a pot of boiling water for 5 minutes, then let them air dry.

- But here's a step you should never skip: Follow the manufacturer's directions precisely when mixing formula. Always check cans to see if formula needs to be diluted: Diluting a formula that shouldn't be diluted, or not diluting one that should be, could be dangerous. Formula that is too weak can stunt growth. Formula that is too strong can lead to an electrolyte imbalance (aka salt poisoning).

- Bottle warming is a matter of taste, namely baby's. There is absolutely no health reason to warm formula before feeding—but babies who get accustomed to having their formula served up warm often come to expect it that way. That's why you might

Do Add-Ins Add Up?

Added in to more and more formulas are more and more ingredients that breast milk has always come by naturally. Among them, DHA and ARA, omega-3 fatty acids that enhance mental and visual development in infants, and probiotics and/or prebiotics, which may promote better digestion and perhaps boost a baby's immune system. Talk to your baby's doctor about which add-ins add up for your little one.

consider starting your baby out on formula that's been mixed with room temperature water or even a bottle right out of the fridge, so he or she gets used to it that way. Then you can save yourself the time and the hassle of warming bottles—something you'll especially appreciate in the middle of the night or when your baby's frantic for a feed. If you do plan to serve a bottle warm, use a bottle warmer or place the bottle in a pot or bowl of hot water or run hot water over it. Check the temperature of the formula frequently by shaking a few drops on your inner wrist—it'll be ready for baby when it no longer feels cool to the touch (it shouldn't be very warm, just body temperature). Once it's warmed, use the formula immediately, since bacteria multiply rapidly at lukewarm temperatures. Never heat formula in a microwave oven—the liquid may warm unevenly, or the container may remain cool when the formula has gotten hot enough to burn baby's mouth or throat.

- Throw out any formula that's left in the bottle for longer than 1 hour after a feeding has started. Once baby has fed from a bottle of formula, bacteria can grow in it, even if it's refrigerated. So as tempting as it might be, don't reuse leftover formula.

- Cover opened cans or bottles of liquid formula tightly and store in the refrigerator for no longer than the times specified on the labels, usually 48 hours (mark with the day and time you opened it so you don't lose track). Opened cans of powdered formula should be covered and stored in a cool, dry place for use within a month.

- Store unopened cans or bottles of liquid formula at temperatures between 55°F and 75°F. Don't use unopened liquid that has been kept for long periods at or below 32°F or in direct heat above 95°F. Also, don't freeze formula or use formula that has been frozen or that shows white specks or streaks even after shaking.

- Keep prepared bottles of formula refrigerated until ready to use. If you are traveling away from home, store previously prepared bottles in an insulated container or in a tightly sealed plastic bag with a small ice pack or a dozen ice cubes (the formula will stay fresh as long as most of the ice is frozen). Don't use premixed formula that's no longer cold to the touch (it'll have to be tossed). Easier options on the go: Take along ready-to-use single serving bottles of formula, bottles of water and single-serving formula packets to mix with them, or bottles that have separate compartments to keep the powder and water apart until you're ready to combine them and feed your baby.

Bottle-Feeding Basics

Need to bone up on bottle-feeding? Whether you'll be feeding formula exclusively, combining it with breast, or using bottles to serve up expressed breast milk, these step-by-step tips should help:

Give notice. Let baby know that "milk's on" by stroking his or her cheek with your finger or the tip of the nipple. That will encourage your baby to "root"— turn in the direction of the stroke. Then place the nipple gently between baby's lips and, hopefully, sucking will begin. If baby still doesn't get the picture, a drop of formula on those sweet lips should clue him or her in.

Make air the enemy. Tilt the bottle so that formula always fills the nipple completely. If you don't, and air fills part of it, baby will be chasing formula down with air—a recipe for gassiness, which will make both of you miserable. Anti-air precautions aren't necessary, however, if you're using disposable bottle liners, which automatically deflate (eliminating air pockets) or if you're using specially designed bottles that keep the formula pooled near the nipple. Keeping baby propped up in your arms instead of lying horizontal can also help.

Start slow. Brand new babies have minimal nutritional needs in their first few days of life—which is good, because they also have minimal appetite (they're usually more eager to sleep than feed). That's why nature's food delivery system makes so much sense (just a teaspoon or so of colostrum is served up at each feed until mama's milk arrives)—and why, if you're delivering those first feeds via bottle, you can expect your newborn to take only tiny amounts of formula. The nursery will probably provide you with 2-ounce bottles, but it's unlikely your little one will drain them at first.

Break for bubbles. A baby who falls asleep after taking just half an ounce or so is probably saying, "I've had enough." On the other hand, if baby doesn't fall asleep but turns away from the bottle fussily after just a few minutes of nipping, it's more likely a matter of gas than overfilling. In that case, don't give up without a bubble. If after a good burping (see page 160), baby still won't budge on the bottle, take that as your signal that the meal is over. (See page 302 for more details on how much formula to feed.)

Check your speed. Be certain that formula isn't coming through the nipple too quickly or too slowly. Nipples are available in different sizes for babies of different sizes and ages. A newborn nipple dispenses milk more slowly, which is usually perfect for a baby who's just getting the hang of sucking (and whose appetite is still tender). Ditto for nipples designed to mimic breastfeeding—they're also slower flow. You can check the speed of the nipples you're using by turning the bottle upside down and giving it a few quick shakes. If milk pours or spurts out, it's flowing too quickly—if just a drop or two escapes, too slowly. If you get a little spray and then some drops, the flow is just about right. But the very best way to test the flow is by observing the little mouth it's flowing into. If there's a lot of gulping and sputtering going on, and milk is always dripping out of the corners of baby's mouth, the flow is too fast. If baby seems to work very hard at sucking for a few moments, then seems frustrated (possibly letting go of the nipple to complain), the flow

is too slow. Sometimes, a flow problem has less to do with the size of the nipple than with the way the cap is fastened. A very tight cap inhibits flow by creating a partial vacuum, so loosening it up a bit may make the formula flow more freely.

Let baby call it quits. When it comes to feedings, your baby's the boss. If you see only 1 ounce has been emptied when the usual meal is 2, don't be tempted to push the rest. A healthy baby knows when to keep feeding and when to stop. And it's this kind of pushing that often leads bottle-fed babies to become too plump—much more often than breast-fed babies, who naturally eat to appetite.

Minimize midnight hassles. If you can afford the premium price, consider using ready-to-serve single-serving bottles at night (just keep them bedside along with clean nipples) so you can skip the midnight bottle prep. Or use a bottle that stores water and formula powder separately. Or invest in a bedside bottle holder, which keeps baby's bottle safely chilled until ready to use and then warms it to room temperature in minutes.

Bottle-Feeding with Love

Whether you've chosen to feed your baby exclusively with formula or to mix it up with breast, the most important ingredient in any feeding session is love. The kind of skin to skin, eye-to-eye contact that's linked to optimum brain development and attachment in a newborn is a built-in feature of breastfeeding. But, it can easily be added to bottle-feeding. To make sure you keep in touch with your baby while you're bottle-feeding:

The Formula for a Happy Baby

Whether you'll be formula feeding your baby exclusively or combining bottle with breast, whether you opted for formula from the beginning or turned to the bottle after a rocky start with breastfeeding (either for you or for baby), feel good about formula feeding. Remember: Breast is best, but filled with the right formula and given the right way, a bottle passes along good nutrition and lots of love—definitely a formula for a happy, healthy baby.

Don't prop the bottle. It may be the easy thing to do—propping the bottle so you can tackle the bills or catch up on Facebook—but it's definitely not a good thing. Not only does propping your baby's bottle mean that you'll both be missing out on quality cuddle time, it increases the risks of choking (even if your baby is in a reclining high chair or infant seat), ear infections, and, once those pearly whites come in, tooth decay.

Go skin-to-skin, when you can. There are piles of research showing the piles of benefits provided by sharing skin-to-skin contact with a newborn—including the fact that so-called "kangaroo care" lifts levels of oxytocin (aka the love hormone), which plays a major role in parent-baby bonding. But you won't need scientists to prove what you'll discover the first time you go skin-to-skin with your baby: that it feels warm, cozy, and generally awesome for you both. So whenever you can, go ahead—open your shirt and nestle your baby close to you when you bottle-feed. To cocoon your cutie even more snugly, tuck his or her body under your shirt or sweatshirt (there are even kangaroo care tops made specifically for skin-to-skin wear). That goes for daddies, too—your baby will love to cuddle cheek-to-chest (and yes, even cheek-to-chest-hair).

Switch arms. Breastfeeding also builds in this feature (alternating breasts means alternating arms), but with bottle-feeding, you'll have to remember to switch. A switch midfeeding serves two purposes: First, it gives your baby a chance to see the world from different perspectives. Second, it gives you a chance to relieve the aches that can develop from staying in one position for so long.

Take your time. A nursing baby can keep suckling on a breast long after it's been drained, just for comfort and sucking satisfaction. Your bottle-fed baby can't do the same with an empty bottle, but there are ways you can supply some of the same satisfactions. Extend the

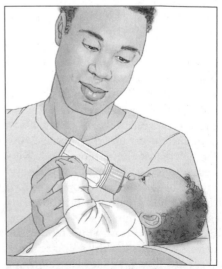

Bottle-feeding pumped milk or formula can give dad and other family members the chance to get close to baby for some quality cuddle time.

pleasure of the feeding session by chatting, singing, or cooing to your baby once the bottle is drained—assuming he or she hasn't dropped off into a milk-induced sleep. The sound of your voice is like music to your baby's ears and makes a feeding session even more special. If your baby doesn't seem satisfied with the amount of sucking each feeding is providing, try using nipples with smaller holes (or slower flow), which will ensure that your baby will get to suck longer for the same meal. Or finish off feedings by offering a pacifier. If your baby seems to be rooting around for more at meal's end, consider whether you're offering enough formula. Increase feeds by an ounce or two to see if it's really hunger that's making your baby fussy.

What You May Be Wondering About

Birthweight

"My friends all seem to be having babies who weigh 8 and 9 pounds at birth. Mine weighed in at a little over 6½ pounds at full term. She's healthy, but she seems so small."

Just like healthy grown-ups, healthy babies come in all kinds of packages—long and lanky, big and bulky, slight and slender. And more often than not, a baby can thank the grown-ups in her life for her birth stats—and her future stats. After all, the laws of genetics dictate that large parents generally have large babies who become large grown-ups, while small parents generally have small babies who become small grown-ups. When dad's large and mom's small (or the other way around), their little ones can be little, big, or somewhere in between.

Mom's own birthweight can also influence her offspring's (if she was born small, her baby's more likely to arrive that way, too). Still another factor is a baby's sex: Girls tend to weigh in lighter and measure up shorter than boys do. And though there is a laundry list of other factors that can affect a baby's size at birth—such as how much weight mom gained during pregnancy—the only factor that matters now is that your baby is completely healthy . . . and likely, every bit as healthy as any newborn chubster.

Keep in mind, too, that some babies who start out small quickly outpace their peers on the growth charts as they start catching up to their genetic potential. In the meantime, enjoy your sweet little bundle while she's still a relatively light load. It won't be long before just hearing the words "Carry me!" from your strapping preschooler will make your back start aching.

Was your baby born small for her gestational age? Check out Chapter 21 for information on low-birthweight babies.

Weight Loss

"I expected my baby to lose some weight in the hospital, but he dropped from 7½ pounds to just over 7 pounds. Isn't that a lot to lose?"

Not to worry. Nearly all newborns check out of the hospital weighing considerably less than when they checked in. In fact, thanks to normal postdelivery fluid loss, babies lose an average of 5 to 10 percent of their birthweight within the first 5 days of life. That loss (essentially, "water weight") is not immediately recouped, since brand new babies initially need and take in very little food. Breastfed babies, who consume only teaspoons of colostrum in those early days of feeding, may lose even more weight than formula-fed babies and may be slower to regain it (which, again, is nothing to worry about). Happily, your newborn is likely to stop losing weight by the time he's 5 days old, and to have regained or surpassed his birthweight by 10 to 14 days—at which point, you'll be able to start posting those weight gain bulletins.

Baby's Appearance

"People ask me whether the baby looks like his mom or his dad. Not sure what to say, since neither one of us has a pointy head, puffy eyes, an ear that bends forward, and a pushed-in nose."

If you've ever wondered why 2- and 3-month-olds are used to play newborns on TV, you've just discovered a key reason: Most babies aren't exactly born photogenic. Beautiful to their parents, of course, but not nearly ready for their close-ups. Instead, most newborns—especially those who arrived via the vagina (C-section babies definitely have an edge in appearance)—have a few wrinkles to work out first, not to mention some puffiness.

As you probably already guessed, the features you're describing weren't inherited from some distant pointy-headed, puffy-eyed, flap-eared relative. They were picked up during your baby's stay in the cramped quarters of your water-filled uterus and during the tight squeeze through your bony pelvis and birth canal during labor and delivery.

Let's break down the features, starting with your precious bundle's unexpectedly pointy head. Believe it or not, nature has your baby's back—if not his just-born looks—in the miraculous design of the fetal head. Since the bones of the skull aren't yet fully formed, a baby's head can be pushed and molded as he's making his descent to and through the exit—allowing for a vaginal birth in most cases, something that wouldn't be possible if his skull were unyielding. That's the upside. The very temporary downside? Being a cone head for a few days or so—after which his head will return to cherubic roundness. Good thing baby beanies are part of the nursery ensemble, right?

The swelling around your baby's eyes is also due, at least in part, to the rough road he took on his fantastic voyage into the world. Another contributing factor might be the antibiotic ointment placed in those precious peepers at birth. And here's one more thought: Some experts speculate that this swelling serves as natural protection for newborns, whose eyes are being exposed to light for the first time. No matter what the cause, puffiness, too, is temporary—lasting just a few days. In the meantime, don't worry that it might interfere with your baby's ability to see mommy and daddy. Though he can't yet distinguish one from another, a newborn can make out blurry faces at birth—even through swollen lids.

The bent ear probably also comes courtesy of the cozy but crowded conditions your baby experienced in his uterine home. As a fetus grows and becomes more snugly lodged in his mother's amniotic sac, an ear that happens to get pushed forward may stay that way even after birth. Again, it's only temporary—and it won't interfere with his being able to hear (or recognize) the sweet music of your voices.

For Parents: Meeting, Greeting, and Bonding

Not only do freshly delivered newborns come equipped with all their senses, they arrive ready to roll them out: to gaze into their parents' eyes, to hear mommy's already familiar voice and identify her uniquely mommy scent, to feel those loving snuggles, to taste that first sip from breast or bottle. They're also extra alert in the hour right after birth, which makes this an especially good time for that first official get-together with their parents—the first cuddle, the first nursing, the first skin-to-skin and eye-to-eye contact. And for parents, well, after 9 months of waiting, that first meet-and-greet is an eagerly anticipated chance to start getting to know their little one. To soak it all in—that flood of emotions, and sensations, and realizations, and expectations—and to start bonding with the newest member of their family.

But what happens if those first moments after birth are nothing but a blur—either because labor was long and hard, delivery was difficult, or baby had to be whisked away quickly for extra care . . . or you just weren't feeling what you thought you'd be feeling? Does missing those moments—or not being able to make the most of them, or not appreciating them as much as you'd hoped you would—matter?

Absolutely not. Just remember, meeting and greeting your baby—whether it's just after birth or hours later—may be a momentous moment, but it's just one of many you'll spend getting to know each other. Yes, it's important, but no more important than the moments, and hours, and weeks, and days, and years that lie ahead. A new beginning, for sure—but really, only the beginning.

The pushed-in nose that may make him look a bit like a baby boxer is also very likely the result of going a long round in your narrow birth canal. It, too, should return to its genetic blueprint. Just remember, baby noses are still a work in progress. Even once your little guy's nose is back to baby normal, the bridge may be broad, almost nonexistent, and the shape often nondescript, making it very different from the nose he'll sport as an adult . . . and meaning it may be a while before you'll know whose nose he has.

Eye Ointment

"Why does my newborn have ointment in his eyes, and how long will it blur his vision?"

There are a lot of factors standing between a newborn baby and a clear view of his surroundings. His eyes are puffy from delivery, still adjusting to the bright lights of the outside world after spending nine months in a dark womb, naturally nearsighted, and, as you've noticed, gooey with ointment. But the ointment serves an important purpose that makes a little increased blurriness well worthwhile—it's administered (as recommended by the AAP and mandated by most states) to prevent a gonococcal or chlamydial infection. Once a major cause of blindness, such infections have been virtually eliminated by this preventive treatment. The antibiotic ointment, usually erythromycin, is mild and not as potentially irritating to the eyes as the silver nitrate drops that were once the treatment of choice.

Portrait of a Newborn

They may be crowd pleasers—espe-cially in a crowd of excited family and friends—but most freshly deliv-ered babies aren't exactly the dimpled, round, button-nosed bundles of cute-ness most parents expect to be handed.

Taking it from the top, babies arrive top-heavy—with their heads looking too large for their body (that head takes up about one quarter of baby's total length). If the trip through the birth canal was a particularly tight squeeze, that head may be somewhat molded—sometimes to the point of being pointy, even "cone" shaped. A bruise might also have been raised on the scalp dur-ing delivery.

Newborn hair may be limited to a sprinkling of fuzz, or so full it looks like it's due for a trim. It may lie flat or stand up straight in spikes. When hair is sparse, blood vessels may be seen as a blue road map across baby's scalp, and the pulse may be visible at the soft spot, or fontanel, on the top of the head.

Many newborns appear to have gone a few rounds in the ring after a vaginal delivery. Their eyes may appear squinty because of the folds at the inner cor-ners, swelling from delivery and, possi-bly, because of the infection-protecting eye ointment gooping them up. Their eyes may also be bloodshot from the pressures of labor. The nose may be flat-tened and the chin unsymmetrical or pushed in from being squeezed through the pelvis, adding to the boxerlike appearance. Babies who arrive by cesar-ean, plucked neatly from the womb, often have a significant temporary edge in the looks department, especially if they didn't go through the compression of labor first.

Because a newborn's skin is thin, it usually has a pale pinkish cast (even in non-Caucasian babies) from the blood vessels just beneath it. Right after deliv-ery, it's most often covered with the remains of the vernix caseosa, a cheesy coating that protects fetuses during the time spent soaking in the amniotic fluid (the earlier a baby arrives, the more ver-nix is left on the skin). Babies born late may have skin that's wrinkled or peeling (because they had little or no vernix left to protect it). Babies born late are also less likely than early babies to be covered with lanugo, a downy prenatal fur that can appear on shoulders, back, forehead, and cheeks and that disap-pears within the first few weeks of life.

A baby's legs and arms, which haven't yet plumped up, may seem more chicken-scrawny than squeez-ably chubby. And finally, because of an infusion of female hormones from the placenta just before birth, many babies—both boys and girls—have swollen breasts and/or genitals. There may even be a milky discharge from the breasts and, in girls, a vaginal discharge (sometimes bloody).

Be sure to capture those newborn features quickly for your baby book or app (as if you'll need to be told to take some pictures!), because they're all fleeting. Most are gone within the first few days, the rest within a few weeks, leaving nothing but darling dimpled cuteness in their place.

The slight swelling and oozy blurriness of your newborn's eyes will last only a day or two. Tearing, swelling, or infection that begins after that may be caused by a blocked tear duct (see page 233).

Bloodshot Eyes

"Why do the whites of my baby's eyes look bloodshot?"

It's not the late hours that newborns keep that often give their eyes that bloodshot look (no, that would be why your eyes will be looking so red for the next few months). Rather, it's a harmless condition that occurs when there is trauma to the eyeball—often in the form of broken blood vessels—during delivery. Like a skin bruise, the discoloration disappears in a few days and does not indicate there has been any damage to your baby's sweet peepers.

By the way, the same can be said for new moms who put in a lot of pushing time and end up temporarily sporting broken blood vessels in and around their eyes.

Eye Color

"I was hoping my baby would have green eyes like her father, but her eyes seem to be a dark grayish color. Is there any chance that they'll turn?"

Will it be baby blues . . . or browns . . . or greens . . . or hazels? It's definitely too early to call now. Most Caucasian babies are born with dark blue or slate-colored eyes, while most dark-skinned infants arrive with dark, usually brown, eyes. While the dark eyes of the darker-skinned babies will usually stay dark, the eye color of Caucasian babies may go through a number of changes (keeping parents guessing) before becoming set somewhere between 3 and 6 months, or even later. And since pigmentation of the iris may continue increasing during the entire first year, the depth of color may not be clear until around baby's first birthday.

Baby's Sleepiness

"My baby seemed very alert right after she was born, but ever since, she's been sleeping so soundly, I can hardly wake her to eat, much less to play with her."

Nine long months of waiting to meet your baby . . . and now that she's here, all she does is sleep? As frustrating as it can be for new parents eager to engage with their little ones, chronic sleepiness is completely normal for brand new newborns—not a reflection on your socializing skills, just a sign that baby's doing what comes naturally. An alert and wakeful first hour after birth, followed by a long stretch of pronounced drowsiness (as long as 24 hours, though she won't sleep for 24 hours straight) is the predictable pattern for newborns—probably designed to give babies a chance to recover from the hard work of being born, and their mothers a chance to recover from the hard work of giving birth. (You will need to make sure that your baby fits feedings into her sleep schedule, however. See page 139 for some waking techniques.)

Don't expect your newborn to become much more stimulating company once those 24 hours of sleepiness are over, either. Here's approximately how you can expect it to go: In the first few weeks of life, her 2- to 4-hour-long sleeping periods will end abruptly with crying. She'll rouse to a semi-awake state to eat, probably doing a fair amount of dozing while she's feeding (shaking the nipple around in her mouth will get

For Parents: Rooming-In

Full-time rooming-in, offered by most hospitals and birthing centers, gives new parents a chance to get to know their newborns while getting some valuable hands-on baby-care experience before they take their little ones home (where there won't be a nurse on call to troubleshoot or offer pointers). And for many parents, it's a wonderful option.

But what happens if you committed to this sleeping arrangement only to realize that you'd actually rather get some sleep? What if what sounded like a dream (baby cuddled contentedly in your arms for hours on end) ends up more of a nightmare (baby's crying inexhaustibly . . . and you're just plain exhausted)?

If you've been without sleep for 48 hours, or if your body has been left limp from a tough labor and delivery, or if you're just more in the mood for sleep than you are for a crying baby, don't feel like you have to stick out around-the-clock rooming-in just because that's what you signed up for (or that's what all the other moms seem to be doing). There's no shame in backing out of rooming-in—at least long enough to catch a nap or a good night's sleep. Ask the nurses to take your newborn off your weary hands in between feeds so you can get the rest you desperately need, and then reevaluate in the morning or after you've had a well-deserved snooze. And don't forget: Round-the-clock rooming-in will begin soon enough at home.

---

her sucking again when she drifts off midmeal). Once she's full, she'll finally fall more soundly asleep, ready for yet another nap.

At first, your little sleepyhead will be truly alert for only about 3 minutes of every hour during the day and less (you hope) at night, a schedule that will allow a total of about an hour a day for active socializing. Maybe not enough for you (after all, how long have you waited to try out your peekaboo prowess?), but it's just what Mother Nature ordered for your baby. She's not mature enough to benefit from longer periods of alertness, and these periods of sleep—particularly of REM (or dream state) sleep—help her grow and develop.

Gradually, your baby's periods of wakefulness will grow longer. By the end of the first month, she'll probably be alert for about 2 to 3 hours every day, most of it in one relatively long stretch,

usually in the late afternoon. Instead of being a round-the-clock cycle, more of her sleep will be concentrated during her evening "naps," which will begin to last longer—instead of being 2 or 3 hours long, some may soon last as long as 6 or 6½ hours.

In the meantime, instead of standing over the bassinet waiting for her to wake for a play session, try hitting your own snooze button. Use her sleeping time to store up a few z's of your own—which you'll need for the days (and nights) ahead, when she'll probably be awake more than you'd like.

Gagging

"My baby just gagged, and then spit up some liquidy stuff—apparently out of nowhere, since I hadn't nursed him recently. What could that be?"

Your baby spent the last 9 months, more or less, living in a liquid environment—where he didn't breathe air but did suck in a lot of fluid. Though his airways were probably suctioned within moments of delivery, additional mucus and fluid may have lingered in his lungs (especially if he was delivered via C-section and didn't have the tight squeeze through the birth canal to help squeeze out more of that mucus). That little bit of gagging is just his way of bringing the rest of that gunk up and out. In other words, it is perfectly normal and absolutely nothing to stress about.

Empty Breasts?

"It's been 2 days since I gave birth to my baby girl, and nothing comes out of my breasts when I squeeze them. She's nursing fine, but I'm worried that she's starving."

Not only is your baby not starving, but she isn't even hungry yet. Infants aren't born with an appetite, or even with immediate nutritional needs. And by the time your baby begins to get hungry for a breast full of milk, usually around the third or fourth postpartum day, you'll almost certainly be able to serve it up.

Which isn't to say that your breasts are empty now. They're dispensing colostrum, a pretty remarkable pre-milk that's custom made for newborns. Colostrum not only provides your baby with all the nourishment she needs (and wants) right now, but also with important antibodies her own body can't yet produce . . . and all of this while helping to empty her digestive system of meconium and excess mucus. But part of the genius of colostrum is how concentrated it is—and how it provides all of those amazing benefits to your baby in tiny amounts. First feedings average less than a half teaspoon, and by the

third day, they max out at less than 3 tablespoons per feeding. What's more, colostrum isn't that easy to express manually—in fact, even a day-old baby, with no previous experience, is better equipped to extract it than you are.

Sleeping Through Meals

"The pediatrician says I should feed my baby every 2 to 3 hours, but sometimes he sleeps for 5 or 6. Should I wake him up to eat?"

Some babies are perfectly content to sleep through meals, particularly during the first few days of life, when they're more sleepy than hungry. But letting a sleeping baby lie through his feedings means that he won't be getting enough to eat, and if you're nursing, that your milk supply won't be getting the jump start it needs. If your baby is a sleepy baby, try these rousing techniques at mealtime:

- Choose the right sleep to wake him from. Baby will be much more easily roused during active, or REM, sleep. You'll know your baby is in this light sleep cycle (it takes up about 50 percent of his sleeping time) when he starts moving his arms and legs, changing facial expressions, and fluttering his eyelids.

- Unwrap him. Sometimes, just unswaddling your baby will wake him up. If it doesn't, undress him right down to the diaper (room temperature permitting) and try some skin-to-skin contact.

- Go for a change. Even if his diaper's not that wet, a change may be just the jolt he needs to wake him for his meal.

- Dim the lights. Though it may seem that turning on the high-voltage lamps

A Newborn State of Mind

It may seem to the casual observer—or the brand new parent—that infants have just three things on their minds: eating, sleeping, and crying (not necessarily in that order). But researchers have shown that infant behavior is actually at least twice as complex as that and can be organized into six states of consciousness. Watch carefully, and you'll see what's on your newborn baby's mind:

Quiet Alert. This is a baby's secret agent state of mind. When babies are in quiet alert mode, their motor activity is suppressed, so they rarely move. Instead, they spend all their energy watching (with their eyes wide open, usually staring directly at someone) and listening intently. This behavior makes quiet alert the perfect time for one-on-one socializing. By the end of their first month, newborns typically spend 2½ hours a day being quiet alert.

Active Alert. The motor's running when babies are in active alert, with arms moving and legs kicking. They may even make some small sounds. Though they'll be doing a lot of looking around in this state, they're more likely to focus on objects than on people—your cue that baby's more interested in taking in the big picture than in doing any serious socializing. Babies are most often in this newborn state of mind before they eat or when they are borderline fussy. You may be able to preempt full-fledged fussiness at the end of an active alert period by feeding or doing some soothing rocking.

Crying. This is, of course, the state newborns are best known for. Crying occurs when babies are hungry, gassy, uncomfortable, bored (not getting enough attention), or just plain unhappy. While crying, babies will contort their faces, move their arms and legs vigorously, and shut their eyes tightly.

might be the best way to jolt baby out of his slumber, it could have just the opposite effect. A newborn's eyes are sensitive to light, so if the room is too bright, your baby may be more comfortable keeping those peepers tightly shut. But don't turn the lights all the way off. A too-dark room will only lull baby back off to dreamland.

■ Try the "doll's eyes" technique. Holding a baby upright will usually cause his eyes to open (much as a doll's would). Gently raise your baby into an upright or sitting position and pat him on the back. Be careful not to jackknife him (fold him forward).

■ Be sociable. Sing a lively song. Talk to your baby and, once you get his eyes open, make eye contact with him. A little social stimulation may coax him to stay awake.

■ Rub him the right way. Stroke the palms of your baby's hands and soles of his feet, then massage his arms, back, and shoulders. Or do some baby aerobics: move his arms, and pump his legs in a bicycling motion (a great trick for releasing gas, too).

■ If sleepyhead still won't rise to the feeding occasion, place a cool (not cold) washcloth on his forehead or rub his face gently with the washcloth.

Drowsiness. Babies are in this state, not surprisingly, when they're waking up or nodding off to sleep. Drowsy babies will make some moves (such as stretching upon waking) and make a variety of adorable but seemingly incongruous facial gestures (that can run the gamut from scowling to surprised to elated), but the eyelids are droopy and the eyes will appear dull, glazed, and unfocused.

Quiet Sleep. In quiet sleep (which alternates every 30 minutes with active sleep) your baby's face is relaxed, eyelids are closed and still. Body movement is rare, with just occasional startles or mouth movements, and breathing is very regular.

Active Sleep. The other half of your baby's sleep time is spent in an active sleep state. In this restless sleep state (which is actually a lot more restful for baby than it looks), eyes can often be seen moving under the closed lids—which is why active sleep is also known as REM, or rapid eye movement sleep. Arms and legs may do a lot of moving around, too, as will that tiny mouth—which may make sucking or chewing motions, or (get ready to melt) even smile. Breathing isn't as regular during active sleep. A lot of brain development is going on—there's an increase in the manufacturing of nerve proteins and neural pathways, and experts believe the brain uses this time to learn and process information acquired while awake. Interestingly, preemies spend more of their sleep time in REM sleep, possibly because their brains need more developing than full termers. Wondering if your sweet little one is having sweet little dreams during his or her REM sleep? It's possible, but hard to know for sure. Some experts say that it's unlikely babies dream due to their limited pool of experiences and their immature brains. Others say babies are probably dreaming about what they've experienced so far in life: the taste of mommy's milk, the touch of dad's hands, the sound of the dog barking, faces baby has seen.

Of course, getting baby up doesn't mean you'll be able to keep baby up—especially not after a few nips of sleep-inducing milk. A baby who's still drowsy may take the nipple, suckle briefly, then promptly fall back asleep, long before he's managed to make a meal of it. When this happens, try:

- A burp—whether baby needs a bubble or not, the jostling may rouse him again.

- A change—this time, of feeding position. Whether you're nursing or bottle-feeding, switch from the cradle hold to the football hold (which babies are less likely to sleep in).

- A dribble—some breast milk or formula dribbled on baby's lips may whet his appetite for his second course.

- A jiggle—jiggling the breast or bottle in his mouth or stroking his cheek may get the sucking action going again, even if he's just doing it in his sleep (babies often do).

- And repeat—some young babies alternate sucking and dozing from the start of the meal to the finish. If that's the case with your baby, you may find you'll have to burp, change, dribble, and jiggle at least several times to get a full feeding in.

For Parents: Have You Heard the One . . .

You haven't even been a parent for 48 hours yet, and already you've been on the receiving end of so much conflicting advice (on everything from umbilical stump care to feeding) that your head's in a tailspin. The hospital staff tells you one thing (or maybe two things, if you count the day nurse and the night nurse), your sister (veteran of two newborns) has a completely different take, both clash with what you seem to recall baby's pediatrician telling you and what you just read on your message board—and let's not even get started on your mother . . . and your mother-in-law. So what's a confused new parent to do—and believe?

The fact is that the facts about baby care—at least, the most up-to-date facts—aren't easy to sort out, especially when everyone (and their mother) is telling you something different. Your best bet when all that contradicting counsel leaves you in doubt about how best to care for your newborn (or when you need a deciding vote you can count on): Stick with the doctor's advice.

Of course, in listening to others (even the pediatrician), don't forget that you've got another valuable resource you can trust—your own instincts. Often parents, even the really green ones, do know best—and usually, much more than they think they do.

It's fine to occasionally let your baby sleep when he's dropped off to dreamland after just a brief appetizer and all efforts to tempt him into his entrée have failed. But for now, don't let him go more than 3 hours without a full meal if he's nursing, or 4 hours if he's formula-fed. It's also not a good idea to let your baby nip and nap at 15- to 30-minute intervals all day long. If that seems to be the trend, be relentless in your attempts to wake him when he dozes off during a feed.

If chronic sleepiness interferes so much with eating that your baby isn't thriving (see page 182 for signs), consult the doctor.

Nonstop Feeding

"I'm afraid my baby is going to turn into a little blimp. Almost immediately after I put her down, she's up, crying to be fed again."

Feed your newborn every time she cries, and baby blimpdom definitely could be on the horizon. After all, babies cry for many other reasons besides hunger, and it may be that you're misreading her signals by serving up a feed each time she fusses (see box, page 144). Sometimes, crying is a baby's way of unwinding for a few minutes before she falls asleep. Put her back to the breast or bottle, and you may not just be overfeeding her but also interrupting her efforts to settle down for a nap. Sometimes, crying after a feed may be a cry for companionship—a signal that baby's in the mood for some socializing, not another meal. Sometimes, crying signals that baby is craving more sucking satisfaction than her meal provided, which means a paci may pacify her—or that she may be having trouble calming herself down, in which case a little rocking and a few soft lullabies may be just what she's fussing for. And sometimes, it's just a simple matter of

Tips for Successful Feeding Sessions

Whether it's a breast or a bottle that will be your newborn's ticket to a full tummy, the guidelines that follow should help make the trip a smoother one:

Zero in on zen. While you're both learning the ropes, you and your baby will have to focus on the feeding, and the fewer distractions from that job, the better. Turn off the TV (soft music is fine), let the phone go to voice mail at baby's mealtimes, and silence those texts and tweets. If you have other children, chances are you'll already be pretty proficient at feeding—the challenge will be keeping your older ones and your new one happy at the same time. Try diverting the older sib set with some quiet activity, like coloring, that they can settle down with at your side, or take this opportunity to read them a story.

Make a change. If your baby is relatively calm, you've got time for a change. A clean diaper will make for a more comfortable meal and less need for a change right after—a definite plus if your baby has nodded off to Destination Dreamland. But don't change before middle-of-the-night feedings if baby's only damp (sopping's another story), since all that stimulation makes falling back to sleep more difficult, especially for infants who are mixing up their days and nights. Does your sleepyhead have trouble staying up for a whole feed? Then changing midfeed might provide just the jolt he or she needs to get that feed finished.

Wash up. Even though you won't be doing the eating, it's your hands that should be washed with soap and water before your baby's meals.

Get comfy. Aches and pains are an occupational hazard for new parents using unaccustomed muscles to tote growing babies around. Feeding baby in an awkward position will only compound the problem. So before putting baby to breast or bottle, be sure you're set up comfortably, with adequate support both for your back and neck and for the arm under baby.

Loosen up. If your baby is tightly swaddled, unwrap that bundle so you can cuddle (preferably skin-to-skin) while you feed.

Cool down a fired-up baby. A baby who's already worked up will have trouble settling down to the business of feeding, and even more trouble with the business of digesting. Try a soothing song or a little rocking first.

Sound reveille. Some babies are sleepy at mealtimes, especially in the early days. If your little one is a dinner dozer, try the wake-up techniques on page 139.

Break for a burp. Midway through each feeding, make a routine of stopping for a burp. Burp, too, any time baby seems to want to quit feeding too soon or starts fussing at the nipple—it may be gas, not food, filling that little tummy. Bring up the bubble, and you're back in business.

Make contact. Cuddle and caress your baby with your hands, your eyes, and your voice. Remember, meals should fill your baby's daily requirements not just for nutrients but for love and attention as well.

Cracking the Crying Code

Sure, crying is a baby's only form of communication—but that doesn't mean you'll always know exactly what he or she is trying to say. Not to worry. This cheat sheet can help you figure out what those whimpers, wails, and shrieks really mean:

"I'm hungry." A short and low-pitched cry that rises and falls rhythmically and has a pleading quality to it (as in "Please, please feed me!") usually means that baby's in the market for a meal. The hunger cry is often preceded by hunger cues, such as lip smacking, rooting, or finger sucking. Catch on to the clues, and you can often avoid the tears.

"I'm in pain." This cry begins suddenly (usually in response to something unexpectedly painful—for instance, the jab of a needle at shot time) and is loud (as in ear-piercing), panicked, and long (with each wail lasting as long as a few seconds), leaving the baby breathless. It's followed by a long pause (that's baby catching his or her breath, saving up for another chorus) and then repeated, long, high-pitched shrieks.

"I'm bored." This cry starts out as coos (as baby tries to get a good interaction going), then turns into fussing (when the attention he or she is craving isn't forthcoming), then builds to bursts of indignant crying ("Why are you ignoring me?") alternating with whimpers ("C'mon, what's a baby got to do to get a cuddle around here?"). The boredom cry stops as soon as baby is picked up or played with.

"I'm overtired or uncomfortable." A whiny, nasal, continuous cry that builds in intensity is usually baby's signal that he or she has had enough (as in "Nap, please!" or "Clean diaper, pronto!" or "Can't you see I've had it with this infant seat?").

"I'm sick." This cry is often weak and nasal sounding, with a lower pitch than the "pain" or "overtired" cry— as though baby just doesn't have the energy to pump up the volume. It's often accompanied by other signs of illness and changes in the baby's behavior (for example, listlessness, refusal to eat, fever, and/or diarrhea). There's no sadder cry in baby's repertoire or one that tugs harder at parental heartstrings than the "sick" cry.

gas (which more feeding would only compound). Bringing up the bubble may bring her the contentment she's craving.

If you've ruled out all of the above scenarios—as well as done a quick check for a dirty or uncomfortably wet diaper—and your baby's still crying, then consider that perhaps she really hasn't gotten enough to eat. Maybe she's settled into a snack-and-snooze habit, drifting off to sleep before she fully fills her belly, and then waking quickly for a

second serving—in which case, the trick will be keeping her awake until she's finished the feed. Or maybe a growth spurt has temporarily sent her appetite into overdrive, and she's letting you know her needs (healthy babies, after all, usually know exactly how much feed they need—even if their parents don't always).

Breastfed babies may feed more often, too, when they're trying to pump up mommy's milk supply—and they usually succeed within a few days. But if your baby is breastfeeding, seems chronically hungry, but doesn't seem to be thriving (she's not gaining weight fast enough or filling her diapers like she should), you may not be producing enough milk (see page 182).

Quivering Chin

"Sometimes, especially when he's been crying, my baby's chin quivers."

Though your baby's quivering chin may look like just another precious ploy to play the cute card, it's actually a sign that his nervous system is age-appropriately immature. As it matures, that quivering chin will disappear—but that's okay, since he'll find plenty of other adorable ways to make you melt.

Startling

"I'm worried that there's something wrong with my baby's nervous system. Even when she's sleeping, she'll suddenly seem to jump out of her skin."

It's startling to parents, but startling is second nature for newborns—one of many very normal (though seemingly peculiar) reflexes babies are born with (see box, page 146). Also known as the Moro reflex, the startle reflex occurs more frequently in some babies than in others, sometimes for no apparent reason, but most often in response to a loud noise, jolting, or a feeling of falling—as when a newborn is picked up or placed down without enough support. Like many other reflexes, the Moro is probably a built-in survival mechanism designed to protect these newborns—in this case, a primitive attempt to regain perceived loss of equilibrium. In a Moro, the baby typically stiffens her body, flings her arms up and out symmetrically, spreads her usually tightly

For Parents: Newly Delivered?

Sure, you're all about how to care for your baby right now—but chances are you have just as many questions about how to care for yourself. For answers on everything you might wonder (and worry) about during your 6-week recovery period—from bloody discharge to hemorrhoids, hair loss to night sweats, exhaustion to depression, that first bowel movement to that first postpartum checkup to the first postpartum period—check out Chapters 17 and 18 in *What to Expect When You're Expecting*.

clenched fists wide open, draws her knees up, then finally brings her arms, fists clenched once again, back to her body in an embracing gesture—all in a matter of seconds. She may also cry out.

While the sight of a startled baby often startles her parents, a doctor is more likely to be concerned if a baby doesn't exhibit this reflex. Newborns are routinely tested for startling, the presence of which is actually one reassuring sign that the neurological system is functioning well. You'll find that your baby will gradually startle less frequently and less dramatically, and that the reflex will disappear fully somewhere between 4 and 6 months. (Your baby may occasionally startle, of course, at any age—just as adults can—but not with the same pattern of reactions.)

Birthmarks

"I've just noticed a raised, bright red blotch on my daughter's tummy. Is this a birthmark? Will it ever go away?"

Newborn Reflexes

Mother Nature pulls out all the stops when it comes to newborn babies, providing them with a set of inborn reflexes designed to protect these vulnerable creatures and ensure their care (even if parental instincts have yet to kick in).

Some of these primitive behaviors are spontaneous, while others are responses to certain actions. Some seem intended to shield a baby from harm (such as when a baby swipes at something covering his or her face, a reflex that is meant to prevent

Fencing reflex

suffocation). Others seem to guarantee that a baby will get fed (as when a hungry newborn roots for a nipple). And while many of the reflexes have obvious value as survival mechanisms, nature's intentions are more subtle in others. Take the fencing reflex. Though few newborns are challenged to a duel, it's theorized that they take this challenging stance while on their backs to prevent themselves from rolling away from their moms.

Newborn reflexes include:

Rooting reflex. A newborn whose cheek is gently stroked will turn in the direction of the stimulus, mouth open and ready to feed. This reflex helps the baby locate the breast or bottle and secure a meal—sort of like a feeding GPS. Your baby will do this for 3 to 4 months, though rooting may persist long after that during sleep.

Sucking reflex. A newborn will reflexively suck when something (for example, a nipple) touches the roof of his or her mouth. This reflex is present at birth and lasts until 2 to 4 months, when voluntary sucking takes over.

They come in all shapes, sizes, textures, and colors, and they don't always show up at birth (sometimes making their appearance in the first few weeks of life), but birthmarks are practically standard issue for newborns—with more than 80 percent of infants sporting at least one. And though some birthmarks will last a lifetime, others will fade fast, and still others will fade over time. Sometimes, a mark will grow a bit before it begins regressing.

How long will a birthmark stick around? When will it start to fade or shrink? That's hard to predict. One thing is for sure: Even a birthmark that's destined to disappear won't vanish overnight. In fact, it will likely fade or shrink so gradually, the changes may be hard for you to notice at all. For that reason, many doctors document birthmark changes by photographing and measuring the mark periodically. If your baby's doctor doesn't, you

Again, it's nature's way of making sure baby scores those feeds.

Startle, or Moro, reflex. When startled by a sudden or loud noise, or a feeling of falling, the Moro reflex will cause the baby to extend the legs, arms, and fingers, arch the back, draw the head back, then draw the arms back, fists clenched, into the chest. Expect this reflex to last around 4 to 6 months.

Palmar grasping reflex. Touch the palm of your baby's hand, and those tiny fingers will curl around and cling to your finger (or any object). An interesting bit of baby trivia: A newborn's grasp may be powerful enough to support his or her full body weight (but no need to test this out). Some more trivia: This reflex curls babies' feet and toes, too, when they're touched. You'll notice the firm grip lasting 3 to 6 months.

Babinski's, or plantar, reflex. When the sole of a baby's foot is gently stroked from heel to toe, the baby's toes flare upward and the foot turns in. This reflex lasts between 6 months and 2 years, after which toes curl downward.

Walking, or stepping, reflex. Held upright on a table or other flat surface, supported under the arms, a newborn may lift one leg and then the other, taking what seem to be "steps." This "practice walking" reflex works best after the fourth day of life and usually lasts around 2 months. Endlessly entertaining to watch, but before you post your apparent prodigy's feats on 2 feet, keep in mind that this reflex doesn't predict early walking.

Tonic neck, or fencing, reflex. Placed on the back, a young baby will assume a "fencing position," head to one side, with the arm on that side extended and the opposite limbs flexed (see illustration). This "en garde" reflex (which may be a baby's way of being "on guard" on his back) may be present at birth or may not appear for at least 2 months, and it usually disappears at about 4 to 6 months (though it varies a lot).

For fun, or out of curiosity, you can try checking your baby for these reflexes—but keep in mind that your results may vary and will probably be less reliable than those of a doctor or other expert. A baby's reflexes may be less pronounced, too, if he or she is hungry or tired. So try again another day, and if you still can't observe the reflexes, mention this to your baby's doctor, who probably has already tested your baby successfully for all newborn reflexes and will be happy to repeat the demonstrations for you at the next well-baby visit.

can do so to keep track (or just for a memento).

Birthmarks usually fit into one of the following categories:

Strawberry hemangioma. This soft, raised, strawberry red birthmark, as small as a freckle or as large as a coaster, is composed of immature veins and capillaries that broke away from the circulatory system during fetal development. It may be visible at birth but typically appears suddenly during the first few weeks of life, and is so common that one out of ten babies will probably have one. Strawberry birthmarks grow for a while but eventually start to fade to a pearly gray and almost always finally disappear completely, sometime between ages 5 and 10. Occasionally a strawberry mark may bleed, either spontaneously or because it was scratched or bumped. If that happens, just apply pressure to stem the flow of blood.

Baby Business

It's hard to believe that a newborn baby will ever have any business to take care of (besides eating, sleeping, crying, and growing). But there are two very important documents that your baby will need periodically throughout life, and both should be registered for now.

One is a birth certificate, which will be needed as proof of birth and citizenship when (and all of these will come sooner than you think) registering for school and applying for a driver's license, passport, marriage license (yes, marriage license!), or Social Security benefits. Usually, the registering of your baby's birth is handled by the hospital, and you receive official notification when the record of the birth is filed. If you don't receive such notification and a copy of the birth certificate within a couple of months, check with the hospital, the local health department, or the state health department to see what's holding it up. (If you gave birth at home, you or your midwife will have to register for the document.) When you do receive the birth certificate, examine it carefully to be sure it's accurate—mistakes are sometimes made. If there are errors, or if you hadn't quite settled on a name for your baby before leaving the hospital and need to add it, call the health department for instructions on how to make the necessary corrections or additions. Once you have a correct birth certificate, make a few copies and file them in a safe place.

The second document that your baby will need is a Social Security card. Though it isn't likely your newborn is going to start holding down a job anytime soon, you'll need the number for other reasons, such as setting up a bank account, investing those cash gifts, obtaining medical coverage, even purchasing U.S. savings bonds. The main reason to get a Social Security number, however, is to claim your baby as a dependent on your income tax return. And, if you bank baby's savings in your own name and Social Security number rather than his or her own, you'll have to pay taxes on the interest at your rate rather than the baby's lower one.

Application for a Social Security number can be made during the birth certificate application process in the hospital. You can simply check a box on the birth certificate information form if you want a Social Security number assigned to your child. The hospital forwards this information to the Social Security Administration, which then assigns the Social Security number and issues the card directly to you. The parent's signature on the birth registration form and the check in the box indicating the parent wants a Social Security number for the child constitute a valid application for one.

Or, you can apply for a Social Security number for your baby at your local Social Security office in person or by mail (you can print out a form at ssa.gov/ssnumber/ss5.htm), submitting a copy of the birth certificate (see, you need it already), plus proof of your own identity, such as a driver's license or passport, plus the Social Security numbers of both parents. If you decide your baby doesn't need a Social Security number now, keep in mind that the law requires one by age 5. Social Security numbers are available free of charge, so never pay anyone for getting a card or number.

Strawberry birthmarks are often best left untreated (even if you're eager for your baby's mark to disappear) unless they continue to grow, repeatedly bleed or become infected, or interfere with a function, such as vision. Treatment (from compression and massage to steroids, surgery, laser therapy, cryotherapy, injections, or oral medications) can sometimes lead to more complications than a more conservative let-it-resolve-on-its-own approach.

Much less common are cavernous (or venous) hemangiomas—only one or two out of every hundred babies has this kind. Often combined with the strawberry type, these birthmarks tend to be deeper and larger, and are light to deep blue in color. They regress more slowly and less completely than strawberry hemangiomas, and are more likely to require treatment (but usually not until a child is older).

Salmon patch, or nevus simplex ("stork bites"). These salmon-colored patches can appear on the forehead, the upper eyelids, and around the nose and mouth, but are most often seen at the nape of the neck (where the fabled stork carries the baby, thus the nickname "stork bites"). They invariably become lighter during the first 2 years of life, becoming noticeable only when a little one cries or exerts herself. Since more than 95 percent of the lesions on the face fade completely, these cause less concern cosmetically than other birthmarks. Those on the neck that don't fade will eventually be covered by baby's hair as it grows in.

Port-wine stain, or nevus flammeus. These purplish red birthmarks, which may appear anywhere on the body, are composed of dilated mature capillaries. They are normally present at birth as flat or barely elevated pink or reddish purple lesions. Though they may change color slightly, they don't fade appreciably over time and can be considered permanent, though treatment with a pulse-dyed laser anytime from infancy through adulthood can improve appearance.

Café au lait spots. These flat patches on the skin, which can range in color from tan (coffee with a lot of milk) to light brown (coffee with a touch of milk), can turn up anywhere on the body. They are quite common, apparent either at birth or during the first few years of life, and don't disappear. If your child has a large number of café au lait spots (six or more), point this out to her doctor.

Mongolian spots. Blue to slate gray, resembling bruises, Mongolian spots may turn up on the buttocks or back, and sometimes the legs and shoulders, of nine out of ten children with African, Asian, or Indian ancestry. These blotchy patches, which can be quite large, are also fairly common in infants of Mediterranean ancestry but are rare in blond-haired, blue-eyed infants. Though most often present at birth and gone within the first year, occasionally they don't appear until later and/or persist into adulthood.

Congenital pigmented nevi. These moles vary in color from light brown to blackish and may be hairy. Small ones are very common. Larger ones, "giant pigmented nevi," are rare but carry a greater potential for becoming malignant later in life. It is usually recommended that large moles, and suspicious smaller ones, be removed (after a baby is 6 months old), if removal can be accomplished easily, and that those not removed be monitored carefully by a dermatologist.

Blotchy Skin

"There are red blotches with white centers on my baby's face and body. Are these anything to worry about?"

They may not be pretty, but they're nothing to worry about, either—just another one of the many surprisingly unsightly skin eruptions newborns can develop (so much for baby-smooth skin, right?). These are actually pretty common, too, and though they come with a scary name (erythema toxicum) and an even scarier appearance (blotchy, irregularly shaped reddened areas with pale centers, sort of like a collection of angry insect bites), these blemishes are, happily, harmless and short-lived. They will vanish within several weeks without treatment. Avoid the temptation to scrub them.

Baby's sporting other funky skin blotches, whiteheads, or pimples? See page 227 for the scoop on these complexion problems.

Mouth Cysts or Spots

"When my baby was crying, I noticed a few little white bumps on her gums. Could she be getting teeth?"

Don't alert the social media yet. While a baby very occasionally will sprout a couple of bottom central incisors six months or so before schedule, little white bumps on the gums are much more likely to be tiny fluid-filled papules, or cysts. These harmless cysts are common in newborns and will soon disappear, leaving gums clear in plenty of time for that first toothless grin.

Some babies may also have yellowish white spots on the roofs of their mouths at birth. Like the cysts, they're fairly common and completely innocuous. Dubbed "Epstein's pearls," these spots will disappear without treatment.

Early Teeth

"I was shocked to find that my baby was born with two front teeth. The doctor says he'll have to have them pulled. Why?"

Every once in a while, a newborn arrives on the scene with a tooth or two. And though these tiny pearly whites may be cute as can be—and fun to show off on Instagram—they may need to be removed if they're not well anchored in the gums, to keep baby from choking on or swallowing them. Such extra-early teeth may be preteeth, or extra teeth, which, once removed, will be replaced by primary teeth at the usual time. But more often they are primary teeth, and if they must be extracted, temporary dentures (which would be fitted once the rest of the primary teeth come in) may be needed to stand in for the missing teeth until their secondary successors come in.

Thrush

"My baby has thick patches of white on the inside of his cheeks. I thought it was spit-up milk, but when I tried to brush it away, his mouth started to bleed."

Sounds like there's a fungus among you—or, more accurately, between you. Though the fungus infection known as thrush is causing problems in your baby's mouth, it probably started in your birth canal as a yeast infection and that's where your baby picked it up. The fungus, called candida albicans, is an organism that normally hangs out in the mouth and vagina and is typically kept in check by other microorganisms. But if you get sick, start using antibiotics, or experience hormonal changes (such as in pregnancy), the balance can be upset, allowing the fungus to grow and cause symptoms of infection.

Since thrush is usually picked up at birth, it's most common in newborns and babies under 2 months. Older babies can also develop thrush if they've been taking antibiotics, have a depressed immune system, or the yeast continues to be passed back and forth between mom and baby during breastfeeding.

How can you tell if your baby has thrush? Look for those trademark elevated white patches, which appear like curds of cottage cheese on the inside of a baby's cheeks, and sometimes on the gums, tongue, roof of the mouth, and even the back of the throat, and touch gently with a gauze-covered finger. If it's thrush, the white patch won't come off very easily, and if it does, you'll find a raw, red patch underneath. Fussiness during feeding or when sucking on a pacifier (baby starts to suck, then turns away in pain) could be another sign of thrush, though some babies don't seem to be uncomfortable with it at all.

If you suspect thrush, contact the doctor, who will likely prescribe an antifungal medication (such as Nystatin), which is applied topically to the inside of the mouth and tongue (be sure to get it on all the white patches in your baby's mouth) multiple times a day for 10 days. In a tough case, Diflucan, which is an oral medication given by dropper, may be prescribed. Some babies with thrush also develop a yeast infection in the diaper region, characterized by an angry red rash. It can be treated with a different prescription antifungal medication specifically for that area.

Are you breastfeeding? Then chances are your baby isn't the only one that yucky yeast is feasting on. Yeast infections are passed back from baby's mouth to mama's nipple (and then back and forth again if both members of the breastfeeding team aren't treated). Symptoms of nipple thrush include

A Milky Tongue

Ever wonder why your baby's tongue is white after a feed . . . or even worried that it might be due to thrush? If a white tongue is your baby's only symptom, his or her milk-only diet is probably the cause. Milk residue often stays on a baby's tongue after feeding but usually dissolves within an hour. Still want to be sure? Simply try to wipe off that white film using a soft, damp cloth. If the tongue is pink and healthy looking after wiping, it's just a matter of milk. Call the doctor if you suspect thrush or if you're just not sure.

extreme soreness and burning, along with a pink, shiny, itchy, flaky, and/or crusty appearance. There may also be sharp shooting pains in the breast during or after feeds.

If you suspect you might have nipple thrush (whether or not you see thrush in your baby's mouth), contact the doctor. Breastfeeding doesn't have to be interrupted if one or both of you have been diagnosed with thrush, but the condition can make feeding excruciating for you—another reason why prompt treatment for both of you is needed. You'll likely be prescribed an antifungal cream that you'll apply to your nipples. If it's practical (for example, if you have the privacy and cooperative weather), you can also try exposing your nipples to sunlight for a few minutes each day, since yeast hates the sun. Probiotics may help speed recovery and keep yeast at bay, and they're safe to take while you're breastfeeding. There are also infant probiotics that the doctor may prescribe for your baby.

To avoid future infections (as well as to prevent reinfection), regularly clean and sterilize pacifiers, bottles, and breast pump parts that touch your nipples (using a microwave sterilizer bag makes this easier). Also helpful: allowing your nipples to completely dry between feedings, changing nursing pads after feedings, and wearing cotton bras that don't trap moisture and washing them daily in hot water (drying them in the sun may provide extra protection). Since antibiotics can trigger a yeast infection, they should be used only when needed—and that goes for both you and baby.

Jaundice

"The doctor says my baby is jaundiced and has to spend time under the bili lights before she can go home. He says it isn't serious, but anything that keeps a baby in the hospital sounds serious to me."

The skin of more than half of babies has begun to yellow by their second or third days—not with age, but with newborn jaundice, caused by an excess of bilirubin in the blood. The yellowing, which starts at the head and works its way down toward the toes, tints the skin in light-skinned newborns and even the whites of their eyes. The process is the same in black- and brown-skinned babies, but the yellowing may be visible only in the palms of the hands, the soles of the feet, and the whites of the eyes. Jaundice is more common in babies of East Asian or Mediterranean descent, though their dark, olive, or yellow-tinged skin may make it more difficult to detect.

Bilirubin, a chemical formed during the normal breakdown of red blood cells, is usually removed from the blood by the liver. But newborns often produce more bilirubin than their immature livers can handle. As a result, the bilirubin builds up in the blood, causing the yellowish tinge and what is known as physiologic (normal) newborn jaundice.

In physiologic jaundice, yellowing usually begins on the second or third day of life, peaks by the fifth day, and is substantially diminished by the time baby is a week or 10 days old. It appears a bit later (about the third or fourth day) and lasts longer (often 14 days or more) in premature babies because of their extremely immature livers. Jaundice is more likely to occur in babies who lose a lot of weight right after delivery, in babies who have diabetic mothers, and in babies who arrived via induced labor.

Mild to moderate physiologic jaundice usually requires no treatment. Usually a doctor will keep a baby with high physiologic jaundice in the hospital for a few extra days for observation and phototherapy treatment under fluorescent light, often called a bili light. Light alters bilirubin, making it easier for a baby's liver to get rid of it. During the treatment, babies are naked except for diapers, and their eyes are covered to protect them from the light. They are also given extra fluid to compensate for the increased water loss through the skin, and may be restricted to the nursery except for feedings. Freestanding units or fiber-optic blankets wrapped around baby's middle allow more flexibility, often permitting baby to go home when her mom is released.

In almost all cases, the bilirubin levels (determined through blood tests) will gradually diminish in an infant who's been treated, and the baby will go home with a clean bill of health.

Rarely, the bilirubin increases further or more rapidly than expected, suggesting that the jaundice may be nonphysiologic (not normal). This type of jaundice usually begins either earlier or later than physiologic jaundice, and levels of bilirubin are higher. Treatment to bring down abnormally high levels of bilirubin is important to prevent a buildup of the substance in the brain, a condition known as kernicterus. Signs of kernicterus are weak crying, sluggish reflexes, and poor sucking in a very jaundiced infant (a baby who's being treated under lights may also seem sluggish, but that's from being warm and understimulated—not from kernicterus). Untreated, kernicterus can lead to permanent brain damage or even death.

Many hospitals monitor the level of bilirubin in babies' blood through blood tests or with a special measurement device (a bilirubinometer) and follow-up visits to ensure that these extremely rare cases of kernicterus are not missed. The pediatrician will also check baby's color at the first visit to screen for non-physiologic jaundice (especially important if mom and baby checked out of the hospital early or if baby was born at home). The treatment of nonphysiologic jaundice will depend on the cause but may include phototherapy, blood transfusions, or surgery. Any visible jaundice that persists at 3 weeks of age should be checked by the pediatrician.

"I've heard that breastfeeding causes jaundice. My baby is a little jaundiced. Should I stop nursing?"

Blood bilirubin levels are, on the average, higher in breastfed babies than in bottle-fed infants, and they may stay elevated longer (as long as 6 weeks). Not only is this exaggerated physiologic (normal) jaundice nothing to worry about, but it's also not a reason to consider giving up on breastfeeding. In fact, interrupting breastfeeding doesn't decrease bilirubin levels, and can interfere with the establishment of lactation. What's more, it's been suggested that breastfeeding in the first hour after birth can reduce bilirubin levels in nursing infants.

True breast milk jaundice is suspected when levels of bilirubin rise rapidly late in the first week of life and nonphysiologic jaundice has been ruled out. It's believed to be caused by a substance in the breast milk of some women that interferes with the breakdown of bilirubin, and is estimated to occur in about 2 percent of breastfed babies. In most cases, it clears up on its own within a few weeks without any treatment and without interrupting breastfeeding. If it doesn't clear up by 3 weeks, check back with the pediatrician.

Stool Color

"When I changed my baby's diaper for the first time, his poop was greenish black. Is this normal?"

This is only the first of many discoveries you'll make in your baby's diapers during the next year or so. And for the most part, what you will be discovering, though occasionally unsettling, will be completely normal. What you've turned up this time is meconium, the tarry greenish black substance that gradually filled your baby's intestines during his stay in your uterus. That the meconium is in his diaper instead of his intestines is a good sign—now you know that his bowels are doing their job.

Sometime after the first 24 hours, when all the meconium has been passed, you'll see transitional stools, which are dark greenish yellow and loose, sometimes "seedy" in texture (particularly among breastfed infants), and may occasionally contain mucus. There may even be traces of blood in them, probably the result of a baby's swallowing some of his mom's blood

The Scoop on Newborn Poop

So you think if you've seen one dirty diaper, you've seen them all? Far from it. Though what goes into your baby at this point is definitely one of two things (breast milk or formula), what comes out can be one of many. In fact, the color and texture of baby poop can change from day to day—and bowel movement to bowel movement—causing even seasoned parents to scratch their head. Here's the scoop on what the contents of your baby's diaper may mean:

Sticky, tarlike; black or dark green. Meconium—a newborn's first few stools

Grainy; greenish yellow or brown. Transitional stools, which start turning up on the third or fourth day after birth

Seedy, curdy, creamy, or lumpy; light yellow to mustard or bright green. Normal breast milk stools

Slightly formed; light brownish to bright yellow to dark green. Normal formula stools

Frequent, watery; greener than usual. Diarrhea

Hard, pelletlike; mucus or blood streaked. Constipation

Black. Iron supplementation

Red streaked. Milk allergy or rectal fissure (a tear around the rectum, usually due to constipation)

Mucousy; green or light yellow. A virus such as a cold or stomach bug

---

during delivery (just to be sure, save any diaper containing blood to show to a nurse or doctor).

After 3 or 4 days of transitional stools, what your baby starts putting out will depend on what you've been putting into him. If it's breast milk, the movements will often be mustardlike in color and consistency, sometimes loose, even watery, sometimes seedy, mushy, or curdy. If it's formula, the stool will usually be soft but better formed than a breastfed baby's, and anywhere from pale yellow to yellowish brown, light brown, or brown green. Iron in baby's diet (whether from formula or vitamin drops) can also lend a black or dark green hue to movements.

Whatever you do, don't compare your baby's diapers with those of the baby in the next bassinet. Like fingerprints, no two stools are exactly alike.

And unlike fingerprints, they are different not only from baby to baby, but also from day to day (even poop to poop) in any one baby. The changes, as you will see when baby moves on to solids, will become more pronounced as his diet becomes more varied.

Pacifier Use

"Will my baby become addicted to the pacifier if she gets one in the hospital nursery?"

Babies are born suckers, which makes pacifiers pretty popular in the hospital nursery—both with the tiny occupants and those who care for them. Not only won't she get hooked from a day or two of pacifier use, but as long as your little sucker is also getting her full share of feeds, enjoying a little between-meal

Going Home

In the 1930s, healthy new babies and their moms came home from the hospital after a whopping 10 days, in the 1950s after 4 days, in the 1980s after 2 days. Then, in the 1990s, insurance companies, in a cost-cutting effort, began limiting hospital stays to just hours. To protect against such so-called drive-through deliveries, the federal government passed the Newborns' and Mothers' Health Protection Act in 1996. The law requires insurance companies to pay for a 48-hour hospital stay following a vaginal birth and 96 hours following a cesarean delivery, though some practitioners and mothers may opt for a shorter stay if baby is healthy and mom is up to going home sooner.

Itching for your own bed and hungry for some real food? The decision to check out early is best made on a case-by-case basis with a physician's input. Early discharge is safest when an infant is full term, is an appropriate weight, has started feeding well, is going home with a parent (or parents) who knows the basics and is well enough to provide care, and will be seen by a practitioner (doctor, nurse practitioner, or visiting nurse) within 2 days of discharge.

If you and your baby are discharged early (or if you delivered at home), make sure you schedule that first checkup within the next 48 hours. In the meantime, watch carefully for signs of newborn problems that require immediate medical attention, such as refusal to eat, dehydration (fewer than 6 wet diapers in 24 hours or dark yellow urine), constant crying, moaning instead of crying, or no crying at all, fever, or red or purple dots anywhere on the skin. Also keep an eye out for signs of jaundice, which include yellowing of the eyes and of the skin in light-skinned babies and yellowing of the eyes, palms of the hands, and soles of the feet in dark-skinned newborns. To run a check for jaundice in your newborn, press down on his or her thigh or arm with your thumb—if the skin turns yellowish instead of white, your little one may be jaundiced. On dark-skinned or Asian babies, the blanch test is done on the inner cheek or lip, or on the palms and soles of the feet.

---

soothing from a soothie is no problem at all. In fact, there are benefits to pacifier use—the AAP suggests that parents consider offering one during sleep to protect against SIDS, a good reason to get baby started on one early (wait too long to introduce the pacifier, and your little one may resist). Nursing mamas can pop the paci, too, without concern about it causing nipple confusion or interfering with breastfeeding—there's no consensus that either is true.

However, if you're concerned about the pacifier satisfying too much of your baby's sucking needs (especially if you're breastfeeding, and particularly if she hasn't been feeding all that well yet), you may decide you'd rather the staff not offer a pacifier when she's in the nursery. Don't be shy about letting them know that you'd prefer to feed her when she cries, or if she's just finished up a feed, use other comfort measures instead of plugging in the paci. If your baby seems to need more between-meal sucking once you're home, and you're considering starting her on a pacifier, see page 219.

A Safe Ride Home

Starting with that first ride home from the hospital—and every ride after that—your baby will have to be properly secured into a properly installed car seat. That's because safety seats, like seat belts, are the law. Not to mention that an unstrapped baby is an unsafe baby. Car crashes are a leading cause of injury and death among children. So even if your destination is literally just a few blocks away (most accidents occur within 25 miles of home and not, as is often believed, on highways), even if you're driving slowly (a crash at 30 miles per hour creates as much force as a fall from a third-story window), even if you're wearing a seat belt and holding your baby tight (in a crash, baby could be crushed by your body or whipped from your arms), even if you're driving very carefully (you don't actually have to crash for severe injuries to result— many occur when a car stops short or swerves to avoid an accident), and even if you're just going from one space to another in the same parking lot, your baby needs to be buckled up safely.

Getting your baby used to a safety seat from the very first ride will help make later acceptance of it almost automatic. And young children who ride in safety restraints regularly are not only safer but also better behaved during drives—something you'll appreciate when you're riding with a toddler.

In addition to checking that a seat meets federal safety standards, be sure that it is appropriate for your baby's age and weight and that you install and use it correctly:

- Follow manufacturer's directions for installation of the seat and securing of your baby. Check before each ride that the seat is properly secured and the seat belts, or LATCH system (see page 54) holding it, are snugly fastened. The car seat should not wobble, pivot, slide side to side, tip over, or move more than an inch when you push it from front to back or side to side—instead, when properly installed it should stay tight. (You'll know the rear-facing infant seat is installed tightly enough if, when you hold the top edge of the car seat and try to push it downward, the back of the seat stays firmly in place at the same angle.) To make sure you've installed the car seat correctly, have it assessed (car seat safety checks are offered at fire and police stations, hospitals, car dealerships, baby stores, and other locations). Keep in mind, however, that only a certified car seat safety technician is likely to be up-to-date on all the latest recommendations. For peace of mind at a price (a relatively small one) you can search locally for a certified car seat technician to install your car seat or check your work at cert.safekids.org.

- Infants should ride in a rear-facing car seat (reclining at a 45-degree angle) until they reach age 2—or until the the weight limit is outgrown (usually around 35 pounds). Experts say that a rear-facing child safety seat does a much better job protecting a young child in a car crash (children under age 2 are 75 percent less likely to be severely or fatally injured in a crash if they are riding rear-facing). That's because in a rear-facing car seat, the child's head, neck, and spine are better supported, making the risk of serious injury much less likely. The majority of kids don't hit that upper weight limit for the car seat until after age 2, but some toddlers may be big enough to be turned forward-facing earlier than age 2. Once baby has outgrown the infant seat, use a convertible seat, which can accommodate larger babies in the rear-facing position.

- Place the infant safety seat, if at all possible, in the middle of the backseat (if there is a LATCH system in the middle seat; if not, then use one of the window seats with a LATCH system). Never put an ordinary rear-facing infant seat in the front seat of a car equipped with a passenger-side air bag—if the air bag is inflated (which could happen even at slow speeds in a fender bender), the force could seriously injure or kill a baby. In fact, the safest place for all children under 13 is in the backseat—older children should ride up front only when absolutely necessary and when safely restrained and sitting as far from the passenger-side air bag as possible.

- Adjust the shoulder harness to fit your baby. The harness slots on a rear-facing safety seat should be at or below your baby's shoulders, and the harness chest clip should be at armpit level. The straps should lie flat and untwisted, and should be tight enough so that you can't get more than two fingers between the harness and your baby's collarbone. Check the instructions to see how the carrying handle should be positioned during travel, if applicable.

- Dress your baby in clothes that allow straps to go between his or her legs. In cold weather, place blankets on top of your strapped-in baby (after adjusting the harness straps snugly), rather than dressing baby in a snowsuit. A heavy snowsuit can come between your baby and an adequately tight harness. See page 53 for more.

- Most infant seats come with special cushioned inserts to keep a very young baby's head from flopping around. If not, pad the sides of the car seat and the area around the head and neck with a rolled blanket—but never underneath baby. And never use inserts that don't come with the car seat. It not only will void the warranty, but it could also make baby unsafe. See page 53.

- For older babies, attach soft toys to the seat with velcro or plastic links (never a cord that's 6 inches or longer). Loose toys tend to be flung around the car or dropped, upsetting baby and distracting the driver. Or use toys designed specifically for car seat use.

- Many infant car seats can lock into shopping carts—something that's sure to be convenient but is also potentially dangerous. The weight of the baby and car seat makes the shopping cart top-heavy and more likely to tip over. So be extra vigilant when placing your baby's car seat on a shopping cart, or, as recommended by the AAP, for optimum safety use a sling, baby carrier, or stroller when shopping.

- The Federal Aviation Administration (FAA) recommends using a child safety seat in flight (secured with the airplane seat belt) until age 4. Most infant, convertible, and forward-facing seats are certified for use on airplanes (see page 521 for more).

- See Chapter 2 for more on choosing an infant safety seat, the types of harnesses available, and other safety information. For specific information about installing your car seat, to find out if your car seat has been recalled, and for other safety information, consult the National Highway Transportation Safety Administration at nhtsa.gov/Safety/CPS.

- The most important rule of car seat safety is: Never make an exception. Whenever the car is moving, everyone in the car should be safely and appropriately buckled up.

ALL ABOUT:
Baby-Care Basics

Put the diaper on backward? Took 5 minutes to get baby positioned for a productive burp? Forgot to wash under the arms at bath time? No sweat. Not only are babies forgiving when it comes to minor baby-care mishaps, but they usually don't even notice. Still, like every new parent, you'll want to do the best job you possibly can taking care of your newborn—even if that personal best is far from parenting perfection. These Baby-Care Basics will help guide you to that goal. But remember, what follows are only suggested ways to care for baby—you'll probably stumble (sometimes literally) on strategies that work better for both of you. As long as it's a safe way to go, go for it.

Diapering Baby

Especially in the early months, the time for a diaper change can come all too often—sometimes hourly during baby's waking hours, sometimes (especially for the breastfed newborn) even more frequently. But while it might not be the best part of your new job (that would be those warm snuggles), it's a necessary one—and in fact, frequent changes (taking place, at the very least, before or after every daytime feeding if baby's wet, and whenever your baby poops) are the best way to keep that sweet but sensitive bottom free of irritation and diaper rash.

You won't have to play diaper detective to figure out when it's time for a change. You'll know when your baby poops—the grunts will clue you in, and if you miss those, you'll get a whiff quick enough. As far as how you can

tell if your little one has peed, it's pretty elementary: Cloth diapers will feel wet, disposables with a liquid-sensitive color changing stripe will give you the sign, and if you have the standard type of disposable, a quick look (and sniff) will tell you what you need to know.

Waking a sleeping baby to change a diaper is hardly ever necessary, and unless baby's very wet and uncomfortable or has had a poop, you don't need to change diapers at nighttime feedings, when the activity and light involved can interfere with baby's getting back to sleep.

To ensure a change for the better whenever you change your baby's diaper:

1. Before you begin to change a diaper, be sure everything you need is at hand, either on the changing table or, if you're away from home, in your diaper bag. Otherwise, you could end up removing a messy diaper only to find out you have nothing to clean the mess with. You will need all or some of the following:

- A clean diaper

- Cotton balls and warm water for babies under 1 month (or those with diaper rash) and a small towel or dry washcloth for drying; diaper wipes for other babies

- A change of clothes if the diaper has leaked (it happens with the best of them); clean diaper wraps or waterproof pants if you're using cloth diapers

- Ointment or cream, if needed, for diaper rash; no need for lotions, baby oil, or powder

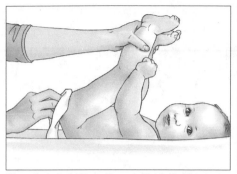

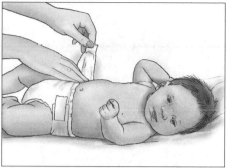

Clean baby's bottom thoroughly, being sure to get into all the creases.

Once that soft tush is completely dry, fasten the clean diaper snugly to minimize leaks.

2. Wash and dry your hands before you begin, if possible, or give them a once-over with a diaper wipe.

3. Have baby entertainment on hand. Live shows are a baby's favorite (cooing, funny faces, songs) backed up by other diversions, which can be a mobile hanging over the changing table, a stuffed toy or two in baby's range of vision (and later, within reach), a music box, a mechanical toy—whatever will hold your baby's interest long enough for you to take off one diaper and put on another.

4. Spread a protective cloth diaper or a changing cloth if you are changing baby anywhere but on a changing table. Wherever you make the change, be careful not to leave baby unattended, not even for a moment, not even before rolling over has been accomplished. Even strapped to a changing table, your baby shouldn't be out of arm's reach.

5. Unfasten the diaper, but don't remove it yet. First survey the scene. If there's a bowel movement, use the diaper to wipe most of it away. Now fold the diaper under the baby with the unsoiled side up to act as a protective surface, and clean baby's front thoroughly with warm water or a wipe, being sure to get into all the creases. Then lift both legs, clean the

buttocks, and slip the soiled diaper out and a fresh diaper under before releasing the legs. Pat baby dry if you used water. Make sure baby's bottom is completely dry before putting on the clean diaper (or any ointments or creams). If you note any irritation or rash, see page 281 for treatment tips. If the umbilical stump is still attached, fold the diaper down to expose the raw area to air and keep it from getting wet, or use newborn diapers that have a special notched top. And be sure to fasten the diaper snugly to minimize leaks, but not so tightly that irritation occurs (telltale marks will warn you that the diaper is too tight).

Got a boy baby? Keep a fresh diaper over that penis for as much of this process as possible, in self-defense. Also, expect to see erections—they happen often during diaper changes, and that's completely normal. Don't be afraid of cleaning under and around the scrotum and penis—just be gentle, of course. Before closing the diaper, try aiming your baby boy's penis down, which will help prevent wetness from creeping up and drenching his clothes.

6. Dispose of diapers in a sanitary way. Used disposable diapers can be folded over, tightly reclosed, and dropped into a diaper pail or the garbage can. Used cloth diapers should be kept in a tightly

An over-the-shoulder hold yields the best burping result for many babies, but don't forget to protect your clothes.

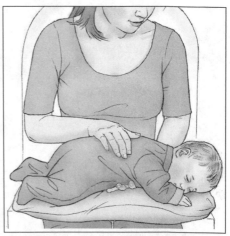

The lap burp position can get the job done with an added bonus: It can be soothing for a colicky baby.

covered diaper pail until wash day or pickup, though you'll probably want to scrape off and flush away anything solid first (a good reason to consider a flushable liner). If you're away from home, they can be held in a plastic bag until you get back.

7. Change baby's clothing and/or sheet as needed.

8. Wash your hands with soap and water, when possible, or clean them thoroughly with a diaper wipe, antibacterial wipes, or hand sanitizer.

Burping Baby

Milk isn't all baby swallows during a feed. Along with that nutritive fluid comes nonnutritive air, which can make a baby feel uncomfortably full before the meal is finished. That's why burping baby to bring up any excess air that's accumulated—every couple of ounces when bottle-feeding, and between breasts when breastfeeding (or midbreast, if your tiny newborn is managing only one breast at a time)—is such an important part of the feeding process.

There are three basic ways to burp a baby—on your shoulder, facedown on your lap, or sitting up—and it's a good idea to try them all to see which gets the job done best for your little one. Though a gentle pat or rub may get the burp up for most babies, some need a slightly firmer hand.

On your shoulder. Hold baby firmly against your shoulder, supporting the buttocks with one hand and patting or rubbing the back (focusing on the left side of baby's body—which is where the stomach is) with the other.

Facedown on your lap. Turn baby facedown on your lap, with that tummy over one leg, head resting on the other. Holding him or her securely with one hand, pat or rub with the other.

Sitting up. Sit baby on your lap, head leaning forward, chest supported by your arm as you hold him or her under the chin. Pat or rub, being sure not to let baby's head flop backward.

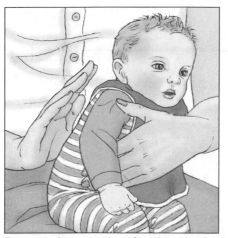
Even a newborn can sit up for a burp, but be sure you're supporting a still wobbly head.

Bathing Baby

Until a baby starts getting down and dirty on all fours, a daily bath definitely isn't needed. As long as adequate spot cleaning is done during diaper changes and after feedings, a bath two or three times a week in the premobile months will keep baby smelling sweet and looking fresh—welcome news if he or she doesn't exactly appreciate those dunks in the tub. Sponging can stand in between baths, as needed. Your little ducky loves the tub? There's no harm in daily dunks, unless dry skin is an issue.

Though just about any time of the day can be the right time for a newborn bath, a before-bedtime slot makes the most sense after all, warm water relaxes, soothes, and induces sleepiness. Plus, as baby starts spending the days getting dirty, nighttime baths will be smart on all fronts—and backsides—while becoming a treasured part of the bedtime ritual. Avoid baths just after or just before a meal, since spitting up could be the result of so much handling on a full tummy, and baby may not be cooperative on an empty one. Allot plenty of undivided time for the bath, so it won't be hurried and you won't be tempted to leave baby unattended even for a second to take care of something else.

The changing table, a kitchen counter, your bed, or the baby's crib (if the mattress is high enough)—or really, any surface that can be easily covered with a waterproof pad or thick towel—are all suitable locations for a sponge bath. Once baby has graduated from sponging to soaking, you can opt for the kitchen or bathroom sink, or a portable tub placed on a counter or in the big tub (though the maneuvering involved when bathing a tiny baby while bending and stretching over a tub can be tricky). Your work surface should be comfortable for you to access and roomy enough to hold all your bath supplies.

A toasty, draft-free room temperature will be most comfy for baby, especially during those early months. Aim for about 75°F to 80°F (a bathroom can be quickly warmed up with shower steam), and turn off any fans and air conditioners until the bath is over.

Have the following ready before undressing baby:

- Warm water, if you won't be within reach of a faucet

- Baby wash and shampoo, if you use it

- Two washcloths (one will do if you use your hand for sudsing)

- Cotton balls for cleaning the eyes

- Towel, preferably with a hood

- Clean diaper, diaper ointment or cream (if you use it), and clothing

The sponge bath. Until the umbilical cord and circumcision site (if any) are healed—a couple of weeks, more or less—tub baths will be taboo, and a washcloth will be your baby's only route

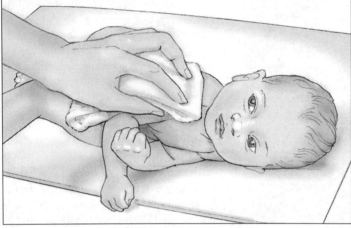

Until the umbilical stump falls off, the sponge bath will help keep your sweetie clean.

Keep a secure grip on your baby in the bathtub. Wet babies are slippery babies.

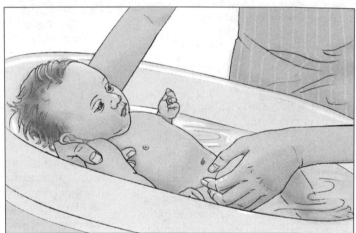

to clean. For a thorough sponge bath, follow these steps:

1. Get baby ready. If the room is warm, you can remove all of baby's clothing before beginning, covering him or her loosely with a towel while you work (most babies dislike being totally bare). If the room is on the cooler side, undress each part of the body as you're ready to wash it. No matter what the room temperature, don't take off baby's diaper until it's time to wash the bottom—an undiapered baby (especially a boy) should always be considered armed and dangerous.

2. Begin washing, starting with the cleanest areas of the body and working toward the dirtiest, so that the washcloth and the water you're using will stay clean. Suds up as needed with your hands or a washcloth, but use a clean cloth for rinsing. This order of business usually works well:

- Head. Once or twice a week, use baby wash or baby shampoo, rinsing very thoroughly. The rest of the time, you can just use water. A careful hold (see illustration on page 164) at the sink's edge can be the easiest and most comfortable way to rinse baby's head. Gently towel-dry baby's hair (for most babies this takes just a few seconds) before proceeding. Cradle cap? See page 253.

- Face. First, using a cotton ball moistened in warm water, clean baby's eyes, wiping gently from the inner corner of the eye outward. Use a fresh ball for each eye. No baby wash is needed for the face. Wipe around the outer ears but not inside. Gently pat dry all parts of the face.

- Neck, chest, and abdomen. Sudsing up is not necessary here, unless baby is very sweaty or dirty. Be sure to get into those abundant folds and creases, where dirt tends to accumulate. Maneuver carefully around the umbilical cord. It's okay to gently wipe away any crust that accumulates around the stump. Pat dry.

- Arms. Extend those little arms to get into the elbow creases, and press the palms to open the fists. The hands will need a bit of baby wash, but be sure to rinse them well before they are back in baby's mouth. Dry.

- Back. Turn baby over on the tummy with head to one side and wash the back, being sure not to miss those neck folds. Since this isn't a dirty area, sudsing probably won't be necessary. Dry, and dress the upper body before continuing if the room is chilly.

- Legs. Extend the legs to get the backs of the knees, though baby will probably resist being unfurled. Dry.

- Diaper area. Follow directions for care of the circumcised or uncircumcised penis (see page 166).

Wash girls front to back, spreading the labia and cleaning with baby wash and water. A white vaginal discharge is normal, so don't try to scrub it away. Use a fresh section of the cloth and clean water or fresh water poured from a cup to rinse the vagina. Wash boys carefully, getting into all the creases and crevices with baby wash and water, but don't try to retract the foreskin on an uncircumcised baby. Dry the diaper area well, and apply ointment or cream if needed.

3. Diaper and dress baby.

The baby-tub bath. A baby is ready for a tub bath as soon as both umbilical cord stump and circumcision, if any, are healed. If baby doesn't seem to like being in the water, go back to sponge baths for a few days before trying again. Here are the steps to take when tub bathing a baby:

1. Before you add the baby, run enough water into the baby tub so that when you place baby into the bath, he or she will be covered with water up to the chest. Test the water temperature with your elbow to be sure it's comfortably warm. Never run the water with baby in the tub, because a sudden temperature change might occur. Don't add baby wash or bubble bath to the water, as these can be drying to baby's skin and also up the chances of a UTI (urinary track infection) and other irritations.

2. Undress baby completely.

3. Slip baby gradually into the bath, talking in soothing and reassuring tones, and holding on securely to prevent a startle reflex. Support the neck and head with one hand unless the tub has built-in support or, if your baby seems to prefer your arms to the tub's support, until good head control develops. Hold baby securely in a semireclining position—slipping under suddenly could result in a scare.

4. With your free hand, wash baby, working from the cleanest to the dirtiest areas. First, using a cotton ball moistened in warm water, clean baby's eyes, wiping gently from the inner corner of the eye outward. Use a fresh ball for each eye. Then wash face, outer ears, and neck. Though baby wash won't usually be necessary elsewhere on a daily basis (unless your baby tends to have all-over poop blowouts), do use it daily on hands and the diaper area. Use it every couple of days on arms, neck, legs, and tummy as long as baby's skin doesn't seem dry—less often if it does. Apply baby wash with your hand or with a washcloth. When you've taken care of baby's front parts, turn him or her over your arm to wash the back and buttocks.

5. Rinse baby thoroughly with a fresh washcloth or by gently pouring water over baby's body.

6. Once or twice a week, wash baby's scalp using baby wash or baby shampoo (or one that's a combo). Rinse very thoroughly and towel-dry gently.

7. Wrap baby in a towel, pat dry, and dress.

Shampooing Baby

This is usually a pretty painless process with a young baby. But to help head off future shampoo phobias, avoid getting even tearless cleanser or shampoo in your baby's eyes. Shampoo only once or twice a week, unless cradle cap or a particularly oily scalp requires more frequent cleanings. When baby is very young and still getting sponge baths, you can do the shampooing over a sink.

A careful hold at the sink's edge can make shampooing a baby who hasn't graduated to tub baths easier.

Once baby has graduated to a baby tub, you can do the shampoo at the end of the bath—right in the tub.

1. Wet baby's hair with a gentle spray of water or by pouring a little water from a cup. Add just a drop of baby shampoo or baby wash (more will make rinsing difficult), and rub in lightly to produce a lather. A foam product may be easier to control.

2. Hold baby's head (well supported) and rinse thoroughly with a gentle spray or 2 or 3 cupfuls of clean water. Be sure to keep baby's head tilted back slightly so the water runs back instead of over baby's face.

Ear Care

Baby ears are pretty much care-free. Not only don't they need to be cleaned, but they shouldn't be—not with your fingers, not with a cotton swab, not even with a washcloth. When you wash your baby's face, you can wipe around the outer ears, but don't venture anywhere near the inside. Worried about wax? Don't be. It's not cute, but it's protective—among other benefits, keeping dirt and debris from traveling into the ear canal. Leave even visible wax alone, and if you're concerned that there's excessive buildup, check with the pediatrician, who can safely remove it if necessary.

Nose Care

As with the inside of the ears, the inside of the nose is self-cleaning and needs no special care. If there's visible mucus, wipe the outside gently, but do not use cotton swabs, twisted tissues, or your fingernail to try to remove goo, gook, or crust from inside the nostrils— you may only push the stuff farther into the nose or even scratch delicate membranes. If baby has a lot of mucus due to a cold, suction it out with an infant nasal aspirator (see page 554).

Nail Trimming

Although trimming a newborn's tiny fingernails may make most new parents uneasy, it's a job that must be done. Little hands with little control and long fingernails can do a lot of damage, usually in the form of scratches on that adorable little face.

An infant's nails are often overgrown at birth (especially if baby arrived late) and so soft that cutting through them is nearly as easy as cutting through a piece of paper. The challenge is getting your baby to hold still for the procedure. Cutting a baby's nails while he or she is sleeping may work if you've got a sound sleeper or if you don't mind inadvertently waking your cutie. Use special baby scissors with rounded tips (so you don't accidentally poke your baby if he or she startles while you're working) or a clipper

designed for the purpose—some even have a built-in magnifying glass to help you get a good view. Still squeamish? Try a baby-size emery board instead. Or do the job when you have a helper available—one of you can hold the baby's hands still (and distract with a song) while the other clips. Want to make trimming even more effortless (and who wouldn't)? Aim to trim after a bath, when the nails are at the softest—and therefore easiest to cut. But don't attempt while baby is still wet and slippery.

When clipping, hold your baby's finger, pressing the fingertip pad down and away from the nail. Gently snip following the natural curve of the fingernail, taking care that you don't go too low and nip the skin. When tending to tiny toes, cut nails straight across. Keep in mind that toenails grow more slowly and therefore require less maintenance.

Though you'll feel awful, try not to worry if you nick your baby's skin—it happens to every well-intentioned mom or dad manicurist. Apply gentle pressure with a clean, lint-free cloth or gauze pad, and the bleeding will soon stop.

Umbilical Stump Care

Think of it as a last souvenir of baby's uterine stay: the umbilical stump. It turns black a few days after birth and can be expected to drop off anywhere between 1 and 4 weeks later. Since healing will happen faster if you keep the area dry and exposed to air, fold diapers down so they don't brush against the scab, and use wrap-style undershirts for now instead of onesies (or use a onesie designed with a special cutout for the stump). Don't swab the stump with alcohol (that might irritate tender skin, and it isn't necessary for healing), but do stick to sponge baths until it has fallen off. If you notice signs of infection (pus or red skin at the base of the cord, see page 221) or if the stump seems painful to the touch, call the doctor.

Penis Care

If your son is circumcised, keep the incision clean and dab it with Vaseline or Aquaphor at each diaper change to keep it from rubbing against the diaper. After the incision heals, just continue to wash with baby wash and water at bath time. For more on care during the recovery period, see page 222.

No special care is needed for an uncircumcised penis. In other words, do not retract the foreskin to clean underneath. It will fully separate from the glans after a few years, at which point it can be pushed back for cleaning.

Dressing Baby

With floppy arms, stubbornly curled-up legs, a head that invariably seems larger than the openings provided by most baby clothes, and an active dislike for being naked, an infant can be a challenge to dress and undress. To dress and undress for success:

1. Select clothes with easy-on, easy-off features in mind. Wide neck openings or necks with snap closings are best. Snaps or a zipper at the crotch make dressing and diaper changes easier. Sleeves should be fairly loose, and a minimum of fastening (particularly up the back) should be necessary. Clothes with lots of give (made of soft, stretchable fabrics) are usually easier to put on and take off.

2. Use protection. To limit wardrobe changes, keep your baby in a bib during and after feeds. Too late for that? Try sponging spit-up spots lightly with a diaper wipe rather than changing baby's outfit.

3. Dress baby on a flat surface, such as a changing table or bed.

4. Talk it up. Consider dressing time a social time, too. Offer a running commentary on what you're doing, punctuating with loud kisses (a smooch for each adorable hand and foot as it appears from the sleeve or pants leg).

Stretch the neck opening of a shirt before putting it over baby's head.

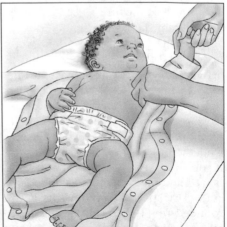

Reach in from the cuff of the sleeve to help get baby's floppy little arms through.

Carefully support baby's neck and back with your arm when lifting your baby.

When snuggling your baby on your shoulder, be sure to keep a supportive hand on that wobbly head.

5. Stretch neck openings with your hands before attempting to squeeze over baby's head. Ease rather than tug tops on and off, keeping the opening as wide as possible in the process and trying to avoid snagging the ears or nose (but don't stress if you do, because you will sometimes). Turn the split second during which baby's head is covered, which might otherwise be scary or uncomfortable, into a game of peekaboo ("Where is Mommy? Here she is!" and "Where is Mia? Here she is!").

6. Instead of trying to shove floppy little arms into sleeves, try to reach in from the cuff of the sleeve (bunching up the fabric if the shirt is long-sleeved), grab hold of your little one's hand, and then gently pull, unfurling the fabric, if necessary, as you bring baby's arm through the sleeve. It'll be more fun if you have a trick up your sleeve, too ("Where is Braden's hand? Here it is!").

7. When pulling a zipper up or down, pull the clothing away from your baby's body to avoid pinching tender skin.

Lifting and Carrying Baby

For the past 9 months, your little one has been carried around in a snug and secure uterine cocoon, moving gently within its cozy confines. Being plucked up, wafted through the open air, and plunked down can therefore be unsettling, especially if baby's head and neck aren't well supported. So aim at lifting and carrying your baby in a way that not only is safe, but feels safe. Can't seem to lose that "but won't baby break?" feeling when you pick up your newborn? Don't worry. Before you know it, carrying your little bundle will become a completely natural experience. In the meantime, these tips can help make both of you feel like baby is in good hands:

Picking up baby. Before you even touch your baby, let him or her know you're coming by making eye contact and saying a few reassuring words (no sneaking up on your sweetie). Then slip one hand under your baby's head and neck, and the other under the bottom, and

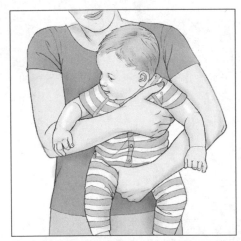

The front hold is a baby fan favorite because it allows a view of the world.

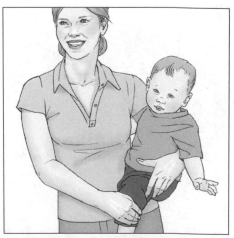

An older baby who can support his or her own weight is a good candidate for the hip hold, which gives mom or dad a free hand.

keep them there for a few moments before actually lifting so that baby can adjust first. Finally, slide the hand under baby's head down the back so that your arm acts as a back and neck support and your hand cradles the bottom. Use the other hand to support the legs, and lift baby gently toward your body, caressing as you go. By bending over to bring your body closer, you'll limit the distance your baby will have to travel in midair—and the uncertain feeling that comes with it.

Carrying baby comfortably. A small baby can be cradled very snugly in just one arm (with your hand on baby's bottom, and your forearm supporting back, neck, and head) if you feel secure that way.

With a larger baby, you both may be more comfortable if you keep one hand under the legs and bottom and the other supporting back, neck, and head (your hand encircling baby's arm, your wrist under the head).

Some babies prefer the shoulder carry, all the time or some of the time. It's easy to get baby up there smoothly

with one hand on the bottom, the other under head and neck. Until baby's head becomes self-supporting, you will have to provide the support. But this can be done even with one hand if you tuck baby's bottom into the crook of your elbow and run your arm up the back with your hand supporting the head and neck.

Even fairly young babies enjoy the front-face carry, in which they can watch the world go by, and many older babies prefer it. Face your baby out, keeping one hand across his or her chest, pressed back against your own, and the other supporting baby's bottom.

The hip carry gives you freedom to use one hand for chores while carrying an older baby resting on your hip. Hold baby snugly against your body with one arm resting his or her bottom on your hip. Avoid this hold if you have lower-back problems.

Putting baby back down. Hold baby close to your body as you bend over to place your little bundle down (again to limit the midair travel), one hand on baby's bottom, one supporting back,

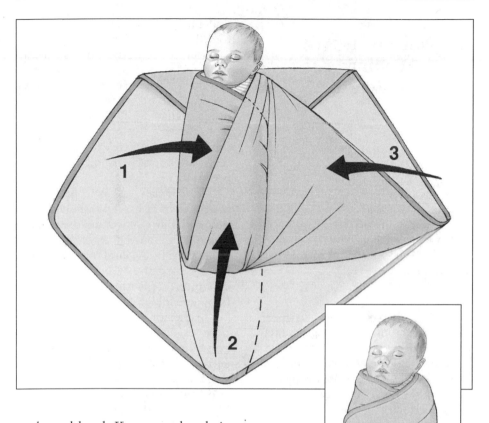

neck, and head. Keep your hands in place for a few moments until baby feels the comfort and security of the surface you're placing him or her on, then slip them out. Finish the transition with a light pat or two and a few reassuring words if baby's awake. (For tips on putting a sleeping baby down without waking him or her, see page 207.)

Swaddling Baby

Remember when your baby first came back from the hospital nursery? He or she was probably wrapped in a neat little package, with only that tiny head poking out—kind of like a baby burrito. That's because nurses know one of the secrets to a happy, calm infant: swaddling. The age-old technique has many benefits. For one thing, it can help your baby feel safe and secure during the transition to life outside the womb and cozy sleeping on his or her back. Swaddling can also prevent your baby from being woken by his or her own startle reflex and keep him or her toasty until the internal thermostat kicks into gear.

Newborn Care, Feeding . . . and Reading?

Can't wait to cuddle up for story-time with your little one? No need to. In fact, the AAP recommends reading to your baby daily, right from birth. You'll be bonding with your baby, nurturing brain development, and creating a ritual that's bound to become a favorite in your family. For more on reading to your baby, see page 424.

So how do you swaddle like a pro? First, spread out a receiving blanket, with one corner pointing up so the blanket is in the shape of a diamond. Fold down the top corner about 6 inches. Your baby's head goes here, with his or her neck on the straight part of the folded-over corner and his or her body extending straight down toward the bottom corner. Take the corner near baby's right arm and pull it over the arm and across baby's body. Lift the left arm, and tuck the blanket corner under baby's back on the left side. Next, fold the bottom corner of the blanket up over baby's body and tuck it into the first fold—under his or her chin. Lift the last corner, bring it over baby's left arm, and tuck it in under the back on the right side. Ta-da: baby burrito! Not a master of the baby burrito or just don't have the patience to perfect? Opt for swaddles with velcro tabs or a zip-up cocoonlike swaddling.

If your baby seems to prefer having freedom of hand movement, wrap below the arms. An added bonus to free hands: Your baby will be able to self-soothe by sucking on those sweet fingers. Because being wrapped up can interfere with development as baby gets older, and because a blanket that a swaddled baby kicks off can pose a safety hazard in the crib, stop swaddling once baby becomes more active (by 3 or 4 months). Be sure, too, that the swaddle isn't too tight . . . and that baby's knees, elbows, and hips are flexed naturally in the usual position for optimal joint development (don't straighten them out before swaddling).

Baby doesn't like being swaddled for sleep? Try a sleep sack or a hybrid swaddle/sack instead.

The First Month

Y ou've brought your baby home and you're giving parenthood everything you've got. Yet you can't help wondering: Is everything you've
got enough? After all, your schedule (and life as you vaguely recall
knowing it) is upended, you're still fumbling over feedings, and you can't
remember the last time you've showered . . . or slept more than 2 hours in
a row.

As your baby grows from a precious but largely unresponsive newborn to a full-fledged cuddly infant,
your sleepless nights and hectic days
will likely be filled not only with pure
joy but also with exhaustion—not to
mention new questions and concerns:
Is my baby getting enough to eat? Why
does he spit up so much? Are these
crying spells considered colic? Will she
(and we) ever sleep through the night?

And how many times a day can I actually call the pediatrician? Not to worry.
Believe it or not, by month's end you'll
have settled into a comfortable routine
with baby, one that's still exhausting
but much more manageable. You'll
also start to feel like a seasoned pro in
the baby-care game (at least compared
to what you feel like today)—feeding,
burping, bathing, and handling baby
with relative ease.

Feeding Your Baby This Month:
Pumping Breast Milk

T his early in the breastfeeding game,
your breasts and your baby probably haven't spent much time apart, and
that's as it should be for starters. But
there will almost certainly come a day
(or a night) when you'll need to (or want
to) be away from your baby during a

feeding—whether you're working, taking a class, traveling, or just out for the
night—and you'll be taking your breasts
with you. How will you catch a breastfeeding break while still making sure
your baby gets the best? Easy: Express
yourself.

Baby Basics at a Glance: First Month

Sleeping. A newborn baby doesn't have much of a pattern to his or her sleep schedule. Baby will be sleeping anywhere from 14 to 18 out of every 24 hours.

Eating. Baby's getting only breast milk or formula at this age:

- Breast milk. Baby will nurse 8 to 12 times during every 24-hour period, taking in a total of anywhere from 12 to 32 ounces of breast milk (if you were counting). That's a feeding roughly every 2 to 3 hours, timed from start of one to start of next. Feed on demand, rather than by the clock.

- Formula. Start with 1 ounce at a time, 8 to 12 times per 24 hours, in the first week or so (for a total of 12 ounces). By the end of the first month, baby will probably take 2 to 3 ounces of formula per 24 hours, or 16 to 32 ounces total. Since formula takes longer to digest than breast milk, you may be able to spread out meals to one every 3 to 4 hours. Even formula-fed newborns are best fed on demand and to appetite, rather than on a schedule.

Playing. A newborn baby doesn't really need any toys (your cuddles and caresses are the best toys for your little one), but since baby can see objects 8 to 12 inches away (the distance to your face as you hold that bundle), a mobile or play gym is a good option for stimulating baby when your arms aren't free. Babies love looking at bold patterns and faces, so if you're able to find a mobile that combines both, even better.

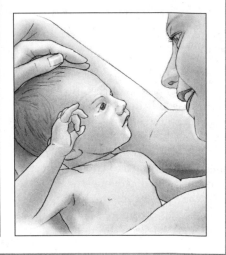

Why Pump?

It's not so much a law of physics as it is a law of busy motherhood: You can't always count on your baby and your breasts being at the same place at the same time. There is a way, however, to feed your baby breast milk (and keep your milk supply up) even if you and baby are miles apart: by pumping (or expressing) milk.

Wondering when you'd need or want to pump? Here are some common reasons:

- Relieve engorgement when your milk comes in

- Collect milk for feedings while you're working

- Provide relief bottles for when you're away from home

- Increase or maintain your milk supply

- Jump-start your milk supply if it's slow coming in

- Store milk in the freezer for emergencies

- Prevent engorgement and maintain milk supply when nursing is temporarily stopped because of illness (yours or baby's) or because you're taking a medication that's breastfeeding-unfriendly

- Provide breast milk for your sick or premature baby in the hospital

- Stimulate relactation if you change your mind about formula feeding

- Induce lactation if you're adopting a newborn

Choosing a Pump

Sure, you can express milk by hand—if you have a lot of time, don't need a lot of milk, and don't mind a lot of pain. But why bother, when pumping makes it so much easier, more comfortable, and more productive to express yourself? With so many breast pumps on the market—from simple manual models that cost a few dollars to pricier electric ones that can be bought or rented—there's one (or more) to fill your needs and fill your baby's supplementary bottles with the best food around.

Before deciding which type of pump suits your expressing style, you'll need to do a little homework:

- Consider your needs. Will you be pumping regularly because you're going back to work or school full time? Will you pump only once in a while to provide a relief bottle (or to relieve engorged breasts)? Or will you be pumping around-the-clock to provide nourishment for your sick or premature baby, who may be in the hospital for weeks or months?

- Weigh your options. If you'll be pumping several times a day for an extended period of time (such as when working full-time or to feed a preterm infant), a double electric pump will probably be your best bet. If you need to pump only occasionally, a single electric, battery, or manual pump will fill your needs (and those few bottles). If you're planning to express only when you're engorged or for a once-in-a-great-while bottle-feeding, an inexpensive manual pump may make sense.

- Investigate. Not all pumps are created equal—not even among those in the same general category. Some electric pumps can be uncomfortable to use, and some hand pumps painfully slow (and sometimes just plain painful) for expressing large quantities of milk. Scout the field by checking websites and stores that carry a wide variety of pumps, considering features and affordability. Ask friends or check out online reviews and posts to see which pumps other moms are pumped up about . . . and which don't make the grade. Or discuss the options with an LC or your baby's doctor.

All pumps use a breast cup or shield (known as a flange), centered over your nipple and areola. Whether you're using an electric or manual pump, suction is created when the pumping action is begun, mimicking baby's suckling (some more efficiently than others). Depending on the pump you use (and how fast your let-down is), it can take anywhere from 10 to 45 minutes to pump both breasts—not surprisingly, higher priced pumps yield speedier results. Here are the general types of pumps on the market:

A double electric pump cuts pumping time in half.

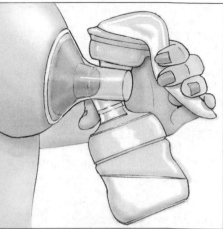

The trigger on a manual pump creates suction with each squeeze of the handle.

Electric pump. Powerful, fast, and usually easy to use, a fully automatic electric pump closely imitates the rhythmic suckling action of a nursing baby. Many electric pumps allow for double pumping—a great feature if you're pumping often. Not only does pumping both breasts simultaneously cut pumping time in half, it stimulates an increase in prolactin, which means you'll actually produce more milk faster. Electric pumps can cost a few hundred dollars, but if you're pumping often, it may be well worth the investment. (Also, when you weigh it against the cost of formula, you'll almost certainly come out ahead.)

Most electric pumps come in portable models that are inconspicuous (the black carrying cases are designed to look like backpacks or shoulder bags). Some pumps also come with a car adapter and/or battery pack (some come with rechargeable batteries) so you don't have to plug them in. There are even some models that have a memory feature that learns your personal pumping rhythm and remembers it for the next time you express. Another feature: Hands-free pumps attach to your bra and allow you to work, play with your baby, blog online, or otherwise be a mommy multitasker while pumping (there are also specially designed bras that allow for hands-free pumping).

Need a pump that's really heavy duty (for instance, because you're pumping full-time for your preemie or trying to relactate)? There are hospital-grade electric pumps you can buy (very expensive) or rent (more cost effective)—often from the hospital you've delivered in or from a lactation center. An LC, the La Leche League, or an online search can help you get connected to a reputable rental company.

Manual pump. These hand-operated pumps are fairly simple to use, moderate in price, easy to clean, and portable. The most popular style is a trigger-operated pump that creates suction with each squeeze of the handle.

Is Your Pump Covered?

Pumped up about preventive care services available to women under the Affordable Care Act? You should be, especially because many (though not all) insurance plans are required to provide breast pumps to new moms at no extra cost, and without co-pays or deductibles. The legislation is designed to ensure that every mom has the opportunity to provide her baby with the ultimate in prevention: breast milk. The catch? Since the law's recommendations aren't specific, coverage varies from health plan to health plan—and there's considerable variation in what sort of pumps are covered. Some plans cover the purchase of manual pumps only, while others exclude hospital-grade pumps, and still others allow moms to rent a pump but not purchase one. Most plans require moms to get the pump from designated vendors (who might not have the model you want), and many plans require that you get a prescription for a pump from your doctor (another hoop to jump through).

Confused? The best thing to do is to contact your health plan to find out what you'll be covered for. Let your insurer know if you're not happy with what's offered. WIC also provides breast pumps and other breastfeeding supplies and support to eligible moms.

Preparing to Pump

Whenever you pump (and no matter what type of pump you're using), there are basic prep steps you'll need to take to ensure an easy and safe pumping session:

- Time it right. Choose a time of day when your breasts are ordinarily full. If you're pumping because you're away from your baby and missing feedings, try to pump at the same times you would normally feed, about once every 3 hours. If you're home and want to stock the freezer with breast milk for emergencies or relief bottles, pump 1 hour after baby's first morning feeding, since you're likely to have more milk earlier in the day. (Late afternoon or early evening, when your milk supply is likely to be at its lowest thanks to exhaustion and end-of-the-day stress, is often an unproductive time to pump.) Or pump from one breast while nursing your baby from the other one—the natural let-down action your body produces for your suckling baby will help stimulate milk flow in the pumped breast as well. (But wait until you're skilled at both nursing and expressing, since this can be a tricky maneuver for a newbie.) Still got extra milk after a feed? Pump whatever baby didn't finish and save it for later.

- Wash up. Wash your hands and make sure that all your pumping equipment is clean. Washing the pump parts immediately after each use in hot, soapy water will make the job of keeping it clean easier. Dishwashers can work well, too. If you use your pump away from home, carry along a bottle brush, bottle wash, and paper towels for washup.

Pumping Shouldn't Hurt

Simply put, pumping shouldn't hurt. If it does, make sure you're pumping correctly, not going over recommended pumping time limits, and that you're treating any soreness or cracking (or other sources of pain, such as infection) you might be having.

Check, check, check to all three—and you're still finding pumping physically painful? The problem may lie with the pump itself (in which case, it might be time for a switch, if that's financially feasible), but it's more likely to be a matter of a too-small (or less often, too large) flange size, a very common problem that's easily fixed. If the flange is the right size, your nipple will move freely in the flange tunnel during pumping, and not much of the areola will be drawn into the tube with the nipple. Check your flange in action next time you pump—and when in doubt, try sizing up or down to see if pumping becomes less of a pain (at least, physically).

- **Set the scene.** Choose a quiet, comfortable environment for pumping, where you won't be interrupted by phones or doorbells and where you'll have some privacy. Cozy up in a chair that allows you to relax in relative comfort. At work, a private office, an unoccupied meeting room, or a designated nursing room can serve as your pumping headquarters. An office restroom is definitely not ideal, and in fact, federal law requires employers in companies with more than 50 employees to provide a private place other than the bathroom for pumping. If you're at home, wait until baby's naptime or when your little one is otherwise occupied—in a swing or infant seat—so you can concentrate on pumping (unless you're pumping while nursing).

- **Chill out.** The more relaxed you are, the more productive a pumper you'll be. So try to chill out for a few minutes first—visualize, use meditation or another relaxation technique, listen to music or a white noise app, or do whatever you find helps you unwind.

- **Hydrate.** Have some water before you get started pumping.

- **Encourage let-down.** Think about your baby, look at baby's photo, and/or picture yourself nursing, to help stimulate let-down. If you're home, giving baby a quick cuddle just before you start pumping could do the trick—or you can pump while your baby sits beside you in an infant seat or swing. If you're using a hands-free pump, you can even try holding your baby while you pump—though many babies won't be too happy about being so near and yet so far from their source of food. Applying hot soaks to your nipples and breasts for 5 or 10 minutes (clearly not so practical at work), taking a hot shower (ditto), doing breast massage, or leaning over and shaking your breasts are other ways of enhancing let-down. A convenient alternative at home or at work: hot/cold packs—packs that you can chill in the freezer before using when you want them soothingly cold or that you can microwave for a few seconds when you want them warm (as in when you want to encourage let-down).

Pumping Practice Makes Perfect

No matter what method of expressing you choose, you may find it difficult to extract much milk the first few times. Consider those initial pumping sessions to be practice—your goal should be to figure out how to use the pump, not necessarily to score large quantities of milk. Milk probably won't be flowing in copious amounts during early sessions anyway, for two reasons: First, you're not producing that much milk yet if your baby is still less than a month or two old. Second, a pump (especially as wielded by a novice pumper) is much less effective in extracting milk than a baby is. But with perseverance (and practice, practice, practice), you'll become a pro pumper in no time.

How to Express Breast Milk

Though the basic principle of expressing milk is the same no matter how you go about it (stimulation and compression of the areola draws milk from the ducts out through the nipples), there are subtle differences in techniques.

Expressing milk by hand. To begin, place your hand on one breast, with your thumb and forefingers opposite each other around the edge of the areola. Press your hand in toward your chest, gently pressing thumb and forefinger together while pulling forward slightly. (Don't let your fingers slip onto the nipple.) Repeat rhythmically to start milk flowing, rotating your hand position to get to all milk ducts. Repeat with the other breast, massaging in between expressions as needed. Repeat with the first breast, then do the second again.

If you want to collect the milk expressed, use a clean wide-topped cup under the breast you're working on. You can collect whatever drips from the other breast by placing a breast shell over it inside your bra. Collected milk should be poured into bottles or storage bags and refrigerated as soon as possible (see page 178).

Expressing milk with a manual pump. Follow the directions for the pump you're using. You might find moistening the outer edge of the flange with water or breast milk will ensure good suction, but it's not a necessary step. The flange should surround the nipple and areola, with all of the nipple and part of the areola in it. Use quick, short pulses at the start of the pumping session to closely imitate baby's sucking action. Once let-down occurs, you can switch to long, steady strokes. If you want to use a hand pump on one breast while nursing your baby on the other,

(Tell) Tales from the Other Side

If you're not double pumping, the breast not being pumped will start getting into the action ahead of time . . . and likely leak accordingly. To avoid a mess, make sure the breast that's being ignored is well packed with breast pads (especially if you'll be going back to your desk after pumping), or take advantage of every drop of milk and collect whatever leaks in a bottle, a clean cup, or a breast shell.

Where Does the Milk Go?

Many pumps come with containers that can be used as storage and feeding bottles, and others allow you to use a standard feeding bottle to collect the milk. Hoping to build up a freezer stash? Special breast milk storage bags are convenient for freezing milk and are less likely to break than disposable bottle liners, which are made of thinner plastic. Some pumps allow you to collect the expressed milk directly into the storage bags, so you can skip the extra step of transferring the milk from bottle to bag before storing—and the risk of spilling any drops of that precious fluid. If you will be transferring, be sure to wash any containers or bottles used for milk collection in hot soapy water or a dishwasher after you're finished transferring the milk from the collection containers to the storage containers.

prop the baby at your breast on a pillow (being sure he or she can't tumble off your lap). You can also use a manual pump to get breasts primed for electric pumping, though that means double the equipment and more work for you, so no need unless you find you have a very hard time getting started with the electric pump.

Expressing milk with an electric pump. Follow the directions for the pump you are using—double pumping is ideal because it saves time and increases milk volume. If you find it helps, you can moisten the outer edge of the flange with water or breast milk to ensure good suction. Start out on

the minimum suction and increase it as the milk begins to flow, if necessary. If your nipples are sore, keep the pump at the lower setting. You might find you get more milk from one breast than the other. That's normal, because each breast functions independently of the other.

Storing Breast Milk

Keep expressed milk fresh and safe with these storage guidelines:

- Refrigerate expressed milk as soon as you can. If that's not possible, breast milk will stay fresh at room temperature (but away from radiators, sun, or other sources of heat) for as long as 6 hours and in an insulated cooler bag (with ice packs) for up to 24 hours.

- Store breast milk for up to 4 days (96 hours) in the back of the refrigerator where temperatures are coolest (though ideally, it's best to use the milk within 2 to 3 days). If you're planning to freeze it, first chill for 30 minutes in the refrigerator, then freeze.

- Breast milk will stay fresh in the freezer for anywhere from a week or 2 in a single-door refrigerator to about 3 months in a two-door frost-free model that keeps foods frozen solid, to 6 months in a freezer that maintains a 0°F temperature.

Quick Tip

Fill breast milk storage containers or bags for the freezer only three-fourths full to allow for expansion, and label with the date (always use the oldest milk first).

Exclusive Pumping

Determined to feed your baby mama's milk but circumstances (say, problems with latching) have made breastfeeding a struggle, or even impossible? There's still a way to give baby the best from the breast: exclusive pumping. It's definitely tougher on moms than nursing is (babies are usually more efficient at extracting mama's milk from the source than a pump is), but pumping all your little one's meals is doable, if you're dogged about it. Here are some tips to keep in mind if you decide to exclusively pump:

- Get a good double pump. Since you'll be spending a lot of one-on-one time with your pump, you'll want one that's efficient—and that works two by two. Doubling up when pumping with a double electric pump will cut back on the time you spend pumping and will actually pump up your milk output.

- Pump often. Pump as often as baby would be eating (every 2 to 3 hours in the early months) to make sure your supply of breast milk becomes established. That includes pumping at least once or twice during the night.

- Pump long enough. To make sure you're stimulating your breasts enough to continue producing milk (and increasing the amount of milk they produce), be sure to pump for around 15 to 20 minutes (that's per breast if you're not double pumping) or until the milk stops dripping at each pumping session (which could

be longer than 20 minutes for some moms). Don't exceed the recommended time limit in hopes of scoring more milk—chances are you'll only score sore nipples.

- Don't drop pumps until your supply's pumped up. It could take anywhere from 6 to 12 weeks until your milk supply is well established. Once it is, you can start dropping some pumping sessions, but if you find your milk supply diminishing, increase pumping frequency until you're back where you want it to be.

- Record . . . or not. Some experts suggest moms record how much milk they're pumping per session. Others recognize that keeping a record (or spreadsheet) is time consuming and can add to the worry. If you're struggling with a low supply, for instance, recording your output will only stress you out, and possibly decrease your supply. Do what works for you.

- Supplement if needed. Sure, your goal is to feed your baby breast milk only, but if your supply is too low, if you're too pooped to pump enough, or if you decide for any other reason that you just can't commit to exclusive pumping anymore, don't feel guilty. Feed your little one with as much breast milk as you can and supplement with formula to fill in as needed (you can even mix breast milk and formula in the same bottle). Remember, every drop of breast milk counts!

Breast Milk at a Glance

It's normal for breast milk to be bluish or yellowish in color. Sometimes it'll even look clear—and that's probably because you've expressed only the foremilk (the hindmilk will usually look thicker and creamier). So if your pumped milk looks thin and watery, it could be because you're not pumping long enough—or the bags or bottles you're pumping into aren't big enough—to get the hindmilk. Expressed milk will also sometimes separate into milk and cream. This, too, is normal. Just swirl gently to mix before feeding (try not to shake, because that could cause a breakdown of some of the milk's valuable components).

- Freeze milk in small quantities, 3 to 4 ounces at a time, to minimize waste and allow for easier thawing.

- To thaw breast milk, shake the bottle or bag under lukewarm tap water; then use within 30 minutes. Or thaw in the refrigerator and use within 24 hours. Do not thaw in a microwave oven, on the top of the stove, or at room temperature—and do not refreeze.

- When your baby has finished a feed, throw out any breast milk that's left in the bottle. Also toss any milk that has been stored for longer than recommended times.

What You May Be Wondering About

"Breaking" Baby

"I know it's a cliché, but I really am afraid of breaking the baby—he seems so tiny and fragile."

Newborns are actually a whole lot sturdier than they appear to their nervous newbie parents. The truth is—and it's one that should keep you from shaking in your slippers every time you get ready to pick up your tiny little bundle—you can't break a baby. That delicate-looking, vulnerable-seeming infant is actually an incredibly resilient, elastic little being—one who's really built to take even the clumsiest care and handling a new parent can dish out.

And here's another happy truth: By the time your newborn turns 3 months old, he'll have gained the weight and control over his head and limbs that will make him seem less floppy and fragile . . . and you'll have gained the experience that will make you feel completely confident as you carry him and care for him.

The Fontanels

"My baby's soft spot on her head seems so . . . soft. Sometimes it seems to pulsate, which really makes me nervous."

That "soft spot"—actually there are two and they are called fontanels—is tougher than it looks. The sturdy membrane covering the fontanels is capable of protecting a newborn from the probing of even the most curious sibling fingers (though that's definitely not something you'd want to encourage), and certainly from everyday care.

These openings in the skull, where the bones haven't yet grown together, aren't there to make new parents nervous about handling their baby (though that's often the upshot) but rather, for two very important reasons. During childbirth, they allow the fetal head to mold to fit through the birth canal, something a solidly fused skull couldn't do. Later, they allow for the tremendous brain growth during the first year.

The larger of the two openings, the diamond-shaped anterior fontanel, is located on the top of a newborn's head, and it may be as wide as 2 inches. It starts to close when an infant is 6 months old and is usually totally closed by 18 months.

This fontanel normally appears flat, though it may bulge a bit when baby cries, and if baby's hair is sparse and fair, the cerebral pulse may be visible through it (which is completely normal and absolutely nothing to worry about). An anterior fontanel that appears significantly sunken is usually a sign of dehydration, a warning that the baby needs to be given fluids promptly. (Call the baby's doctor immediately to report this sign.) A fontanel that bulges persistently (as opposed to a little bulging with crying) may indicate increased pressure inside the head and also requires immediate medical attention.

The posterior fontanel, a smaller triangular opening toward the back of the head less than half an inch in diameter, is much less noticeable and may be difficult for you to locate (and no need to try). It's generally completely closed by the third month but may be closed

---

What Month Is It, Anyway?

Trying to figure out what month baby's in—and which one you should be reading right now? Here's how it works: The "First Month" chapter covers your baby's progress from birth to the first-month birthday, the "Second Month" chapter gives you the lowdown on your 1-month-old until he or she turns 2 months old, and so on. The first year blow-by-blow ends as baby blows out those first birthday candles.

---

at birth or shortly after. Fontanels that close prematurely (they rarely do) can result in a misshapen head and require medical attention.

Having Enough Breast Milk

"When my milk came in, my breasts were overflowing. Now that the engorgement is gone, I'm not leaking anymore. Does that mean I'm not making enough milk?"

Since the sides of your breasts don't come marked with ounce calibrations (and aren't you pretty glad they don't?), it's virtually impossible to tell at a glance how your milk supply is holding up. Instead, you'll have to look to your baby. If he seems to be happy, healthy, and gaining weight well, you're producing enough milk—which the vast majority of moms do. Leaking like a faucet or spraying like a fountain are more common early on, when supply often exceeds demand (though some moms continue to leak and spray, and that's normal, too). Now that your baby has caught up to your flow, the only milk that counts is the milk that goes into him.

True problems with supply happen, but they're pretty uncommon. If at any time your baby doesn't seem to be getting enough milk, more frequent nursing plus the other tips on page 78 should help you boost your supply. If they don't, check with the doctor.

"My baby was nursing about every 2 or 3 hours and seemed to be doing really well. Now, suddenly, she seems to want to nurse every hour. Could something have happened to my milk supply?"

Unlike a well, a milk supply rarely dries up if it's used regularly. In fact, the exact reverse is true: The more your baby nurses, the more milk your breasts will produce. And right now, that's what your hungry little girl—who's probably going through a growth spurt that's spurring her appetite into overdrive—is counting on. Growth spurts most commonly happen at 3 weeks, 6 weeks, and 3 months, but can occur at any time during an infant's development. Sometimes, even a baby who's been sleeping through the night begins to wake for a middle-of-the-night feeding during a growth spurt. Simply put, your baby's active appetite is likely her way of ensuring that your breasts will step up milk production to meet her growth needs. (See page 78 for more on these so-called cluster feedings.)

Just relax and keep your breasts handy until the growth spurt passes. Don't be tempted to give your baby formula (and definitely don't consider adding solids) to appease her appetite, because a decrease in frequency of nursing would cut down your supply of milk, which is just the opposite of what the baby ordered. Such a pattern—started by baby wanting to nurse more, leading to mom doubting her milk supply, prompting her to offer a supplement, followed by a decrease in milk production—is one of the major causes of breastfeeding being ditched early on.

Sometimes a baby begins to demand more daytime feedings temporarily when she begins to sleep through the night, but this, too, shall pass with time. If, however, your baby continues to want to nurse hourly (or nearly so) for more than a week, check her weight gain (and see below). It could mean she's not getting enough to eat.

Baby Getting Enough Breast Milk

"How can I be sure my breastfed son is getting enough to eat?"

When it comes to bottle-feeding, the proof that baby's getting enough to eat is in the bottle—the empty bottle. When it comes to breastfeeding, figuring out whether baby's well fed takes a little more digging . . . and diaper diving. Luckily, there are several signs you can look for to reassure yourself that your breastfed baby is getting his fair share of feed:

He's having at least 5 large, seedy, mustardy bowel movements a day. Fewer than 5 poops a day in the early weeks could mean he's not getting enough to eat (though later on, around age 6 weeks to 3 months, the rate could slow down to one a day or even one every 2 to 3 days).

His diaper is wet when he's changed before each feeding. A baby who pees more than 8 to 10 times a day is getting adequate fluid.

His urine is colorless. A baby who is not getting enough fluids passes urine that is yellow, possibly fishy smelling, and/or contains urate crystals (these look like powdered brick, give the wet diaper a pinkish red tinge, and are normal before breast milk comes in but not later).

You hear a lot of gulping and swallowing as your baby nurses. If you don't, he may not be getting much to swallow. Don't worry, however, about relatively silent eating if baby is gaining well.

He seems happy and content after most feedings. A lot of crying and fussing or frantic finger sucking after a full nursing could mean a baby is still hungry. Not all fussing, of course, is related to hunger. After eating, it could also be related to gas, an attempt to poop or to settle down for a nap, or a craving for attention. Or your baby could be fussy because of colic (see page 210). Keep in mind, however, that no crying at all in a newborn (or very little crying) can be a red flag—a possible sign that baby is not thriving (babies should cry). See page 208 for more.

You experienced engorgement and your breasts feel full in the morning. Engorgement is a good sign you can produce milk. And breasts that are fuller when you get up in the morning and after 3 or 4 hours without nursing than they are after a feed indicate they are filling with milk regularly—and also that your baby is draining them. If baby is gaining well, however, lack of noticeable engorgement shouldn't concern you.

You notice the sensation of let-down and/or experience milk leakage. Different women experience let-down differently (see page 75), but feeling it when you start feeding indicates that milk is coming down from the storage ducts to the nipples, ready to be enjoyed by your baby. Not every woman notices let-down when it occurs, but its absence when baby's not thriving is a red flag.

Filling Out

Most babies start to fill out by 3 weeks, looking less like scrawny chickens and more like softly rounded babies. In most cases, you can expect a breastfed baby to regain his or her birthweight by 2 weeks and then gain roughly 6 to 8 ounces a week for the next couple of months. Formula-fed babies usually gain weight faster in the beginning.

Worried your baby's not filling out fast enough? Remember that your eyes are not necessarily a reliable gauge of your baby's weight gain—after all, you get to see your little one every day, so you're less likely to notice growth than those who see baby less often. Still have doubts? Call the doctor's office and ask if you can bring your baby in for a drive-by weigh-in. Don't try to weigh your baby on a home scale—even if you do the weigh-yourself-with the baby and then weigh-yourself-without maneuver. Home scales are not sensitive enough to pick up those ounces and half ounces that matter so much to a newborn's weight.

You don't get your period during the first 3 months postpartum. If you're breastfeeding exclusively, you're not likely to get your period, particularly in the first 3 months. If you do, it's possible you may not be producing enough milk.

"I thought that breastfeeding was going pretty well, but the doctor says my baby girl isn't gaining weight quickly enough. What could be the problem?"

Breastfed babies typically don't pack on the ounces as fast as their formula-fed friends, and that's not

Supplemental Nursing System

Here's how the SNS works: A bottle filled either with pumped breast milk or formula hangs around your neck. Narrow flexible tubes leading from the bottle are gently taped onto your breasts, extending slightly past the nipples. As your little one nurses at the breast, he or she gets the supplement through the tube along with any milk that comes from your breasts. It's win-win, since baby gets the nutrition he or she needs and your breasts get the stimulation they need.

That is, when it works according to plan. Some moms find their babies fuss over or even reject feeding from a breast that has a tiny tube hanging off it (it could make it uncomfortable or difficult for some babies to latch on properly). If you find your baby is struggling to nurse when you're using the SNS, have a lactation consultant watch your technique and offer advice and tips on how to make using the SNS easier and better, if possible.

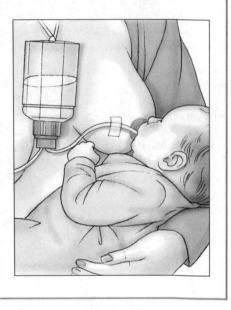

usually a concern. It's also the reason why charts that use formula-fed babies to gauge average growth have fallen out of favor. It's a good idea to make sure the one your pediatrician is using to gauge your baby's gain is based on breastfed averages (the World Health Organization, or WHO, chart is). Occasionally, however, a baby truly doesn't thrive on breast milk alone, at least not from the start, and there are several possible reasons why. Identify what's holding up your baby's weight gain, and chances are you'll be able to find a fix for the problem, so she can continue nursing and start gaining weight faster:

Possible problem: You're not feeding baby often enough.

Solution: Increase feedings to at least 8 to 10 times in 24 hours, and try never to go more than 3 hours during the day or 4 at night between feedings. That means waking up a sleeping baby so that she won't miss dinner or feeding a hungry one even if your slowpoke just finished a meal an hour earlier. If your baby is "happy to starve" (some newborns initially are) and never demands feeding, it means taking the initiative yourself and setting a busy feeding schedule for her. Frequent nursings will not only help to fill baby's tummy (and fill out her frame), they will also stimulate your milk production.

Possible problem: Baby's not draining at least one breast at each feeding, or you're switching breasts too early in a feed. The result: Your baby doesn't get the rich, higher-calorie hindmilk that's intended to fill (and fatten) her up, and she doesn't gain enough weight.

Solution: Make sure your baby finishes one breast (10 to 15 minutes minimum should do the trick sufficiently) before you offer the second. That way she'll be able to quench her thirst with foremilk but still cash in on the calories in the hindmilk. Let her nurse for as long (or as little) as she likes on the second breast, and remember to alternate the starting breast at each feeding.

Possible problem: Your baby is considered a sluggish or ineffective suckler (called a "lazy" suckler by the experts). This may be because she was preterm, is ill, or has abnormal mouth development (such as a cleft palate or tongue or lip tie; see pages 4 and 188). The less effective the suckling, the less milk is produced, setting baby up for failure to thrive.

Solution: Until she's a strong suckler, she will need help stimulating your breasts to provide adequate milk. This can be done with a breast pump, which you can use to empty the breasts after each feeding (save any milk you collect for future use in bottles). Until milk production is up to snuff, your doctor will very likely recommend supplemental bottle-feedings of formula (given after breastfeeding sessions) or the use of a supplemental system, or SNS (see box, facing page). The SNS has the advantage of simultaneously stimulating your production while supplementing your baby's supply.

If your baby tires easily while feeding, you may be advised to nurse for only a short time at each breast (be sure to pump the rest later to empty the breast of the hindmilk and to keep up your milk supply), then follow with a supplement of expressed milk (which will contain the all-important and calorie-rich hindmilk) or formula given by bottle or the supplemental nutrition system, both of which require less effort by the baby.

Possible problem: Your baby hasn't yet learned how to coordinate her jaw muscles for suckling.

Solution: A baby who hasn't quite yet mastered the art of the suckle will also need help from a breast pump to stimulate her mama's breasts to begin producing larger quantities of milk. In addition, she will need lessons in improving her suckling technique— the doctor may recommend you get hands-on help from an LC and possibly even a pediatric occupational or speech therapist. While your baby is boning up on her technique, she may need supplemental feedings (see above). For further suggestions on improving suckling technique, contact your local La Leche League.

Possible problem: Your nipples are sore or you have a breast infection. Not only can the pain interfere with your desire to nurse, reducing nursing frequency and milk production, but it can actually inhibit milk let-down—especially if you're tensing up.

Solution: Take steps to heal sore nipples or cure mastitis (see pages 78 and 86).

Possible problem: Your nipples are flat or inverted. It's sometimes difficult for a baby to get a firm hold on such nipples. This situation sets up the negative cycle of not enough suckling, leading to not enough milk, to even less suckling, and less milk.

Solution: Help baby get a better grip during nursing by taking the outer part of the areola between your thumb and forefinger and compressing the entire area for him to suckle on. Use breast shells between feedings to make your nipples easier to draw out.

Possible problem: Some other factor is interfering with milk let-down. Let-down is a physical function that can be inhibited as well as stimulated by your state of mind. If you're stressed out about breastfeeding (or in general), not only can let-down be stifled, but the volume and calorie count of your milk can be diminished.

Solution: Try to de-stress before and during feeds by playing soft music, dimming the lights, using relaxation techniques, or meditating. Massaging your breasts or applying warm soaks also encourages let-down, as does opening your shirt and cuddling baby skin-to-skin during feeds.

Possible problem: Baby's become frustrated at the breast—due to problems on her side or yours. The frustration leads to fussing, which leads to tension for you, which leads to more frustration and fussing for baby, and a cycle begins, sometimes sabotaging breastfeeding.

Solution: Seek the hands-on help of a lactation consultant, if possible, to get any latching, positioning, or other problems resolved so both you and baby can stay calm and on task. Try to relax yourself and your baby as much as possible before feeds (see above tip)—and always begin feeds before your baby starts showing hunger cues (and is more likely to become frantic at the breast).

Possible problem: Your baby is getting her sucking satisfaction from a pacifier. Babies are born to suck, but too

---

Timing Is Everything

A reminder: Like labor contractions, intervals between feedings are timed from the beginning of one to the beginning of the next. So a baby who nurses for 40 minutes starting at 10 a.m., then sleeps for 1 hour and 20 minutes before eating again, is on a 2-hour schedule, not a 1-hour-and-20-minute one.

---

much sucking on a nonnutritive pacifier can sabotage your baby's interest in breastfeeding.

Solution: Save the pacifier for only when baby sleeps (or put it aside for now)—instead, breastfeed baby when she seems to want to suck.

Possible problem: Your baby's appetite is dampened by supplementary water.

Solution: Giving your breastfed baby a supplementary bottle of water is a no-no before 6 months, since it not only supplies nonnutritive sucking but can also decrease her appetite and, in excess, dangerously dilute blood sodium levels. See page 193 for more on supplementary water.

Possible problem: You're not burping baby between breasts. A baby who's swallowed air can stop eating before she's had enough because she feels uncomfortably full.

Solution: Bringing up the air will give her room for more milk. Be sure to burp baby between breasts (or even mid-breast if she's a slow feeder) whether she seems to need it or not—more often if she fusses a lot while nursing.

Possible problem: Your baby is sleeping through the night. An uninterrupted night's sleep is great for you, but not necessarily for your milk supply. If baby is going 7 or 8 hours a night without nursing, your milk may be diminishing, and supplementation may eventually be needed.

Solution: To make sure this doesn't happen, you will have to wake your little sleepyhead (and yourself) at least once in the middle of the night. She shouldn't be going longer than 4 hours at night without a feeding during the first month.

Possible problem: You're stomach sleeping. Yes, you earned it after so many months of side sleeping. But when you sleep on your tummy, you also sleep on your breasts—and all that pressure on your breasts can cut down on milk production.

Solution: Turn over, at least partway, to take the pressure off those mammary glands.

Possible problem: You've returned to work. Returning to work—and going 8 to 10 hours without breastfeeding or pumping during the day—will definitely decrease milk supply.

Solution: One way to prevent this is to express milk at work at least once every 4 hours you're away from baby (even if you're not using the milk for feeding).

Possible problem: You're doing too much too soon. Producing breast milk requires a lot of energy. If you're expending yours in too many other ways and not getting enough rest, your breast milk supply may diminish.

Solution: Try a day of almost complete bed rest, followed by 3 or 4 days of taking it easy, and see if your baby isn't more satisfied (hey, you'll feel better, too).

Possible problem: There are bits of placenta left in your uterus. Your body won't accept the fact that you've actually delivered until all the products of pregnancy have left the building—and that includes the entire placenta. If fragments remain, your body may not produce adequate levels of prolactin, the hormone that stimulates milk production.

Solution: If you have any abnormal bleeding or other signs of retained placental fragments, contact your practitioner at once. A dilatation and curettage (D&C) could put you and your baby on the right track to successful breastfeeding while avoiding the danger a retained placenta can pose to your own health.

Possible problem: Your hormones are out of whack. In some women, prolactin levels are too low to produce adequate amounts of milk. Other women have thyroid hormone levels that are off, causing a low milk output. And in still others, insulin deregulation can be the cause of a low milk supply.

Solution: Speak to your doctor or endocrinologist. Tests can determine the problem, and medications and other treatments can get you back up and regulated, hopefully getting your milk production back up and running, though the process will likely take time, and supplementation with formula may be necessary at least in the short term.

Once in a while, even with the best efforts, under the best conditions, and with the best support and professional advice, it turns out a mom can't provide all the milk her baby needs. A small percentage of women are simply unable to breastfeed exclusively, and a small few can't breastfeed at all. The reason may be physical, such as a prolactin

Tongue-Tied

Ever hear the term "tongue-tied"? It's often used to refer to someone who's too shy, excited, or embarrassed to get words out. But tongue-tie is actually a very real hereditary medical condition that affects up to 2 to 4 percent of infants, and in some cases can impact their ability to breastfeed successfully.

Known in doctor speak as ankyloglossia, this hard-to-pronounce congenital condition means that the frenulum—the band of tissue that connects the bottom of the tongue to the floor of the mouth—is too short and tight. The result? The tongue's movements are restricted, and your baby may have difficulty nursing.

How can you tell if your little one is tongue-tied? If baby is unable to stick out his or her tongue fully, or if that little tongue looks heart shaped, it could mean that it is "tied." Another clue: When your baby sucks on your finger, his or her tongue doesn't extend over the gum line as it should.

Most tongue-tied babies—usually those whose frenulums are attached farther back in the mouth—have no problem breastfeeding. But if your baby can't use his or her tongue efficiently enough to suck strongly on your nipple and areola, he or she may not be getting enough milk—and slow weight gain and extra fussiness may result. What's more, if the frenulum is so short that the tongue can't extend over the lower gum, your baby may end up compressing your nipple with his or her gums instead of the tongue, and that can cause nipple soreness, pain, clogged ducts, and a host of other problems for you. You'll know that your little one's tongue-tie is causing breastfeeding problems if you hear a clicking sound when he or she nurses or if your baby loses the nipple again and again during a nursing session, which happens because he or she can't extend the tongue enough to get a good grip.

If you think tongue-tie might be the cause of your baby's breastfeeding problems—or even if you aren't sure and only suspect that might be the problem—have your baby checked out by the pediatrician or an LC. If your baby's tongue-tie is truly causing feeding problems, the doctor can clip the frenulum to loosen it and allow the tongue to move freely. Called a frenotomy, the clipping is an extremely quick in-office procedure causing little pain—though not all pediatricians perform it and you might need to be referred to a specialist.

Baby's tongue-tie isn't causing feeding problems? No need to be concerned. In most cases the frenulum recedes on its own during the first year, and causes no long-term issues with feeding or speaking.

Similar to tongue-tie is the less common lip-tie, which involves the upper lip and gum. The upper lip also has a connective tissue attachment called the maxillary labial frenum (you can feel yours if you run your tongue between your upper lip and top of the gum) and if that tissue is short and tight, or if it attaches farther down the gum or even between where the front teeth will eventually come in, it may cause breastfeeding problems as well. That's because in some cases a lip-tie may restrict the movement of the upper lip, making it harder for baby to latch on properly. You can tell if your baby has a lip tie just by lifting his or her upper lip and seeing where it attaches. If it's high up, it's normal. If it's attached low on the gum and you're having trouble nursing (you won't necessarily), check in with an LC who can show you specific positional techniques to help make breastfeeding a success or advise you on a procedure to revise the lip-tie.

deficiency, insufficient mammary glandular tissue, markedly asymmetrical breasts, or damage to the nerves going to the nipple caused by breast surgery (more likely to be the case if you've had a reduction than an augmentation). Or it could be due to excessive stress, which can inhibit let-down. Or, occasionally, it may not be pinpointed at all.

If your baby isn't thriving, and unless the problem appears to be one that can be cleared up in just a few days, her doctor is almost certain to prescribe supplemental formula feedings (see page 92)—possibly with a formula designed for supplementation. Not to stress. What's most important is adequately nourishing your baby, not whether you give breast or bottle. In most cases when supplementing, you can have the benefits of the direct parent-baby contact that nursing affords by letting baby suckle at your breast for pleasure (hers and yours) after she's finished her bottle, or by using a supplemental nursing system. Often, a baby can return to exclusive breastfeeding (or the combo; see page 90) after a period of supplementation—a goal that's definitely worth trying for.

Once a baby who is not doing well on the breast is put on formula temporarily, she almost invariably thrives. In the rare instance that she doesn't, a return trip to the doctor is necessary to see what is interfering with adequate weight gain.

Nursing Blisters

"Why does my baby have a blister on his upper lip? Is he sucking too hard?"

For a baby with a hearty appetite, there's no such thing as sucking too hard—though you of tender nipples may disagree. Nursing blisters, which develop on the center of the upper lips of many newborns, both breast- and bottle-fed, do come from vigorous sucking—but they're nothing to worry about. They have no medical significance, cause no discomfort to your baby, and will disappear without treatment within a few weeks to months. Sometimes, they even seem to disappear between feedings.

Feeding Schedule

"I seem to be breastfeeding my new daughter all the time. Should I think about getting her on a schedule?"

One day, your little one will be ready to eat by the clock. But for now, the only schedule that matters is the one her tummy sets for her—and it goes like this: "I'm empty, you fill me. I'm empty again, you fill me again." It's a schedule that's built on demand—not on timed intervals—and it's the very best way for a breastfed baby to feed. While bottle-fed newborns can do well on a 3- or 4-hour schedule (in other words, because formula is so filling, they will usually demand another feeding only when 3 to 4 hours have passed), breastfed infants need to eat more often. That's because breast milk is digested more quickly than formula, making a baby feel hungry again sooner. On-demand breastfeeding also ensures that mom's milk supply keeps pace with baby's growing appetite, which fuels baby's growing body—and nurtures a successful breastfeeding relationship.

So breastfeed as often as your little eating machine demands during these early weeks. Just keep three things in mind as you do. One, new babies tend to nod off before they're finished filling their tanks. Making a concerted effort to keep your baby awake at the breast until she's had a full meal will keep her from waking up hungry an hour later.

Double the Trouble, Double the Fun

Got your hands—and both arms—full with twins? While you probably had many months to prepare for your new life with a double blessing, the reality of life with two babies can hit like a ton of bricks—and a ton of dirty diapers. That is, unless you know how to contain the chaos—and how to handle (and enjoy) this doubly challenging time:

Double up. Do as much as possible for your babies in tandem. That means waking them at the same time so they can be fed together, wearing them in a sling together, walking them in the stroller together. Double burp them together across your lap, or with one on your lap and the other on your shoulder. When you can't double up, alternate. At an early age, daily baths aren't necessary, so bathe babies on alternate nights. Or bathe them every second or third night and sponge in between. Putting them foot to foot or swaddled side by side in the same crib during the early weeks may help them sleep better. But check with the pediatrician, since some experts warn that prolonged tandem sleeping can increase the SIDS risk once the twins are able to roll over.

Split up. The work, that is. When both parents are around, divide the household chores (cooking, cleaning, laundry, shopping) and the babies (you take over one baby, your spouse the other). Be sure that you alternate babies so that both get to bond with both parents. And of course, accept all the help you can get, from any willing source.

Try the double-breasted approach. Nursing twins can be physically challenging but eliminates fussing with dozens of bottles and endless ounces of formula—plus, it'll leave more room in your doubly stretched budget (formula feeding two babies can cost a couple of small fortunes). Since trying to breast-feed only one baby at a time can turn into a 24/7 nursing marathon, try feeding them simultaneously (it's a good thing breasts come in pairs!). You can prop your twosome on a twins feeding pillow in the football position with their feet behind you (see page 66), or with their bodies crossed in front of you. Alternate the breast each baby gets at every feeding to avoid creating favorites and mismatched breasts should one baby turn out to be a greedier suckler than the other, or to avoid one baby getting less to eat if one breast turns out to be a less productive provider. If you find it too difficult to breastfeed your twins exclusively, you can nurse one while you bottle-feed the other—again alternating from feeding to feeding.

Plan to have some extra hands on hand, if you're bottle-feeding. Bottle-feeding twins requires either an extra set of hands or great ingenuity. If you find yourself with two babies and just two hands at feeding time, you can sit on a sofa between the babies (prop them up on pillows or a twins feeding pillow) with their feet toward the back and hold a bottle for each. Or hold them both in your arms with the bottles in bottle-proppers raised to a comfortable height by pillows. You can also occasionally prop the bottle for one in a baby seat (but never lying down) while you feed the other the traditional way or put both of them in their infant seats side by side and feed them at the same time. Feeding them one after the other is another possibility, but you'll be spending twice as much time feeding them—and will have half as much time to get anything else done. Back-to-back feeds will also put the babies on somewhat different napping schedules if they sleep after eating, which can be good if you'd like some time alone with each, or bad if you depend on that tandem sleeping time to rest or get other chores done.

Don't split z's. Sleep will necessarily be scarce for the first few months, but it will be scarcer if your babies are always waking at different times during the night. Instead, when the first cries, wake the second (if he or she isn't already awake) and feed them both. Any time that both members of your darling duo are napping during the day, catch a few winks yourself—or at least try to put your feet up.

Double up on equipment. When you don't have another pair of hands around to help, utilize such conveniences as baby carriers (you can use a large sling for two babies, use two slings, or tote one baby in a carrier and one in your arms), baby swings, and infant seats. A play yard is a safe playground for your twins as they get older, and because they'll have each other for company, they will be willing to be relegated to it more often and for longer periods than a singleton would. Select a twin stroller to meet your needs, and don't forget that you will need two car seats. Put both in the backseat of the car.

Keep twice as many records. Who took what at which feeding, who was bathed yesterday, who's scheduled for today? Unless you keep a log or use an app, such as the What to Expect app, to keep track, you're sure to forget. Also make note in a permanent record book of immunizations, illnesses, and

so on. Though most of the time, the babies will both get everything that's going around, occasionally only one will—and you may not remember which one.

Go one-on-one. Though it won't be easy (at least in the beginning), there are ways to find that special one-on-one time with each baby during the day. When you're better rested yourself, stagger naptime—put one baby down 15 minutes before the other—so you can devote some individualized attention to the one who's awake. Or take only one on an errand and leave the other one with a sitter. Even everyday baby care—diaper changes or getting the babies dressed—can be a chance to bond with each of your twins.

Be doubly alert once your twins are mobile. You'll find, as your babies begin crawling and cruising, that what one of them doesn't think of in the way of exploits, the other will. So they will need to be watched twice as carefully.

Double up on support. Other parents of twins will be your best source of insights and tips, so be sure to tap in to them. Don't know anyone in the same double boat? Start hanging out on twin message boards online (check out WhatToExpect.com).

Expect things to get doubly better. The first 4 months with twins are the most challenging. Once you begin to work out the many logistics, you'll find yourself falling into an easier rhythm. Keep in mind, too, that twins are often each other's best company. Many have a way of keeping each other busy that parents of demanding singletons envy—and that will free you up more and more in the months and years to come.

Two, babies cry for reasons other than feelings of hunger. Getting to know her cries (see page 144) will help you figure out whether she's really in the market for a meal, or for a cuddle, some rocking, or a nap—and that will cut down on feeds she doesn't need. And three, once in a while, a baby's frequent feeding—especially if she never seems satisfied, isn't gaining weight, or shows other signs that she's not thriving—can mean she's not getting enough to eat (see page 182). If you're concerned that's the case with your baby, check in with the doctor.

Once your milk supply is well established, usually at about 3 weeks, you can start stretching the time between feedings. When your little one wakes crying an hour after feeding, don't rush to feed her. If she still seems sleepy, try to get her back to sleep without nursing her. If she seems alert, try some socializing. Or a little massage. Or a change of position or point of view. If she's fussy, try wearing her, rocking her, walking with her, or offering her the pacifier. If it's clear she's really hungry, go ahead and feed her—again, just make sure she takes a full meal instead of a nip-and-nap snack bar approach.

In time, those round-the-clock feeds will become a thing of the sleep-deprived past—and feedings will start coming at more reasonable intervals—2 to 3 hours, and eventually, 4 or so. Still on-demand for her, but far less demanding for you.

Changing Your Mind About Breastfeeding

"I've been breastfeeding my son for 3 weeks, and I'm just not enjoying it. I'd like to switch to a bottle, but I feel so guilty."

Not having fun breastfeeding yet? That's pretty common, given the bumpy start that so many brand new breastfeeding teams get off to (sore nipples . . . latching on problems . . . both of those and more?). Usually, even the rockiest road leads to a smooth ride by the middle of the second month—at which point, breastfeeding becomes a walk in the park, and typically, an enjoyable one at that. So it might make sense to hold off on your decision until your baby is 6 weeks old—or even 2 months. If by then you're still finding breastfeeding a drag, you can quit or consider doing the combo (supplementing with formula instead of breastfeeding exclusively). Your baby will have received many of the benefits of breastfeeding, and you'll have given breastfeeding your best shot. Which means you can win-win when you ultimately wean-wean. Another option that some moms prefer: pumping their baby's meals and feeding from a bottle.

Decided that you don't have it in you to wait on quitting? Grab a bottle of formula and get busy. For tips on bottle-feeding with love, see page 131.

Too Much Formula

"My baby loves his bottle. If it were up to him, he'd feed all day. How do I know when to give him more formula or when to stop?"

Because their intake is regulated both by their appetite and by an ingenious supply-and-demand system, breastfed babies rarely get too much—or too little—of a good thing. Bottle-fed babies, whose intake is regulated instead by their parents, sometimes do—if they drink too much formula, that is. As long as your baby is healthy, happy, wetting his diapers regularly, and gaining adequate weight, you know he's getting enough formula. In other words, if your little one is eating to his appetite (even if that appetite is huge), there's nothing to be concerned about. But if his bottle becomes the liquid equivalent of an all-you-can-eat buffet—refilled even when he's full—he can easily get too much.

Too much formula can lead to a too chubby baby (which, research shows, can lead to a too chubby child and a too chubby adult). But it can also lead to other problems. If your baby seems to be gaining weight too quickly, or if he seems to be spitting up a lot (more than normal, see page 197) he might be taking more ounces than his tiny tummy can handle at this point. Your baby's pediatrician will be able to tell you what his rate of gain should be, and how much formula (approximately) he should be getting at each feeding (see page 302 for guidelines of how much formula to feed). If he does seem to be taking too much, try offering smaller-volume feedings, and stop when baby seems full instead of pushing him to finish. If he's fussy after a feed, consider that he may just need a burp—not a second serving. Or serve up some comfort or entertainment instead (babies cry for reasons other than hunger; see page 144 to help decode your baby's cries). Keep in mind, too, that it may just be the sucking (not the formula that comes with it) that he's craving. If your baby's a natural-born sucker, consider offering a pacifier after he's had his fill of formula, or help him find his fingers or a pacifying fist to suck on.

Supplementary Water

"I'm wondering if I should be giving my son a bottle of water."

When it comes to feeding, newborn babies have just two options—and so do the parents who feed them: breast milk or formula. For the first 6 months or so, one or the other (or a combo of the two) will provide your baby with all the food and fluids he needs, no water necessary. In fact, adding supplementary water to a baby's already all-liquid diet isn't only unnecessary, in excess it can be dangerous—possibly diluting his blood and causing serious chemical imbalances (just as adding too much water when preparing formula can). If your baby's breastfeeding, water can also satisfy his appetite and his need to suck—possibly sabotaging breastfeeding and weight gain.

Once your sweetie has started solids, offering sips of water from a cup (babies can't get too much water from a cup, only a bottle) will be fine—and good practice for the days when all his drinks will come from a cup instead of your breasts or a bottle. If the weather's really hot, some pediatricians will okay sips of water for a formula-fed baby before solids are started, but do check first.

Vitamin Supplements

"We've heard a lot of different opinions about vitamin supplements. Should we give our baby one, and what kind should we give him?"

When it comes to deciding whether or not to give your baby a vitamin supplement (and which kind to give), it's the pediatrician's opinion that matters most. That's because your baby's doctor will take into account not only the ever-evolving research and recommendations on vitamin supplements, but your little one's unique needs.

If your little one is exclusively or partially breastfed, he'll be getting most of the vitamins and minerals he needs from breast milk (assuming you're eating a good diet and taking a daily prenatal vitamin or one designed for

For Parents: Getting Everything Done

Take the responsibility of caring for a newborn baby for the first time. Add in the days and nights that seem to blur together as one endless feeding. Plus a few too many visitors, a generous helping of postpartum hormonal upheaval for mom (and some for dads, too), and, possibly, a fair amount of home clutter accumulated during your stay in the hospital or in the last days of pregnancy—when you could barely move, never mind clean. Throw in the inevitable mountain of gifts, boxes, wrapping paper, and cards to keep track of. It's only natural to feel that as your new life with baby begins, your old life—with its order and cleanliness—is crumbling around you.

As hard as it may be to believe now, your inability to keep up with both new baby and house during the first weeks or months in no way predicts your future success at the juggling act called parenthood. Things are bound to get better as you get more sleep, become more adept at all those baby-care tasks, and learn to be a little more flexible. It will also help to:

Get help. If you haven't already arranged for household help—paid or unpaid—and taken steps to stream-line housekeeping and cooking chores, now's the time to do so. Also be sure that there is a fair division of labor (both baby care and household care) between parents, if there are two.

Get your priorities straight (before you straighten up). Is it more impor-tant to get the vacuuming done while baby's napping or to put your feet up and relax? Is it really essential to clean out the fridge, or would going for a stroll with the baby be a better use of your time? Keep in mind that doing too much too soon can rob you of the energy to accomplish anything well, and that while your house will someday be clean again, your baby will never be 2 days, or 2 weeks, or 2 months old

again. In other words: Stop (cleaning) and smell the babies.

Get organized. Have a million to-do's floating through your sleep-deprived head? Write them down. First thing every morning (or before you crash every night), make a list of what needs to be done. Divide your pri-orities into three categories: chores that must be taken care of as soon as possible, those that can wait until later in the day, and those that can be put off until tomorrow, or next week, or indefinitely. Assign approx-imate times to each activity, taking into account your personal biological clock (are you useless first thing in the morning, or do you do your best work at the crack of dawn?) as well as your baby's (as best you can determine it at this point).

Though organizing your day with lists doesn't always mean that every-thing will get done on schedule (in fact, for new parents it rarely does), it will give you a sense of control over what may now seem like a completely uncontrollable situation. You may even find, once you've made your list, that you actually have less to do than you thought. Don't forget to cross off or delete completed tasks for a satisfying

breastfeeding moms). But he'll defi-nitely fall short on vitamin D, which is why pediatricians recommend that breastfed babies get 400 IU a day of

vitamin D in the form of a supplement (probably A-C-D, which combines vitamins A, C, and D), starting in the first few days of life. And while he'll feeling of accomplishment. And don't worry about what's not crossed off—just move those items to the next day's list.

Another good organizational trick of the new parent trade: Keep a running list of baby gifts and their givers as they're received. You think you'll remember that your cousin Jessica sent that darling blue-and-yellow onesie set, but after the seventeenth onesie set has arrived, that memory may be dim. And check off each gift on the list as the thank-you note is sent, so you don't end up sending two notes to Aunt Karen and Uncle Marvin and none to your boss.

Get simplified. Take every shortcut you can find. Make friends with frozen vegetables and healthy frozen entrées, your local salad bar, the pizza delivery guy, online grocery and diaper shopping.

Get a jump on tomorrow tonight. Once you've bedded baby down each night and before you collapse, summon up the strength to take care of a few chores so that you'll have a head start on the next morning. Restock the diaper bag. Measure out the coffee for the coffeepot. Sort the laundry. Lay out clothes for yourself and the baby. In 10 minutes or so you'll accomplish what would take you at least three times as long with the baby awake. And you'll be able to sleep better (when your little one lets you) knowing that you'll have less to do in the morning.

Get out. Plan an outing every day with your little one—even if it's just a walk around the mall. The change of pace and space will allow you to return to Casa Chaos somewhat refreshed.

Get to expect the unexpected. The best-laid plans of parents often (actually, very often) go awry. Baby's all bundled up for an outing, the diaper bag is ready, your coat is on, and suddenly the distinct gurglings of an explosive poop can be heard from under all baby's gear. Off comes coat, bunting, diaper—10 minutes lost from an already tight schedule. To allow for the unexpected, try to build extra time into everything you do.

Get the joke. If you can laugh, you're less likely to cry. So keep your sense of humor, even in the face of total disorder and utter clutter—it'll help you keep your sanity, too.

Get used to it. Living with a baby means living with a certain amount of mayhem most of the time. And as baby grows, so will the challenge of keeping the mayhem in check. No sooner will you scoop the blocks back into their canister than he or she will dump them back out again. As fast as you can wipe mashed peas off the wall behind the high chair, your baby can redecorate with strained peaches. You'll put safety latches on the kitchen cabinets, and your one-baby demolition derby will figure out how to open them, covering the floor with your pots and pans.

And remember, when you finally pack your last child off to college, your house will be orderly once again—and so empty and quiet that you'll be ready to welcome the pandemonium (and even the dirty laundry) they bring home on school vacations.

---

score enough iron from your breast milk in the first 4 months, levels can diminish after that point—which is why the pediatrician is likely to add an iron supplement to the mix (1 mg/kg per day, probably in an A-C-D supplement with iron added) at least until iron-rich solids (like fortified cereals, meat, and

Whites, Colors, and Baby's?

Tired of separating your baby's laundry (especially because the loads, like the clothes, are so tiny)? Here's a happy laundry alert: Most babies probably don't need their clothes washed separately from the rest of the family's, with special baby laundry soaps. Even the high-potency detergents that really get clothes clean, eliminating most stains and odors (the kind babies are very good at generating), aren't irritating to most infants when well rinsed. (Rinsing is most thorough, and stain-fighting powers are most effective, with liquid detergents.)

To test your baby's sensitivity to your favorite laundry detergent, add one item that will be worn close to baby's skin (such as a t-shirt) to your next family load, being careful not to overdo the detergent or underdo the rinse. If that tender skin shows no rash or irritation, go ahead and wash baby's clothes with yours. If a rash does appear, try another detergent, preferably one without colors and fragrances, before deciding you have to stick with a baby laundry formula.

Love the smell of baby laundry detergent? Go ahead, make your day—and your whole family's laundry—smell baby fresh.

green vegetables) are introduced. As an added precaution, the pediatrician may suggest that your little one stay on an iron supplement throughout the first year. The added benefit of combining iron with vitamin C (either in a supplement or with food): The vitamin C helps with iron absorption.

If your little one is exclusively bottle-fed, chances are he's getting most of the nutrients he needs through formula—though he may fall short on vitamin D until he's consistently drinking enough to meet his daily quota (he'd have to down a minimum of 32 ounces, something he's not likely managing yet). To fill the gap, the pediatrician may recommend giving your baby a vitamin D supplement (probably in the form of A-C-D drops) at least in the short term. Later, once your baby gets serious about solids and starts drinking less formula, the doctor may suggest adding iron as well, again probably in an A-C-D with iron formula.

Ask the pediatrician for recommendations on what supplements your baby needs (if any), and when. Happily, most infant vitamin drops are tasty, and many (though far from all) babies have no problem taking them. It might be easier to give the drops right before a feed, when your baby's apt to lap them up (from hunger)—or you may find him more receptive after a feed. A tasteless powdered supplement can be substituted for the drops if your baby takes a bottle (you mix them right into formula or breast milk—just make sure your baby drinks the whole bottle to get the full dose). The powder can also be mixed with solids once they're started (but again, only if you can count on baby finishing that bowlful).

If your baby has health problems, was premature, or if you're breastfeeding and think your diet might be lacking some important vitamins and minerals (say, if you're a vegan and you're not getting enough B_{12}, zinc, or calcium), the doctor might recommend additional supplements for your baby. Preterm infants who are breastfed will likely be prescribed an iron supplement of 2 mg/kg daily, starting at 1 month of age and continuing until their intake of iron-rich foods fills the requirement for this essential mineral.

What about fluoride? Babies under 6 months don't need fluoride supplementation, and older babies need it only if there isn't adequate fluoride in the water supply or if they don't drink tap water (bottled water doesn't contain it). Ask your baby's doctor for specific recommendations. Keep in mind that with fluoride, as with most good things, too much can be bad. Excessive intake while the teeth are developing in the gums, such as might occur when a baby drinks fluoridated water (either plain or mixed with formula) and takes a supplement, can cause fluorosis, or mottling ("chalk marks" appearing on the teeth). Excessive intake can also occur if excessive amounts of fluoridated toothpaste are used. See page 363 for more information.

Spitting Up

"My baby spits up so much that I'm worried she's not getting enough to eat."

Although it seems as if your little one is literally losing her lunch (and

---

Quick Tip

Keep a small plastic bottle of water mixed with a little baking soda handy for spit-up spot cleaning. Rubbing a cloth moistened with the mixture on spots will keep them from setting and will eliminate most of the odor. Or carry a to-go spot remover. Or use a diaper wipe. And definitely get in the habit of pretreating spots when it's time for laundry.

---

breakfast, and dinner, and snacks), she's almost certainly not. What looks like a lot of spit-up probably amounts to no more than a tablespoon or two of milk, mixed with saliva and mucus—certainly not enough to interfere with your baby's nourishment. If your baby's growing well, peeing and pooping plenty, and thriving, there's no need to cry over spit-up milk—or to worry about it.

Doctors are fond of saying that spit-up is a laundry problem, not a health problem. It's smelly and messy, but it's normal—and so common. Most babies spit up at least occasionally, and many spit up with every feeding. The reason for this malodorous mayhem? Newborns have an immature sphincter between the esophagus and stomach, which allows food to back up—even more easily, since they spend most of their time lying flat on their backs or semireclining. They also have excess mucus and saliva that needs to be cleared—and up and out is the most effective way for an infant to ship that goop out. Often, they spit up because they eat too much (especially if they're bottle-fed and mommy or daddy is pushing more ounces than a tiny tummy can handle), or because they're getting too many air bubbles with their milk (particularly if they were crying before the feed or didn't get burped enough during it). Later, teething babies often gag and spit up thanks to all the drool they're producing.

Most babies stop spitting when they start sitting, usually at about 6 months. The introduction of solids (also at about 6 months) can help limit spit-up, too—after all, it's easier to spit up an entirely liquid diet. Until then, there's no sure way to stop the spitting up (though a bib for your baby and a burp cloth for you should prevent some of the mess), but you can cut down on the frequency:

- Keep bubbles at bay by minimizing air gulping during mealtimes (don't feed her when she's crying, and try to calm her down before feeds).

- Put gravity in your corner by feeding her with her upper body elevated (as upright as is comfortably possible).

- Tilt bottles so that the liquid (not air) fills the nipple, or use bottles that don't allow air to enter the nipple.

- Avoid bouncing her around while she's eating or just afterward. You'll be less likely to bring up the works if you keep her relatively still.

- Break for burps often enough—at least once, halfway through her feedings (if you wait until the end, one big bubble can open the floodgates). If she's a slow eater or seems fussier than usual, break more frequently.

- Keep her upright as much as possible after meals.

Most babies are "happy spitters"—in other words, the spitting doesn't bother them in the slightest (though the same probably can't be said for their parents), and it doesn't affect weight gain or growth. Some babies may have discomfort with spitting—or may be gassy or have other signs of reflux without spitting—and the doctor might diagnose it as gastroesophageal reflux disease or GERD (see page 569).

If your baby's spitting is accompanied by prolonged gagging and coughing or associated with poor weight gain, if it seems severe, or if the vomit is brown or green in color or shoots out 2 or 3 feet (projectile vomiting), call the doctor. These could indicate a medical problem, such as an intestinal obstruction or pyloric stenosis (see page 570).

Blood in Spit-up

"When my 2-week-old spit up today after I breastfed her, there were some reddish streaks that looked like blood in with the curdled milk. Now I'm really worried."

Any blood that seems to be coming from your newborn, particularly when you've found it in her spit-up, is bound to worry you. But before you panic, try to determine whose blood it actually is. If your nipples are cracked, even very slightly, it's probably your blood, which baby could be sucking in (and then spitting up) along with the milk each time she nurses.

If your nipples aren't obviously the cause (they may be, even if you can't see the tiny cracks), or if you're not breastfeeding, call your pediatrician to help you figure out the source of the blood in your baby's spit-up.

Milk Allergy

"My baby is crying a lot, and I'm wondering if he might be allergic to the milk in his formula. How can I tell?"

As eager as you might be to uncover a cause (and an easy cure) for your baby's crying, it's not likely the milk that's to blame. Milk allergy may be the most common food allergy in infants, but it's a lot less common than most people believe (only about 2 to 3 in 100 babies will develop a true allergy to milk). And when a baby is allergic to milk, other symptoms will accompany the crying.

A baby who is having a severe allergic response to milk will usually vomit frequently and have loose, watery stools, possibly tinged with blood. Less severe reactions may include occasional vomiting and loose, mucousy stools. Some babies who are allergic to milk may also have eczema, hives, wheezing, and/or a nasal discharge or stuffiness when exposed to milk protein.

Unfortunately, there's no way to test for milk allergy, except through trial and error—but don't try anything (including a change of formula) without the doctor's advice. If there is no history of allergy in your family, and if your baby doesn't have any symptoms other than crying, the doctor will probably suggest that you treat the crying spells as ordinary colic (see page 210).

If there is a family history of allergies or your baby has symptoms of milk allergy other than crying, the doctor may recommend a trial change of formula, from regular cow's milk formula to hydrolysate (in which the protein is partly broken down or predigested). If the symptoms disappear, it's likely your baby is allergic to milk (though sometimes it can just be a coincidence), and you'll probably be told to keep him on the hydrolysate formula for now. Happily, milk allergies are eventually outgrown, so at some point the pediatrician may recommend a reintroduction of cow's milk formula, or after a year, whole milk. If symptoms don't return when you switch back, your baby either wasn't really allergic in the first place or has outgrown the allergy (at which point you can bring on the dairy products without worry).

A switch to soy formula usually isn't recommended when a true milk allergy is suspected, since a baby who's allergic to milk is often allergic to soy as well.

Very rarely the problem is an enzyme deficiency—an infant is born unable to produce lactase, the enzyme needed to digest the milk sugar lactose. Symptoms of congenital lactose intolerance include gas, diarrhea, bloated stomach, and failure to gain weight. A formula containing little or no lactose will usually resolve the problem.

If the problem is not traced to milk allergy or intolerance, it's probably best to stay with—or switch back to—a cow's milk formula, since it is the better breast milk substitute (though the doctor may suggest one for sensitive stomachs).

Sensitivities in Breastfed Babies

"I'm breastfeeding exclusively, and when I changed my baby's diaper today, I noticed some streaks of blood in his bowel movement. Does that mean he's allergic to my breast milk?"

Babies are virtually never allergic to their mother's milk, but in rare cases, a baby can be allergic to something in his mom's diet that ends up in her milk—often cow's milk proteins. And it sounds as if this might be the case with your very sensitive infant.

Symptoms of such an allergy, known as allergic colitis, may include blood in baby's stool, extreme fussiness, lack of (or minimal) weight gain, and vomiting and/or diarrhea. Your baby could have one or all of these symptoms. Researchers suspect that some babies may become sensitized to certain foods mother eats while baby is still in utero, causing allergies after birth.

Although cow's milk and other dairy products are common culprits in these reactions, they're not the only ones. Others include soy, nuts, wheat, and peanuts. A quick check with your baby's doctor will probably lead you to this course of action: To determine what in your diet is causing your baby's allergy, try eliminating a potential problem food for 2 to 3 weeks. Baby's symptoms may ease during the first week after you've eliminated a food from your diet, but for a sure call, wait the full 2 to 3 weeks to confirm that you've found the culprit.

Occasionally, no correlation between foods and allergic symptoms is found. In that case, your baby might just have had a gastrointestinal virus that caused the streaks of blood in his stool. Or there might be small cracks or fissures in his anus that caused the bleeding. Another possibility: Baby may have swallowed your blood if your nipples are cracked—and that blood can exit in spit-up or poop (sometimes the blood can give poop a black tinge instead). Monitoring by your baby's doctor should solve the mystery.

Bowel Movements

"I expected 1, maybe 2, bowel movements a day from my breastfed baby. But she seems to have one in every diaper—sometimes as many as 10 a day. And they're very loose. Could she have diarrhea?"

Most breastfed infants seem bent on beating the world record for dirtying diapers. But not only is a prolific poop pattern not a bad sign in a breastfed newborn—it's a very good sign. Since the amount that's coming out is related to the amount going in, lots of movements a day in the first 6 weeks means your baby's getting plenty of nutrition from your breast milk.

In the early days, breastfed babies usually have—on average (and average being the operative word here)—one poopy diaper per day of life. In other words, on day 1 of her life, she'll poop once, and on day 2 she'll poop twice. Fortunately, this pattern doesn't usually continue past the fifth or so day of life. After day 5, the average breastfed newborn will poop about 5 times per day. What counts as a BM worth counting? Any poop bigger than the size of a quarter can be added to your tally (if you're keeping track, that is). Some babies—like yours—will poop more (sometimes even once per feeding), some less (though consistently infrequent poops in the first few weeks can mean a baby's not getting enough to eat). By 6 weeks the poop pattern of breastfed babies may start to change, and you may notice your baby skipping a day (or two . . . or even three) between BMs. Or not. Some babies will continue to poop up a storm, filling their diapers several times a day or more throughout the first year. It's not necessary to continue keeping count after 6 weeks as long as baby is happy and gaining weight. The number may vary from day to day, and that's perfectly normal, too.

Normal, also, for breastfed infants is a very soft, sometimes even watery, stool. But diarrhea—frequent stools that are liquidy, smelly, and may contain mucus, often accompanied by fever and/or weight loss—is less common among babies who dine on breast milk alone. If they do get it, they have fewer, smaller movements than bottle-fed babies with diarrhea and recover more quickly, probably because of the infection-fighting properties of breast milk.

Explosive Bowel Movements

"My son's poops come with such force and such explosive sound, I'm beginning to think there's something's wrong with my breast milk."

A breastfed newborn is rarely discreet when it comes to pooping. But the

Flat Out, the Best Way to Sleep

With all the significant health and safety benefits of back-to-sleep come a couple of relatively minor drawbacks. One—that newborns sleep less cozily on their backs—can be minimized by swaddling, which will keep your baby bug snug and secure in a back-sleeping position. Another—that babies who sleep on their backs are more likely to develop flat or bald spots from always facing the same direction—can be prevented with a flip. Alternate your infant's position for sleep (head at one end of the crib one night, the other next). Because babies tend to focus on the same spot in a room (say,

a window) when they're on their backs, flipping their position will ensure that one side of the head won't get all the pressure—and that will make flattening or balding on that side less likely. If, in spite of your efforts, your baby's head flattens (plagiocephaly) or a bald spot develops, don't worry—chances are these problems will go away on their own. Rarely a special headband or helmet will be prescribed to correct a case.

Putting baby on her tummy to play when she's awake (and watched) will minimize flattening while allowing her to develop muscles and practice gross-motor skills.

noisy barrage that fills the room as your little one fills his diaper is completely normal. While giggle inducing (for parents), and sometimes a bit embarrassing (in public), these explosive movements and the surprising variety of sounds that punctuates their passing are just a result of gas being forcefully expelled from an immature digestive system. Things should quiet down in a month or two.

Passing Gas

"My baby passes gas all day long—very loudly. Could she be having tummy troubles?"

The digestive exclamations that frequently explode from a newborn's tiny bottom (otherwise known as farts) are, like those explosive poops, perfectly normal. Think of it like new plumbing, which it essentially is. Once your newborn's digestive system works out the kinks, the gas will pass more

quietly and less frequently, if not less pungently.

Constipation

"I'm wondering if my formula-fed baby is constipated. He's been averaging only one BM every 2 or 3 days."

When it comes to constipation, frequency isn't what counts—consistency is. Formula-fed babies aren't considered constipated unless their poops are firmly formed or come out in hard pellets, or if they cause pain or bleeding (from a fissure or crack in the anus as a result of pushing a hard poop). If your baby's movements are soft and passed without a struggle (even if they arrive only once every 3 to 4 days), he's not constipated. No need to jump to constipation conclusions, either, if he grunts, groans, and strains when he poops. That's standard pooping practice for babies, even when passing soft poop, probably because their anuses aren't strong or coordinated enough for easy elimination. Not to mention that young babies, who usually poop lying down, get no help from gravity.

If your baby really does seem to be constipated, check with the doctor for confirmation and a treatment plan, if necessary. Don't use any at-home remedies without medical advice.

For breastfed babies, constipation is rare, but infrequent poops in the early weeks can be a sign that an infant isn't getting enough to eat (see page 182).

Sleeping Position

"I know my baby's supposed to sleep on her back, but she seems so uncomfortable that way. Wouldn't she sleep better on her tummy, or at least on her side?"

There are no two ways about it: Back sleeping is a must for your baby's safety. Research has shown that compared with tummy sleepers, back sleepers have fewer fevers, fewer problems with nasal congestion, and fewer ear infections, and are no more likely than tummy sleepers to spit up during the night (or choke on their spit-up). But by far the most important reason why back sleeping is crucial: Placing babies to sleep on their backs sharply reduces the risk of crib death (Sudden Infant Death Syndrome, or SIDS).

Start your baby sleeping on her back (without any sleep positioners or wedges, both of which are considered unsafe) right away, so that she'll get used to and feel comfortable in that position from the beginning. Some babies fuss more on their backs at first—that may be because they feel less cozy and secure, since they can't cuddle up against the mattress. They

may startle during sleep more on their backs, too, and that can lead to more frequent wake-ups (see page 145 for more on startling). Swaddling your little one for sleep (or putting her in a sleep sack) will help ease startling and help make her more comfy—and content—on her back.

The incidence of SIDS is highest in the first 6 months, although the recommendation of "back to sleep" applies for the whole first year (and applies no matter who's putting baby to sleep, so make sure anyone who cares for your baby follows this recommendation). Once baby starts rolling over, however, she may decide that she prefers a tummy

Safe Sleeping

The safest way to place your baby down to sleep is on his or her back. Babies placed on their stomachs to sleep are at greater risk of SIDS. But safe sleeping is about more than just sleeping position. It's also about where your baby sleeps and what's in the crib or bassinet with him or her. Bottom line: Never place baby on soft bedding (firm mattresses only, with no "pillow-top"), or in a crib (or parents' bed) with pillows, comforters or fluffy blankets, bumpers, or stuffed animals because of the risk of suffocation. Also especially unsafe for sleep: beanbag chairs, waterbeds, gliders, recliners, armchairs, and sofas—anything upholstered. And the best place for baby to sleep in the early months? In your room, next to your bed—in his or her own crib or bassinet. See page 270 for more on SIDS and safe sleeping.

Is Silence Golden When Baby Is Sleeping?

Should silence rule when baby is sleeping? Should you tiptoe around the house when he's snoozing? Put your phone to vibrate when she's napping? Ask visitors to knock on the door instead of use the doorbell? Go full-on librarian, shushing the dog and anyone who tries to speak above a whisper?

Maybe not. These typical techniques for keeping a sleeping baby sleeping might work in the short term, but may backfire in the long term—when you discover that your little one can't sleep in the real world, a world where phones and doorbells ring and dogs bark. Plus, it may not be necessary—or even productive.

Just how much noise, and what kinds of noise, a newborn can sleep through depends partly on the sounds he or she became accustomed to before birth (say, that barking dog) and partly on individual temperament. Some babies are much more sensitive to stimulus than others, but others can't sleep without some background noise (after all, the uterus your little one is used to was a pretty noisy place). So take cues from your baby in figuring out how far you must go to protect him or her from noise during naps and at night. If a baby turns out to be especially sound-sensitive during sleep, it's probably wise to silence the phone, to change the doorbell to a less shrill ring, and to turn down the volume around the house. Avoid these tactics, however, if baby sleeps through everything.

position for sleep—still, continue to put your baby down on her back and let her decide about flipping.

And don't forget the flip side of back to sleep: tummy to play. See page 236 for more.

No Sleeping Pattern

"My baby wakes up several times a night to feed, and I'm exhausted. Shouldn't she be getting into a regular sleeping pattern by now?"

As much as you and your aching body (and dark-circled under-eyes) would love a full night's sleep, you'll have to wait a little longer before you can clock one in. Babies aren't expected to sleep through the night in the first month, for a couple of reasons. One, with so much growing to do—and such a small tank to fuel up with—most still need at least one (and usually more) feeds to get them through the night. This holds especially true for breastfed newborns, who need frequent feeds even at night—making sleeping through the night an impossible dream for the first 3 months or so. Weight plays a role, too—a small baby will need to feed more often than a large one, and will continue to need during-the-night feeds until she catches up in the pounds department. Trying to start a sleep schedule too soon could not only interfere with the establishment of a mom's milk supply, but also affect baby's growth. Another reason for answering your baby's midnight (and 3 a.m.)

Better Sleep for Baby

Any sleep sound good to you right now (preferably at night)? You can optimize your baby's sleep potential (and thus, yours) with these soothing sleep strategies, many of which re-create some of the comforts of home in the womb:

Keep it cozy. The wide open spaces of a crib can be an unsettling setting, making your tiny newborn feel isolated, vulnerable, and far removed from the cozy confines of mommy's womb. So consider putting your baby to sleep in a snugger space that better approximates the uterine home just left behind—a cradle, a bassinet, or a play yard that has a bassinet top. For added coziness, swaddle your infant or use a sleep sack.

Control for temperature. After 9 months of perfect climate control, being too warm or too cold can disturb a baby's sleep (and overheating can be a risk factor for SIDS). So keep baby and the room temperature just right (touch the nape of baby's neck to check on comfort).

Rock-a-bye, baby. In the uterus, your baby was most active when you were resting—when you were up and on the go, your baby slowed down, lulled by the motion. Out of the womb, movement still has a soothing effect. Rocking, swaying, and patting will help get your baby to sleep. A vibrating pad that can be slipped under the crib mattress can continue the rocking motion once you've put your baby down.

Sound it out. The uterus is a noisier place than you'd think. For months, your baby slept to the sound of your heartbeat, the gurgling of your tummy, and the ambient sound of your voice—which can make sleeping without some background noise tricky now. So try the hum of a fan or a white noise machine, the soft strains of baby-friendly tunes from a musical mobile or app, or one of those baby soothers that imitate uterine or heartbeat sounds.

Wait out those whimpers. Research suggests that a parent's proximity during baby's sleep may reduce the risk of

---

calls, whether she's breastfed or bottle-fed, small or large: She is just beginning to learn about the world, which is still a new and somewhat scary place. The most important lesson she needs to learn now isn't how to sleep on a schedule, but that when she cries, you'll be there to comfort her—even in the middle of the night, when you're understandably beyond beat, and even when she's up for the fourth time in 6 hours.

Though you may find it hard to believe right now, your little one will one day sleep through the night—and so will you.

Restless Sleep

"Our baby seems so restless and noisy when he sleeps. Is there a way to get him to sleep more soundly?"

Sleeping "like a baby" sounds pretty peaceful—but the truth is, baby sleep rarely is. While newborns do sleep a lot (16 hours a day on average), they also wake up a lot in the process. That's because much of their sleep is REM (rapid eye movement), a light, active sleep phase with dreaming, a lot of restless movement, and sometimes startling—and for babies, a lot of noise.

SIDS—which is why experts recommend room sharing for the first 6 to 12 months. The only downside with this arrangement: You'll be more likely to pick up your baby at the slightest stirring. For better sleep all around, wait out those whimpers and pick your little one up only once it's clear he or she is awake and ready for a feed or attention.

Make bedtime routine. Since your newborn will fall asleep most of the time while nursing or bottle-feeding, a bedtime routine might seem unnecessary. But it's never too early to get in the bedtime routine habit—and while you're at it, a naptime routine, too. Later it can become more involved (and include a nightly bath which isn't necessary yet), but for now it can simply come as a series of predictable steps designed to unwind your little one: Dim the lights, speak in hushed tones, add a little soft music, cuddle quietly, give a gentle massage, maybe even read a story. The breast or bottle can be last on the agenda for babies who still fall asleep that way, but can come earlier for those who have already learned to doze off on their own.

Don't nix naps. Some parents try to solve nighttime sleeping problems by keeping their babies awake during the day, even if the baby wants to sleep. The problem with this strategy: Overtired babies sleep more fitfully than well-rested ones. It's fine to limit the length of daytime naps if your little one is still mixing up days and nights—but don't nix those much-needed naps altogether.

See the light of day. Infants exposed to afternoon sunlight tend to have a better night's sleep, so try an after-lunch stroll.

Know when to quit the crutches. For now, as your newborn adjusts to sleep on the outside (instead of snuggled in your cozy womb), a little extra comfort—in the form of soothing motion, white noise, or music—can go a long way in encouraging better sleep. Just be ready to wean baby off these comforting sleep crutches later in the first year (usually by about 6 months or so).

When you hear your baby fuss or whimper at night, it's probably because he's finishing a REM period.

As he gets older, your baby's sleeping patterns will mature. He will have less REM sleep and longer periods of the much sounder, deeper "quiet sleep," from which it's harder to wake him. He will continue to stir and whimper periodically, but less frequently.

In the meantime, if you're sharing a room with your noisy little sleeper (as recommended by AAP for SIDS prevention), keep in mind that picking him up at every midnight murmuring will disrupt his sleep (and yours). Instead, wait until you're sure he's awake and ready for a feed or comfort—a steady cry will clue you in.

Mixing Up of Day and Night

"My 3-week-old sleeps most of the day and wants to stay up all night. How can I get her to reverse her schedule so we all can get some rest?"

Got a little baby vampire on your hands—partying all night, sleeping all day? That's not surprising, given that just 3 weeks ago, your baby lived in the dark round the clock. It was also in your womb that she became accustomed to snoozing the day away (since that's when you were most active, knocking her out with rocking)—and kicking her heels up at night, when you were lying down, trying to rest. Happily, her nocturnal ways are only temporary, and as she adjusts to life on the outside, she'll stop mixing up her days and nights—likely on her own, probably within the next few weeks if not sooner.

If you'd like to help speed her realization that nighttime is the preferred sleep time (not the preferred party time), a little gentle persuasion may do the trick. Start by limiting her daytime naps to no more than 3 or 4 hours each. Although waking a sleeping infant can be tricky, it's usually possible. Try changing her diaper, holding her upright, burping her, rubbing under her chin, or massaging her feet. Once she's somewhat alert, try a little interaction to stimulate her: Talk to her, sing lively songs, or dangle a toy within her range of vision, which is about 8 to 12 inches. (For other tips on keeping baby awake, see page 139) Don't, however, try to keep her from napping at all during the day, with the hope that she'll sleep at night. An overtired, and perhaps overstimulated, baby is not likely to sleep well at night.

Making a clear distinction between day and night may help, too. Wherever she naps, avoid darkening the room or trying to keep the noise level down. When she wakens, ply her with stimulating activities. At night, do the opposite. When you put baby to bed, strive for darkness (use room-darkening shades), relative quiet, and inactivity. No matter how tempting it may be, don't play with or do a lot of socializing when she wakes up during the night, don't turn on the lights or the TV while you're feeding her, avoid unnecessary diaper changes, and keep communications to a whisper or softly sung lullabies.

Baby's Breathing

"Every time I watch my newborn sleep, her breathing seems irregular, her chest moves in a funny way, and frankly it frightens me. Is something wrong with her breathing?"

Not only is that kind of breathing during baby sleep normal, but so are you for worrying about it (that's what new parents do).

A newborn's normal breathing rate is about 40 breaths each minute during waking hours, but when your sweetie sleeps, it may slow down to as few as 20 breaths per minute. Her breathing pattern during sleep is also irregular, and that's normal (if stress-inducing to you). Your baby might breathe fast, with repeated rapid and shallow breaths, lasting 15 to 20 seconds, and then pause (that is, stop breathing—and this is where it gets really scary), usually for less than 10 seconds (though it might seem forever to you), and then, after that brief respiratory respite, breathe again (which is generally when you can start breathing again, too). This type of breathing pattern, called periodic breathing, is standard during sleep for babies, and is due to your baby's immature (but, for her age, developmentally appropriate) breathing control center in the brain.

You may also notice your baby's chest moving in and out while she is sleeping. Babies normally use their diaphragms (the large muscle below the lungs) for breathing. As long as your baby doesn't seem to be working hard to breathe, shows no blueness around the lips, and resumes normal shallow breathing without any intervention, you have nothing to worry about.

Half of a newborn's sleep is spent in REM (rapid eye movement) sleep, a time when she breathes irregularly, grunts and snorts, and twitches a lot—you can even see her eyes moving under the lids. The rest of her slumber is spent in quiet sleep, when she breathes very deeply and quietly and seems very still, except for occasional sucking motions or startling. As she gets older, she will experience less REM sleep, and the quiet sleep will become more like the non-REM sleep of adults.

In other words, what you're describing is normal baby breathing. If, however, your baby takes more than 60 breaths per minute, flares her nose, makes grunting noises, looks blue, or sucks in the muscles between the ribs with each breath so that her ribs stick out, call the doctor immediately.

"Everybody always jokes about parents standing over their baby's crib to hear if he's breathing. Well, now I find myself doing just that—even in the middle of the night."

Anew parent standing over a baby's crib checking for breathing does seem like good stand-up material—until you become a new parent yourself. And then it's no laughing matter. You wake in a cold sweat to complete silence after putting baby to bed 5 hours earlier. Could something be wrong? Why didn't he wake up? Or you pass his crib and he seems so silent and still that you have to poke him gingerly to be sure he's okay. Or he's breathing so hard, you're sure he's having trouble breathing. You . . . and all the other new parents.

Not only are your concerns normal, but your baby's varied breathing patterns when he snoozes are, too. It'll probably take a while, but eventually you will become less panicky about whether he's going to wake up in the morning—and more comfortable with both you and him sleeping 8 hours at a stretch.

Still, you may never totally be able to abandon the habit of checking on your child's breathing (at least once in a while) until he's off to college and sleeping in a dorm—out of sight, though not out of mind.

Wondering if those breathing monitors—the ones that clip on to your baby's diaper or slip under the mattress and then sound an alarm when there's been no movement for 20 seconds—will bring the peace of mind you're looking for? They might—and many parents are able to sleep more soundly thanks to the security of knowing their sweet sleeper's breathing is being monitored. But before you shell out the big bucks for these devices, keep in mind that the number of false alarms they give may actually cause more anxiety than they are supposed to prevent, and many parents, fed up with the repeated false alarms, end up switching the devices off altogether. What's more, there's no evidence that these monitors prevent SIDS.

Moving a Sleeping Baby to a Crib

"Every time I try to put my sleeping baby down in her crib, she wakes up."

She's finally asleep after what seems like hours of nursing on sore breasts, rocking in aching arms, lullabying in an increasingly hoarse voice. You edge cautiously to the crib, holding your breath and moving only the muscles that are absolutely necessary. Then, with

Babies Are Supposed to Cry

Some cry more than others, but all newborns cry—and they're supposed to. After all, that's how babies make sure they get their needs met (think of it as survival of the loudest). So a baby who's not doing much crying at all—who seems content most of the time, whether or not those needs are being met—may be telling you something else entirely: that he or she is not strong or healthy enough to cry. If your baby is doing very little crying after the first couple of days of life—especially if he or she isn't demanding the most basic of needs, regular feeds—check in with the doctor without delay. You may just have a very laid-back little one on your hands (and in that case you'll have to stay on top of those needs even if he or she doesn't demand them), or your baby may not be thriving, in which case getting the right medical attention is vital.

a silent but fervent prayer, you lift her over the edge of the crib and begin the perilous descent to the mattress below. Finally, you release her, but a split second too soon. She's down—then she's up. Turning her head from side to side, sniffing and whimpering softly, then sobbing loudly. Ready to cry yourself, you pick her up and start all over.

If you're having trouble keeping a good baby down, wait 10 minutes until she's in a deep sleep in your arms, then try:

A high mattress. You'll find it much easier to place your baby in her crib if you set the mattress at the highest possible level (at least 4 inches from the top of the rail). Just be sure to lower it by the time your baby is old enough to sit up. Or start out using a bassinet or cradle or a play yard with a bassinet insert, which may be easier to lift a baby into and out of.

Close quarters. The longer the distance between the place where baby falls asleep and the place where you are going to put her down, the more opportunity for her to awaken on the way. So feed or rock her as close to the cradle or crib as possible.

A seat you can get out of. Always feed or rock your baby in a chair or sofa that you can rise from smoothly, without disturbing her.

The right side. Or the left. Feed or rock baby in whichever arm will allow you to put her in the crib most easily. If she falls asleep prematurely on the wrong arm, gently switch sides and rock or feed some more before attempting to put her down.

Constant contact. When baby is comfortable and secure in your arms, suddenly being dropped into the open space of a mattress can be startling—and result in a rude awakening. So cradle baby all the way down, back first, easing your bottom hand out from under just before you reach the mattress. Maintain a hands-on pose for a few moments longer, gently patting if she starts to stir.

A lulling tune. Hypnotize your baby to sleep with a traditional lullaby (she won't object if you're off-key or don't actually know all the words) or an improvised one with a monotonous beat ("aah, aah, ba-by, aah, aah, ba-by") or with a few rounds of "shh." Continue as you carry her to her crib, while you're putting her down, and for a few moments afterward.

Putting Crying on Hold

It's a credo for newborn crying: When your baby cries, you come running. But what if baby cries when you're in the middle of rinsing shampoo out of your hair . . . or draining boiling water from a pot of pasta . . . or unclogging the toilet that's about to overflow . . . or finishing a text to your boss . . . or finishing, um, a little business in the bedroom? Do you need to drop everything to pick up your crying baby? Of course not—letting a baby cry for a minute or 2 or even 5 every now and then isn't harmful, as long as he or she can't get into trouble while waiting for you, and especially if your usual response time is prompt.

Even taking a 10- to 15-minute break during a particularly trying crying marathon won't hurt—and it might help both of you get through this challenging phase of babyhood. In fact, some experts suggest building those breaks in if you're dealing with a particularly tough case of colic: setting up a routine in which you let baby cry for those short intervals in a safe place like the crib, picking him or her up and trying to comfort for another 15 minutes, then putting him or her down and repeating. Clearly, don't try this if it seems to make the colic worse or if it's something you just don't feel comfortable doing.

If she begins to toss, sing some more, until she's fully quieted.

A rock till she drops off to dreamland. One of the benefits of a rockable cradle or bassinet—you can continue that soothing rocking once she's down for the count. Another option: a vibrating mattress pad designed to be slipped under the crib mattress that runs for a half hour or so—long enough, hopefully, for your sweet little one to fall deeply to sleep.

Crying

"I know babies are supposed to cry—but ever since we came home from the hospital with our baby, she's been crying. A lot."

Most parents do a fair amount of high-fiving at the hospital—pretty certain that they scored the one baby on the block who hardly cries. But that's because few babies do a whole lot of crying in their first hours of life, when they're still catching up on their rest and recovering after delivery. Fast-forward a couple of days—usually right about the time that parents bring their bundle of joy home—and baby usually changes her tune. And that's not surprising. Crying is, after all, the only way infants have of communicating their needs and feelings—their very first baby talk. Your baby can't tell you that she's lonely, hungry, wet, tired, uncomfortable, too warm, too cold, or frustrated any other way. And though it may seem impossible now, you will soon be able (at least part of the time) to decode your baby's different cries and know what she's crying for (see page 144).

Some newborn crying, however, seems entirely unrelated to basic needs. In fact, 80 to 90 percent of all babies have daily crying sessions of 15 minutes to an hour that are not easily explained—or decoded. These periodic

You Can't Spoil a Newborn

Worried about spoiling your newborn by always responding so quickly to those cries? Don't be—it isn't possible to spoil a baby in the first 6 months. Responding promptly to crying won't make your baby more demanding—in fact, quite the opposite is true. The faster your newborn's needs are met, the more likely he or she is to grow into a more secure, less demanding child.

crying spells, like those associated with colic, a more severe and persistent form of unexplained crying, most often occur in the evening. It may be that this is the most hectic and stressful time of day in the home—everybody's tired, everybody's hungry (and mom's milk supply may be at its lowest level of the day), everybody's done, done, done and that goes for baby, too. Or it may be that after a busy day of taking in and processing all the sights, sounds, smells, and other stimuli in her environment, a baby just needs to unwind with a good cry. Crying for a few minutes may even help her nod off to sleep.

Hang in there. As your baby becomes a more effective communicator—and as you become more proficient at understanding her—she will cry less often, for shorter periods, and will be more easily comforted when she does cry. Meanwhile, even if your baby's crying doesn't seem to reach colicky proportions (and fingers crossed, it won't), the same strategies that help with colic may help restore calm—see the next question.

Colic

"I'm almost afraid to consider that our baby has colic—but with all this crying, I can't imagine what else it might be. How do I know for sure he's colicky?"

Call it colic, call it extreme crying . . . call it miserable. And, call it common, too, because if misery loves company, parents of colicky babies have quite a pity party going on. It's estimated that 1 in 5 babies have crying spells, usually beginning in late afternoon and sometimes lasting until bedtime, that are severe enough to be labeled colic. Colic differs from ordinary crying (see previous question) in that baby seems inconsolable, crying turns to screaming, and the ordeal lasts for 3 hours, sometimes much longer, occasionally nearly round-the-clock. Most often colicky periods recur daily, though some babies take an occasional night off.

Doctors usually diagnose colic based on the "rules of three": at least 3 hours of crying, at least 3 days a week, lasting for at least 3 weeks—but of course, some babies are colic over-achievers, crying far more hours and days and weeks. The baby with a textbook case of colic pulls his knees up, clenches his fists, and generally moves his legs and arms more. He closes his eyes tightly or opens them wide, furrows his brow, even holds his breath briefly. Bowel activity increases, and he passes gas. Eating and sleeping are disrupted by the crying—baby frantically seeks a nipple only to reject it once sucking has begun, or dozes for a few moments only to wake up screaming. But few infants follow the textbook description exactly—different babies do colic differently, and sometimes the same babies do colic differently on different days.

Colic generally begins during the second or third week of life (later in preterm infants), and usually gets as bad as it's going to get by 6 weeks. Though colic may feel as though it will never end, it will typically start to taper off at 10 to 12 weeks (light at the end of the tunnel!). By 3 months (later in preterm babies), most colicky infants seem to be miraculously cured—with just a few continuing their problem crying through the fourth or fifth month or (shudder) beyond. The colic may stop suddenly—or end gradually, with some good and some bad days, until they are all good.

Though these daily screaming sessions, whether they're marathons or shorter sprints, are usually called "colic," the word is really just a catch-all term for problem crying—the problem being, there's no solution to it besides the passing of time. There isn't a clear definition of exactly what colic is or how (and if) it differs from other types of extreme crying. But when it comes down to it—do definitions and differences really matter when your baby's crying for hours on end, and you're powerless to calm him down? Realistically, probably . . . not so much.

What might help—at least a little—is to know that colic isn't your fault, or anyone else's fault. While the exact causes of colic remain a mystery, what experts do know is that it isn't the result of genetics, anything that happened during pregnancy or childbirth, or parenting skills (or lack of them, in case you're wondering). Here are some theories of what's behind all that crying:

Overload. Newborns have a built-in mechanism for tuning out the sights and sounds around them, which allows them to eat and sleep without being disturbed by their environment. Near the end of the first month that mechanism disappears, leaving babies (and their brand new senses) more vulnerable to the stimuli in their surroundings. With so many sensations coming at them, some infants become overwhelmed, often (not surprisingly) at the end of the day. To release that stress, they cry—and cry and cry. Colic ends when the baby learns how to selectively filter out some environmental stimuli and in doing so, avoid a sensory overload. If you think this might be the cause of your baby's colic, the try-everything approach (rocking, bouncing, driving, swinging, singing) may actually make things worse. Instead, watch how your baby responds to certain stimuli and steer clear of the offending ones (if baby cries harder when you rub or massage him, limit that kind of touching during colic—instead, try wearing your baby or using a swing once he's old enough).

Immature digestion. Digesting food is a pretty demanding job for a baby's brand new gastrointestinal system. As a result, food may pass through too quickly and not break down completely, resulting

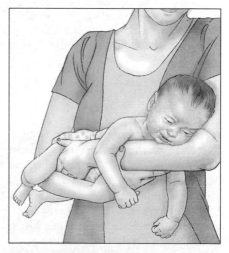

The colic hold puts comforting pressure on a newborn's gassy tummy.

For Parents: Surviving Colic

There's no question that parents get the worst of colic. Though it can safely be said that even hours and hours of daily crying doesn't seem to hurt a baby, it certainly does leave its mark on mom and dad. Listening to a baby's screams is irritating and anxiety-provoking (yes, even when you love that baby with all your heart). Objective studies show that it's linked to a rise in blood pressure, a speeding up of the heartbeat, and changes in blood flow to the skin—in other words, it can take a physical and emotional toll. To cope with colicky crying that just won't quit, try the following:

Break it up. If you're the one who's been left holding the crying baby 7 nights a week at colic time, the strain is bound to wear on you, your health, and your relationships with your baby and with others. If there are two parents at home during baby witching hours, make sure colic duty is divided up equally between the two of you (an hour on, an hour off, a night on, a night off, or whatever arrangement you find works best). A fresh set of arms (and a different rocking rhythm, and a different singing voice) sometimes induces calm in a crying baby, which may make switching off frequently your best bet.

Then, try to make sure you take an occasional break together. If you can find a babysitter or a family member who's patient and experienced with crying babies, go out for dinner (even if you're breastfeeding, you should be able to squeeze in a meal), hit the gym, or just take a long, quiet walk.

If you're the only parent in the house either all or some of the time (or as often happens, all of the colic time), you'll need to call on help even more often—coping with a crying infant for hours a day every day is a lot for any one person to handle. No help in sight? Keep reading.

Take a break. Sure, it's important to respond to crying, which is an infant's only way of communicating. But every once in a while, it doesn't hurt to give yourself a break from your baby—and your baby a break from you. Try the strategy described in the box on page 209, and use those 10 or 15 minutes to do something relatively relaxing: Do a few yoga poses, watch a little TV, listen to some music. Hopefully, you'll be a little less ragged and a little more refreshed when you pick up baby again for round two (or three, or four)—and that will do you both some good.

in pain when gas is passed. When gas seems to be pulling the colic trigger, there are medications that may help (see box, page 214). When it's the type of formula that might be the culprit, a change (in consultation with the pediatrician) to one that is more easily tolerated or digested may be in order. Much less likely, it could be something in a breastfeeding mom's diet that's triggering the colic. To find out if that's the

case, you can try eliminating common offenders in your diet (caffeine, dairy, cabbage, broccoli) to see if that makes a difference over a couple of weeks.

Reflux. Research has found reflux may sometimes trigger the excessive crying of colic. Reflux irritates the esophagus (much like heartburn in an adult), causing discomfort and crying. If reflux seems to be the cause of the colic in

Tune out. To lessen the effect of your baby's wails, use earplugs or noise-canceling headphones—they won't block out the sound entirely, just dull it so it won't be so wearing. Or tune in to some iTunes—the music will not only soothe you (and if you're lucky, baby), it'll also give you a rhythm to move to.

Get physical. Exercise is a great way to work off tension, something a crying baby will give you plenty of. Work out at home with baby early in the day, head to the gym that has child-care services, or take the baby for a brisk walk outdoors when fussy hour hits—it may help calm you both. And always keep a stress ball nearby, for times when you need to knead.

Talk about it. Do a little crying yourself—on any willing shoulder: your spouse's, the pediatrician's, a family member's, a friend's. Or vent on social media. Talking about the colic won't cure it, but you may feel a little better after sharing—especially if you share with others in the same rocky boat (or who've been in the same boat—and weathered the storm). Just knowing you're not alone in the world of inconsolable babies can make a world of difference.

If you really feel violent, get help. Almost everyone finds a constantly crying baby hard to take, sometimes even hard to love—and that's completely normal (you're only human, just like your baby). But for some, endless crying becomes more than they can cope with. The result is sometimes child abuse. You may be even more likely to cross that line if you're suffering from untreated (and possibly undiagnosed) postpartum depression. If your thoughts of hurting your baby are more than fleeting, if you feel like you're about to give in to the urge to hit or shake your baby or harm him or her in any way, get help immediately. Put your baby in a safe place and get on the phone right away with your spouse, a friend or relative, the doctor, or someone else who can help you. Or bring your baby over to a neighbor's house and ask for help. Even if your powerful feelings don't lead to child abuse, they can start eroding your relationship with your baby and your confidence in yourself as a parent unless you get counseling (and if you're suffering from postpartum depression or psychosis, appropriate treatment) quickly. Don't wait it out—get the help you need now.

your baby, some of the treatment tips on page 571 may help.

Exposure to smoking. Several studies show that moms who smoke during or after pregnancy are more likely to have babies with colic. Secondhand smoke may also be a culprit. Though the link exists, it is unclear how cigarette smoke might cause colic. (The bottom line for loads of more significant health reasons:

Don't smoke or let anyone else smoke around the baby.)

What's reassuring about colic (besides that it doesn't last forever) is that babies who have these crying spells don't seem to be any the worse for wear . . . though the same can't always be said for their parents. Colicky babies thrive, usually gaining as well or better than babies who cry very little, and are no

Prescription for Colic

Looking for a colic cure you can count on while you're counting the days until your cute little crier has crossed the 3-month threshold—hopefully leaving colic behind? Unfortunately, there are no prescriptions or potions—traditional or homeopathic or complementary and alternative—that are guaranteed to stop the crying. There are, however, a few that doctors sometimes suggest—if only to offer parents desperate for "anything." In most cases the evidence that they work doesn't add up, and if parents see an improvement, it's most likely because babies with colic improve after a few months anyway. Here are some treatments that have plenty of anecdotal evidence, but not much in the way of science, to back them up:

Antigas drops. Colicky babies are often extra gassy (whether they're gassy because they're crying or they're crying because they're gassy—or both—isn't clear), and studies show that reducing the gas may reduce the discomfort (and the crying). So, simethicone drops, the same antigas ingredient found in many adult preparations (formulated for babies under such brand names as Mylicon and Phazyme), are often recommended for relief. Two trials comparing crying duration, however, found no difference between babies treated with simethicone drops and those not treated. Ask the doctor whether these drops might help relieve your baby's symptoms.

Probiotics. Something else to ask the doctor about: probiotic drops, which may reduce crying in some colicky babies, probably because they can ease tummy troubles. Again, research has yet to consistently back this up.

Gripe water. In the category of "little evidence, lots of anecdotes," gripe water, a combination of herbs and sodium bicarbonate in drops, is touted for its baby-soothing benefits. Anecdotally, many parents swear by gripe water, but no reliable studies have shown its effectiveness in reducing colic symptoms. Check with your baby's doctor for a recommendation.

Chiropractic. The theory behind this treatment is that when a baby's spine is misaligned, it can lead to digestive issues and discomfort. Gentle manipulation of the spine is supposed to remedy this, though the clinical evidence hasn't backed that up. Plus, some doctors say chiropractic on infants isn't safe—so definitely get the pediatrician's advice (and a referral to a qualified practitioner) before booking this kind of treatment.

Herbs. Herbal remedies, such as fennel extract, or herbal tea (chamomile, licorice, fennel, balm mint, and so on), given by dropper, may be somewhat effective in relieving symptoms of colicky babies, but not significantly, according to studies. Check with the pediatrician before using any herbal remedy.

Just remember, as desperate as you might be for a problem crying panacea, don't give your baby any medication, herbal or otherwise, without talking to your baby's doctor first. And really, the best prescription for colic isn't treating the baby, but rather treating the parents—finding ways to relieve your stress from all that crying (see box, page 212) and reminding yourself that colic isn't harmful to your baby—and that it will pass (promise!).

more likely to have behavioral problems than other children later on. They're often more alert as babies (which is probably part of their problem, since they take in more of the kind of stimuli that ends up overwhelming them), and better problem solvers as toddlers. Looking for a solution for this problem? There really isn't one—besides the passing of time—but in the meantime, check out the strategies for dealing with colic on the pages that follow.

Coping with Crying

"My baby just won't stop crying . . . and I need help helping her (and me)."

There's nothing more frustrating than trying to console an inconsolable baby—especially when you've been trying, trying, trying . . . and baby's still crying, crying, crying. But the truth is, not all soothing strategies work on every baby, and few work on every baby every time—but chances are you'll find at least a couple in the following list of tricks that will work on your baby some of the time. Just give each a fair shot before you switch to another (and don't pull out too many tricks at one time, or you'll overload baby's circuits—and step up the crying you're trying to stop):

Respond. Of course you know that responding to your baby's cries is important—but put yourself in her little booties for a moment, and you'll see just how important. Crying is a baby's only way of communicating her needs—but it's also her only way of wielding any control at all over a vast and bewildering new environment: She cries, you come running to her side—powerful stuff when you're otherwise completely powerless. Though it may sometimes seem the definition of pointless in the

short term (you come, she still cries), responding promptly to your baby's cries will, studies show, reduce her crying in the long run. In fact, babies whose parents responded to them regularly and promptly in infancy cry less as toddlers. What's more, crying that's been left to intensify for more than a few minutes becomes harder to interpret—the baby becomes so upset, even she doesn't remember what started all the fuss in the first place. And often, the longer baby cries, the longer it takes to stop the crying.

Assess the situation. Even a colicky baby who does a lot of unexplained crying can cry for a reason, too. So always check to see if there's a simple and fixable cause for crying. The usual suspects: Your baby's hungry, tired, bored, wet or poopy, too warm, or too cold, or needs food, a nap, some rocking, some attention, a change of position, a new diaper, to be swaddled.

Do a diet check. Be sure your baby isn't always crying because she's always hungry. Lack of adequate weight gain or signs of failure to thrive can clue you in. Increasing baby's intake (pumping up your milk supply if you're breast-feeding) may eliminate excessive crying. If baby is bottle-fed, ask the doctor whether the crying might be due to an allergy to her formula (though this isn't very likely unless crying is accompanied by other signs of allergy). If you're breastfeeding, consider doing a check of your own diet, since there's the very slight possibility that the crying might be triggered by baby's sensitivity to something you're eating. Test more common culprits, like dairy, caffeine, or gas-producing vegetables like cabbage, by removing them one at a time from your diet and seeing if there's an improvement in baby's symptoms. You can add them back in one at a time to narrow down the culprit or culprits, if any.

Get close. In societies where babies are always worn or toted in carriers, there isn't as much crying or fussiness. This traditional wisdom seems to translate well in our world, too. Research has shown that babies who are worn or carried for at least 3 hours every day cry less than babies who aren't toted as often. Not only does wearing or carrying your baby give her the pleasure of physical closeness to you (and after 9 months of constant closeness, that may be just what baby's crying for), but it may help you tune in better to baby's needs.

Swaddle. Being tightly wrapped is very comforting to many newborns, especially during those fussy periods, since it offers the same warm, snug security they grew accustomed to in the womb. A few, however, intensely dislike swaddling. The only way you'll know which holds true for your baby is to give swaddling a try the next time colic begins (see page 169).

Take a clue from kangaroos. Like swaddling, kangaroo care—cuddling your baby close to you, cocooned under your shirt or zipped into a sweatshirt skin-to-skin, heart-to-heart—gives many babies a sense of comforting security. Just keep in mind that, as with swaddling, some babies prefer more freedom of movement and will resist being held tightly.

Rhythmic rocking. Most babies find comfort (and calm) from being rocked, whether in your arms, a carriage, a vibrating or swaying infant seat, a baby swing (when baby's old enough), or being worn while you walk or sway. Some babies respond better to fast rocking than to slow—but don't rock or shake your baby forcefully, since this can cause serious whiplash injury. For some babies, rocking side to side tends to stimulate, rocking back and forth to calm. Test your baby's response to different kinds of rocking.

A warm-water bath. A bath can soothe some babies—though bath-haters may just scream louder when they hit the water.

Soothing sounds. Even if your singing voice has a fingernails-on-the-blackboard effect on others, your baby will probably love it . . . and be lulled by it. Learn whether your baby is soothed by soft lullabies, sprightly rhymes, or rock ballads or pop tunes, and whether a hushed, high-pitched, or deep voice is the ticket to calm. But don't stop at singing. Many babies are calmed by other sounds as well—the hum of a fan, vacuum cleaner (you can wear your baby while you vacuum—combining motion with sound, and getting your floors clean at the same time), or clothes dryer (try leaning your back against the dryer while you're wearing your baby to get a nice vibration with the machine's purr). Also soothing: a repeated "shh" or "ahhhhh, ahhhhh," a white noise machine, or an app that plays nature sounds—like the wind blowing through trees or waves breaking on the beach.

Massage. For babies who like to be stroked—and many do—massage can be very calming, especially if you give it while you're lying on your back, baby on your chest. (See page 251 for tips on baby massage.) Experiment with light and firmer strokes to make sure you're rubbing your baby the right way. Your baby's not buying the massage? Don't push the rub— some little ones are touch averse when they're fussy.

Add a little pressure. On baby's tummy, that is. The "colic carry" (see illustration, page 211) or any position that applies gentle pressure to baby's abdomen (such as across your lap, with belly on one knee and head on the other), can relieve discomfort that might be contributing to the crying. Some babies prefer being upright on the shoulder, but again with pressure on their bellies while their backs are being patted or rubbed. Or try this gas reliever: Gently push baby's knees up to his or her tummy and hold for 10 seconds, then release and gently straighten them. Repeat several times. Alternatively, you can bicycle baby's legs gently to relieve any gas pain.

Satisfy with sucking. Sucking doesn't always have to come with a meal—and in fact, newborns sometimes need to suck just for sucking's sake. Using the breast or bottle to satisfy your baby's need for extra sucking can lead to a cycle of too much feeding, too much gas, and too much crying. When your baby's fussy but not hungry, try a pacifier (that's why they call them soothies) or your pinkie. Or help your little one find her fist to suck on.

Comfort with consistency. Even babies who are too young for a schedule can be calmed by consistency—singing the same song, swaddling the same way, rocking at the same speed in the same direction, playing the same white noise sounds. Consistency is likely to pay off with soothing techniques, too. Once you find what works, stick with it most of the time, and try not to switch around too much from one strategy to the other during the same crying jag.

Get out of the house. Sometimes, just a change to an outdoor location will magically change a baby's mood. Add motion, and you've got a really powerful soothing potion. So take your baby for a walk in the stroller or in a sling or carrier, or strap her into the car seat for a drive (but turn around and head home if the crying continues in the car—otherwise it could distract you from the road).

Control air. A lot of newborn discomfort is caused by swallowing air during feeds. Discomfort leads to crying—and crying leads to more swallowed air, a cycle that you definitely want to break when you can. Babies will swallow less air during feeds if they're properly latched on during breastfeeding or slightly upright during bottle-feeding. The right-size nipple hole on a bottle will also reduce air intake. Be sure it isn't too large (which promotes gulping of air with formula) or too small (struggling for formula also promotes air swallowing). Hold the bottle so that no air enters the nipple (or choose one that controls for air), and be sure to burp baby frequently during feedings to expel swallowed air. Sometimes a change of nipple or bottle can significantly reduce crying.

Start fresh. As new as your newborn is to the world, she's wise beyond her days when it comes to picking up your feelings. If you're struggling for hours to soothe your baby, you're bound to be stressed out—and she's bound to sense it and be stressed out by it. The result? More crying, of course. If you can, periodically hand baby off to another pair of loving arms so you can both get a stress break and a fresh start. Have no one to relieve you? Try putting your baby down in a safe place for a few minutes (see box, page 209).

Excise excitement. Having a new baby to show off can be fun—everyone wants to see the baby, and you want to take her everywhere to be seen. You also want to expose baby to new experiences in stimulating environments. That's fine for some babies,

For Parents: Helping Siblings Live with Colic

So, let's recap the last few weeks as it appears to your older (but still very young) child. First, mommy disappears for a couple of days and then returns (super tired and achy) with her arms full of a strange little bundle that's too small to play with but apparently not too small to take up everyone's lap and attention . . . or to be gifted with a steady stream of toys. The baby cries a lot, and just when it seems like there's no way anything could possibly cry any more or any louder, this red-faced creature starts to cry even more and even louder. Screaming, shrieking, howling for hours on end—not to mention, during the hours of the day that were always big sib's favorite: dinner with mommy and daddy, bath and story time, cuddles. All of which seem to have gone out the window suddenly (and big sib probably, by now, not-so-secretly wishes that baby would follow out the window). Instead of being a time for eating, sharing, and quiet play, early evening turns into a time of disrupted meals, frantic pacing and rocking, and distracted, irritable parents.

You can't make colic easy on your older child any more than you can make it easy on yourself (in fact, it's bound to be a little harder, since your firstborn can't grasp that colic is a "phase"). But you can help ease the toll little sib colic can take if you:

Show and tell. Explain, on your older child's level, what colic is—that it's baby's way of getting used to being in a new and strange world, which can be a little scary at first. Reassure him or her that most of the crying will stop once the baby learns more about the world and figures out other ways of saying, "I'm hungry," "I'm tired," "My tummy hurts," "I need a cuddle," "I'm scared." Show the brand new big sib a photo of himself or herself crying as a newborn, and then as a smiling older baby and toddler—this might

help illustrate that there's hope for this newborn.

Play the no-blame game. Little children tend to blame themselves for everything that goes wrong in a home, from mommy and daddy's arguing to a new baby's crying. Explain that all this crying is nobody's fault—that all babies cry when they're new.

Load up on love. Dealing with a colicky baby can be so distracting—especially in the context of an already busy day—that you may forget to do those special little things that show a toddler or older child you care. Even during the worst of the storm, make sure you break from the pacing and rocking occasionally to give your older son or daughter a reassuring hug. If baby is soothed by walks outdoors, put the little crier in a carrier and take a stroll

too stimulating for others (particularly young ones). If your baby is colicky, limit excitement, visitors, and stimulation, especially in the late afternoon and early evening.

Check with the doctor. While the odds are that your baby's daily screaming sessions are due to normal crying or

colic, it's a good idea to talk the situation over with the doctor—if only to get some reassurance and maybe a few extra soothing strategies. Describing the crying (its duration, intensity, pattern, any variation from the norm, and any accompanying symptoms) will also help the doctor rule out any underlying medical condition (like reflux or a with your older child—or head to the playground (you can push the swing wearing a sling). The new baby will be lulled, and your older child will feel loved.

Divide the baby, conquer the sibling rivalry. When both parents are home, try taking turns walking the floor with the baby during colic marathons, so that your older child is usually getting the attention of at least one parent. Another option: One parent can take baby out for a ride in the stroller or the car (the motion often helps subdue the colic) while the other parent spends some quality quiet time at home with your older son or daughter. Or one of you can take your big kid out to dinner (for pizza with a side of peace and quiet) or, if it's still light out, for an early evening excursion to the playground while the other toughs it out at home with The Screamer.

Put baby on mute. Okay . . . you can't mute your little crier, but you can help muffle baby's wails so big bro or sis can catch a break from the constant background crying. Gift your older child with soundproofing earmuffs and set him or her up with a book to look at, crayons to scribble with, play clay to pound on. Or let your big kid listen to an audiobook with low volume headphones that dampen the sound of baby's cries. Or let your older child listen to music with headphones in another room (again, keep the volume low so as not to damage your big kid's ears) to help drown out baby's howling.

Preserve the rituals. Routines are comforting to young children, and when they're disrupted, it can be enormously unsettling—especially during times when life is more unsettled than usual (as when there's a new, crying baby in the house). Do your best to make sure your older son or daughter's treasured rituals don't fall victim to your baby's colic. If bedtime has always meant a leisurely bath (complete with bubbles and splashing), a cuddlefest, and two stories, strive for a leisurely bath, cuddlefest, and two stories every night, even when colic's in full swing. Dividing the colic duty will, hopefully, make those routines possible more often than not.

Go one-on-one. Even if it's only half an hour a day—maybe during your newborn's best nap of the day, probably before daily colic kicks in—try to schedule some special one-on-one time to spend with your older child, without screeching baby sibling tagging along. Play teddy bear picnic, bake muffins, paint a mural (on an extra-large piece of paper), put together a puzzle, start an egg carton garden. Have other stuff to do while you have a chance? Chances are, there's nothing more important.

---

milk allergy) that could be triggering the crying.

Wait it out. Sometimes nothing relieves colic but the passing of time. And while that time may seem to stretch on forever—especially if your baby's colic is a daily struggle—it may help to remind yourself (over and over and over again): This, too, shall pass—usually by the time baby's 3 months old.

Pacifier

"My baby has crying jags in the afternoon. Should I give him a pacifier to comfort him?"

It's easy, it's quick, and for many babies it turns on the comfort and turns off the tears more reliably than a dozen hoarse choruses of "Rock-a-Bye Baby." There's no denying a pacifier can work remarkably well at comforting your baby and calming his crying (especially if he has a strong need to suck but hasn't yet figured out how to get his fingers in his mouth). But should you pop that binky into your baby's mouth at the first whimper? Here's a look at some pacifier pros and cons:

Pros

- A pacifier could save your baby's life. Talk about a powerful positive: Research has linked pacifier use to a decreased risk of SIDS. Experts believe that babies who suck on pacifiers may not sleep as deeply and wake more easily than babies who don't, making them less susceptible to SIDS. Another theory is that sucking on a pacifier might help open up air space around a baby's mouth and nose, which ensures he gets enough oxygen. Because of the reduced SIDS risk, the AAP suggests that pacifiers be used for babies under age 1 at naptime and bedtime (assuming your baby will take one—not all babies will).

- The pacifier is in the parent's control. That can be a good thing when nothing but plunking that pacifier in your baby's mouth will generate calm. Plus, unlike the thumb, which is in baby's control, when you decide it's time for your baby to give up the binky, you're the one who'll be able to pull the plug (whether your little one will put up a fight is another issue).

Cons

- If a baby gets attached to a binky, the habit can be a hard one to break—especially once your baby turns into a more inflexible toddler (when the continuing use of pacifiers is linked to recurrent ear infections and, later, to misaligned teeth).

- A paci can become a crutch for the parents. Plunking that pacifier in your baby's mouth can become just a little too easy and a lot more convenient than trying to figure out the reason for the fussing or if there might be other ways of placating him. The result may be a baby who can be happy only with something in his mouth, and who is unable to comfort himself any other way.

- Being paci dependent can mean less sleep for everyone, because babies who learn to go to sleep with a pacifier might not learn how to fall asleep on their own—and they might put up a sniffly fuss when the binky gets lost in the middle of the night (requiring weary mom or dad to get up and pop it back in each time baby wakes up). Of course, though inconvenient, this is a pretty minor con compared with the significant pro of safer sleep for pacifier-using newborns.

What about nipple confusion or pacifiers interfering with breastfeeding? Contrary to popular belief, there is little evidence that pacifiers cause nipple confusion. And as far as throwing a monkey wrench into long-term nursing for your little monkey, the data doesn't bear that out either. In fact, some research shows that limiting the pacifier for newborns actually decreases the rate of exclusive breastfeeding. Still, there's no doubt that your milk supply is dependent on your baby's suckling—which means that spending too much time with a mouth full of binky can mean too little time spent with a mouth full of breast, which can mean too little stimulation for your milk supply.

The bottom line on binkies? Make moderation your motto. Consider bringing on a paci at sleep times (as recommended) and at fussy times (when your baby really seems to need relief . . . and so do you). Give one a try, also, if your little one has such a strong need for sucking that your nipples have become human pacifiers or if baby is taking too much formula because he's not happy without a nipple in his mouth. Just don't overuse it—especially if binky time is cutting down on feeding time or socializing time. Remember, it's hard to coo or smile when you're sucking. And try not to use it as a substitute for parent-provided attention or comfort.

Most important, be sure to use the pacifier safely. Never attach one to the crib, carriage, playpen, or stroller, or hang it around your baby's neck or wrist with a ribbon, string, or cord of any kind—babies can be strangled this way. Be sure to size up the pacifier as baby grows (and ditch the soft hospital paci) so it doesn't become a choking hazard. And have in mind a plan to ditch the pacifier down the road once your baby is approaching his first birthday, at which point the pros will start to be outweighed by the cons—and your little one will be better off trying to figure out how to self-soothe in other ways.

Healing of the Umbilical Cord

"The cord still hasn't fallen off my baby's belly button, and it looks really awful. Could it be infected?"

Healing belly buttons almost always look worse than they actually are—even when they're healing normally. Not surprising when you consider what an umbilical stump is—the remnants of the gelatinous, blood-vessel-filled cord that spent months nurturing and nourishing your baby but is now yucky, gross, and without a doubt, overstaying its welcome—not to mention, preventing the much-anticipated appearance of your baby's adorable belly button. (It pretty much goes without saying that there's nothing adorable about an umbilical stump.)

The cord stump, which is shiny and moist at birth, usually turns from yellowish green to black, starts to shrivel and dry up, and finally falls off within a week or two—but the big event can occur earlier, or even much later (some babies don't seem to want to give theirs up). Until it does drop off, keep the site dry (no tub baths) and exposed to air (turn diapers down so they don't rub). When it does fall off, you might notice a small raw spot or a small amount of blood-tinged fluid oozing out. This is normal, and unless it doesn't dry up completely in a few days, there is no need for concern.

Unsightly though that cord stump might be, it's unlikely that it's infected—especially if you've been taking care to keep it dry. But be sure to keep a close eye on your baby's healing stump if he was born premature or at a low birthweight, or if the stump falls off early, since research suggests these may increase the risk of a belly button infection.

If you do notice pus or a fluid-filled lump on or near your baby's umbilical-cord stump and a reddish hue around the stump, check with your baby's doctor to rule out infection, which is rare. Symptoms of an infection may also include abdominal swelling, a foul-smelling discharge from the infected region, fever, bleeding around the umbilical-cord stump, irritability, lethargy, and decreased activity. If there is an infection, antibiotics can be prescribed to clear it up.

Umbilical Hernia

"Every time she cries, my baby's navel seems to stick out. What does that mean?"

It probably means that your baby has an umbilical hernia—which (before you start worrying) is absolutely nothing to worry about.

Prenatally, all babies have an opening in the abdominal wall through which blood vessels extend into the umbilical cord. In some cases (for black babies more often than white), the opening doesn't close completely at birth. When these babies cry, cough, or strain, a small coil of intestine bulges through the opening, raising the navel and often the area around it in a lump that ranges from fingertip to lemon size. While the lump might look a little scary (and sound even scarier when you hear it's a hernia), it's likely to resolve on its own eventually, without any intervention. Small openings usually close or become inconspicuous within a few months, large ones by age 2. In the meantime, the best treatment for an umbilical hernia is usually no treatment at all. So definitely don't listen to old-schoolers and others who tell you to tape or bind the hernia down.

Circumcision Care

"My son was circumcised yesterday, and there seems to be oozing around the area today. Is this normal?"

Not only is a little oozing normal, it's a sign that the body's healing fluids are heading to the site to begin their important work. Soreness and, sometimes, a small amount of bleeding are also common after a circumcision and nothing to be concerned about.

Using double diapers for the first day after the procedure will help to cushion your baby's penis and also to keep his thighs from pressing against it—but this isn't usually necessary later. Usually, the penis will be wrapped in gauze by the doctor or mohel (a ritual circumciser of the Jewish faith). Check with your baby's doctor about continuing care—some doctors recommend putting a fresh gauze pad, dabbed with Vaseline, Aquaphor, or another ointment, on the penis with each diaper change, while others don't think it's necessary as long as you keep the area clean. You'll also need to avoid getting the penis wet in a bath (you probably won't be dunking your baby yet anyway, because the umbilical cord is not likely to have fallen off at this point) until healing is complete. Clearly it will get wet when he pees, and that's not a problem as long as you change diapers as needed.

Swollen Scrotum

"Our son's scrotum seems disproportionally huge. Should we be concerned?"

Probably not. Testicles—as you probably know—come encased in a protective pouch called the scrotum, which is filled with a bit of fluid to cushion them. And thanks to exposure to mom's hormones in utero and a little bit of normal genital swelling at birth, a newborn's testicles can look rather large—especially next to his baby-size penis. In some babies the swelling doesn't go down a few days after birth, likely the result of an excessive amount of fluid in the scrotal sac. Called hydrocele, this condition is nothing to worry about since it gradually resolves during the first year, almost always without any treatment.

Ask about your little man's parts at the next doctor's visit, just to be sure it isn't an inguinal hernia (see page 254), which can either resemble a hydrocele or occur along with it. An exam can quickly determine whether the swelling is due to excess fluid or if there is a hernia involved—or both—or whether it's just baby scrotum business as usual. If you notice swelling that seems painful, tenderness, redness, or discoloration, contact the doctor right away.

Hypospadias

"We were just told that the outlet in our son's penis is in the middle instead of the end. What will that mean?"

Every so often, something goes slightly awry during prenatal development of the urethra and the penis. In your son's case, the urethra, the tube that carries urine (and after puberty, semen), doesn't run all the way to the tip of the penis but opens elsewhere. This condition is called hypospadias and is found in an estimated 1 to 3 in 1,000 boys born in the United States. First-degree hypospadias, in which the urethral opening is at the end of the penis but not in exactly the right place, is considered a minor defect and requires no treatment. Second-degree hypospadias, in which the opening is along the underside of the shaft of the penis, and third-degree hypospadias, in which the opening is near the scrotum, can be corrected with reconstructive surgery.

Because the foreskin may be used for the reconstruction, circumcision (even ritual circumcision) is not performed on a baby with hypospadias who will require surgery.

Occasionally, a girl is born with the urethra opening at the wrong place, sometimes into the vagina. This, too, is usually correctable with surgery.

Swaddling

"I've been trying to keep my baby swaddled, like they showed me in the hospital. But she keeps kicking at the blanket, and it gets undone. Should I stop trying?"

Just because swaddling is standard procedure in the hospital doesn't mean it has to be standard procedure at home—especially if your baby's not a fan. Most newborns do love that cocooned feeling of being all wrapped up in a tight little bundle, and will sleep better on their backs when swaddled—especially because they'll startle less. Swaddling also helps ease colic in many babies. But even with all those potential perks, some babies just don't see it that way. For them, being wrapped up is too restrictive, and they'll fight it every time. A good rule: If swaddling seems to feel good to your newborn, do it. If it doesn't, don't. But before you give up on swaddling your little one altogether, see if using a velcro swaddler might keep her from kicking it off, or opt for a zip-up cocoonlike swaddler or a sleep sack (there are also hybrids—swaddlers that have velcro tabs on top and a sack on the bottom). Or try leaving her arms unwrapped to see if that gives her the freedom of movement she seems to crave (and giving her access to her fingers for the comfort she craves) while still providing her with extra stability on her back during sleep.

Once babies become more active, they usually start kicking off or squirming out of their swaddles, no matter what kind. That's a sign to call it quits on swaddling—especially during sleep, since a kicked-off blanket poses a suffocation risk. Continued swaddling can also keep a baby from practicing motor skills—so once a baby stops needing that snug cocoon (usually around 3 to 4 months, though some babies crave the

Outings with Baby

Never again will you be able to leave the house empty-handed—at least not when baby's along. And while you won't always need all these items when you head out with your little one, it's a good idea to pack these essentials in your diaper bag when you're out and about:

A changing pad. If your diaper bag doesn't have one, pack a waterproof pad. You can use a towel or a cloth diaper in a pinch, but they won't adequately protect carpeting, beds, or furniture when you're changing baby away from a changing table.

Diapers. How many depends on how long your outing will be. Always take at least one more than you think you'll need—you'll probably need it if you don't.

Diaper wipes. A small convenience pack is easier to carry than a full-size container, and especially convenient if you can refill it. Or you can use a small ziplock plastic sandwich bag to tote a mini-supply. Wipes aren't just for bottoms, by the way—use them to wash your own hands before feeding baby and before and after changes, as well as for wiping spit-up and baby-food stains from clothing, furniture, or your baby (or you).

Plastic bags. You'll need these for disposing of dirty disposable diapers, particularly when no trash can is available, as well as for carrying wet and soiled baby clothes home.

Formula, if you're bottle-feeding. If you're definitely (or possibly) going to be out past the next feeding with a bottle-fed baby, you'll have to bring a meal along. No refrigeration will be necessary if you take along an unopened single-serving bottle of ready-to-use formula, a bottle of water to which you'll add powdered formula, or a bottle that stores both powder and water separately until you're ready to shake and serve. If, however, you bring along formula you've prepared at home, you'll have to store it in an insulated container along with a small ice pack or ice cubes.

Burp cloths. As any veteran parent knows, a burp cloth can spare you (and others who hold your baby) smelly shoulders.

---

swaddle for longer), it's time to unwrap your baby burrito for good.

Keeping Baby the Right Temperature

"I'm not sure how many layers I need to put on my baby when I go out with him."

Once a baby's natural thermostat is properly set (within the first few days of life), he doesn't need to be dressed any more warmly than you dress yourself. So, in general (unless you're the type of person who's always warmer or colder than everyone else), choose clothing for him that's smaller and cuter, but not heavier, than what you're wearing. If you're comfy in a t-shirt, your baby will be, too. If you're chilly enough for a sweater, your baby will need one as well. Jacket for you? Jacket for your baby.

Still unsure if you've bundled your little bundle just right? Don't check his hands for confirmation. A baby's hands

A change of baby clothes. Baby's outfit is picture-perfect and you're off somewhere special. You arrive, lift your bundle of cuteness from the car seat, and find a pool of loose, mustardy stools has added the outfit's "finishing touch." Just one reason why it's wise to carry along an extra—or two extra—sets of clothing. And while you're thinking about clothing, carry along a sun hat when the sun is shining and a cold weather hat when the weather calls for it.

An extra blanket or sweater. Between seasons? When temperatures fluctuate unpredictably, an additional layer will come in handy.

A pacifier, if baby uses one. Carry it in a clean plastic bag or use one that comes with a cover. Consider packing a spare, too, as well as paci wipes to clean pacis that get dropped (they will).

Toys. For a very young baby, bring along something to look at in the car seat or stroller (mirrors can be magic). For older babies, lightweight toys they can swat at, poke at, and mouth will fill the bill.

Sunscreen. If there's no shade available, use a small amount of baby-safe sunscreen on baby's face, hands, and body (recommended even on babies under 6 months) year-round. Even in winter, snow's glare and sun's rays can combine to cause serious burns.

A snack (or two, or three) for baby. Once solids are introduced, bring along baby food (no refrigeration is needed before it's open, no heating up is needed before serving) if you'll be out during mealtime. Include a spoon stashed in a plastic bag (save the bag to bring the dirty spoon home in), a bib, and plenty of paper towels. Later, you can tote a selection of finger foods such as puffs or rice cakes to pull out as needed. And while you're at it, pack a snack for you, too, especially if you're a breastfeeding mama.

Other must-haves. Depending on your baby's needs, you may want to carry diaper rash ointment or cream, bandaids (especially once baby has started crawling or walking), and any medication your baby is due to be dosed with while you're out (if refrigeration is required, pack with an ice pack in an insulated container).

and feet are usually cooler than the rest of his body, because of his immature circulatory system. You'll get a more accurate reading of his comfort by checking the nape of his neck or his arms or trunk (whichever is easiest to reach under his clothing) with the back of your hand. Too cool? Add a layer. Too warm? Peel one off. If he seems extremely cold to the touch, or dangerously overheated, see page 587.

Don't take the fact that your baby sneezes a few times to mean he's cold either—he may sneeze in reaction to sunlight or because he needs to clear his nose. But do listen to your baby. Babies will usually tell you that they're too cold (the same way they tell you most everything else) by fussing or crying. When you get this message (or if you're just not sure whether you've dressed him appropriately), run that temperature check with your hand and adjust as needed.

The one part of a baby that needs extra protection in all kinds of weather is his head—partly because a lot of heat

Taking Baby Out

Running a cabin fever, but sticking close to home because you're worried your newborn's not ready for the great outdoors (or the great superstore)? Assuming you're up to a field trip yourself (those first couple of postpartum weeks can be pretty grueling), feel free to plan your first escape from home. A healthy, full-term baby is hardy enough to handle any number of excursions—whether it's a stroll in the park or a trip to the market.

When you take baby out, dress him or her appropriately, protect him or her from weather extremes, and always take along an extra covering if there's a possibility of a change for the cooler in the weather. If it's windy or rainy, use a weather shield on the stroller. If it's very chilly or extremely hot and humid, limit the amount of time your baby spends outdoors. Avoid more than brief exposure to direct sunlight, even in mild weather. And, most important, if your outing is in a car, be sure your baby is properly harnessed in a rear-facing infant car seat.

In the first 6 to 8 weeks, do consider a little crowd control—particularly during flu season. Limit exposure to large indoor gatherings—even big family parties where Pass the Baby might be played, exposing your little one to germs.

---

is lost from an uncovered head (especially a baby's head, which is disproportionately large for his body), and partly because many babies don't have much protection in the way of hair. On even marginally cool days, a hat is a good idea for a baby under a year old. In hot, sunny weather, a hat with a brim will protect baby's head, face, and eyes—but even with this protection (plus sunscreen), exposure to full sun should be brief.

A young baby also needs extra protection from heat loss when he's sleeping. In deep sleep, his heat-producing mechanism slows down, so in cooler weather, bring along an extra blanket or covering for his daytime nap in the stroller. If he sleeps in a cool room at night, a toasty blanket sleeper or sleep sack will help him stay warm (quilts and comforters are unsafe coverings for a sleeping baby). Don't, however, put a hat on baby when you put him to sleep indoors, since it could lead to overheating. Ditto for overbundling, particularly when baby is sleeping (do the nape of the neck check again).

When it comes to dressing baby in cold weather, the layered look is not only fashionable, it's sensible. Several light layers of clothing retain body heat more efficiently than one heavy layer, and the outer layers can be peeled off as needed when you walk into an overheated store or board a stuffy bus, or if the weather takes a sudden turn for the warmer.

Touchy Strangers

"Everybody wants to touch our son—the cashier at the pharmacy, perfect strangers in the elevator, random people in line at the ATM. I'm always worried about germs."

There's nothing that cries out to be squeezed more than a new baby. Baby cheeks, fingers, chins, toes—they're all irresistible. And yet resist is just what you'd like others (especially others who are strangers) to do when it comes to your newborn.

Understandably you're touchy about all that uninvited touching—and legitimately concerned about your baby being on the receiving end of so many germs. After all, a very young infant is more susceptible to infection because his immune system is still relatively immature and he hasn't had a chance to build up immunities. So, for now at least, politely ask strangers to look but not to touch—particularly when it comes to baby's hands, which usually end up in his mouth. You can always blame it on the doctor: "The pediatrician said not to let anyone outside the family touch him yet." As for friends and family, ask them to wash their hands before picking up baby, at least for the first month (keep hand sanitizer handy so they can use it before you hand over your baby). Anyone with sniffles or coughs should stay away. And skin-to-skin contact should obviously be avoided with anyone who has a rash or open sores.

No matter what you do or say, expect that every once in a while your baby will have some physical contact with strangers. So if a friendly neighbor tests your child's grasp on his finger before you can stop the transaction, just pull out a diaper wipe and discreetly wash off baby's hands. And be sure to wash your own hands after spending time outdoors and before handling your baby. Germs from outsiders (and from door handles or shopping carts) can easily be spread from your hands to your baby.

As your baby gets older, it will not only be safe to lift the hygiene bubble—it'll be smart. Your little one will need to be exposed to a variety of garden-variety germs in order to start building up immunities to those common in your community. So after the first 6 to 8 weeks, plan to loosen up a little and let the germs fall where they may.

A Summer Rash

It's what many babies are wearing every summer season: heat rash. Also known as prickly heat, its tell-tale tiny red spots on the face, neck, armpits, and upper torso are caused when perspiration builds up because of clogged sweat-gland ducts. Though the rash usually fades on its own within a week, you can treat baby with a cool bath, but avoid powders or lotions that can further block the sweat from flowing. Call the doctor if pustules, increased swelling, or redness develop.

Baby Breakouts

"My baby seems to have little whiteheads all over his face. Will scrubbing help clear them?"

Though you may be surprised—and a little bummed—to find a sprinkling of tiny whiteheads on your sweetie's face where you expected to see baby-soft skin, these blemishes, called milia, are very common (affecting about half of all newborns), temporary, and definitely not a sign of pimple problems to come. Milia, which occur when small flakes of dead skin become trapped in tiny pockets on the surface of your little one's skin, tend to accumulate around the nose and chin, but occasionally show up on the trunk, arms, and legs, and even on the penis. The best treatment? Absolutely no treatment at all. As tempting as it may be to squeeze, scrub, or treat milia, don't. They'll disappear spontaneously, often within a few weeks but sometimes not for a few months or more, leaving your son's skin clear and smooth—that is, unless he comes up against another common baby complexion challenge: infant acne (see the next question).

Baby's Skin Color

Wondering when your mixed-race baby or baby of color will actually turn the color he or she is meant to be? Babies who are destined to be dark-skinned are usually born with light skin—often a shade or two lighter than their color will end up. It could take weeks or months—or in some cases, a few years—before your little cutie shows his or her true colors. Looking for a sign of how pigmented he or she will be eventually? Some parents swear that the ears will clue you in—check out the top of your baby's tiny ears and you'll notice they're darker than the rest of your newborn's skin tone. There's a good chance he or she will end up being close to that color.

"I thought babies were supposed to have beautiful skin. But my 2-week-old girl seems to be breaking out in a terrible case of acne."

Does your baby have more pimples than an eighth grader? Just when she seems ready for her close-up—head rounding out nicely, eyes less puffy and squinty—here comes infant acne. This pimply preview of puberty, which affects about 40 percent of all newborns, usually begins at 2 to 3 weeks (right about the time you were going to schedule that first formal portrait) and can often last until baby is 4 to 6 months old. And believe it or not, as with adolescent acne, hormones are believed to be mainly to blame.

In the case of newborns, however, it's not their own hormones that are probably prompting the pimple problems, but mom's—which are still circulating in their systems. These maternal hormones stimulate baby's sluggish oil glands, causing pimples to pop up. Another reason for infant acne is that the pores of newborns aren't completely developed, making them easy targets for infiltration by dirt and the blossoming of blemishes.

Infant acne isn't the same as newborn milia—the acne is made up of red pimples, while milia are tiny whiteheads. They both, however, call for the same treatment: absolutely none—that is, beyond patience (though some suggest that dabbing the affected area with breast milk can help speed the healing process—and there's no reason not to try that at home if you're breastfeeding). Don't squeeze, pick, scrub with soap, slather with lotions, or otherwise treat your newborn's acne. Just wash it with water two or three times daily, pat it dry gently, and it will eventually clear, leaving no lasting marks—and that beautiful baby skin you've been waiting for in its place. And just in case you're already worrying about your little one's middle school yearbook photos, know that infant acne doesn't predict future pimple problems.

Skin Color Changes

"My baby suddenly turned two colors—reddish blue from the waist down and pale from the waist up. What's wrong with her?"

Watching your baby turn color before your eyes can be unsettling, to say the least. But there's nothing to worry about when a newborn suddenly takes on a two-tone appearance, either side to side or top to bottom. As a result of her immature circulatory system, blood has simply pooled on half of your baby's body. Turn her gently upside down (or over, if the color difference is side by side) momentarily, and normal color will be restored.

You may also notice that your baby's hands and feet appear bluish, even though the rest of her body is pinkish. This, too, is due to immature circulation and usually disappears by the end of the first week.

"Sometimes when I'm changing my new baby, I notice his skin seems to be mottled all over. Why?"

Purplish (sometimes more red, sometimes more blue—it depends on the color of your baby's skin) mottling of a tiny baby's skin when he's chilled, crying, or even (in some babies) all the time isn't unusual. These transient changes are yet another sign of an immature circulatory system, visible through baby's still very thin skin. He should outgrow this colorful phenomenon in a few months. In the meantime, when it occurs, check the nape of his neck or his midsection to see if he is too cool. If so, add a layer of clothing or raise the thermostat. If not, just relax and wait for the mottling to disappear, as it probably will in a few minutes.

Hearing

"My baby doesn't seem to react much to noises. She sleeps right through the dog's barking and my older son's tantrums. Could her hearing be impaired?"

It's probably not that your baby doesn't hear the dog barking or her brother screaming, but that she's used to these sounds. Although she saw the world for the first time when she exited the womb, it wasn't the first time she heard it. Many sounds—from the music you played, to the honking horns and screeching sirens on the street, even

---

How Loud Is Too Loud?

Most babies love music—but that doesn't mean you should pump up the volume, especially when you're in an enclosed area, like the car. A baby may cry when music (or another noise) is too loud, but don't rely on your little one's complaints to tell you when to turn down the sound. A baby's ears, in fact, don't have to be "bothered" to be harmed.

According to the National Institute for Occupational Safety and Health, more than 15 minutes of exposure to 100 decibels is unsafe for an adult. And noise that is hazardous to an adult is even more dangerous to a baby because of the thinner skull and smaller ear canal, which makes the sound pressure entering the ear greater. In fact, an infant might perceive a sound as 20 decibels louder than an adult or older child does, making a toy that emits 90 decibels of sound seem more like 110 decibels to your little one's tender ears—equal to the noise of a power mower, chain saw, or subway train. The bottom line on sound: It's too loud if you can't talk easily over it. Turn it down, or take your baby to a quieter place quickly.

Even white noise machines that are meant to soothe baby with background sounds can be harmful to tiny ears if they're played too loud or positioned too close. To play it safe, place any white noise far from baby's crib, and set volume to low.

---

to the whir of the blender if you were an expectant fan of smoothies—penetrated the walls of her peaceful uterine home, and she became accustomed to them.

Keeping Baby Safe

Babies look pretty fragile, but they're actually pretty sturdy. They don't "break" when you pick them up, their heads don't snap when you forget to support them, and they weather most minor falls without major injury.

Still, babies can be vulnerable, and in ways that parents wouldn't necessarily think. Even a newborn seemingly too tiny to get into trouble sometimes does—rolling off a changing table or a bed long before he or she is mobile. To protect your baby from injuries that don't have to happen, be sure to follow all of these safety tips all of the time:

- In the car, always buckle your baby into a rear-facing infant car seat no matter how far you're going or how fast or slow you'll be driving—and no matter how much baby is crying. Wear a seat belt yourself, and make sure whoever's doing the driving does, too—no one's safe unless the driver is. And never drink and drive (or drive when you're very tired or taking medication that makes you sleepy), text while driving, or talk on a phone that's not hands-free while driving, or let baby ride with anyone who does. (See page 156 for more on car seat safety.)

- Always keep one hand on baby at bath time while you suds and rinse with the other. If you bathe baby in a large tub, put a small towel or cloth at the bottom to prevent slipping.

- Never leave your baby unattended on a changing table, bed, chair, or couch—not for a second. Even a newborn who can't roll over can suddenly extend his or her body and fall off. If you don't have safety straps on your changing table, you should always keep one hand on your baby.

- Never put baby in an infant (or car) seat or carrier on a table, counter, dryer, or any other elevated surface, or leave baby unattended in a seat on any surface, even the middle of a soft bed or sofa (where suffocation is a risk should baby tip over).

- Never leave a baby alone with a pet, even a very well-behaved one.

- Never leave baby alone in a room with a sibling who is under 5 years old. A game of peekaboo affectionately played by a preschooler could result in tragic suffocation for an infant. A loving but overly enthusiastic bear hug could crack a rib.

- Don't leave baby alone with a sitter who is younger than 14, or one you don't know well or whose references you haven't checked. All sitters should be trained in infant safety and CPR (and so should all family members who might be caring for your baby, you included).

Most babies will react to loud noise—in early infancy by startling, at about 3 months by blinking, at about 4 months by turning toward it. But those sounds that have already become a part of the background of a baby's existence may elicit no response—or one so subtle, you might miss it, like a change in her position or activity.

Still concerned about your baby's hearing? Try this little test: Clap your hands behind her head and see if she startles. If she does, you know she can hear. If she doesn't, try again

- Never jiggle or shake your baby vigorously (even in play) or throw him or her up into the air.

- Never leave baby alone at home, even while you go for the mail, move the car, or check the laundry in the apartment building basement. It takes only seconds for an accident to happen.

- Never leave a baby or child alone in a vehicle, not even for a moment. In hot (or even mild) weather, even keeping the windows down might not prevent the baby from succumbing to heatstroke. During winter months, snow can block a car's exhaust pipe, and warming up a car can cause carbon monoxide to back up into the car. A baby left alone in a car during cold weather is also at risk of hypothermia. In any weather, a baby left unattended can be quickly snatched.

- Never take your eyes off your baby when you're shopping, going for a walk, or sitting at the playground. A baby in a stroller or shopping cart makes an easy target for abduction.

- Remove any strings, cords, or ribbons longer than 6 inches from gowns, hoodies, and other baby clothing.

- Avoid using any kind of chain or string on baby or on any of baby's toys or belongings—that means no necklaces, no strings for pacifiers or rattles, no religious medals on chains, and no ribbons longer than 6 inches on cribs or cradles, or anywhere else for that matter. Be sure, too, that baby's crib, play yard, and changing table are not within reach of electrical cords (which present double danger), cords from phones or chargers, or venetian blind or drapery cords. All of these items can cause accidental strangulation.

- Don't place filmy plastics, such as dry-cleaner bags or other plastic bags, on mattresses, the floor, or anywhere baby can get at them.

- Never leave an unattended infant within reach of pillows, stuffed toys, or plush items, or let baby sleep on a sheepskin, plush-top mattress, beanbag, waterbed, or a bed wedged against the wall. Always remove bibs and any hair ties or barrettes before putting baby down to sleep.

- Consider keeping a fan on in baby's room during sleep. Research suggests that the circulating air may reduce the risk of SIDS.

- Remove crib gyms and mobiles once baby can get up on hands and knees (around 4 to 6 months).

- Do not place baby on any surface next to an unguarded window, even for a second, and even when baby's asleep.

- Use smoke detectors and carbon monoxide detectors in your home, and install them according to fire department recommendations.

later—children (even newborns) have a wonderful way of ignoring or blocking out their environment at will, and she may have been doing just that. A repeat test may trigger the response you're looking for. If it doesn't, try to observe other ways in which your baby may react to sound: Is she calmed or does she otherwise respond to the soothing sounds of your voice, even when she isn't looking directly at you? Does she respond to singing or music in any way? Does she startle when exposed to an unfamiliar loud noise?

If your baby seems never to respond to sound, check in with the doctor. Most newborns are screened routinely for hearing problems before leaving the hospital (see page 124), so it's likely that yours was screened and found to be fine—but it's always best to ask if you're not sure whether your baby was screened or what the results were. The earlier hearing deficit is diagnosed and treated, the better the long-range outcome.

Vision

"I put a mobile over my baby's crib, hoping the colors would be stimulating. But he doesn't seem to notice it. Could something be wrong with his eyesight?"

It's more likely there's something wrong with the mobile—at least, where it's located. A newborn baby focuses best on objects that are between 8 and 12 inches away from his eyes, a range that seems to have been selected by nature not randomly, but by design—it being the distance at which a nursing infant sees his mother's face. Objects closer to or farther away from a baby lying in his crib will be nothing but a blur to him—though he'll fixate on something bright or in motion even in the distance if there's nothing worth looking at within his range of vision. Your baby will also spend most of his time looking to his right or left, rarely focusing straight ahead or overhead in the early months. So a mobile directly above his crib isn't likely to catch his attention, while one hung to one side or the other may. But even a mobile hung in the right place may not move your baby, at least not right away. Most babies don't pay attention to mobiles at all until they're closer to 3 to 4 weeks or even older, and others will always find something better to look at.

Even though your newborn's vision is a work in progress (it will take several months for his focus to mature, and he won't be able to perceive depth well until 9 months), he still loves to look. And gazing at the world is one of the best ways he has of learning about it. So what should you give him to look at besides his favorite sight—you? Most young babies like to study faces—even crudely drawn ones, and especially their own in crib mirrors (though they won't recognize them as their own until well after their first birthday). Anything with high contrast, such as patterns of black and white or red and yellow, will capture more attention than subtle ones, and simple objects will score more than complex ones. Light is a baby mesmerizer—whether it's from a ceiling track, a lamp, or a window (especially one through which light is filtered via the slats of blinds).

Vision screening will be part of your baby's regular checkups. But if you think your baby doesn't seem to be focusing on well-located objects or faces or doesn't turn toward light, mention this to his doctor at the next visit.

Crossed Eyes

"The swelling is down around my baby's eyes. Now she seems cross-eyed."

What looks like crossed eyes is probably just extra folds of skin at the inner corners of those precious peepers. If that's the case, which it usually is with newborns, the skin will retract as your baby grows, and her eyes will probably begin to seem more evenly matched. During the early months, you may also notice that your baby's eyes don't work in perfect unison all the time. These random eye movements mean she's still learning to use her eyes and strengthening her eye muscles. By

3 months, coordination should be much improved.

Check with the pediatrician if you don't notice any improvement in her eye coordination, or if her eyes always seem to be out of sync. If there is a possibility of true crossed eyes (strabismus, in which the baby uses just one eye to focus on what she's looking at, and the other seems aimed anywhere), consultation with a pediatric ophthalmologist is in order. Early treatment is important, because so much that a child learns she learns through her eyes, and because ignoring crossed eyes could lead to "lazy" eye, or amblyopia (in which the eye that isn't being used becomes lazy, and consequently weaker, from disuse).

Teary Eyes

"At first, there were no tears when my baby cried. Now her eyes seem filled with tears even when she's not crying. And sometimes they overflow."

Tiny tears don't start flowing out of the tiny eyes of newborns until close to the end of the first month. That's when the fluid that bathes the eye (aka tears) is produced in sufficient quantity by the glands over the eyeballs. The fluid normally drains through the small ducts located at the inner corner of each eye, and into the nose (which is why a lot of crying can make your nose run). The ducts are particularly tiny in infants, and in about 1 percent of babies—yours included—one or both are blocked at birth.

Since a blocked tear duct doesn't drain properly, tears fill the eyes and often spill over, producing the perpetually "teary-eyed" look even in happy babies. But the clogged ducts are nothing to worry about. Most will clear up by themselves by the end of the first year without treatment, though your baby's doctor may show you how to gently massage the ducts to speed up the process or suggest you drop a little breast milk into the eye to help clear the clog. (Always wash your hands thoroughly first before using massage. If baby's eyes become puffy or red, stop massaging and tell the doctor.)

Sometimes, there is a small accumulation of yellowish white mucus in the inner corner of the eye with a tear duct blockage, and the lids may be stuck together when baby wakes up in the morning. Mucus and crust can be washed away with water and cotton balls. A heavy, darker yellow discharge and/or reddening of the whites of the eye, however, may indicate infection or another condition that requires medical attention. The doctor may prescribe antibiotic ointments or drops, and if the duct becomes chronically infected, may refer your baby to a pediatric ophthalmologist. Call the doctor if a tearing eye seems sensitive to light or if one tearing eye looks different in shape or size from the other.

Sneezing

"My baby sneezes all the time. He doesn't seem sick, but I'm afraid he's caught a cold."

New babies have plenty to sneeze at besides colds. For one thing, sneezing is a protective reflex that allows your baby to clear out amniotic fluid and excess mucus that might be trapped in his respiratory passages. Frequent sneezing (and coughing, another protective reflex) also help him get rid of foreign particles that make their way into his button nose from his environment—much as sniffing pepper makes many adults sneeze. Your baby may also sneeze when exposed to light, especially sunlight.

First Smiles

"Everybody says that my baby's smiles are 'just gas,' but she looks so happy when she does it. Couldn't they be real?"

No new parent wants to believe that baby's first smiles are the work of a passing bubble of gas—not a wave of love meant especially for mommy or daddy. But scientific evidence so far seems to back up this age-old buzz kill: Most babies don't smile in the true social sense before 4 to 6 weeks of age. That doesn't mean that a smile is always "just gas." It may also be a sign of comfort and contentment—many babies smile as they are falling asleep, as they pee, or as their cheeks are stroked.

When baby does reveal her first real smile, you'll know it (your baby will engage her whole face in the smile, not just her mouth), and you'll melt accordingly. In the meantime, enjoy those glimpses of smiles to come—undeniably adorable no matter what their cause.

Hiccups

"My baby gets the hiccups all the time. Do they bother him as much as they do me?"

Some babies aren't just born hiccupers, they're hiccupers before they're born. And chances are, if your baby hiccuped a lot on the inside, he'll hiccup plenty in the first few months on the outside, too. What causes those hiccups? One theory is that they're yet another in baby's repertoire of reflexes. Another theory is that infants get hiccups when they gulp down formula or breast milk, filling their tummies with air. Later on, giggles may bring on the hiccups. Whatever the trigger, hiccups don't bother your baby. If they bother you, try letting your baby breastfeed or suck on a bottle or pacifier, which may quell the attack.

ALL ABOUT:

Baby Development

First smiles, first coos, first time rolling over, first unassisted sit, first attempt at crawling, first steps. Your little one's first year is a baby book of momentous milestones just waiting to be filled out. But when will your little one reach those milestones, you wonder? Will that first smile come at an impressively early 4 weeks . . . or a wait-for-it 7? Will your baby roll ahead when it comes to rolling over—or lag behind? Sit out crawling? Or run circles around the babies in the neighborhood before they've even pulled up to a stand? And is there anything you should do—or can do—to speed up your baby's progress on the developmental road ahead?

The truth is that while every baby is born tiny and cute, each develops differently—at a pace that seems less influenced by nurture than hardwired by nature. Every little one comes programmed with a timetable of development that specifies the arrival of many important skills and achievements. And while parents can definitely nurture along the schedule that nature has already set (or hold baby back from meeting those milestones by withholding nurture), many of the spaces in that developmental baby book were filled out before your baby was even born.

Infant development is usually divided into four areas:

The Pattern of Development

How will your baby grow and develop physically? Only your baby's DNA knows for sure—and it isn't telling. But here's something you can count on and look for while you're waiting to fill in those blanks. While every baby develops physically at a different rate, each child's development—assuming it isn't being held back by environmental or physical factors—follows the same basic patterns. First, a baby develops from the top down, from head to toes. Babies lift their heads up before they can hold their backs up to sit, and hold their backs up to sit before they can stand on their legs. Second, they develop from the trunk outward to the limbs. Children use their arms before they use their hands, and their hands before they use their fingers. Physical development also progresses, not surprisingly, from the simple to the complex.

Social. Babies arrive a little lump-like—but happily, they don't stay that way for long. By 6 weeks, most babies express their first truly social skill: smiling. But even before that, they're priming for a life of engagement and interaction with other humans (starting with mommy and daddy)—making eye contact, studying faces, and tuning in to voices. Some babies are more socially outgoing from the start, while others are naturally more serious and reserved—personality traits that come courtesy of their genes. Even so, the more social stimulation a baby receives, the faster those social skills will develop. A major delay in social development that goes beyond individual differences in personality could indicate a problem with vision or hearing, or another developmental issue that may need some watching. It could also be a product of baby's environment—maybe because he or she isn't getting enough eye contact or smiles or conversation or close cuddling that's needed to develop socially.

Language. A little one who's working a large vocabulary at an early age or who speaks in phrases and sentences way before his or her baby peers is probably going to have a way with words. But the tot who relies on pointing to make a point or grunts to make a request well into the second year may catch up and do just as well or even better later on. Since receptive language development (how well baby understands what is said) is a better gauge of progress than expressive language development (how well baby actually speaks), the little one who says little but understands much isn't likely to be experiencing a developmental delay. Again, very slow development in this area occasionally indicates a vision or hearing problem and should be evaluated.

Large motor development. Some babies seem physically active (make that, perpetually in motion) from the first kicks in the womb. Once born, they keep packing a physical punch—holding their heads up at birth, crawling by 6 months, walking by 9 months. But many slow starters make quick strides later on, steadily catching up and even gaining on those early movers and shakers. Very slow starters, however, should be evaluated to be certain there are no physical or health obstacles to normal

Making Time for Tummy Time

Keeping your baby safe means never forgetting "back to sleep." But keeping your baby on target with developmental milestones means also remembering the flip side of back-to-sleep: tummy-to-play. The AAP recommends tummy time play with your baby two to three times a day for about 3 to 5 minutes (though you may need to start out with fewer minutes and may find you can work up toward more). Special mats are available, but a blanket and (if you want) a soft, rolled towel under baby's chest will work just as well. The best—and coziest—place for your baby to do tummy time right from the start? Lying on your tummy or chest. Remember: back-to-sleep, tummy-to-play.

Baby hates tummy time? Check out page 250 for tips on making it more enjoyable for your little one.

development (which early intervention can often overcome fast).

Small motor development. Reaching for, grasping, and manipulating objects—everything your baby does with those adorable fingers and hands—is considered small motor development, but it's no small task. Coordinating those early movements between eyes and hand isn't easy for babies—which means your little one will eye that rattle long before he or she can grasp it with those tiny hands (and finally, figure out how to shake it). Early eye-hand coordination may predict your baby will be good with his or her hands—but a baby who takes longer to fine-tune fine motor development isn't necessarily going to be "all thumbs" later on.

What about your baby's smarts? Don't overthink it—or even give it a first thought—at this tender age. Most indicators of intellectual development (creativity, sense of humor, and problem-solving skills, for example) don't even come into play—or into your child's play—until at least the end of the first year. Think of them as intellectual gifts just waiting to be unwrapped. While DNA means your baby arrives hardwired with certain strengths, nurturing all sides of your little one means you'll be helping him or her reach (or exceed) that baked-in intellectual potential. And among the best ways to nurture your newborn's brain power are the simplest and most intuitive ways: making eye contact with your baby, talking and singing to your baby, and reading to your baby early (starting from birth) often (making it a treasured daily ritual right from the beginning).

Another thing to keep in mind while your baby's busy making milestones: The rate of development in different areas is usually pretty uneven. Just as some adults are social butterflies and others are physical busy bees, different babies have different strengths, too, and may zoom ahead in one area (smiling at 6 weeks or talking up a storm at a year) but lag behind in others (not reaching for a toy until 6 months or not walking until a year and a half).

Something else to remember: Babies tend to concentrate on learning one skill at a time, and while they're learning it, they're laser-focused on it—which often means that already mastered skills or skills they've been dabbling in will be temporarily shelved. A baby may be blasé about babbling when he's practicing pulling up. Or she may be sidetracked from sitting when she becomes all-consumed with crawling. Once a skill is mastered, another moves to center stage—and your baby may even seem to forget the last skill while forging ahead on the next. Eventually, your little one will be able to integrate all those various skills—new, old, and yet to be conquered—and use each spontaneously and appropriately. Even then, some skills will be left behind—because, well, your baby has moved on.

No matter what your little one's rate of development ends up being—no matter how quickly those spaces in that baby book (or app) get filled out, and in what order—what is accomplished in the first year is nothing short of amazing. Never again will so much be learned so quickly.

With the emphasis on quickly—since the first year will be over a lot faster than you'd probably imagine right now. Keep an eye on your baby's development, but don't let watching that timetable (or the timetable of the baby down the block) keep you from enjoying the incredible days, weeks, months, and years of growing and developing that lie ahead. And don't

Today's Slower Babies

Something you should definitely keep in mind when that compulsion to compare gets the best of you (and it will): Babies today are developing later in some major gross motor skill categories than they used to. Not because they're less naturally precocious, but because they're spending less time on their tummies. Putting babies to sleep on their backs dramatically reduces the risk of SIDS, but it also temporarily slows motor development in some babies. With little opportunity to practice those skills babies used to practice on their tummies (such as crawling), more babies are accomplishing these skills later. Many are even skipping the crawling stage entirely (which is no problem, since it's not considered a developmental must-do).

forget, your baby is one of a kind. For a developmental timeline, see page 106.

CHAPTER 7

The Second Month

Chances are there have been plenty of changes around your house in the last month—not counting all those diaper changes (too many to count anyway). Changes in your baby, who's steadily progressing from cute-but-unresponsive to active-and-alert, who's sleeping a little less and interacting a little more. And changes in you, as you evolve from fumbling rookie to semi-seasoned parenting pro. After all, just weeks into your new gig, you're probably an old hand at one-handed diapering, have burping (baby) down pat, and can latch that little mouth onto your breast in your sleep . . . and often do.

But while life with baby may be settling into a somewhat more predictable (though still exhausting) routine, there will be lots to keep you guessing (and making frequent calls to the doctor)—like crying spells, cradle cap, and diaper contents, to name a few. So the challenges of caring for a newborn continue—but happily, the perks of parenting are soon to be multiplied. This month you'll be getting a reward for all those sleepless nights and all that floor walking: your baby's first truly social smile!

Feeding Your Baby: Introducing the Supplemental Bottle

Sure, breastfeeding's ideal—the very best way to feed a baby. But as easy and practical as it can be, it does have its logistical limitations, the most significant one being that you can't breastfeed your baby unless you're with your baby. And that's where the bottle often comes in.

Thinking of skipping the bottle? Some exclusively breastfeeding moms

Baby Basics at a Glance: Second Month

Sleeping. Your baby is slowly starting to understand the difference between day and night, meaning more of those z's will be caught when it's dark outside. Still, baby will spend plenty of each day napping, and total sleep hours won't change much from last month. Expect baby to sleep 14 to 18 hours (in a 24-hour day), with about 8 to 9 hours at night and 7 to 9 hours during the day (in about 3 to 5 naps).

Eating. It's an all liquid diet for your little one:

- Breast milk. Baby will nurse 8 to 12 times every 24-hour period, taking in a total of 12 to 36 ounces of breast milk. Feeding may start to spread out a little now—every 3 to 4 hours, though demand feeding is still the way to go, especially for the breast-fed set.

- Formula. Baby will be drinking about 3 to 6 ounces of formula 6 to 8 times per 24 hours, for an approximate total of 18 to 32 ounces of formula. Want a better estimate? Multiply your baby's weight by 2.5.

The answer will give you an idea of roughly how many ounces of formula to feed over a 24-hour period.

Playing. Baby's starting to smile this month (yay!) and showing excitement when people are nearby. Mobiles and play gyms are still favorite toys for little ones, but you can also add small stuffed animals and rattles to the mix. Wrap baby's tiny fingers around the rattle and he or she will probably keep a tight grip on it—at least for a minute or so. Gently shake baby's hand so the rattle makes noise. Another new toy for baby this month: a baby-safe soft-framed mirror. Your little one will have no idea who he or she is looking at, but will be fascinated by that adorable face staring (and smiling) back nonetheless.

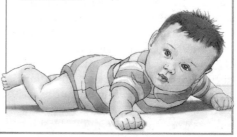

do—ultimately saving themselves and their babies a step in the weaning process (arguably the toughest one: giving up the bottle). But skipping the bottle entirely relies on staying within arm's reach of your baby for all those first-year feeds—an organizational feat that many breastfeeding moms can't manage. Planning (or hoping) to be away from your baby during at least some feedings during the first year—whether for a 40-hour workweek or a 3-hour dinner date twice a month? Or just want to keep your options open, so

you can have some feeding flexibility? Then plan on introducing a bottle, if you haven't already.

What's in the Bottle?

Breast milk. Filling a bottle with expressed breast milk is usually uncomplicated (once you're a pumping pro) and allows you to feed your baby a breast-milk-only diet—even when your breasts and baby aren't in the same place at the same time.

Bottle-Free

Thinking about going bottle-free? As long as you can organize your life and your lifestyle to fit a bottle-free first year, there's no need to bring on the bottle (or to push it if baby just won't take the bottle bait). That said, it's always good to have a backup plan—and a backup supply of breast milk in case of an emergency (you're called out of town unexpectedly, for instance, or you're temporarily taking medication that isn't safe for breast-feeding babies). So consider pumping and freezing a small stash of breast milk just in case (you may need to replace the emergency cache as it expires; see page 178 for time limits on frozen breast milk).

Formula. Supplementing with formula is obviously as easy as opening a bottle or a can—and many moms find they can successfully combine breastfeeding and formula feeding (there's even formula that's specially designed for supplementation). But offering formula too soon, before breastfeeding is well established (usually by around 6 weeks), can create problems with your milk supply, so it's best to hold off on supplemental formula until then, unless it's medically necessary. And some moms choose not to introduce formula at all, either because they're determined to breastfeed for a year or longer (studies show a link between formula supplementation and early weaning) or to try avoiding an allergy to cow's milk formula when there's a family history of allergies.

Winning Baby Over

Ready to offer that first bottle? If you're lucky, baby will take to it like an old friend, eagerly latching on and lapping up the contents. Or, maybe more realistically, your breast fan may take a little time to warm up to this unfamiliar food source. Keeping these tips in mind will help win baby over:

- Time it right. Wait until your baby is both hungry (but not frantically so) and in a good mood before giving a bottle for the first time.

- Hand it over. Your baby is more likely to accept the first few bottles if someone other than you offers them—preferably when you and your milk aren't within sniffing distance.

- Keep it covered. If you have to offer that first bottle yourself, it may help to keep your breasts under cover. Bottle-feed braless or in a thin or low-cut t-shirt, and your baby will be too close to the goods.

- Pick the right nipple. Some breastfed babies take to any shape bottle nipple the first time it's offered. Others balk at the unfamiliar shape and texture that feels very different from mama's own. If your baby resists a particular nipple after several tries, try one with a different design (for instance, one that mimics the shape and pliability of a human breast and nipple). If your baby takes a pacifier, a nipple that's similar in shape and feel may do the trick.

- Dribble some on. To help baby figure out what's in the bottle, shake a few drops onto the nipple before offering it.

- Warm it up. Your nipples come already warmed, bottle nipples do not. Try dipping the nipple in warm water just before offering it, to take off the chill. Warming the bottle contents (whether you're serving formula or expressed breast milk) may help, too—though it's not necessary if baby is fine with room temperature or even straight-from-the-fridge.

- Be a sneak. If you keep meeting bottle resistance, sneak it in during sleep. Pick up baby toward the end of a nap, and offer the bottle before your little dreamer is fully awake. Hopefully, he or she will be too sleepy to notice. Once you've gained sleepy acceptance, you can try when baby's alert.

Making the Introduction

When to begin. Some babies have no difficulty switching from breast to bottle and back again right from the start, but most do best with both if the bottle isn't introduced until at least 2 to 3 weeks. Earlier than this, bottle-feedings may interfere with the successful establishment of breastfeeding (not so much because of so-called "nipple confusion," but because your breasts won't be stimulated enough to pump up supply). Wait much later than this,

Supplementation Myths

Myth: Supplementing with formula (or adding cereal to a bottle) will help baby sleep through the night.

Reality: Babies sleep through the night when they are developmentally ready to do so. Bringing on bottles of formula or introducing cereal prematurely won't make that bright day (the one when you'll wake up realizing you had a full night's sleep) dawn any sooner.

Myth: Breast milk alone isn't enough for my baby.

Reality: Exclusively breastfeeding your baby for 6 months provides him or her with all the nutrients your little one needs. After 6 months, a combo of breast milk and solids can continue nourishing your growing baby well without adding formula.

Myth: Giving formula to my baby won't decrease my milk supply.

Reality: If you choose to do the combo (see page 90), go for it. But if you're hoping to breastfeed exclusively (or even mostly), it's important

to remember that any time you feed something other than breast milk to your baby (formula or solid food), your milk supply drops. It's a simple supply-demand calculation: The less breast milk your baby takes, the less milk your breasts make. But waiting until breastfeeding is well established can minimize the effect of those diminishing returns from supplementary bottles.

Myth: Breastfeeding is an all or nothing proposition.

Reality: You want to breastfeed your baby but aren't sure you're willing to do it exclusively (or perhaps you're unable to do it exclusively). Combining breast milk and formula isn't only possible, for some moms and their babies it's the best of both worlds, and it's definitely a whole lot better than giving up on breastfeeding altogether. So feel good about doing the combo, making sure to fit in enough breastfeedings so your milk supply doesn't drop too much and remembering that any amount of breast milk your baby gets is a bonus.

Mix It Up

Don't have enough expressed milk to make up a complete bottle? No need to throw all that hard work down the drain. Instead, mix formula with the expressed milk to fill the bottle. Less waste— and your baby will be getting enzymes from the breast milk that will help digest the formula better.

and baby might reject rubber nipples in favor of mama's soft, warm, familiar ones.

How much breast milk or formula to use. Breastfeeding automatically controls intake—allowing baby to eat to appetite, not to the specified number of ounces you're pushing. Bring on the bottle, and it's easy to succumb to the numbers game. Resist. Give your baby only as much as he or she is hungry for, with no prodding to finish any

particular amount. Remember—there are no absolutes when it comes to how much formula or breast milk to feed your little one at each meal. The average 9-pounder may take as much as 6 ounces at a feeding, or less than 2. Looking for a little more guidance? A very rough general rule of thumb is to take your baby's weight and multiply it by 2.5—that's the total number of ounces to feed your baby over the course of a 24-hour period. See page 302 for more.

Getting baby used to the bottle. If your schedule will require you to regularly miss two feedings during the day, switch to the bottle one feeding at a time, starting at least 2 weeks before you plan to go back to work or school. Give your baby a full week to get used to the single bottle-feeding before moving on to two. This will help not only baby adjust gradually, but your breasts, too, if you'll be supplementing with formula instead of pumping and feeding breast milk. The ingenious supply-and-demand mechanism that controls milk

Supplementing When Baby Isn't Thriving

Most of the time, breast milk alone provides all the nourishment a tiny body needs to grow and thrive on. But once in a while, a mom's breast milk supply just can't keep up with all of her baby's needs—no matter how she tries to pump it up. If the doctor has recommended offering supplementary formula because your baby isn't doing well on breast milk only, following that advice will most likely get your little one back on track soon. But how do you beef up your milk supply

while you're beefing up your baby with formula, so you can eventually fill all of your baby's nutritional needs without supplementation? The best solution may be using a supplemental nutrition system (SNS), shown on page 184, which provides a baby with the formula he or she needs to begin thriving while stimulating mom's breasts to produce more breast milk. SNS not working for you? Check out the other tips for pumping up your milk supply on page 93.

production will cut back the amount as you do, making you more comfortable when you're back on the job or in class.

Keeping yourself comfortable. If you plan to give a bottle only occasionally—say for your Saturday date night or for a weekly class—feeding baby thoroughly (or expressing) from both breasts before heading out will minimize uncomfortable fullness and leakage. Make sure your baby won't be fed too close to your return (less than 2 hours is probably too close) so you can breastfeed as soon as you get home . . . and before you burst.

Even if you'll be supplementing with formula, keep in mind that you'll probably need to express milk if you will be away from your baby for more than 5 or 6 hours, to help prevent clogging of milk ducts, leaking, and a diminishing milk supply. The milk can be either collected and saved for future feedings or tossed.

What You May Be Wondering About

Smiling

"My son is 5 weeks old and I thought he would be smiling real smiles by now, but he doesn't seem to be."

Cheer up . . . and smile. Even some of the happiest babies don't start true social smiling until 6 or 7 weeks of age. And once they start smiling, some are just naturally more smiley than others. How will you be able to tell a real social smile from those early gas-passing ones (or those "I just peed and it feels so good" ones)? Easy: by the way the baby uses his whole face to smile, not just his mouth—and by the way that tentative, gummy grin instantly melts your heart into a puddle of slush.

That first smile (and all the smiles that follow) will be worth waiting for. Just remember, while babies don't smile until they're ready, they're ready faster when they're talked to, played with, kissed and cuddled, and smiled at . . . a lot. The more you smile at your baby, the faster he'll be matching you grin for grin.

Cooing

"My 6-week-old baby makes a lot of breathy vowel sounds but no consonants at all. Is she on target speechwise?"

With young babies, the ayes (and the a's, e's, o's, and u's) have it. It's the vowel sounds they make first, somewhere between the first few weeks and the end of the second month. At first the breathy, melodic, and insanely cute cooing and throaty gurgles seem totally random. But then you begin to notice they're directed at you when you talk to your baby, at a stuffed animal who's sharing her play space, at a mobile beside her that's caught her eye, or at her own reflection in the crib mirror. These vocal exercises are often practiced as much for her own pleasure as for yours—babies actually seem to love listening to their own voices. And while she's at it, your sweet talker is also conducting a series of verbal experiments, discovering which combinations of throat, tongue, and mouth actions make what sounds.

How Do You Talk to a Baby?

Your baby's a sponge for your mother (and father) tongue—soaking up every syllable that's spoken around him or her. That said (and said, and said again), your little one's speech will develop faster and better if you nurture it. Here are some of the many ways you can talk your baby into talking:

Do a blow-by-blow. Don't make a move, at least when you're around your baby, without talking about it. Narrate the dressing process: "Now I'm putting on your diaper . . . here goes the t-shirt over your head . . . now I'm pulling up your pants." In the kitchen, put your spin on salad making—and don't forget to toss the conversation back to your baby. During the bath, dish on soap and rinsing, and explain that a shampoo makes hair shiny and clean. Baby doesn't get it? Of course not—but that's not the point. Blow-by-blow descriptions help get you talking and baby listening—and ultimately, understanding.

Ask a lot. Don't wait until your baby starts having answers to start asking questions. The questions can be as varied as your day: "Would you like to wear the red pants or the green ones?" "Isn't the sky a beautiful blue today?" "Should I buy green beans or broccoli for dinner?" Pause for an answer (one day your baby will surprise you with one), and then supply the answer yourself, out loud ("Broccoli? Good choice").

Give baby a chance. Studies show that infants whose parents talk with them rather than at them learn to speak sooner. Give your baby a chance to get in a coo, a gurgle, or a giggle. In your running commentaries, be sure to leave some openings for baby's comments.

Keep it simple—some of the time. It's fine to recite the Gettysburg Address if you want (baby will love listening to anything), but as he or she gets a bit older, you'll want to make it easier to pick out individual words. So at least part of the time, make a conscious effort to use simple sentences and phrases: "See the light." "Bye-bye." "Baby's fingers, baby's toes." "Nice doggie."

Put aside pronouns. It's difficult for a baby to grasp that "I" or "me" or "you" can be mommy, or daddy, or grandma, or even baby, depending on who's talking. So most of the time, refer to yourself as Mommy or Daddy and to your baby by name: "Now Daddy is going to change Madison's diaper."

Raise your pitch. Most babies prefer a high-pitched voice, which may be why female voices are usually naturally

---

For you, this adorable cooing is a welcome step up from crying on the communication ladder—and just the first step of many. By about 3 to 4 months, baby will begin adding laughing out loud, squealing, and a few consonants to her repertoire. The range for consonant vocalizations is very broad—some babies make a few consonant-like sounds in the third month, others not until 5 or 6 months, though 4 months is about average.

"Our baby doesn't seem to make the same kind of cooing sounds that his older brother made at 6 weeks. Should we be concerned?"

higher pitched than male voices—and why most mom (and dad) voices instinctively climb an octave or two when they talk to their newborns. Try raising your pitch when talking directly to your baby, and watch the reaction. (A few infants prefer a lower pitch, so experiment to see which appeals to yours.)

Bring on the baby talk . . . or not. If the silly stuff ("Who's my little bunny-wunny?") comes naturally to you, babble away in baby talk—after all, babies eat it up. If you'd prefer to keep it simple yet dignified, that's fine also. Even if you're big on baby talk, try not to use it exclusively. Toss some more adult (but still simple) English into your baby-side chats, too, so that your little one won't grow up thinking all words end with y or ie.

Be present (tense). As your little one's comprehension develops, stick more to the here and now—what baby can see or is experiencing at the moment. Young babies don't have a memory for the past or a concept of the future—and a change in tense won't make sense for many months to come.

Ape your little monkey. Babies love the flattery that comes with imitation, so be a mommy or daddy mimic. When baby coos, coo back. Answer that breathy "ah" with an equally breathy "ah." Not only will you be playing baby's soon-to-be favorite game, but you'll be reinforcing those first attempts at talking,

and that will only encourage more of the same . . . and better.

Set it to music. Don't worry if you can't carry a tune—babies don't know their sharps from their flats, and they don't much care. Your baby will love your singing whether it's pitch perfect or off-key, rock or rap, techno or R&B, or a horrible hybrid. Remember some nursery rhymes from your own nursery days? Even young infants will be engrossed by Mother Goose. (Drawing a blank? Let Google jog your memory, or make up some silly ditties of your own, with hand gestures for double the fun.) Develop a playlist—you'll soon see which songs rock your baby's world most. And sing them again and again.

Read aloud. It's never too early to begin reading some simple board books out loud. In fact, the AAP recommends reading daily to baby from birth. Craving some adult-level reading material? Share your love of literature (or recipes or gossip or politics) with your little one by reading what you like to read, aloud. The words will go over your baby's head—but straight into those ears (and that brain).

Take your cues from baby. Everyone needs some quiet time—newborns included. When your baby tunes out, turns away, or cranks up the crankies, that's a signal that his or her verbal saturation point has been reached, and that it's time to give your voice (and baby's ears) a rest.

There's no comparison when it comes to your baby, or at least there shouldn't be. That's because no two babies share the same developmental schedule, even when they share the same pair of parents—and even when it comes to something as seemingly simple as cooing. About 10 percent of babies produce their first

coos before the end of the first month and another 10 percent not until nearly 3 months—while the rest commence cooing somewhere in between. Either way, your baby's still well within the norm, even if he's lagging a little behind his brother.

And speaking of brothers, it could be that you're so busy in your fuller

Understanding Your Baby

It'll probably be almost a year before your baby speaks that first recognizable word, 2 years or more before words are strung into phrases and then sentences, longer still before most of those sentences are easily comprehensible. But long before your baby is communicating verbally, he or she will be communicating in a variety of other ways. In fact, look and listen closely now, and you'll find that your baby's already trying to speak to you—not in so many words, but in so many behaviors, gestures, and facial expressions.

There is no dictionary of baby communication that can translate what your baby's saying (though there are apps that claim to). To really understand your baby, you'll need to sit back and watch. Observation will speak louder than words—and will speak volumes about your little one's personality, preferences, needs, and wants months before word one is actually spoken.

Watch: Does your baby wiggle and fuss uncomfortably when she's undressed before her bath? Maybe it's the cold air on her naked body that's making her squirm—or maybe it's just the sensation of being naked. Keeping her covered as much as possible before lowering her into the bath may ease her discomfort.

Or does your baby always make coughing sounds right around the time he's ready for a nap? Coughing might be your baby's heads-up that he's getting sleepy—an early warning to clue you in before early fatigue melts down into crankiness.

Or does your baby frantically stuff her fist into her mouth when she's due for a feeding, before she starts wailing loudly? That could be her hunger cue—her first message to you that she's ready to eat (the second message, crying, will make the feeding much more difficult for both of you to accomplish). By observing your baby's behaviors and body language, you'll notice patterns that will start to make sense—and will help you make sense of what baby's telling you.

Taking the time to watch, listen to, and discern your baby's nonverbal cues won't only make your job of providing care easier, but it'll make your baby's job of taking on the world easier. Knowing that what he or she has to say matters will boost not only your baby's language development, but also his or her confidence, sense of security, and emotional maturity, not only now, but in the lifetime that lies ahead.

house that you're not really noticing your new baby's verbal achievements—or that you're not spending as much time cultivating coos as you did in round one (as often happens with second babies). Or that between your older son and the rest of the family making so much noise, your littlest one can't get a coo in edgewise (also common when baby makes four or more). Take a little more time to focus on engaging your new baby in conversation, and you may well be rewarded with the coo you've been waiting for.

If it seems to you over the next several months that your baby consistently—in spite of extra encouragement—falls far below the monthly milestones in the first year timeline (see page 106), speak to his doctor about your concerns. A hearing evaluation or other tests may be in order to rule out a delay.

A Second Language

"My wife wants to speak Spanish (her native language) to our baby so he picks it up early on. I'd love for him to learn a second language, but wouldn't it be less confusing to learn one at a time?"

If babies can be considered sponges for language, then babies in bilingual households can be considered extra-absorbent sponges. So let the soaking up begin. Most experts agree that speaking two languages to your baby from the start allows your little one to "acquire" a second language along with the first as opposed to merely "learning" it, as would be the case if it were introduced later. That's a powerful distinction, since it's the difference between being a native speaker in two languages and merely being fluent in a second language. What's more, teaching your little guy Spanish now capitalizes on the bilingual head start he received in utero (from the sixth month of pregnancy on, when your wife spoke Spanish, your son heard it).

Some suggest that learning two languages at once can slow a child in both, but if it does, that would be only a very temporary blip in his verbal development (balanced out by the significant benefits of being bilingual and having a natural affinity for learning languages likely to last a lifetime).

Either way, no need to roll out Rosetta Stone. There are a couple of simple approaches to helping your baby learn two languages in the time most babies learn a single language. Probably the most effective: You speak English exclusively to your baby while mom speaks Spanish exclusively to him. A somewhat less effective approach: A grandparent, sitter, or au pair can speak Spanish while you both speak English. And probably the least practical of the approaches (which probably would slow down English skills considerably): You both speak Spanish (assuming you are fluent—anyone who speaks to your baby in Spanish should be fluent in it), and your baby picks up English at daycare, preschool, or from a sitter.

As for curriculum, keep it natural. Teach a second language to your baby as you teach the first—through talking, reciting nursery rhymes, and singing; reading books, playing games, and watching movies; visiting friends and relatives who speak it; and if possible, visiting places where the language is native (especially if it is your wife's homeland, since you'll be imparting a sense of heritage along with those language skills). Later, you can consider a bilingual preschool program or playdates with other bilingual children to reinforce the acquired language skills.

At first, your baby will go through some periods of mixing his two languages (both equally new)—and that will be incredibly cute, but it shouldn't be concerning. Eventually your son (and hijo) will be able to keep his two languages equal . . . but separate.

Baby Won't Sleep on Back

"I know I should put my baby to sleep on his back to protect against SIDS, but he sleeps terribly that way. Once, when I put him on his tummy to play, he fell asleep and took his longest nap ever. Is it safe to switch?"

Often babies know what's best for them. But unfortunately, they don't usually get it right when it comes

Making the Most of the First Three Years

Your baby won't remember much about the first 3 years of life, but according to researchers, those 3 years will have a huge impact on the rest of his or her life—in some ways, more than any of the years that follow.

What makes those first 3 years—years filled primarily with eating, sleeping, crying, and playing—so vital to your child's ultimate success in school, in a career, and in relationships? How can a period of time when your little one is so clearly unformed so clearly influence the formation of the full-size human being he or she will eventually become? The answer is fascinating, complex, and still evolving—but definitely food for new-parent thought.

Research shows that a child's brain grows to 90 percent of its adult capacity during those first 3 years—granted, a lot of brainpower for someone who can't yet tie his or her shoes. During these 3 phenomenal years, brain "wiring"—when crucial connections are made between brain cells—takes place. By the third birthday (likely, before your little one can read word one), about one thousand trillion connections will have been made.

With all this activity, however, a child's brain is very much a work in progress at age 3. More connections are made until age 10 or 11, but by then the brain has started specializing for better efficiency, eliminating connections that are rarely used (this pattern continues throughout life, which is why adults end up with only about half the brain connections a 3-year-old has). Changes continue to take place well past puberty, with important parts of the brain still continuing to change throughout life.

While your baby's future (like his or her brain) will be far from fully shaped at age 3, a whole lot of molding will have gone on—in large part, thanks to the nurturing you'll be busy doing. Research shows that the kind of care a child receives during those first 3 years helps determine how well brain connections are made, how much that little brain will develop, and how content, how confident, and how capable of handling life's challenges that child will be. And that's where you (and your loving arms) come in.

Feeling a little overwhelmed by the responsibility that's been handed to

to sleeping position. Most babies naturally prefer the tummy position for sleep—it's more comfortable, it's cozier, and it makes them less likely to startle and less likely to wake themselves up. All of which makes for a sounder night's sleep and a longer, more restful nap.

But clearly, tummy sleeping isn't best for baby. It's linked to a much higher incidence of SIDS—particularly in babies who aren't used to being on their tummies (because, like yours, they started out on their backs from birth). Most babies get used to the back position quickly, especially if they've never known another sleeping position, others continue to fuss a bit on their backs, and a few, like yours, don't seem able to settle down for a good night's sleep when they're tummy up. Almost all babies would sleep more soundly on their tummies given the chance, which is one of the possible reasons why experts suggest SIDS is more likely to strike tummy-sleeping babies. Because you in a neat, sweet, swaddled little package? Don't be. Most of what any loving parent does intuitively (with no training, and without the addition of flash cards or educational apps) is exactly what your child—and your child's brain—needs to develop to his or her greatest potential. In other words, it doesn't take rocket science to help today's baby become tomorrow's rocket scientist (or science teacher . . . or doctor . . . or Internet entrepreneur). It's much simpler than that. Consider:

- Every bit of nurturing you do—all that touching, holding, cuddling, hugging, and responding, all that reading, talking, singing, eye contact, and cooing—helps build your baby's brainpower and boost his or her social and emotional skills. And for most parents, nurture is second nature.

- Every time you meet your little one's basic needs now and in those early years to come (your baby gets fed when hungry, changed when wet, held after a scare), you're helping him or her develop trust, empathy, and self-confidence—all key ingredients to a healthier emotional and social future. Kids who know they're cared for and cared about have fewer behavioral problems and stronger relationships.

- Healthier kids are happier, smarter kids. Regular medical care ensures your little one will be screened for any medical or developmental issues that could slow intellectual, social, or emotional growth (early intervention can help make all the difference). Regular exercise boosts brainpower, too—as does getting enough z's (babies do a lot of their developing while they sleep). And eating regularly (and well) fuels all the growth and development that goes on in those early years.

- You're helping to shape, not trying to manipulate. It's easy for encouragement to cross the line to pushing— but when in doubt, check with your baby. Babies should always be the last word (even before they've spoken their first word) on how much stimulation is enough and how much is too much. Take your cues from your little one—who, when it comes to getting what he or she needs, can be wise beyond even your years. Watch and listen carefully, and you'll almost always know what's best for your baby.

infants sleep more deeply on their tummies, their arousal responses are muted, possibly preventing them from waking up during episodes of sleep apnea and resuming normal breathing patterns. That's why you'll need to have your baby's back when it comes to sleep position.

The first thing you should do is discuss the problem with your pediatrician. He or she might want to look into why your baby dislikes the back position so much. It's rare, but occasionally a baby has a physical or anatomical reason that makes being on his back unusually uncomfortable. Much more likely, your baby just plain doesn't like the way it feels. If that's the case, try some of these tips for keeping your baby happy on his back:

- Swaddle for sleep. Research shows that infants who are swaddled before they're put on their backs cry less— and sleep better. Wrapped into a tight little bundle, they're also less likely to startle and be woken up by those normal, jerky movements. But don't swaddle once your baby is active enough to kick off the swaddling blanket (loose bedding in the crib poses a safety hazard). Some babies manage to wriggle from their wrapping as early as the second month, though if your little one stays put, you can keep swaddling. Sleep sacks (or a swaddle-sack hybrid) can't be kicked off, so they're considered safer longer. Also make sure the room is cool enough when you're swaddling (and that you haven't overbundled baby in the swaddle or sack), since overheating is another risk factor for SIDS.

- Prop it up. Try propping up the head of the mattress slightly (with a pillow or rolled blanket *under* the mattress) so baby isn't flat on his back—at an incline, he may be inclined to sleep longer. But don't prop baby with any pillows or other soft bedding inside the crib.

- Pass up positioners. If you're thinking about using a positioner or wedge (or rolled blankets) to keep baby on his back or side, think again. Experts agree that any type of sleep positioner or wedge is unsafe and should never be used. Not only don't positioners and wedges prevent SIDS (as manufacturers claim), but they also pose a serious suffocation risk.

- Back up your position. Slowly train your baby to be more comfortable sleeping on his back. If falling asleep in that position is tough for him, try rocking him to sleep before transferring him to the crib once he's asleep (on his back).

- Stick with it. Consistency almost always pays off when it comes to babies. Eventually, he'll probably get used to sleeping on his back.

Once your baby can roll over by himself, chances are he'll flip over into his preferred sleeping position even when you've put him down on his back, and that's okay (see page 358).

Trouble with Tummy Time

"My baby hates tummy time. How do I get him to like it?"

You can lead a baby to his tummy, but often, it's hard to make him happy on it. For a lot of little ones, tummy time can seem like torture time—particularly before they've developed the muscles they need to lift their heads out of that awkward face plant position. Still, just a few minutes of tummy play a few times a day will give your baby the opportunity to flex a different set of muscles than he'll work on his back—muscles he will eventually need in order to master a variety of skills, including sitting up. To make tummy time less torture and more fun, try these tricks (and don't forget, tummy time should always be closely supervised):

- Put him tummy down on your chest while you do your sit-ups. Add some funny faces and silly noises with each rep. Every so often, lift him, airplane style, and then return him for a belly touchdown.

- Lie on your bellies together, side by side or face-to-face, on a comfy surface—just make sure it's not so cushy that your baby can't push up easily. Then entertain him with a special toy or just coo at each other.

- Give him a lift—on a specially designed tummy time pillow or spinner. A tummy time mat can also keep things interesting.

- Add a mirror image. A baby-safe floor mirror will provide him with a distracting image of himself. Vary the position—in front of him, then to either side.

- Vary locations—and the view from his tummy. Try the family room for a minute or two in the morning, your bedroom in the afternoon.

- If he enjoys a good rubdown, try massaging him while he's on his belly. He may relax long enough to clock in some solid tummy time.

- Have someone else try tummy time with him—believe it or not, he may already be sensing too much performance pressure from you.

- If he won't take the belly bait, give him a belly break—and try again later. There's no good reason to force tummy time when he's screaming for release—and there's a very good reason not to (he'll only resist more the next time). A minute or two (or whatever his limit seems to be) is plenty to start, with the goal of gradually stretching each tummy time session by a few seconds until you've worked up to a solid 5 minutes.

- In between tummy time sessions, make sure he gets lots of other opportunities to work his muscles. Too many stints cooped up in a stroller, car seat, or bouncy seat can keep him from getting a move on.

Baby Massage

"I've heard that massaging a baby is good for her, but I have no idea how to do it."

Everybody craves a soothing rubdown every now and then, and most babies are no exception. A gentle massage not only feels good to newborns, it does their little bodies good, too. Of the five senses, touch is the one that's most developed at birth—and research suggests that stimulating the sense of touch through massage comes with enormous benefits.

What kinds of benefits? It's well known that preemies who are massaged regularly grow faster, sleep and breathe better, and are more alert. But massage also appears to help full-term babies thrive—possibly strengthening the immune system, improving muscle development, stimulating growth, easing colic, alleviating tummy troubles and teething pain, promoting better sleep patterns, stimulating the circulatory and respiratory systems, and decreasing stress hormones (yes, babies have those, too). And, just as cuddling does, massage boosts parent-baby bonding. Plus, massage isn't relaxing for just your baby—giving one can help you find your own inner zen, too (and who can argue with that?).

Here's how to rub your little one the right way:

Pick a time that's relaxing for you. The massage won't have the soothing effect you're after if your cell is ringing, dinner's burning on the stove, and you have two loads of laundry going. Choose a time when you're unhurried and unlikely to be interrupted.

Pick a time that's relaxing for baby. Don't massage baby when she's hungry (she won't enjoy the belly rubs if her belly's empty) or too full (she'll likely spit up). Right after a bath is a perfect time, when baby has already started to relax (unless bath time is a high stress time). Before playtime is another possibility, since babies have been shown to be more focused and attentive after a massage.

Set a relaxing scene. The room you select for the massage should be quiet and warm, at least 75°F (since baby

For Parents: A Father's Touch

Think only mom has that special touch when it comes to baby? Not so. Research shows that a dad's touch has an equally positive effect on a baby's health, well-being, and development (massage has been linked to fewer sleep problems and better digestion in babies, among many other physical and emotional perks). And baby's not the only one who stands to gain from a daddy's touch. Fathers who learn to soothe their babies through massage see their own stress levels drop, get a parental self-esteem boost, and develop deeper bonds with their newborns that continue through childhood. The proof is in the hormones: Dads release as much of that nurture hormone, oxytocin, as moms do when they get close to their babies through touch.

will be undressed except for a diaper). Dim the lights to reduce stimulation and enhance relaxation, and add soft music if you like. You can sit on the floor or bed and lay baby on your lap or between your open legs, using a towel, a blanket, or a pillow covered by a towel or blanket under her. While you work, talk or sing softly.

Lubricate, if you like. Sure, you don't need oil to rub your little one the right way, but it'll be more enjoyable for both of you if your hands glide easily over your baby's body. Use a natural baby massage oil, or reach for straight-up coconut, canola, corn, olive, grape seed, apricot, avocado, or safflower oil. These oils are easily absorbed into a baby's skin—and easily digested when your little one sucks on her hands or fingers. Use only a dab, and stay away from baby oil or mineral oil—they clog the pores. And nix nut oils, too, because of the potential for allergies. Warm the oil or lotion a little between your hands before you start rubbing baby.

Experiment with techniques. In general, babies prefer a gentle touch—but usually not so light that it's ticklish. As you work, always keep one hand on your baby. Here are a few ideas to get you started:

- Gently place both of your hands on either side of your baby's head and hold for a few seconds. Then stroke the sides of her face, continuing down the sides of her body to her toes.

- Make tiny circles on baby's head with your fingers. Smooth baby's forehead by gently pressing both hands from the center outward.

- Stroke baby's chest from the center outward.

- Stroke baby's tummy from top to bottom using the outer edge of one hand, then the other, in a circular motion. Then, let your fingers do the walking across your baby's tummy.

- Gently roll baby's arms and legs between your hands or use firmer, deep strokes to "milk" those sweet limbs. Open those curled-up hands and massage those little fingers.

- Rub baby's legs up and down, alternating hands. When you get down to the feet, massage them, uncurling and stroking baby's toes.

- Turn baby on his tummy, and stroke his back from side to side, then up and down.

Another smart tip from the infant massage playbook: Stroking away from the heart (from shoulder to wrist, for example) is relaxing, and therefore better suited for pre-nap or pre-bedtime massages. Stroking toward the heart (from wrist to shoulder) is more stimulating and better suited for when your baby will be awake and active. You can also do a combo.

Take your cues from baby. No one likes to be massaged when they're not in the mood, and that's true for babies as well. If baby turns away or cries when you lay your hands on, save the session for later. And remember, you don't have to give a full-body massage every time. If your baby decides enough's enough after you've rubbed only her legs and feet, that's okay, too.

Cradle Cap

"I wash my daughter's hair every day, but I still can't seem to get rid of the flakes on her scalp."

There's definitely nothing cute about cradle cap—but happily, there's nothing permanent about it, either. Cradle cap, a seborrheic dermatitis of the scalp that's very common in young infants, usually begins in the first 3 months and may linger as long as a year (though more often, it runs its flaky course by 6 months)—but it doesn't predict a lifetime of dandruff. Mild cradle cap, in which greasy surface scales appear on the scalp, often responds well to a brisk massage with mineral oil or petroleum jelly to loosen the scales, followed by a thorough shampoo to remove them and the oil. There are also natural shampoos and treatments specially made for baby cradle cap—and different products work for different babies. That natural wonder product, breast milk, may also ease the flakes. Check with the doctor if your baby has a case that won't respond to any of these treatments (with heavy flaking and/or brownish patches

and yellow crustiness), which may benefit from the daily use of an antiseborrheic shampoo that contains selenium or salicylic acid (there are some no-tear brands). Since cradle cap usually worsens when the scalp sweats, keeping it cool and dry may also help—so skip the hat unless it's sunny or cold out and then remove it when you're indoors or in a heated car.

Sometimes cradle cap goes away, then returns—in which case, bringing back the same treatment should bring back that downy, flake-free scalp. When cradle cap is severe, the seborrheic rash may spread to the face, neck, or buttocks. If this happens, the doctor will probably prescribe a topical cortisone cream or ointment.

Crooked Feet

"Our son's feet seem to fold inward. Will they straighten out on their own?"

Your little one's feet definitely wouldn't stand out in a crowd of newborns. Most babies appear bowlegged and pigeon-toed, and for good reason: One, the cramped quarters in the uterus often force one or both feet into odd positions, resulting in a rotational curve in the legs. When a baby emerges at birth, after spending several months folded up in that position, the feet are still bent or seem to turn inward. In the months ahead, as your baby's tootsies enjoy the freedom of life on the outside—and as he learns to pull up, crawl, and then walk—his feet will begin to straighten out.

The doctor has probably already checked your baby's feet to make sure all is well, but another check to ease your mind won't hurt—so ask at the next well-baby visit. Keep in mind, too, that it's routine for the doctor to keep an eye on the progress of a baby's feet to make sure they straighten out as he grows—which yours almost certainly will without any treatment.

Undescended Testicles

"My son was born with undescended testicles. The doctor said that they would probably drop down from his abdomen by the time he was a month or two old, but they haven't yet."

The abdomen may seem a strange location for testicles, but it isn't. The testicles (or testes) in males and the ovaries in females both develop in the fetal abdomen from the same embryonic tissue. The ovaries, of course, stay put. The testes are scheduled to descend through the inguinal canals in the groin, into the scrotal sac at the base of the penis, somewhere around the eighth month of gestation. But in 3 to 4 percent of full-term boys and about one-third of those who are preterm, they don't make the trip before birth. The result: undescended testicles.

Because of the migratory habits of testicles, it's not always easy to determine that one hasn't descended. Normally, the testicles hang away from the body when they are in danger of overheating (protecting the sperm-producing mechanism from temperatures that are too high). But they slip back up into the body when they are chilled (protecting the sperm-producing mechanism from temperatures that are too low) or when they are handled (again protective, to avoid injury). In some boys the testes are particularly sensitive and spend a lot of time sheltered in the body. In most, the left testicle hangs lower than the right, possibly making the right seem undescended. For that reason, the diagnosis of undescended testicle or testicles is made only when one or both have never been observed to be in the scrotum, not even during a warm bath.

An undescended testicle causes no pain or difficulty with urinating, and as your doctor assured you, usually moves down on its own. By age 1, only 3 or 4 boys in a thousand still have undescended testicles, at which point surgery (a minor procedure) can easily put them in their proper place.

Penile Adhesion

"My baby was circumcised, and my doctor says he's developed a penile adhesion. What does that mean?"

Whenever tissues of the body are cut, the edges will stick to the surrounding tissue as it heals. After the foreskin of the penis is removed during a circumcision, the circular edge remaining tends to stick to the penis as it heals. If a significant amount of foreskin remains after the circumcision, it, too, can stick to the penis during the healing process, causing the foreskin to reattach. This penile adhesion is not a problem as long as it's gently retracted periodically to prevent it from becoming permanently attached. Ask the doctor how you should do this or if it's really necessary to do at all. When boys, even baby boys, have erections (which they do all the time), the sticking skin surfaces are pulled, helping to keep them apart without any intervention.

In rare cases, the bridge of skin permanently attaches, and a urologist may eventually need to separate the skin and remove the remaining piece of foreskin to prevent the problem from recurring.

Inguinal Hernia

"The pediatrician said that my twin boys have inguinal hernias and will have to have surgery. Is this serious?"

Hernias aren't unusual in newborns, particularly boys, and especially those born prematurely (as twins often are). In an inguinal hernia, a part of the intestines slips through one of the inguinal canals (the same channels through which the testes descend into the scrotum) and bulges into the groin. The hernia is often first noticed as a lump in one of the creases where the thigh joins the abdomen, usually when a baby is crying or very active (it often retracts when he's calm). When the section of the intestines slips all the way down into the scrotum, it can be seen as an enlargement or swelling in the scrotum, and may be referred to as scrotal hernia. Should you notice a lump in your baby's groin, report it to the doctor as soon as possible.

A hernia doesn't usually cause any discomfort, and while it must be treated with surgery, it isn't considered serious or an emergency (which means you can relax). Doctors usually recommend repair as soon as the hernia is diagnosed—assuming the baby is strong and healthy enough to undergo surgery. The surgery is usually simple and successful, with a very short (sometimes one day) hospitalization. Only very rarely does an inguinal hernia recur after surgery, though in some little ones, another hernia occurs on the opposite side later on.

If a diagnosed infant inguinal hernia is not treated, it can lead to the herniated section becoming "strangulated"— pinched by the muscular lining of the inguinal canal, obstructing blood flow and digestion in the intestines. Call the doctor immediately if you notice any of the symptoms of strangulation (crying in pain, vomiting, not having bowel movements, and possible shock). If the doctor can't be reached, take the baby (or babies) to the nearest emergency room. Elevating baby's bottom slightly and applying an ice pack while en route to the ER may help the intestine to retract, but don't try to push it back in by hand.

ALL ABOUT:
Stimulating Your Baby's Senses

Welcome to the world, baby—a world of sights, sounds, smells, tastes, touches, and textures, some of them comforting, some of them confusing, all of them stimulating to an infant's brand new set of senses. How do you help your little one make sense of those senses—and of the big, sometimes overwhelming world around him or her? Chances are you're already helping plenty, without even trying (or knowing what you're doing—after all, you're new at this, too). Most nurturing comes naturally—which means you'll instinctively give your baby's senses the workout they need to develop to their greatest potential. Just remember, it's a process—one that's just getting started, and one you should never rush or push. Here are a few ways to stimulate your brand new little bundle's brand new little senses. (Also see "Making the Most of the First Three Years," page 248.)

The sense of taste. Right now you don't have to go out of your way to stimulate this sense. Your baby's taste buds get a buzz at every meal on breast or bottle. But as your little one gets bigger, "tasting" will become a way of exploring, and everything within reach (sometimes edible . . . more often, not) will end up being mouthed. Resist the temptation to discourage this—except, of course, when what goes into your baby's mouth is toxic, sharp, dirty, or small enough to choke on.

The sense of smell. In most environments, an infant's keen smelling apparatus gets plenty of workouts. There's breast milk or formula, dad's shaving cream, Rover scampering nearby, the flowers in the park, the bagel you're toasting. Unless your baby shows signs of being supersensitive to odors, think of all these scents as yet another opportunity to learn about the environment.

The sense of sight. Babies can see from the moment they're born—if a bit fuzzily—and are able to learn from their sense of sight right from the start. Through their eyes they learn very quickly to differentiate between objects and human beings (and between one object or human being and another), to interpret facial expressions (mommy's smile!), body language (daddy's open arms!) and other nonverbal cues, and to understand a little bit more every day about the world around them.

What's visually stimulating to your newborn (besides your face)? In general, sharp contrasts and designs that are bold and bright catch a very little one's eyes more than ones that are soft, delicate, or nuanced. Black and white and other strong color contrasts are favored for the first 6 weeks or so, while pastels and other colors become appealing later on.

Many objects, toys among them, can be visually stimulating to your baby. Just keep in mind that more is not more—your baby may become overwhelmed and overstimulated if there are too many toys or other objects competing for his or her visual attention:

- Mobiles. Hang mobiles no more than 12 inches (the distance at which newborns see best) over your little one's face, on one side or the other of baby's line of vision, rather than straight above (most babies prefer to gaze toward the right, but check to see if yours has a preference). Musical mobiles, an age-old nursery favorite, stimulate two senses at the same time.

- Other things that move. You can move a rattle, a stuffed animal, a finger puppet, or other bright toy across baby's line of vision to encourage tracking of moving objects. Position baby in front of a fish tank (or a crib aquarium, or a dream catcher that's caught a breeze). Or blow bubbles for baby.

- Stationary objects. Babies spend a lot of time just looking at things—and that's time well spent. Geometric patterns or simple faces in black and white, hand-drawn or store-bought, are early favorites—but baby will probably also be fascinated by everyday objects you wouldn't glance at twice (like a cut-glass vase shimmering in the sunlight).

- Mirrors. Mirrors give babies an everchanging view, and babies usually love looking at themselves in one—and socializing with the cutie looking back, even though they have no clue yet who that cutie is. Be sure to use unbreakable, baby-safe mirrors, and hang them on the crib, in the stroller, beside the changing table, in the car. Or place your baby in front of a mirror (or beside it) for tummy time entertainment.

- People. Babies delight in looking at faces close up (especially at that magical 8 to 12-inch range), so spend lots of time getting your face in baby's face. Later, you can also show baby family photos, pointing out who's who.

- Books. Show baby simple pictures of babies, children, animals, or toys, and identify them. The drawings should be clear and sharply defined without a lot of extra (for a baby) detail. Boldly illustrated board books are perfect for this.

- The world. Very soon your baby is going to take an interest in seeing beyond that little button nose. Provide plenty of opportunity to see the world—from the stroller, or car seat, or by carrying your baby face forward once he or she has good head control. Add commentary, too, pointing out cars, trees, people, and so on. Baby's tuning you out? Time to turn off your tour guide mode.

The sense of hearing. Hear this: It's through the sense of hearing that your baby will learn language, about cadence and rhythm, about feelings (including empathy), about danger—and about much more that goes on in the world around him or her. Let your baby's ears hear all about it through:

- The human voice. This, of course, is the most significant sound in a new infant's life, so use yours a lot—talk, sing, and babble to your baby. Try lullabies, nursery rhymes, silly lyrics you create yourself. Imitate animal sounds, especially ones your baby regularly hears, such as the barking of a dog or the meowing of a cat—or go to town with Old MacDonald's whole farm. Most important, parrot the sounds baby makes to reinforce those verbal efforts. And read to your baby early and often.

- Sounds around the house. They're nothing new to you (in fact, you've probably become pretty adept at tuning them out), but household sounds can be captivating to a young baby: the hum of the vacuum cleaner or the dryer, the whistle of the teakettle or the splash of running water, the crinkling of paper or the tinkling of a bell or wind chime. One sound that baby's better off not hearing around the house: the TV. Try to keep it off when baby's awake.

- Rattles and other toys that make gentle sounds. You don't have to wait until your baby is able to shake a rattle to get rolling. In the early months, you can shake while baby watches and listens, put the rattle in baby's hand and help shake it, or attach a wrist rattle. Coordination between vision and hearing will develop as baby learns to turn toward sound. An activity center that baby can swat or kick at and activate sounds from (if inadvertently) can be entertaining to those ears, too.

- Musical toys. Music is music to your baby's ears, no matter what the source—a music box, a teddy that plays tunes, a musical activity center for the crib, a play mat that makes musical sounds. Toys that do triple duty (make music, provide visual stimulation, and offer practice with fine motor skills), such as a brightly colored toy that plays a sound when squeezed or pushed, are three times the fun, though baby will need your help with the squeezing or pushing for now. Avoid toys that make very loud noises that can damage hearing, and don't place even moderately noisy ones right by baby's ear. Also be sure that the toys are otherwise safe for baby (no strings attached, no batteries that can work their way out of the toy and into baby's mouth).

- Background music. All of life is a sound track for your baby's eager ears, but why not add some background music, too? Play a medley of

Early Learning Made Simple

Simply put, it's the simple things in your baby's new life that mean the most and have the greatest impact on development. Here's all you need to know to help your baby learn all he or she needs to know about the world right now (and hint: It's a lot easier than you'd think).

Love your baby. Here's a baby-brain-power-boosting no-brainer: Nothing helps a baby grow and thrive as much as being loved unconditionally. You may not always be in love with your baby's behavior (say, when a 4-hour colic bout or a string of sleepless nights or a feeding strike brings you to the edge), but you'll always love your baby, no matter what—and that's what will make your baby feel safe and secure, no matter what.

Relate to your baby. Yes, your baby is, well, a baby—and you're an adult. But that doesn't mean you can't relate to each other. Take every opportunity to talk, sing, or coo to your baby—while you're changing a diaper, giving a bath, shopping for groceries, or driving the car. These casual yet stimulating exchanges aren't meant to instruct (baby's way too young for that), but to interact. A few choruses of "The Farmer in the Dell" will go a lot further in making a brighter baby than any educational toy or program. And speaking of toys, don't forget your little one's favorite plaything—the one that will give him or her the biggest development boost of all: you.

Get to know your baby. Learn what makes your baby happy or miserable, excited or bored, soothed or stimulated (or overstimulated)—paying more attention to that feedback than to the advice of any book, website, app, or expert (remember, your baby is the expert when it comes to getting what he or she needs). Gear stimulation to your one-of-a-kind baby. If being loud and raucous rocks the baby boat, entertain with soft sounds and gentle play. If going easy on his or her senses at playtime puts your little one to sleep, pump up the party with a little more baby-appropriate action.

Give your baby space. Of course your baby needs attention, and lots of it—just remember, it is possible to get too much of that good thing. When stimulating attention crosses that fine line to hovering, your baby misses opportunities to tune out of the Parent Channel (all peekaboo, all the

music in your home—anything from classical to classic rock to country, R&B to reggae, tango to techno—and base encores on what genres baby responds to best. Try tot tunes, too—the more repetition in the choruses (and the sillier), the better. And as you stimulate baby's sense of hearing, protect it, too, by keeping the volume down (if it's too loud to talk over, it's too loud, period).

The sense of touch. Sight and hearing may get all the buzz, but touch is one of a baby's most indispensable senses—invaluable in exploring and learning about the world. It's through touch that a baby learns the softness of mommy's face and the relative roughness of daddy's, that the dog's ear and the teddy bear's belly feel velvety, that air blowing from a fan feels tickly, that water feels warm and wet, that nothing feels better time) and to tune in other interesting sights and sounds in his or her environment—the friendly-looking fuzzy caterpillar on the infant seat toy bar, the pattern of light and shadow cast by the blinds, his or her own fingers and toes, an airplane overhead, a fire engine down the street, the dog barking next door. By all means engage your baby—just not on an endless loop. Sometimes, just for a change of pace and a taste of independence, just get baby and toy together, then watch them get acquainted.

Follow the leader. Make sure your baby, not you, is in the lead. If he's got his eye on the mobile, no need to mobilize the crib mirror. If she's content batting at the activity board, no reason to bring on the rattle. Of course, your baby won't be endlessly self-entertaining (realistically, he or she will max out after a moment or two), which means that you'll be directing most of the activities for now, but don't forget who's ultimately in charge of playtime ... and learning time.

Let your baby take the lead, too, in deciding when to end a play session— even if it's before the rattle is reached for. Your baby will tell you, "I'm over this" by turning away, fussing, or crying. That's your signal to switch off the stimulation.

Time it right. A baby is always in one of six states of consciousness: deep (or quiet) sleep, light (or active) sleep, drowsiness, quiet wakefulness, active wakefulness, or fussiness and crying. It's during active wakefulness that you can most effectively encourage physical feats and during quiet wakefulness that you can best nurture other types of learning (see pages 260–261). Also keep in mind that infants have very short attention spans—so when your baby seems to lose interest in your moo-if-you're-a-cow routine after just a fleeting moment of focus, it's only because he or she has run out of concentration.

Cheer your baby on. Nothing motivates like positive reinforcement. So don't hold back the applause, the cheers, the hugs, and the smiles when your baby practices or accomplishes a new skill. No need to bring down the house—just to let your baby know: "I think you're awesome!"

Apply no pressure. There's no overstating it: Pressure doesn't have a place in early learning, especially this early on. Don't get caught up in developmental milestones—get caught up, instead, in your baby's sweet smile and those breathy coos aimed at you. So relax, enjoy, and think of the time you spend stimulating your baby as fun first, foremost ... and really, only.

than a cuddle, and that those who care for him or her are loving (that's the message you send with every tender touch).

You can provide more varied touching experiences for your baby with:

- A loving hand. Try to learn how your baby likes to be handled—firmly or lightly, quickly or slowly. Most babies love to be caressed and kissed, to have their tummies tickled or razzed by

your lips, to have you blow gently on their fingers or toes. They love the difference between mommy's touch and daddy's, the playful way a sibling hugs, the expert ease of grandma's rocking. And skin to skin (kangaroo care) is always in.

- Massage. Preemies who are massaged for at least 20 minutes daily gain weight faster and do better overall

Developing the Fun Way

You can't help but help your baby develop—it's what parents do intuitively (with all that talking, singing, holding, cuddling, and of course all those games of "clap hands" and "stinky feet"). Here's a roundup of infant development and how to nurture your little one's progress the fun way—which for babies is the only way:

Social development. Your baby becomes a social being long before ever hitting the playground or joining a playgroup—mostly thanks to you, your baby's first, most important, and most favorite playmate. It's through interacting with you (and watching you interact with others) that your baby begins to learn giving and taking, caring and sharing, treating others the way you'd like to be treated, and all the rules of social engagement (including using those magic words, and practicing those p's and q's). Don't buy that baby's paying attention yet? Just wait: A few years from now, you'll hear your example echoed in that tiny voice as your little one plays with friends or talks to adults.

Toys that help babies with social development include stuffed animals, animal mobiles, and dolls—watch your baby cooing with the animals prancing on a play mat or revolving on a mobile, and you'll see how.

Small motor development. Right now your baby's hand movements are totally random, but in a couple of months, those tiny hands will move with more purpose and control. You can help develop those purposeful movements by giving your baby's hands plenty of freedom—don't always keep them tucked into a blanket or swaddled or covered in mitts. Look for toys that don't require a lot of dexterity, that baby can manipulate inadvertently (shaking a wrist rattle or swatting at an activity board), and eventually, that those tiny hands and fingers can grasp and pick up (offer those from the side, since young babies usually won't reach for objects that are directly in front of them). Give your baby ample opportunity for "hands-on" experience with the following:

- Rattles that fit small hands comfortably. Start with wrist rattles, then move on to those with two handles or grasping surfaces, which will eventually allow a baby to pass the rattle from hand to hand, an important skill. Rattles a baby can mouth will help bring relief when teething begins.

- Play gyms or bars (they fit across a stroller, play yard, or crib) that have a variety of parts for baby to grab hold of, spin, pull, and poke. Avoid any, however, with strings more than 6

than those who aren't. But your baby doesn't have to arrive early to benefit from a loving touch—all babies do. Discover the kind of strokes your baby enjoys most, and avoid those that seem to annoy (see page 251 for tips).

- Fabric fun. Try rubbing a baby's skin with different textures (satin, silk, terry cloth, velvet, wool, faux fur, cotton) so he or she can get to know how each feels. Put baby tummy down (while supervised) on surfaces with different textures: the living room inches long, and take down any gym once your baby is able to sit up.

- Activity boards that require a wide range of hand movements to operate. Your baby may not be able to intentionally maneuver the toy for a while, but even a young infant can sometimes set it in motion accidentally. In addition to the spinning, dialing, pushing, and pressing skills these toys encourage, they teach the concept of cause and effect. Lights, sounds, and movements will captivate your little one.

Large motor development. For your baby, getting a move on depends on freedom of movement—after all, a baby who's always cooped up in a swing, baby seat, jumper, or stroller, or swaddled in a blanket or bunting, will have little chance to flex those mini muscles and practice those big motor moves. Change your baby's position often during the day (from propped in a sitting position, to tummy-down, to tummy-up) to maximize the opportunities for different kinds of physical activity. As baby's motor skills (and head control) rev up, put your little mover through the paces by making movement interactive: Gently pull baby to a sitting position (and give a kiss when he or she arrives), "fly" him or her in your arms to encourage those cute arms and legs to wiggle, or give your little one a ride by lying on your back, placing him or her facedown lengthwise on your shins, and slowly lifting your legs (knees bent) up and down. As baby gets closer to the rolling stage (around 3 to 4 months) give rolling over a boost—and a little motivation—by placing a favorite toy or eye-catching object at baby's side. Chances are your rock and roller will turn to the side a bit—and then you can give a little help by nudging baby all the way over (sweet success!).

Intellectual development. Everything your baby sponge soaks up through those budding senses boosts brainpower, but your baby will learn the most from you—and, once again, from interactions that come naturally. Talk to your infant a lot, right from the start. Give names to objects, animals, and people your baby sees. Identify your eyes, nose, and mouth (and baby's hands, fingers, feet, and toes). Detail the groceries you're plucking from the shelf and plunking into your cart. Read nursery rhymes and simple stories, showing your baby the illustrations as you go. Expose your little one to a variety of settings (stores, the museum, the park). Even at home, vary your baby's point of view: Hold baby near a window or in front of a mirror, lay baby in the middle of the living room carpet to survey the action or in the middle of the bed (supervised) to watch you fold the laundry, or park the swing in the kitchen while you make yourself a snack.

carpet, a towel, dad's sweater, mom's shirt, the wood floor—the possibilities are limitless.

- Toys with texture. Offer playthings that have interesting textures: a plush teddy bear and a coarse-haired stuffed doggie, hard wooden blocks and soft stuffed ones, a rough wooden bowl and a smooth metal one, a silky pillow and a nubby one.

CHAPTER 8

The Third Month

This month, baby's finally starting to discover that there's way more to life than eating, sleeping, and crying. Not to say that babies this age don't do plenty of all of these (colicky infants generally keep up the late afternoon and early evening crying bouts until month's end)—just that they've expanded their horizons to interests beyond. Like their own hands—as far as 2- and 3-month-olds are concerned, the most fascinating toys ever invented. Like staying awake for longer stretches of play during the day (and hopefully, staying asleep for longer stretches at night). Like keeping mommy and daddy entertained with adorable live performances of smiles, gurgles, squeals, and coos that make parenting well worth the price of admission. And with that said, enjoy the show!

Feeding Your Baby: Breastfeeding and Working

You're ready to go back to work, but maybe you're not ready to stop breastfeeding. After all, the benefits of continued breastfeeding—from the physical (better health for baby) to the emotional (built-in close contact with baby before and after work)—can be well worth any extra effort you'll need to make to make breastfeeding and working work. Luckily, once you get the hang of pumping on the job, you'll realize that being a breastfeeding, employed mother may not be such hard work after all.

You'll definitely have your hands full getting ready for your return to work—and not just full of baby. There's plenty of prep work to be done before your nursing and pumping plan is ready to roll out. Here's what you need to know to make breastfeeding and work . . . work:

Bring on the bottle. If you haven't already, get busy with the bottle— even if you won't be heading back to work for a while. Typically, the older

Baby Basics at a Glance: Third Month

Sleeping. While your cutie's ever more alert, sleep is still job one. Naps continue to take up a considerable chunk of daylight hours—a total of around 4 to 8 hours a day, usually divided among 3 or 4 daytime snoozes. Add in 8 to 10 hours of nighttime z's (not necessarily scored all in one stretch yet, of course), and you can expect your baby to sleep about 14 to 16 hours per 24-hour day, though some babies will sleep more, some less.

Eating. It's all liquid, all the time when it comes to baby's menu. Keep in mind that bigger babies tend to drink more than smaller babies,

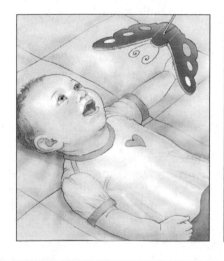

though smaller babies may still tend to eat more often.

- Breast milk. Expect to nurse your little suckler around 8 to 10 times in a 24-hour period, though some babies may be nursing more often, and that's perfectly fine. Demand still rules the day—and night. Though you won't be able to measure the amount going in (unless you're pumping every meal), your baby will be drinking somewhere between 15 and 32 ounces of breast milk a day.

- Formula. Your bottle-drinker will likely be taking in around 4 to 6 ounces at every meal. How many meals? Around 6 a day—for a total of 24 to 36 ounces of formula a day.

Playing. Babies in their third month are still captivated by high-contrast patterns and bright colors—so bring out the brightly hued play yard toys, infant play gyms, mobiles, and anything else your baby can bat at. A soft ankle or wrist rattle allows your little one to experiment with sounds that he or she can make. It's also time to add a (baby-safe) mirror to baby's play space, if you haven't already. Though babies this age don't realize they're looking at themselves in the mirror, they do find their own reflections fascinating and may even smile at that fellow cutie in the mirror!

and wiser babies get, the less open they are to the bottle bait-and-switch. Once you've made the introduction, get baby used to taking at least one bottle feeding a day—preferably during what will soon be your working hours.

Get pumping. Your first day back on the job will be stressful enough (even if

you can find your shoes and your keys) without adding the strain of figuring out how to use a breast pump. So begin pumping a few weeks before you're due back at the office. That way, not only will you be a more confident pumper, but also you'll have started collecting a stash of frozen milk by the time you start collecting paychecks. Didn't manage to get the head start you were hoping for? Don't let that stop you from moving ahead with your plan—you can play catch-up by pumping more frequently.

Do a couple of trial runs. With childcare in place (if that's feasible), rehearse your workday game plan, doing everything as you would if you were really going to work (including expressing milk away from home), but leave the house for just a couple of hours the first time, longer the next. Finding out now about problems that might pop up is a lot better than finding out the morning you're due back on the job, and it'll give you time to figure out how they can be handled.

Start off slow. If you're going back to a full-time job, you might try returning on a Thursday or Friday to give yourself a chance to get started, see how things go, and reevaluate as needed over the weekend. Beginning with a short week will also be a little less overwhelming than starting out with 5 days ahead of you.

Work part-time. If you can swing a part-time schedule, at least at first, you'll be able to spend more time strengthening breastfeeding links. Working 4 or 5 half days is more practical than 2 or 3 full ones for several reasons. With half days, you may not have to miss any feedings—and certainly no more than one a day. You'll have little trouble with leakage (your clothes will thank you), and probably won't have to do any on-the-job pumping (which means you'll actually get to drink coffee on your coffee break). Best of all, you'll spend most of each day with your baby. Working nights is another option that interferes very little with breastfeeding, especially once baby is sleeping through the night, but it can seriously interfere with two other very important commodities: rest and romance.

Scope out your workplace. Once you're back on the job, finding the time and the place to pump can be a bit of a challenge, depending on your workplace. The logistics will be easier if you work in a large company that is required by law to accommodate working breastfeeding moms or at a smaller company that's enlightened enough to do this voluntarily. See the box, facing page, for more.

Keeping these tips in mind can help you succeed, too.

- Dress for pumping success. Wear clothes that are convenient for pumping, or even designed for breastfeeding moms. Be sure your work tops can be lifted or opened easily for pumping at work, and that they won't be stretched out of shape or wrinkled by being pulled up or open. Whatever you wear, line your nursing bra with breast pads to protect your clothing, and carry an extra supply of pads in your bag to replace wet ones.

- Look for privacy. If you're able to pump behind the closed door of your office, awesome. Privacy problem solved. If not, look for an unused office or conference room, or a clean corner in the bathroom lounge. Keep in mind that if you're employed in a large company, the law's on your side when it comes to providing an appropriate place for pumping.

- Be consistent. Schedule permitting, try to pump at the same times every day—as close as possible to the times you would be feeding your baby if you were home. That way your breasts will come to anticipate pumping (as they would anticipate nursing) and fill up with milk like clockwork.

- Plan for storage. Store freshly pumped milk in the refrigerator, clearly marked with your name. Or bring a cooler

Making the Workplace Nursing-Friendly

The days of sneaking breast pumps down the hall to the ladies' room and hiding milk stashes where they won't be poured accidentally into someone's coffee are gone—at least in many mom-friendly workplaces. As companies realize that policies that make working parents happier usually make them more productive on the job, more and more corporate lactation programs have begun springing up across the country. Companies with these programs make lactation rooms available for their employees, complete with comfortable chairs, pumps, refrigerators, and even access to a lactation consultant, making it a breeze to mix business with baby feeding. These programs benefit not only the mom (because she's less stressed) and baby (because of the health benefits of breast milk) but also the company. It doesn't take an MBA to do the math: A happy mama plus a healthy baby equals more productivity . . . and a better bottom line for all.

Even if your company hasn't gotten with the corporate lactation program, the government may pick up some of the slack. Federal law requires any company with more than 50 employees to provide breastfeeding moms with sufficient break time during the workday to pump milk for their babies, up to age 1. The employer must also provide a private place, other than a bathroom, for breastfeeding employees to do their pumping.

---

from home with ice packs, or use the cooler that came with your pump. See page 178 for more on storing breast milk.

- **Use promptly.** When you get home, refrigerate the pumped milk, and have the care provider feed it to your baby the next day. This way you should always have a full day's supply in the fridge.

- **Schedule in breastfeeding, too.** Breastfeeding on schedule will help keep your milk supply up—as well as give you and baby that special together time. Breastfeed before going to work in the morning and as soon as you come home in the afternoon or evening. To make sure your baby will be in the market for a breast on your return, ask the care provider not to feed your baby during the last hour of the workday, or to feed baby just enough to take the edge off hunger.

- **Take a vacation from bottles on weekends.** To pump up your milk supply, use weekends and holidays as time for exclusive nursing. Try to go bottle-free as much as possible then, or any other day you're home.

- **Schedule smart.** Arrange your schedule to maximize the number of nursings. Squeeze in two feedings before you go to work, if possible, and two or three in the evening. If you work near home and can either return during lunchtime for nursing or have the sitter meet you somewhere for a drive-by nursing session with baby (even at your workplace, if you can arrange it), go for it. If your baby is in daycare, nurse when you arrive there in the morning, or in your car before you go in, if that works better. Also try nursing your baby at pickup time, instead of waiting until you get home.

- Stick close to home. If your job entails travel, try to avoid trips that take you away from home for more than a day, at least in the early months. If opting out of travel's not an option, try to express and freeze a big enough milk stash to last while you're away (with extra for backup), or get your baby used to formula before you plan to go. For your own comfort (you won't want to be lugging engorged and leaky breasts through airports and to client meetings) and to keep up your milk supply, take along a breast pump and express milk every 3 or 4 hours. When you get home, you may find your milk supply somewhat diminished, but more-frequent-than-usual nursings, along with a little extra rest, should pump it back up.

- Work from home if you can work it out. If you're lucky enough to have a flexible job that allows you to work from home part-time, an obliging employer, and a sitter to watch baby (or a low-maintenance baby who makes multitasking a breeze), you'll be able to nurse as needed on those home workdays.

- Keep your priorities straight. You won't be able to do everything—and do it well. Keep your baby and your relationship with your spouse (and any other children you have) at the top of the list. Your job—especially if it means a lot to you, either financially, emotionally, or professionally—will probably also have to make the top of the list, but be relentless about cutting energy-saving corners everywhere else.

- Stay flexible. A (relatively) calm and happy mom is more valuable to her baby's well-being than being exclusively breastfed. Though it's entirely possible you'll be able to continue providing all of your baby's milk (as many working moms do), it's also possible that you won't. Sometimes the physical and emotional stresses of mixing work and breastfeeding can do a number on a mom's milk supply. If your baby isn't thriving on breast milk alone, try nursing more frequently when you're at home and pumping more often at work. If you find you still can't keep up with working and pumping (or if it's just wearing you down), it might be best to supplement breast milk with formula (you can choose one designed for supplementation).

What You May Be Wondering About

Time for a Schedule?

"I have no idea how to plan my day because my baby's eating and sleeping is so unpredictable. Should I put him on a schedule?"

Look a little closer at your baby's day—it's probably more predictable than you'd think. Like many typical 2-monthers, it may go something like this: He wakes up around the same time each morning (give or take 15 minutes here or there), feeds, perhaps stays awake for a short period, takes a nap, wakes again for lunch, follows with another nap, feeds, then has a fairly long period of wakefulness late in the afternoon, capped off by a meal and a nap in the early evening. That

Happy to Be . . . Schedule-Free?

Not one for schedules altogether? If your little one thrives without a schedule (he or she seems perfectly content, active, and interested by day, and sleeps well at night) and you do, too (you don't mind putting baby's needs first, even when it means that other areas of your life will take a backseat), then a system of on-demand all-the-time can work well. Attachment parenting (see box, page 269) says that responding to your baby's every need, whenever that need arises, allows you to better understand your baby and foster that all-important trust—the foundation of good parent-child communication. That nursing baby whenever he cries for food (even if he just finished eating), letting her sleep (or stay up) whenever she wants to, and wearing (or carrying) baby as much as possible during the day (or on demand) allows an infant to feel secure and valued as a human being—with the added bonus of less fussing and crying. So there's no need for a set of routines or a flexible schedule in your baby's life if it doesn't fit with the way you want to parent.

Remember, if it doesn't work for you, it doesn't work. Parent the way you feel works best for your baby and your family (as long as it's safe and healthy), and you're doing what's best.

A few things to keep in mind if you plan to parent on demand, schedule-free. First, some babies crave schedules right from the start. They become cranky when feedings are late or over-tired when naps and bedtimes are delayed. If your baby reacts unhappily to your unscheduled days and nights, it may be that he or she needs a little more structure, even if you don't. Second, remember that every child is different, and some can end up being quite different from their parents. There's always the possibility that a child raised without a schedule may end up creating a schedule to meet his or her needs, and the child who's raised by the clock may turn out to be the one who finds that schedules never fit. Finally, if you choose to parent on demand, make sure that both parents (if there are two) are happy to be a schedule-free party of three.

last nap runs past your bedtime? You might wake him for a nightcap feeding, maybe about 11 p.m. (or as late as an exhausted parent like you can keep your eyes open). And then, hopefully, baby goes back to sleep again until early morning, since some babies this age can sleep 6 hours at a stretch, and sometimes more.

Or maybe your baby's schedule seems a bit more erratic, yet still (strangely enough) somewhat consistent. Say he wakes up at 6 a.m., feeds, and goes back to sleep for an hour or 2. Once awake, he may be content to play

for a while before nursing, but once he starts nursing, he wants to nip nonstop for the next 3 hours. After a 20-minute nap (barely enough time for you to suds up in the shower . . . hopefully enough time to rinse), he's up again for hours, with just one nursing period and another 5-minute nap. He nurses again at about 6 p.m. and by 7 p.m. is sound asleep, and he stays that way until you rouse him for a top-off feed before you turn in. His isn't the traditional 3- or 4-hour schedule, but there's still a consistent pattern of sleep-wake-eat to his day.

Your baby's routine seems even more random than that? Believe it or not, he's probably following a more organized and consistent internal clock than it seems—you just have to dig a little deeper to find it. Keeping a journal—or making notes on the What to Expect app—can help you uncover clues.

Whichever pattern your little one falls into (and there are just about as many patterns as there are babies), he's most likely got a rhythm—and a schedule all his own. Follow it as best you can, and you'll be able to create some semblance of a schedule in your own day. Ready for a little more of a schedule, and sense your baby is, too? Even at this tender age, it's possible to begin modifying your baby's already rhythmic internal clock to meet his needs within the framework of a daily routine—a flexible (not rigid) timetable based on your newborn's natural eating and sleeping patterns, his inborn personality (some little ones naturally seem to need more structure, some less), and of course, what feels right to you. Good for you, clearly (so you can plan your day . . . if not set your watch), good for baby (since predictability, for most little ones, breeds comfort).

Not sure how to introduce some semblance of structure into your baby's life? Begin organizing your little one's day with bedtime. A predictable bedtime routine is easy to establish, soothing on both sides, and best of all, the long-term payoff potential—a baby who ultimately learns to fall asleep like clockwork—is huge. (To read more about bedtime routines, see page 355.) Incorporate consistent patterns into other parts of your baby's day, too: A wakeup ritual of cuddles in your bed, followed by a feed in the glider, followed by a walk in the stroller. Midmorning tummy time on the mat, midafternoon back-and-forth babble session in the bouncer, early evening massage and Mozart followed by a mellow read of *Goodnight Moon,* a round of This Little Piggy with every diaper change, a chorus of "Rubber Duckie" at each bath.

No matter how you incorporate structure (or how much structure you incorporate), remember that any routine will need to evolve, and keep evolving, to meet your baby's needs as he gets older. Remember, too, that you'll also have to keep it flexible . . . and keep it real. After all, life with a baby—even one who's on a schedule—is hardly ever predictable.

Baby Falling Asleep While Feeding

"I know I should be putting my baby down awake so she learns to fall asleep on her own, but how is that even possible if she always falls asleep nursing?"

It's an idea that sounds good in theory: Put a baby to bed when she's still awake, so she'll develop the most essential of all healthy sleep habits right from the start—being able to fall asleep on her own. In practice, it's an idea that's not exactly compatible with reality. There's just very little you can do to keep a feeding baby awake if she wants to sleep. And if you could wake her up, would you really want to?

Teaching your baby to fall asleep without help from breast (or bottle) can more practically wait until baby is older—between 6 and 9 months—and nursing less often. And if the habit hangs on, it can definitely be kicked after your baby is weaned.

When you do get the chance (your little one gets groggy during a feed but doesn't fully pass out), consider putting her down for a nap or at bedtime while she's still awake—not so awake that drifting off will be difficult, but in a state of drowsy readiness. A little rocking, nursing, or lullabying can usually bring a baby to this state—just try not to continue the comforting action to the point of sound sleep.

Waking Up for Nighttime Feeds

"So many of my online friends have babies who've been sleeping through the night since they were 6 weeks old, but mine is still waking up and eating as often as he did when he was first born."

Your parent pals may be lucky, but they're not typical. Though some babies no longer need night feedings by the third month (and sometimes sooner), most 2- or 3-month-old babies, particularly breastfed ones, still need to fill their tummies once or twice during the night.

Three or four (or more) middle-of-the-night chow-downs, on the other hand, are typically too much of a good thing at this point—and for most babies, definitely not a necessary thing. Gradually reducing the number of late-show feedings baby's getting won't only help you get more rest now, it's an important first step in preparing him to

---

Attached to Attachment Parenting . . . or Attached Without It?

Do you wear your baby by day, snuggle next to your baby by night? Believe there's no such thing as too close for comfort . . . and that comfort comes from staying close? Plan on letting baby lead the way when it comes to sleep, and breastfeeding until your little one's ready to call it quits (even if that means breastfeeding a preschooler)? Feel that there's never a good reason—or a reasonable amount of time—to let your baby cry, or even fuss? That consistently and immediately meeting your little one's needs best meets your needs? Then attachment parenting—aimed at building the strongest attachment possible between mom, dad, and baby, and setting the stage for secure relationships later in life—may be the perfect parenting approach for you.

Or maybe you're attached to certain aspects of attachment parenting, but not to others. Maybe some principles of attachment parenting don't mesh comfortably with your lifestyle, your personality, the realities of your workday—or maybe even your baby. Happily, the philosophy behind attachment parenting (that babies thrive emotionally when they're receiving quality care consistently) is pretty intuitive—and easily adapted to fit any family. In other words, babies feel attached less because of a parenting technique than a parent's unconditional love. With that basic premise as the foundation for everything you do, it doesn't really matter whether you switch up baby wearing with baby strollers, breast with bottle, co-sleep or stay close (with baby in a bedside bassinet)—or opt to have baby sleep in his or her own room, in a crib. Whether you connect completely to attachment parenting right from the start, sample first before settling on it (or most of it), or pick and choose (and adapt) from a variety of parenting styles to create your very own—what works best for you, your baby, and your family is always what's best.

Preventing Sudden Infant Death Syndrome (SIDS)

Though it's the major cause of infant death, the risk of SIDS is actually very small for the average baby (about 1 in almost 2,000). And thanks to preventive steps that more and more parents are taking (see below), that risk is getting smaller still.

SIDS most often occurs in babies between 1 and 4 months, with the vast majority of deaths occurring before 6 months. Though it was once believed that victims were "healthy" babies randomly stricken, researchers are now convinced that SIDS babies only appear healthy and actually have some underlying defect or defects that predisposes them to sudden death. One hypothesis is that the control in the brain that is usually alerted when breathing conditions are dangerous is underdeveloped in these babies. Another theory: SIDS may be caused by a defect in the heart or a faulty gene involved in managing breathing and heart rate. What is known for sure is that SIDS isn't caused by vomiting, choking, or illnesses. Nor is it caused by immunizations.

There is a somewhat higher SIDS risk for preterm or low-birthweight babies, as well as for babies of women who had poor prenatal care and those who smoked during pregnancy. But many risk factors for SIDS are also related to a susceptible baby's environment. They include tummy sleeping, sleeping on soft or loose bedding or with pillows or toys, being overheated during sleep, or exposure to tobacco smoke. The good news is that these risks can be avoided. In fact, there has been a 50 percent decrease in the number of SIDS deaths since the AAP and other organizations initiated the "Back to Sleep" campaign in 1994.

You can reduce the SIDS risk significantly for your baby with these measures:

- Use a firm mattress and tightly fitting bottom sheet for baby's crib . . . and nothing else. No loose bedding, pillows, blankets, bumpers, fluffy quilts, sheepskins, or soft toys. Don't use devices designed to maintain sleep position (such as wedges) or to reduce the risk of rebreathing air—many have not been sufficiently tested for their safety, and none has been shown to be effective at reducing the risk of SIDS.

sleep food-free through the night later on. Here's how:

- Increase the size of the bedtime feeding. Many sleepy babies nod off before they've totally filled their tanks for the night. Try restarting yours with a burp or a jiggle or a little socializing, and continue feeding until you feel he's really had enough. Don't be tempted to add solids to baby's diet (or put cereal in your baby's bottle) before he's developmentally ready in hopes of buying extra hours of sleep. Not only will it not work (there's no more nutritionally dense food for a baby this age than breast milk or formula), giving solids usually isn't recommended until 6 months.

- Top off before you turn in. Rousing your baby for a late-evening meal (aka a dream feed) may fill him up enough to last him through your own 6 or 8 hours

- Put baby to sleep on his or her back—every single time. Make sure all of baby's providers, including babysitters, daycare workers, and grandparents, are instructed to do this, too.

- If your baby falls asleep in a car seat, stroller, swing, carrier, or sling, move him or her to a firm sleep surface as soon as possible.

- Never allow your baby to get overheated. Don't dress baby too warmly for bed—no hats or extra clothing or blankets (use a temperature-appropriate sleep sack or swaddle instead)—and don't keep the room too warm. To check for overheating, touch the nape of baby's neck or the tummy—it shouldn't feel hot (hands and feet normally feel cooler to the touch, so they're not a reliable gauge).

- Consider running a fan in baby's room. Circulating air may reduce the risk of SIDS.

- Offer a pacifier at sleep times, even if baby doesn't use it during the day. (Don't worry if baby spits it out during the night or refuses to take it.)

- Don't allow anyone to smoke in your home or near your baby.

- Continue to breastfeed your baby—researchers report a lowered risk of SIDS among breastfed babies.

- Consider sharing a room with your baby. Studies show a lowered risk of SIDS among babies who sleep in the same room as their parents. Babies who share a bed with their parents, however, are at greater risk of SIDS and suffocation and entrapment death, so if you do choose to co-sleep with your baby, you'll need to be sure that sleeping conditions in your bed are as safe as possible, see page 274.

- Be sure your baby is up-to-date with all vaccines. There is evidence that suggests that immunization reduces the risk of SIDS by 50 percent.

If, even after taking all these preventive measures, you're still nervous about the risk of SIDS, you may feel more secure if you learn infant rescue techniques and CPR. Also make sure that babysitters, grandparents, and anyone else who spends time alone with your baby knows these lifesaving techniques. That way, if your baby ever does stop breathing, for any reason, resuscitation can be attempted immediately (see page 598).

of shut-eye. Even if he's too sleepy to take a full meal, he may take enough to hold him an hour or two longer than he would have gone without a snack. Of course, if your baby begins waking more often once you've started this strategy, discontinue it. It could be that being woken up by you makes him more prone to waking himself.

- Make sure baby's getting enough to eat all day long. If he isn't, he may be using those night feedings to catch up on calories—after all, he's busy growing up a storm. If you think this might be the case, consider nursing more frequently during the day to stimulate milk production (also check the tips on page 93). If your baby's on the bottle, increase the amount of formula you give at each feeding. But never force-feed. And be aware that for some babies, feeding every couple of hours during the day sets up a pattern they continue around the clock. If your baby seems to have fallen into such a schedule, you might want to go for longer, less frequent feedings instead, assuming he's growing well.

■ Wait a little longer between feedings. If he's waking and demanding food every 2 to 3 hours (necessary for a newborn, but not usually for a thriving 3-month-old), try to stretch the time between feedings, adding half an hour each night or every other night. Instead of jumping to get him at the first whimper, give him a chance to try to fall asleep again by himself—he may surprise you. If he doesn't, and fussing turns to crying, try to soothe him without feeding him—pat or rub him, sing a soft, monotonous lullaby, or turn on a musical crib toy or white noise app. If the crying doesn't stop after a reasonable time (for however long you feel comfortable letting him fuss), pick him up and try soothing him in your arms by rocking, swaying, cuddling, or singing. If you're breastfeeding, the soothing tactics have a better chance of success if dad's on duty, since a breastfeeding infant who sees, hears, or smells his source of food is not easily distracted from eating. Keep the room dark, and avoid a lot of conversation or stimulation.

If baby doesn't fall back to sleep and still demands feeding, feed him—but by now you've probably stretched the interval between feedings by at least half an hour from the previous plateau. The hope is that baby will reach a new plateau within the next few nights and sleep half an hour longer between feedings. Gradually try to extend the time between meals until baby is down to one nighttime feeding, which he may continue to need for another few months, especially if he's breastfed or growth is on the slow side.

■ Cut down the amounts at the nighttime feedings you want to eliminate. Gradually reduce the number of minutes he spends nursing or the ounces in his bottle. Continue cutting back a little more each night or every other night.

■ Increase the amount offered at the night feeding you are most likely to continue (for now). If your baby is getting up at midnight, 2 a.m., and 4 a.m., for example, you may want to cut out the first and last of these feedings. This will be easier to do if you increase the amount your baby takes at the middle one, either from breast or bottle. A nip from the breast or a couple of ounces from the bottle is not likely to knock him out for long. See the tips for keeping a sleepy baby awake for feeding on page 139.

■ Don't change your baby's diaper during the night unless it's poopy or uncomfortably sopping.

■ Listen before you leap. Room sharing provides safer sleep, but probably not sounder sleep. Parents tend to pick up their babies more when they're close by, leaping to feed when there's really no need. Keep your baby in your room for safety's sake, but try to remember that a fussy baby isn't always a hungry baby.

Metabolically speaking, babies can usually get through the night without a feeding once they've reached about 11 pounds, yet far from all actually do—especially those who've tipped that scale at an early age. But by 4 months, you can rest assured (and hopefully rest more at night) that your little one doesn't need any middle-of-the-night feedings at all. If the night-waking habit continues into the fifth or sixth month, you can begin to suspect that your baby is waking not because he needs to eat during the night, but because he's become used to eating during the night. See page 349 for tips on getting an older baby to sleep through the night.

Breathing Lapses

"My premature baby had occasional periods of apnea for the first few weeks of her life, and I'm worried about it possibly putting her at risk of SIDS."

Breathing lapses are very common in premature babies—in fact, about 50 percent of those born before 32 weeks gestation experience them (see page 626). But this "apnea of prematurity," when it occurs before the baby's original due date, is totally unrelated to SIDS, and it doesn't increase the risk of SIDS or of apnea, itself, later. So unless your baby has serious episodes of apnea after her original due date, there's no cause for concern, monitoring, or follow-up. Even in full-term babies, brief lapses in breathing without any blueness, limpness, distress, or need for resuscitation are normal. They're not believed by most experts to be a predictor of SIDS risk.

"Yesterday afternoon I went in to check on my baby, who seemed to be taking a very long nap. He was lying in the crib absolutely still and blue. I grabbed him and he started breathing again—but I'm terrified it'll happen again."

Your baby experienced what's called an "apparent life-threatening event," but as frightening as that sounds (and as understandably terrifying as the experience was for you), it doesn't mean that his life is in danger. While a single episode of prolonged apnea

Breathing Emergencies

Though very brief (under 20 seconds) periods of breathing lapse can be normal, longer periods—or short periods in which a baby turns pale or blue or limp and has a very slowed heartbeat—require medical attention. If you have to take steps to revive your baby, call the doctor or 911 immediately. If you can't revive your baby by gentle shaking, try rescue techniques (see page 598), and call or have someone else call 911. Try to note the following to report to the doctor:

- Did the breathing lapse occur when baby was asleep or awake?

- Was baby sleeping, feeding, crying, spitting, gagging, or coughing when the event occurred?

- Did baby experience any color changes, turning pale, blue, or red in the face?

- Did baby need resuscitation? How did you revive him or her, and how long did it take?

- Were there any changes in baby's crying (higher pitch, for example) before the breathing lapse?

- Did baby seem limp or stiff, or was he or she moving normally?

- Does your baby often have noisy breathing? Does he or she snore?

(when breathing stops for more than 20 seconds) does put an infant at slightly increased risk for SIDS, there's a 99 percent chance that the risk will never become reality.

Still, be sure to call your baby's doctor to report what happened. It's likely the doctor will want to evaluate, test, and monitor your baby in the hospital. The evaluation often uncovers a specific treatable cause for such an event—an infection, a seizure disorder, GERD (gastroesophageal reflux disease), or an airway obstruction—that can be treated, eliminating the risk of future problems, and hopefully putting your mind greatly at ease.

If the cause is undetermined, or if there seems to be an underlying heart or lung problem, the doctor may recommend putting your baby on a device that monitors breathing and/or heartbeat at home. The monitor is usually attached to the baby with electrodes or is embedded in his crib, play yard, or bassinet mattress. You, and anyone else who cares for your baby, will be trained in connecting the monitor as well as in responding to an emergency with CPR. While the monitor won't give your baby absolute protection against a recurrence, it may help your doctor learn more about his condition and help you feel less helpless.

Bed Sharing

"I've heard a lot about the benefits of co-sleeping. And with all the night waking our baby does, it seems like sharing a bed would mean more sleep for her and us."

For some families, a family bed (aka co-sleeping) is an unequivocal and cuddly joy. For others, it's just a convenience (whatever gets you through the night, right?). For still others, it's a total nonstarter (babies sleep in cribs, grown-ups sleep in bed . . . end of bedtime story).

For some, there is no debate—or even room for discussion. Those who advocate against bed sharing point to a variety of reasons, chief among them safety (a parent's bed can be a plushy

land mine of pillows, pillow tops, featherbeds, headboards, and other suffocation and entrapment risks). They also point to problems with sleep habits (babies who get used to sleeping between mom and dad may have trouble sleeping on their own later on), less sound sleep (for parents when there's a baby in the bed, for babies when their parents are too quick to comfort during normally restless baby sleep), and possibly less intimacy for adults in the bed (adults-only snuggles and more can be elusive for a couple whose baby has literally come between them).

Co-sleeping advocates feel just as strongly about a family bed—considered a key component of attachment parenting. They believe it cultivates emotional bonds, boosts a little one's sense of security, and makes it easier to breastfeed and otherwise offer comfort. They also maintain that co-sleep is safer sleep (though the AAP and other safety experts point to research that shows the opposite).

While there's no shortage of theories and certainly no shortage of opinions on the issue, the decision of whether to have your baby join you in bed or sleep solo in her bassinet or crib—like so many decisions you'll make in your tenure as parents—is a very personal one. And it's a choice best made when you're wide awake (read: not at 2 a.m.) and with your eyes wide open to the following considerations:

Baby's safety. In this country, where sleeping accommodations are usually pretty cushy, keeping baby safe in mommy and daddy's bed takes extra precautions. The Consumer Product Safety Commission has linked the family bed to numerous infant deaths, and the AAP discourages bed sharing (while encouraging room sharing), citing a two- to threefold increase in SIDS risk

From Bassinet to Crib

It's likely your little one started his or her sleeping life in a bassinet since it's the perfect size for a tiny body used to a tight space. And since bassinets are less bulky than cribs, they're easier to fit in your bedroom—the safest place for a newborn to sleep, according to the AAP. But when will your baby outgrow his or her snug sleeping quarters?

There's no hard-and-fast rule about the bassinet-to-crib transition, and in fact, as long as your baby is sleeping well in the bassinet, there's no reason to make a switch. Unless he or she has outgrown the bassinet, that is. Check the weight limitations on the bassinet. Some are as low as 10 pounds, though most can accommodate a 20-pound infant. Don't have the manual handy because the bassinet was a hand-me-down? Err on the side of caution and move your baby to a crib when he or she is 15 pounds. Got a lightweight on your hands? Weight considerations aside, most babies tend to outgrow the bassinet by the time they are 3 to 4 months old . . . or about the time they are able to move around a lot. By then, the bassinet's confines are usually too confining for your little mover and shaker. Not to mention that all that moving and shaking (flipping over, for instance, or getting up on hands and knees) could make the bassinet less safe for your active cutie. The fact that bassinets are shallow makes them even more dangerous once baby is able to sit up.

Your little one may look lost the first time you plop (make that, gently place) him or her in the big crib, but at the rate your baby is growing, he or she will grow into that crib fast enough.

in even low-risk infants who co-sleep. Proponents of co-sleeping, however, point out that there is an innate connection between a co-sleeping mother and child, possibly because of the hormone response activated when the mother is in close proximity to her child, making a mom who co-sleeps more keenly aware of her child's breathing and temperature throughout the night, and allowing her to respond quickly to any significant changes. Not surprisingly, the hormone response is also responsible for the lighter sleep that moms who co-sleep generally experience.

If you choose to co-sleep, make sure your bed and bedding meets the same safety criteria looked for in a crib. A firm mattress (not a pillow top or waterbed) is a must, as are tight-fitting sheets. Skip the feather bed, avoid plush comforters, be sure blankets don't cover baby, keep pillows out of baby's creeping or rolling reach (make sure baby is closer to your chest and abdomen, not your head), and check for entrapment dangers (headboard slats should be no farther apart than 2⅜ inches, and there should be no gaps between the mattress and the frame). Never put baby on a bed that's next to a wall (she could slip between bed and wall and become entrapped) or leave her in a position where she could roll off the bed (this can happen long before a baby actually learns to roll over) or allow her to sleep with a parent who has been drinking or smoking, is under the influence of drugs, is taking medication that induces deep sleep, or is just a very deep sleeper. Never let a toddler or preschooler sleep directly next to

For Parents:
To Work or Not to Work?

For many new parents, there's no choice to make—whether it's due to tight finances or a fast-track career path, returning to work is a given . . . not an option. But even if you have the choice, it's not necessarily a clear one—especially since there's no clear-cut research showing substantial long-term benefits or risks for children whose parents work outside the home over those who have at least one parent home . . . or vice versa. Should you stay home or should you go back to work now? You may find the answer in the following questions:

What are your priorities? Consider carefully what's most important in your life. Clearly your baby and your family will top the list, but what about financial security? Your career path? Home ownership, vacations, and other potential perks of having a two-income family? Is there room for all of those priorities in your life right now—or will something have to give? What can you give up most easily?

Which full-time role suits your personality best? Are you happy as a mama or daddy clam at home all day with your baby? Does pulling the baby shift 24/7 soothe you? Or does it make you antsy? Do you miss your job, crave adult conversation, need a little more stimulation than rounds of "All Around the Mulberry Bush" can provide? Will you be able to leave worries about your baby at home when you go to your job and worries about your job at the office when you're home with your baby? Or, will an inability to compartmentalize your life keep you from doing your best at either job?

Are you comfortable with your child-care choices? No one can take your place, of course, but can you find a person (or group situation) you'll feel comfortable with as a stand-in for you while you work? For more on choosing a care provider for your baby, see page 287.

Is there enough of you—and enough of your energy—to go around? You'll need plenty of emotional and physical stamina to rise with a baby, get yourself ready for work, put in a full day on the job, then return to the demands of your baby and home once again (though you'd also need plenty of energy to be a stay-at-home parent). On the other hand, many new parents—particularly those who really love their work—find time at the office rejuvenating, a respite that allows them to reenter each night refreshed and ready to tackle the very different challenges of baby care. Just don't forget to factor your relationship with your partner into the equation (does baby plus job equal little couple time—or can you schedule in all three?).

How stressful are your job and your baby? If your job is low stress and your baby's a piece of cake to care for, the duo may be relatively easy to handle. If your job is high pressure and your

your baby. And never smoke, or allow anyone else to smoke, in the family bed, since this can increase the risk of SIDS (as well as fires).

A couple's consensus. Make sure you're both on board with the family bed before you bring baby on board your bed—and factor in both your feelings and your baby is, too, will keeping your lid on be an option—or are you the type to boil over?

Will you get enough help? Will your partner be doing half the share of baby care, shopping, cooking, cleaning, and laundry? Are you able to afford outside help to take up the slack or to reduce the load for both of you? Or are you confident that you can balance the demands of work with the demands of home (say, by not being so demanding of yourself)?

What is your financial situation? How will working—or not working—affect your family's finances? Are there ways of cutting back so that the loss of your income won't hurt so much? If you go back to work, how much of a dent will job-related costs (clothes, commuting, childcare) make in your income? Will you lose needed and essential benefits if you don't work?

How flexible is your job? Will you be able to take time off if your baby or your babysitter is sick? Or come in late or leave early if there's an emergency at home? Does your job require long hours, weekends, and/or travel—and how will you feel spending extended time away from the baby?

How will not returning to your job affect your career? Might putting your career on hold indefinitely set you back when you return to the working world—and if so, are you willing to take the risk? Are there ways to keep yourself in touch professionally during your at-home years without making a full-time commitment? Will one of you be less affected than the other professionally by a stint at home?

Is there a compromise position? Full-time working doesn't work for you—but neither does full-time staying at home? Maybe there's a creative compromise you can tap into. Depending on your workplace, your experience, and your skills, the possibilities might include a sabbatical from your current job, working part-time, job sharing, freelancing, project-based or consulting jobs, telecommuting, a compressed workweek, or a compressed workday. Another possibility: Two part-time parents can cover full-time childcare.

And speaking of compromise, there's likely to be some in any choice you make—and realistically, some second thoughts, too . . . and even a few regrets. After all, no matter how committed you might be to staying home, you're bound to feel a twinge or two when talking to friends still pursuing their careers. Or, as committed as you are to returning to work—you're sure to have a tug at your heart passing parents and their babies on the way to the park while you're on your way to the office. Mom and dad misgivings are normal—and so common, few parents escape them entirely. Check in with friends and social media buddies trying to balance their lives in your conflicted work shoes (or unsure at-home sneakers) and you'll see.

That said, if misgivings keep multiplying and second-guessing leads to serious doubts about whether you've made the right decision, consider reconsidering. No decision is final—and no decision that's right for you is wrong (or the other way around).

partner's. Key considerations: Will having baby between you in bed come between you as a couple? Will parent cuddle time be preempted by baby cuddles? And what about sex? (Yes, you can have sex in other locations than the bed—but will you have the energy as busy new parents to get busy anywhere else?)

Sleep—yours and baby's. For some parents, not having to get out of bed for midnight feedings or to calm a crying baby is reason enough to co-sleep. For breastfeeding moms, being able to nurse without having to be fully awake is a real plus. The flip side: Though they may never have to leave their beds at night, the sleep co-sleepers do get may be more broken up and, although emotionally satisfying, less physiologically satisfying (parents and children who co-sleep tend to sleep less deeply and sleep less overall). Also, co-sleeping babies wake more often, sleep fewer hours, and may have trouble learning how to fall asleep on their own, a skill they'll eventually need.

Sleep plans for the future. In making your decision about the family bed, consider how long (ideally) you'd like the arrangement to continue. Sometimes, the longer it lasts, the tougher the transition to solo sleeping. Switching a 6-month-old over to a crib is usually a relative breeze, but moving a baby who's approaching her first birthday may be a little more trying—and weaning a toddler or preschooler from your bed can be a tougher sell still. Some children will vacate the family bed voluntarily (or with a minimum of coaxing) at about age 3, others aren't ready to move on until they start school (or are nudged out, whichever comes first). Happy just playing the family bed by ear? As always, what works best for your family is best.

Whether or not you decide to share your bed with baby at night, you'll still enjoy bringing her in for early morning feedings or cuddling fests. As your little one gets older, you can continue to make family togetherness (if not a family bed) a favorite ritual on weekend mornings.

Early Weaning

"I'm going back to work full-time at the end of the month, and I'm thinking about weaning my baby before I do. Will it be hard on her?"

A 3-month-old is, in general, a pretty agreeable and adaptable sort. Even with a budding personality all her own, she's still far from the opinionated older baby she'll eventually evolve into. And not only is she less likely to play favorites, she's not developmentally ready to play the memory card—what's here today can be gone tomorrow, without her missing it much . . . even if it's her mama's beloved breasts. As much as she loves breastfeeding (and what's not to love?), she probably won't cling to it as much as she would a year or so from now.

In other words, weaning now will probably be a relative piece of cake. Before you decide to opt out of breastfeeding entirely, though, consider that it may be easier than you think to continue once you've returned to work—at least for a few months, and even for the entire first year, which is considered ideal. Another option: doing the combo. Read all about making breastfeeding and working work, starting on page 262.

Convinced you're ready to make the switch from breast to bottle now? First—if you haven't already—you'll need to make sure your little one is acclimated to her new source of nourishment: the bottle. It's probably best to fill the bottles with formula at this point, so your milk supply will begin to taper off. Be persistent when offering the bottle, but don't push it. Try giving the bottle before the breast at each feed—and if your baby rejects the bottle the first time, try again at the next feeding. (See page 238 for more tips on introducing the bottle, especially if

The Longer the Better

It's no news that breastfeeding is best for babies—and that even a little breast milk goes a long way when it comes to giving your baby the healthiest start in life. Six weeks of nursing, after all, can offer substantial benefits. But what is news—big news—is the research showing that longer is better, and that those substantial benefits increase substantially for every month longer a baby is nursed in the first year. Which is why the AAP recommends that breastfeeding continue, ideally, for at least the first year of life. The many benefits of longer breastfeeding include:

Fewer battles with the bulge. The longer a baby is breastfed, the less likely he or she is to join the rapidly growing ranks of overweight children, teens, and adults.

Fewer tummy troubles. Everyone knows that breast milk is more easily digested than formula. But research has shown that infants who are fed only breast milk for the first 6 months have a lower risk of developing gastrointestinal infections than infants who are supplemented with formula beginning at 3 or 4 months. Another digestive plus for older breastfed babies: Those who are nursed while solids are introduced are less likely to develop celiac disease, a digestive disorder that interferes with the normal absorption of nutrients from food.

Fewer ear troubles. Studies have found that babies who are exclusively breastfed for longer than 4 months suffer from half as many ear infections as their formula-fed peers.

Less to sneeze at. Babies nursed for 6 months are much less likely to have problems with allergies of all kinds.

Higher IQ. Many studies have pointed to a link between continued breastfeeding and higher IQ, as well as higher scores on verbal and nonverbal intelligence tests. This connection may have as much to do with the mommy baby interaction that's built into breastfeeding as the breast milk itself (a good reason to keep that interaction during feeds strong if you're feeding formula).

A lower SIDS risk. The longer babies are breastfed, the lower their risk of SIDS.

Of course, though the benefits of continued breastfeeding are compelling, not every mom will choose to or be able to keep nursing for as long as is recommended. So it's important to keep in mind that while longer may be better, some breastfeeding is still definitely better than none.

---

you're having trouble selling the store-bought nipple.)

Keep trying until she takes at least an ounce or two from the bottle. Once she does, substitute a meal of formula for a nursing at a midday feeding. A few days later, replace another daytime breastfeeding with formula, increasing the number of total ounces. Making the switch gradually, one feeding at a time, will give your breasts a chance to adjust with a minimum of really uncomfortable engorgement. Eliminating the early morning and late evening feeds last may make sense, since that will give you the option of hanging on to them for as long as you'd like, even once you've started back to work—assuming your milk supply holds out, and your baby's still interested. Those are, after all, typically the most emotionally gratifying feeds of the day.

Being Tied Down by Breastfeeding

"I was happy with my decision to skip bottles with my baby . . . until I realized it's almost impossible to have a night out without him. And now he won't take a bottle, even of pumped milk."

Breastfeeding is hands down the easiest way to feed your baby—that is, if you're with him. Step out for the night, and the logistics get a little complicated. After all, it's hard to do dinner and a movie when baby's got to eat, too—and your date's scheduled to last longer than the window between two feeds.

You can always try, try, and try again with the bottle (keeping in mind that he may be more likely to accept a mama substitute when mama's not around). If you still don't succeed, opt for a movie or dinner—or order up dinner and Netflix at home instead for now.

Once baby starts going for longer stretches at night between feeds and starts filling his tummy with solids and drinks from a cup, too (usually around month 6), getting a night out will no longer be an impossible dream—assuming you can secure a sitter. In the meantime, if you have a special event you'd like to attend that will keep you from home for more than a few hours, try these tips:

- Take baby and sitter along, if there's an appropriate place for them to hang out while they're waiting. That way baby can nap in a stroller while you

enjoy the event, slipping out to nurse as needed.

- If the event is out of town, consider taking the family along. Either bring your own sitter or hire one where you will be staying. If the place where you're staying is near enough to the event, you can pop in at feeding time.

- Adjust baby's bedtime, if possible. If your baby doesn't usually go to bed until after 9, and you need to leave at 7, try to get him to cut down on his afternoon nap and put him to bed a couple of hours early. Be sure to give him a full nursing before you leave, and plan on feeding him again when you return home, if necessary.

- Leave a bottle of expressed milk and hope for the best. If your baby wakes up and is really hungry, he may take the bottle. If he doesn't take it, well, that's what you pay a good sitter the big bucks for—just make sure you prepare her for the possibility of a fussy baby, and be ready to feed as soon as you get home. Keep your cell phone handy, and be prepared to cut dinner off at the entrée and run home to feed baby.

Fewer Bowel Movements

"I'm concerned that my baby may be constipated. She's exclusively breastfed and has always had six or eight bowel movements a day—but lately she's been having just one, and sometimes she even misses a day."

Don't be concerned . . . be grateful. This slowdown in production isn't only normal, but it will send you to the changing table less often. Definitely a change for the better.

Many breastfed babies start having fewer bowel movements somewhere between 1 and 3 months of age. Some will even go several days between movements. That's because as babies get bigger, their bowels get bigger and longer, too, allowing waste to hang out longer before exiting. What's more, fluid is better able to be absorbed, resulting in fewer, larger poops. Other babies will continue their prolific poop production as long as they are nursing, and that's normal, too. What's regular . . . is what's regular for her.

Constipation is rarely a problem for breastfed babies—and what's more, infrequency isn't a sign of it. Hard, difficult-to-pass stools are (see page 563).

Diaper Rash

"I change my baby's diaper frequently, but she still gets diaper rash—and I have trouble getting rid of it."

Diaper rash is typically triggered by a combination of moisture (too much), air (too little), friction (rubbing against those soft folds of skin), and irritants (think everything from urine and stool to the ingredients in disposable diapers, wipes, bath products, and laundry detergents). And since that pretty much sums up what your baby's bottom is exposed to most of the day and night, it's no wonder she (like a third of her comrades-in-diapers) isn't sitting on a pretty bottom. You can expect diaper rash to remain a potential problem as long as your little one is in diapers, but don't be surprised if things get worse before they get better. Often, when a more varied diet is introduced, what comes out the other end is even more irritating to baby's tender skin, leading to redness and rash. Exacerbating the rash is aggressive and frequent cleansing of that often dirty diaper area. You may also notice the rash is worse where urine concentrates in the diaper, toward the bottom with girls and the front with boys.

There are many different types of diaper rash, from the more common chafing dermatitis (redness in areas of high friction) to candidal dermatitis (bright red rash in the crease between the abdomen and the thighs), seborrheic dermatitis (a deep red rash with yellow scales) to impetigo (large blisters or crusts that weep, then ooze yellowish fluid before crusting over) and intertrigo (a red area of skin that might ooze white to yellowish gunk).

The best cure for your sweet pea's garden-variety diaper rash is prevention (see page 158). Too late for that? The following may help eliminate your baby's simple diaper rash, as well as help ward off recurrences:

Less moisture. To reduce moisture on that tender skin, change your little one's diaper often—preferably (at least for now) right after she pees or poops.

More air. After you've cleaned her up, but before you've replaced the diaper, give her bottom some bare air time (just make sure the surface you choose to let her enjoy the breeze on is covered with an absorbent pad or towels in case she springs an unexpected leak). No time for air time? Blow on her bottom or use the clean diaper to fan her bum dry. Also, try to leave a little breathing room in the diaper when it's on. You want your baby's diaper snug enough to prevent leaks but not so tight that it rubs and chafes. If she's in cloth diapers, use breathable diaper wraps.

Fewer irritants. You can't do much about the pee and poop that rubs her bottom the wrong way (besides change her frequently), but you can avoid adding extra irritants to the mix. Make sure all the products that touch your baby's tush are gentle and unscented (that goes for wipes, too). When baby's really rashy, try to skip the wipes and instead dab her bottom clean with warm water and cotton balls, or even a soft washcloth.

Different diapers. If your baby has a recurrent diaper rash, consider switching to another type of diaper (from cloth to disposables or vice versa, from one type of disposable to another) or another brand of wipes to see if the change makes a difference.

Blocking tactics. Spreading a thick, protective layer of ointment or cream (A&D, Desitin, Balmex, Boudreaux's Butt Paste, Aquaphor, or whatever your baby's doctor recommends) on baby's bottom after cleaning it at changing time will prevent urine from reaching it and irritating the rash further. Make sure, though, that before you spread the ointment or cream on baby's bottom, her skin is completely dry (trapped moisture beneath the barrier cream will only make diaper rash more likely—or make a bad diaper rash worse).

If a rash doesn't clear up or at least start improving in a day or two, or if blisters or pustules appear, check in with the doctor, who may prescribe a topical antifungal cream or ointment, a steroid cream, or, much less likely, an oral antibiotic.

Penis Sore

"I'm concerned about a red, raw area at the tip of my baby's penis."

Thought diaper rash only shows up on your baby's sweet bottom? Not always. That red area on your little one's penis is probably nothing more than a localized diaper rash—and it's pretty common. But just because it's common doesn't mean you should ignore it. Left untreated such a rash can occasionally cause swelling, and in rare instances, that swelling can make it difficult for a baby to pee. So do everything you can to get rid of the rash, following the tips for treating diaper rash in the previous answer. And if you're using home-laundered diapers, switch to a diaper service or disposables until the rash goes away. The rash is staying put? If two or three days of home treatment doesn't help, put in a call to the doctor.

Still Jerky Movements

"When my son tries to reach for something, he can only swat at it—and his movements are so random, not coordinated. Is that normal?"

Though it has come a long way from the days when you felt tiny twitches in your uterus, your baby's nervous system is still young and inexperienced, and it hasn't worked out all its kinks. When his arm whips out in the direction of a toy but doesn't land anywhere near its target, it may seem random—but it's actually a normal stage in infant motor development. Soon he'll gain more control, and the purposeful, clumsy batting will be replaced with more skilled, coordinated reaching movements. And once he gets to the stage when nothing within that cunning reach is safe again, you may look back fondly on a time when he looked but wasn't able to touch.

Leaving Baby with a Sitter

"We'd love a night out alone, but we're afraid of leaving our baby with a sitter when she's so young."

Jogging with Baby

Eager to get back on the running trails . . . and hoping to take baby with you? Better think twice before you lace up your sneakers and strap your little one into that baby carrier. While running might be great for your body, it's not good for a young baby's body. Any type of activity that bounces a baby too vigorously (such as jogging with him or her in a front or back baby carrier or when an adult tosses a baby in the air) can result in serious injuries. One dangerous possibility is a type of whiplash (similar to the kind you can get from a car crash). Because your baby's head is heavy in proportion to the rest of his or her body and the neck muscles are not fully developed, self support for the head is poor. When a baby is shaken roughly or energetically bounced up and down, the head whipping back and forth can cause the brain to rebound again and again against the skull. Bruising of the brain can cause swelling, bleeding, pressure, and possibly permanent neurological damage with mental or physical disability. Another possible injury is trauma to the delicate infant eye. If detachment or scarring of the retina or damage to the optic nerve occurs, lasting visual problems, even blindness, can result. Such injuries are rare, but the damage can be so severe that the risk is certainly not worth taking.

So do your running while pushing baby in a stroller, instead. There are specially designed jogging strollers with extra springs to cushion baby from the bouncing motion (just check the stroller's age and weight minimums to make sure he or she is big enough to enjoy the ride safely)—and that's a better bet when getting back into shape.

Go to town . . . and soon. Assuming you're going to want to spend some time alone together (or just alone) during the years to come, getting your baby used to being cared for by someone besides you will be an important part of her development. And chances are the earlier she starts making the adjustment, the easier. Infants 2 and 3 months old definitely recognize their parents, but out of sight usually means out of mind. And as long as their needs are being met, young babies are generally happy with any attentive person. By the time babies reach 9 months (much sooner in some babies), many begin experiencing what is called separation or stranger anxiety—not only are they unhappy being separated from mom or dad, they're also very wary of new people. So now's the perfect time to bring a babysitter into baby's life—and a little adults-only fun into yours.

At first you'll probably want to take only short outings, especially if you're nursing and have to squeeze your dinner in between baby's meals. What shouldn't be short, however, is the time you spend choosing and preparing the sitter, to ensure your baby will be well cared for. The first night, have the sitter come at least half an hour early. That way sitter and baby can meet, and you can do any baby briefing (how your little one likes to be rocked, what calms her down when she's fussy) that makes you feel more comfortable. (See page 287 for tips on choosing childcare.)

For Parents:
The New Face of Fatherhood

If you're like most dads these days, you're able to change a diaper with your eyes closed (and often do when you're on diaper duty at 2 a.m.). And you're a pro at producing a burp (baby's, not yours). And you can rock your whimpering baby with one arm while simultaneously checking last night's scores or today's market prices on your smartphone with the other. Not only do you have this parenting thing down pat, but—it turns out—you can't get enough of it. So much so, that you're wondering whether you could make this new job called fatherhood a full-time one—especially if there are circumstances that have you questioning whether a return to the workforce makes financial or practical sense.

Maybe your partner brings home the bigger paycheck or has the more stable job. Maybe maintaining a two-salary household doesn't stack up to the cost of childcare—or you're more comfortable keeping childcare in the family. Or maybe you just can't imagine sitting at a desk all day when your heart's at home with your baby.

Stay-at-home dads, known in social media circles by the somewhat unfortunate acronym SAHD (there's nothing sad about a stay-at-home dad), are a growing trend—around 2 million dads are primary caregivers for their kids these days, either full-time or part-time. And as the sight of a dad snuggling his cutie in a baby carrier while pushing a shopping cart filled with groceries has become more common-place, society—and even the media—has become more accepting of this new reality, even embracing it. Still, this switch in traditional roles is not without its challenges, and you're sure to face a few bumps along the stay-at-home parenting road—some similar to those felt by moms, but others unique to you and fellow SAHDs.

Here are some strategies to navigate those challenges so you can get the most out of your stint as stay-at-home dad:

Find other SAHDs. Stay-at-home parents—both moms and dads—often feel isolated. After all, the transition from interacting with adults all day (in full sentences) to interacting with a newborn whose communication skills are limited to breathy coos or high-pitched wails can be difficult—you may have someone to talk to, but no one to talk with. That sense of isolation may extend to playgrounds and playgroups, which tend to be mom-heavy (or even mom-exclusive), leaving SAHDs who'd like to become involved feeling out of the loop. Instead of staying on the outside looking in to stay-at-home social circles, try being more proactive in reaching out and connecting. Look for SAHD groups in your area (or create one yourself). Turn to online dad groups for advice, support, and a place to vent with guys who have also traded in their briefcase for a diaper bag. Don't write off the mamas, though. Mingling with SAHMs—who are dealing with many of the same parenting challenges as you are—can also be part of your support system.

Trust yourself. If you're taking over for mom after her maternity leave has elapsed, you may find yourself wondering what she would do in a certain situation, how she would handle this feeding issue or that crying jag. Sure, it makes sense to tap into any baby lessons she has already learned, and to segue into full-time daddy care with a minimum of major changes in schedule and parenting protocol (babies typically aren't fans of change). But it's just as important that you carve out your own care-giving identity, rather than just trying to morph into hers. Mom may have that special touch when it comes to massage, but your colic hold is all yours—and so epically effective, you may need to think about a patent. Just remember, parenting doesn't always come naturally to moms or dads. Learning the ropes of baby care takes time, and how much time it takes is completely unrelated to a parent's gender. It's a job that's best learned on the job. Listen to that little voice inside (instincts—you have them, too!), and you'll discover everything you need to know, and gain the confidence you need to trust yourself.

Make sure you and mom are on the same page. Setting clear expectations up front will reduce conflict and the potential for resentment (as when one parent feels he or she is carrying the heavier load). So talk about it. Together decide which chores fall to which parent—even charting them at first to make sure responsibilities are accounted for equitably. Is one parent doing the grocery shopping, the other doing the cooking? Is baby laundry all you, picking up the dry cleaning all her? Is breakfast duty a joint effort, bath time a job for two, too? Who does nights, and who does what on weekends? Be specific, but also be prepared to be flexible as baby's needs change, or when schedules shift or roles evolve. Open communication and compromise are both key to a successful parenting partnership, but especially when roles are being defined (or redefined). Speak up, too, if you find mom tends to micromanage too much, even as she leaves you home with the ultimate

(if cutest) responsibility. Remind her gently but as needed that her input is welcome, but that she'll need to hover less and trust you more, allowing you to make your own decisions and (like any parent) make your own mistakes. But don't get so carried away running with the responsibility that you start feeling like you run the parenting show entirely. This is a partnership, after all.

Find time for yourself. Everyone needs some "me" time occasionally to prevent burnout, and SAHDs are no exception. Look for ways to give yourself a break while still caring for your little one, such as taking advantage of the gym's free babysitting services so you can stay in shape while staying on dad duty, taking up a hobby that you can do with baby in tow, or volunteering with baby.

Look to the future. Your job as dad may be a full-time one now, but that doesn't mean you shouldn't consider what the future might look like. Continue to network with colleagues and stay up-to-date as things change in your area of expertise. Now (while baby's still taking naps) might also be a good time to take an online course or two to expand your future career horizons, or just keep your skills strong.

Own it. Even with the number of SAHDs on the rise, you'll still get plenty of curious looks at the playground, and clueless comments ("Cool dude, you're off every day!"). But don't let outdated, unenlightened social views (reinforced by ridiculous media images of hopelessly hapless dads) get you down. No matter what brought you to your status as stay-at-home dad (financial or otherwise), you've made a decision that works for you and your family—and you should be proud to call yourself a SAHD.

Never Shake a Baby

Some parents assume that shaking a baby is safer than hitting as a way to let off steam when they're frustrated or angry (at the nonstop crying, for instance) or as a way to discipline their little one (such as when baby won't sleep or stop crying). But that's an extremely dangerous assumption to make. First of all, babies are too young to be disciplined effectively. Second

of all, physical discipline of any kind (including spanking) is never appropriate (see page 466 and *What to Expect the Second Year* for appropriate and effective ways of disciplining a toddler). But, most important of all, shaking, jostling, or vigorously bouncing a baby (whether in anger or fun) can cause serious injury or death. Never, ever shake a baby.

Just not ready to go to town without baby? Some parents are just as happy taking their little ones along on date night, and if you've got a go-with-the-flow kind of baby, that's fine, too. See the next question.

"We take our baby with us everywhere—and we actually like it that way. But some comments we've gotten make us wonder if we're going to make her too dependent on us."

When you're a newborn, there's no such thing as being too dependent, especially when it comes to the two people in the world you're most dependent on: your mommy and your daddy. And that's the way it's supposed to be—being within cuddling distance of a loving parent makes a baby feel loved.

If you're more comfortable taking baby along for the ride wherever you go, go ahead—and as for the comments, remember the rule you probably relied on a lot when it came to unsolicited pregnancy advice: in one ear, out the other (smile and nod optional). Just also keep in mind that babies—even the sweet, adorable baby you can't get enough of—aren't always welcome in every environment or at any occasion

(four-star restaurants, movie theaters, wedding receptions that specify "no children"). For that reason and others, it might be smart to get your baby adjusted to being left with a babysitter occasionally—especially before stranger anxiety rears its unfriendly head in the second half of the first year.

"We always have the babysitter come after our baby's asleep for the night—it seems easier to sneak out. But now we're rethinking that decision—especially because we sometimes want to go out earlier."

Since they're basically born yesterday (or a couple of months before yesterday), newborns are pretty easy to sneak out on. Leave your baby when he's sleeping, and not only is he not likely to notice—but even if he does notice when he wakes up, a cuddle or a bottle or both will likely placate him quickly ("What was I upset about again?"). But fast-forward not too far ahead, and you'll find a very different scenario unfolding. Your baby may still be easy to sneak out on, but he won't be so easy to placate should he wake up to find a stranger in your place. He also may start to feel less secure about your comings and goings. As his memory power increases, he may worry about you disappearing at any moment (cue clinging). And he'll certainly become mistrustful of anyone who tries to stand in for you, whether during the day or at night.

So reconsidering your strategy now—and occasionally getting your evening started earlier, so you can leave your still-awake baby with your carefully chosen sitter—is definitely a smart move.

ALL ABOUT:
The Right Childcare for Baby

Does the thought of leaving your precious, sweet, and oh-so-new bundle in someone else's care have you second-guessing whether you should ever leave your baby at all? Of course it does—especially the first time. After all, it's probably taken you—the people who love that little one more than anyone else in the world—weeks (maybe months) to figure out how your baby works: what cries mean what, what calming techniques work and which don't, what sounds soothe and what sounds stress, the best way to pat out a burp. How can you expect someone else to pick up your baby's signals as sensitively and intuitively as you do? Be as caring, as concerned, as attentive, as responsive, as reliable as you? As focused on (okay, make that a tad obsessed with) your newborn? As capable of providing the stimulation that will make your baby's brainpower and muscle skills grow? Able to concede that mom and dad know best when it comes to babycare philosophies (even if those philosophies are in direct contradiction with those practiced by the caregiver on her own babies or other people's babies) or at least, to accept that you're the last word on sleep, feeding, discipline . . . all of the above and more?

Separating from your little one—whether for a 9-to-5 job or a Saturday-night dinner and a movie—will never be easy, especially the first few times you head out the door and leave your baby behind. But knowing that you've left your precious, sweet, and oh-so-new bundle in the best possible hands will help ease your mind, your stress . . . and, yes, maybe even some of the inevitable guilt.

In-Home Care

Nobody can take your place with your baby, not ever . . . not even close. Mommy or daddy care is the best care there is. But most experts agree that the next best thing to having a parent at home caring for a child is having a parent substitute (a nanny, babysitter, au pair) at home providing that care.

The advantages of in-home care are many. Baby stays in familiar surroundings (complete with the comforting consistency of his or her own crib, high chair, and toys), isn't exposed to lots of other baby germs, and doesn't have to do any commuting. Instead of competing for attention with a roomful of other little ones, baby has one-on-one care—and a good chance of building a strong relationship with a single care provider.

There are some potential drawbacks, though. Topping the list: cost. At-home care is usually the most expensive kind of childcare—especially if you choose a professionally trained nanny, possibly less so for an au pair, a college student, or someone with minimal experience. If the care provider is sick, unable to come to work for other reasons (for instance, a sick child of her own), or suddenly quits, there's no automatic backup system. A wonderfully strong attachment between the babysitter and an older baby may prove not so wonderful if the sitter leaves suddenly, or if mom or dad develops more than a mild case of envy. And, finally, some parents find that having someone else in their home all day cramps their style and intrudes on their privacy—especially if that someone is living in.

Starting the Search

Finding the ideal care provider can be a time-consuming process, so if you can, allow as much as 2 months for the search. There are several trails you can take to track her (or him) down:

Online. There are plenty of resources online to help jump-start your search—from agencies you can hook up with to help-wanted databases. Be sure to get recommendations from friends or colleagues who have used a particular online resource before logging on.

The baby's doctor. Probably no one else you know sees as many babies—and parents—as your baby's doctor. Ask him or her for nanny recommendations, check the office bulletin board for notices put up by care providers seeking employment (some pediatricians require that references be left at the reception desk when such notices are posted), or put up a notice of your own. Ask around the waiting room, too.

Other parents. Don't pass one by—at the playground, at a postpartum exercise class, at cocktail parties and business meetings, in line for coffee—without asking if they've heard of, or have employed, a good care provider. Ask around on local message boards, like the ones on WhatToExpect.com.

Your local community center, library, house of worship, preschool. Post on and check out the bulletin board, as well as the message boards online.

Teachers of toddlers and preschoolers. Early childhood teachers may be open to babysitting on nights and weekends, or may know of other experienced childcare workers.

Nanny agencies and registries. Trained and licensed (and usually expensive) childcare workers and nannies are available through these services—and selecting a care provider this way usually eliminates a lot of guesswork and legwork. (But always interview and check references and background yourself, anyway.) You may have to pay a membership fee to access an agency or registry, and sometimes an agency percentage.

Babysitting services. Screened babysitters are available through these services, many of them listed online, for full-time, part-time, or occasional work.

A local hospital. Some hospitals offer babysitting referral services. Generally, all sitters referred have taken a babysitting course offered by the hospital, which includes baby CPR and other first-aid procedures. At some hospitals and nursing schools, nursing or medical students may be available for babysitting jobs.

Local parent papers. Check for ads run by care providers seeking employment, and/or run an ad yourself.

Babysitter Checklist

Even the best trained, most experienced babysitter needs instructions (after all, every baby and every family has different needs). Before you leave your baby in someone else's care, make sure she's familiar with the following:

- How your baby is most easily calmed (rocking, a special song, a favorite mobile, a ride in the sling)

- What your baby's favorite toys are

- That your baby should sleep on his or her back, with no pillows, positioners, blankets, soft toys, bumpers, or comforters

- How your baby is best burped (over the shoulder, on the lap, after feeding, during feeding)

- How to diaper and clean baby (do you use wipes or cotton balls? An ointment for diaper rash?) and where diapers and supplies are kept

- Where extra baby clothes, sheets, and towels are kept

- How to give the bottle, if your baby is bottle-fed or will be getting a supplement of formula or expressed milk

- What your baby can and can't eat or drink (making it clear that no food, drink, or medicine should be given to your baby without your okay or the doctor's)

- The setup of your kitchen, the baby's room, and so on, and any other pertinent facts about your house or apartment (such as how the security system operates, and where fire exits are located)

- Any habits or characteristics of your baby that the sitter might not expect (spits up a lot, poops frequently, cries when wet, falls asleep only with a light on or when being rocked)

- The habits of any pets you may have that the babysitter should be aware of, and rules concerning your baby and pets

- Baby safety rules (see page 230)

- Who is cleared by you to visit when you are not at home, and what your policy is on visitors

- Where the first-aid kit (or individual items) is located

- Where a flashlight is located

- What to do in case the fire alarm goes off or smoke or fire is observed, or if someone who hasn't been cleared by you rings the doorbell

You should also leave the following for the babysitter:

- Important phone numbers (your cell, the baby's doctor, a neighbor who will be home, local family members, the hospital emergency department, the Poison Control center, the building superintendent, a plumber or handyman)

- The address of the nearest hospital and the best way to get there

- A signed consent form authorizing medical care within specific limits, if you can't be reached (this should be worked out in advance with baby's doctor)

It's helpful to combine all the information necessary for caring for your baby—for instance, phone numbers, safety and health tips—in one place (a notebook, say), or use *The What to Expect Baby-Sitter's Handbook*.

College employment offices. Part-time or full-time, year-round or summer help may be found through local colleges. Early childhood education or nursing students would make ideal candidates.

Senior citizen organizations. Lively seniors can make terrific sitters—and surrogate grandparents at the same time. Just make sure they've received training on new-school baby care, first aid, and safety.

Au pair or nanny organizations. These services can provide families with a live-in au pair (usually a young person from a foreign country who wants to visit or study in the United States for a year or so) or with a well-trained nanny.

Settling on a Job Description

It'll be easier to find the right care provider if you know what you're looking for. So before you start sorting through job candidates, settle on a job description. Be as detailed as possible. Baby care will be job one, of course, but will you be adding other responsibilities, such as laundry and light cleaning? (Be wary of overloading a care provider with chores that might distract her attention from your baby.) Also decide how many hours a week you'll need her to work, whether the hours will have to be flexible, and how much you'll pay—both as basic salary and for overtime. Consider, too, whether you will need her to drive or have other specialized skills.

Sifting Through the Possibilities

You won't want to spend endless days interviewing clearly unqualified candidates, so sift them out first via email and phone. If there's no resume to work from, ask candidates for their full name, address, phone numbers, age, education, training, and experience (this may

actually be less important than some other qualities, such as enthusiasm and natural ability). Also ask each applicant about salary and benefit requirements (check beforehand to see what the going rate is in your area; 2 weeks of paid vacation a year is a standard perk). Detail the job description, and ask why she wants the job. Set up a personal interview with those applicants who sound promising.

Interviewing the Finalists

Even the most exhaustive resume won't tell you everything you need to know—and neither will phone conversations or email or text exchanges. For the full scoop on your childcare candidates, you'll need to hold in-person interviews, preferably in your home. Phrase questions so that they require more than a yes or no answer (it doesn't mean much when you get a "yes" to "Do you like babies?"). For example:

- Why do you want this job?

- What was your last job, and why did you leave it?

- What do you think a baby this age needs most?

- How do you see yourself spending the day with a baby this age?

- How do you see your role in my baby's life?

- Will you be fully supportive of my continuing to breastfeed (i.e., on board with using expressed milk for bottles, timing feeds so they don't interfere with after-work breastfeeding sessions)? This is important, of course, only if you are breastfeeding and intend to continue.

- When my baby starts getting more active and getting into everything, how will you handle it? How do you believe babies and toddlers should be disciplined, if at all?

- How will you get to work on a daily basis? In bad weather?

- Do you have a driver's license and a good driving record? Do you have a car?

- How long do you envision staying with this job?

- Do you have children of your own? Will their needs interfere with your work? Will you be able to come to work, for instance, when they're home sick or off from school? Allowing a caregiver to bring her children along has some benefits and some drawbacks. On the one hand, it gives your child the chance to be exposed to the companionship of other children on a daily basis. On the other hand, it gives your child more of a chance to be exposed to all of these extra germs on a daily basis. Having other children to care for may also affect the quality and quantity of attention the caregiver can give your own baby. It may also result in greater wear and tear on your home.

- Will you cook, shop, or do housework? Having some of these chores taken care of by someone else will give you more time to spend with your baby when you're at home. But if the care provider spends a lot of time with these chores, your baby may not get the attention and stimulation he or she needs.

- Are you in good health? Ask for evidence of a complete physical exam, up-to-date immunizations (including the flu shot and a Tdap booster), and a recent negative TB test. Ask, too, about smoking habits (she should be a nonsmoker), and alcohol and drug use. A drug or alcohol abuser will probably not be forthcoming with this last information, but be alert for clues, such as restlessness, agitation, dilated pupils, tremors, chills, sweating, slurred speech, poor concentration, and bloodshot eyes. Of course, many of these symptoms can be signs of illness (mental or physical) rather than drug abuse. In either case, should they show up in a childcare worker, they should concern you. You will also want to avoid someone with a medical condition that could interfere with regular attendance at work or the ability to do the job.

- Have you recently had, or are you willing to take, baby CPR and first-aid training?

Though you'll be asking the questions, the job applicant shouldn't be the only one answering them. Ask these questions of yourself, based on your observations of each candidate, and answer them honestly:

- Did the candidate arrive for the interview well groomed and neatly dressed? Though you probably won't require a freshly starched nanny's uniform on the job, dirty clothes, hair, and fingernails are all hygiene red flags.

- Does she speak English (or whatever your primary language is)? How well? Obviously, you'll want someone who can communicate with your baby and with you (especially if you speak only English), but there are some benefits to a babysitter who has a working understanding of English but isn't a native speaker—she might be able to teach your baby a second language at a time when baby is ripe for learning one (see page 247).

- Does she seem to have a sense of orderliness that's compatible with your own? If she has to rummage through her handbag for 5 minutes for her references and you're a stickler for organization, you'll probably clash. On the other hand, if she seems compulsively neat and you're compulsively messy, you probably won't get along either.

- Does she seem reliable? If she's late for the interview, watch out. She may be late every time she's due to work. Check this out with previous employers.

- Is she physically capable of handling the job? She'll need to be fit enough to carry your baby around all day now, and to chase your toddler later.

- Does she seem good with your baby? The interview isn't complete until the applicant spends some time with your baby so that you can observe their interaction or lack of. Does she seem engaged (making eye contact, cooing at your cutie), patient, kind, interested, really attentive, and sensitive to your baby's needs? Nurturing? Find out more about her childcare style from previous employers.

- Does she seem intelligent? You'll want someone who can teach and entertain your child the way you would yourself, and who will show good judgment in difficult situations.

- Are you comfortable with her? Almost as important as the rapport the candidate has with your baby is the rapport she has with you. For your baby's sake, there needs to be constant, open, comfortable communication between a chosen caregiver and you. Be certain this will be not only possible, but easy.

- Were there any red flags in her comments and questions? Asking, "Does the baby cry a lot?" might reflect impatience with normal infant behavior. Silence may speak volumes as well (the candidate who never says anything about liking babies and never comments on yours may be telling you something).

If the first series of interviews doesn't turn up any candidates you feel good about, don't settle—try again. If it does, the next step in narrowing down your selection is to check references. Don't take the word of a candidate's friends or family on her abilities and reliability—ask for the names and contact information of previous employers, if any, or if she doesn't have much work experience, those of teachers, clergy, or other more objective judges of character. You might also consider hiring an employee-screening firm to do a thorough background check (some, but not all, agencies do thorough prescreens). The prospective employee's permission is needed to do this.

Getting Acquainted

Would you be happy being left alone to spend the day with a perfect stranger? Probably not. And the same could likely be said about your baby, too (less so in the early months, when any loving pair of arms will do—more so once baby becomes more parent-centric). To ease the transition to a new care provider, make sure she's no stranger (no matter how perfect) to baby. Before you leave them alone together for the first time, introduce baby and babysitter so they can get to know each other.

Your prospective care provider should spend at least a full paid day with you and your baby, getting to know him or her, but also becoming familiar with your home, your parenting style, and your household routines. That will give you a chance to make suggestions, and her a chance

Is He Manny Enough for the Job?

If it's true what they say (and it is) that there's nothing that a mom can do that a dad can't do equally well if not better (besides breastfeed, that is), then it's also true that there's nothing that a female nanny can do that a male nanny can't do equally well if not better. Which is why more and more men are signing up to provide childcare—and why more and more parents are hiring them as nannies. In fact, this newer breed of childcare providers even has a name: manny. Though still a minority in the childcare business, the ranks of qualified mannies are growing fast. Who says a good manny is hard to find?

to ask questions. It will also give you a chance to see the care provider providing care—and a chance to change your mind about her if you don't like what you see. Just be careful about judging the babysitter on your baby's initial reaction to the caregiver—at least early on, when, depending on his or her stage of development, a strong preference for you (especially when you're around) is normal. Instead, look to the sitter's reaction to your baby's reaction. (Is she patient, calm, and cajoling while trying to win over baby's affections—or does she seem stressed and spooked?) It's also a good idea to leave the sitter with your baby for a short time that first day—and if your schedule is flexible, to leave for a half day next time or at least before you leave for a full day.

Your baby will probably adjust to a new care provider most easily when he or she is under 6 months old, and may take much longer once stranger anxiety appears on the scene (usually sometime between 6 and 9 months; see page 442).

Trying Before Hiring

It's always smart to hire a childcare provider on a trial basis so that you can evaluate her performance before committing for the long term—and not to keep this arrangement to yourself. It's fairer to her and to you if you make clear in advance that the first 2 weeks or month on the job (or any specified period) will be provisional. During this time, observe your baby. Does he or she seem happy, clean, and alert when you come home? Or more tired than usual, and more cranky? Does it seem a diaper change has been made fairly recently? Important, too, is the care provider's frame of mind at day's end. Is she relaxed and comfortable? Or tense and irritable, obviously eager to hand back your bundle? Is she quick to tell you about her day with the baby, reporting achievements as well as any problems she's noted—or does she routinely tell you only how long the baby slept and how many ounces of the bottle were emptied, or, worse, how long the baby cried? Does she seem mindful of whose baby she's caring for, respectful of your decisions, and accepting of your feedback (and constructive criticism, if any, of her care)? Or does she seem to feel that she's in charge now? Does it appear that she ignored basic safety protocol (you instructed her that there be nothing in the crib but your baby—but you returned home to find a rolled blanket on each side of your sweet bundle . . . and a plush toy, too)?

The Business of Hiring a Nanny

Hiring a nanny comes with its share of paperwork. By law, you are required to apply for federal and state household employment tax ID numbers and to pay half of your nanny's Social Security and Medicare payments, as well as her unemployment taxes. Make sure, too, that the person you hire is legally allowed to work in this country (hiring an illegal immigrant is against the law)—there's a form to complete to verify employment eligibility. A lot of trouble, true, but there are perks for abiding by the law (besides avoiding hassles with the IRS for noncompliance). If your company offers a flexible spending account, you may be able to get a tax break on the money you use to pay for childcare.

If you're not happy with the new caregiver (or if she's clearly not happy with the job), start a new search. If your evaluation leaves you uncertain, you might try arriving home early and unannounced to get a look at what's really happening in your absence. Or you could ask friends or neighbors who might see the babysitter in the park, at the supermarket, or walking down the street how she seems to be doing. If a neighbor reports your usually happy baby is doing a lot of crying while you're away, that should be a red flag. Another option: Consider video surveillance with a "nanny cam" (see box, page 296).

If everything and everyone seems to be fine except you (you're anxious every time you leave your baby, you're miserable while you're away, you keep looking for fault in a babysitter who's doing a good job), it's possible that it's the childcare arrangement, not the childcare provider, that isn't working out. Maybe you can find an alternative to full-time outside-the-home work or school that allows you to stay at home with your baby part or all of the day—or maybe a group care situation will actually suit you and your baby best.

Group Daycare

A good daycare program can offer some significant advantages. In the best of them, trained personnel provide a well-organized program specifically geared to a baby's development and growth, as well as opportunities for play and learning with other babies and children. Because such facilities are not dependent on a single provider, as in-home care is, there is generally no crisis if a teacher is sick or leaves, though your baby may have to adjust to a new one. And when the daycare is licensed, there may be safety, health, and in some cases even educational monitoring of the program. It is also usually more affordable than in-home care, making it not only the best option but also the only option for many parents.

The potential disadvantages for babies, however, can also be significant. First of all, not all programs are equally good. Even in a good one, care is less individualized than it is in a baby's own home, there are more children per caregiver, and teacher turnover may be high. There is less flexibility in scheduling than in a more informal setting, and if the center follows a public school calendar, it may be closed on holidays when you're working. The cost, though typically less expensive than good in-home care, is still usually fairly high, unless subsidized by government or private sources (as in corporate daycare). Possibly the greatest disadvantage is the germ spreading that goes on in daycare centers. Since many employed parents don't have another option when their children have colds and other minor ills, they often send them to the center anyway—which is why babies who attend them end up with more than their share of ear infections and other bugs. The unexpected upside to all this early extra germ exposure: often, a toughened immune system (and fewer colds and infections) later on in childhood.

Certainly, there are some excellent daycare facilities—the trick may be finding such a facility in your area that you can afford and that has space for your baby.

Where to Look

You can get the names of local daycare facilities (which may be nonprofit, cooperative, or for profit) through recommendations from friends and local message board buddies whose parenting style is similar to yours, by searching online resources for lists of childcare referrals or referral services, by checking with the state regulatory agency (the state health or education department should be able to refer you), or by asking around at work. You can also ask your baby's doctor for suggestions. Once you have a few possibilities, you'll need to start evaluating them.

What to Look For

Daycare centers range in quality from top of the line to bottom of the barrel, with most falling in the middle range. Online reviews from other parents may give you some clues to the quality of a particular facility, but you'll also want to dig deeper. To best evaluate a center you're considering, look for the following:

Licensing. Most states license daycare facilities, checking them for sanitation and safety but not for the quality of care. Some states, however, don't even have adequate fire and sanitation regulations. (Check with your local fire and health departments if you have any questions.) Still, a license does provide some safeguards—and is always preferable to unlicensed care.

A trained and experienced staff. The head teachers, at least, should have degrees in early childhood education, and the entire staff should be trained and experienced in caring for infants, as well as trained in first aid and rescue techniques (such as CPR). The staff turnover should be low—if there are several new teachers each year, beware.

A healthy and safe staff. Ask if (or ask to see proof that) all caregivers are up-to-date on immunizations and have had complete medical checkups, including a TB test, and thorough background checks.

A good teacher-to-baby ratio. There should be at least 1 staff person for every 3 infants. If there are fewer, a crying baby may have to wait until someone is free to offer comfort.

Moderate size. A huge daycare facility might be less well supervised and operated than a smaller one—though there are exceptions to this rule. Also, the more children, the more chance for the spread of illnesses. Whatever the size of the facility, there should be adequate space for each child and no overcrowding.

Keeping an Eye on the Sitter

Do you ever wonder what really goes on when you're not at home? Does the nanny spend all day providing your baby with loving, nurturing care . . . or texting and watching TV? Does she coo, cuddle, and dote on your infant, or leave him or her strapped in an infant seat or crying in the crib? Does she follow your instructions to the letter, or throw them out the window the moment you're out the door? Is she the Mary Poppins you hoped you hired, or the nanny that nightmares are made of—or more likely someone in between?

To make sure the babysitter they've chosen is close to everything they think she is, or to determine if she's far from it (especially if some red flags have been raised), more and more parents are turning to so-called "nanny cams"—hidden video surveillance to watch those who are watching their children. If you're considering installing such a system, consider the following first:

The equipment. You can either buy or rent cameras, or hire a service that will set up an elaborate surveillance system throughout your home (you can also ask your home security company if they can set it up for you). The least expensive option—a single camera hidden in a room your baby and the babysitter are likely to spend the most time in—can provide you with a glimpse of what goes on while you're away, but it won't give you a full picture (abuse or neglect might be occurring in a different room, for instance). A wireless camera hidden inside a stuffed animal is more expensive but is also more inconspicuous, and since it can be moved from room to room, you'll be able to view different rooms on different days. A system that monitors the entire home will obviously offer the clearest picture of your baby's care but is much more expensive.

Separation of age groups. Infants younger than 1 year should not be mixed with toddlers and older children, for safety, health, attention, and development reasons.

A loving atmosphere. The staff should seem to genuinely like little ones and enjoy caring for them. Children should look happy, alert, and clean. Be sure to visit the facility unannounced in the middle or toward the end of the day, when you will get a more accurate picture of what the center is like than you would first thing in the morning. And be wary of any program that does not allow unannounced parent visits.

A stimulating atmosphere. Even a 2-month-old can benefit from a stimulating atmosphere, one where there is plenty of interaction—both verbal and physical—with caregivers, and where age-appropriate toys are available. As children become older and developmentally advanced, there should be plenty of appropriate toys to play with, as well as exposure to books, music, and the out-of-doors. The best programs include occasional "field trips" to a park, a supermarket, a fire station, a museum, or other places a baby might go with a stay-at-home parent.

Parent involvement. Are parents invited to participate in the program in some way, and is there a parent board that makes policy? Will you be required to

Keep in mind, too, that how well the surveillance works will depend on how well you survey it. You'll need to be committed to recording at least several days a week (daily would be best) and watching the video recordings regularly, or monitoring baby and caregiver in real time on your desktop at work or by using an app. Otherwise you might not catch abuse or neglect until days after it occurs.

Your rights—and your nanny's. Laws regarding covert video recording vary from state to state, though in most cases it's considered legal to videotape a care provider at work in your own home without her knowledge. Your equipment supplier should be able to inform you about the legal considerations in your state. The ethical issues are another matter—and very much open for debate. Some parents believe that a nanny cam is necessary for their child's safety, and that outweighs any ethical concerns. Other parents feel that nanny cams are an invasion of the sitter's privacy, and that introducing one implies a fundamental lack of trust. Of course, you can make surveillance a condition of the job, and you can inform the nanny ahead of time that your security system records your home at all times, so it's likely she'll be watched as well. This way, if she accepts the job, she's also accepting the video monitoring.

Your motivation. If you're just eager for some peace of mind, a nanny cam might just buy it. On the other hand, if you're already feeling uncomfortable enough about the childcare provider you've hired that you're compelled to spy on her with a nanny cam, perhaps that person shouldn't be in your home at all. In that case, you might be wiser to trust your instincts, save your money, and find your baby a sitter you have confidence in

If you do decide to install a nanny cam, don't use it as a way of screening prospective childcare providers. Any babysitter should be thoroughly screened before she's left home alone with your baby.

participate—and if so, will the requirements fit in your schedule?

A compatible philosophy. Are you comfortable with the daycare center's philosophy—educationally, religiously, ideologically? Check its mission statement (if it has one) to know for sure.

Good napping conditions. Most babies, in daycare or at home, still take a lot of naps. There should be a quiet area for napping in individual cribs, and little ones should be able to nap according to their own schedules—not the school's.

Security. The doors to the facility should be kept locked during operating hours, and there should be other security measures in place (a parent or visitor sign-in sheet, someone monitoring the door, requesting ID when necessary). The center should also have a system in place for pickups that protects children (only those on a list approved by you should be able to pick up your baby).

Strict health and sanitation rules. In your own home, there's less reason to worry about your baby mouthing everything within reach—but in a daycare center full of other little ones, each with his or her own set of germs, there is. Daycare centers can become a focus for the spread of many intestinal and upper respiratory illnesses. To minimize germ spreading and safeguard the health of the children, a well-run daycare center

How's the Childcare?
Check with Your Child

No matter which childcare choice you make, be alert to any of these red flags in your baby: new problems with feeding and sleep, sudden changes in personality or mood, clinginess, and fussiness that's not linked to teething, illness, or any other obvious cause. If your baby seems unhappy or not to be thriving physically, developmentally, or emotionally, check into your childcare situation—it may need a change.

will have a medical consultant and a written policy that includes:

- Caregivers must wash hands thoroughly after changing diapers. Hands should also be washed after helping children use the toilet, wiping runny noses or handling children with colds, and before feedings.

- Diapering and food preparation areas must be entirely separate, and each should be cleaned after every use.

- Feeding utensils should be washed in a dishwasher or be disposable (bottles should be labeled with the babies' names so they aren't mixed up).

- Bottles and food should be prepared under sanitary conditions.

- Diapers should be disposed of in a covered container, out of the reach of children.

- Toys should be rinsed often with a sanitizing solution, or a separate box of toys kept for each child.

- Stuffed animals and other toys that can be machine-washed, should be frequently.

- Teething rings, pacifiers, washcloths, towels, brushes, and combs should not be shared.

- Immunizations must be up-to-date for all babies, as well as for caregivers (including seasonal flu vaccines and boosters).

- Little ones who are moderately to severely ill, particularly with diarrhea, vomiting, fever, and certain types of rashes, should be kept at home (this isn't always necessary with colds, since those are contagious before that button nose even starts running) or in a special sick-child section of the facility. When a baby has a serious contagious illness, all parents of children in the center should be notified by the center.

- There should be a policy about giving children medication.

Also check with the local health department to be sure there are no outstanding complaints or violations against the center.

Strict safety rules. Accidental injuries, mostly minor, are not uncommon in daycare facilities (after all, they can also happen at home). But the safer the facility, the safer your baby will be. Be sure the center follows the same safety and childproofing rules you follow at home (see page 391). Make sure, too, that the toys they use are age-appropriate (and kept separate for different ages) and that the center stays up to date on and complies with recalls on toys, furniture, and baby gear.

Careful attention to nutrition. All meals and snacks should be wholesome, safe, and appropriate for the ages of the children being served. Parental instructions regarding formula (or breast milk), foods, and feeding schedules should be followed. Bottles should never be propped.

Home Daycare

Many parents feel more comfortable leaving a baby in a family situation in a private home with just a few other children than in a more impersonal daycare center, and for those who can't afford or arrange for a sitter in their own homes, home daycare is often the best choice.

There are many advantages to such care. Family daycare can often provide a warm, homelike environment at a lower cost than other forms of care—and depending on the provider, can be a nurturing option as well. Because there are fewer children than in a daycare center, there is less exposure to infection and more potential for stimulation and individualized care

(though this isn't a given). Flexible scheduling—early drop-off or late pickup when that's necessary—is often possible.

The disadvantages vary from situation to situation. Since most (but not all) home daycare facilities are unlicensed, there may be no oversight of health and safety protocol (though conscientious providers will follow optimum protocol anyway). Some home providers may be untrained in childcare or safety and CPR, or lacking in professional experience. Backup care may be a considerable issue if the provider becomes ill (or her children do). And though the risk may be lower than in a larger daycare facility, there is always the possibility of germs spreading from child to child, especially if sanitation is lax. See the section on group daycare, starting on page 294, for tips on what to look for and look out for when checking out home daycare.

Corporate Daycare

A common option in other developed countries for many years, daycare facilities in or adjacent to a parent's place of work are much less

---

Safe Sleeping and Sitters

If you're leaving a young infant in the care of someone else—whether a sitter, grandparent, friend, or daycare provider—be sure he or she is aware of (and can be counted on practicing) safe sleep practices, including back-to-sleep, tummy-to-play. Your baby should sleep and nap on his or her back on a safe surface and under safe conditions, and should spend some constantly supervised wakeful time on his or her tummy.

Sick-Baby Workdays

No parent likes to see his or her baby sick, but the working parent particularly dreads that first sign of fever or upset stomach. After all, caring for a sick baby when you've got another full-time job to do may present many challenges—the central ones being who will take care of the baby, and where.

Ideally, either you or your spouse should be able to take time off from work when your baby is sick, so that you can offer that care yourself at home—as anyone who's ever been a sick child knows, there's nothing quite the same as having your mommy or daddy around to hold your hot little hand, wipe your feverish brow, and administer specially prescribed doses of love and attention. Next best is having a trusted and familiar sitter or another family member you can call on to stay with your baby at home. Some daycare centers have a sick-child infirmary, where a little one is in familiar surroundings, surrounded by familiar faces. There are also special sick-child daycare facilities, both in homes and in larger freestanding centers, sprouting up to meet this need—but in these, of course, a baby has to adjust to being cared for by strangers in a strange environment when he or she is least able to handle change. In order to keep parents on the job, some corporations actually pay for sick-childcare, such as time in a sick-child daycare center or hiring a sick-baby nurse to stay with the child at home (which will also require adjustment to an unfamiliar caregiver).

common in the United States, though more family-friendly companies are recognizing the perks of offering such a service. It's an option many parents would choose if they had it.

The advantages are extremely attractive. Your child is near you in case of emergency, you can visit or even breastfeed during your lunch hour or coffee break, and since you commute with your child, you spend more time together. Corporate facilities are usually staffed by professionals and well equipped. Best of all, knowing your child is nearby and well cared for may allow you to give fuller attention to your work. The cost for such care, if any, is usually low.

There are some possible disadvantages. If your commute is a difficult one, it may be hard on your baby—and hard on you if there's a lot of struggling on and off of buses or subways with diaper bags and strollers, or if you travel by car and have a baby who always cries in the car seat. Sometimes seeing you during the day, if that's part of the program, makes each parting more difficult for your baby, especially during times of stress. And visiting, in some cases, may take your mind from your work long after you're back at your desk.

Corporate daycare, of course, should meet all the educational, health, and safety standards of any childcare facility. If the one set up by your employer doesn't, then speak to those responsible for the facility about what can be done to make the program better and safer. Rallying other parents around the cause may help, too.

Babies on the Job

Take Your Baby to Work Day—every day? It's far from a common—or logistically realistic—option, but for a few parents, it's in the mix of childcare choices. It works best if you have flexibility on the job, the cooperation and support of your coworkers, a space in your office for a portable crib and other baby paraphernalia, and a baby who's not a big crier. Ideally, you should also have a sitter on the spot, at least part of the time, or be able to multitask easily—otherwise, baby may actually end up getting less attention and stimulation than he or she might in another childcare situation. Keeping baby on the job usually works best, too, if the atmosphere in the workplace is relaxed—a high stress level won't be good for baby. When it does work, this kind of situation can be perfect for the breastfeeding mom or for any parent who wants to stay on the job and keep baby close by.

CHAPTER 9

The Fourth Month

Someone's all smiles this month—and as a result, chances are you'll be, too. Your adorable little one is just entering what might be considered the golden age of babyhood—a period of several (maybe more) enchanted months when happiness reigns during the day, more sleep is happening at night, and independent mobility has yet to be achieved (which means your baby will continue to stay pretty much where you plop him or her down, limiting mischief and mayhem—enjoy this while it lasts). Sociable and interested, eager to strike up a cooing conversation, to watch the world go by, and to charm anyone within a 10-foot radius, babies this age are an undeniable delight to be around.

Feeding Your Baby: Formula Amounts

When you're breastfeeding, figuring out whether your baby's getting the right amount to eat is a pretty simple calculation—if enough's coming out, enough's going in. With bottle-feeding, there's some higher math to do. While there's no magic formula for how much formula to pour into each bottle, how much you can expect your little one to drink, or how much will get the sitter through the day or you through the week, there are general guidelines you can look to. Not surprisingly, a lot depends on your baby's weight, age, and, once solids are introduced, how much he or she is eating.

- Infants under 6 months (those not supplementing with solids) should be taking about 2 to 2½ ounces of formula per pound of body weight over a 24-hour period. So, if your baby weighs 10 pounds, that would translate to approximately 20 to 25 ounces

Baby Basics at a Glance: Fourth Month

Sleeping. Is there a full night's sleep in your near future? Some (but certainly not all) babies are able to sleep longer stretches at night (think 6 to 8 hours at a time) by the fourth month. Total nighttime sleep will be approximately 9 to 10 hours. You should still expect two to three daytime naps (each about 1½ to 2 hours). Baby's total sleep per 24-hour day? Around 14 to 16 hours.

Eating. Not much has changed since last month in terms of baby's diet (still liquids only).

- Breast milk. You'll be nursing around 6 to 8 times in a 24-hour period (you should find there are fewer middle-of-the-night feedings), and baby will be drinking somewhere between 24 and 36 ounces of breast milk a day . . . if you are keeping tabs.

- Formula. Your bottle drinker will likely be drinking around 5 to 7 ounces of formula 4 to 6 times per day for an average total of 24 to 32 ounces of formula a day.

Playing. What's baby playing with now? Play gyms and play yard toys are still fan favorites, but baby will also love to play with sensory toys—toys that trill or squeak or tweet or rattle when pressed or shaken—this month, and for many months to come. Watch how baby loves the entertainment an activity mat provides! Baby's reaching for toys now, so look for playthings that he or she can grasp on to. Soft books with high-contrast patterns and colors are hot items now, too. Read to your little one and watch how captivated he or she is by the pictures as you turn the pages. Also still captivating: mirrors that capture your cutie's image for his or her own viewing pleasure. Finally, toys that play music (especially in reaction to your baby's movements, such as a kickable keyboard) will be music to your little one's ears now, so be sure to add them to your baby's playthings.

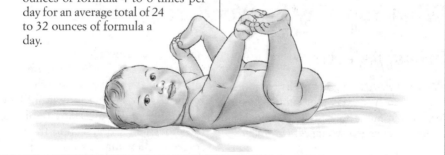

of formula a day. In a 24-hour period, you'll be feeding your baby around 3 to 4 ounces about every 4 hours.

- Babies under 6 months generally don't need more than 32 ounces of formula a day. Once solids are added to the mix, the number of formula ounces can be scaled back a bit.

- Most babies start off with 2 to 4 ounces per feeding during the first month and increase that amount by about 1 ounce per month until they reach 6 to 8 ounces per bottle. As your tiny one's tummy gets bigger and is able to hold more food at one sitting, he or she will probably drink fewer bottles a day with more formula in

What About This Month?

Looking for more information on how much formula to feed in a particular month? Check out the "Baby Basics at a Glance" boxes in the beginning of each chapter.

each bottle. The average 6-month-old, for instance, could be consuming 4 or 5 bottles of 6 to 8 ounces each day.

But because these are just rough guidelines, and because every baby is different (and even the same baby's needs are different on different days), you shouldn't expect your infant to follow this formula for formula precisely. How much your baby needs to take may vary somewhat—from day to day and feeding to feeding—and may differ significantly from the needs of baby buddies the same age. Keep in mind, too, that your baby's consumption won't just depend on weight, but on age, too. A large 6-week-old, for example, probably won't be able to drink as much as a small 3-month-old—even if they weigh about the same.

Most of all, remember that bottle-fed babies, just like breastfed babies, know when they've had enough—and enough, for a young infant, is like a feast. So take your cues from baby's hunger and feed to appetite instead of to a specified number of ounces. As long as your baby is gaining enough weight, is wetting and dirtying enough diapers, and is happy and healthy, you can be sure you're on target. For more reassurance, check with your baby's pediatrician on formula intake.

What You May Be Wondering About

Breast Rejection

"My baby was doing great at the breast—now, suddenly, he has pretty much been refusing to nurse for the past 8 hours. Could something be wrong with my milk?"

Something is probably wrong—though not necessarily with your milk. Temporary rejection of the breast, also called a nursing strike (even in non-union babies), is not unusual and almost always has a specific cause, the most common of which are:

Mom's diet. Have you been indulging in garlicky pesto? Feasting your chops and chopsticks on General Tso's chicken? Honoring Saint Patrick with corned beef and cabbage? If so, your baby may simply be protesting the spicy and/or strong flavors you've been seasoning his milk with. If you figure out what turns your baby off, avoid eating it until after you've weaned him. Many babies, on the other hand, don't mind the strong spices in their mama's milk, especially if they became accustomed to those flavors in utero through highly flavored amniotic fluid. In fact, some especially relish the taste of breast milk that comes with a kick.

A cold. A baby who can't breathe through a stuffy nose can't nurse and breathe through his mouth at the same time—understandably, he opts for breathing. If your baby has been stuffed up, gently suction baby's nostrils with an infant nasal aspirator. Is that snot too crusty? Soften it first with saline spray.

Teething. Though most babies don't start struggling with teeth until at least 5 or 6 months, a few begin much earlier, and an occasional baby actually pops a pearly or two in the first 4 months. Nursing often puts pressure on swollen gums, making suckling painful. When budding teeth are the cause of breast rejection, a baby usually starts nursing eagerly, only to pull away in pain.

An earache. Because ear pain can radiate to the jaw, the sucking motions of nursing can make discomfort worse. See page 556 for other clues to ear infection.

Thrush. If your baby has this yeast infection in his mouth, breastfeeding may be painful. Be sure the condition is treated so that the infection isn't passed on to you through cracked nipples or spread elsewhere on baby (see page 150).

Slow let-down. A very hungry baby may grow impatient when milk doesn't flow immediately (let-down can take as long as 5 minutes to occur in some nursing moms), and may push away the nipple in frustration before let-down begins. To avoid this problem, express a little milk before you pick him up, so that he'll get something for his efforts the moment he starts to suck.

A hormonal change in you. A new pregnancy (unlikely now if you're nursing exclusively, more possible if you've started your baby on supplemental formula feedings) can produce hormones that change the taste of breast milk, causing baby to reject the breast. So can the return of your period, which again isn't usually an issue until partial weaning begins.

Your stress level. Maybe you're stressed because you've recently returned to work. Maybe it's because it's bill-paying time, or because the dishwasher just broke again. Maybe it's just because you've had a really bad day. Whatever the reason, if you're worried or upset, you may be communicating your tension to your baby, making him too unsettled to settle down for nursing. Try to relax yourself before offering the breast.

Distraction . . . in baby. As your little one becomes ever more alert, he may start realizing there's more to life than mommy's breasts. Ever more easily distracted by the world around him, he may struggle to get a look at it, even as you're struggling to feed him. If that seems to be the case with your curious little cutie, try breastfeeding in a quiet, darkened, boring location.

Once in a while, there appears to be no obvious explanation for a baby's turning down the breast. Like an adult, a baby can be "off his feed" for a meal or two. Fortunately, this kind of hiatus is usually temporary. In the meantime, these suggestions may help you ride out the nursing strike:

- Don't try substitutes. Offering a bottle of formula when your baby balks at the breast could exacerbate the problem by decreasing your milk supply. Most nursing strikes, even longer-term ones, last only a day or two.

- Try some breast in a bottle. Express some milk and give it to your baby in a bottle if he continuously rejects the breast (though this won't work if it's something in the milk that's bothering him). Again, the strike is likely to last only a day or two, after which your baby will be ready to take milk from the source again.

- Try, try again. Even if he rejects it for a few feedings, chances are he'll surprise you and start right back where he left off.

- Slow down on solids. If you've started your baby on solid food, he may be eating too much, curbing his appetite for breast milk. At this age, breast milk is still more important than any solids (in fact, solids aren't usually recommended until 6 months), so cut down on the amount of solids you're feeding and always offer the breast first.

If rejection of nursing continues beyond a day or two, if you're concerned your baby isn't getting enough to eat, or if it occurs in connection with other signs of illness, check in with the doctor.

Wriggling at Changing Time

"My baby won't lie still when I'm changing her—she's always trying to turn over. How can I get her to cooperate?"

Realistically, you can't count on much diaper-changing cooperation at this increasingly active stage, and (sigh!) you'll likely see less and less as the months go by. Not surprisingly. After all, your baby turtle is both frustrated by being immobilized on her back, and bored with diaper business as usual—a combo that can set off a tussle with each change. The tricks: Be quick (have all the diapering supplies ready and waiting before you lay baby on the table) and provide distractions (a mobile above the changing table or any toy to occupy her hands and, hopefully, her interest). Engaging your baby in a song or a cooing conversation or a few belly raspberries may also divert her long enough to get the job done. Or try a change of diaper-changing locale—on a towel on the living room floor, for

example, or in the middle of your bed (don't leave her side for a moment, of course).

Propping Baby

"I'd like my baby to see what's going on around him when he's in the stroller, but he doesn't sit yet. Is it okay to prop him up?"

There's no need for your little one to take the world lying down anymore. As long as your baby can hold up his head well and doesn't crumple, slump over, or slide down when propped up, he's ready—and probably eager—for the props. Besides providing a welcome change of position, sitting affords your baby an expanded view of the world. Instead of just the sky or the inside of the stroller, an upright baby can see people, stores, houses, trees, dogs, other babies in strollers, older children, buses, cars—and all the other amazing things that inhabit his growing universe. He's also likely to stay happy longer than he would lying down, which will make outings more fun for both of you. Use a

A prop up will give your baby a new view of the world.

specially designed head support to help keep your baby's head upright when propped. Using a supportive shopping cart cover can keep him propped while you shop, too (just make sure it's designed for his age and size).

He'll also welcome props at home. Use specially designed propping pillows and let him play from a different vantage point. You'll know he's had enough of his more upright position when he starts to complain, wriggle, or slump down (it's hard work, after all).

Fussing in Baby Seat

"I really need to keep my baby in the infant seat once in a while so I can get things done. But she fusses as soon as I put her in."

Some babies are perfectly content to sit in an infant seat and watch the world (and their parents) go by. Others—usually those born with more get-up-and-go than they are able to get up and go with yet—are bored and frustrated by stints in the seat. Your baby may be among those who resist such confinement—in which case keeping her content in infant seats may be ever-challenging. To give yourself a fighting chance:

- Limit the captivity. Reserve the infant seat for times when you absolutely need your baby safely confined and near you (as when you're attempting a shower).

- Try a change of scenery. An infant seat with a view is less likely to provoke instant rejection. Place the seat on the floor in front of a mirror (she may enjoy interacting with her reflection) or in a safe spot next to you (there's nothing more fascinating than a parent in action).

- Add some entertainment. A toy bar can turn an ordinary infant seat into a personal entertainment center, particularly if toys are rotated to keep interest up and boredom from setting in. If toys seem to make baby fussier, it may be because she's overtired or overstimulated, in which case removing the entertainment may calm her.

- Make a motion. Turning on the rocking motion may soothe your baby while she's in the seat (though some babies are actually upset by the movement, so as always, take your cues from her reaction). Or put her in a bouncer that allows her to make her own motion.

- Let her loose. While younger infants are often satisfied to sit, older ones begin craving some freedom of movement. So instead of plunking her in the infant seat, try placing her on a blanket or play mat—tummy down—in the middle of the floor. This may not only placate her, but give her a chance to practice her rolling-over and creeping skills (though once she's mobile, you'll have to stay by her side for safety's sake).

- Consider a different approach. It's possible your baby has outgrown the infant seat, both physically and developmentally. If you need to keep her in one place sometimes, try a play mat/ gym or a well-stocked play yard.

Unhappy in Car Seat

"My baby cries every time I strap him into the car seat—I dread getting into the car as much as he does."

Though the purr of the car's engine and the motion of driving are both soothing and sleep-inducing to many infants (some will drop off to dreamland the moment the ignition powers on), not all babies agree that getting there is half the fun—especially when getting there means being strapped into a car seat. Rest assured that your son's not the only confinement-phobic baby on the block. Fussing in the car seat is common, particularly once babies become more active—and especially since facing the rear can be lonely and boring. To keep everyone happier on the road:

- Create a diversion. If your baby starts to struggle the moment he spies the car seat, keep him busy while you're buckling him up. Start singing a favorite song or holding up a favorite toy for him to look at as you attempt the dreaded procedure. With any luck, he won't notice what you're doing until the dirty work's done.

- Make him comfortable. Harness straps should be tight enough to ensure safety (you shouldn't be able to fit more than two fingers between baby and harness), but not so tight that they pinch or dig into baby's skin. Straps that are too loose, in addition to being unsafe, may also allow your tiny passenger to slide around, which may add to his discomfort. And if he still doesn't fill up the whole car seat, use the insert that came with the seat (not an aftermarket one) specially designed for smaller babies to make him more comfortable and less apt to flop from side to side. Also check the temperature in the backseat to make sure it's not too hot or too cold, and that there are no vents blowing directly on him.

- Block the sun. Most babies dislike having the sun in their eyes—which means you may have it made if baby's in the shade. Pull up the canopy on the seat, or invest in car shades to block the sun.

- Drive him with distraction. Play soothing music, lively songs for you to sing along with, or baby's favorite nature sound app. Load up with car-safe toys that can't be dropped (attach them safely to the seat with links or use ones that attach with velcro) and rotate them often so baby won't get bored. Place a specially designed mirror on the seat back in front of him (the view from a rear-facing car seat would bore anyone to tears). Not only will the reflection entertain him, but if you position the mirror in the right way, you'll be able to see his adorable face in your rearview mirror.

- Let him know you're there. It's lonely in the back. So do a lot of talking and singing (yes, even over the crying). The sound of your voice may eventually calm him down.

- Try a little companionship. When two adults are in the car, one can buckle in next to baby and offer some live entertainment and reassurance. Older siblings can do the same (all children under the age of 13 should ride in the backseat, anyway).

- Give it time, but don't ever give in. Eventually, your baby will come to accept the car seat (though he may never actually enjoy the ride in it). But caving on the car seat—even once, even just for a short ride—is not only incredibly dangerous (it takes only a moment for a crash to occur and for an unrestrained child to be injured or killed) but a strategic error, since it opens the door to future wiggle room.

Thumb Sucking

"My little one has taken to sucking her thumb. At first I was happy because it was helping her sleep better, but now I'm afraid it's going to become a habit I won't be able to break her of later."

It isn't easy being a baby. Every time you latch on to something that gives you the comfort and satisfaction you're searching for, somebody wants to take it away from you.

Virtually all babies suck on their fingers at some time during the first year of life—many even begin their habit in the womb. That's not surprising. An infant's mouth is important not just for eating, but for exploration and pleasure, too (as you will soon discover, when everything baby picks up makes a beeline to her mouth). But even before a baby can reach for objects, she discovers her hands. The first time, the hands may make it to the mouth by random chance, but baby quickly learns that a mouthful of fingers feels really good. Soon she's mouthing on her fingers regularly. Eventually, many babies decide that the thumb is the most efficient and satisfying finger to suck on (maybe because it's the easiest one to isolate) and switch from finger mouthing to thumb sucking. Some stick with one or two fingers, others prefer a whole fist (particularly while teething) . . . or even a two-fisted approach.

At first you may think the habit is cute, or even be grateful that your baby has found a way to pacify herself without your help. But then you start to wonder, and maybe worry—is this a habit that'll be hard to break? Or one that will lead to the orthodontist's office?

Well, stop worrying and start letting your baby feast on those fingers. There is no evidence that thumb sucking—if it stops by age 5—does damage to the alignment of permanent teeth. And nearly 80 percent of kids give up the thumb by age 5 (95 percent by age 6), usually on their own. Those who use it to help themselves get off to sleep or to comfort themselves in times of

---

Suck on This

Babies are known to suck on anything they can get their cute little mouths near—a nipple, their thumb, and you (your finger, your shoulder . . .). You might be extra tasty to your little one, but is your skin safe for baby chomping? After all, you applied body lotion after your shower this morning and some sunscreen later in the day before you headed out. Is baby getting a mouthful of more than he or she bargained for? Possibly. Though lotions and sunscreens wear off the longer you wear them, there's probably some residue left on your body. Which means your little chomper is likely sucking on some of that residue (and more, if he or she's mouthing you soon after application). If you can, switch up your products to baby-friendly ones that are as pure as possible (share your baby's products to save time, space, and money). Or wash or diaper wipe the lotions off before you hold baby.

---

stress hang on to the habit longer than those who are just in it for the oral gratification.

In the meantime, let your baby suck away. Be sure, however, that if she's breastfed, she isn't sucking her thumb to compensate for suckling she isn't getting at the breast. If she seems to want to nurse a little longer at each feeding, let her. And if thumb sucking is keeping her from using her hands for other explorations, occasionally remove her finger from its sucking station long enough to play a finger or hand game (This Little Piggy, pat-a-cake, or eyes-nose-mouth, for instance) or to help her shake a rattle.

Chubby Baby

"Everybody admires my chubby little baby. But I'm a little concerned that she's getting too fat. She's so round, she can hardly move."

With dimples on her knees and her elbows, a belly to rival any Buddha's, an extra chin to chuck, and an endearing amount of pinchable flesh on her cheeks, she's the picture of baby cuteness from head to chubby toes. Yet is the plump baby also the picture of health? Or is she on her way to becoming a fat child . . . and an obese adult?

It's a good question—and one that's being studied a lot these days. Research already shows that babies who put on weight speedily in their first 6 months may be at an increased risk of obesity as early as age 3. But even without the benefit of research, there are clearly disadvantages to extreme chubbiness early on. The baby who is too plump to budge may become the victim of a vicious cycle of inactivity and overweight. The less she moves, the chunkier she gets; the chunkier she gets, the less she can move. Her inability to move makes her frustrated and fussy, which may lead her parents to overfeed her to keep her happy. If she stays overweight through age 4, the odds that she will be an overweight adult increase greatly.

But—and this is a big but (and an adorable dimpled butt)—before you jump to any conclusions, be sure she is actually overweight and not rounded just right. Since babies haven't developed much muscle yet, even a slim one will sport significant padding—and that's as it should be. For a more accurate assessment, take a look at your baby's weight in relation to her length (see the charts, pages 116–119). If both are moving up quickly but on a similar curve, you probably just have a bigger-than average baby on your hands. If her weight seems to be moving up faster than her length, check with the doctor. She may be picking up too many pounds too quickly.

Should chubby babies go on a diet? Absolutely not. At this age she doesn't need to lose weight but rather to slow down the rate of gain, if she's off the charts. As she grows taller she will slim down—something most little ones do anyway, thanks to their increased activity (think nonstop running around).

Here's how to make sure your baby stays healthy—and at a healthy bottom line—throughout the first year:

■ Let appetite rule. Babies are born knowing how to regulate their appetites: They eat when they're hungry, stop when they're full. But that system can be easily disrupted by parental prodding to take those last few ounces of formula, to finish those last few bites of cereal. So let your little one call the shots—and call it quits—when it comes to feedings.

■ Feed for hunger's sake only. A baby who's fed not only when she's hungry but also when she's hurt or unhappy, when mom or dad is too busy to play with her, or when she's bored in the stroller will continue to demand food for the wrong reasons (and as an adult may eat for the same wrong reasons). Instead of feeding her every time she cries, try first to figure out whether she's crying for food. Offer comfort with a cuddle, not an extra feed (and if she needs extra sucking between meals or after a feed, offer a pacifier). When you're too busy to play with her, prop her in front of a mobile or an activity bar instead of propping her up with a bottle. Occupy her with a toy or a song in the supermarket instead of occupying her with food.

Hold the Juice

There's nothing more wholesome for a baby than a bottle of juice, right? Actually, that's wrong. Studies show that infants who fill up on juice—any fruit juice—may get too few nutrients. That's because juice (which isn't much of a step up nutritionally from sugar water, containing calories but none of the fat, protein, calcium, zinc, vitamin D, or fiber that babies need) can drown tender appetites for the breast milk or formula that should be the mainstay of a baby's diet in the first year of life. Too much juice can also cause diarrhea and other chronic tummy troubles, as well as tooth decay (a problem that's especially common among babies who take bottles or sippy cups of juice to bed or suck on them all day long). What's more (sometimes a lot more), the mainly empty calories in juice can lead to overweight.

The AAP recommends that fruit juice not be given at all to infants younger than 6 months. But even after 6 months, avoid giving any juice at bedtime, and give it only from a cup and only in small amounts during the day (no more than 4 to 6 ounces total daily for children up to the age of 6). Mixing the juice at least half-and-half with water will help ensure that your little one won't down too much, will minimize the effects on tummy and teeth, and will help prevent an early taste for sweet beverages. Or skip the juice entirely—it's definitely not a must-serve. Ultimately, your little one will be better off eating fruit than drinking it.

Your choice of juice matters, too. White grape, studies show, is less likely to trigger tummy troubles than that baby-standard, apple, especially for babies who suffered from colic. Later on, look for juices that have something to offer besides calories—added calcium and vitamin C, for instance.

- Wait on solids. Giving solids too soon, especially to formula-fed infants, can lead to overweight. Go slow when you do get the green light on solids from your baby's doctor, and offer them on a spoon, not in a bottle. Adding cereal to a bottle can add too many calories too easily. Be sure, too, that as you add more solids, the amount of breast milk or formula your little one gets goes down.

- Don't get juiced. Because it's sweet and easy going down, babies can chug far too many calories too fast in the form of juice. Babies under the age of 6 months shouldn't get any juice at all—and once it's introduced, it should be watered down and limited (see box above). Another important rule: Never offer juice in a bottle—wait for the cup instead.

- Make sure you're not underdiluting formula. Always check the label when you're mixing formula to make sure you're not inadvertently adding too little water—which can increase the calorie count per ounce of formula considerably, not to mention make it too salty.

- Get your baby moving. When you change her diaper, touch her right knee to her left elbow several times, then the reverse. With her grasping your thumbs, use your other fingers to hold her forearms, so she can "pull

A Baby Workout

Baby's not even officially crawling . . . or walking . . . or jumping—yet. But even though your little one isn't on the go, it doesn't mean it's too early to start him or her on the road to lifelong fitness. Here's how:

Fit in fitness. Every little bit of baby-moves counts, so get your little one going whenever you can. At playtime, pull him to a sitting position (or a standing one, when he's ready), gently raise her hands over her head and down to that roly-poly tummy, hold him up in the air with your hands around that adorable middle, and watch him flex those arms and legs. Add some activity into those endless diaper changes, too, by "bicycling" those chubby legs in a rhythmic way. And speaking of rhythm, add some of your own beat to your little one's exercise routines with a rocking tune.

Don't fence baby in. Is your little one always strapped into a stroller or an infant seat or snuggled into a sling? A baby who's given little opportunity to get moving may well become a junior member of the couch potato club—and, if those sedentary habits stick, possibly even a lifelong member. Be sure to give your budding gym rat plenty of freedom of movement—on a play mat on the floor or in the center of a large bed (with constant supervision, of course). For instance, watch him or her inch around, exploring by hands and mouth, pushing that bottom up in the air, raising head and shoulders, stretching those tiny arms and legs, kicking those feet, and trying to turn over (help your rock and roller practice by slowly turning him or her over and back again).

Keep it informal. No need to sign up for a formal baby movement class to get your little one moving anytime

up" to a sitting position. Let her "stand" on your lap—and bounce, if she likes. (See the box above for more on baby workouts.)

- Thinking of turning on the tap to slow your baby's weight gain? Though offering water to an overweight older baby may help curb extra calories, check with the doctor before giving water to one who's younger than 6 months.

Thin Baby

"All the other babies I see are roly-poly, but mine is long and thin. The doctor says he's doing just fine and I shouldn't worry, but I do."

Though they might not win as many diaper commercial roles as their roly-poly peers, slender babies are usually just as healthy—sometimes healthier. As long as he's content, alert, and otherwise thriving—and his weight, even if it's at the lower side of average, is keeping pace with his height—your lean little one is likely following his genetic blueprint, and in mommy and/or daddy's slimmer footsteps.

If you sense that your baby's not gaining enough because he's not getting enough to eat—and the baby's doctor confirms your hunch—you'll need to step up your feeding efforts so he can step up his weight gain. If you're breastfeeding, try the tips on page 182. If you're bottle-feeding, the doctor may soon, or even ever. Babies, given the opportunity, get all the exercise they need naturally. But if you eventually opt to sign up for a baby gym program (if only to give your little one a chance to try things he or she might not be able to try at home), check for the following before you hand over your credit card:

- Do the teachers have good credentials?

- Is the type of movement in the class safe for babies? Are classes just for babies or is it a mixed-age class? Baby-only is best, obviously.

- Do the babies seem to be having fun? Look for lots of eager, happy faces.

- Is there plenty of age-appropriate equipment for your baby to play with? For instance, brightly colored mats, inclines to creep up, balls to roll, and toys to shake.

- Are babies given plenty of opportunity to do their own thing? Circle

activities are fun, but classes should allow for plenty of free play.

- Is music an integral part of the program? There's nothing like bopping and moving to a beat—even for a baby.

- Does the class setting (and diaper-changing areas) seem clean?

Let baby set his or her pace. Call it quits when baby tells you it's time to quit (indifference or fussiness should clue you in).

Keep baby energized. Once solids are introduced, load up baby with the right kinds of food so he or she has the energy needed to get a move on.

Get yourself moving. Remember: The apple doesn't fall far from the tree, and neither does the couch potato tot. The best way to teach your little one the importance of exercise is to get yourself moving, too. Set a fit example, and you'll likely find your little one following in your running shoes.

suggest diluting the formula a little less, or adding a small amount of extra powdered formula or rice cereal to the mix (don't try this without doctor's approval, and be sure to follow directions on measurements precisely). Once solids get the green light, focusing on foods that are denser in calories and nutrients (e.g., avocado) can also help fill out your Slim Jim.

Also make sure that your little guy is feeding frequently enough—he should be eating a minimum of 5 times a day (more if he's breastfeeding). Some babies are too busy or too sleepy to demand regular meals, and others skimp on feeds because they're just as content to suck on a pacifier. If your baby is a mealtime slacker, you'll

have to take the initiative to make sure he brakes for feedings—even if that means cutting short a marathon daytime nap, interrupting a fascinating encounter with the crib gym, or unplugging the paci. If he's easily distracted, try feeding in a dark, quiet space.

Heart Murmur

"The doctor says my baby has a heart murmur but that it doesn't mean anything. Still, it sounds scary to me."

Hearing the words "heart murmur" can definitely make a new parent's heart skip a beat—and that's understandable. But happily, it's also unnecessary. The vast majority of heart murmurs are completely harmless and clinically insignificant. Most, in fact, do mean absolutely nothing . . . and that means that they're absolutely nothing to worry about.

So what is a heart murmur, and why is it not worrisome? It's abnormal heart sounds caused by the turbulence of the flow of the blood through the heart. The doctor can often tell if an abnormality is likely responsible for the murmur by the loudness of the sounds (from barely audible to almost loud enough to drown out normal heart sounds), by their location, and by the type of sound—blowing or rumble, musical or vibratory, for example.

Usually—and it sounds as though the doctor has already found this to be the case with your baby's—the murmur is the result of normal turbulence of blood flow due to the shape of the heart as it grows. This kind of murmur is called "innocent" or "functional," and is usually picked up by stethoscope at a routine doctor's visit. No further tests or treatments or limitations of activities are usually necessary. More than half of all babies will have an innocent murmur sometime during their lives, and it is likely to come and go throughout childhood. But the existence of the murmur

will be noted on your baby's record so other doctors who examine him at a later date will know it has always existed. Very often, when the heart is fully grown (or sometimes earlier), the murmur will disappear.

Occasionally, the pediatrician will ask a pediatric cardiologist to double-check that a baby's murmur is normal, which it's most often confirmed to be.

Black Stool

"My baby's last diaper was filled with a blackish BM. Could that means she's having a problem with her digestion?"

More likely she's been having an iron supplement. In some children, the reaction between the normal bacteria of the gastrointestinal tract and the iron in a supplement causes the stool to turn dark brown, greenish, or black. A change in poop color (usually to a dark green) can also happen if you recently started your breastfed baby on iron-fortified formula. There's no medical significance in this change, and no need to be concerned by it. If your baby has black stools and isn't taking a supplement or hasn't recently switched from breast milk to formula, check with her doctor.

ALL ABOUT:
Playthings for Baby

Walking into a toy store (or browsing toys on a baby store site) is like walking into a carnival in full swing. With every aisle or page bombarding the senses with its selection of eye-catching playthings for your bundle of joy, it's hard to know where to start and when to stop. So how can you make sure you don't succumb to the prettiest

packages and the most alluring gimmicks, and end up with a huge collection of the wrong toys for your baby? Check out the following before you head to the checkout:

Is it age-appropriate? The right toy will help your baby perfect skills already learned or help develop new ones just about to be tackled. How will you know if it's the right toy for your little player? Take a look at the toy's package. Those age-appropriate recommendations are there for two good reasons: first, to help you meet your baby's developmental needs, and second, to keep your little one safe. So while you might be taken in by that darling dollhouse, best to hold off until all that itty-bitty furniture no longer poses a choking hazard (and your baby has the manual dexterity to have fun playing with it). Giving your baby toys before he or she is ready for them has yet another disadvantage: It's possible that by the time baby is actually developmentally ready, the toys will be yesterday's boring news.

Is it stimulating? Not every toy has to bring your baby one step closer to that college acceptance letter—after all, babyhood (and childhood) are times for just plain fun, too. But your baby will have more fun with a toy if it's stimulating to the senses: sight (a mirror or a mobile), hearing (a music box, a rattle, or a bear with a bell in his belly), touch (a baby gym bar or activity board), or taste (a teething ring or anything else that's mouthable). As your baby grows, you'll want toys that help him or her learn hand-eye coordination, large- and small-motor gross- and fine-motor control, the concept of cause and effect, color and shape identification and matching, spatial relationships, and those that stimulate social and language development, imagination, and creativity.

Is it safe? Toys are responsible for more than 100,000 injuries a year, so when choosing playthings for your baby, you'll want to make safety tops on your list. In general, do your toy shopping at reputable stores and sites and choose toys that have been made recently by reputable toy manufacturers. Avoid

"antique" or vintage toys (the kind that you might pick up at a garage sale or flea market, or discover in grandma's attic) and noncommercial toys (say, made by craftspeople and sold at a farmers market or local shop)—or put them out of baby's reach until he or she is old enough to play with them without mouthing them or pulling them apart. Bargain stores may also sell imported toys that are unsafe (and often imported from countries where regulations are nonexistent). Specifically, look for:

- Age guidelines. Follow the recommendations from the toy's manufacturer on age appropriateness. These guidelines are there for safety reasons, not for educational readiness. If the toy you've bought used (or received handed down) has no packaging, check the age guidelines on the company's website. If it's so old that it's now off the market, play it safe: Don't let your baby play with it.

- Sturdiness. Steer clear of a toy that breaks or falls apart easily—it's an injury waiting to happen.

- Safe finish. Be sure that the paint or other finish is lead-free and isn't toxic. Keep up to date on toy recalls (cpsc .gov/recalls) to make sure you don't have unsafe toys in your house.

- Safe construction. Toys with sharp edges or breakable parts are unsafe.

- Washability. Bacteria love to put down roots on toys that can't be washed—and that could be a big problem for your little one, who likely puts everything (including bacteria-laden toys) in that adorable mouth. So look for toys that can be washed and disinfected.

- Safe size. Toys that are small enough to pass through a small-parts tester or a toilet paper tube, or that have small

Suitable for Cuddling

Nearly every stuffed animal your baby will encounter will be lovable and huggable. Here's how to make sure those teddies, giraffes, bunnies, and doggies are as safe as they are cute:

- Eyes and noses on animals should not be made of buttons or other small objects that could fall off (or be pried or chewed off) and pose a choking hazard. Screen for buttons elsewhere, too (such as on a teddy bear's suspenders).

- No wire should be used to attach parts (such as elephant ears). Even if the wire is covered with fabric, it could be chewed off or worn off and pose a puncture hazard.

- No strings should be attached—that goes for bows around the bunny's neck, a leash on the dog, a string on a pull toy, and so on—that are longer than 6 inches.

- Look for sturdy construction— seams and connections that are tightly sewn. Check periodically for wear that could allow stuffing to come out (which would pose a choking hazard).

- All stuffed animals should be washable, and should be washed periodically so germs don't collect on them.

- Never place stuffed animals in baby's bassinet or crib—they can pose a suffocation hazard.

removable parts or parts that can be broken off, present a serious choking hazard. Ditto toys with pieces that can be chewed off once teeth have poked through.

- Safe weight. Got a toy that's heavy? Keep it away from your lightweight. Heavy toys can cause an injury if they fall on your baby.

- No strings attached. Toys (or anything else) with strings, cords, or ribbons longer than 6 inches are a strangulation risk. Attach toys to cribs, play yards, and elsewhere with plastic links, which have the added bonus of being bright and fun to play with. Or buy toys that attach with velcro.

- Safe sound. Loud sounds can damage baby's hearing, so look for toys that have gentle sounds rather than sharp, loud, or squeaky ones, and ones that can have the sound lowered or turned off completely.

For more on choosing developmentally-appropriate toys for your baby, go to WhatToExpect.com.

CHAPTER 10

The Fifth Month

Your little one's the life of the party these days—and you're invited to enjoy every moment. And what's not to enjoy? During the fifth month, your baby continues being endlessly entertaining company, picking up new crowd-pleasing tricks almost daily, never seeming to tire of social interaction—especially with his or her favorite companion, you. Even better: With a (relatively) longer attention span, the interaction's a lot more dynamic than it was even a couple of weeks ago. Watching that little personality unfold is fascinating, as is baby's growing captivation with the expanding world around him or her. Baby's doing more than looking at that world now—he or she is touching it, too, exploring everything that's within reach with those hands, and everything that can fit (and many things that can't) with that mouth . . . possibly including those feet. Foot in mouth? That's standard practice for still phenomenally flexible babies.

Feeding Your Baby: Thinking About Solids

Chances are you've heard a conflicting message or two . . . or five . . . about when to start spooning up solids, all of them spooning up confusion: Start at 4 months! Definitely not before 6 months! You didn't start yet? No wonder your baby's not sleeping through the night!

Want the real dish on what's the right time for solids? First, listen to the experts. The AAP recommends holding off on feeding solids until your baby is 6 months old (and if you feel the need to start earlier to definitely wait until your little one is at least 4 months old).

Next, tune in to your baby. While most babies are ready for solids somewhere within those widely accepted guidelines (4 to 6 months), your little one's individual development definitely tops the list when deciding whether or not it's time to graduate to a more varied diet.

Baby Basics at a Glance: Fifth Month

Sleeping. Your baby will still be sleeping 15 hours—on average—each day. Those hours will likely be split between daytime naps (3 to 4 hours over two to three naps) and nighttime sleep (around 10 to 11 hours each night—though baby's likely to wake up once or twice during those 10 hours).

Eating. Baby is still on a liquid-mostly diet. (Though some parents choose to begin solids during the fifth month, most doctors recommend waiting until the half-year mark.)

- Breast milk. Count on an average of 5 to 6 feeds a day—though some babies nurse lots more than that. Baby will be drinking somewhere between 24 and 36 ounces of breast milk a day.

- Formula. You'll be bottle-feeding an average of 5 times a day, around 6 to 8 ounces of formula per bottle for a total of 24 to 36 ounces of formula a day.

- Solids. Most doctors recommend starting solids at 6 months. But if you're spooning up solids sooner, remember that baby doesn't need much more than 1 tablespoon of baby cereal mixed with 4 to 5 teaspoons of breast milk or formula once or twice a day, or the equivalent in fruit or vegetables if you've started with those foods. Breast milk or formula should still be the mainstay of baby's diet.

Playing. Baby's discovered how much fun his or her hands can be, both as playthings themselves and because they can manipulate objects and toys. So give baby toys he or she can grasp, mouth, and eventually, pass from hand to hand. If baby's still horizontal (not sitting), the play gym will still be fun, though try to switch out some of the dangling toys for interest. Activity bars on your little one's infant seat will provide loads of fun, as will squeaky rubber toys that can be squeezed, banged against the floor, or mouthed (especially when baby starts teething). Soft stuffed animals may become baby's favorites at this age, so be sure to provide your cuddly cutie with some cuddly cuties of his or her own. And as baby spends more and more time on his or her tummy, a fun activity mat can still provide lots of entertainment.

Though you might be eager to hop on the feeding bandwagon sooner rather than later (It's fun! It's cute! He'll sleep better! She'll cry less!), there are plenty of reasons why starting a baby on solids too soon isn't smart. First, a very early introduction to solids can occasionally trigger allergies. Second, a young baby's digestive system—from a tongue that pushes out any foreign substance placed on it, to intestines still lacking many digestive enzymes—is unready developmentally for solids. Third, solids aren't necessary early on—babies can fill all their nutritional needs for the first 6 months of life from breast milk or formula alone. Bringing on the solids too soon can also undermine future eating habits (baby may reject those spoonfuls initially simply because he or she isn't ready, then may reject them later because of previous parental pushing). And fourth, especially in formula-fed babies, early introduction of solids can lead to obesity later on in childhood and beyond.

On the other hand, waiting too long—say, until 8 or 9 months—can also lead to potential pitfalls. An older baby may resist being taught the new (and challenging) tricks of chewing and swallowing solids, preferring to cling to the tried-and-true (and easy) methods of tummy filling: breastfeeding or bottle-feeding. And, like habits, tastes may be tougher to change at this point. Unlike the more pliable younger baby, an older baby may not be as open to opening wide for solids when milky liquids have long monopolized the menu.

To decide if your baby is ready for the big step into the world of solid foods at 4 months, not till 6 months, or somewhere in between, look for the following clues—and then consult the doctor:

- Your baby can hold his or her head up well when propped to sit. Even strained baby foods should not be offered until then. Chunkier foods should wait until a baby can sit well alone, usually not until 7 months.

- The tongue thrust reflex has disappeared. This is a reflex that causes young infants to push stuff out of their mouths (an inborn mechanism that helps protect them from choking early on). Try this test: Place a tiny bit of baby-appropriate food thinned with breast milk or formula in your baby's mouth from the tip of a baby spoon or your finger. If the food comes right back out again with that tiny tongue, and continues to after several tries, the thrust is still present and baby isn't ready for spoon-feeding.

- Your eager beaver reaches for and otherwise shows an interest in table foods. The baby who grabs the fork out of your hand or snares the bread from your plate, who watches intently and excitedly with every bite you take, may be telling you he or she's hungry for more grown-up fare.

- Baby is able to make back-and-forth and up-and-down movements with the tongue. How can you tell? Just watch carefully.

- Your little one is able to open wide, so that food can be taken from a spoon.

For more on starting solids when the time comes, see page 343.

What You May Be Wondering About

Teething

"How can I tell if my baby's teething? She's drooling and biting on her hands a lot, but I don't see anything on her gums."

You may not be able to predict exactly when the teething fairy will fly in for a first visit (or future ones), but a number of signs can signal that she's on her way. Just which signs (and how uncomfortable they are) vary wildly from little

Tooth Eruption Chart

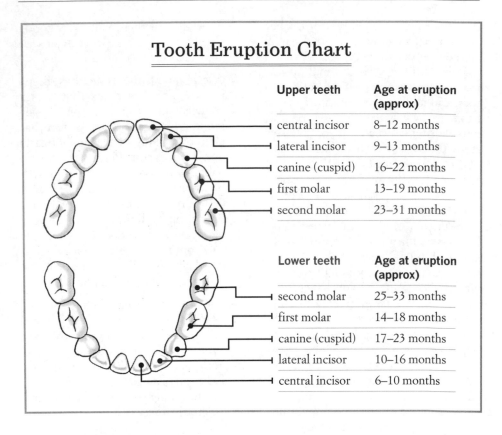

Upper teeth	Age at eruption (approx)
central incisor	8–12 months
lateral incisor	9–13 months
canine (cuspid)	16–22 months
first molar	13–19 months
second molar	23–31 months

Lower teeth	Age at eruption (approx)
second molar	25–33 months
first molar	14–18 months
canine (cuspid)	17–23 months
lateral incisor	10–16 months
central incisor	6–10 months

teether to little teether. For one baby, teething means lots of discomfort and big-time tears, while another baby might breeze to a mouth full of teeth without a complaint. Still, you can expect to see at least some, and maybe many, of the following symptoms (some of which can precede the actual appearance of a tooth by as much as 2 or 3 months):

Drooling. Does drool rule at your house? Since teething stimulates drooling, the faucet can start flowing early (usually anywhere from about 10 weeks to 3 or 4 months)—and often. Some babies drool buckets throughout their teething tenure.

Chin or face rash. The constant drip of saliva on those sweet cheeks and chin, around baby's mouth and neck, even on the chest area, can trigger chapping, chafing, dryness, redness, and rashes. Try to keep the areas as dry as possible by patting away the drool gently (and changing wet t-shirts quickly), create a moisture barrier with Vaseline or Aquaphor, and moisturize with a gentle skin cream as needed. Have some nipple cream on hand (like Lansinoh)? It's great for protecting tender baby skin, too.

Coughing. All that drool can make babies gag and cough (you'd choke, too, with a mouthful of spit). And as long as your little gagger isn't showing any other signs of cold, flu, or allergies, it's nothing to stress about.

Biting. Those pearly whites poking through those tender gums may be teeny tiny, but the pain and discomfort they cause can be plenty big. Counterpressure, aka biting, can bring the sweet relief your little teether is seeking. Teething babies will gum down hard on whatever they can find, from their own fists and fingers, to teething rings and rattles, to your nipples, shoulder, fingers . . . even your cheeks.

Pain. The inflammation of tender gum tissue can cause what seems like terrible pain to some babies, while others barely seem to notice. First teeth usually hurt the most (as do the molars, because they're just plain bigger), although most babies eventually get used to what teething feels like and aren't quite so bothered later on.

Irritability. Get ready for the crankies. Your baby's mouth will ache as that little tooth presses on the gums and pokes up to the surface, and not surprisingly, it'll probably make her feel fussy. Some babies are cranky for just a few hours, but others can stay crabby on and off for days or even weeks.

Feeding fussiness. Uncomfortable, cranky babies may seek comfort in a breast or bottle only to find that the suction of suckling makes tender gums feel worse. For that reason, teething babies may be fussy feeders—and frustrated ones. Babies on solids may also be off their feed. If your baby refuses several feedings in a row, check with the pediatrician.

Diarrhea. Doctors usually won't go on record saying so (since actual diarrhea isn't something to write off in a wee one), but to hear most parents tell it, loose poop happens when babies are teething, probably from all that swallowed drool. It may or may not happen with your teething baby, but make sure to report any diarrhea (liquidy, runny stools—not seedy mustardy ones) to your baby's doctor if it lasts more than two bowel movements.

Elevated temperature. Another symptom that doctors are reluctant to link to teething is a slight increase in temperature—especially since the first teeth often pop in around the same time babies start to lose some of the immunity protection they acquired through mom, making them more susceptible to infections and bugs. But like inflammation anywhere else in the body, inflamed gums can sometimes produce low-grade fever (less than 101°F, measured rectally). Treat it like any other low-grade fever—with a call to the doctor if it lasts for 3 days, sooner if it is accompanied by other worrisome symptoms. And definitely don't dismiss a higher fever as teething related.

Wakefulness. The teething fairy doesn't work only the day shift—she can work plenty of miserable mischief at midnight, too. In fact, like many pains, teething pain may be more bothersome to your baby in the evening hours—possibly disrupting nighttime slumber (even if she previously slept through). The wake-ups may be just momentary, so before offering comfort, see if she can settle herself back to sleep. If she's still restless, soothe her with patting or lullabies, but avoid a return to nighttime feedings if she's already given them up (these habits can continue long after teething pain has left the building).

Gum hematoma. Teething can trigger bleeding under the gums, which looks like a bluish lump. It's nothing to worry about and can heal faster (and feel better) with the help of a cold compress (a frozen washcloth can work wonders, but don't put ice directly on the gum).

Ear pulling and cheek rubbing. Teething babies may tug furiously at their ear or rub their cheek or chin. The reason? Gums, ears, and cheeks share nerve pathways, and so an ache in the gums (especially from erupting molars) can travel elsewhere. But since ear infections can also trigger ear yanking and cheek rubbing, do check with the pediatrician if you suspect your baby may be bothered by more than just teething (for example, if it's accompanied by a fever, not just a slight elevation in temperature).

"My baby seems to be in so much pain from teething. What can I do to help him?"

If you could, you'd take your baby's pain on for him. Since you can't, try these time-tested teething remedies to take at least some of the pain away:

- **Something to chew on.** Babies will chomp down on just about anything they can get their gums on when they're teething. That's because the gumming action provides soothing counterpressure. But not all little ones are fans of teething rings, or devotees of the same type of ring. Some like their teething toys soft and pliable, some like them harder. Some prefer plastic (some soft, some hard), others wood, others cloth. A textured, bumpy surface can offer more relief than a smooth one, a shape that fits neatly into that little mouth may score more points than one that is big and bulky, and squeaky sounds can offer a dose of distraction—but again, let your baby vote on the winner.

- **Something to rub against.** Some of the best teething tools are the ones attached to your baby's hands—those yummy fingers, of course. But your bigger, stronger fingers can actually be even more effective pain relievers. Wash one thoroughly (and trim any sharp nails), and use it to firmly massage your baby's sore spots. Just don't be surprised if your baby barracuda bites down.

- **Something cold.** Chilling your baby's gums numbs them—while easing inflammation and swelling. Keep a stash of teething rings in the freezer, try a frozen wet washcloth (you can store a supply of these in the freezer, too, each in a single layer separated by wax paper). If your baby has started solids, you can serve a feeder filled with frozen banana, applesauce, or peaches, or chilled avocado—and if he is over 6 months, you can also offer a bottle or sippy of ice cold water. Still on breast milk or formula only? Those can be frozen and provided in a feeder for his gumming pleasure as well.

- **Something to ease pain.** Still searching for teething relief? You can occasionally break out the baby acetaminophen (once your little one is over 6 months, you can opt for baby ibuprofen). The FDA warns against using benzocaine-based teething gels to numb pain, so don't turn to these or to homeopathic teething tablets or gels without the doctor's advice. A safer natural way to soothe? Soak a washcloth in chamomile tea (which calms inflammation), wring it out, freeze, then let baby suck on it. He's not a fan of cold? Just skip the freezer part and hand over a wrung-out wet washcloth at room temperature. Or try rubbing some room-temperature chamomile tea directly on those achy gums.

Chronic Cough

"For the last 3 weeks my baby has had a little cough. He doesn't seem sick, and he doesn't cough in his sleep—he almost seems to be coughing on purpose. Is this possible?"

Even as early as the fifth month, many babies have begun to realize that nothing beats an admiring audience. So when a baby discovers that a little cough—either triggered by teething or discovered when he was experimenting with sounds—gets a lot of attention, he may continue coughing just for its effect. As long as he's otherwise healthy and seems in control of the cough rather than vice versa, ignore it. Though your little performer may never lose his flair for the dramatic, he will probably give up this attention-getter as he (or his audience) becomes bored with it.

Ear Pulling

"My baby has been pulling at her ear a lot. She doesn't seem to be in any pain, but I'm worried that she might have an ear infection."

Babies have a lot of territory to discover—some of it on their own bodies. The fingers and hands, the toes and feet, that diaper area, and another curious appendage, the ear, will all be targets of exploration at one time or another. Unless your baby's pulling and tugging at her ear is also accompanied by crying or obvious discomfort, fever, fussiness, food refusal, and/or other signs of illness (see page 556 if it is), it's very likely that it's a sign of curiosity, not a symptom of ear infection. Some babies may also fuss with their ears when teething (a result of the pain that's referred from sore gums to the ear) or when they're tired. Redness on the outside of the ear isn't a sign of infection, just a result of all that rubbing. If you suspect your baby's sick—or if ear pulling continues unexplained—check with the doctor.

Naps

"My baby is awake more, much more, during the day and I'm not sure—and I don't think he is either—how many naps he needs, or how long each one should be."

Remember when you brought your little bundle home from the hospital? You'd stand over the bassinet all day, watching his sweet slumber, wondering when your cutie would wake up so you could play and cuddle with him. Fast-forward a few months, and now you're aching for a nap (or at least a few minutes off baby duty)—and wondering when he'll take one, too, and how long the snooze will last.

Though the typical baby in the fifth month takes 3 or 4 pretty regular naps of an hour or so each during the day, some babies thrive on 5 or 6 naps of about 20 minutes each, and others on two longer ones of 1½ or 2 hours. The number and length of naps your baby takes, however, are less important than the total amount of shut-eye he gets (about 14½ to 15 hours a day on average during the fifth month, with wide variations from baby to baby), and how well he does on the sleep he gets. Longer naps are more practical for you—nobody needs to tell you this—because they allow you longer stretches in which to get things done. Another reason to encourage longer daytime naps? A catnapper during the day may follow the same pattern at night, waking up again and again. Getting your little one used to longer daytime naps may increase the chances for a better night's sleep for you.

Here are a few strategies to use to try to extend nap time:

Choose a good napping location. Comfort is key to a longer nap, so make sure your baby drifts off in a place where

For Parents: Carving Out Couple Time

Love cuddling your little one—but wondering when you're ever going to have a chance to cuddle someone your own size again? No surprise there. When your arms are always full of baby, your days and nights filled with feedings, and a few minutes of sleep understandably trump a few minutes of romance, it's hard to fit in some just-for-two time. But while babies need a whole lot of nurturing, your relationship does, too. How do you shift your twosome from back burner to front and center and keep sexy alive when baby makes three? Start by thinking of romance in terms of quality, not quantity.

Grab a few minutes together every day. Put aside just-for-two time—or, let's face it, you'll never take it. Start a morning cuddle policy—even if it's just a quick hug before you both leap out of bed. Make a nightly date for a late dinner, or a snack, or a sofa snuggle once baby's tucked in. And try to end every night with a hug and a good-night kiss. Why should babies get all the bedtime loving?

Be touchy. There's no better way to keep connected than through touch. So reach out and touch your partner as often as you can—even if it's fleeting,

it's effective. A pat on his butt when he's changing baby's. A sneaky squeeze while she's getting dressed. A smooch, a hug, a hand on his knee for no reason at all. Remember, sex isn't the objective—or realistically, the likely end game. Intimacy is.

Schedule regular couple time. It's time to start dating each other again. Pick a date night—whether it's once a week or once a month—and put it on the calendar so you can't punk out. Can't spring for a sitter? Swap child care with other new parents or enlist a willing relative. At the very least, nab some tender time without leaving the nest: Download a movie, order takeout, and do some heavy cuddling on the couch.

Don't forget your mate. There's no question that your baby's needs come first right now—but that doesn't mean your partner has to feel like a distant second. So give your mate your full-on attention when you can—even if it means finishing up the cuddle with your big sweetie before picking up your little sweetie. And don't forget that three can be cozy company, too—try a three-way cuddle and you'll see why.

---

he can happily snooze for a solid while (his crib, that is, as opposed to your shoulder). Of course, occasional naps in the stroller or car seat are inevitable and fine, but don't substitute those spots for the crib (or pack-and-play) on a regular basis.

Choose a good naptime. As always, the best time to schedule a snooze is when baby is getting sleepy but not once he's crossed that fine line to overtired. So look for those snooze clues—they're

his body's way of telling you it's time for a nap.

Think ahead. A little advance planning can translate into many more minutes asleep, so avoid these surefire nap killers: an empty tummy (he'll probably wake up too soon . . . and crabby), a very wet or full diaper (try to put him down with a clean one if possible), a too warm or too cool environment (or an outfit that's too heavy or too light for comfortable sleep).

Ease into nap mode. It's hard to drift off to dreamland when you've just been scooped up from your toys and swept off to your crib. Instead, allow a little buffer time for your baby, so he can wind down, mellow out, and get in a sleepier state of mind. Set a sleepy mood, too, by dimming lights, putting on some soothing music, and giving your baby a relaxing massage. The more alert and active your little one becomes, the more transition time he'll need before naps.

Run interference. If your baby wakes (or cries) 20 minutes into his nap, try to encourage a longer snooze by offering some gentle strokes and soothing words—without picking him up. If soft music is the key to summoning his sandman, put it on to help him fall back asleep (or turn on the white noise). Once he realizes that play is not in the plan right now, chances are he'll drift off once again.

Increase baby's awake time. By 4 or 5 months, you can expect your baby to be able to stay up for 2 to 3 hours at a stretch. And the longer your baby is awake between naps, the longer he's likely to sleep once he goes down. Try any of the infant-stimulating ideas on pages 255 and 369 to increase stay-awake time—so you can consolidate stay-asleep time.

Though many babies regulate themselves pretty well when it comes to getting their quota of sleep, not every baby gets as much as he needs. How can you tell if your little one is cashing in on that quota or falling short? Look to his mood—a baby who's mostly happy is most likely getting enough nap time, while one who's chronically cranky probably isn't. Your baby sleeps very little, yet seems perfectly content, active, and alert? He may just be one of those babies who need less shut-eye.

Eczema

"My baby has begun to break out in a red rash on her cheeks. It must be itchy, because she keeps trying to scratch it."

What's smooth, silky, soft . . . and suddenly dry, flaky, and rashy red all over? Baby skin that has been hit by eczema, that's what. Eczema usually appears in patches, starting at about 2 to 4 months, in very visible places, such as those chubby cheeks, behind the ears, and on the scalp. Then it typically spreads south to the elbow creases, behind the knees, and sometimes even to the diaper area. The flaky skin gets redder, and small pimples pop up, fill with fluid, and then burst. Baby eczema isn't pretty, and yes, it's very itchy for your little one. Happily, however, it isn't dangerous or contagious, and it usually resolves itself.

Eczema is the term doctors use to describe both atopic dermatitis (a typically inherited chronic condition more common among babies with a family history of allergies, asthma, and eczema) and contact dermatitis (when skin comes in contact with an irritating substance). With contact dermatitis, the rash usually clears when the irritant is removed (a stubborn case can be treated with hydrocortisone cream or ointment). Treatment for atopic dermatitis that doesn't go away on its own includes hydrocortisone cream or ointment and possibly antihistamines to reduce the itching.

On the home front, it's important to:

- Keep baby's nails short to prevent scratching. You may be able to prevent her from scratching while she's sleeping by covering her hands with a pair of socks or mittens (built into some long-sleeve sleepers).

- Gently pat drool away whenever you see it, because excessive wetness can set off an eczema outbreak.

- Limit baths to no longer than 10 or 15 minutes, and use an extra-mild soap-less cleanser (Aveeno or Cetaphil, for example) only as needed. Occasionally, sprinkle a pinch of baking soda, a handful of uncooked rolled oats (not instant), or colloidal oatmeal (made specifically for baths) into baby's bath water (put the oatmeal in a sock or fine mesh bag to contain it). All are natural eczema treatments.

- Limit dips in chlorinated pools and salt water.

- Pat—don't rub—skin dry, and apply plenty of rich hypoallergenic moisturizer (like Aveeno, Eucerin, Lubriderm, or Aquaphor) after baths, when skin is still damp.

- Minimize exposure to extremes in temperature, indoors and out. Think layers when dressing your little one so you can remove one or more if things get too toasty (sweating can reboot the eczema cycle).

- Use a cool-mist humidifier (clean it frequently to prevent bacteria or mold buildup) to prevent dry indoor air. But don't overdo the humidity in your home, because it can lead to mold and mildew, common allergy and asthma triggers.

- Dress your baby in the softest cotton knits (rather than wool or synthetics), avoiding clothes that are scratchy against sensitive skin. Wash new clothes as needed to soften them up before baby wears them.

- When your baby plays on carpeting, which can irritate the skin, too, place a cotton sheet under her.

- Switch to detergent that's fragrance-free and meant for sensitive skin.

- Eliminate any food that seems to trigger a flare-up or a worsening of the rash—sometimes just topical exposure to an irritating food (she smears tomato sauce on her face) can set off a reaction.

- Ask the pediatrician about probiotics, which have been shown in some studies to reduce the incidence and severity of eczema in some babies.

Food Allergies

"How will I know if my son is allergic to certain foods? It seems everyone's baby has some sort of allergies these days."

About 8 to 10 percent of children under 18 have food allergies—with the most common offenders being milk, eggs, nuts and peanuts, soy, and wheat. Those babies with a family history of allergies tend to be the ones most at risk of developing allergies—so if you or your spouse (or both of you) have allergies, asthma, or eczema, chances are higher that your baby will have allergies, too.

A baby becomes allergic to a substance when his immune system becomes sensitized to it by producing antibodies. Sensitization can take place the first time his body encounters a substance or the hundredth time. But once it does, antibodies rev into action whenever the substance is encountered, causing any one of a wide range of physical reactions, including runny nose and eyes, headache, wheezing, eczema, hives, diarrhea, abdominal pain or discomfort, vomiting, and, in severe cases, anaphylactic shock.

Not every adverse reaction to a food or other substance, however, is an allergy. What appears to be an allergy may sometimes be an enzyme deficiency that triggers an intolerance. Babies with insufficient levels of the enzyme lactase, for example, are unable to digest the milk sugar lactose, and so they react badly to milk and milk products. And those with celiac disease are unable to digest gluten, a substance found in many grains, and so they appear to be allergic to those grains. The workings of an immature digestive system or such common infant problems as colic may also be misdiagnosed as allergy. If you suspect a food allergy, consult with your doctor or a pediatric allergy specialist. They can do tests to help determine whether your baby has a true food allergy or other issue (such as lactose intolerance).

There's not much you can do to prevent allergies in your little one if he's predisposed to having them, though studies do show that breastfeeding your baby for at least 6 months and ideally a year or longer will help keep allergies at bay. For high-risk formula-fed babies, a hydrolysate formula may be recommended over regular formulas (including soy-based ones). When it comes to solid food introduction, it was once common to delay giving a baby certain foods like dairy, eggs, seafood, and nuts in the hopes of staving off allergies, but the AAP no longer recommends that since the data shows that holding off on certain foods does not prevent food allergies. Most pediatricians do say, however, that you can lower your baby's risk of developing food allergies if you wait until he's 6 months old (instead of 4 months) to start solids. Not so sure what's best for your baby? Check in with the doctor.

If a true allergy exists, you'll need to keep your baby away from the offending food (sometimes just touching it or even inhaling its scent can be dangerous). You'll need to become an expert at reading labels and screening foods at playgroup, plus you'll want to come up with a response plan in case your baby is accidentally exposed to the offending food. Be sure to share this plan with anyone who cares for your baby, including regular childcare providers, occasional babysitters, and family members, so they'll know what to do in case of an emergency.

The good news is that food allergies are often outgrown during early childhood. Experts say that 80 to 90 percent of egg, milk, wheat, and soy allergies disappear by age 5.

Baby Swing

"My baby loves being in her infant swing—she can spend hours in it. How much time can I allow her to spend swinging?"

Being in the swing of things is entertaining and soothing for baby, and convenient for you when your arms are otherwise occupied, but it does come with a downside. Too much swinging can prevent your baby from practicing important motor skills, such as creeping, crawling, pulling up, and cruising. It can also cut down on the amount of contact your baby has with you—both physical (the kind she gets from being held by you) and social (the kind she gets from playing with you).

So keep on swinging, but with restrictions. First, limit swinging sessions to no longer than 30 minutes at a time, twice a day. Second, place the swing in the room you'll be in and keep interacting with your baby even as she swings—play peekaboo behind a dish towel while you're making dinner, sing songs while you're checking your Facebook page, swoop down for an occasional cuddle while you're talking on the cell. If she tends to fall asleep in the swing (who can blame her?), try to complete the transfer to the crib before she nods off—not only so that her head doesn't droop, but so that she'll learn to fall asleep without motion. And, third, keep these safety tips in mind whenever she swings:

- Always strap baby in to prevent falls.

- Never leave your baby unattended while she's in the swing.

- Keep the swing at least arm's length away from objects that your baby can grab on to (such as curtains, floor lamps, drapery cords), and away from dangerous items a baby can reach for (such as outlets, the oven or stove, or sharp kitchen utensils). Also keep the swing away from walls, cabinets, or any surface your baby might be able to use to push off from with her feet.

- Once your baby reaches the manufacturer's weight limit recommendation, usually 15 to 20 pounds, pack up the swing.

Jumpers

"We received a jumping device, which hangs in the doorway, as a gift for our baby. He seems to enjoy it, but we're not sure if it's safe."

Jumpers come in the doorway variety (it attaches to the upper doorway frames and allows for swinging and jumping) and the stand-alone combined activity jumper (it looks like a stationary activity center but has springs and an open bottom to allow for jumping). Most babies are ready and eager for a workout long before they're independently mobile—which is why many enjoy the acrobatics they can perform in a baby jumper. So allow your bouncing baby to jump for joy, but be aware that some pediatric orthopedic specialists warn that too much jumper use might cause certain kinds of injuries to bones and joints. What's more, baby's exhilaration with the freedom of movement

a jumper affords can quickly turn to frustration as he discovers that no matter how—or how much—he moves his arms and legs, he's destined to stay put in the doorway or in his jumper station.

If you do opt to use the doorway jumper, make sure your doorways are wide enough. And no matter which type of jumper you use, remember, as with any baby-busying device (a stationary walker or a swing, for example), that its purpose is to meet your baby's needs, not yours. If he's unhappy in it, take him out immediately. Even if your baby seems to love it, limit jumper use to no more than 30 minutes, twice a day. And never leave your baby unattended in the jumper—even for a moment.

The Challenging Baby

"Our baby is adorable, but she seems to cry so easily. Everything seems to bother her—noise, bright light, being even a tiny bit wet. Is it something we're doing wrong? We're going crazy trying to cope."

Pregnant daydreams are pink-and-blue collages of a contented infant who coos, smiles, sleeps peacefully, cries only when she's hungry, and grows into a sweet-tempered, cooperative child. Challenging children—those inconsolable babies and kicking, screaming toddlers—clearly don't make the daydream. If they do, they belong to another parent—one who did it all wrong and is paying the price.

And then, for so many parents like you, reality does a number on that particular fantasy. Suddenly, it's your baby whose behavior is challenging—who's crying all the time, who won't sleep, or who seems perpetually unhappy and dissatisfied no matter what you do . . .

long after she should have outgrown colic or other newborn fussiness. Which makes you wonder, "What did we do wrong?"

The reassuring answer is: absolutely nothing, except maybe pass on some contributing genes, since a challenging temperament appears to have much more to do with nature than nurture. What's more (and even more reassuring): You're far from alone in the challenge of having a challenging baby—more than 25 percent of parents do. Knowing that you have company can help immeasurably—as can commiserating, venting, and swapping tips and insights with parents who feel your frustration. (Look for parents who can relate on the message boards at WhatToExpect.com.)

Something else that can help a lot: knowing how to adapt your little one's environment so that it's a better (and more soothing) fit for her challenging temperament. First, you'll need to figure out exactly where the challenge lies with your baby. Here are some types of challenging temperaments (keep in mind, there may be overlap between categories for your baby), as well as some techniques for coping with them:

The low-sensory-threshold baby. A wet diaper, a tight t-shirt, a high neckline, a bright light, a scratchy sweater, a cold crib—any or all of these may stress out a baby who seems to be extra sensitive to sensory stimulation. In some little ones, all five senses (hearing, vision, taste, touch, and smell) are very easily overloaded—in others, just one or two. Helping a low-sensory-threshold baby means trying to keep the general level of unnecessary sensory stimulation down, as well as avoiding those specific things that bother her, such as:

- Sound sensitivity. As much as is practical (remember, you still have to live in the house, too) lower the sound

level in your home. Keep the TV and all other sound systems low, adjust all telephone rings to low or vibrate, and install carpets and curtains, where possible, to absorb sound. Speak or sing to your baby softly, experimenting with pitch to see which are most appealing to her sensitive ears, and watch for her reaction to musical or other sound-producing toys, too. If outside noises seem to be a problem, try a white-noise machine or app or an air cleaner in baby's room to block them out.

- Light or visual sensitivity. Use room-darkening shades or curtains where baby sleeps so the light won't disturb her, filter out bright sunlight in her stroller with a cover, and avoid turning on bright lights wherever she is. Try not to expose her to too much visual stimulation at once—give her just one toy to play with at a time, and keep it simple. Select toys that are soft and subtle in color and design rather than bright and busy.

- Taste sensitivity. If your baby is breastfed and has a bad day after you've eaten garlic or onions, consider that she's not keen on the flavor your milk has picked up. If she's bottle-fed and seems cranky a lot, try switching to a formula with a different taste (ask the doctor for a recommendation). When you introduce solids, let her sensitive palate be your guide—respect that she may reject strong flavors entirely (though don't always assume it).

- Touch sensitivity. With this princess-and-the-pea-like syndrome, your baby might lose her cool as soon as she wets her diaper, become frantic when she's dressed in anything but the softest fabric, scream when she's dunked in the tub or put down on a too-chilly mattress, struggle when you tie her shoes over wrinkled socks. So dress her for comfort (cotton knits with smooth seams and buttons, snaps, labels, and collars that won't irritate because of size, shape, or location are ideal), adjust bathwater and room temperatures to levels that keep her happy, and change diapers frequently (or change the diapers you're using to ones that are softer and more absorbent).

A small percentage of babies are so oversensitive to touch that they fuss in a sleep sack, try to break free of a kangaroo hold, and even resist cuddling, especially skin-to-skin. If that sounds like your little one, do a lot of your caressing and interacting with words and eye contact rather than actual physical touching. When you do hold your baby, learn which way seems least annoying (tight or loose, for example). Observe closely to see what feels good and what doesn't. And most of all, don't take her preferences personally—remember, this is nature talking, not nurture.

- Smell sensitivity. Unusual odors aren't likely to bother a very young infant, but some babies begin to show a negative reaction to certain scents before the end of the first year. The aroma of frying eggs, the smell of a diaper rash cream, the fragrance in a fabric softener or a lotion, can all make a smell-sensitive baby restless and unhappy. If your baby seems sensitive to smells, limit her exposure to strong odors when you can, and go fragrance-free as much as possible.

- Stimulation sensitivity. Too much stimulation of any kind seems to trigger trouble for some infants. These babies need to be handled gently and slowly. Loud talk, hurried movements, too many toys (particularly very stimulating ones), too many people around, too much activity in a day can all be stressful. By watching your baby's reactions carefully, you'll be able to ease her sensory load before she hits overload. To help your stimulation-sensitive baby sleep better, avoid active play just before bedtime, substituting a soothing, warm bath followed by quiet storytelling or lullabies. Soft music may help her settle down, too.

The active baby. Babies often send the first clue that they're going to be more active than most right from the womb—suspicions are confirmed soon after birth, when swaddles are kicked off, diapering and dressing sessions become wrestling matches, and baby always ends up at the opposite end of the crib after a nap. Active babies are a constant challenge (they sleep less than most, become restless when feeding, can be extremely frustrated until they're able to be independently mobile, and are always at risk of hurting themselves), but they can also be a joy (they're usually very alert, interested and interesting, and quick to master milestones). While you don't want to curb your active baby's enthusiasm and adventurous nature, you'll definitely want to take steps to keep her safe as she takes on her environment, as well as learn ways to calm her for eating and sleeping:

- Be especially careful never to leave your active baby on a bed, changing table, or any other elevated spot even for a second—she may figure out how to turn over very early, and sometimes just when you least expect it. A restraining strap on the changing table is essential, of course, but don't rely on it if you're more than a step away from your extra wriggly wee one.

- Adjust the crib mattress to its lowest level as soon as your baby starts to sit alone for even a few seconds—the next step may be pulling up and over the sides of the crib.

- Don't place your active baby's infant seat anywhere except on the floor— she may be capable of overturning the seat. And of course, baby should always be strapped in.

- Learn what slows down your active baby—massage, soft music, a warm bath. Build such quieting activities into your baby's schedule before feeding and sleeping times.

The irregular baby. At about 6 to 12 weeks, just when other babies seem to be settling into a schedule and becoming more predictable, an irregular baby seems to become more erratic. Not only doesn't she fall into a schedule on her own, she's not interested in any you may have to offer.

Sound like your baby? Instead of following her chaotic lead or trying to impose a very rigid schedule that goes against her erratic nature, try to find a comfortable middle ground. To put a modicum of order in her life and yours, try as much as possible to build a schedule around any natural tendencies she might have (as hard to spot as they might be). Keep a diary to uncover any hints of a recurring time frame in your little one's days, such as hunger around 11 a.m. every morning or fussiness after 7 p.m. every evening.

Try to counter any unpredictability with predictability. That means trying, as much as possible, to do things at the same times and in the same ways every day. Nurse in the same chair when possible, give baths at the same time each day, always soothe by the same method (rocking or singing or whatever works best). Try scheduling feedings at roughly the same times each day, even if your baby doesn't seem hungry, and try to stick to the schedule even if

she is hungry between meals, offering a small snack if necessary. Ease rather than force your baby into more of a structured day. And don't expect true regularity, just a little less chaos.

Nights with an irregular baby can be the toughest challenge of all, mostly because she may not differentiate them from days. You can try the tips for dealing with night-day differentiation problems (see page 205), but it's very possible they won't work for your baby, who may want to stay up throughout the night, at least initially. To survive, you may need to alternate night duty or share split shifts with your parenting partner (if you have one) until things get a bit more predictable, which they eventually will with some calm persistence.

The poor-adaptability or initial-withdrawal baby (aka the "slow-to-warm-up" baby). These babies consistently reject the unfamiliar—new objects, people, foods. Some are upset by change of any kind, even familiar change such as going from the house to the car. If this sounds like your baby, try setting up a daily schedule with few surprises. Feedings, baths, and naps should take place at the same times and in the same places, with as few departures from baby's routine as possible. Introduce new toys and people (and foods, when baby is ready for them) very gradually. For example, hang a new mobile over the crib for just a minute or two. Remove it and bring it out again the next day, leaving it up for a few minutes longer. Continue increasing the time of exposure until baby seems ready to accept and enjoy the mobile. Introduce other new toys and objects in the same way. Have new people spend a lot of time just being in the same room with your baby, then talking at a distance, then communicating close up, before they make an attempt at physical

iBaby

Has your smartphone already become your baby's toy of choice? Does she coo over YouTube—or babble up a storm in answer to the talking heads on TV? Does he giggle with glee when a swipe of your iPad makes images flash and icons dance? In a world where a handheld is hardly ever out of arm's reach, it's hard to keep your little one from becoming wired by wireless. But is all of that exposure to electronic media good for your tiny techie? Check out the answers on page 509.

---

contact. Later, when you introduce solids, add new foods very gradually, starting with tiny amounts and increasing portion size over the span of a week or two. Don't add another food until the last is well accepted. Try to avoid unnecessary changes when making purchases—a new bottle with a different shape or color, a new gadget on the stroller, a new style of pacifier.

The high-intensity baby. You probably noticed it right at the beginning—your baby outcried every other newborn in the nursery. Her louder-than-average crying, the kind that can frazzle even the steadiest nerves, played on a loop when you got home . . . and hasn't stopped. You can't flip a switch and turn down the volume on your baby, of course, but turning down the volume of noise and activity in the environment may help tone your little one down a bit. Also, you will want to take some purely practical measures to keep the noise from bothering family and neighbors. If possible, soundproof your baby's room by insulating the walls with insulating board or padding, adding carpeting, curtains, and anything else that will absorb the sound. You can try earplugs, a white-noise machine, or a fan or air conditioner to reduce the wear and tear on your ears and nerves without totally blocking out your baby's cries. As the amount of crying your baby does lessens in the months ahead, so will this problem, but your little one will probably always be louder and more intense than most.

The negative or "unhappy" baby. Instead of being all smiles and coos and dimpled joy, some babies just seem serious all the time, even grumpy. This is no reflection on a baby's parents or their parenting skills (unless, of course, depression or other issues in the home are leaving the baby emotionally or physically neglected), but it can have a profound impact on them. They may find it difficult to bond with their unhappy baby, and may even stop trying.

If nothing seems to make your baby happy, check with the doctor to rule out any medical explanation. Then do your best (and it won't always be easy) to be loving, caring, nurturing, and particularly, happy around your baby, secure in the knowledge that the grumpiness is just his or her temperament at work. Chances are that as your baby learns other ways of self-expression (besides crying), the general unhappiness will diminish, though he or she may always be the "serious" type.

In the meantime, you may find it helpful to seek support and coping strategies from other parents who have a chronically unhappy baby, as well as to turn to the pediatrician for help (and possibly, to a developmental pediatrician or an early childhood behavioral specialist).

Before you decide that your baby is definitely one of the challenging ones, consider whether the extra fussiness isn't due simply to a longer-lasting case of colic or an allergy to formula or a sensitivity to something in your diet, if she's breastfed. Not getting enough sleep (day, night, or both) can also make a baby extra-cranky, as can teething. Check in with the doctor, too, to rule out any physical causes that might need treatment (like acid reflux, for instance).

If your baby does turn out to be very challenging by nature, it won't be easy taking the extra steps to keep her calm and relatively happy—but it will almost always be worth the effort. Keep in mind, however, that you won't always be able to put her unique needs first (she's sensitive to bright lights and noise, but you have to take her with you to a family Christmas celebration). That's fine, too—life must go on even now that your life includes a challenging baby—though you may have to deal with the crying consequences once the party's over.

Most important, keep in mind that while temperament is hardwired by nature, it's not carved in stone. Challenging characteristics can change, mellow, and sometimes even seem to disappear over time, and parents can learn strategies to help their little ones adapt. What's more, those challenging traits can often be channeled to turn a liability into an asset.

Need some help coping with your challenging baby on a daily basis? Look for support from those who know—especially other parents who share your challenges (ask around online—you're sure to find plenty). Your baby's pediatrician can also provide you with strategies, as well as refer you (if necessary) to a developmental pediatrician or an early childhood behavioral specialist who can help you better help your baby.

ALL ABOUT:
A Safe Environment for Your Baby

It's a big, beautiful, exciting world out there, and for your newborn, who has gone from the controlled cocoon of your womb to the protective embrace of your arms, it's been a pretty safe one so far, too. But as your little one's world opens up—and as he or she starts opening up wide for a wider array of edibles (and inevitably, nonedibles), begins exploring with curious hands, and (before you know it) masters mobility on all fours, and then on two feet—the safety of his or her environment gets a little sketchier. From the air your baby breathes, to the food he or she eats, the toys he or she plays with, and the grass

Safe Baby Products

Wondering about the safety of the lotions, shampoos, and soaps you use on your baby's tender skin? See page 38 for the lowdown on safe baby products.

A Greener Clean

Every time you wipe down the changing table, bathroom, or kitchen counter with a product that contains lots of chemicals, you leave a little bit of toxic residue behind. For a safer, greener clean, consider switching to natural cleaning methods and nontoxic cleansers—they'll get the job done and keep your baby safe. To screen for green, look for products with these terms on their labels: biodegradable, plant-based, hypoallergenic, formulated without dye or synthetic fragrance, nonflammable, does not contain chlorine, phosphate, petroleum, ammonia, acids, alkalized solvents, nitrates, or borates. There are even green nursery cleaning products to choose from.

Or make your own all-natural cleaners: Mix vegetable-based liquid soap with a few drops of lavender essential oil for an all-purpose household cleanser. Mix baking soda and water into a thick paste to get stains off tiles, countertops, and clothing. Mix 2 cups of water, 3 tablespoons of liquid soap, and 20 to 30 drops of tea tree oil to knock out germs on surfaces without resorting to strong products such as bleach. Mix 2 tablespoons of white vinegar with 1 gallon of water and put it in a spray bottle to shine your mirrors and windows. Use club soda or (would you believe?) cornmeal to soak up spills on carpets (just dab the club soda on with a towel or let the cornmeal soak up the spill and then vacuum it all up). Mop your floors with a mixture of ¼ cup white vinegar and 30 ounces of warm water. Unclog your drains with ½ cup of baking soda followed by 2 cups of boiling water (though for stubborn clogs try chasing the baking soda with a ½ cup of vinegar).

he or she may nibble on, the world is still mostly safe, for sure (especially with you or other vigilant caregivers on duty)—but with more exploration comes more exposure to risk.

Other factors increase a growing baby's exposure, too. Little ones have smaller body size (which means that a small dose of a toxin will have a larger impact). They touch almost everything, and most of what they touch also ends up in their mouths. They spend more time on the ground (on carpets that have been treated, grass that's been sprayed). And finally, since they have more lifetime ahead of them—and more developing to do—there's more opportunity for toxins to be stored and potentially do harm.

What's an environmentally concerned parent to do? Read up on how to go green for your little sprout . . . without going crazy.

Clearing the Air

To make sure the air you and your baby breathe at home is safe, keep these unsafe sources of air pollution out:

Tobacco smoke. Secondhand smoke (and thirdhand smoke—the kind that lingers on clothes of smokers) is super unsafe for babies. Little ones exposed to smoking on a regular basis are more susceptible to SIDS, asthma, tonsillitis, respiratory infections, ear infections, and bacterial and viral infections severe enough to land them in the hospital. Children of smokers score lower on tests of reasoning ability and vocabulary and have an increased risk down the road of developing lung cancer. Plus, it sets an example no parent would like followed. Children who see someone they love smoke are more likely to become smokers themselves, with all the serious risk for a shortened life span that the habit involves. So kick butt . . . and kick smokers out of your home.

Carbon monoxide. Take the following steps to keep this colorless, odorless, tasteless, but treacherous gas (it's fatal in high doses) out of your home:

- Keep your heating system in good working order.
- Don't use charcoal fires or propane heaters indoors.
- Be sure that gas stoves and other gas appliances are properly vented (install an exhaust fan to the outdoors to draw out fumes) and adjusted (if the flame isn't blue, have the adjustment checked).
- Never use a gas stove for heating any part of your home.
- Never leave fireplace fires to smolder (douse them with water). Clean chimneys and flues regularly.
- Never leave a car idling, even briefly, in a garage that is attached to your home (open the garage door before starting the car).
- Cool off an overheated car before closing the garage door.

Most important: Install a carbon monoxide detector (read the instructions carefully to determine the correct location for installation), which will warn you of increasing levels before they became dangerous.

Rethinking Your Home Decor

Once your little rug rat starts crawling, he or she will spend more time on the floor—and on your wall-to-wall carpet—than anywhere else. But even when your babe is in your arms, the quality of your carpet is what counts. Many carpets are made with chemicals that pollute the air in your home. The padding and adhesive glue used to lay carpets can also irritate a baby's sensitive skin. So if you can, consider swapping to more bare floors (a plus: They're easier to keep clean) and do your best to manage existing carpet by vacuuming often and deep cleaning on a regular basis to remove contaminants, leaving less to circulate in your air. If you're having new carpet installed, choose one with low VOC (volatile organic compound) emission, or a "green" carpet.

When it comes to furniture, look for formaldehyde-free furniture or "exterior grade" pressed-wood products, which emit noxious fumes at a lower rate. If your furniture has formaldehyde (or more likely, you're not sure), no need to redecorate—unless you were looking for an excuse to, anyway. Just increase air circulation (open those windows whenever possible), get a dehumidifier to lower the humidity in your house and keep fumes from "hanging" in the air, and stock up on baby-safe houseplants (see page 336).

Miscellaneous fumes. Fumes from some cleaning products, from aerosol sprays, and from painting-related materials can be toxic. So, always use the least toxic products you can find,

Purify with Plants

Bring nature indoors and your baby will breathe easier . . . literally. Air-cleaning plants don't just make your rooms look pretty, they detox your home by removing pollutants like ammonia (found in cleaning products) and formaldehyde (found in furniture). An assortment of 15 to 20 plants should do the trick in a 2,000-square-foot home. Rather than scattering single plants around, create group displays in each room for maximum air-cleaning effect. Some good antitoxin and relatively nontoxic choices: spider plants, philodendrons, and rubber plants. Put all houseplants out of reach or block them with a gate to keep your baby from nibbling on leaves or toppling over pots.

Don't have a green thumb? Never met a plant you didn't kill? An air filter or purifier can remove indoor air pollutants, too, and is especially valuable if someone in the family has allergies. There are various technologies to choose from, among them HEPA (high-efficiency particulate air) filters—long considered the gold standard in air purification, though they use a lot of energy and need to be changed often (look for one that doesn't emit ozone)—and UV-C light, and ionic filtration (which charges airborne particles and collects them on plates with opposite charges).

and use any questionable products in a very well-ventilated area. Most important: Use these products only when your little one isn't nearby. And remember to store all household products safely out of reach of curious little hands.

Radon. You can't smell it, taste it, or see it, and you won't know it's there at all unless you test for it. But radioactive radon gas can cause lung cancer, and it can enter your home through cracks in the floors and walls or even through your tap water. Testing is the only way to know if your home has elevated radon levels. You can buy a test kit at most hardware stores (they're inexpensive and the test is easy to perform), or if you're buying or selling a home, it may be worth the extra cost to hire a pro to perform the test. If necessary, radon-reduction systems can then bring the amount of radon down to a safe level.

Testing the Waters

Water, water everywhere—but is it safe for your baby to drink? To be sure, test the waters.

Tap water. Most water in this country is perfectly safe for sipping right out of the tap, but quality can vary from community to community, and even from home to home. If you're unsure about how safe the water that's flowing from your faucet is, check with your local water supplier or health department, the Environmental Protection Agency (epa .gov), or a consumer advocacy group. Even if your baby isn't yet drinking water from a sippy cup, contaminants in tap water can be passed through your breast milk (if you drink the water) or show up in formula (if you're using the water to mix with formula)—and with baby's small body mass, relatively low levels of contaminants can be potentially harmful. Particularly dangerous for a baby or young child is lead, which can leach from lead pipes or brass faucets and may affect brain development. How can you tell if your water is passing through lead pipes, and possibly contaminated? Lead pipes are soft (you can scratch them pretty easily with a key) and dull gray in color. If you can't get to your pipes to see or scratch them—or if you have any reason to believe there's lead in your water supply—get your water tested by a lab that's certified by the EPA or your state. Another contaminant that can be very harmful to babies: nitrates. A qualified lab can test for nitrates in tap water as well.

The best way to detox your tap? Buy a home water filter (such as a reverse osmosis filter) that removes contaminants—especially lead or nitrates, if they've shown up in your water supply. Change the filter as recommended. You can also hire a professional company for water treatment, which may include adjusting the pH of your water supply in order to reduce the lead content. Running water for 30 seconds before using it for drinking or cooking also helps reduce lead levels—and since hot water contains more lead, use only cold water for drinking, cooking, and preparing baby formula.

If your water supply isn't fluoridated, the pediatrician will prescribe fluoride drops starting at age 6 months to protect your baby's teeth (see page 364).

Bottled water. Has your family gone bottled because of concerns about the safety of your local water supply (or for convenience, or for the taste)? The problem is, water that comes from a bottle isn't necessarily safer than water that comes from the tap (and in fact, some bottled water actually comes from a tap—just not your tap). Still, it should be at least as safe, since bottled water is regulated by the Food and Drug Administration (FDA), which requires the same water quality standards established by the Environmental Protection Agency (EPA) for tap water. To check the purity of a particular brand, contact the National Sanitation Foundation (nsf.org), or check the label of the bottle for NSF certification. Also look for bottles that don't contain BPA. Most brands use polyethylene soda bottles (with the recycling code "1" on the bottom), which are not made with BPA.

If you do choose bottled water for your baby, you'll also want to factor in fluoride. Unlike most tap water, many

A Safer Walk on the Wild Side

Be extra careful if your baby wants to get up close and personal with the goats and sheep at the petting zoo or farm. Though they're cute and cuddly, these animals can also carry the dangerous E. coli bacteria, which they can pass on to little petters. E. coli infection causes severe diarrhea and abdominal cramps, and in some cases it can be fatal. So be sure you wash your baby's hands with soap and water or with an antibacterial wipe or gel after any petting session. If you didn't take these precautions in previous visits but your baby didn't have any subsequent symptoms, there's no need to worry. Just take the precautions next time.

The Dirty Dozen . . . and the Clean Team

Wondering whether organic produce is worth the premium price you pay for it? When it comes to your baby, it may be, at least in some cases. Organic foods are guaranteed by the U.S. Department of Agriculture to be free of toxic pesticides, fertilizers, hormones, antibiotics, and genetic modifiers. While they don't promise greater freshness or improved nutritional benefits (unless they're locally grown, in which case both perks may apply), eating them will reduce your baby's exposure to potentially harmful chemicals—definitely a big plus.

Of course, an all-organic policy comes with a big bottom line, as well as, in some cases, less availability. If you have to pick and choose, here's something to consider. Certain fruits and veggies (aptly called the dirty dozen) have been identified as the ones *most* likely to contain pesticides if they're conventionally grown—so whenever possible, opt for organic on these (whether fresh, frozen, or in ready-to-serve baby food): apples, bell peppers, celery, cherries, imported grapes, nectarines, peaches, pears, potatoes, raspberries, spinach, and strawberries. Maxed out your budget avoiding the dirty dozen? Turn to the clean team. These five fruits are the *least* likely to have pesticide residues when they're conventionally grown: avocados, bananas, kiwi, mangoes, and pineapple. The vegetables *least* likely to have pesticides: asparagus, broccoli, cabbage, corn, eggplant, onions, and sweet peas.

bottled waters contain no fluoride, which babies over the age of 6 months need to protect their teeth (see page 197 for more on fluoride).

Checking the Food Chain

Whole grains? Check. Fruits and veggies? Check. Healthy fats, like olive oil, avocados, and almond butter? Check. Bacteria, pesticides, and other assorted chemicals? You might want to . . . check. As you introduce your little one to a variety of nutritious foods, it's smart to consider the less wholesome substances that might be hitching a ride to your baby's mouth with those first (and future) bites. Taking sensible steps to protect babies and small children from potentially harmful chemicals in the food chain is an especially smart precaution, since tiny bodies absorb more of these chemicals relative to their size, and because little ones have more years ahead during which those absorbed chemicals can affect them. Here are some tips for keeping meals safe as baby begins climbing the food chain:

- Go green in the produce aisle. Organic produce isn't necessarily more nutritious, but it won't contain the high levels of chemical residues that often cling to the surfaces of conventional varieties. Your budget won't allow for all organic produce, all the time—or availability is limited where you live and shop? Spend the extra bucks on organic when you're shopping for produce that's more likely to contain higher levels of pesticides (the so-called "dirty dozen" named in the box above), and save cash buying conventional when you're shopping for the "clean team" (produce that's least likely to be contaminated). In general, fruit that has a thicker peel (like bananas, melons, mangoes, and citrus) and veggies that you plan to peel are safer bets. When buying fruits and veggies fresh, look for locally grown produce in season, which tends to be safest since large quantities of chemicals aren't needed to preserve it during shipping or storage. Also safer are foods with heavy protective husks, leaves, or skin (such as avocados) that keep out pesticides. Produce that doesn't look perfect (has blemishes) may also be safer, since it's usually chemical protection that keeps foods looking beautiful. In most instances, conventional produce from the U.S. is less contaminated than imported varieties.

- Whether you buy organic or conventional produce, you still have to scrub it thoroughly when you get home to remove bacteria—either with a produce wash or regular soap and water (or even plain running water).

- Opt for organic dairy, eggs, meat, and poultry. Cows, pigs, and chickens raised on conventional factory farms are given lots of antibiotics and hormones to keep them healthy or to help them produce more milk (and you probably don't want your family members getting secondhand doses

of either). So if your budget allows, opt for organic meat and poultry (and baby food made from them), as well as organic eggs, and organic yogurt and other dairy products. And while baby isn't eating a hunk of beef quite yet, it's not too early to think ahead. Consider reaching for grass-fed beef instead of the regular (less healthy) corn-fed version, and limit your family's intake of animal fat, because the fat is where chemicals (antibiotics, pesticides, and so on) are stored. Trim fats from meat, and trim fat and skin from poultry.

- Never serve your baby unpasteurized (raw) dairy products, juice, or cider. These can contain dangerous bacteria that can cause life-threatening illness in babies and young children.

- Fish selectively. Fishing for a healthy source of baby brain-building nutrients? Research shows that regularly feeding fish can boost IQ. Just stick to varieties that are considered safest, including haddock, hake, pollack, ocean perch, whitefish, wild salmon, tilapia, flounder, trout, sole, shrimp, and scallops. Skip any fish with high levels of mercury, including shark, swordfish, king mackerel, and tilefish. Skip fresh tuna, too. If tuna's on the menu, reach for canned chunk

Food Hazards in Perspective

Though it makes sense to avoid chemicals in your family's diet when you can, fear of additives and chemicals can so limit the variety of foods your family eats that it interferes with good nutrition. It's important to remember that a well-balanced, nutritious diet, high in whole grains and fruits and vegetables will not only provide the nutrients needed for growth and good health, but will also help to counteract the effects of toxins in the environment. So limit chemical intake when practical and affordable, but there's no need to drive yourself and your family crazy while you're at it.

In the Know About GMOs

An apple that doesn't turn brown after it's sliced may sound like the best thing since . . . well . . . sliced whole-grain bread. But the way growers are getting produce to stay pristine may not be all that appetizing once you bite a little deeper. Genetically engineered foods and plants (known in the food business as GMOs, for Genetically Modified Organisms) contain DNA from other animals or plants in order to give foods more desirable traits—like staying fresher longer or being able to thrive on a steady diet of weed killer and pesticides. Problem is, because the FDA doesn't require GMO foods to be labeled as such, it's hard to know whether the food you're feeding your little one is made with genetically modified ingredients or not.

One thing that's growing—besides those genetically modified crops—is the controversy over their safety, with organizations and industries on both sides of the argument firmly planted in their position. Not willing to wait out the debate—or to take a chance with your little one's health by serving up GMOs? Look for foods that are labeled "USDA organic"—they'll be free of GMOs, as well as questionable additives or chemicals. Or check for certification by the Non-GMO Project. And stay tuned, because many states are passing legislation that requires labeling of GMO foods, which means it may soon be easier to shop for non-GMO foods.

light tuna, which contains less mercury than albacore (white) tuna, and limit weekly intake to no more than 1 ounce per 12 pounds of baby's weight. Also steer clear of fish from contaminated waters (whether ocean or lake). That may mean going wild with your salmon (farmed salmon tends to contain more of the chemical contaminant PCB) but farmed with your trout (some wild trout comes from contaminated lakes). If you go fishing (or you've been gifted with recreationally caught fish), check with area health or fish and game departments about whether it's safe for young children to eat fish pulled from those waters. Whenever you serve your baby fish, trim away the skin before you cook it (since contaminants collect on the skin) and prefer baking, broiling, grilling, or poaching over frying, so that any chemicals seep out of the fish and can be discarded.

- Most smoked or cured meats, such as hot dogs, bologna, and bacon, have nitrates and other chemicals in them—which means they should be served to babies rarely, if at all. (The fact that they are high in sodium and animal fat, and likely contain any number of unnamed animal parts as well, is yet another reason to keep them off baby's menu.) Ditto for most smoked fish. If you do buy processed meats, look for those that are made from organic or grass-fed animals, are processed without nitrates, and contain less sodium.

- Subtract additives and pass over processed. Opt for foods that are as close to their natural state as possible, and read ingredients to screen for chemical additives you shouldn't be adding to your little one's diet (including artificial colors, flavors, and sweeteners, and pretty much anything you can't pronounce). Reach for "real" foods instead as they become age-appropriate (real fruit instead of fruit snacks, real juice instead of juice drinks, real cheese instead of processed cheese).

Banishing Bugs

Ants. Roaches. Mice. Termites. While chemical pesticides protect your home from those creepy crawlies, they also spell danger to your sweet little crawler. An insect trap can irritate delicate skin (or do worse, if it ends up in baby's mouth). Spray or gel pesticides can nestle deep in carpets and other fabrics, releasing harmful toxins into the air. So how do you get bugs to bug off without resorting to baby-unfriendly chemicals? Try:

Blocking tactics. Install window and door screens (don't leave unscreened windows and doors open) and screen or otherwise close off entry points for insects and vermin.

Sticky insect or rodent traps. Not reliant on killer chemicals, these snare crawling insects in enclosed boxes (roach traps) or containers (ant traps), flies on old-fashioned flypaper, and mice on sticky rectangles. Because human skin can stick to their surfaces, these traps must still be kept out of the reach of children or put out after they are in bed at night and taken up before they are up and around in the morning. From a purely humane standpoint, these traps have the disadvantage of prolonging the death of their victims.

Baited traps. These traps do contain a poison, but it gives off no chemical fumes and is enclosed in the trap, making it more difficult for a baby to reach. Still, place the traps out of your child's reach.

Box traps. The tenderhearted can catch rodents in box traps and then release them in fields or woods far from residential areas, though this isn't always easy. Because the trapped rodents can bite, the traps should be kept out of the reach of children or put out and carefully monitored when children are not around.

BPA in Food Containers

Bisphenol A (BPA), a chemical that may be toxic to humans and may adversely affect brain development, is found in many polycarbonate plastic products. Happily, the FDA doesn't allow baby bottles and sippy cups to contain BPA because of the potential effects of the chemical on the brain, on behavior, and on the prostate gland in infants and young children. And most baby toys and teethers made from plastic are BPA-free (check labels to be sure). But some plastic containers and plastic cups not marketed specifically for children may still contain BPA.

Children, because they're less able to metabolize or absorb the chemicals that end up in their systems, and because they're still growing and developing, and because they do a lot of drinking and snacking from plastic containers, may be most vulnerable to BPA exposure. Which is why it's wise to avoid buying or using products with BPA. How can you tell if a plastic container contains BPA? Simply look for a number on the bottom. If it says "7," it likely contains BPA. The number "1" on bottled water means the bottle is made from polyethylene plastic and does not contain BPA.

Lead Can Lead to Trouble

Many homes built before 1978 still harbor paint with high concentrations of lead beneath layers of newer applications. As paint cracks or flakes, microscopic lead-containing particles are shed. These can end up in household dust and on a child's hands, toys, clothing—and eventually, of course, in the mouth.

Check with the EPA's National Lead Information Center (epa.gov/lead) for information on testing the paint in your home for lead. If testing shows there is lead, it'll need to be either completely removed by a professional trained in hazardous waste removal or covered with an approved sealant.

But lead paint doesn't lurk just on painted walls. Older toys, some new imported ones, and furniture can also be painted with lead. Keep up to date with furniture and toy recalls by going online to the Consumer Product Safety Commission (cpsc.gov) or the CDC (cdc.gov/nceh).

What's so dangerous about lead? Large doses of lead can cause severe brain damage in children. Even relatively small doses can reduce IQ, alter enzyme function, retard growth, and damage the kidneys, as well as cause learning and behavior problems, and hearing and attention deficits. Most doctors will do a finger-prick (or heel-stick) test for lead at around 12 months, but you can ask for an earlier screening if you live in a high-risk area or in a pre-1960s building, if your water supply is contaminated with lead, if a sibling, housemate, or playmate has been diagnosed with high blood levels of lead, if you or another adult in your home has a job or hobby involving lead exposure, or if you live near an industry that is likely to release lead into the air, soil, or water.

If testing shows that your child has high lead levels in his or her blood, it may be helpful to consult with a specialist in treating this problem. Chelation therapy and the use of iron and calcium supplementation may be recommended to remove the lead and prevent the damage it can cause.

Safe use of chemical pesticides. Virtually all chemical pesticides—including boric acid—are highly toxic. If you opt to use them, do not spread them (or store them) where your baby can get to them or on food-preparation surfaces. Always use the least toxic or more "green" substance available for the job. If you use a spray, keep your child out of the house while spraying and for the rest of the day, if possible. Better still, have the spraying done while you're away from home. When you return, open all the windows for a few hours to air out your home, and be sure to clean your countertops and other flat surfaces thoroughly.

To find information on safer pest control, contact Beyond Pesticides, beyondpesticides.org; the National Pesticide Information Center, npic.orst .edu; or the Environmental Protection Agency (EPA), epa.gov/pesticides.

Wondering about how to keep your outdoor garden pest-free and also safe for your little one? Get information on outdoor pest control from the EPA, epa.gov/pesticides/lawncare; from the National Institute of Environmental Health Sciences, niehs.nih.gov; and from growsmartgrowsafe.org.

CHAPTER 11

The Sixth Month

B aby is personality plus these days—and it's a personality all his or her own. Socializing with mom, dad, and just about anyone who passes by the stroller or carrier is still high on baby's list of favorite activities, and you'll find the long sentences of babble, punctuated by giggles and squeals, more and more fascinating—to you and your little one. Games of peekaboo delight baby, as does shaking a rattle or anything else that makes noise. The passion for exploration continues, and extends to your face, which baby will pull at as if it were a favorite toy (your hair, jewelry, and glasses aren't safe from those little fingers for now). At some point this month it'll be time to break out the bib and high chair and spoon up that momentous first bite of solids.

Feeding Your Baby: Starting Solids

I t's the moment you've been waiting for . . . or soon will be. Somewhere between 4 and 6 months—with the pediatrician's official go-ahead—your baby will be ready to take on a brand new feeding frontier: solids. And you'll want to be ready, too, for that momentous first meal. But as you prepare (Spoon, check! Bowl, check! Bib, check! Video to record it all, check!), remember that as exciting as those debut bites of solids will be, your little one won't be ready to turn in the breast or bottle yet. While first feeds are fun—and an important foundation for the lifetime of eating that lies ahead—they're more about gaining

experience than piling up nutrients. Breast milk or formula will continue to provide most of your baby's nutritional requirements until the end of the first year.

First Feedings— and Beyond

R eady . . . set . . . splat! A sense of timing—and a sense of humor—are key when you introduce solid foods to your baby. Here are some rules to feed by:

Time it right. The "perfect" time of day to feed your baby is whatever time

Baby Basics at a Glance: Sixth Month

Sleeping. How much sleep will baby be getting this month? Those sleep numbers haven't changed much from last month: around 15 hours on average, with about 10 or 11 of them coming at night, and 3 to 4 hours during the day, split up into two or three naps.

Eating. Baby's still eating similar amounts as last month, though solids may be added to the mix this month.

- Breast milk. Count on an average of 5 to 6 feeds a day—though some babies nurse lots more than that. Baby will be drinking somewhere between 24 and 36 ounces of breast milk a day.

- Formula. You'll be bottle-feeding an average of 4 to 5 times a day, around 6 to 8 ounces of formula per bottle, for a total of 24 to 32 ounces of formula a day.

- Solids. If you're starting solids this month, you'll be starting small: about 1 tablespoon of baby cereal (mixed with a small amount of breast milk or formula—enough to thin to a soupy consistency) twice a day, or the equivalent in fruit or vegetables (also a small amount thinned down to start). Feed to appetite, but expect the amount baby takes to increase

gradually, up to 4 tablespoons per meal as baby gets used to solids and expresses an eagerness for more.

Playing. Is baby starting to sit? That new position will give your cutie a whole new perspective when playing. Best bets this month include action/reaction toys (such as ones that light up or play music), toys that encourage crawling (cars or trains or balls that roll), picture books a baby can look at on his or her own or on your lap, roly-poly toys (they right themselves when rolled over), activity toys, play gyms, and anything baby can safely mouth (teething toys or soft blocks, for instance).

works for both of you. If you're breast-feeding, you might try solids when your milk supply is at its lowest (probably late afternoon or early evening). On the other hand, babies who wake up bright eyed and eager might be happy to sample solids for breakfast. Experiment: Offer a first course of formula or breast milk to whet that appetite, then bring on the solids. Or try an appetizer of

solids followed by a main course of milk. Start with one meal per day, then move up to two (probably a morning and evening meal) for the next month or so.

Monitor baby's mood. As trying as those first feedings may be for you, they're even more of a challenge for your little one. So keep in mind that a baby who's cheerful and alert is more likely to open wide for an incoming spoon, and one who's cranky or getting sleepy may want only breast (or bottle). If your baby is firmly in the fussy camp, be flexible—you might want to skip solids at that meal and try them next time.

Don't rush. Food is never fast when it comes to babies—you'll be surprised at how long it takes to get one little spoonful into that little mouth (and ultimately down the hatch). Give yourself and your baby plenty of time for feedings—and have plenty of patience, too. You will need it.

Sit pretty. Holding a squirming baby on your lap while trying to deposit an unfamiliar substance into an unreceptive mouth is a perfect script for disaster. Before your baby actually takes bite one, let him or her practice sitting in the high chair or feeding seat for a couple of days, adjusting the height of the tray or seat so it fits just right. And don't forget how wiggly your little worm can be—*always* fasten the safety straps, including the one around the crotch. If baby can't sit up at all in such a chair or seat, it's probably a good idea to postpone solids a bit longer.

Gear up. Skip the silver spoon Aunt Marlene sent—a silicone, plastic, or corn-based model with a small, soft bowl is much easier on tender gums. Count on having several on hand during feedings (one for you, one for baby, a spare when one lands on the floor) to foster baby's sense of independence and to avoid power struggles (yes, those happen even at this age). For you, choose one with a long handle for maneuverability (experiment with both a deeper and shallower bowl to see which is easier to deposit food from). For baby, a short, curved handle is easier for tiny fingers to grip and will avoid

a self-inflicted eye poke. And while you're gearing up, don't forget to put a bib on (on baby, that is—your bib is optional). A word to the wise: Get your baby into the bib habit right from the start or you'll face big-time resistance later. It can be made of soft plastic, cotton, or paper—as long as it's big enough to cover the chest and belly, you're good to go. Also consider a diaper-only dress code for meals early on, room temperature allowing, unless your baby dislikes being undressed.

Make some introductions. Before even attempting to bring spoon to mouth, put a dab of the food on the table or high chair tray and give baby a chance to examine it, squish it, mash it, rub it, maybe even taste it. That way, when you do approach with the spoon, what you're offering won't be totally unfamiliar.

Ease in. For someone who's brand new to the concept of spoon feeding—and unfamiliar with textures and tastes beyond liquid and milky—solids can come as something of a shock. So ease in. Start by gently placing about a quarter teaspoon of food on the tip of baby's tongue. If that's swallowed, place the next quarter teaspoon a little farther back. At first, expect almost as much food to come out as goes in. Eventually your little one will get the hang of spoon feeding—and respond with a wide-open mouth.

Count on rejection. Even bland tastes can be an acquired taste for a brand-new solids eater. Babies may reject a new food several times or more before they decide to like it. So don't push when baby snubs what the spoon is delivering, but do try, try again another day.

Invite imitation. What your baby monkey sees, he or she may be more likely to do. It's an old parent trick but a goodie: Open up wide and take a pretend taste

Feeding Baby Safely

Feeding your baby isn't only about feeding healthy foods. It's also about making sure the food you buy, prepare, and serve your little one is as safe as can be. Happily, with just a few precautions and a lot of common sense, you'll be all set when it comes to food safety—now and as your baby's menu expands:

- Always wash your hands with soap and water before feeding baby. If you touch raw meat, poultry, fish, or eggs (all of which harbor bacteria) during the feeding, wash your hands again. Obviously, wash them, too, if you blow your nose or touch your mouth.

- Store dry baby cereals and unopened baby food jars and pouches in a cool, dry place away from extremes of heat (over the stove, for example) or cold (as in an unheated basement).

- Wipe the tops of baby food jars or pouches with a clean cloth or run them under the tap to remove dust before opening.

- Make sure the button is down on safety lids before opening a jar for the first time—when opening, listen for the "pop" to make sure the seal was intact. Discard or return to the store any jar that has a raised button or that doesn't pop. Make sure the cap on an unused pouch is sealed before opening it for the first time.

- Whenever you use a can opener, make sure it's clean. When you can't get it clean or it starts to look rusty, it's time to toss it.

- Remove one serving at a time from a jar of baby food with a clean spoon, or squeeze out spoonfuls from a pouch (don't let baby suck food out of the pouch if you want to save leftovers). If baby wants a refill, use a fresh spoon to scoop it out of the jar or squeeze again. Don't feed baby directly out of a baby food jar unless it's the last meal from that jar, and don't save a bowl of food that baby's eaten from for the next meal, since enzymes and bacteria from baby's saliva will cause it to spoil more quickly. If you're using a pouch, be sure the top of the pouch doesn't touch a used spoon when you're squeezing out the food.

- After you've taken a serving out of a jar or pouch, recap the remainder and refrigerate until it's needed again. If juices and fruits haven't been used within 3 days, and everything else within 2 days, toss them. Have a hard time keeping track of what you opened when? Start labeling.

from the spoon—and don't forget to smack your lips and relish your make-believe bite enthusiastically ("yummy, yummy!").

Know when enough is enough. Realizing when to stop feeding is as important as knowing when to start. A turned head or a clenched mouth are sure signs that baby is finished with this meal. Forcing a baby to eat is always a lost cause—and can actually set up future food fights.

First Foods—and Beyond

It's chow time, baby! While everyone agrees that the perfect first liquid for baby is mother's milk, there's no consensus on the perfect first solid. Should

- Try to mix only one serving at a time of baby cereal (it's fast and easy, so no need to prep in advance), though if you've made more than baby can eat (assuming you haven't double-dipped a spoon that's been in baby's mouth), you can store it in the refrigerator for a few hours (longer than that and it gets too thick and dry).

- It's not necessary to heat baby food (baby won't care if it's room temperature or cold), and it's an extra step you can easily skip. But if you do, heat only enough for one meal and discard any uneaten heated portion. You can place the baby food in a heat resistant dish over simmering water or place the pouch in hot water to warm it (but you'll have to throw out any leftovers once the pouch has been warmed). Or less ideally, you can use the microwave, keeping these important caveats in mind: First, make sure the dish is microwave safe. Second, heat for only 5 seconds, then stir, and test the temperature of the food on your wrist. If it's still cold, heat for another 5 seconds, then stir, then test—continuing with this pattern until the food is slightly warm. Keep in mind that though the container may stay cool, the contents continue to heat for a few minutes after you take it out of the microwave, and may be hot enough to burn baby's mouth.

- When preparing fresh baby foods, be sure utensils and work surfaces are clean. Keep cold foods cold and warm foods warm. Don't keep opened food at room temperature for more than an hour. See page 380 for tips on storing homemade baby food.

- Cook eggs well before serving. Raw or undercooked eggs can harbor salmonella. (To be extra safe, you can use pasteurized eggs.)

- Make sure all juice, milk, cheese, and other dairy products you serve your baby are pasteurized (never "raw") to prevent bacterial infection.

- When tasting during food preparation, use a fresh spoon each time you taste, or wash the spoon between tastings.

- When in doubt about the freshness of a food, throw it out.

- When out and about, carry any open jars, pouches, or containers of anything that needs refrigeration in an insulated bag packed with ice or an ice pack if it will be more than an hour before you serve it. Once the food no longer feels cool, you'll have to toss it. Better still, pack unopened food that doesn't require refrigeration (but be careful never to store it in extreme temperatures, like in a hot car).

it be whole-grain oatmeal or brown rice cereal? Perhaps it's best to start with veggies. Or maybe fruit is the way to go at first. Something obvious (like sweet potatoes) or something less conventional (like avocado)? Though there's no one right answer, there are some that are better than others, so it's always best to ask the doctor to recommend a first food.

No matter what's on the menu, the texture of your baby's very first spoon-fed solids should be super smooth and practically dripping off the spoon (strained, pureed, or finely mashed foods thinned with breast milk or formula as needed). As your tiny gourmand becomes a more experienced eater, gradually reduce the liquid you add, and thicken and then slightly chunk up the texture. Here are some good first food choices:

Eat Well with WIC

If you qualify, the WIC program can help you afford healthy food for your baby. WIC gives eligible moms vouchers to buy healthy food at local supermarkets. Find out more at fns.usda.gov/wic.

Cereal. If you start with baby cereal, pick a single-grain, iron-enriched whole-grain variety, like brown rice, whole-grain oat, or whole-grain barley. To prepare, mix a small amount of baby cereal with formula, breast milk, or even water to create a creamy "soup." Don't sweeten the taste by adding things like mashed bananas, applesauce, or juice—first, because it's best to introduce only one food at a time, and second, because it's better for baby to acquire a taste for plain before you sweeten the cereal pot.

Vegetables. Veggies are tops in nutrition and unlikely to trigger allergies. Start with milder yellow or orange options such as sweet potatoes, squash, and carrots before moving on to peas and green beans, which have slightly stronger flavors. If your baby rejects what you've got, try again tomorrow and the next day and the next. Some babies need to be introduced to a new food four or five (or more) times before they'll accept it, so perseverance is key.

Fruit. Delicious, digestible first fruits include finely mashed bananas or baby applesauce, peaches, or pears. For something completely different, and completely baby-friendly, start with smoothed-down mashed or pureed ripe avocado—it's creamy, yummy, and loaded with healthy fats.

Expanding Baby's Repertoire

Once your baby is lapping up those first foods, you can expand the menu. But keep these pointers in mind:

Stay solo . . . and go slow. Most doctors recommend a one-at-a-time policy when introducing new foods. So unless your baby's doctor has suggested a different course for bringing on different courses, serve up new foods alone—or in combo with other foods that have already tested well. Offer a new menu item for 3 to 5 days before you bring on another—that way, if your little one shows signs of an allergy or sensitivity (excessive gassiness, diarrhea or mucus in the stool, vomiting, a rough rash on the face, particularly around the mouth, a runny nose and/or watery eyes or wheezing that doesn't seem to be associated with a cold, unusual night wakefulness or daytime crankiness), you'll be able to figure out which food triggered it. No adverse reaction? Then you can keep the item on the menu and move on to the next new food.

If you think your baby may be sensitive to something you've served, wait about a week before trying the food again (though if the reaction was severe, check with the doctor before ever serving that food again). If you get a similar reaction two or three times in a row, you can probably conclude there's a sensitivity. Eliminate that food from baby's diet for several months, then try it again when your pediatrician gives the green light. If your baby seems to react to almost every new food you offer, or there's a history of allergies in your family, check in with your doctor.

Keep food choices simple . . . and separate. Ready to serve up a combo platter? Go ahead—but keep the selections separate at first, so baby gets to sample each flavor on its own (mush the peas and carrots together and your little one may never know the joy of just plain peas). After single foods have been savored, feel free to mix things up. Create your own yummy melange with favorite flavors, or try packaged combos in jars or pouches, but read the labels to screen for ingredients your baby isn't ready for (like added sugar or salt).

Check the no-serve list. While doctors used to recommend waiting on certain foods until after the first birthday to reduce the risk of allergies, there is some evidence that introducing highly allergenic foods early may actually prevent food allergies. Check with the doctor for a list of green-light and red-light foods. Many doctors give the go-ahead on wheat, eggs, chocolate, citrus fruits, tomatoes, strawberries, and even smooth almond or peanut butter during the first year, while others say to hold

---

No Honey for Your Little Honey

Honey may be sweet, but not when it comes to your little sweetie. Honey (or foods made with honey) needs to stay off the menu for the first year because it may contain the spores of Clostridium botulinum—bacteria that is harmless to adults but can cause botulism in babies. This serious though rarely fatal illness can cause constipation, weakened sucking, poor appetite, and lethargy and can even lead to pneumonia and dehydration.

---

off on some—or even all. Definitely off the menu this year are unsafe foods like honey (see box, above), foods that can be choking hazards, like nuts, chunky nut butters, and raisins (see page 431), and cow's milk (see page 433).

What You May Be Wondering About

Getting Baby to Sleep Through the Night

"My baby won't go to sleep without my nursing her—and then she still gets up twice a night and won't go back to sleep without more feeds or rocking. Will we ever get any sleep?"

Doing the zombie shuffle from your bed to your baby's crib and back again night after night can get old fast. But here's the thing: It's not the night waking that's the problem. Even the best snoozers (those who sleep through the night) actually wake up several times during the night—everyone does. But a lifetime of good sleep for your baby will depend on her learning how to fall asleep and fall back to sleep solo—on her own, unassisted by you. If you're ready to renounce your position as your baby's personal sandman and your baby's ready (even if she doesn't know it yet) to give up night feeds and a helping hand getting back to sleep, then this is a good time to start sleep teaching—so you and baby can hang up

For More Z's, Try C for Consistency

Last night you toughed out 20 minutes of crying, but tonight you're worn down after 2—tomorrow is another night, after all. Understandable—you're only human, and you're a sleep-deprived human at that—but unfortunately, inconsistency will get you nowhere when it comes to sleep teaching. So give the strategy a chance to work before you conclude it's not working. If you don't stick with it long enough to see a difference, you'll never know whether the method's a failure or your follow-through is. Stick with it consistently for a solid 2 weeks before you give up entirely.

those midnight calls and dial in a good night's sleep. (On the other hand, if you'd like to continue answering baby's calls—or you're just plain opposed to sleep teaching on principle—there's no need to stop. See page 353 for more.)

Before you begin sleep teaching (aka sleep training), you'll need to take a close look at baby's sleep habits, including whether she's napping too much or too little during the day (see page 323). Another important first step will be weaning baby off middle-of-the-night feedings (see page 269). And if baby's been falling asleep at the breast or bottle, establish a bedtime routine (see page 355) that puts the bedtime feeding before the bath and other rituals and well before when she actually needs to fall asleep. That way, you'll be able to put her in the crib awake, which will help her begin the process of

learning how to fall asleep on her own instead of relying on her current sleep crutch, feeding.

Sleep teaching will, unfortunately, involve some tears (likely on both sides of the crib) and a certain amount of tough love. But the truth is, for those parents desperate and determined to get that good night's sleep sooner rather than later, letting an older (say, 5- or 6-month-old) baby cry it out—widely known in social media circles as CIO—almost always works. Here's why: By 6 months babies are wise to the fact that crying often results in being picked up, rocked, fed, or if they're really lucky, all three—pretty good motivation to keep on wailing. But once they get the message that mom and dad are not buying what they're selling, most will give up the crying game, usually within 3 or 4 nights.

If you feel comfortable trying the crying-it-out method on your baby (and not everyone does—so don't feel obligated to try sleep training if it doesn't feel right for you and your baby), there are two things you should know about it: First, it's not as harsh as it sounds—and you can (and most definitely should) modify the amount of crying you let your baby do to fit your comfort level. Some parents are okay letting baby cry for a set period of time, while other parents will feel more comfortable without prescribed crying times and will prefer to return to baby for a reassuring rub based on gut, not the clock.

Second, the crying-it-out approach is definitely harder on you than it is on your baby. Remember this (especially as you're sitting outside her door, thinking you're the worst parent in the world): A few minutes (or even more than a few minutes) of whimpering, fussing, or even crying to self-soothe won't hurt her in the short or long term—and it definitely won't scar her for life. And ultimately—if you can stand it—you're doing her a favor by helping her learn to fall asleep (and fall back to sleep) on her own, a life skill she'll need her entire life.

Up to sleep training? Here's what you do:

- Watch for those snooze clues. Eye rubbing or a clockwork case of the crankies, for instance, will help clue you in to when your baby is feeling tired. Anticipating your baby's natural sleepy times at both naptime and bedtime will allow you to get your baby into sleep mode before she gets overtired. Being aware of those sleep cues is a crucial step in this process, since overtired babies—ones who skip naps altogether, just catch brief catnaps, or don't get enough sleep at night—have a harder time settling down for daily naps and when it's time to go to bed at night. And, they are more likely to sleep fitfully and wake in the wee hours—undermining your sleep training efforts.

- Initiate the naptime/bedtime routine. At bedtime have a calm and quiet (approximately) 30- to 45-minute routine that includes a warm bath, massage, and final feeding before you put your baby down in her crib (see page 355). While you shouldn't go through the same 30-minute routine at naptime, some sort of abridged version (a book, a lullaby, and a sweet cuddle or a little massage, for instance) during the day will help signal to your little one that it's naptime—and time to sleep. The most important thing to remember about these pre-sleep routines? Be consistent (and persistent) about it.

- Choose the right sleep location. Lay baby down in her crib or another setting that's conducive to a long sleep.

Watch Your Response Time

CIO isn't your MO (or even in your DNA)? Still, try not to rush to baby's side at the first whimper. Babies make all kinds of noises—including crying—or even wake momentarily during the light phase of sleep, only to fall back to sleep on their own. Others whimper regularly (and briefly) before settling down for the night (or during night wakenings) as a way of comforting themselves. If you come a-running, you may actually be waking your about-to-nod-off baby, and that's not in anyone's best interest. So unless there's some full-fledged wailing coming from that crib, wait a few minutes to see if your little snoozer drifts back to dreamland solo.

At night the crib is the most obvious place for sleep, but get into the habit of putting her in the crib (or a pack-and-play) for daytime naps as well. There are plenty of reasons why your baby shouldn't get into the habit of sleeping in the stroller or swing for naps—and for sure not at bedtime.

- Put baby down awake. Remember, the whole point of sleep teaching is to get your little one to fall asleep on her own. If you rock or nurse her to sleep and then transfer her from your arms to the crib when she's already snoozing, the lesson's not learned. Not to mention that she'll associate falling asleep with being rocked or nursed—and those sleep association habits will be hard to break. The sleep teaching that you're doing will allow her to form new sleep associations—ones

Worked Up . . . and Throwing Up

You've committed to sleep training and are prepared for the crying that comes with it. But what happens when what starts as crying ends up with . . . throwing up? It's true that a small number of babies get so worked up from crying that they actually vomit. Clearly, crying-induced vomiting is a laundry concern (and a case for waterproof crib mattress covers)—but happily, it isn't generally a health concern. So what to do? You can stick with the plan (allowing for cleanups, of course) for 3 or 4 days to see if the throwing up lets up, which it usually does. If it doesn't (or you're not up to the midnight cleanups), you could put sleep training efforts on hold for a few weeks, then try again to see if the vomiting reoccurs or not. You might also want to consider whether feeding your little one too much too close to bedtime might be triggering the upchucks. Try switching the order of the bedtime routine so breast or bottle (or any bedtime snacks) comes at the beginning instead of the end. And of course, to rule out any medical concerns, check in with the doctor if the vomiting continues.

that give her the self-soothing tools that will enable her to fall asleep without your help. So . . . put her down awake, give her a gentle rub, then softly recite a consistent goodnight phrase and leave the room. That means leave the room immediately, without waiting for her to fall asleep.

- Cue the crying. You can expect some fussing and—you knew it was coming—crying. And here's where you make the decision to either stay tough and continue with the sleep teaching or choose a different path. If you want to sleep teach, there will be crying. There are different ways to respond to the crying (see below), but if you think there's no way you can stand by for even a moment while your precious one wails, then sleep teaching isn't for you (see box, facing page).

- Respond . . . or not. Now that your baby is crying, there are a few ways you can respond. Some experts suggest you let baby cry until she tires herself out and falls asleep from exhaustion. Others suggest you set a time limit on the crying—a full 5 minutes (it'll seem much longer), for instance—before you go back in. Or you can be less regimented about sticking to a clock and go with your gut instead (perhaps your gut is telling you to respond after 2 minutes, for instance). When you do go back in, repeat the original routine—a quick pat, a gentle good-night, a phrase that reminds her it's time to go to sleep. Replace the pacifier (if you use one), and go. It may be better for dad to head in at this point if mom is associated with feedings and comfort.

Another variation on the same concept, which works better for some older babies and is more comfortable for some parents, is to reassure your baby from a chair near her crib until she falls asleep each evening (again, without picking her up). Move the chair a little farther away each night, until you're at the doorway. Finally, move out the door—at which point, baby should be able to fall asleep without you present. Keep in mind, however, that for some babies,

Sleeping Through the Night . . . Together

Don't feel the need to push the independent sleep agenda so soon—or to give up night feedings yet? Not a fan of letting your baby cry, even a little? Prefer to have your precious bundle positioned conveniently beside you rather than having to drag yourself out of bed to dispense doses of comfort? Believe that happiness (in the middle of the night) is a warm baby? Another strategy for getting your baby to sleep through the night is arguably (at least in the short term) the easiest of them all: sleeping together. What else is in it for you and baby? Proponents say it's the best way to foster positive sleep associations and discourage negative ones. The presence of parents—their touch, smell, and sound—gives babies a reassuring message that falling asleep or resettling back into deep sleep is safe and secure. Instead of fearing them, so the theory goes, bed-sharing babies come to embrace sleep and the dark.

Sharing a bed with your baby doesn't mean that you're giving up on the idea of independent sleeping entirely (all kids eventually learn to sleep on their own, and some do so voluntarily by the time they're 3), just that you're shelving it until you and baby feel ready to tackle it. Do keep in mind, however, that some co-sleepers have a harder time weaning themselves off the nighttime company than others. Also remember that it's always best for both parents to be on board the co-sleeping bed—which can start to get crowded when the little one isn't so little anymore (or is a restless sleeper).

While there are plenty of positives to sleep sharing, there can also be risks if you don't follow these rules for safe co-sleeping: Make sure your mattress is firm, keep comforters and pillows away from baby, make sure there are no cracks or crevices baby could get stuck in (like between the mattress and the wall or the headboard), never smoke in (or near) bed, and never co-sleep after you've been drinking or have taken a sedative. For more on safer co-sleeping, see page 274.

parents won't be out of mind unless they're out of sight—in that case, this approach will definitely not work.

- And repeat. Repeat the process you've chosen for as long as baby cries, extending the time you leave her alone by about 5 minutes (or again, what your gut says) each time until she falls asleep. Stretch the time she spends on her own by a few more minutes the second night and again on the third. Keep in mind that sleep teaching at naptime will have to be slightly modified, since 30 minutes of crying and there goes baby's naptime. Consider setting a limit of a total of 10 or 15 minutes of crying (and responding), for instance, before resorting to giving up on the nap altogether or using another means of getting baby to sleep. The good news is that by the end of the first week of nighttime sleep teaching, naptimes should be smoother as your little one comes to understand that when she's placed in her crib, it's time to sleep.

- Reap the reward. You'll likely find your baby's crying jags diminish steadily over 3 nights, and—drumroll, please—virtually disappear somewhere between the fourth and seventh night, replaced perhaps by a

It's All in the Timing

One major change or stress in your baby's life at a time is plenty. If baby's already dealing with one—whether it's teething, mom going back to work, a new babysitter, or a bout with a stuffy nose or an ear infection—wait until things have settled down again before launching any sleep-through-the-night campaign. It makes sense to wait, also, if you're planning a family trip in the near future (travel is almost certain to derail your efforts).

Keep in mind that even babies who have mastered sleeping through the night may begin waking again during times of change or stress, or after a disruption of schedule (during a trip or a busy holiday season). Night waking may also start up again when a baby has just passed a major developmental milestone—such as learning to crawl or walk—since baby's compulsion to practice the new skill may interfere temporarily with sleep. A refresher course of sleep teaching may be all your little one needs to get back to sleep business as usual.

bit of fussing or short burst of tears. The next sound you're likely to hear: nothing . . . except maybe a tiny, blissful snore. Sure, there'll be plenty of nights, even after the initial sleep teaching period, when your baby will fuss (perhaps loudly) or cry (even louder) at first, but give it a chance. Once your baby learns how to soothe herself to sleep each night (and almost all babies do in time)—perhaps by sucking her thumb or a pacifier, or by rocking herself, turning her head, or changing position, or even by whimpering—she'll be able to drift off to dreamland solo at bedtime and drift back to dreamland when she wakes during the night. And Mission Sleep Teach will be accomplished.

Does that mean you'll never face another night of broken sleep? Maybe . . . maybe not. There may be nights even after your sweetie has started to sleep through the night when she'll put up a sleep fuss. Whether it's a case of sleep regression (common when a baby's busy trying to conquer a new skill; see page 417) or just a case of temporary teething pain, avoid sliding back into old routines of rocking or nursing, which will undermine all the hard work you both did. Instead, sticking to the consistent strategy that helped her sleep train in the first place will help ease her over this bedtime blip.

What Will the Neighbors Think?

"We live in an apartment, and our baby's room shares a wall with the next apartment. We'd like to try some sleep teaching, but we're honestly afraid of what the neighbors will think about her crying."

It's hard enough for you to listen to your baby crying in the middle of the night—but what about the neighbors? If you live in an apartment or otherwise within earshot of the folks next door, letting your little one cry for any amount of time during the night may seem decidedly unneighborly. Here's how to make a sleeper out of your baby without making enemies out of your neighbors:

■ Give fair warning. Let your neighbors know what's in store ahead of time (rather than at 3 a.m., when they call to complain). Tell them your plan (to teach baby how to sleep through the night by letting her cry for short periods each night) and how long you think it will take (hopefully not more than a week).

- Apologize in advance . . . and if that doesn't work, buy forgiveness. Chances are, they won't be thrilled at the prospect of broken sleep (after all, broken sleep comes with your territory as new parents—not theirs). Neighbors who have little ones of their own (and have done their own share of walking the floor with screaming infants) may be empathetic—and may even offer some coping suggestions. Other neighbors may be less understanding—and who can blame them? Apologies may be accepted more graciously if accompanied by a small disturbing-the-peace offering (a bottle of wine, a basket of fruit and cheese, a box of chocolates—or, in tough cases, all three). If your neighbors have a sense of humor (which they hopefully do), you might offer up a set of earplugs or a pair of earmuffs.

- Close the windows. Make sure baby's cries can't travel out an open window and down the street.

- Take some muffling measures. Hang blankets on the wall in baby's room or over any windows that are adjacent to the neighbor's. If possible, put baby's crib in a carpeted room or place an area rug under it to better insulate sound.

- Don't feel too bad. Some amount of noise comes with apartment or townhouse living—chances are you've put up with your share of yapping dogs, slamming doors, midnight footsteps, blaring music, and crack-of-dawn vacuum cleaners. A good neighbor (hopefully the kind you have) will be just as tolerant of your crying baby.

A Bedtime Routine

"We'd like to give our baby boy a bedtime routine, but we're not sure how to go about it."

Whether you're co-sleeping or sleep teaching, every good night's sleep begins with a good bedtime routine. A predictable, comforting sequence of nightly activities when it's nearly time for bed will give your baby a heads-up that it's time to put his sweet head down, gently leading him to the land of nodding off. It bridges that transition from the buzz of the day to the lull of the night, helping your increasingly busy little one go from 60 to zero with less fuss. What's more—a lot more—a bedtime routine provides a chance to bond with your little bundle at the end of a long day. After all, the time spent snuggling, singing lullabies, and quietly reading are some of the coziest—and calmest—you'll get to spend with your baby.

To allow enough time for a satisfying and successful bedtime routine, get things rolling about 30 to 45 minutes before you'd ideally like your little one to hit the sheets. Though bedtime routines should be consistent from night to night, you can be flexible in developing one that works for you and your baby, incorporating all or some of the following. But first things first: Get ready to get your baby sleepy. Creating a sleep-inducing atmosphere—dimming the lights, turning off the TV, powering down the phone—will help set a relaxing tone. Then move on to:

A bath. After a day of cleaning the floor with his knees, massaging his scalp with mashed banana, and rolling in the grass, baby probably needs a bath. But the evening bath does more than get a baby clean—it's also relaxing. Warm, soothing waters wield magical,

For Parents:
Baby's Sleeping Through . . . How About You?

It's perhaps one of parenting's greatest ironies: No sooner than baby starts sleeping through the night, then you're up all night with insomnia. It doesn't happen to every sleep-deprived parent who suddenly scores the ultimate baby sleep prize (sleeping through the night), but it happens. And if it's happening to you, you might be ready to try crying yourself to sleep (if only you could).

Post-sleep-teaching insomnia seems inherently unfair, but it also makes sense, at least biologically. While you were busy setting your baby's sleep habits straight, you were also busy wreaking havoc on your own, throwing your internal clock for a loop . . . a loop of sleeplessness. Add in the lighter sleep you've become accustomed to since your demanding bundle of joy arrived, and it's no wonder you're lying in bed waiting for whimpers and wails that never come—and a sandman who never arrives.

Happily, you can straighten out your own sleep habits using some of the same tricks you used to straighten out your little one's. Most important will be a bedtime routine. Instead of falling into bed (as natural an inclination as it is for new parents), ease yourself into it. Dim the lights, play soft music, take a warm bath, have a light snack (with a milk chaser, which actually helps you catch those z's faster), have sex or some quiet cuddles with your big sweetie—anything you find relaxing. Taking a magnesium supplement, which relaxes your muscles, can also help summon slumber. Try to avoid TV, tablets, your phone—anything that might wire you and that emits a bright light—for about 30 to 60 minutes before bed. Some research suggests that bright light exposure before sleep can disrupt body rhythms and suppress the release of melatonin, the sleep-promoting hormone.

Be consistent in the hour that you begin your bedtime routine and the order in which you play it out—just as you are with your baby—so your body begins to get acclimated to the idea that the routine will end in sleep. And though it may seem obvious, skip the caffeine in the afternoon and evening hours—it can stay in your system for as long as 8 hours, fueling that frustrating cycle of sleeplessness.

---

sleep-inducing powers, so don't waste them by giving baby a bath earlier in the day. You might also want to try baby bedtime bath wash or lotion enriched with lavender and chamomile, known for their soothing and relaxing properties.

A massage. If your baby enjoys a good rub, now would be a great time to relax him with one. Research suggests that babies who are massaged before bed produce more of the sleep-inducing hormone melatonin. Use a soothing scented oil or lotion for extra sleepy benefits. For tips on baby massage, see page 251.

Breastfeeding or a bottle of formula. A nightcap can fill your baby's tummy till morning. Don't forget to brush baby's teeth (if he has any) afterward, or to wipe them with a tooth wipe or washcloth. If your baby tends to fall asleep during this feeding and you'd rather he didn't, do it a bit earlier (such as before the bath) and keep the noise and activity level high. Later, when your baby is closer to the end of the first year, you can opt to add a bedtime snack.

A story. After your baby's been diapered and pajamaed, settle down together into a glider, a comfortable chair, or the sofa with a book or two and some snuggles. Any book will do, but bedtime classics like *Goodnight Moon* or *Guess How Much I Love You* often become family favorites. Read in a soft, soothing tone rather than a lively, animated voice. Or just look at the pictures together.

A song, a cuddle. Sing quiet songs and lullabies, cuddle, but save rougher fun (such as "I'm gonna get you" kissing games or tickling sessions) for daytime—after all, once baby's motor is turned on, it's hard to turn off.

Good-byes. Take a good-night tour—saying night-night to stuffed animals, siblings, mommy, and daddy. Share good-night kisses all around, say, "I love you" or "good night, sleep tight" (or anything else you'd like to say—just make it short, sweet, and predictable), put baby down tenderly, stroke his hair or his cheek gently for a moment or two, add a few quiet rounds of "shhh," and then make your exit (unless you're all going to sleep together).

Still Using a Pacifier

"Should I be taking the pacifier away now that my baby is 6 months old, before she gets too attached?"

There's no need to give up the binky at bedtime—in fact, it's a good idea for baby to be put to bed with her pacifier, since research has shown that this may reduce the risk of SIDS. But it might be wise to try limiting pacifier use

to when your sweetie's sleeping. This way, it won't interfere with socializing and vocalizing during the day. And start thinking ahead—while it isn't necessary to wean your baby off the paci at her first birthday (use of it isn't likely to harm teeth until age 2 to 3), it's definitely an opportune time to ditch the binky for good. As you've guessed, the more entrenched the paci habit is, the harder it is to kick.

Early Rising

"At first we were grateful that our son was sleeping through the night. But with him waking up like clockwork at 5 every morning, we almost wish he'd wake up in the middle of the night instead."

With a night waker, at least there's the promise of another few hours of sleep once baby settles down again. But with a baby who greets his parents alert and energetic, ready and eager to start every day when even the roosters are still snoozing, there's no hope of further rest until night falls once more. Let's just say . . . it's a rude awakening.

It probably isn't realistic to expect your baby to sleep in past 6 or 7 (at least not until he's a teenager, at which point you'll probably have to drag him out of bed each morning just to get him to school on time). But it may be possible to reset your little alarm clock at least a bit later:

Keep out the dawn's early light. Some babies (like some adults) are particularly sensitive to light when they're sleeping. Especially when the days are longer, keeping baby's room dark can buy a little extra sleep for everyone. Invest in room-darkening shades or lined curtains, to prevent an early sunrise from waking baby.

Keep the traffic out. If your baby's window faces a street with a lot of traffic in the early morning hours, the noise could be waking him too soon. Try keeping his window closed, hanging a heavy blanket or curtains at the window to help muffle sound, or moving him, if possible, to an off-street room. Or use a fan or a white-noise machine to drown out street noises.

Keep baby up later at night. Sometimes, too early to bed (say, 6 p.m.) can mean too early to rise. So try putting your baby to bed 10 minutes later each night, until you've gradually postponed his bedtime an hour or more. To make this work, it will probably help to move his naps and meals forward simultaneously and at the same pace. On the other hand, sometimes a too late bedtime can result, paradoxically, in a too early riser. If that seems to be the case with your little one, try a somewhat earlier bedtime.

Keep baby up later during the day. Some early risers are ready to go back to sleep in an hour or two. Early naps lead to early bedtime, which inevitably continues the cycle of early waking. To break the cycle, postpone baby's return to the crib by 10 minutes more each morning until he's napping an hour or so later, which may eventually help him to extend his night's sleep.

Keep naps down. A baby needs only so much total sleep—an average of 14½ hours at this age, with wide variations in individual babies. Maybe yours is getting too much sleep during the day and thus needs less at night. Limit daytime naps, cutting one out or shortening all of them. But don't cut out so much daytime sleep that your baby's actually overtired (and less likely to sleep well) by bedtime. And if he seems not to be napping enough during the day,

consider that the key to longer night sleeps might be longer day sleeps.

Keep him waiting. Don't rush to greet him at the first call from the crib. Wait 5 minutes first. If you're lucky, he may cuddle up and go back to sleep, or at least amuse himself while you catch a few more moments of rest.

Have entertainment standing by. If keeping the room dark doesn't help, try letting a little light seep through so that he can play while he waits for you. An attached crib soother, crib mirror, or crib keyboard may keep him busy for a few minutes.

Keep him waiting for breakfast. If he's used to eating at 5:30 a.m., hunger will continue to be his early wake-up call—and yours. Gradually postpone the first feed by a few minutes each day, so that he's less likely to wake up early for it.

Tried it all but your baby still won't sleep in? It may be your baby's just an early morning person, even if you are definitely not. In that case, you may have no choice but to rise—if not shine—early, too. That is, at least until he's old enough to get up and make his own breakfast.

Flipping During the Night

"I always put my baby on her back to sleep. But now that she knows how to roll over, she flips over and sleeps on her stomach. Should I keep flipping her back?"

Now that your baby has learned to flip, there's no point in trying to keep her on her back—and happily, no reason to worry if you can't. Experts agree that a baby who is able to change positions easily is at a significantly decreased risk for SIDS. That's because the high-risk period for SIDS has generally passed by the time a baby can turn over. It may also be because a baby who has developed the strength and mobility to roll onto her tummy has developed the maturity to sense trouble when she's sleeping—and she's better equipped to protect herself from whatever it is about tummy sleeping that increases SIDS risk.

You can—and according to experts, you should—keep putting your baby to bed on her back until her first birthday. But don't lose any sleep over her position if it changes during the night (or even as soon as you've put her down). Be sure, however, that her crib is safe—continue to follow the tips for preventing SIDS on page 270, such as using only a firm mattress and avoiding pillows, blankets, bumpers, comforters, and plush toys.

Bathing in the Big Tub

"Our baby is far too big now for his infant tub. But I'm nervous about washing him in our bathtub—and he seems to be, too. The one time I tried it, he screamed so much, I had to take him out. So now what?"

Taking the plunge into the family bathtub (especially a deep soaking tub) may seem an intimidating step for both baby and you. After all, he's still such a little—and slippery—fish for such a big pond. But if you're careful about preventing accidents (see box, page 360) and easing baby's fears (and yours), the big tub can turn into a water wonderland for an older baby, and bath time into a favorite (if wet) family ritual. To make sure the transition to deeper waters is smooth sailing for baby, see the basic tips on bathtub bathing on page 163, and try the following:

Let your baby test the waters in a familiar boat. For a few nights before he graduates from it, bathe him in his baby tub placed in the empty grown-up tub (if you haven't already). This way, the big tub won't seem quite so big when it's filled with water—and him.

Take a dry run. If he's sitting well and is willing, put him in the tub (on a large bath towel or a safe bath seat so he doesn't slip) without water and with a pile of toys. That way he can become used to the tub while it's dry—and hopefully discover how much fun playing in it can be. If the room is warm enough and he's a baby who doesn't mind being naked, let him play in there undressed. Otherwise, keep his clothes on. If he seems reluctant, try climbing into the tub with him to keep him company. As in any bathtub situation, don't leave his side for a moment.

Use a stand-in. While someone else holds baby, give a demonstration bath to a washable doll in the bathtub, with a comforting running commentary each step of the way. Make it look as if everybody involved is having a good time.

Test the waters. Don't go deep—the water should come up to waist-high for baby when he's sitting. The temperature should be warm, but not hot (a bath thermometer is the easiest way to ensure a comfortable and safe temperature).

Avoid the big chill. Babies dislike being cold, and if they associate being chilled with being bathed, they may balk at bathing. So be sure that the bathroom is comfortably warm—if it's too chilly, you can try steaming it up first by running a hot shower. Don't remove baby's clothes until the tub is filled and you are ready to slip him into it. Have a large, soft towel—hooded is best—ready to wrap him in as soon as you lift him from the water. Dry baby thoroughly,

Safe Big-Bath Bathing

To make sure tubby time is not only fun but safe, follow these important tips:

Wait until baby's a sitting duck. You'll both be more comfortable with big-tub bathing if your baby's capable of sitting unassisted, or with only minimal support.

Take a safe seat. A wet baby is a slippery baby, and even a solid sitter can take a slide in the tub. And though a momentary slip under the water wouldn't be physically harmful, it could generate a longer-term fear of baths. (Of course, if he slips and you're not there, the consequences could be much more serious.)

Though most experts recommend *against* using a bath seat for safety's sake, some parents choose to use one as an alternative to the old one-hand-on-baby-at-all-times maneuver. If you do decide to use a bath seat, be sure you use one that meets the safety standards issued by the Consumer Product Safety Commission (CPSC) in 2010. These tougher standards include stricter stability requirements to prevent the bath seat from tipping over, tighter leg openings to prevent children from slipping through, and a larger permanent warning label alerting parents and caregivers that bath seats are not safety devices and that infants should never be left unattended in a bath seat.

If you're not using a bath seat, be sure the tub bottom is lined with a rubber tub mat or skidproof stick-ons to prevent slipping—wet baby bottoms are slippery bottoms.

Be prepared. Towel, washcloth, baby wash, shampoo, tub toys, and anything else you'll need for baby's bath should be on hand before you put baby in the tub. If you do forget something and you have to get it yourself, bundle baby in a towel and take him or her with you. Also prepare by removing everything from tub-side that's potentially dangerous in baby's curious hands, such as soap, razors, and adult body wash and shampoo—not to mention sponges and products used for cleaning the tub.

Be there. Your baby needs adult supervision every moment of every bath—and will continue to for the first 5 years of bathing. Never leave your little one in the tub unattended, even in a baby seat, even for a second (he or she could slip out or climb out). Keep this startling statistic in mind when the phone or doorbell rings, a pot boils over on the stove, or anything else threatens to take your attention away from your baby: 55 percent of accidental infant drownings take place in the bathtub.

Don't overfill. Water should come to baby's waist when sitting.

Do the elbow test. Your relatively toughened-up hands are much more tolerant of heat than a baby's sensitive skin. So test the water with a bath thermometer, your elbow, or the inside of your wrist before dunking baby. While it should be comfortably warm, it should not be hot. Turn the hot water tap off first, so that any drips from the faucet will be cold and baby won't be scalded. Setting the hot water at 120°F or below will also prevent scalds. A safety cover on the tub spout will protect baby from burns and bumps.

being sure to get into the creases, before unwrapping and dressing him.

Launch a fleet of fun. Make the tub a floating playground for your baby so that he'll be diverted while you take care of bathing business. Specially designed tub toys (particularly those that bob atop the water, like a rubber ducky) and bath books are great, but you don't need pricey water toys to make a splash—plastic containers of all shapes and sizes will provide a boatload of fun. To avoid mildew buildup on tub toys, towel them off after use and store them in a dry container or a mesh bag. Clean water-retaining bath toys at least once a week with a mixture of 1 part bleach to 15 parts water (be sure to rinse well) to reduce any buildup of bacteria or mold.

Let baby make a splash. For most babies, splashing is a large part of bath-time fun, and the wetter a baby can make you, the happier he'll be. But while he almost certainly will like to make a splash, he may not like to be the target of one. Every baby is different, but many have been turned off to the tub with a single playful splash.

Use the buddy system. Some babies are more amenable to a bath if they've got company. Try climbing into the tub with your baby, but at bath temperatures geared to his comfort. Once he becomes adjusted to these baths-for-two, you can try him solo.

No swimming right after eating. It makes sense not to bathe your baby directly after meals, because the increase in handling and activity could cause spit-ups.

Don't pull the stopper until baby is out of the tub. Not only can it be a physically chilling experience to be in an emptying tub, it can be psychologically chilling, too. The gurgling sound can frighten even a young infant, and an older baby or toddler who sees the water rushing down the drain may fear that he's going down next.

Be patient. Eventually, your little minnow will take to the tub. But he'll do it faster if he's allowed to do it at his own pace, and without parental pressure.

Bottle Rejection in a Breastfed Baby

"I'd like to give my baby an occasional bottle of pumped milk to free me up a little, but she refuses to drink it. What can I do?"

Your baby wasn't born yesterday. And unlike a relative newcomer, she's developed a strong sense of what she wants, what she doesn't want, and how she can best go about getting things her way. What she wants: your nice, soft, warm nipples. What she doesn't want: a factory-made substitute. How she can best go about getting things her way: crying for the former and rejecting the latter.

Waiting this long to introduce a bottle into your baby's life has turned the odds against you—the introduction is better made no later than 6 weeks (see page 238). But it's still possible that you'll be able to win her over by following these tips:

Feed her on an empty stomach. Many babies will be more receptive to the bottle as a source of food when they're in the market for something to eat. So try offering the bottle when your baby is really hungry—she may just take the bottle bait.

Or feed her on a full stomach. With some babies, offering a bottle when they are looking for a breast just plain makes them mad. If this is the case with your baby (and you'll find out only through trial and rejection), don't offer the bottle when she's at her hungriest. Instead, offer it casually between nursings. She may be more in the mood to experiment and more open to a snack.

Don't let her see you sweat. Instead of acting as though there's a lot at stake (even if there is), act as if the bottle issue is no biggie, no matter what her response.

Let her play before she eats. Before attempting to get down to business with the bottle, let her get her hands on it. If she's had a chance to explore it on her own, she may be more likely to let it into her life and, hopefully, into her mouth. She may even put it there herself—as she does everything else.

Banish your breast. And the rest of you, when the bottle is launched. A breastfed baby is more likely to accept a bottle from those lacking lactation equipment—in other words, anyone but mom. It may also help if you and your breasts are out of smelling distance. At least until bottle-feeding is well established, even the sound of your voice may spoil baby's appetite for a bottle.

Try a favorite fluid. It's possible that baby's objecting not to the bottle but to the fluid inside it. Some infants will take to a bottle better if it's filled with familiar breast milk, but others, reminded of breast milk's original source, are more open to another beverage. If your baby's doctor has okayed water, give that a whirl first.

Sneak it in during sleep. Have your bottle giver pick up your sleeping baby and try to offer the bottle then. After a few weeks, your little stubborn bottle snubber may open wide when wide awake, too.

Know when to surrender—temporarily. Don't let the bottle become the object of a battle, or your side doesn't stand a chance of winning. As soon as your baby raises objections to the bottle, take it away (again, like you could care less) and try again another day, and then another. Offer the bottle once every few days for at least a couple of weeks before you consider giving up entirely.

Even if baby never ends up budging on the bottle, don't give up hope. There's another alternative to your breasts: the cup. Many babies can master a cup by 6 months or so and happily take supplementary feedings from it (see page 410), and most become skilled enough cup drinkers by the end of the first year to be weaned directly from the breast to the cup—which saves the extra step of weaning from the bottle.

Baby-Bottle Mouth

"I have a friend whose baby's front teeth had to be pulled because of tooth decay. How can I prevent this from happening to my son?"

There's nothing cuter than a first grader whose grin reveals an adorable space where his two front teeth used to be. But losing baby teeth early to decay (so-called baby-bottle mouth) isn't so cute. It also doesn't just affect a baby's smile. It's painful, can lead to infection if not treated, and can result in problems with eating and speech development.

So you're smart to think prevention—and happily, baby-bottle mouth is completely preventable. It occurs most often in the first 2 years of life, when teeth are most vulnerable, and most frequently as a result of a baby's falling asleep regularly with a bottle (or much less often, a breast) in his mouth. The sugars in whatever beverage he's sipping (formula, fruit juice, even breast milk) combine with bacteria in his mouth to erode that brand new enamel and decay the teeth. The dirty work is done during sleep when the production of saliva, which ordinarily dilutes food and drink and promotes the swallowing reflex, slows dramatically. With little swallowing occurring, the last sips baby takes before falling asleep pool in his mouth and cling to his teeth for hours.

Some babies are more susceptible to baby-bottle mouth because of a genetic predisposition. So, if you or your partner get lots of cavities, that might put your little one at greater risk. That said, any baby can get tooth decay in those first precious pearlies under the right—or, in this case, the wrong—conditions. To avoid baby-bottle mouth:

- Once your baby's first teeth come in, don't put him to bed for the night or down for a nap with a bottle of formula or breast milk. Give the bottle before you put him down, and if it's nighttime, brush his teeth after the feed. If he takes a bottle to bed, fill it with water only, which won't hurt his teeth (and if it's fluoridated, will help strengthen them). Avoid juice in bottles altogether.

- Use bottles for feeds, but not for pacifying. All-day nipping (crawling around with a bottle, or always having it handy for sips while playing) can be as harmful to the teeth as nighttime sucking. Bottles should be considered part of a meal or snack and like these should routinely be given in the appropriate setting (your arms, a baby seat, a high chair or other feeding chair) and at appropriate times.

- Dilute even 100 percent fruit juice at least half-and-half with water, and serve it in a cup instead of a bottle (or skip the juice altogether). Avoid drinks with sugar added, such as cranberry juice cocktail, fruit punches, or fruit drinks.

- Drop the bottle at 12 months, as recommended by the AAP.

- Whatever goes for bottles goes for sippy cups as well, which also allow fluids to pool in a baby's mouth—so set similar limits with sippies. Straw cups or regular cups (as they're introduced) are a better dental bet.

- While baby-bottle mouth is far less common among breastfed babies, be wary of all-night nipping at the breast, too, once teeth arrive.

Brushing Baby's Teeth

"My baby just got her first tooth. The doctor said I should start brushing it now, but that seems silly."

Those tiny pearls that bring so much pain before they arrive and so much excitement when they first break through the gums are going to fall out during the early and midschool years, to be replaced by permanent teeth. So why take good care of them now?

For several very good reasons. Since they hold a place for the permanent teeth, decay and loss of these first teeth can deform the mouth permanently. Not to mention that your baby will need these primary teeth for biting and chewing for many years—so it's important they are as healthy as can be. Healthy teeth are also important for the development of normal speech. Finally, and probably most important, getting your baby in the brushing habit early will make it second nature by the time that second set of teeth comes in.

The first teeth can be wiped clean with a damp gauze pad or washcloth, or a tooth wipe or finger brush designed for infants, or you can brush them with an infant toothbrush. Less is more when it comes to traditional bristle brushes—choose one with no more than three rows of very soft bristles, and swap for a new one when it gets rough around the edges (which will happen pretty quickly if baby likes to chomp down during brushing). Or opt for a flexible brush with silicone bristles—these are gentler, more durable, and offer a soothing gum massage during teething bouts. They're also dishwasher safe (so they're easier to keep clean). Some come with a wide handle or a silicone shield to keep baby from pushing the brush too deep into her mouth.

Aim for brushing or wiping teeth after meals and at bedtime. Be gentle, since baby teeth are soft and gums are tender. Lightly brush or wipe the front of the tongue, too (going too far back can trigger gagging), since it can harbor germs.

What about toothpaste? According to the American Academy of Pediatric Dentistry (AAPD), it's a good idea to start brushing baby teeth with cavity-preventing fluoride toothpaste right from the start—instead of waiting until age 2, as was previously recommended. But remember that size very much matters. To avoid overdosing a baby or toddler on fluoride, use just a rice-grain-size smear of toothpaste, graduating to a pea-size blob at age 3. Experts say those quantities probably won't generate mottling of the teeth, even if your little one swallows some paste (she will). In the second year you can start trying to teach her the fine art of spitting.

Though brushing is the first line of defense against tooth decay, there are other preventive steps you can take to ensure a lifetime of healthy teeth, such as those listed in the previous question, as well as:

- Limiting refined carbs (bread, crackers, and teething biscuits made with white flour) in your little one's diet since they quickly turn into sugar on your baby's pearly whites, posing as much of a cavity risk as candy. Whole grains aren't only more nutritious, but they're also better for baby's teeth.

- Setting limits on bottles and sippy cups (see previous answer).

- Checking up on your baby's mouth and teeth. The doctor probably does a check at each well-baby visit—and unless there are signs of decay or other issues, that's likely all she needs now. The American Academy of Pediatric Dentistry recommends a visit to the dentist (a pediatric dentist or a regular dentist who sees children) around the first birthday—and an early visit can help get your little one acclimated to dental checkups—but if all is well and she's getting her teeth checked regularly by her pediatrician, it's fine to hold off until your little one turns 3.

- Asking about fluoride. Most babies over 6 months get all the fluoride they need from fluoridated drinking water (and a smidge of fluoride toothpaste). If your baby doesn't, ask the doctor about whether you should add a fluoride supplement.

Cereal Snubbing

"Our baby loves eating vegetables and fruits, but he doesn't seem to like cereal. Does he need to eat cereal?"

It's not the cereal that babies need, it's the iron it's fortified with. For the formula-fed set, cereal snubbing isn't an issue, since these babies fill their requirement for this vital mineral every time they drink a bottle. Nursing babies, however, need another source of iron once they've reached the 4-month mark. Fortunately, while fortified baby cereals are a very popular alternative source of iron (at least, among the majority of beginning eaters and their parents), they're not the only one. Breastfed

Iron: It's Elementary

Thanks to iron-fortified formula and baby cereals, as well as recommendations that breastfed babies get daily iron supplements, anemia (a low supply of protein in the red blood cells) isn't very common—only 4 to 12 percent of babies become anemic in the first year. But because the only way to diagnose the condition in babies is with a blood test, the AAP recommends that babies get tested between 9 and 12 months, and between 6 and 9 months for premature infants, who are at higher risk for anemia (because they didn't have time before birth to lay down sufficient reserves).

Full-term babies are generally born with stores of iron built up during the last few months of pregnancy that carry them for the first few months of life. After that, as babies continue to require the mineral in large quantities to help expand their blood volume to meet the demands of rapid growth, they need a source of iron in the diet, such as iron-fortified formula (for bottle-fed babies) or iron-fortified baby cereal. And though breastfeeding exclusively for the first 4 to 6 months is considered the best way to nourish your baby, and the iron in breast milk is very well absorbed, breastfeeding alone does not ensure adequate iron intake after 4 months (which is why supplementation is recommended at least until iron-rich foods are introduced into the diet; see page 193).

Keep in mind that though your baby will be tested for iron-deficiency anemia, it's important you take steps to help prevent it (the blood test isn't always perfect), so try the following:

- Be sure that if your baby is bottle-fed, he or she is getting a formula fortified with iron.

- Be sure that if your baby is breastfed, he or she is getting an iron supplement after 4 months and at least until iron-rich foods are introduced (and eaten regularly).

- As your baby increases his or her intake of solids, be sure to include foods rich in iron, preferably served up with foods rich in vitamin C to boost absorption (see page 449).

cereal spurners can easily fill their requirement with an iron supplement.

And before you close the pantry door on all cereal, you might want to try offering baby another variety that you haven't introduced yet—barley, perhaps, or oat. It's possible that his more adventurous taste buds naturally prefer a slightly stronger taste (rice is definitely the blandest of the bunch). Whatever cereal you choose, whole grain is the best bet nutrition wise, and tastier, too. Or consider mixing a small amount of cereal with one of the fruits he enjoys (no need to sweeten the cereal deal with fruit, however, for a baby who already enjoys it straight up).

A Vegetarian or Vegan Diet

"We're vegans and plan to raise our daughter the same way. Can our diet provide enough nutrition for her?"

Your little sprout can grow up to be just as healthy as any milk-drinking or meat-eating tot—and with the right food choices, maybe even healthier. Just remember to:

- Breastfeed your baby. Continuing to breastfeed for at least a year, if possible, will ensure that your infant will get all the nutrients she needs for the first 6 months and most of what she needs for the first year—assuming you're getting all the nutrients you need (including folic acid and vitamin B_{12} in a supplement) to produce high-quality breast milk. If you're not breastfeeding, be certain that the soy formula you choose is one recommended by your baby's doctor.

- Supplement. Check with your baby's doctor to see whether your baby should be getting any additional vitamin supplements above the ones recommended for all babies.

- Be selective. Serve only whole-grain cereals, breads, rice, and other grains once your baby has graduated to them. These provide more of the vitamins, minerals, and protein ordinarily obtained from animal products than their refined varieties do.

- Turn to tofu. Use tofu and other soy-based products to provide added protein when your baby moves on to solids. When the pediatrician gives the okay, brown rice or quinoa cooked until it is fairly soft, mashed chickpeas or other beans and peas, and high-protein or whole-grain pastas can also be added to the diet as sources of protein. And don't forget to bring on the edamame. Cooked until very soft and shelled, served pureed at first, mashed later, these soybeans are tasty and full of protein.

- Concentrate on calories. Growing babies need plenty of calories to grow on, and getting enough fuel is more difficult on a diet that's limited to plant food. Keep an eye on baby's weight gain to make sure she's taking enough calories. If it seems to be slacking, boost her breast milk intake and focus on higher-calorie plant foods, such as avocados.

- Don't forget the fat—the good fat, that is. Vegans who never eat animal products at all have to look elsewhere for good fats like omega-3 fatty acids—avocados, canola and flaxseed oil, and, when introduced, nut butters.

Changes in Bowel Movements

"Since I started my breastfed baby on solids last week, his poops have been more solid—which I would expect—but they are also darker and smellier. Is this normal?"

Sadly, the sweet-smelling poop party is over once you invite solids into your baby's diet. Party-pooping solids change a breastfed baby's stools from soft, mustardy, and mild to thick, dark, and smelly seemingly overnight—not necessarily a diaper change for the better, but a completely normal one. Expect your baby's stools to become increasingly adultlike as his diet does—though a breastfed baby's may remain somewhat softer than a bottle-fed's until weaning.

"I just gave my baby carrots for the first time, and her next bowel movement was bright orange."

What goes in must come out. And in babies, with their immature digestive systems, it sometimes doesn't change very much in the process. Once they start solids, their stools seem to vary movement to movement, often reflecting the most recent meal in color or texture. Later, foods not chewed thoroughly—especially those that are harder to digest—may come out whole or nearly so. As long as bowel movements don't also contain mucus and aren't unusually loose, which might signal gastrointestinal irritation (and the need to withhold the offending food

Elimination Communication

Eager to get started on Project Potty now, while your baby is still, well, a baby? You're not alone. One toilet-training trend that's getting a lot of playground press is called "elimination communication"—essentially very early potty lessons for the new-to-diapers set (aka infants).

How can you turn your baby into a potty prodigy, if you so choose? First, become attuned to your little one's pooping and peeing schedule. Babies usually pee when they wake up, some time after a feeding, and at regular intervals between feedings. Pooping also tends to occur at fairly regular intervals throughout the day—usually after a feeding. Then you'll want to watch your baby closely for those elimination signs (you know what they are: the grunts, the red face, the pursed lips, the look of concentration, becoming still for a minute, maybe a little shivery shudder). The more attuned you are to your little one's pooping and peeing schedule, the easier it'll become to spot those signs. As soon as you know your baby's about to go, hold him or her over the potty and make a specific sound (such as "pssss") to cue your baby that it's time to pee. Pretty soon, your little one will associate the position and sound with the need to pee. Do the same with pooping and a different sound (like a grunt).

Not all experts agree that babies this young have the muscle control necessary to truly be "potty trained," and some worry that starting the potty learning process so early could set up unrealistic expectations on the part of the parents as well as a potential for struggles between parent and child. But if you're up for and eager for super-early training, go for it—just be prepared to spend lots of time on the project. Remember, it'll be labor-intensive for you, requiring you to have very quick reflexes and a super flexible schedule. But when it works, elimination communication allows diapers to be ditched much earlier than what's currently the norm (around age 3).

Your baby seems stressed out by your campaign to potty train? That's a sign to back off for now. There's plenty of time to hop on the potty train.

for a few weeks), you can continue her newly varied diet without concern.

Walkers and Stationary Play Centers

"My daughter seems very frustrated that she can't get around yet. She's not content to lie in her crib or sit in her infant seat, but I can't carry her all day. Can I put her in a walker?"

Life can be frustrating when you're all revved up with no place to go (or at least no way to get there without a grown-up's help). These frustrations often peak when an eager-to-get-going baby's able to sit fairly well but unable to get around on her own (by crawling, creeping, cruising, or whatever method she's first able to come up with). The obvious solution used to be a walker—a seat set inside a table framework on four wheeled legs that allowed babies to zoom happily around the house long before they achieved independent mobility. But because walkers have been the cause of too many injuries requiring medical treatment (from head injuries caused by falls to burns that result from

The 30-Minute Rule

Some babies are quick to set their own limits on the time they spend in activity centers, jumpers, and swings—often too quick for the parents who crave a little break from toting their little ones. But others can't get enough of that swinging, bouncing, jumping, and swiveling stuff, and they'll entertain themselves happily in their activity centers for as long as they're allowed. Yet babies can get too much of these good things—even if they don't realize they can. To make sure your little one gets lots of opportunities to flex different muscles—and get a different perspective—limit sessions in all of these baby entertaining gadgets to no more than 30 minutes at a time, and try not to exceed a total of an hour a day.

scooting over to an open oven door or to a toaster that can be pulled down by its cord), and many more that are kissed-and-made-better at home, they are no longer recommended, and in fact, the AAP has called for a ban on the manufacture and sale of all mobile walkers (they're already banned in Canada).

A somewhat satisfying, safer substitute for a walker is a stationary activity center (like the ExerSaucer), which allows baby some movement (a little one can bounce, rock, and swivel) without the risks of a mobile walker. They're also pretty entertaining, with most providing a bouncy seat that spins and a selection of toys to play with—often including light and sound features. Still, they don't come without a downside. First, a baby whose frustrations lie in not being able to get aound without

hitching a ride from mom or dad isn't likely to be any less frustrated in a walker that doesn't move. She might even become more frustrated once she realizes that the stationary variety moves only in circles ("I'm moving, but I'm not getting anywhere!"). What's more, research shows that babies who spend too much time in a stationary play center (as in a walker, infant seat, or swing) may be slower to sit, crawl, and walk, since they don't get as much opportunity to flex the muscles necessary to practice and master those skills. In fact, babies use a different set of muscles to stay upright in a stationary activity center than they do to stay upright for walking. And because they can't see their feet in an activity center, they're deprived of the visual clues that would help them figure out how their bodies walk through space (a key part of learning how to walk). Finally, they don't learn how to balance themselves, and how, when balance fails them, to fall and pick themselves back up—also vital steps in becoming a solo walker.

If you do choose to use an ExerSaucer or other stationary activity center, follow these tips for keeping baby both content and safe while she's in it:

Test-drive before you buy. The best way to find out if your baby's ready for a stationary activity center is to let her try one out. If you don't have a friend whose baby has one, go to a store and let your baby try out a floor model. As long as she seems happy and doesn't slump, she's ready to take it for a spin (or a bounce).

Watch her "activity." Stationary activity centers aren't a substitute for supervision, any more than swings, jumpers, infant seats, or bouncers are. Leave your baby in her ExerSaucer only when she can be watched—and don't place it anywhere near something she shouldn't touch or reach for (like the cord on a phone charger or a hot cup of coffee).

Limit her "activity." For most babies, 5 or 10 minutes in the activity center and they're more than ready for another activity—and clamoring to get out. A few will be happy to bounce, spin, and play for far longer, but it's best to limit even a completely content activity center activist to no more than 30 minutes per session. Every baby needs to spend some time on the floor, practicing skills—such as lifting her belly off the ground while on all fours—that will eventually help her to sit and crawl. She needs the opportunity to pull up on coffee tables and kitchen chairs in preparation for standing and, later, walking. She needs more chances to explore and handle safe objects in her environment than any confined seat (even a really fun one) allows. And, she needs the interaction with you and others that free play requires and allows.

Don't delay packing away. The activity center, that is. As soon as your baby starts getting ready to start taking on crawling or cruising, pack away the ExerSaucer and let her practice her floor exercises—the ones that will eventually help her stand up and deliver

those first steps, ending her frustrating era of immobility for good. Keeping her cooped up in an activity center not only won't help speed those steps, but its continued use may cause confusion, because standing in an activity center and standing and walking solo require different body movements.

Pre-Walking Shoes

"My baby's not walking yet, of course, but her outfits look so much cuter with shoes. Is there a certain kind I should look for?"

Socks, booties, or, weather permitting, bare feet are best for your baby at this stage of development—offering room to breathe, stretch, and flex. Still, there's nothing wrong with outfitting her tiny tootsies in something a little more styling on special occasions (or cold ones)—as long as it's the right kind of style. Since your baby's feet aren't made for walking (at least not yet), the shoes you buy shouldn't be, either. Shoes for infants should be lightweight and made of a breathable material (leather, cloth, or canvas—but not plastic), with soles so flexible that you can feel baby's toes through them (hard soles are a baby shoe must-not-do). For tips on choosing shoes once baby is walking, see page 473.

ALL ABOUT:
Stimulating Your Older Baby

Already peekabooed and pat-a-caked out? Blown so many raspberries, your cheeks hurt? This little piggy has cried "wee, wee, wee" one too many times in your home? Then there's good news: Though these timeless newborn games will probably still get lots of play

in the months to come, your older baby is game to take on a more sophisticated playlist—not to mention, take on more of the play.

No more lying back while you do all the work. Your baby is ready to be an active participant instead of a passive audience—engaging, interacting, exploring, and learning by doing. Ready to coordinate senses that were once used one at a time—seeing what's being touched, looking for what's being heard, touching what's being tasted. Ready—and eager—for more challenges, more excitement, more stimulation.

Here's how you can help:

Large motor skills. Physical skills take practice, practice, practice—which your baby can't get while cooped up in a stroller or a bouncer. So let your little one loose, and provide lots of opportunities that allow him or her to develop the large motor strength and coordination eventually needed for sitting, crawling, walking, climbing, throwing a ball, riding a scooter, and more. Change up baby's position often—from back to tummy, from propped-up to prone, from the crib to the floor—so he or she will have the chance to practice all kinds of physical feats. During tummy time, place an object just out of baby's reach to encourage him or her to stretch for it. Let baby lie on his or her back with those cute tootsies within kicking distance of an activity gym (a musical one that makes noise every time a kick makes contact provides even more satisfaction). Grab a stability or birthing ball and place baby on top—either sitting (with your hands firmly holding him or her) or lying tummy down (ditto) for balance practice. And then, as your baby seems ready (you won't know until you try), provide the opportunity to do the following:

- Pull to sitting

- Sit in a "frog" position (like a tripod)

- Sit upright, propped with pillows if necessary

- Stand on your lap and bounce

- Pull to standing, holding on to your fingers

- Pull to standing in a crib or play yard, or on other furniture

- Lift up on all fours

Small motor skills. At your baby's fingertips is a world of essential skills just waiting to be mastered (and lots of ones that are just plain fun, too)—from eating, to painting and crayoning, to writing, to brushing teeth, to buttoning a shirt, to putting on socks . . . to pouring magical tea for a favorite teddy. But first, those tiny fingers and hands will need to develop the dexterity necessary to grab on to life's challenges, big and small. Again, opportunity rocks—babies who are given lots of chances to use their hands a lot (yes, even to smear oatmeal in their hair), to manipulate objects of all kinds, to touch, explore, and experiment (not to mention mouth everything they can) with those 10 determined digits, and flex those small-muscle groups will develop dexterity faster. To help, offer:

- Activity cubes, boards, or tables: A variety of activities gives baby plenty of practice flexing those small motor skills, though it will be months before most babies can conquer them all. Activity gyms also offer plenty of small motor fun, as baby progresses from swatting at the hanging toys to making contact (score!) to grabbing on.

- Blocks: Simple cubes of wood, plastic, or cloth, large or small, are appropriate at this age. Your little one will grab and eventually pick them up, learning how to knock them together and make music (at least to his or her ears!). Though babies this age don't yet have the dexterity to stack blocks (and other stacking toys), they get their kicks by unstacking.

- Soft dolls and stuffed animals: Handling them builds dexterity. As your cutie gets bigger, dolls with different textures and features (buttons, zippers, laces) will excite the senses and help improve small motor dexterity.

- Finger foods: As they're introduced into baby's diet, finger foods can help build pincer grasp skills. Oat circles, soft peas and carrots, and other small, but safe to eat foods will help baby learn how to use his or her thumb and index finger to pick up bite-size morsels. Until then, foods that can be palmed (whole-grain breadsticks, cubes of cheese, chunks of soft melon)—once they've been introduced—will help develop small motor skills.

- Real or toy household objects: Babies usually love real or toy cell phones, mixing spoons, measuring cups, strainers, pots and pans, paper cups, and empty boxes.

- Balls: of varying sizes and textures, to hold, to squeeze, to swat at, that light up or make sounds. They are especially fun once baby is able to sit up and roll them or crawl after them.

- Stacking containers: first to just hold and drop, then to try to clang together, then to actually stack one into the other (though it'll be quite some time before baby's able to manage that skill!).

- Finger games: At first you'll be the one to play clap hands, pat-a-cake, The Itsy-Bitsy Spider, and similar games, but before you know it, baby will be playing along. After you do a demonstration or two, assist baby with the finger game while you sing along (don't be surprised if baby pulls your hands into his or her mouth).

Social skills. The middle of the first year is a very sociable time for most babies. They giggle, laugh, squeal, and communicate in a variety of other ways (like kicking their little legs when they're excited) and will share eye contact and a smile with anyone who's within cooing distance (whether it's an admirer in the park or a stranger at the supermarket or their own image in the mirror). Now, before stranger anxiety starts to rear its fearful head (that's usually later in the first year), is the perfect time to nurture the budding social butterfly in your baby, to go places where you'll see people (of all ages), to let your little life of the party interact and be interacted with. Let your baby learn from your social experience, too. Teach through example a simple greeting like "hi," and model some of the other basic social graces, such as waving bye bye, blowing a kiss, and saying thank you. Remember, you're just planting seeds now, so no pushing is needed. Feeling a little more socially ambitious? Consider joining a playgroup. The babies won't group play, per se, but they'll definitely get a kick out of watching each other—excellent, if not required, practice for the years of socializing ahead.

Cognitive skills. Comprehension is beginning to dawn—and it's pretty exciting stuff. Names (mommy's, daddy's, siblings') are recognized first, followed by basic words ("no," "bottle," "bye-bye," for example), and pretty soon after, simple, often-heard sentences ("Do you want to drink?" or "Make nice to the doggie"). This receptive language (understanding what they hear) will come well before spoken language, but it's huge—transforming a baby's perspective on the world ("Now I get it!"). Other types of intellectual development are also on the horizon. Many years ahead of that first math class, your baby is actually taking the first steps (though it won't seem so at first) toward acquiring the skills of

How Do You Speak to Your Baby Now?

Now that your baby hovers on the brink of learning your language, what you say to him or her takes on new meaning. You can help your baby's language skills along in the following ways:

Slow down. When baby is starting to try to decode your language (which is just jargon to those tiny untrained ears), fast talk will slow those efforts. To give your baby the chance to begin picking out words, speak slowly, clearly, and simply.

Focus on single words. Continue your running commentaries, but begin emphasizing individual words and simple phrases commonly used in baby's everyday life. At feeding time, when you say, "I'm putting cereal in the bowl," hold up the cereal and add, "Cereal, here is the cereal." Hold up the bowl, and say, "bowl." Always pause to give baby plenty of time to decipher your words before going on to say more.

Downplay pronouns. Pronouns are still confusing for your baby, so stick to "This is Daddy's shoe," and "That is Gray's shoe."

Emphasize imitation. Now that the number of sounds your baby makes is growing, so is the fun you can have imitating each other. Whole conversations can be built around a few consonants and vowels. Baby says, "ba-ba-ba-ba," and you come back with an animated "ba-ba-ba-ba." Baby replies, "da-da-da-da," and you respond, "da-da-da-da." If baby seems receptive, you can try offering some new syllables ("ga-ga-ga-ga," for example), encouraging imitation. But if the role reversal seems to turn baby off, switch back again. In not too many months, you'll find your baby will begin trying to imitate your words—without prompting.

Talk it up. Talk to your baby about everything—and anything—as you go

---

rudimentary problem solving, observation, and memorization—concepts that appear simple to you but are complex for your baby. You can help by:

- Playing games that stimulate your baby's brain (see page 444) and help explain concepts: cause and effect (fill a cup with water in the tub and let baby turn it over) and object permanence (cover a favorite toy with a cloth and then have baby look for it or play peekaboo behind your hands, a book, a menu). Point out: This teddy is soft, that coffee is hot, the car goes fast, you're sleepy, the ball is under the

table. While using objects, describe what they're for: This broom is for sweeping, this chair is for sitting on, this towel is for drying, a book is for reading. At first your words will be meaningless to baby, but eventually, with lots of repetition, the concepts will start to crystallize.

- Tuning your child in to the world of sounds. When a plane goes by overhead or a fire engine speeds down the street, sirens screaming, point them out to baby: "That's an airplane" or "Do you hear the fire engine?" Emphasizing and repeating the key about your day together. Be natural in your conversation, but with a baby-friendly inflection—as feels comfortable to you, that is. See page 486 for more on talking to your baby.

Build a repertoire of songs and rhymes. Ever find yourself tuning out after too many rounds of "Wheels on the Bus?" While it's mind numbing to you, repetition is music to your baby's ears, which pick up more and more from the same-old, same-old. It doesn't matter if you lean on Mother Goose, Dr. Seuss, or your own creativity—what counts is consistency.

Bank on books. There's a world of words in even the simplest board books—open up that world by opening up books often with your baby. As you read, do plenty of pointing out of single objects, animals, or people. Start asking, "Where is the dog?" and eventually baby will surprise you by placing a pudgy paw right on Spot.

Wait for a response. Though baby may not be talking yet, he or she is beginning to process information, and will soon start having a response to what you say—even if it's just an excited squeal (when you've proposed a walk in the stroller) or a pouty whimper (when you've announced it's time to come off the swing).

Be commanding. In time, your baby will learn to follow simple commands such as "kiss Grandma," or "wave bye-bye," or "give Mommy the dolly" (add "please" if you want the word to eventually come naturally to baby). But keep in mind that baby won't follow through on your requests for months to come, and even when he or she begins to, the response won't be consistent or immediate (baby may wave bye-bye, but not until 5 minutes after your friend has left the building). Don't show disappointment when baby doesn't perform. Instead, help your little one act out your request (waving bye-bye yourself) while waiting for him or her to catch on . . . typically not until closer to the first birthday.

words ("airplane," "fire engine") will also help with word recognition. Do the same when you turn on the vacuum or the water in the bathtub, when the teakettle whistles or the doorbell or phone rings. And don't overlook those favorite funny noises—razzes on baby's belly or arm, clicks with your tongue, and whistles are all educational, too, encouraging imitation, which in turn encourages language development.

■ Encouraging curiosity and creativity. Give your child a chance to experiment and explore—whether that means pulling up tufts of grass in the garden, smearing applesauce all over his hair or her t-shirt, or squeezing out a wet washcloth in the tub. A baby will learn volumes more through experience than through instruction, and this kind of play and exploration is absolutely free. So step back and let your baby call the shots by choosing what to play with and how.

CHAPTER 12

The Seventh Month

Still a social animal—with a serious charm offensive and a smile that happily just won't quit—your baby is also beginning to notice that there's a fascinating world beyond your adoring face, just waiting to be explored. And explore it your baby will—that is, as soon as he or she figures out how to get around in it. Which is just a matter of time—since the days of being able to plop your baby down in the middle of the floor, secure that he or she will stay there, are numbered. It may be weeks or it may be a month or two or more, but before you know it, baby will likely be twisting, rolling, creeping, and crawling from one end of the room to the other (though some babies opt out of all fours and skip straight to two feet, especially if they haven't spent much time on their tummies). With independent mobility just around the corner (and with it, access to such dangerous baby temptations as the stairs, the dishwasher, and the glass coffee table), it's time to do a thorough childproofing of your home if you haven't yet.

Feeding Your Baby: Ready-Made or Homemade Baby Foods

Will the spoon you'll be piloting into your eager baby's tiny mouth be filled with store-bought baby food or heaped with the homemade kind? Or perhaps a combination of both? The choice of what to serve your new eater is yours (and hint: all of these choices are good ones).

Baby Basics at a Glance: Seventh Month

Sleeping. Your baby should be logging in around 9 to 11 hours of sleep each night and 3 to 4 hours of sleep during the day, probably split up into a morning and afternoon nap. That's a total of around 14 hours during each 24-hour day.

Eating. Though baby has probably starting eating solids now, most nutritional requirements are still being filled via breast or bottle.

- Breast milk. Your baby will feed around 4 to 6 times a day (some babies will nurse more often . . . possibly way more). Baby will be drinking somewhere between 24 and 30 ounces of breast milk a day, though as more solids are added to the diet, that amount will decrease.

- Formula. Your baby will probably drink 4 to 5 bottles a day, filled with 6 to 8 ounces of formula, for a total of 24 to 30 ounces per day. As more solids are added to the diet, baby will feed on less formula.

- Solids. How much will your baby eat, solids-wise? For a newbie eater, think about 1 to 2 tablespoons (or less) each of cereals, fruits, and vegetables (as they're introduced), twice a day. Once baby gains eating experience, total intake may range anywhere from 3 to 9 tablespoons of cereal, fruit, and vegetables each (or less) per day, over 2 to 3 feedings. Just remember: Baby's the boss when it comes to intake. Let appetite rule the high chair.

Playing. Baby will love to play with action/reaction toys (ones that light up or play music when baby presses a button, for instance), stacking toys (ones with different-size rings or multicolored cubes, though baby won't be able to stack them properly yet), toys that encourage crawling (cars, trains, balls that roll, light up, make music) roly-poly toys (they right themselves when rolled over), and toys that encourage pulling up to standing (make sure they're sturdy!). Don't forget to keep a rotating stock of colorful board books for baby to page through with you, and on his or her own.

Ready-Made Baby Food.

Ready-made baby food—available in classic jars, boxes, convenient pouches, and single-serving frozen cubes—comes with a price, but also with a lot of perks. First, it's usually just as nutritious for your little one as homemade, especially when it comes to the simple fruit and veggie purees you're likely to premiere with. Sometimes, they're more nutritious—at least when it comes to out-of-season fruits and veggies. All first-stage food labels list wholesome, totally recognizable ingredients (buy a pouch of peaches,

Squeezing the Best from Food Pouches

They're the ultimate in convenience, plus they're often filled with good-for-your-baby food—from just plain peaches to wholesome blends of grains, veggies, fruits, spices, and even meat. But to make sure you're squeezing all the benefits out of food pouches without serving up any risks, keep these two tips in mind.

First, squeeze the food directly onto the spoon only if you know your baby is going to finish the contents of the entire pouch in one sitting. If one pouch will cover two (or more) meals, you're best off squeezing the right size portion into a bowl and spooning the contents from the bowl into your baby's mouth the old-fashioned way. More dishes to wash this way, yes, but it protects your baby from bacterial contamination, which can occur when you touch the top of the pouch onto the spoon that baby's already mouthed, and then store the pouch for later use.

Second, though it's certainly easy for baby to suck the yummy contents directly from the pouch as you (or later, he or she) squeeze, it's not a great habit to get into. Your newbie eater is already a proficient sucker (think of all that breast milk or formula he or she has been downing since birth) and needs to learn how to eat solids the big boy or girl way—from a spoon (and eventually, a fork). Then, of course, there's the potential for contamination if your baby sucks on a pouch, drops it, then picks it up hours or days later. Plus, there's a limit to what can be eaten from a pouch (really chunky foods—the next step to a varied diet—can't be, and neither can table foods). Occasionally letting your little pouch potato suck up a meal directly from the container is fine—say, when you're out and about and don't have a spoon at the ready. Just try not to make it baby food business as usual—instead, spoon up the practice your eager eater needs to master conventional feeding.

for instance, and you'll probably get nothing but peaches). The pureed varieties are the perfect consistency for beginners, and single-ingredient starter foods make it easy to screen for allergies. While homemade foods may vary in taste and texture from batch to batch, store-bought is consistently consistent in both—plus, they're manufactured under uber-sanitary conditions that would be hard to reproduce in your home, meaning its safety is hard to beat. And best of all, store-bought baby food is easier for you—just open and serve. What about additives and pesticides? There are plenty of organic baby food brands, and even those brands that aren't certified are usually free of additives and test low on pesticide residues.

It's when your baby gets older that you'll need to pay closer attention to what's inside that jar or pouch or box. Commercially prepared foods for older babies and toddlers can contain added sugar and refined grains. Screen labels for ingredients that your baby doesn't need (like sugar) and those that your little one should have (like whole grains) and you'll be able to fill your shopping cart and your baby's belly with only the healthiest options.

Once your little chomper is able to handle softly cooked, mashed, coarsely chopped, or flaked foods from the family menu, it's smart to open up your baby's culinary horizons instead of always opening up a jar or a pouch. That's because offering table foods earlier on—rather

Food for Thought

Could the food that fills your baby's tummy also build his or her brain? That's the idea behind commercial baby foods that are enriched with DHA and ARA, brain-boosting fatty acids that are found naturally in breast milk and added to some formulas.

How effective these foods are in increasing a child's brainpower is still being researched, but since such fatty acids are also heart-healthy, there's certainly no harm—and potentially plenty of benefits—in choosing them for your baby. The only downside: These foods, like the specially fortified formulas, can be pricey. Also remember, a food that's less than wholesome without added DHA is still a food that's less than wholesome once it's been added. So don't assume a food with added DHA (or any fortification) makes the nutritional cut without first checking out the rest of the ingredients. And whenever you can, add healthy fatty acids to your baby's diet by adding foods that contain them naturally (see page 449).

than sticking with commercially prepared baby foods—is more likely to produce a more amenable eater (in other words, one who eats what the rest of the family is eating). Still, you probably won't want to retire baby foods entirely—they're convenient to have on hand even for older babies and toddlers when you're on the road or out and about, or when a restaurant menu (or the family menu) isn't exactly baby friendly.

Homemade Baby Foods

Not pressed for time? Feeling motivated? Like the idea of doing it yourself? While commercial baby foods are better than ever, preparing your baby's meals from scratch—some or all of the time—is a wonderful option, and sometimes a less pricey one. Here's what you need to know:

The gear. You'll need something to grind or puree baby's food. You can use a blender, food processor, or immersion blender—equipment you likely have at home already—or you can opt for gadgets designed specifically for baby food

prep: a hand-turned food mill (which usually has different blades for different textured foods), a baby food grinder (which usually doesn't), or an all-in-one baby food maker (which both steam cooks and then purees the food). Of course, you can also go low tech with just a fork—especially when you're preparing easily mashable foods like

Pesticides on Produce

Worried about exposure to pesticides from the foods your little one eats (or will eat)? You can opt for organic fruits and veggies (they're grown pesticide-free; see page 338) or you can use a produce wash or simple soap and water to wash off any pesticide residue on the outside of the produce (though that'll get rid of only surface pesticides, not pesticide that might have seeped below the skin) before making any baby food.

Baby Food Stages

Wondering which jar or pouch to buy at which age? Luckily, it's as easy as 1-2-3—literally. Every baby food label is clearly marked with a 1, 2, or 3, instantly telling you what stage and age that food is for (some labels go into even more detail, including what level of motor development matches up with each stage). This easy navigation tool means there's no guessing whether the food inside that pretty packaging is perfect for your baby:

- Stage 1 (4 to 6 months +): Single-ingredient pureed fruits and vegetables (though spice, usually cinnamon, may also be included)

- Stage 2 (6 months +): Pureed blends of fruit, veggies, grains, and proteins in various combinations

- Stage 3 (9 months +): Combinations of chunky fruit, veggies, grains, and proteins

avocados, bananas, or butternut squash. Even lower tech (though hard to clean): a mesh feeder that baby can suck on (fill with any soft, age-appropriate fruit or veggie). These also come in easier-to-clean plastic.

Food prep. Wash and then bake, boil (use as little liquid as possible), or steam produce (vegetables and hard fruits like apples and plums, for instance) before pureeing or grinding. Peel and pit (or strain) as needed, and then puree in a blender, grinder, or food mill, adding liquid (water, breast milk, formula) as needed to get the desired consistency for your baby (the older baby gets, the less liquid you will need to add). Going with the grain? Cook grains and then puree or grind them, thinning with liquid as needed. Bringing on the poultry and meat? Puree trimmed and skinned meats and poultry either alone or with other already-introduced foods (veggies, for instance) for an all-in-one meal. Want to make your own baby cereal? Simply grind organic short-grain brown rice in a blender or a clean spice or coffee grinder until it is finely ground. At mealtime, sprinkle 2 tablespoons

of the brown-rice powder over a cup of boiling water and whisk until thick and creamy. Serve warm, not hot. If you like, cook this tummy-filling favorite with breast milk or formula instead of water for added nutrition. (Do remember, though, that this homemade cereal isn't fortified with all-important iron, like store-bought baby cereal is.) As baby gets older and has been introduced to more foods, simply give him or her what's on the menu for the rest of the family—mash it up, blend it, or puree it to the right consistency.

Weaning from the Breast

Wondering when it's time to retire your breasts as baby's food source? While it's best to wait until your baby is at least 1 year old before quitting breastfeeding, some moms find they need to (or want to) wean earlier. For the scoop on when and how to wean, see page 490).

Baby-Led Weaning

Not into the whole baby food thing? Think there must be a better way to start your little one on solids without messing around with mush? Popular in the U.K. and gaining traction in the U.S. is "baby-led weaning"—where babies (6 months old or older) jump straight to finger foods as soon as solids are introduced, bypassing purees and mush. It's called baby-led because that's what the premise is—letting your little one self-feed the healthy foods he or she wants to eat, right from the start (which is why this works only for a baby who's at least 6 months old and capable of self-feeding). And it allows babies to learn how to chew (really, gum) first, then swallow. No mush, no purees, no food processor, no spoon feeding into your little one's mouth, no bowls to be flung. You do the cooking and prep work, baby does the rest. It also prevents parents from pushing food, since babies are in control of how much food gets transported to their mouths.

Baby wants your toast? Hand it over. Junior wants to snack on the banana you're munching on? Give him a chunk and let him gum away. That chicken you're chewing on (and she's reaching for)? Offer her a portion. Dinner for mom and dad is steamed cauliflower and salmon? No reason baby can't dig in. Cut up a cucumber, steam a carrot until it's soft, chunk up some mango, proffer some pasta, parcel out pieces of peaches . . . you name it. As long as it's soft and/or crumbly, cut into small, manageable pieces (baby fist–size), and not on the list of foods that pose choking risks (see page 431), it's on the baby-led weaning menu.

Do keep in mind that while there won't be any mush with baby-led feeding, there will be plenty of mess—and that's all good. For baby it's mainly about the experience of eating, of exploring tastes and textures, or discovering what happens when he flings a chunk of pear or she smushes a hunk of sweet potatoes between her fingers.

Worried your new eater will turn into a new gagger? It'll happen—especially in the first few weeks of baby-led weaning—as baby tries to maneuver unfamiliar lumps in his or her mouth. But it's important to remember that gagging is actually a safety response to food traveling too far back into the mouth—and it's not choking, which is silent. When babies gag, they're actually handling the problem themselves, and it's best just to stay calm (or at least look calm) and wait until it passes. The gagging will ease up as baby learns to cope with the solids and the lumps. Just be sure to keep a careful watch on your little one as he munches away (constant supervision is a must when you're feeding this way), make sure baby is always sitting in his or her high chair before you hand over the food, and know what to do in case of choking (see page 594). Also offer up small amounts of food so baby doesn't try to wolf down too much too quickly.

Wondering if baby-led weaning is right for your baby? Run the idea by your little one's pediatrician for an opinion. Look to your baby, too—some babies like taking the feed lead, others don't. Keep in mind, too, that baby-led weaning, like so many parenting philosophies, isn't an all-or-nothing proposition. You can choose baby-led feeding some of the time, alternating with spoon feeding or adding to it (baby eats a chunk of banana, you spoon in some yogurt).

High Chair Safety Tips

Feeding baby safely doesn't just mean introducing new foods gradually. In fact, feeding safety begins even before the first spoon is filled—when baby first takes a seat in the high chair. To help make sure every mealtime passes safely, follow these rules:

- Never leave a baby unattended in a feeding chair. Have the food, a sippy cup of water, bib, paper towels, spoon, and anything else necessary for the meal ready so that you won't have to leave your little one alone while you retrieve them.

- Always fasten all the safety or restraining straps, even if your baby seems too young to climb out. And though many seats have crotch guards to prevent sliding out the bottom, don't forget to fasten the strap between the legs to prevent baby from climbing out.

- Keep all chair and eating surfaces clean (wash with soapy water and rinse thoroughly). Babies won't think twice about picking up a decaying morsel from a previous meal and munching on it.

- Always be certain slide-off trays are safely snapped into place—an unsecured one could allow a lunging and unbelted baby to go flying out head first . . . or at least have a bad scare.

- Check to be sure that a folding-type chair is safely locked into the open position and won't suddenly fold up with baby in it.

- Place the chair away from any tables, counters, walls, or other surfaces that baby could possibly kick off from—causing the chair to tumble backward.

- To protect baby's fingers, know where they are before attaching or detaching the tray.

- Use a hook-on seat only on a stable wooden or metal table. Do not use it on glass-topped or loose-topped tables, tables with the support in the center (baby's weight could topple it), card tables, aluminum folding tables, or on a table leaf. If your little one can rock the table, the table isn't stable enough. Be certain any locks, clamps, or snap-together parts are securely fastened before putting your baby in the seat, and always take your baby out of the seat before releasing or unfastening it.

Add flavor the healthy way. Be sure to keep the lids on the sugar bowl and salt shaker—it's always best to give food to babies straight. After all, baby taste buds are just developing, their sweet tooth hasn't yet been activated, and they still don't care a lick about salt—so why flip the switch early? But that's not to say you can't season with healthy herbs and spices (see page 430). Cinnamon, for instance, is a high chair favorite, and adds extra pizzazz to sweet potatoes, carrots, fruit, and more.

Store it. DIY purees will last in the fridge up to 4 days or in the freezer for 3 months max. Store homemade baby food in single-serving containers or ice-cube trays for easy-to-serve portions that you can thaw overnight in the fridge or in a microwave (at the "defrost," not "cook," setting—and be sure to mix and test the temperature before serving to your baby).

Safety. Be sure to follow the safe food prep tips on page 346.

What You May Be Wondering About

Picking Up Baby

"I pick up my baby the minute he cries, and end up carrying him around with me much of the day. Am I spoiling him?"

Your arms may be weary—but until your baby starts getting around on his own, they're his only ticket to ride. They're also his favorite ticket to comfort when he's cranky, to entertainment when he's bored, to company when he's lonely. Plus, they're his favorite place in the world to spend time.

Still, while all the holding in the world can't possibly spoil your little one (and withholding holding can even make him more clingy), there are some good reasons why you might want to slow down on your pickups, at least somewhat. Playing "baby taxi"—picking up your tiny passenger the moment you're hailed by a wave of that little arm or a whimper of boredom—can leave you "on duty" throughout your baby's waking hours. What's more, carrying baby around the clock not only prevents you from getting things done, it can prevent him from getting things done. In your arms your baby doesn't have the opportunity to practice skills—such as creeping and crawling—that'll eventually allow him to get around without a free ride. It also doesn't give him a chance to flex his fledgling muscles of independence in other important ways, such as learning how to keep himself entertained and enjoy his own good company—even if it's only for a few fleeting moments.

So what should you do the next time your little one whimpers for a pick-me-up?

- First consider: Is it a call for a ride, or a call for attention? Has it been one of those days, when you're spending most of your time playing catch-up on chores (or going app happy) instead of playing with your baby? Your baby may be hitting you up for some face time (something he needs in generous, regular doses) as much as for the arm time.

- Next, run a comfort check. Is his diaper dirty? Is it feeding time? Is he thirsty? Tired? You've satisfied all those needs? Proceed.

- Move him to a new location: the play yard if he was in the bouncer, the play mat if he was in the play yard, propped up sitting if he was on the play mat. A change of scenery may satisfy his wanderlust.

- Create a new diversion. With an age-appropriate attention span of mere minutes (if that), you'll need to regularly rotate your little guy's selection of toys or other diversions. Just remember, more is not more to a baby . . . it's only overwhelming. Keep the new selections to a manageable number—two or three at a time is plenty.

- Try a drive-by. He's still pleading for a pickup? Instead, try swooping in for a moment of face time. Plop down beside him and show him how to stack some blocks, point out the "eyes-nose-mouth" on his stuffed dog, push the buttons on his pop-up toy. Getting him started may keep him going, if only for a few minutes.

- Keep him waiting. You've tried everything, but the calls for a pickup keep

Facing-Front Facts

Wearing your baby snuggled against your chest is undeniably yummy (just smell that sweetness!). It's also convenient (or more like indispensable) when you'd like your baby close and your hands free. What's more, those snuggles are important for your baby, both emotionally and physically.

But at some point, your baby may signal that he or she is eager for a little more freedom of movement and a lot more perspective—at least, more than a parent's chest can offer. The inward-facing position, as perfect as it is for young babies, may get old fast after 6 months or so. Especially when there's something interesting to see—say, at the aquarium, the zoo, or the park (dog ahead! birds overhead! flowers on your left!). Enter the front-carrying position—which, depending on the carrier you've been using for inward-facing, may mean flipping your baby to front-facing, or, if your carrier doesn't offer a facing-out option, investing in a multipurpose carrier that does.

That is, unless you've heard some unsettling reports on carrying a baby facing forward—in which case you may be understandably hesitant to make the switch. Maybe you've heard that carrying your baby facing forward in a baby carrier is unsafe for your little one's hips and spine. Or that it could be overstimulating. Or under-nurturing.

Happily, there isn't any scientific evidence to support those theories— at least, once a baby is old enough (usually at about 5 or 6 months) to appreciate a front-facing view of the world—and smart enough to tell you how much front-facing is too much. To set the record straight, here are some front-facing facts:

Myth: Facing forward in a baby carrier places too much stress on your baby's crotch and lower spine because it shifts his or her center of gravity.

Fact: A baby's body isn't like an adult's. In fact, baby's head is much larger relative to body size, making the weight distribution very different from that of an adult. Consequently, what may seem uncomfortable (or dangerous) for an adult (being "dangled by the crotch") doesn't apply to an infant. In fact, with a baby, the brunt of his or her body weight isn't felt in the seat, but rather is distributed throughout the upper back, neck, and head. There are no studies demonstrating that forward-facing carrying puts too much stress on a baby's spine when baby's legs are spread out and hips are spread apart, as per the manufacturer's instructions. And despite the increase in parents using forward-facing carriers, there has not been a corresponding increase in spine and crotch injuries among infants.

Myth: Forward-facing baby carriers can cause hip dysplasia.

Fact: Hip dysplasia, a condition where the bones of the hip joints do not align correctly, is congenital (meaning it's present from birth), though it usually isn't diagnosed until later in infancy. The theory that baby carriers cause

coming in? Try to delay the inevitable for a minute or two. Go about your business casually, singing, chatting, and smiling as you do. Have him wait for his ride a little bit longer each time. But don't have him wait so long that whimpers escalate to wails (and he starts to think of playing solo as a hip dysplasia is not supported by any studies or scientific evidence, and most experts agree the carriers don't (and can't) cause that condition. And again, even with an increase in the use of front-facing baby carriers, there hasn't been a corresponding increase in hip dysplasia cases. In fact, when used properly (making sure your baby is held in the carrier with his or her legs spread out as per the manufacturer's instructions, and/or choosing a carrier that has a structured bucket seat, ensuring that the correct squat-leg sitting position is maintained even in the front-facing position), the hips are abducted (held apart), and that's the ideal way to keep your baby's hips developing properly.

Myth: The best way to prevent hip problems in a baby is to wear baby in a sling.

Fact: Slings come with a slew of benefits—but they, like other carriers, can do harm if they're not used correctly. Studies show that when babies are carried papoose-style (with legs together) or in a sling with their legs straight and together, or when babies are swaddled tightly with their legs pulled straight and together, there's an increased risk of improper hip development. Luckily, minimizing that risk is as easy as proper positioning. When you put your baby in a sling (or swaddle), make sure you leave room to allow the hips and knees to move freely. Also remember, switching positions ensures not only a different vantage point for baby, but an opportunity for him or her to flex different bones, muscles, joints, and ligaments—so they all get the workout they need.

Myth: The forward-facing position can result in baby being overstimulated by the view and unable to nuzzle into your body to avoid looking at something overwhelming. Plus, you won't be able to tune in when your baby's upset or stressed out because he or she is facing out.

Fact: Whether you're strolling down the street or the aisles of a supermarket, it's a busy world out there—sometimes too busy for a young baby, whose brand new circuits can easily be overloaded by stimuli. Once babies have clocked in 5 or 6 months on the planet, however, many are not only ready but eager to absorb more of their surroundings. Facing a parent's chest is still comforting and cozy, but it may not always provide enough of the stimulation an older baby's in the market for. Switching off between an inward-facing position and an outward-facing one allows your little one to cash in on both the comfort he or she still needs and the interesting sights and sounds he or she now wants. Stay tuned in to your baby while you're carrying him or her front-facing, and you'll be able to notice signs that he or she is uncomfortable or overstimulated, tired, or zoning out (crying, turning the head away, fussing). That's your cue to flip baby around to inward-facing. Keep front-facing time limited to periods your baby can handle, be sure to interact while he or she is facing out (point out those interesting sights and sounds, sing or chat, squeeze those little hands and stroke those chubby legs, and of course, plant plenty of kisses on that sweet head), and you'll both enjoy the ride—without any developmental downside.

punishment, which it isn't). Return to his side, reassure him, play with him, cuddle him, pick him up if necessary, and then start the process over again.

Not getting far (or even across the room) without being hailed by that pint-size passenger? The reality is, most babies won't play for more than

For Parents: Only-for-You Behavior

The babysitter says your baby's an angel—feeds like a pro, naps like a champ, smiles for miles. Which makes the wailing that starts the minute the sitter walks out the door (or the minute you walk out of daycare with that angel in your arms) all the more disheartening, leaving you to wonder, "Is it me?"

Actually, it is you—and that's a good thing. The fact that most older babies (and toddlers . . . and even older children) are more likely to crank up the crankies with their parents than with other care providers is a sign of comfort and security. Your love is a sure thing—something your little one can count on receiving in spades even when those true-blue colors show through.

Timing may also have something to do with the meltdown. Your homecoming probably coincides with what's typically a baby's fussiest time of the day—early evening—when fatigue, overstimulation, and hunger can get the best of even the most cheerful cherub. After a hard day on the job and possibly a difficult commute, you may be frazzled on your return,

too—something baby's keen mood radar is sure to pick up on. Your high stress level intensifies your baby's, and his or hers reinforces yours—and pretty soon you've both got a bad case of the crabbies. Add the distraction factor—understandably, you have more things to focus on when you walk in the door than your baby (like changing your clothes or starting dinner)—and you're keying up for baby's cries for attention by the time you've dropped your keys. Are you nursing on reentry? Your milk supply may be at its lowest point of the day, definitely not a high point for your hungry baby. And finally, change isn't something that all babies believe in—especially older ones—which means that this changing of the guardians may be unsettling in and of itself.

To ease the transition when you return home each night, try the following tips:

- Don't come home to a hungry, tired baby. Have feeds timed so you'll both have a chance to unwind before it's time to refill (just make sure, if you're breastfeeding, that your baby

a few minutes on their own, and even very independent ones need frequent changes of scenery and toys. Another reality? There may be more to life than your arms, but it's still the good life for your baby.

Using a Back Carrier

"Our baby is getting too big to lug around in a front baby carrier. Is it safe to use a back carrier?"

Once your baby can sit independently, even briefly, he's ready to graduate to a back carrier. There are front carriers that switch to a back-carrying position, where baby is safely nestled against your back and shoulders, and there are frame-backpack-type carriers that typically perch baby higher up (better for viewing the world). Assuming your back's up for the heavy lifting and baby is up for the adventure, there's no reason not to use a back carrier if you'd like. Some parents won't have sucked down a bottle right before you arrive home with full breasts—instead, have the care provider offer a solids snack to take the edge off that tender appetite without sabotaging it entirely). Same when it comes to sleep. A nap later in the afternoon may also help keep the crankies at bay, but make sure baby's not napping so late that he or she won't be able to settle down at a reasonable hour.

- Relax before you return. If you've been stuck in traffic for an hour, sit in your car and do a few relaxation exercises before you walk in the door. Instead of spending your commute on the bus or train doing last-minute work on your iPad, use the time to empty your mind of worries and fill it with thoughts that soothe you—say, the image of a frozen drink on a warm beach.

- Relax when you return. Don't rush to start dinner or fold laundry the moment you put down your bag or briefcase. Instead, take 15 minutes to unwind with your baby, offering cuddles and your completely undivided attention, if possible. If your baby seems to be the kind who hates

transitions, don't rush the babysitter out the door, either. Reinsert yourself into your baby's day gradually, so that he or she can get used to the idea that a change is about to take place. When baby adjusts to you both being there, then the babysitter can exit.

- Include baby in your to-dos. Once you're both feeling more relaxed, tackle the things you need to do—but include baby. Plunk baby in the middle of your bed (supervised) or on the floor while you change your clothes. Hold baby on your lap while you answer a text. Sit baby in the high chair with a few toys while you start dinner, chatting with your cutie as you chop vegetables.

- Don't take it personally. Almost all parents who work outside the home experience the homecoming meltdown. Those who have children in daycare may experience it at pickup time, on the way home, or when they arrive home. In fact, stay-at-home moms and dads may find themselves facing a similar end-of-the-day challenge, even if they've spent that whole day at home with their babies. Happy hour . . . it isn't.

find back carriers awkward and a strain on the muscles, while others love their convenience. Some babies are thrilled by the height and the bird's-eye view a frame-backpack carrier affords, others are unnerved by the precarious perch. To find out whether a back carrier is right for you and your baby, flip your three-in-one carrier (three being front, hip, and back positions) to the back, or, if you're considering a frame backpack, take him for a test ride in a friend's or in a store floor sample before buying.

If you do use a back carrier, always be certain baby is fastened in securely. Also be aware that the position allows a baby to do a lot more behind your back than sightseeing—including pulling cans off the shelves in the supermarket or plucking (and then munching) leaves off shrubs and trees in the park. Keep in mind, too, that you'll have to judge distances differently when baby's in a higher backpack-type carrier—for example, when you back into a crowded elevator or go through a low doorway.

Not Sitting Yet

"My baby hasn't started sitting up yet, and I'm worried that she's slow for her age."

Far from all babies are sitting pretty by the time they've reached the 6-month mark—and that's because sitting is just one of the many developmental milestones that can be mastered on a time line that has a very wide "normal" range. While the "average" baby sits unsupported somewhere around 6½ months, some very normal babies sit as early as 4 months and others as late as 9 months. Which means your little one has a long way to go before she reaches the outer limits of that normal range—and that you have no reason to stress yet about her lagging behind.

What can you do to speed up your sweetie's sitting schedule? Not much. Babies are programmed by genetic factors to sit—and to accomplish other major developmental skills—at a certain age. But there are ways to avoid slowing sitting—for instance, by providing plenty of supported sitting practice. A baby who is propped up often at an early age—in an infant seat, a stroller, or a high chair, gets the hang of hanging out in a sitting position before she's able to support herself, and may sit sooner. On the other hand, a baby who spends a majority of her time lying on her back or in a baby carrier or sling, and is rarely propped to sit, may sit very late. In fact, babies in other cultures who are constantly worn in baby carriers often stand before they sit, so accustomed are they to the upright position. Chubbier babies may also have a harder time with sitting (it's not so easy to balance all that weight—and roly-poly babies often roll right over when they try). A larger-than-average head may also tip a baby over when she tries to sit up.

As long as you're giving your baby plenty of opportunities to practice her sitting skills, chances are she'll take her seat within the next 2 months. If she doesn't, and/or if you feel she's not on track developmentally in other ways, talk to her doctor.

Biting Nipples

"My baby now has two teeth and seems to think it's fun to use them to bite me when she's breastfeeding. How can I break her of this painful habit?"

Biting sucks—especially when it's your nipples that are being gnawed on instead of sucked on. But babies often bite the nipples that feed them, and it's a habit that can start even before those first teeth poke through. Your little nipper's nibbling may have started when she was seeking counterpressure for teething pain. Or it could have happened inadvertently—she became distracted during nursing, but didn't let go of the nipple entirely . . . and then clamped down. Or she may have just been experimenting with her mouth. She bites, you let out a yelp, she giggles at your reaction, you giggle back, and suddenly she's discovered an entertaining new game that she can't wait to play again. Having teeth to bite with ups the ante—it's more satisfying to her, elicits more of a reaction from you. One thing that's clear is that a baby can't bite and suck at the same time, so if she's nipping at your nipples, she's not feeding anymore (and that could be why most biting happens toward the end of a nursing session).

How can you nip the nipping habit in the bud before she becomes too fond of it, and before she has enough chompers to do much damage? First, pay attention to your baby during feeding sessions and watch for signs of boredom or distraction. Either can provoke

Room Sharing Now

Thinking of moving your baby roommate out of your bedroom—so you both can get more sleep (and you can have more privacy)? While room sharing makes sense in the first months of a baby's life (and is actually recommended for safer sleep by the AAP until the risk of SIDS has subsided), three can start to feel like a crowd as the second half of the first year rolls around. It can also be more difficult to attempt sleep teaching when baby's in the same room.

Happy with your rooming-in policy, and in no hurry to send your baby packing to the nursery? Sharing a room—or a bed—well into childhood is convenient and enjoyable for many families. But if a family bedroom is not your long term plan, this is probably a good time to settle your little one into a room of his or her own.

Only have one bedroom—or you have more children than bedrooms? Then continuing to room share may be your only option. If you want a separation even when you're not separated, consider a divider—either a screen or a heavy curtain hung from a ceiling track (it's also a good sound insulator). Or partition off a corner of the living room for the baby and do your late-night TV watching or talking in the bedroom.

If your baby will have to share with another child, how well the sleeping arrangement works out will depend on how well the two sleep. If either one or both are light sleepers with a tendency to issue wake-up calls during the night, you may all be in for a difficult period of adjustment until each has learned to sleep through the other's wakings. Again, a partition may help muffle the sounds while providing the older child with privacy.

---

a bite, so if you see one of the warning signs, you can prevent biting before it happens. Another preventive tip: If your baby is biting at the beginning of a nursing session (less common, but it can happen when your little one is teething), offer a teething toy or cold washcloth before you latch baby on to take a bite off the pain and hopefully prevent a bite into you.

If your little one takes a nip, the best response is a firm, no-nonsense, low-drama-mama statement of the rule ("no biting" and "biting hurts Mommy") as you remove the offending fangs from their target. Get her attention with an all-business tone, but don't yell or scream in pain—and definitely don't giggle. Your baby will either find your overreaction funny (which will only bring on a repeat performance) or be scared by your outburst (which could lead to crying or even refusing to nurse). Baby won't let go? Slip your finger between baby's gums so you can pull away more gingerly. If that doesn't work, pull baby close to your breast. Your little chomper will automatically let go to open her mouth and uncover her nose to breathe. Once she's off the breast, offer her something she can bite on—a teething toy, pacifier, or something chilled, for example—and tell her it's okay to sink her pearly whites there. You can also try distracting her with a song, a toy, or a visit to the window to see the cars outside. Be consistent with this routine and eventually it'll sink in: Sinking your teeth into mommy isn't so much fun after all.

For Parents: Dinner and a Baby

Have reservations about eating out with your baby? Actually, the restaurant may, too—that is, if you don't come prepared. Before you secure a table for two and a high chair, check out these restaurant survival tips:

Call ahead. Not just for those reservations (or to find out if the coast is clear—you won't want to choose a restaurant with a wait), but to find out what baby supplies and accommodations are on hand. For instance, are there high chairs? Clip-on feeding chairs? Booster seats probably won't work until baby's closer to a year old. You'll probably be bringing some baby food along, but it doesn't hurt to ask if the kitchen is flexible when it comes to ordering. For instance, will they serve up pint-size portions without charging a full-size price? Will the chef tailor foods to tiny tots (mash potatoes without salt and pepper, serve fish without sauce)? Children's menus may sound like a good idea, but they are often heavy on hot dogs and other baby-unfriendly fare.

Listen carefully when you call. Not just to the answers to your questions, but to the attitude they're served up with, which can speak volumes about how welcome you and your baby will really be.

Get an early start. Plan to dine on baby's schedule, not yours, even if that means being the earliest birds to catch the early bird special. Another plus to early eating: The waitstaff isn't frazzled yet, the kitchen isn't fried, there are fewer diners to annoy with baby's cup banging.

Ask for a quiet table in the corner. Not for the romance, obviously (which definitely won't be on the menu), but so that your group won't offend fellow diners or get in the way of harried waitstaff. You'll also appreciate the privacy if you'll be spending much of the meal breastfeeding.

Make it snappy. Even four-star dining can fizzle into fast food when baby's at the table. So it makes sense to prefer quick-paced eateries, where more time can be spent eating than waiting. Order the entire meal promptly (hopefully you've scanned the menu app before sitting down), and ask that baby's food (if you've ordered for your littlest diner) be brought out as soon as possible.

Come prepared. Gone are the days when you could leave for a restaurant with just your credit card. You'll also need to pack:

- A high chair cover is optional, but it will make your baby's seat at the table more comfortable, snugger,

Teeth Coming in Crooked

"My baby's teeth are coming in crooked. Does this mean that he'll eventually need braces?"

Don't schedule that appointment with the orthodontist yet. The way those first baby teeth come in is not usually an indication of smiles to come. In fact, baby teeth often appear crooked, particularly the front bottom ones, which frequently form a V when and of course, more hygienic (plus easier to clean up afterward).

- A bib to keep baby clean, as well as some wipes. If the restaurant is carpeted, a splat mat to spread under baby's chair will be appreciated by those who will have to pick up the mess after you're finished.

- Toys, books, and other diversions. Don't take them out, however, until they're needed (baby will probably be content to play with a spoon, flirt with the waitstaff, and point at the light fixtures for the first few minutes), and then bring them on one at a time. No more tricks in your bag? Try a game of peekaboo with the menu or a napkin.

- Jarred or pouch food, if junior's not on the table variety yet, or if you fear there won't be any baby-friendly offerings on the menu, or just to supplement what's offered.

- Snacks, especially finger foods that will keep those fingers (and that attention) occupied. Nibbles can also be a lifesaver when the meal takes longer than expected to arrive or when baby gets bored with table food. But hold these in reserve, too, until they're needed.

If you don't see it, ask for it. Just because it's not on the menu doesn't mean it's not in the kitchen. Good choices, depending on what's been introduced so far, include cottage cheese, whole-wheat bread or rolls, cheese, hard-boiled egg (crumbled), hamburger (cooked through and crumbled), chicken (minced), soft fish (cooked through, flaked, and carefully screened for bones), mashed potato or sweet potato, peas or beans (mash them), soft-cooked pasta, well-cooked carrots, cauliflower, broccoli or green beans, and ripe avocado, melon, banana, and mango.

Keep baby seated. Even if the restaurant is mostly empty, letting your baby explore the floor is never a good idea. It's dirty down there—plus it's too easy for a waitperson to be tripped up by a baby underfoot, or for your baby to discover and mouth something unsafe or to grab on to a tablecloth.

Be sensitive to those around you. Maybe the table next to you can't get enough of your baby's adorable antics. Or maybe it's occupied by a couple who's spending good money on a sitter to get away from their little ones for the night. Either way, be quick to exit for a stroll if baby is crying loudly, practicing those ear-piercing shrieks, or otherwise disturbing the peace of the restaurant.

Know when to call it a meal. When baby's had his or her fill and has begun flinging what's left at the next booth, it's time to ask for the check. And consider: An extra big mess might call for an extra big tip.

---

they poke through. The top front teeth may also seem huge in comparison to those below. And in some babies, the top teeth come in before the bottom teeth, but that's also nothing to worry about.

By the time your baby reaches 2½,

he'll likely be the proud owner of a full set of baby teeth—20 in all. And though they'll probably have evened out by then in proportion and formation, especially because baby's tongue is always pushing against the inside surfaces of the new teeth, helping them

Look Who's Talking

Think those adorable "ah-oh-ah"s are just baby babble? They're actually the beginnings of spoken language—baby's first attempts at figuring out how the other half (the adult half, that is) speaks. And it's a process that started at a month or two with baby's breathy vowel-filled coos. Keep a close listen as those vowel sounds make way to consonant-vowel sounds. When babies begin experimenting with consonants, they usually discover one or two at a time and repeat the same single combination (ba or ga or da) over and over and over—like the cutest little broken record ever. The next week, they may move on to a new consonant-vowel combo, seeming to have forgotten the first. They haven't, but since their powers of concentration are limited, they usually work on mastering one thing at a time. They also love repetition—after all, practice, practice, practice is how they learn, learn, learn.

Following the two-syllable, one-consonant sounds (a-ga, a-ba, a-da) come singsong strings of consonants (da-da-da da-da-da), called "babble," at 6 months on the average (though some babies begin babbling by 4½ months, others not until 8 months or later). Also at 8 months, many babies can produce wordlike double consonants (da-da, ma-ma, ha-ha), usually without associating any meaning with them until 2 or 3 months later. Heads-up: "da-da" typically comes before "ma-ma," not a product of preference (try telling dad that), but a product of development (d's are easier for babies to articulate than m's). It won't be until much later, often not until 4 or 5 years of age—occasionally even later—that your little one will conquer all his or her consonants.

to grow into even rows, don't worry if they haven't. Crooked baby teeth don't predict crooked permanent teeth.

Tooth Stains

"My daughter's two teeth seem to be stained a grayish color. Could they be decaying already?"

Chances are, what's keeping your baby's pearly whites gray isn't decay, but iron. Some children who take a liquid vitamin and mineral supplement that contains iron develop staining on their teeth. This doesn't harm the teeth in any way and will disappear when your child stops taking liquid vitamins and begins taking chewables. In the meantime, brushing your baby's teeth or cleaning them with a tooth wipe or gauze right after giving her a supplement will help minimize staining.

On the other hand, if your baby hasn't been taking a liquid supplement, and especially if she's been doing a lot of sucking on a bottle of formula or juice at bedtime, the discoloration might suggest decay. It could also be the result of trauma, or a congenital defect in the tooth enamel. Discuss this with her doctor or a dentist.

ALL ABOUT:

Making Home Safe for Baby

Imagine a fragile day-old baby (the one you were always afraid of "breaking"). Now put that newborn next to a chubby, sturdy 7-month-old (the one who's getting heavier and heavier to carry). And now guess which one of these babies is more vulnerable, more likely to be injured? Actually, it's the older baby who's at greater risk for injury, thanks to all those emerging skills he or she is or will soon be acquiring—from sitting to creeping to crawling, rolling over to pulling up, cruising to (before you know it) walking, not to mention handily reaching for (and grasping, pulling, tugging, and mouthing) just about anything within reach, and many things that seem beyond reach. That's because even though babies in the second half of the first year have a far more advanced set of motor skills than newborns do, their judgment hasn't yet caught up to their on-the-go abilities . . . a gap that won't begin to close for many years to come. Which makes your older baby a prime candidate for accidental injuries.

Fortunately, though a baby on the move may be an accident waiting to happen, there are plenty of steps you can take to keep those accidents from happening. In fact, most accidents (and accidental injuries) are preventable. With a little know-how, some smart injury-prevention steps, and a lot of vigilance, you can significantly reduce the odds of bumps, boo-boos, and worse.

Babyproofing Around the House

Until now, your baby has seen your home mostly from your arms—at your eye level. Now that he or she is beginning to get a look at it from all fours (or on that cute little bottom), you'll have to begin looking at it from that perspective, too. So get down on the floor—and down on your hands and knees—to survey your home for potential trouble spots, and make changes as necessary:

Windows. To make sure your little one can't take a tumble out above-ground-level windows, install metal window guards that attach to the sides of the window frame and have bars no more than 4 inches apart. Or install a locking device on double-hung windows that prevents the lower window from opening more than 4 inches. Screens and storm windows aren't secure enough, so they can't be relied on to keep a baby from tumbling out. However you child-secure your windows, make sure you can open them quickly in an emergency, as in case of fire. Fire and rescue officials recommend that you use releasable window guards on at least one window in every room—they will allow for an escape in the event of a fire but still provide protection against falling.

As an extra precaution, never place furniture that your baby can climb on in front of a window. And if you have a window seat, make sure the window it's under is always locked or is protected by a window guard.

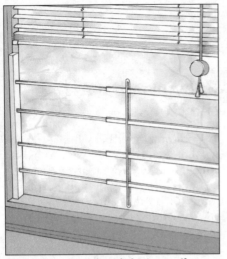

Window guards and cord shorteners (for venetian blind or drapery cords) make windows safer for babies.

Window blind cords. Your safest bet is to use cordless window coverings throughout the house, especially in your baby's bedroom. If you have blinds with cords and you can't replace them, it's absolutely vital to keep those cords (which are strangulation hazards) out of your baby's reach. Tie up cords on wall hooks so your baby can't become entangled. Eliminate looped pull cords (found on blinds and shades manufactured before 1995) and install cord stops on all pre-2001 horizontal blinds and corded shades using directions from the Window Covering Safety Council (windowcoverings.org).

Never place a crib, bed, other furniture, or large toy that a child can climb on within reach of window coverings.

Doors. Install doorstops and door holders (that hold the door open) to protect curious fingers and hands from getting caught in slamming doors or door hinges. Install gates at doorways to unsafe areas, and always keep an eye on your baby to make sure he or she doesn't scale the gates.

Stairs. Prevent a tumble down the stairs by installing sturdy safety gates at the top of the stairs and at the bottom. Don't use a pressure-mounted gate at the top of the stairs (a child can push against it, dislodge it, and tumble down the stairs). Consider putting the lower gate three steps from the bottom, so your little one has a small, safe area to practice stair-climbing skills (skills vital to keeping your baby safe in the future).

Keep steps clear of toys, shoes, and anything else that could trip up your baby (or anyone else). Carpeting on the stairs may improve footing and help minimize injury in case a fall does occur. A plush, well-padded carpet or a thick nonskid area rug at the foot of each staircase should also cut down on bumps and bruises.

Banisters, railings, and balconies. Be sure that balusters (the upright posts) aren't loose and that the distance between them on stairs or balconies is less than 3 inches, so a baby can't get stuck or slide through. If the gap is wider, consider a temporary safety "wall" of plastic or firm mesh (usually available at stores that sell child-safety equipment) along the length of a balcony.

Your baby's crib. Babies don't usually have the height or climbing skills necessary to scale the sides of a crib—but that doesn't mean they absolutely can't. So adjust the mattress to its lowest position and remove bulky toys, pillows, bumper pads (all things that shouldn't be in the crib anyway), and anything else that could be used as a stepping-stone to freedom. Also be sure not to string any toys (such as a crib gym) across the top of the crib. Never place a crib next to a window, near a heating vent or radiator, close to a floor lamp, or within reach of a heavy piece of furniture.

Safe Gates

Sometimes the only way to keep your baby away from danger is to make it inaccessible—and that's why safety gates can be indispensable. Use them to keep your baby in a room that's safe, or out of a room that's not. Also use them at the bottom of steps and at the top of steps.

Gates can be portable (these usually have to be released and moved for anyone to get through the doorway) or permanent (these usually stay in place, but swing open after unlatching), depending on your needs. Both varieties are generally adjustable to fit different door-frame sizes and can vary from 24 to 32 inches in height. If you are installing a permanent gate (which you definitely should at the top of the stairs), be sure to screw it into wooden wall studs or use drywall anchors to prevent toppling under the pressure of an eager-to-escape baby (drywall or plaster alone won't hold the screws securely). Choose models with Plexiglas or fine mesh (if the mesh is flexible, it will be even harder for your baby to pull up on the gate) or those with vertical slats (no more than 2⅜ inches apart). Avoid using a hand-me-down gate, because older models (like accordion gates) are often unsafe. Any gate you use should be sturdy, with a nontoxic finish, no sharp parts, no parts that can catch little fingers, and no small parts that can break off and be mouthed. Follow installation directions exactly.

Your baby's portable crib or play yard. A play yard or portable crib (if you use one) should have fine mesh sides (openings of less than ¼ inch) or vertical slats no more than 2⅜ inches apart. Always be sure the play yard/crib is fully open before putting your baby in it, and never leave it partly opened—it could close up on a child who climbs into it.

Toy chests. In general, open shelves and bins are safer for toy storage. But if you still prefer to use a chest, look for one that has a lightweight lift-off lid or a safe hinged lid—one that doesn't snap closed automatically when released. The hinge should allow the lid to remain open at any angle to which it is lifted. If you have an old toy chest that doesn't meet these requirements, remove the lid permanently (and remember that an old toy chest might be painted with lead-based paint, another serious safety concern). There should also be air holes in the body of the box (drill a couple on each side, if there aren't any) just in case a small child climbs in and becomes trapped.

Kick Butt

Nothing you can buy in a baby store, splurge on in a toy store, or sock away into a savings account can match the gift to your baby of growing up in a smoke-free environment. Babies who are around parents (and other caregivers) who smoke have a greater risk of SIDS, respiratory illnesses (colds, flu, bronchiolitis, asthma), and ear infections during the first year of life. Not only are the children of smokers sick more often than children of nonsmokers, but their illnesses also last longer. And it's not just secondhand smoke that's harmful. Thirdhand smoke (from smoke that lingers on clothes of smokers) may be just as damaging to a child's health.

Perhaps worst of all, kids of smokers are more likely to become smokers themselves. So quitting may not only keep your child healthier in childhood, it may also keep him or her alive and well longer. And if that's not motivation enough, keep this in mind, too: By quitting, you'll be giving your baby the gift of healthier parents.

Like all furniture children spend a lot of time around, a toy chest should have rounded corners or corner padding.

Unstable furnishings. Put away lightweight, rickety, or unstable chairs, tables, or other furniture that might topple if leaned on or pulled up on until your baby is sure-footed enough not to need furniture for support. Climbers, too, need to be protected from furniture they can pull down easily.

Heavy furniture. Bracket heavy furniture (such as dressers, bookcases, entertainment units, and shelves) to the wall with safety straps, L-brackets, screws, or even heavy-duty velcro to prevent it from tipping over onto a baby. Place heavy items on the bottom shelves of bookcases instead of up high, so the unit is bottom heavy and therefore more stable. Secure to the wall any television that you place on top of furniture—even flat screen TVs, since they can topple over and fall on baby.

Dresser drawers. Open drawers are an open invitation to babies learning to pull up. Keep dresser and cabinet drawers closed so your child will be less likely to pull up on them, possibly upending an unstable dresser. Place heavier items in lower dresser drawers to keep the dresser bottom heavy and less likely to tip over.

Loose knobs on furniture or cabinets. Secure any loose knobs that are small enough to be swallowed, cause choking, or get stuck in your baby's mouth.

Sharp edges or corners. The sleek coffee table with the glass top was so chic last year, but once your baby can pull up and cruise, it's more dangerous than stylish. Cushion sharp table corners and edges with bumpers that can soften the impact if your baby knocks into them. The same bumpers work on any sharp edges throughout the house (such as fireplace hearths and low windowsills).

Electrical cords. Move them behind furniture so that your baby will be less tempted to mouth or chew on them (risking electric shock) or tug at them (pulling computers, lamps, or other heavy items down). If necessary, fasten the cords to the wall or floor with electrical tape or specially designed gadgets or protective covers that hide the wires. Do not use nails or staples, and do not run cords under carpets, where

Yeng, J
6329

Monday, October 28, 2019

they can overheat. Don't leave an appliance cord plugged into an outlet when the cord itself is disconnected from the appliance—not only could this cause major shock if the cord becomes wet, but serious mouth burns could result if it's mouthed.

Electrical outlets. It's important to cover electrical outlets to prevent your little one from inserting an object or probing its mysteries with a drooly finger. But the small plug-in caps that are sometimes used can easily end up in your baby's mouth. Instead, use removable caps that cover both outlets and/ or are too big to be a choking hazard) or replace the outlet cover itself with one that has a sliding safety latch. Or place heavy furniture in front of outlets. If you use multiple-outlet power strips, look for ones that are child-safe or ones with childproof cases.

Lamps and light fixtures. Don't place a lamp where a baby could touch a hot bulb (to be extra-safe, choose cool-touch bulbs when possible), and don't leave a lamp or other light fixture without a bulb within your baby's reach—probing an empty socket might be irresistible to your child but very unsafe.

Fireplaces, heaters, stoves, furnaces, and radiators. Put up protective grills, covers, or other barriers to keep small fingers away from fire and hot surfaces. Remember, too, that most of these surfaces stay hot long after the heat has been turned off or the fire has died down.

Ashtrays. There are multiple reasons not to allow smoking in your home, ever. Here's another one: A baby who reaches into a used ashtray can get hold of a hot butt or sample a mouthful of ashes and butts. Always keep ashtrays out of a baby's reach.

Texting While Parenting

Could technology diminish your ability to properly supervise your little one? Experts say yes, and they point to the sharp uptick in injuries and accidents among young children whose parents are driven to distraction by their smartphones or tablets or minis when they should be watching their little ones instead.

Research shows that parents are more absorbed in their mobile devices than they think—and though people report they are paying attention to what's going on around them when they're texting or posting, it turns out the opposite is true. Clearly the estimated 11 hours per day parents spend on digital media cuts into important social interaction time with little ones, but it can also put those little ones at risk for accidental injury.

So be a smart and attentive parent and prevent such so-called device distraction: Fight the urge to multitask with your mobile— texting, photosharing, emailing— when you're supposed to be watching (or playing or interacting with) your cutie. Remember, all it takes is a split second for your baby to get into trouble. That text or tweet can wait until baby's naptime.

Trash containers. Switch from open wastebaskets and recycling containers to ones that are covered and inaccessible to curious little hands.

Exercise equipment. Great for getting in shape, but potentially dangerous for your baby. Don't let your baby anywhere near bikes, elliptical machines, rowing machines, treadmills, weights,

Red Light Greenery

Your baby might not be eating leafy greens at the table yet, but that doesn't mean he or she would pass on the chance to chomp a handful or two of leaves off the house and garden plants. Problem is, some common plants are poisonous or at the very least cause stomach upset when eaten. So keep all plants out of reach (and always assume babies can reach farther than you think) and farm out potentially harmful plants to friends who don't have small children, at least until your baby is more mindful of what belongs in his or her mouth. And just in case, know the botanical names of all your plants, so if your baby does take a nibble of one, you'll be able to identify the plant in question for the doctor or Poison Control.

The following is a list of some (but not all) of the more common poisonous houseplants:

Amaryllis	Elephant's ear	Mistletoe
Arrowhead vine	English ivy	Myrtle
Azalea	Flamingo flower	Oleander
Caladium	Foxglove	Oxalis
Clivia	Holly	Peace lily
Devil's ivy	Ivy	Poinsettia
Dumb cane	Jerusalem cherry	Umbrella tree

and weight machines, and if possible keep rooms that store them inaccessible. Every piece of equipment comes with its own safety risks, and all (especially those with moving parts) are extremely tempting to curious babies. Keep equipment unplugged when not in use by an adult (and make sure to keep the plug out of reach). Be sure, too, that any safety straps or other long straps on exercise equipment are tied up and completely out of reach for a baby (they could pose a strangulation risk). Ditto if you exercise with a jump rope or strap—always store it out of baby's reach.

Tablecloths. Best to leave your table bare when there's a baby afoot and crawling around. Plan B: Use short tablecloths with little or no overhang so your baby can't pull them (and everything on the table) down. Or hold longer tablecloths securely in place with clasps that are designed to keep outdoor tablecloths from blowing away in windy weather (though an intrepid baby can reach even a short or secured tablecloth to pull it down). Placemats can be a good alternative to long tablecloths, but remember that a curious baby can pull down a placemat, too—so if it's set (with china or hot coffee, for instance), be sure your baby is carefully supervised and kept away from the table.

Houseplants. Keep them out of reach, where your child can't pull them down or sample the leaves or dirt. Best to keep poisonous plants out of your home entirely (see the box this page).

Hazardous objects. Keep all hazardous household objects out of the reach of your baby by storing them in drawers, cabinets, chests, or closets with childproof latches, on absolutely out-of-reach shelves, or behind closed doors your baby absolutely can't open. When you're using hazardous items, be sure your child can't get at them when you turn your back, and always put away these dangerous items as soon as you've finished with them:

- Pens, pencils, and other pointed writing implements. When it's time for scribbling, use chunky nontoxic crayons or washable markers.

- Assorted small items, including thimbles, buttons, marbles, or pebbles (like the ones often used in potted plants and flower arrangements), coins, safety pins, and anything else a child might possibly swallow or choke on.

- Jewelry. Most risky: beads and pearls (which can be pulled off the strand and swallowed), and small items like rings, earrings, and pins. Some inexpensive imported children's jewelry may also contain toxic metals, which means mouthing them could be dangerous.

- Strings, cords, ribbons, belts, ties, scarves, measuring tapes, or anything else that could get wrapped around a child's neck.

- Sharp implements such as knives, scissors, needles and pins, knitting needles, letter openers, wire hangers, and razors and razor blades (don't leave these on the side of the tub or sink or dispose of them in a wastebasket your baby could get into).

- Matches and matchbooks, lighters, cigarettes, anything that can light a fire.

- Toys meant for older kids. Keep out of the reach of babies: building sets with small pieces or dolls with small accessories; large trikes, bikes, and scooters; miniature cars and trucks; and anything with sharp corners, small or

breakable parts, or electrical connections. Whistles can also be a hazard—a young child could choke on a tiny toy whistle and on the small ball inside any whistle if it comes loose.

- Button batteries. The disk-shaped type used in watches, calculators, hearing aids, and cameras are easy to swallow and can release hazardous chemicals into a child's esophagus or stomach. Store new, unused batteries in an inaccessible place in their original packaging rather than loose. Keep in mind that "dead" batteries are as hazardous as fresh ones; dispose of them promptly and safely. Know what kind of batteries you are using. If your baby swallows one, call the National Button Battery Ingestion Hotline at 202-625-3333 or Poison Control (800-222-1222) immediately. Keep regular batteries inaccessible to your baby as well.

- Lightbulbs. Small bulbs, such as those used in nightlights, are particularly easy for a baby to mouth and break. Use an LED nightlight (it won't get hot) or a nightlight made specifically with infants and children in mind (the bulb won't be accessible).

- Glass, china, or other breakables.

- Perfumes, toiletries, cosmetics of all kinds. They are potentially toxic.

- Vitamins, medicines, and herbal or homeopathic remedies, both topical and oral.

- Lightweight or filmy plastic bags, such as produce bags, dry-cleaning bags, and packaging on new clothing, pillows, and other items—they can suffocate a baby or young child. Remove clothing from dry-cleaning bags and new items from their plastic wrap as soon as you get them home, then safely recycle or dispose of the plastic.

No Gun
Is a Safe Gun

Accidents involving young children and the guns they find at home are completely preventable. Not by hiding the weapons (children are capable of seeking out and finding, or simply stumbling upon, just about anything their parents try to hide). Not by locking up the guns (all it takes is forgetting to secure the lock just once). Not by teaching children to stay away from guns (curiosity can easily erase parental warnings and overwhelm a young child's underdeveloped impulse control). But by keeping guns out of your home, period. And by keeping your little one out of homes where guns are kept.

Young children are impulsive and incurably inquisitive, perfectly capable of pulling a trigger on a gun, but not capable of comprehending the possible consequences of that seemingly innocent action. Keeping a gun in the home, whether you think your baby or toddler can get to it or not, is leaving open the very real possibility of tragedy. The AAP and numerous safety organizations strongly urge: Don't do it.

If you must keep a gun at home, keep it locked up, inaccessible, and unloaded. Store the bullets in a separate locked location (even very young children have figured out how to load a gun). And buy a trigger lock or other device to prevent accidental discharge.

- Cleaning materials and other household products, even those that are environmentally friendly or "green."

- Shoe polish. If your little one gets into it, the results can be messy—and harmful if it's ingested.

- Mothballs. They're toxic as well as a choking hazard. Opt instead for cedar blocks (not small cedar balls, which can be popped into a curious mouth). If you do use mothballs, store them in an area not accessible to your baby, and air clothing and blankets out thoroughly (until the odor has dissipated) before using them.

- Tools of a trade or hobby: toxic paints, paint thinners, sewing and knitting supplies (including thread and yarn), woodworking equipment, and so on.

- Fake food. Apples, pears, oranges, and other food made of wax, papier-mache, rubber, or any other substance that isn't safe for children tempted to taste them (a candle that smells and looks like an ice-cream sundae, a child's eraser that smells and looks like a strawberry).

- Guns (see the box on this page).

Babyproofing in the Kitchen

Since families generally spend a great deal of time in the kitchen, babies do, too. To ensure that your kitchen is baby-safe, take the following precautions:

- Rearrange storage areas. Try to move anything that should be off-limits to your little one to upper cabinets and drawers. This includes glassware and dishes that are breakable, food wrap boxes with serrated edges, sharp knives, utensils with slim handles that can poke an eye, skewers, graters, peelers, bag clips, and appliances with intricate gears that can pinch little fingers (like an eggbeater, nutcracker, or can opener), cleaning products, alcoholic beverages, medicines, anything in a breakable container, or potentially dangerous

Happy, Safe Holidays

Holidays are always more magical, more wondrous, more fun through a little one's eyes—but to make sure the celebrations are as safe as they are festive, keep these holiday safety tips in mind during every season:

- Don't take a holiday from safety. Assess holiday decorations for safety as you would any other household objects. Examine them for breakability, small parts, toxicity, choking hazards (fake snow, for instance), and size (tiny tree ornaments or dreidels, for example, are unsafe) and place anything unsafe high, out of the reach of young children. Avoid decorations that resemble candy or food that may tempt a young child to try to eat them.

- Light safely. Be sure any decorative lights you use are UL-approved and are installed according to instructions. Check cords from lights used in previous years to be sure they are not frayed. And never ever allow your baby (or toddler or preschooler) to play with lights—even when they are unplugged.

- Get that glow the safe way. Place lighted candles where children can't reach them and away from curtains and paper decorations. Keep nearby windows closed so a breeze won't fan the flames. Never leave lighted candles on a table draped with a cloth that a baby can pull off, and be sure to carefully blow out the candles before going to bed or leaving the house. Keep jack o' lanterns or luminarias unlit, or light them with a glow stick instead of a candle.

- Give the gift of safety. Don't leave potentially unsafe gifts under a tree or arranged anywhere else accessible to your baby. Be sure gift wrapping bows or ribbons are not easily accessible to your baby's reach, and clear away all wrappings, bags, and gift decorations promptly after gifts are opened.

- When trimming a full-size tree, make sure your baby can't pull down on the hanging lights or branches and topple it over. Or safer still, trim a tabletop tree that baby can enjoy from a safe distance. And in the interest of fire safety, purchase either a fire-retardant artificial tree or the freshest tree you can find (the needles should bend, not break), then have a couple of inches sawed off the trunk and set it up in a water-filled tree stand (but make sure your baby can't get into the water). Or opt for a live tree you can later plant or donate to a local park (though keep your baby away from the soil).

- Leave fireworks to the pros. Don't try to create your own fireworks display. Even Class C fireworks, labeled "safe and sane" by sellers, are potentially dangerous, as are sparklers. So, as recommended by the AAP and many safety organizations, never use fireworks or sparklers at home, especially near children. Get your fireworks fix at public events (and if you do and will be close to the loud display, be sure to use child-size noise muffling earmuff/headphones to protect your baby's delicate ears).

foods (nuts, hot peppers, bay leaves, sticky or hard candy, jars of peanut butter). Keep child-safe pots and pans, wooden and plastic utensils, unopened food packages that would be safe if opened, and dish towels and cloths in the more accessible lower cabinets and drawers.

Not a Do-It-Yourselfer?

Just don't have the time, the inclination, or confidence to babyproof your home (and feeling pretty overwhelmed about the prospect after reading over this section)? Consider hiring a professional to do the job for you. Childproofing services do it all—from fire and electrical safety to latches of every variety. They'll investigate your home for potential dangers and take all the appropriate precautions for you—securing furniture, cabinets, and doors, installing window guards, gates, and alarms, scanning for choking, poisoning, and burn hazards, checking wiring, safeguarding your pool, and more.

Does peace of mind come with a price? Absolutely—these services can be expensive. To make sure you're getting a service that knows its stuff, look for one that's HHT (Home Hazards Test) certified and belongs to the International Association for Child Safety (IAFCS). For more information, go to iafcs.org.

- Install child-guard latches on drawers or cabinets that house dangerous items or items you don't want your baby to touch, even if you believe these cabinets are inaccessible to your baby. What your baby cares to go after and to what lengths (and heights) he or she will go to get it will change over time (and depends on your baby, and eventually your toddler), so your storage arrangement may have to change as well. Reassess periodically and as needed—and always overestimate your baby's resourcefulness, strength, and skill.

- Use back burners of the range for cooking, when possible, and always turn the handles of pots toward the rear. If the burner controls are on the front of the range, snap on commercial stove-knob covers. Appliance latches can keep conventional and microwave ovens inaccessible. Remember that the outsides of some ovens (and other appliances, such as toasters, coffeemakers, and slow cookers) can get hot enough to cause burns and can stay hot long after they've been turned off—so keep them out of reach of baby.

- Keep the dishwasher locked between uses, and be careful when you're loading and unloading—it takes only a second for a baby to reach for something sharp or breakable. Keep dishwasher detergents (especially those colorful and appealing-to-baby dishwasher pods) out of reach of babies.

- Keep sponges out of reach. One bite of a sponge can turn into a choking hazard—plus used sponges can harbor plenty of bacteria.

- Keep the refrigerator off-limits to your baby by installing an appliance latch. Also avoid small refrigerator magnets: They are often appealing and—since they may be choking hazards—dangerous. By the way, all magnets are unsafe for baby and downright dangerous if swallowed, so be sure to keep them out of baby's reach.

- Don't sit your baby on a countertop. Besides the potential for a tumble, those curious fingers could quickly end up reaching for something they shouldn't (like a knife or a toaster).

- To avoid spills that burn, don't carry your baby and a hot beverage or dish at the same time. Be careful, too, not to leave a hot cup or dish at the edge of a table or counter, near your baby's high chair, or anyplace else where small hands can reach it.

- Keep garbage and recycling in tightly covered containers that your little one can't open and rummage through, or under the sink behind a securely latched door.

- Clean up all spills promptly—they make for slippery floors.

- Store kitchen detergents, scouring powder or soap pads, silver polish, and all other potentially toxic kitchen supplies out of your baby's reach.

- Don't store food and nonfood products (like cleaning products) together. It's too easy to confuse or inadvertently switch them.

- Don't leave a cleaning or utility bucket or other container of water standing around and within reach of your baby. A baby can drown in just a couple of inches of water.

Babyproofing in the Bathroom

The bathroom is full of fascination for a curious child, but it's also full of potential risk, which means your baby should always be closely supervised in it. One way to keep it off-limits is to put a hook and eye or other latch or lock high up on the bathroom door, and to keep it latched when not in use. But don't count on locks—inevitably, there will be times when the door is left open. Make your bathroom baby-safe, too, by taking the following precautions:

- If the tub isn't nonslip, apply nonslip decals or use a rubber bath mat.

- Use nonskid bath rugs on the floor to minimize falls and to cushion your baby when they do occur.

- Latch all bathroom drawers and cabinets. Among the many bathroom staples you should keep behind latched doors: medications (including over-the-counter or homeopathic ones), vitamins, mouthwash, toothpaste, hair products, skin care products, cosmetics, razors, scissors, tweezers, clippers, and bathroom cleaning products (including the toilet bowl brush and the plunger).

- Never use a hair dryer or other electrical appliance near your baby when he or she is in the bath or playing with water. Always unplug and safely store the hair dryer, curling iron, and other small electrical appliances when they're not being used. Keep in mind, too, that the cords themselves present a strangulation hazard. For optimum safety, put these appliances away promptly after using (and don't put them down for a moment when you're using them around your baby—or use them while you're holding baby).

- To prevent severe or lethal shocks, make sure all outlets in the bathroom (and kitchen) have code-mandated ground fault circuit interrupters (they'll have the little reset buttons).

- Keep the water temperature in your home set no higher than 120°F to help minimize accidental scalding. Young children have thin skin, so water at 140°F can give a child a third-degree burn—serious enough to require a skin graft—in just 3 seconds. If you can't adjust the heat setting (if you live in an apartment house, for example) install an anti-scald safety device (available from plumbing supply stores) in the tub, which will slow water to a trickle if it reaches a dangerously

There's No Substitute for Supervision

You've latched and locked, capped off and padded, checked and rechecked—your home is officially babyproofed. Time to relax? Not completely. Though thorough baby-proofing is a very important first step in keeping your little one safe, you've still got your work cut out for you. Constant adult supervision (keeping your baby within either eye- or ear-shot at all times) is vital even when you've got all your babyproofing bases (and outlets) covered.

high temperature. For additional safety, always turn on the cold faucet before the hot and turn off the hot faucet before the cold. And routinely test bathwater temperature with your elbow or whole hand, swishing it around to make sure the temperature is even throughout, before putting your baby in. Or invest in a tub thermometer (sold with other baby bath supplies). If you're planning to install new bathroom faucets, a faucet with a single control is safer than separate hot and cold faucets.

- Consider a protective cover for the tub spout to prevent bumps or burns should a child fall against it.

- Never leave your baby in the tub unattended, even in a special tub seat (most aren't recommended, anyway, since kids can topple over in them). This rule should be strictly followed until your child is at least 5 years old.

- Never leave any amount of water in the tub when it's not in use. A small child

at play can fall into the tub and drown in just a couple of inches of water.

- When the toilet isn't being used, keep the lid closed with suction cups or a safety latch made for this purpose. Again, just those couple of inches of water pose a drowning risk to a small child who topples in.

Babyproofing in the Laundry Room

While your washer, dryer, detergent, stain remover, and other laundry products are indispensable when there's a baby in the house, they could be harmful in little hands. To reduce that risk:

- Limit access to the laundry room or area. If it has a separate door, keep it closed and latched. If not, secure the area with a gate, if possible.

- Keep the washer and dryer doors closed when you're not loading or unloading. If your machine gets very hot during use, make sure your baby can't touch it.

- Keep bleach, detergents, stain removers, dryer sheets, and other laundry products in a latched cabinet and store them promptly again after using. When containers are empty, rinse them thoroughly, then place them in a baby-inaccessible recycling or trash bin. Detergent and stain removing pods are especially appealing to little ones, and easy for them to pop into their mouths—make sure those are never within reach.

Babyproofing in the Garage

Most family garages (and green-houses, workshops, sheds, and hobby areas) are chock-full of toxic products, sharp objects, and other potential hazards:

- If your garage is attached to your house, keep the door between the two locked at all times. If the garage is separate, keep the garage door closed. And, keep any vehicles in the garage locked, too.

- If you have an automatic garage door, be sure that it's one that automatically reverses if it hits an obstacle (such as a small child). All automatic doors manufactured after 1982 are required to have this safeguard—if yours doesn't, get a retrofit kit to upgrade your door. Adding a resilient rubber strip along the bottom of the door offers additional protection because it has a cushioning effect. Check your garage door periodically by lowering it onto a heavy cardboard box or another expendable item to be sure the reverse feature is still operating. If it isn't, disconnect the opener until it's been repaired or replaced.

- Store paints, paint thinners, turpentine, pesticides, weed killers, fertilizer, antifreeze, windshield washer fluid, and other car-care products in an out-of-reach cabinet. All hazardous products should be stored in their original containers so that there is no mistaking their contents. Be sure the directions for their use and safety warnings are visible. If you aren't sure what's in a particular container, dispose of it as you would hazardous waste.

- As an extra precaution, don't let your baby loose in the garage (or a workshop or other dangerous space), even for a moment. Carry your baby to and from the car.

Outdoor Safety

Though most injuries to infants occur in the home, serious ones can also occur in your own backyard, or someone else's, at the local playground, or on the street. Clearly, you can't baby-proof the world (though there will be times when you'll wish you could), but you can easily prevent most outside-the-home accidents:

- Never let a baby play outdoors alone or snooze in a stroller or car seat outside alone.

- Check public play areas before letting your baby loose. Be alert for dog poop, broken glass, cigarette butts, and anything else baby shouldn't touch.

- Be sure that porch and deck railings are sturdy (check them regularly for deterioration or damage) and spaced so that young children can't stick their heads through or fall through the sides. Any outdoor area with a precipitous drop should be inaccessible to young children.

- Don't allow your baby to crawl around in deep grasses or anywhere poison ivy, poison oak, or poison sumac might lurk, or where he or she might sneak a snack on some poisonous plant. This is also the kind of locale where ticks may be biting (see page 409). Keep an eye on baby, too, when he or she is in the stroller or playing near flowers, leaves, shrubbery, or pine needles. Baby can easily grab a handful of leaves or petals and stuff them into his or her mouth (or get pricked by a pine needle).

- If you have a sandbox, keep it covered when it's not in use (to keep out animal droppings, leaves, blowing trash, and so on). If the sand gets wet, let it

Poison Control

Every year, some 1.2 million children in the U.S. accidentally ingest a hazardous substance—and that's not surprising. Children, particularly very young ones, often explore their environment orally—which means that anything they pick up may go right into their mouths. They don't stop to consider whether a substance or object is safe or edible—or whether it's toxic. Their unsophisticated taste buds and sense of smell don't warn them that a substance is dangerous because it tastes or smells bad.

If your baby ever ingests something you think might be harmful (or you suspect that he or she might have), call Poison Control at 800-222-1222 immediately.

To protect your baby from accidental poisoning, follow these rules:

- Lock all potentially poisonous substances out of reach and out of sight of your baby. Even crawlers can climb up on low chairs, stools, or cushions to get to things left on tables or counters.

- Follow all safety rules for administering medicines (see page 549). Never call medicine "candy" or take medicine in front of your child.

- Purchase products that have child-proof packaging, when possible—but don't rely on it to keep your baby from getting them open. Store them where baby can't access them at all.

- Make a habit of closing all containers tightly and returning hazardous substances to safe storage immediately after each use. Don't put a hazardous cleanser or a bottle of detergent down even for a moment while you answer an email or the door.

- Store food and nonfood items separately and never store nonedibles in empty food containers (bleach in an apple juice bottle, for example).

---

dry out in the sun before covering. When filling the sandbox, be sure to use play sand or ordinary beach sand. And always carefully supervise a baby in a sandbox, ending the play session if baby starts to sample the sand or throw it.

- If you have an outdoor fireplace, fire pit, or barbecue grill, make sure to keep your baby away from it while it's in use. The fire should be attended by an adult from the moment it's lit until it's been doused and is completely cool. With a charcoal grill, supervise until the coals, if any, have cooled and been disposed of (remember that coals that aren't doused with water stay hot for a long time after the fire itself is out). If you use a tabletop grill, be sure to set it on a stable surface that your baby can't reach or overturn. If you have a propane grill, make sure your child can't access the controls, gas tubing, or tank valve.

- In hot weather, always check metal parts on playground equipment, strollers and car seats, and outdoor furniture before letting your baby come in contact with them. Metal can get hot enough, especially in a scorching sun, to burn a young child severely with just a few seconds of contact. Blacktop or asphalt can also get hot in the sun, so don't let your baby crawl on it or toddle on it barefoot on very hot days.

Children learn very early where their food comes from, and will assume that what they see is what they'll get without wondering why the "juice" isn't golden or the "jelly" isn't purple.

- Never leave alcoholic beverages within your baby's reach, and keep all wine and liquor bottles in a locked cabinet or bar (if you store any in the refrigerator, make sure they're kept at the back of the highest shelf). Any amount of alcohol, no matter how small, can be harmful to your little one. Ditto for mouthwash, which often contains alcohol.

- Always choose the less hazardous household product over the one with a long list of warnings and precautions. Still, be aware that even "green" products can be unsafe, so keep those out of your baby's reach as well.

- When discarding potentially poisonous substances, empty them down the toilet—unless they can harm the septic system or pipes, in which case follow label directions for disposal. Rinse the containers before discarding (unless the label instructs otherwise) and put them out in a tightly covered recycling bin or trash can immediately.

- To help everyone in your household think "danger" when seeing a potentially poisonous product, put "poison" stickers on the product containers. If you can't locate commercially printed labels (some poison centers can provide "Mr. Yuk" labels), simply put an X of black tape on each product (without covering instructions or warnings). Explain to your family that this mark means "danger." Regularly reinforce the message, and eventually your child will also come to understand that these products are unsafe.

- Be alert for repeat poisonings. A child who has ingested a poison once is statistically likely to make the same mistake again within the year.

- Keep wading pools and any other water catchments (ponds, fountains, birdbaths) inaccessible to babies, even if the water is only an inch or two deep. When they're not in use, keep wading pools overturned, stored away, or covered, so they don't fill with rainwater.

- Enclose a swimming pool with a fence that is at least 5 feet high on all sides, separating the pool from the house. Entrances to the pool should be kept locked at all times. Gates should open away from the pool and be self-closing, with a self-latching lock that is well out of reach of children. An alarm that signals the gate has been opened offers additional protection. Remember, too, to avoid leaving toys around or in the pool that might attract a baby or toddler.

- Be sure that outdoor play equipment is safe. It should be sturdily constructed, correctly assembled, firmly anchored, and installed at least 6 feet from fences or walls. All screws and bolts should be capped to prevent injuries from rough or sharp edges. Check for loose caps periodically. Avoid S-type hooks for swings (the chains can pop out of them) and rings or other openings that are between 5 and 10 inches in diameter, since a child's head might become entrapped. Swing seats should be of soft materials to prevent serious head injuries. The best surfaces for outdoor play areas are 12 inches of sand, mulch, wood chips, or a shock-absorbent material, such as composition rubber mats.

Teaching Your Baby to Be Safe

Injuries are much more likely to happen to someone who's susceptible to them. And of course, babies easily fall (and trip, and bump, and reach) into that category. Your goal as a parent is to reduce this susceptibility as much as you can.

Injury-proofing your baby's environment and supervising constantly are very good places to start—but don't stop there. To keep your little one safe, you'll also have to start injury-proofing your little one. How? By teaching what's safe and what's unsafe (and why), and establishing (and modeling) good safety habits.

Begin by building and using a vocabulary of warning words that your baby will come to associate with dangerous objects, substances, and situations (ouch, boo-boo, hot, sharp) and phrases ("don't touch," "that's dangerous," "be careful," "that's an ouch," "that could give you a boo-boo"). The red flags will sail right over your little one's head at first, like everything else you're trying to teach. But in time and with consistent repetition, your baby's brain will begin to store and process this vital information— until one day, it becomes clear that your lessons have taken hold. Begin teaching your baby now about the following:

Sharp or pointy implements. Whenever you use a knife, scissors, razor, or other sharp implement, be sure to remind your baby that it's sharp, that it's not a toy, and that only mommy and daddy (or other grown-ups) are allowed to use it. Illustrate more tangibly by pretending to touch the point of the implement,

saying "ouch," and pulling your finger away quickly in mock pain.

Hot stuff. Even a 7- or 8-month-old will begin to catch on when you consistently warn that your coffee (or the oven, a lit match or candle, a radiator or heater, a fireplace) is hot and shouldn't be touched. Very soon the word "hot" will automatically signal "don't touch" to your baby—though impulse control to avoid touching anyway will come much later. Illustrate the concept by letting your baby touch something warm, but not hot enough to burn, such as the outside of your coffee cup after it has cooled down. Continue pointing out what's hot and shouldn't be touched. Be particularly careful to provide the "hot . . . don't touch" warning with something new in your home—like a new toaster or oven.

Steps. True, it's necessary to protect crawlers and new walkers from serious falls by securely gating all staircases in the home. But it's also necessary to help your child learn how to navigate steps safely. The child who has no experience with steps, who knows nothing about them (except that they are off-limits), is at greatest risk of a tumble the first time an open stairway is discovered. So put a gate at the top of every stairway of more than three steps in your home—going downstairs is much trickier for the beginner than going up, and so much more dangerous. Downstairs, put the gate three steps up from the bottom so that your child can practice going up and down under controlled conditions.

Electrical hazards. Electrical outlets, cords, and appliances are all appealing to curious babies. And it's not enough to use distraction every time you catch your baby on the way to probing an unprotected outlet, or to hide all the visible cords in your home—it's also

Afraid of Heights? Not Yet.

You'd think that human infants would come with a wariness of heights—instinctively staying away from cliffs, edges, and ledges that might threaten their survival. But research shows that babies don't have that natural instinct until about 9 months (or until they've had enough self-locomotion experience under their belts). Babies younger than that—even newbie crawlers and scooters—have no problem going over the edge of a bed, a changing table, or even the top of a staircase. In fact, studies show that when infants are placed near a virtual drop-off—a glass-covered table that reveals the floor beneath—they seem to be enthralled by the drop-off, not fearful of it. It's only after they have enough experience getting around on their own that they develop a fear and instinctive avoidance of ledges and heights. Which means that you can't rely on biology to protect your little one from falling down a flight of stairs or off a changing table. Keep in mind, however, that even though biology says 9-month-olds should instinctively steer clear of ledges, their natural instincts don't always kick in fast enough to keep them safe. Another reason why it's so important to childproof your house and be extra vigilant around stairs, changing tables, and other high perches—whether your little one is 9 months, or 2 years.

necessary to repeatedly remind of the "ouch" potential.

Tubs, pools, and other watery attractions. Water play is fun and educational, so encourage it. But also encourage a healthy respect for water. Teach your baby basic water-safety rules, including: It's dangerous (and not allowed) to get into any water (a tub, a pool, a pond, a fountain, for example) without a parent or another grown-up. But remember, you can't sufficiently "waterproof" a young child, not even with water wings and swimming lessons (see box, next page), so never leave a baby alone near water, even for a moment. Always be within arm's reach of your little one.

Choking hazards. When your baby puts something in his or her mouth that doesn't belong there (a coin, a pencil, a big sib's little LEGO), take it away and explain, "Don't put that in your mouth. It can give you a boo-boo." Teach your baby that food should be eaten while sitting, and (ultimately) chewed and swallowed before talking.

Baby-unfriendly substances (including beverages). You're always meticulous about locking away household cleansers, medicines, and so on. But at a party, one of the guests leaves his vodka and cranberry on the coffee table. Or you're at your parents' house, and your father, who's been trying to clear a clogged sink, leaves the drain cleaner on the bathroom counter. You're asking for trouble if you haven't begun to teach your baby the rules of substance safety. Always supervise your baby carefully, but also start repeating these important messages, over and over and over again:

■ Don't eat or drink anything unless your parent or another grown-up you know well gives it to you. This is clearly a nearly impossible concept for a baby to grasp, but repetition will make it stick—though realistically not for at least a year, possibly several.

- Medicine and vitamin pills are not candy, though they are sometimes flavored to taste that way. Don't eat or drink them unless your parent or another grown-up you know well gives them to you.

- Don't put anything in your mouth that isn't food.

- Only grown-ups are allowed to use cleaning products and dishwasher detergent. Repeat this every time you scrub the tub, wipe down the countertops, or load the dishwasher.

Street hazards. Begin teaching street smarts now. Every time you cross a street with your baby, explain about "stop, look, and listen," about crossing at the green (or the corner or the crosswalk), and about waiting for the "walk" (or green) light. If there are driveways in your neighborhood, be sure to explain that it's necessary to stop, look, and listen before crossing them, too. Explain that drivers can't see little children so little children have to hold the hand of someone big when crossing. Point out the curb as the line a child must never go beyond on his or her own.

It's a good idea to hold hands on the sidewalk, too, but many new toddlers revel in the freedom of walking on their own. If you permit this (and you probably will want to, at least some of the time), keep up with and keep a sharp eye on your child.

Be sure, too, to start pointing out that it's not okay to leave the house or apartment without you or another adult your baby knows well.

It's also important to teach your baby not to touch garbage in the street— broken glass, cigarette butts, food wrappers. But don't make your child afraid of touching anything at all—it's okay to touch flowers (preferably without

---

Swimming Lessons

Eager to turn your little one into a wee water baby—a pint-size swimmer? Hold on to that eagerness until your baby is at least a year old. While there is some evidence suggesting that children over age 1 may be less likely to drown if they've had formal swimming lessons, the AAP recommends against swim class for babies in their first year.

What about classes that claim to "drown-proof" infants? It actually isn't possible—baby swim classes can give parents a false sense of security when their little ones are around water, putting them at greater risk. Though young children float naturally because they have a higher proportion of body fat than adults, skills learned in an infant swim class aren't likely to help during a life-threatening situation. And infant swim lessons don't make children better swimmers in the long run than lessons taken later on in childhood. What's more, classes where babies are submerged come with other potential risks: Water intoxication (ingesting too much water, which creates an imbalance of electrolytes), plus an increased risk of infections like diarrhea (because of germs swallowed along with pool water), swimmer's ear (because of water entering the ear), and skin rashes. Bottom line: It's smart to skip the lessons for now, though feel free to bring your baby into the pool with you (safely in your arms above water) to help him or her get used to the water and for lots of splashing fun.

Don't Let the Bugs Bite

Even though most insect bites are harmless, the itching they can cause can definitely bug your baby, so it makes sense to protect against bugs and their bites. (For treating bites, see page 577.)

All insects. Once your baby is over 2 months, you can use insect repellents (choose one made for children and wash it off once you're back indoors):

- Bug sprays with the chemical DEET offer the best defense. The AAP cautions against using any repellent with more than 30 percent DEET on kids. Your safest bet: Stick with 10 percent DEET. Apply after sunscreen.
- Repellants with citronella and cedar can help ward off bugs, but not as well as DEET. Reapply often because protection doesn't last long. Products containing oil of lemon eucalyptus should not be used on children under 3 years.
- Permethrin is a chemical that kills ticks and fleas (not mosquitoes) on contact, so it can protect against Lyme disease. It can only be applied to clothing—never to skin. Protection lasts for several washings.

- Picaridin reportedly lasts as long as 10 percent DEET, but the AAP has held back their stamp of approval pending long-term studies.

Bees. Keep your baby out of flower beds, and avoid serving baby sticky, sweet snacks outside. When you do, wipe fingers and face promptly so bees aren't attracted to your sweet baby.

Mosquitoes. Their bites are mostly just itchy, but occasionally mosquitos can spread infectious diseases. Protect your baby by staying indoors at dusk when mosquitoes are swarming, screening doors and windows, and covering the stroller with a net as needed.

Deer ticks. Deer ticks can carry Lyme disease and Rocky Mountain spotted fever, so it's especially important to cover as much of your child's body as possible with clothing and apply an insect repellent when in areas where ticks are prevalent. Check your child for ticks nightly and remove ticks right away if you spot them (see page 577).

picking them), trees, store windows, elevator buttons, and so on.

Car safety. Be certain that your baby not only becomes accustomed to being buckled into a car seat, but understands why it's essential: "You can get a bad boo-boo if you don't buckle up." Also explain the other auto safety rules: why it's not safe to throw toys or play with door locks or window buttons.

Playground safety. Teach swing safety: Never twist a swing, push an empty swing, or walk in front of or behind a moving one. Address slide safety, too:

Never climb up the slide from the bottom or go down headfirst, always wait until the child ahead of you is off the slide before going down, and when you reach the bottom, move right out of the way. (Avoid going down a slide with your baby on your lap. Many babies are injured that way.)

Pet safety. Teach your child how to interact safely with pets—and to keep away from other animals. Set an example by always asking the owner first before petting a dog or other animal. Practice safe petting on stuffed animals.

CHAPTER 13

The Eighth Month

S even- and eight-month-old babies are busy babies, and getting busier by the day. Busy practicing skills they've already mastered or are on the brink of mastering (like crawling) and skills they're eager to master (such as pulling up). Busy playing—which, with greater dexterity in those chubby little fingers and hands, is at least twice as much fun, and, with greater ability to focus, is at least twice as absorbing. Busy exploring, discovering, learning, and, as a budding sense of humor emerges, laughing out loud . . . a lot. This month, baby continues to experiment with vowels and consonants and may even string together those combos you've been waiting for ("ma-ma" or "da-da") by month's end. Comprehension is still very limited, but baby's starting to pick up the meaning of a few words—fortunately, "no," a word that will come in handy in the months to come, will be one of the first understood . . . if not often complied with.

Feeding Your Baby: Drinking from a Cup

T hough at this point your cutie is likely quite content with the breast or bottle (or a combo), now is a great time to get cracking on the cup, too. An early start on sipping means your little one will be a cup pro when weaning rolls around (of course breastfeeding can continue as long as both of you like, but experts recommend you break any bottle habit at 12 months). In the meantime, a cup can be a fun and convenient (if initially messy) source of fluids for your baby.

Baby Basics at a Glance: Eighth Month

Sleeping. Not much difference from last month when it comes to sleeping patterns. Your baby will probably be getting 9 to 11 hours of sleep each night and 3 to 4 hours of sleep during the day, broken up into two naps. That's a total of around 14 hours during each 24-hour day.

Eating. Most of baby's nutrition still comes from those all-important liquids, breast milk and formula—even as greater quantities of solid foods are eaten.

■ Breast milk. Your baby will nurse about 4 to 6 times a day (some babies will nurse more often). Baby will be drinking somewhere between 24 and 30 ounces of breast milk a day, though as more solids are added to the diet, baby will drink less.

■ Formula. Your baby will probably down 3 to 4 bottles a day, filled with 7 to 8 ounces of formula, for a total of about 24 to 30 ounces per day (though some babies will continue to drink smaller bottles more often). As more solids are added to the diet, baby will drink less.

■ Solids. As baby becomes a more experienced eater, expect anywhere from 4 to 9 tablespoons of cereal, fruit, and vegetables each per day, spread out over 2 to 3 meals (though some

babies eat less than that, and that's nothing to worry about—just let baby's appetite be your guide). As protein foods (like meat, chicken, fish, and tofu) are added, baby may eat anywhere from 1 to 6 tablespoons of these per day. Whole-milk yogurt and cheese provide protein, too, and are baby faves.

Playing. Your baby's really starting to get a move on, so choose toys that get him or her moving (toys on wheels that your baby can push across the room while crawling or scooting, balls that baby can roll, musical toys that get baby rocking and rolling). Toys that encourage your little one to pull up to standing (such as an activity table or a sturdy push toy that won't roll away) are always well received, as are sorting and building toys, toys with buttons, levers, and dials (like busy boards, activity cubes, and bead mazes), toys that make sounds when pulled, squeezed, shaken, or bopped, blocks and stacking toys, and of course stuffed animals. Don't forget that regular household items can also stand in as toys: plastic containers, wooden spoons, and plastic measuring cups can keep your cutie just as entertained . . . sometimes more!

Sippy Sense

Who doesn't love a sippy cup? They're practically spillproof and unbreakable, so there's no crying over spilled milk (or juice), fewer cleanups, and less laundry. Plus they're portable. Unlike other cups and glasses, they can be used in the car, at play, in the stroller, and—here's the biggie for busy parents—without supervision.

But research has pointed to some potential pitfalls in sippy cup use, too—especially for older babies. Because they're more like a bottle than a cup in the way liquid is extracted from them (it's a slower process, allowing the liquid to spend more time pooling in the mouth and on teeth), extended, frequent use can lead to tooth decay . . . at least, once teeth have arrived. This is especially true if the sippy cup is used (as it so often is) between meals, and even more likely a risk if it's carried around all day by an older baby for round-the-clock nipping (the way a bottle might be). Another problem when they're carried around all day is that they become a breeding ground for bacteria (particularly if the cup gets dumped in a toy pile one day and retrieved and drunk from again the next day). What's more, a baby drinking all day from a sippy cup full (or a bottle full) of juice may drown his or her appetite for food and/or take in too many mostly empty calories (or even suffer from chronic diarrhea). As if that's not enough, some experts suggest that exclusive sippy cup use may slow speech development. The theory goes that the sippy method of drinking—unlike drinking from a regular cup or with a straw—doesn't give the mouth muscles the workout they need.

Still, sippy cups offer a terrific transition from breast or bottle to traditional cups, minimize mess, and are an undeniable convenience on the road. To eliminate the potential risks that go along with those benefits:

- **Don't be exclusive with a sippy.** Make sure your baby also has the opportunity to learn the fine art of sipping from a spoutless cup—and then use both, rather than going full-on sippy. Once baby gets a bit older (beginning at about 8 to 9 months old), introduce a cup with a straw. Not only does sucking from a straw require complex movements of the mouth and jaw, giving them the workout they need to develop well, but straws send the liquid on a fast track to being swallowed instead of letting it pool in the mouth. Win-win for speech and teeth.

- **Limit sippy sipping to meal and snack times.** Don't let your baby crawl around with the sippy cup, and don't always use a sippy to soothe your baby in the car or stroller. Limits help protect teeth and speech, prevent overdosing on juice, and keep sippy use from slipping into sippy abuse.

- **Fill it with water.** If the sippy becomes a comfort object (much as a bottle can), don't deny the comfort, but fill it with water, which won't harm those teeth—and if it's fluoridated, will help protect them.

- **Know when to stop.** Once your little sipper can drink easily from a regular cup or a straw cup, ditch the sippy.

Here's how you can make the introduction to the cup successful:

- **Let your baby sit pretty.** It's definitely easier to sip if you can sit—and your baby will be less likely to gag on those sips if he or she is able to sit well . . . all alone or propped up.

- **Protect all concerned.** Teaching your baby to drink from a cup won't be neat—you can expect more to drip down the chin than into the mouth. So until your little sipper picks up some skills, keep him or her covered with a large bib during drinking lessons.

- **Consider timing.** Babies are more open to just about every new experience when they're in a jolly mood, have had a recent nap, and aren't cranky from hunger. Try offering sips at a time your little one isn't used to having a breast or bottle—say, as a side with solids.

- **Choose right.** Certain features will make those first sipping experiences easier and less messy for everyone. Look for a cup that's sturdy, spillproof (so you'll be in the clear when it's tossed off the high chair—and it will be), weighted on the bottom (so it won't tip over), and easy to grab (try a small baby-size cup). Most babies like cups with handles, but experiment until you find the right match. If you opt for a plastic cup, choose one that's BPA-free (current FDA regulations don't allow children's drinking cups to contain BPA, but one that's a hand-me-down might). Of course, if your little one tries to grab your glass of water at dinner, there's no harm in letting him or her take a supervised swig (you hold it, your little one sips it). Baby will learn to drink from a variety of cups faster if he or she tries several sooner.

  A cup with a spouted lid (known in baby and toddler circles as a "sippy cup") offers a nice transition from sucking to sipping, though babies who've taken a bottle may take to a sippy cup more easily than those accustomed to a human nipple. There will be less spillage to worry about with a sippy than with a regular cup, too (and none at all with a spillproof variety, a definite perk). Still, there are benefits to switching off between a sippy cup and a regular cup—and to eventually swapping out the sippy for a straw cup (see box, page 414).

- **Fill it with the familiar.** Your baby might take to the cup more readily if it's filled with a familiar fluid, like breast milk or formula. Or your little one may balk at an old favorite coming from a strange new source. In that case, move on to water. If water's not winning, switch to diluted fruit juice (which you can introduce after 6 months).

- **Go slow.** For someone who's been suckling from a breast or sucking from a bottle his or her whole life, sipping from a cup is a whole new experience. So let your baby take some time getting acclimated to the cup (touch it, inspect it, even play with it). Then try holding the cup to baby's mouth, tipping it a little, and letting a few drops trickle in. Remember to pause for a swallow before offering more—otherwise your newbie cup drinker might gag (he or she may also be too surprised at first to swallow—which means that the fluid may trickle right back out of baby's mouth). Your baby doesn't seem to get it? Hold the cup near your mouth and pretend to take a drink ("Mmm! That tastes good!").

- **Invite participation.** He reaches out for the cup? Let him grab hold while you help him guide it. She wants to hold it herself? Let her—even if she can't quite figure out what she's supposed to do with it.

Straw Savvy

Is your little sipper having a hard time sucking it up . . . from a straw? Figuring out how to drink from a straw is a challenge for most babies. It requires the use of different muscles and more sophisticated motor movements than sucking from a nipple or even from a spouted sippy cup—and most little ones don't really have all that coordination down pat until the eighth or ninth month at least. Even then, the mechanics can be tough for your munchkin to master. Still, since straws come with so many benefits, it's an effort worth making (they're better than sippy cups for baby's mouth, jaw, and language development, and easier on tiny teeth). And it'll be a little easier with some straw savvy.

First you'll want your baby to recognize that the straw is a way to extract liquid from a cup. To help make that association, demonstrate. Place a straw in a glass of water, cover the end of the straw with your finger, lift the straw out of the cup, and then release your finger, showing your baby how water comes out. Try this a few times and then switch to releasing the water (making sure it's only a small amount to avoid any unsettling gagging) into baby's mouth.

Got your baby's attention with that trick? Next, fill a ziplock bag with water, leaving some air in it. Poke a small hole in the air pocket large enough to fit a straw, and put a short straw into the bag. Bring the straw to baby's mouth and give the bag a gentle squeeze so a small amount of fluid gets into his or her mouth. Bingo—straw-drink connection made. A juice pouch can essentially teach the same lesson, but it will be a sticky lesson, for sure.

Now it's time to lay the foundation for sucking from a straw. Cut a regular disposable straw very short (so not a lot of sucking effort is needed to extract fluid) and put it in a cup of water (or breast milk or formula). Hold the straw (and the cup), bring it to baby's mouth, and let him or her suck the liquid out. Increase the length of the straw a little at a time over the next couple of days.

Some babies will catch on quickly. Others may need a wee bit more practice. If that's the case with your little one, go back to lifting the straw with liquid in it out of the cup, this time placing another finger on the bottom of the straw to trap the fluid inside. Bring the top of the straw to baby's mouth and encourage sucking. Baby will get a little liquid, and hopefully, the concept. Keep putting more and more water into the straw so baby is sucking more and more through the straw. Then go back to putting the straw directly into the cup and letting baby take a drink.

If your baby is a slow study on straws (and not to worry—many babies are), hold off on introducing spill-free straw cups until he or she has gotten the hang of straw drinking from a regular cup. That's because no-spill straw cups often require stronger sucking to get the goods—and that can lead to frustration, and baby giving up on the straw too soon. A cup that is valve-free and has a weighted straw can make the sucking easier.

■ Take no for an answer. If your little one turns away, that's the signal that enough is enough (even if it hasn't been any at all). All systems "no"? Put the cup away until the next meal or, if your baby is really resistant, until another day.

What You May Be Wondering About

Baby's First Words

"My baby has started saying 'ma-ma' a lot. We were all excited until someone told us that she's probably just making sounds without understanding their meaning. Is that true?"

Remember when that first wave of contentment washed across your little one's face, and your heart told you it was a smile meant just for you—even as your head told you it was "just gas"? Ultimately, it didn't matter—your baby was on her way to a lifetime of sweet smiles, by now something she's likely already made a significant down payment on. Same with her first "ma-ma" or "da-da." It's hard to pinpoint just when a baby makes the transition from mimicking sounds without meaning (saying "ma-ma" because she's practicing her m's) to speaking meaningfully (saying "da-da" because she's calling her daddy). And ultimately, that distinction doesn't matter either at this point. The important thing is that your baby is vocalizing and attempting to imitate sounds she hears, and that means she's on her way to a lifetime of talking.

When the first real word is spoken varies a great deal in babies, and is, of course, subject to less-than-objective parental interpretation. According to the experts, the average baby can be expected to say what she means and mean what she says for the first time anywhere between 10 and 14 months. But before you let developmental data rain on your parade of parental pride, hear this: A small percentage of babies say their first meaningful word as early as 7 or 8 months. Other perfectly normal tots don't utter a single recognizable word until midway through their second year, at least as far as their parents can tell. Very active babies may be more focused on conquering motor skills than becoming a motormouth.

Of course, long before a baby speaks her first words, she will learn to understand words (aka receptive language). Your baby's receptive language development begins the moment you speak your first words to her (actually before, since she began hearing your voice in utero). Over time, she starts to sort out individual words from the jumble of language around her, and then one day, about the middle of the first year, you say her name and she turns around. She's recognized a word! Pretty soon after she should begin to understand the names of other people and objects she sees daily, such as mommy, daddy, bottle, cup, cracker. In a few months, or even earlier, she may begin to follow simple commands, such as "Give me a bite," or "Wave bye-bye," or "Kiss Mommy." This comprehension moves ahead at a much faster pace than speech itself and is an important forerunner to it. You can nurture both receptive and spoken language development every day in many ways (see page 486).

Signing with Baby

"Some of my friends are using baby signs to communicate with their babies—and it seems to work. I'd like to try with my baby, but want to be sure it won't slow down his speech."

Your baby may be a born communicator, but that doesn't mean you'll always understand what he's trying to

Baby Signs, Baby Smarts?

Do baby signs signal a smarter future for your baby? Not necessarily. Though a baby who's able to sign definitely has an easier time communicating early on (as do his parents with him), research hasn't pointed to a lasting language edge. Once a child can speak and be understood, the verbal gap between signing babies and those who skip signs seems to diminish and eventually disappear. The bottom line on signs: Sign away to help baby communicate now, not to boost SAT scores later.

say, especially in the first and second year, when communication (and comprehension) gaps between a little one and the parents who struggle to understand him can be pretty gaping. That's where "baby signs" step in.

Why sign up for baby signs? For one thing, signing lets your baby express his needs without needing words (words that are still beyond his ability to speak). Better communication leads to smoother interactions and fewer frustrations (for both of you)—but it also boosts baby's confidence as a communicator ("they get me!"), which spurs his motivation to keep communicating, first through signs, then through a mixture of signs and sounds, ultimately through words.

Will signing slow down speech? Research shows it doesn't—and in fact, for some babies signs can speed spoken language development, since it promotes interaction between parent and baby. Signing with your baby means you'll be spending more time talking

with him, too—and there's no better way to help him learn to speak than speaking to him.

If you'd like to use baby signs, here's how:

- Sign on early. Begin using signs as soon as your baby shows an active interest in communicating with you—preferably by 8 or 9 months, though there's no harm in getting into the signing habit earlier, or even later. Most babies will start signing back somewhere between 10 and 14 months.

- Sign as needed. The most important signs to develop and learn will be the ones your baby needs to express his everyday needs, such as being hungry, thirsty, and sleepy.

- Sign what comes naturally. Develop a natural sign language that works for you and your baby. Any simple gesture that fits a word or phrase well can work: Flapping arms for "bird," scratching under the arms for "monkey," hands together and supporting a tilted head for "sleep," a rubbed belly for "hungry," a cupped hand placed up to the mouth for "drink," a finger touched to the nose for "smell," a palm facing up and then a curling in of the fingers for "more," arms up for "up," palm facing down and then lowering hand for "down," and so on.

- Follow your baby's signs. Many babies invent their own signs. If yours does, always use the signs of his design, which are more meaningful to him.

- Sign him up. If you want to go more formal, sign you and your baby up for a class that covers it (many hospitals, community centers, and other organizations offer classes), or look for books or online resources that teach baby sign language, many of which use the formal signs from American Sign Language (ASL).

- Sign consistently. By seeing the same signs over and over, your baby will come to understand them and imitate them more quickly.

- Speak and sign at the same time. To make sure your baby learns both the sign and the spoken word, use both together.

- Sign up the whole family. The more people in your baby's life who can speak his language, the happier he'll be. Siblings, grandparents, care providers, and anyone else who spends a lot of time with your baby should be familiar with at least the most important signs.

- Know when to sign off. Signing, like all forms of communication, should develop naturally and at a little one's own pace, without any pressure. If your baby seems frustrated by the signs, resists using them, or shows signs of sign overload, don't force the agenda. The idea is to reduce frustration for both of you, not add to it.

While signing can make life a little easier during the preverbal stage, it's definitely not necessary—either for your relationship with your baby or his language development. So sign on to baby signs if you're feeling it, but if you're not (or baby's not), don't feel compelled to keep it up. Communicate with your little one any way that works and feels comfortable to you both (inevitably, some nonverbal communication will make its way into the mix on baby's side, whether it's gestures like pointing or assorted grunts and squeals—all

Sleep Regression

You've prided yourself on having a baby who sleeps through the night and naps well during the day. Until recently, that is. All of a sudden your good snoozer is turning into a bad dream—nightly wake-ups, difficulty settling down for naps. Who's the imposter in your little one's crib—and where did your sleeping sweetie disappear to?

Welcome to sleep regression—a perfectly normal blip on the sleep radar many babies experience, typically at 3 to 4 months, 8 to 10 months, and 12 months, though it can happen at any time. Night waking may start up again during a growth spurt, or when baby is passing through a developmental stage (like learning how to flip, sit, crawl, or pull up). It makes sense: The compulsion to practice an exciting new skill can make your baby restless—a reality that, in turn, can leave you restless and pining for the days when your little one slept reliably through the night.

Happily, sleep regression is temporary. Once your little one acclimates to his or her new mobility, sleeping patterns should return to baseline (at least until the next major developmental milestone appears). Until then, stay consistent with the bedtime routine, treat these new wakenings as you did when your baby was younger (see page 349), and be sure your baby is getting enough sleep during the day to make up for the lost sleep at night (it'll be even harder for an overtired baby to settle down). And then keep repeating to yourself that probably already familiar mantra of parenting: "This, too, shall pass."

Different Ways of Crawling

For a baby eager and determined to get from one place to another, function definitely trumps form. As long as your baby is attempting to get around on her own, it doesn't matter how.

of which can be surprisingly effective). Eventually, the words will flow—and the communication gap will close.

Crawling

"My baby has started to scoot around on her tummy but won't get on all fours. Is this considered crawling?"

Crawling styles vary—and since there are no "must-dos" when it comes to crawling, it doesn't really matter how your little rug rat is getting around. In fact, moving around on the belly, or creeping, is usually a precursor to hands and knees mobility (aka crawling)—though some babies stick to creeping and never get up on all fours at all.

Some babies start crawling (or creeping or scooting) as early as 6 or 7 months (especially if they've spent plenty of supervised playtime on their bellies), but most don't get their crawl on until closer to 9 months or later. More babies are crawling later these days (because of less time spent on their tummies). Late crawling (or no crawling at all; see next question) is not cause for concern as long as other important developmental milestones are being reached (such as sitting—a skill babies must master before they can tackle crawling). Many begin crawling backward or sideways, and don't get the hang of going forward for weeks. Some scoot on one knee or on their bottom, and others travel on hands and feet, a stage that many babies reach just before walking. The method a baby chooses to get from one point to another is much less important than the fact that she's making an effort to get around on her own. (If, however, she does not seem to be using both sides of her body—arms and legs—equally, check with her doctor.)

Baby's Not Crawling

"My son hasn't shown any interest in crawling yet. Is that a problem?"

No crawling? No problem. Crawling isn't a must-do for the diaper set. It's actually considered an optional skill, and isn't even included on most developmental assessments. And while those who opt out of crawling are limited in mobility, they are limited only briefly—until they figure out how to pull up, to cruise (from chair to coffee table to sofa), and finally to walk. In fact, many babies who never take to all fours end up on two feet earlier than their contentedly crawling comrades.

Some babies don't crawl because they haven't been given the chance. So limit the time your baby spends confined in a stroller, bouncer, baby carrier, play yard, and/or ExerSaucer or lying on his back, and give him plenty of opportunities for supervised tummy time so he can practice raising himself on all fours. Encourage him to get moving on hands and knees by putting a favorite toy, a mirror, or an interesting object (like your face or a rolling ball) a short distance ahead of him. Got a hard, slippery floor or scratchy carpet? Roll out a yoga or exercise mat for his tummy time, or cover his knees to provide traction and comfort.

In the next few months, one way or another, your baby will be taking off—and off into trouble. And you'll be left wondering what the rush was.

Baby Making a Mess

"Now that my daughter is crawling around and pulling up on everything, I can't keep up with the mess she makes. Should I try to control her—and the mess—better, or give up?"

Messes may be your worst enemy, but they're an adventurous baby's best friend. Sure, it's a pain in the neck (and lower back) to clean up after your mess-making munchkin, but curbing the clutter can also curb her curiosity. Letting her roam—and mess—freely (but safely) allows her to flex her brainpower, her muscles, and her budding sense of independence. Bottom line: It's impossible to keep your house as neat as it was prebaby, and it's sort of pointless to try. You'll be a lot less frustrated—and overwhelmed—if you accept this new, messier reality instead of trying to fight it. But that doesn't mean you have to wave the Swiffer of surrender entirely. Here's how to reach a sane compromise between clean and clutter:

Start with a safe house. While it may be okay for her to scatter socks on the bedroom floor or build a house of napkins on the kitchen tile, it isn't okay for her to clang bottles together to see what happens or rummage around the loose change in your bag. So before you let your baby roam at home, be sure it's safe for her and from her (see page 391).

Contain the chaos. You'll be a lot happier if you try to confine the mess to one or two rooms or areas in the home. That means letting your baby have free run only in her own room and perhaps the kitchen or family room—wherever you and she spend the most time together. Use closed doors or baby-safe gates to define the areas. If you have a small apartment, of course, maintaining baby-free (and mess-free) zones like that may not be realistic.

Also reduce the potential for mess by wedging books in tightly on shelves accessible to your baby, leaving a few of her indestructible books where she can reach them and take them out easily. Seal the more vulnerable cabinets and drawers with childproof safety locks (especially those that contain breakables, valuables, or hazards), and keep most knickknacks off low tables, leaving only a few you don't mind her playing with. Set aside a special drawer or cabinet for her in each room she frequents to call her own, and fill it with plastic cups, plates, and containers, wooden spoons, stacking cups, and empty boxes.

Setting limits will not only help save your sanity but also help your baby's development. Little ones really do thrive when limits are set for them—plus, they will eventually teach her the important (though initially elusive) lesson that other people, even parents, have possessions and rights, too.

Let her make a mess in peace. Don't complain constantly about the mess she's making. Remember, she's expressing her natural curiosity ("If I turn this cup of milk over, what will happen?" "If I take all these clothes out of the drawer, what will I find underneath?"), and that's healthy.

Play it safe. An exception to a let-the-mess-fall-where-it-may attitude should be made when it presents a safety risk. If baby spills her juice or empties the dog's water bowl, wipe it up promptly. Also pick up sheets of paper and magazines as soon as baby is through with them, and keep traffic lanes (stairways, especially) clear of toys, particularly those with wheels, at all times.

Set aside a sanctuary. You won't always be able to keep up with the mess, but space in your home allowing, try to preserve a clutter-free zone of your own, even if it's no more than a nook. Then, at the end of every day, you'll have a haven to escape to.

Restrain yourself. Try not to follow your happy little hurricane around as she wreaks havoc, putting away everything she takes out. This will frustrate her, giving her the sense that everything she does is not only unacceptable but essentially pointless. And it will frustrate you if she immediately reclutters what you've uncluttered. Instead, play pickup once a day, twice tops.

Involve her in cleanup. Don't do your major cleanups with her underfoot. But do pick up a couple of things with her at the end of each play session, making a point (even if she's not old enough to get the point) of saying, "Now, can you help Daddy pick this monkey up and put it away?" Hand her one of the blocks to put back into the toy basket, give her a plastic container to return to the cabinet or some crumpled paper to throw into the recycling bin, and applaud each effort. Though she will be messing up a lot more often than she'll be cleaning up for years to come, these early lessons will help her to understand—eventually—that what comes out must go back in.

Eating Off the Floor

"My baby is always dropping her cracker on the floor and then picking it up and eating it. What's the real deal on the 5-second rule?"

If the world is your baby's oyster these days, it's also her own personal buffet table. Clearly she doesn't consider what germs her cracker may have picked up on the floor before she munches—and clearly she doesn't care. And neither should you, at least not most of the time. Sure, there are germs on the floor at home—no matter how hygienically hyper you are—but not in significant numbers. And for the most part, they're germs your baby has been exposed to before, particularly if she frequently plays on the floor, which she should. That means they're usually not harmful, and in fact by challenging her immune system to flex its muscles, routine germ exposure may help beef up her resistance. Even germs that she picks up (literally) from the floor of your neighbor's house or at the day-care center can help on this front. So stay calm and carry on when you catch her eating off the floor (even if it's obviously not clean enough to eat off of). No need to launch germ warfare with antibacterial rinses or wipes, or leap over the sofa to confiscate the cracker in question if it has overstayed the 5-second rule.

Speaking of that 5-second rule, it's time to debunk it. Germs will win the race, no matter how quickly you're able to retrieve the dropped item. Bacteria can attach itself to dropped food within milliseconds (though the longer the food in question stays on the floor or other bacteria-laden surface, the higher the transfer of germs). So the question then is not how long the cracker has spent on the floor (face it, it'll have bacteria on it), but rather will that bacteria make your baby sick. And that depends on the condition of the surface (where it is, if it's wet, what's been there before, and so on).

So leap if you must to intercept a damp object that she's picked up off the floor and is about to munch on—that day-old cracker she sucked on for hours, the pacifier soaking in a puddle of juice, or the banana chunk that's been decomposing under the high chair since last week—because bacteria multiply rapidly on wet surfaces. Also unhealthy (and unsuitable for consumption, 5 seconds or not) are objects picked up from the ground outdoors, where less-benign germs (those from dog poop, for instance) make their unwholesome home. Before letting your baby pop a dropped pacifier, bottle, or teether back into her mouth when you're outside, wash it with soap and water, or clean it with a paci wipe.

Floor picnics won't be safe, however, if there is lead paint in your home, since it can be ingested by your baby along with anything else she eats (or mouths) off the floor. If you have lead paint in your home (possible in homes built before 1978, when lead paint was outlawed) and it hasn't been abated yet, make sure you have it professionally taken care of now. In the meantime, intercept those dropped crackers before they reach her mouth. See page 342 for more on lead exposure.

Eating Dirt— and Worse

"My son puts everything in his mouth. Now that he plays on the floor so much, I have less control over what goes in. Should I be concerned?"

Into the mouths of babes goes anything and everything that fits: dirt, sand, dog food, insects, dust balls, rotten food, even the contents of a dirty diaper. Though it's obviously best to avoid his sampling from such an unsavory selection, it's not always possible. Few babies get through the creepy-crawly stage without at least one oral encounter with something his parents consider creepy (or even crawly). Some can't even get through a single morning.

But you've got a lot less to fear from what's unsanitary than from what's used to sanitize. A mouthful of dirt isn't likely to hurt anyone, but even a lick of some cleansers can cause serious damage. You can't keep everything out of baby's inquisitive grasp, so don't worry about the occasional bug or clump of dog hair that finds its way into his mouth (if you catch him with the cat-about-to-swallow-a-canary look, squeeze his cheeks to open his mouth and sweep the object out with a hooked finger). Concentrate instead on keeping toxic substances away from your curious cutie.

You should also be very careful not to let your baby mouth items small enough to swallow or choke on—buttons, bottle caps, paper clips, safety pins, pet kibble, coins, and so on (see page 397). Before you put your baby down to play, survey the floor for anything that's less than 1⅜ inches in diameter (about the diameter of a toilet paper tube) and remove it.

Getting Dirty

"My daughter would love to crawl around at the playground if I let her. But the ground is so dirty, I'm not sure I should."

Break out the stain remover, and break down your resistance to letting your baby get down and dirty. Babies who are forced to watch from the sidelines when they'd really like to be in the scrimmage are likely to stay spotless but unsatisfied. Besides, little ones are thoroughly washable. The most obvious dirt can be washed off with diaper wipes while you're still at the playground or in the backyard, and ground-in dirt will come off later in the bath. So steel your sensitive sensibilities and, checking first to be sure there's no broken glass or dog droppings in her path, allow your little sport a carefully supervised crawl around. If she gets into something really dirty, give her hands a once-over with a diaper wipe and send her on her way again. And of course, always tote an extra outfit in the diaper bag—just in case you really need to clean up her act.

Discovering Genitals

"My baby has recently started touching her vagina whenever her diaper is off. Should I try to stop her?"

Your baby is only doing what comes naturally (touching something that feels good to touch), so there's no need to stop her. This interest in girl or boy parts is as inevitable and healthy a phase of a baby's development as was her earlier fascination with her mouth, fingers, and toes—or as ears and nose will be later (if they aren't already). Some babies start these down-south explorations by midway through the first year, others not until year's end—while still others may not appear as interested, and that's just as normal. Keep in mind that though the vagina (or penis) is technically a sexual organ, there's absolutely nothing sexual about this kind of self-touching. It's as innocent as your baby is.

But what about when she touches her vaginal area and then those same fingers head right to her mouth? Is that unsanitary? No need to worry. All the germs that are in a baby's genital area are her own and pose no threat. But definitely intercept before hands that have touched a poopy diaper area head toward the mouth. The fecal-oral route is something you want to derail, since serious infections can result. Another hand-genital action you should stop in its tracks: your little girl probing her girl parts with very dirty . . . and germy . . . hands. Those germs could cause a vaginal infection, so be sure to wash your little one's hands often to keep them clean. Boy parts are not susceptible in the same way, but clean hands are always a good idea, for boys or girls.

When your little one gets old enough to understand, you'll be able to explain that this part of her body is private, and that though it's okay for her to touch it, it's best if she touches herself in private—and that it's not okay to let anyone else touch it (except a doctor).

Erections

"When I'm diapering my baby, he sometimes gets an erection—and I'm wondering if that's normal at his age."

Erections come with the territory when you have a penis—in fact, boy fetuses even have them in utero. Though they're definitely not sexual yet, they're the normal reaction to touch of that sensitive sexual organ—as are a little girl's clitoral erections, which are less noticeable but probably as common. A baby may also have an erection when his diaper rubs against his penis, when he's nursing, when you're washing him in the bathtub, in response to air—or just randomly. All baby boys have erections, and some have them more often than others. In other words, it's boy business as usual—and absolutely nothing to worry about.

Play Yard Time

"When we bought our play yard a couple of months ago, our baby just couldn't seem to get enough time in it. Now she screams to get out after only 5 minutes."

As your baby has grown, so has her perspective from inside the play yard. A couple of months ago, the play yard was vast and endlessly entertaining—her own personal amusement park. Now she's beginning to realize that there's a whole world—or at least a family room—out there, and she's game to take it on. The four mesh walls that once enclosed her paradise are now her barriers to freedom, keeping her on the inside looking out.

So don't fence her in. Take your baby's hint and start using the play yard sparingly and only as needed—for instance, when you need her penned up for her own safety while you mop the kitchen floor, put something in the oven, or pick up her toys (though be sure not to leave her unattended in the play yard—she should always be in your view). Limit her time to no more than 10 to 20 minutes at a stretch, which is about as long as an active 7- or 8-month-old will tolerate it anyway—or should be expected to. Rotate her stock of toys frequently so she won't become bored too soon, especially if she's outgrown any toy accessories the yard came with. Just keep large toys out, since an extremely agile and resourceful baby may be able to use them to climb to freedom. Also avoid hanging toys across the top of the play yard.

If she protests before she's done her time, try giving her some novel playthings—a metal bowl and a wooden spoon, perhaps, or a clean, empty plastic bottle or two (without the cap)—anything she doesn't usually play with in this setting. If that doesn't work, parole her as soon as you reasonably can.

"My son could stay in the play yard all day if I let him, but I'm not sure I should."

Some easygoing babies seem perfectly content to be cooped up in the play yard, even late into the first year—and it's fine for your little guy to play in one place, to a point. It's also important for him to see the world from a different perspective than he can spy from the confines of his four mesh walls, and to flex the muscles that will eventually allow him to explore that world on all fours, then two feet. So even if he's not actively demanding his freedom, let him free on the floor in between play yard stays. If he's hesitant at first, help him transition to those wide-open spaces by sitting with him. Set him up with a few favorite toys, or cheer on his attempts at crawling. Gradually, help him adjust to more floor time, less yard time.

Left- or Right-Handedness

"I've noticed that my baby picks up and reaches for toys with either hand. Should I try to encourage him to use his right?"

It's common for babies to appear ambidextrous, freely alternating between hands until they decide which is more . . . handy. In fact, babies usually don't start playing hand favorites until about 18 months at the earliest, and most don't settle on one until at least the second birthday—though some kids keep their parents guessing for several years beyond that.

Statistically speaking, your baby (and 90 percent of his baby buddies) will probably end up preferring the right hand—only 5 to 10 percent of people are lefties. A lot has to do with genetics—when both parents are lefties, there's more than a 50 percent chance their children will also be left-handed. When just one parent is left-handed, the chance of a child being left-handed drops to about 17 percent, and when neither parent is left-handed, it's down to 2 percent.

Wondering if you should try nudging your little one to use one hand over the other? Hands off. Since it's nature, not nurture, at work here, nothing you do would work anyway. Research suggests that pushing a child to use the hand he's not genetically programmed to use can lead to problems later with hand-eye coordination and dexterity. (Have you ever tried to write with the "wrong" hand? Imagine how tough it would be if you had to use that hand consistently.) Time will tell whether you've got yourself a righty or a lefty on your hands—all you need to do is sit back and watch nature take its course.

If your baby strongly favors one hand over the other before he turns 18 months, let the doctor know. In rare cases, such an early and consistent preference can signal a neurological problem.

Reading to Baby

"I'd like my daughter to be a reader, like I am. Is it too early to start reading to her?"

It's never too early to start raising a reader—even though your baby may be more wiggle worm than bookworm at first, or do more chewing on the corners of books than looking at their pages. But soon enough she'll begin to pay attention to the words as you read them (first to the rhythm and sounds of the words, later to their meanings) and to the illustrations (enjoying the colors and patterns at first and later relating

Storytime will become everyone's favorite time.

Baby Books

Which kinds of books are best for your little reader? Choose books with:

- Sturdy construction that defies destruction. Sturdiest are books with laminated cardboard pages with rounded edges, which can be mouthed without breaking down and turned without tearing, or those made of waterproof, tear-resistant material. Soft cloth books are good, too, though page turning can be tricky. A plastic spiral binding on a board book is a plus—it lies flat when open, and baby can play with the fascinating spiral design (make sure it's flexible, not rigid, so little fingers can't be pinched). Vinyl books are good for bath time, one of the few times little ones will sit still long enough for a reading session. To keep these free of mildew, dry thoroughly after each bath, and store in a dry place.

- Lots of pictures. Illustrations or photos should be simple, clear, bright, and show relatable subjects and situations: familiar animals, cars and trucks, other babies and children. Try flipping through family photos, too.

- Simple, uncomplicated text. Rhymes are music to a baby's ears and have the best chance of holding that fleeting attention (the sounds are appealing even if comprehension is still limited). One-word-on-a-page books are good, too, especially if you use the word to create a sentence: "Banana—bananas are yummy and sweet."

- Audience participation. Books with flaps to lift or textured patches to touch get extra points—because they encourage learning about textures and stimulate games like peekaboo, but also because they help make reading fun and interesting. Keep in mind that such features can be fragile, so you may want to supervise touching of books that include easy-to-tear flaps and tabs.

the pictures to known objects). And before you know it, your baby will look forward to storytime as much as you do. Here's how you can nurture a love of reading:

Be a reading role model. Are you hooked on books? Not surprisingly, readers are more likely to raise readers (much as TV watching tends to run in the family). So let your baby catch you with your nose behind a book or e-reader often—or at least, as often as you realistically can. Steal a moment or two while your little one's playing to read a few pages—reading out loud can

help make the connection even stronger. Keep books around the house, and point out often, "This is Daddy's book" or "Mommy loves to read books."

Learn to read baby-style. When reading to a baby, style (tempo, tone, inflection) matters even more than the words do. So go slowly, but go to town with your delivery—with the lilting singsong voice babies lap up and exaggerated emphasis in the right places. Stop at each page to point out what's going on in the pictures ("Look at the little boy sitting on the hill," or "See the puppy playing?") or to show her animals or people ("That's a cow—a cow says 'moo'" or "There's a baby in a crib—the baby's going night-night").

Make reading a habit. Build reading into baby's daily routine, doing a few minutes at least twice a day, when she's alert and when she's already been fed. Before naptime, after lunch, after bath, and before bed are all good reading times. But keep to the schedule only if baby's receptive—don't push a book on her when she's in the mood to practice crawling or make music with two pot covers. Reading should be fun—never a drag.

Keep the library open. Store destructible books on a high shelf for parent-supervised reading sessions, but keep a small (to prevent baby from being overwhelmed) rotating (to prevent baby from becoming bored) library of babyproof books where she can reach and enjoy them. Sometimes a baby who resists being sat down for a reading session with mommy or daddy will be happy to "read" to herself, turning pages and looking at pictures at her own pace. Ditto for e-readers. Allow her the supervised opportunity every so often to look at electronic books, many of which are interactive.

ALL ABOUT:
Putting the Super in Baby

No doubt you've heard about the flashy educational toys sure to boost your baby's brain development and send those fine motor skills soaring off the charts. The apps that'll have your 7-month-old channeling Einstein and Mozart (not to mention reading on a fourth-grade level by age 2). The classes practically guaranteed to turn out a pint-size prodigy. And now you're wondering: Should I be buying (and signing my child up for) these whiz-baby products and services?

You may want to read this first. Though it might be possible—and let's face it, even a little satisfying—to teach an infant a wide variety of skills (including how to recognize words) long before they are ordinarily learned, the majority of experts agree that there's no evidence that intense early learning actually provides a long-term advantage over a more traditional timetable of learning patterns. In fact, studies show

that so-called reading programs for babies don't teach babies how to read at all.

Interestingly, early learning programs touted to beef up brainpower and speed language development may have a very different effect. Research has shown that infants fed a steady diet of educational videos, computer programs, and apps actually know fewer words than those who have less screen time—probably because excessive screen time preempts valuable one-on-one time with mom and dad, which is when babies do their best language learning.

In other words, your baby should be spending his or her first year being a baby, not a student. And babyhood comes with quite a course load of its own—not just intellectual but emotional, physical, and social as well. During these exciting 12 months, babies have to learn to build attachments to others (to mommy, daddy, siblings, babysitters), to trust ("When I'm in trouble, I can depend on Mommy or Daddy to help me"), and to grasp the concept of object permanence ("When Daddy hides behind the chair, he's still there, even though I don't see him"). They need to learn to use their bodies (to sit, stand, walk), their hands (to pick up and drop, as well as to manipulate), and their minds (solving problems such as how-to-get-that-truck-from-the-shelf-I-can't-reach). They'll need to learn the meanings of hundreds of words and, eventually, how to reproduce them using a complicated combination of voice box, lips, and tongue. And they'll need to learn something about feelings—first their own, then those of others. With so many lessons lined up already, it's likely that academic add-ons might overload baby's circuits, maybe even leaving some of these important areas of learning (including those critical emotional and social ones) to lag.

How do you make sure you're fully nurturing all the many amazing sides of your baby's development, so he or she can reach that personal best at a rate that's personally appropriate? Not necessarily by signing up for classes or ordering online educational programs, but by standing by to offer plenty of encouragement and support as your baby tackles the ordinary (but extraordinary!) tasks of infancy. By nurturing baby's natural curiosity about the big world at large (whether it's a dust ball on the floor or a cloud in the sky). By providing a stimulating variety of settings to soak up (stores, zoos, museums, gas stations, parks). By talking about people you see ("That man is riding a bicycle," "Those children are going to school," "That woman is a police officer who can help us"), and by describing how things work ("See, I turn on the faucet and water comes out"), what they are used for ("This is a chair. You sit in a chair"), and how they differ ("The kitty cat has a long tail and the pig has a little curly one"). Offering your baby an environment that's language rich (by spending plenty of time talking, singing songs, and reading books) will boost language skills immeasurably—but keep in mind that it's more important for your baby to know that a dog says "woof," can bite and lick, has four legs, and has fur all over than to be able to recognize that the letters d-o-g spell dog.

If your baby does show an interest in words, letters, or numbers, by all means nurture that interest. But don't pass on the playground so you and baby can spend all your time with a pile of flashcards (or a tablet's worth of apps). Learning—whether it's how to recognize a letter or how to throw a ball, two things your baby can learn just as easily and probably more effectively on a playground as in a class setting—should be fun. And at this tender age, learning should come from doing, which is always how little ones learn best.

The Ninth Month

There just aren't enough waking hours in the day for a busy 8-month-old who's on the go—or attempting to be on the go. Baby's not only a mover and shaker, but a budding comedian who'll do anything for a laugh, an avid mimic who delights in copying sounds you make (warning: all sounds), and a born performer. ("And for an encore, I think I'll do another round of fake coughs—always a crowd pleaser!") That amazing noggin's starting to make sense of complex concepts that previously caused it to draw a blank, making for more sophisticated interactions and play. Case in point, object permanence: "Mommy's not really gone when she peekaboos from behind a diaper . . . she's just goofing on me." But all this new maturity doesn't come only with more fun and games—it can also come with stranger anxiety. Once happy in just about any pair of cozy arms, many 8-month-old babies suddenly become pretty picky about the company they keep. Only mommy, daddy, and maybe a favorite sitter need apply.

Feeding Your Baby: Finger Foods

Has the novelty of feeding your baby pureed mush worn off already? You're not the only one fed up with spoon-feeding. Your baby probably is, too. Witness his willfully clenched lips . . . or the way she turns her head away just at the critical moment (splat!) . . . or how his pudgy hands intercept and overturn the spoon just before it reaches its destination (more splat!).

Happily, it's time to serve up a change—and introduce a new utensil to the feeding mix: baby's fingers. Most eager beaver babies are able to trade in that spoon and trade up for finger foods by the time they are 7 to 8 months old. And once they discover that foods of all kinds can be transported to their mouths by hand (and fingers), self-feeding becomes the name

Baby Basics at a Glance: Ninth Month

Sleeping. Babies this age sleep an average of 10 to 12 hours per night and take two naps during the day, each around 1½ to 2 hours long, for a total of 14 to 15 hours each day.

Eating. Breast milk and formula are still the most important part of baby's diet, but baby's taking in more and more solids each day.

- Breast milk. Your baby will nurse around 4 to 5 times a day (some babies will nurse more often). Baby will be drinking somewhere between 24 and 30 ounces of breast milk a day, though as more solids are added to the diet, baby will drink less.

- Formula. You baby will probably down 3 to 4 bottles a day, filled with 7 to 8 ounces of formula, for a total of 24 to 30 ounces per day. As more solids are added to the diet, baby will drink less.

- Solids. As baby becomes a more experienced eater, expect anywhere from 4 to 9 tablespoons of cereal, fruit, and vegetables each per day, spread out over 2 to 3 meals. As protein foods are added, baby may eat anywhere from 1 to 6 tablespoons of meat, chicken, fish, tofu, eggs, or beans per day. More grains (like quinoa or brown rice) and dairy products (cheese or yogurt) may also add protein to baby's repertoire.

Playing. Baby will continue to play with toys that encourage pulling up to standing (look for sturdy ones that won't tip over), sorting and stacking toys (different-colored foam blocks, for instance, or rings of different sizes), toys with buttons, levers, and dials (like busy boards or activity cubes and tables), toys that make sounds when baby presses a button or pulls on a short string, balls large and small, foam blocks, stuffed animals, and books. Toys that encourage language development (toys that "talk" or respond to words) are a nice addition at this age.

of the game . . . and ultimately, the only game in town.

But the transition from spoon to fingers won't happen overnight. It's a process—a process that can be messy and frustrating on both sides of the high chair. Even if your baby has spent much of his or her young life trying to take on the world by mouth, trying to figure out the mechanics of maneuvering food

to mouth is challenging. Most babies start out by holding their food in their fists, not having learned yet to coordinate individual fingers for pickup and transport. Some learn to open the hand flat against the mouth, while others put their food down and pick it up again with more of it exposed—strategies that can consume a lot of time but often don't result in the consuming of

Spice It Up

Looking to spice up your baby's diet? Consider adding spices and herbs (such as cinnamon, nutmeg, basil, mint, and garlic) to baby's meals. Remember, if you're breastfeeding, your little one has already been experiencing the spicier side of life thanks to the spiced-up foods you eat.

much food. As your baby perfects the pincer grasp (usually between 9 and 12 months), his or her ability to hold smaller objects (like peas and small pasta shapes) between thumb and forefinger will improve—considerably expanding the menu and the amount of self-feeding that can practically be done.

Best Finger Foods

Which first finger foods should you hand over to your baby? Look for consistency that can be gummed before swallowing or that will dissolve easily in the mouth—no chewing should be necessary (whether or not your little one has been visited by the tooth fairy). Start with foods that have been well received in pureed form on a spoon, serving them up in manageable cubes or chunks—pea-size for firmer items, marble-size for softer foods. Good choices include:

- Whole-grain bread, bagel, or toast, rice cakes or other crackers that become mushy when gummed

- Cubes of whole-grain French toast, waffles, or pancakes

- Oat circle cereals, baby puffs

- Tiny cubes of cheese, or shredded cheese

- Small cubes of tofu

- Ripe avocado slices

- Chunks of ripe banana, very ripe pear, peach, apricot, cantaloupe, honeydew, kiwi, and mango

- Blueberries (squish them first so they're not whole)

- Small chunks of cooked-to-tender carrot, white or sweet potato, yam, broccoli or cauliflower florets, and peas (cut in half or crushed)

- Flakes of baked or poached fish (but screen carefully for bones)

- Soft meatballs (cooked in sauce or soup so they don't get crusty)

- Small pieces of cooked chicken or turkey

- Well-cooked pasta of various sizes and shapes (break up before or cut after cooking, as necessary)

- Well-cooked smashed beans and lentils

- Scrambled or hard-cooked eggs

To serve finger foods, scatter four or five pieces onto an unbreakable plate or directly onto baby's feeding tray, and add more as baby eats them. Beginning eaters confronted by too much food, especially all in one spot, may respond either by trying to stuff all of it into their mouths at once or by sending it all to the floor with one high chair–clearing swipe—a good reason to serve it up slowly. As with other foods, finger foods should be fed only to a baby who is seated, and not to one who is crawling, cruising, or toddling around.

Are those yummy soft finger foods (that mango, that avocado, the tofu) slipping and sliding in your baby's pudgy fingers? Grind Cheerios or other whole-grain cereal, wheat germ, or whole-grain crackers into a fine powder and then coat the foods with the "dust." It'll make it easier for your little one to grab hold of and munch on (plus it'll boost the health factor of the foods).

Moving Up from the Mushed

Finger foods shouldn't be the only new delicacies on your baby's menu. You can also start to add more texture to the foods you spoon-feed your little one. You can turn to store-bought "stage 3" foods or mash baby's meals from what you serve the family: Instead of strained applesauce, consider serving the chunky variety. Serve smashed baked sweet potato instead of pureed. Spoon up thicker oatmeal instead of the thin baby kind. Think about mashed small-curd whole-milk cottage cheese or ricotta, scraped apple

Crackers that get mushy in the mouth are perfect for newbie self-feeders.

or pear (scrape tiny bits of fruit into a dish with a knife), mashed or coarsely pureed cooked fruit with the skin removed (apples, apricots, peaches, and plums, for example), and soft-cooked vegetables (such as carrots, sweet and white potatoes, cauliflower, and winter squash). Watch out for strings from fruits (such as bananas and mangoes) and vegetables (such as broccoli, string beans, and kale), and sinew or gristly bits from meats. And be sure to check fish very carefully for bones that might be left after mashing.

Off the Finger Food Menu

Because of the danger of choking, don't give your baby foods that won't dissolve in the mouth, can't be mashed with the gums, or can be easily sucked into the windpipe. Avoid uncooked raisins, whole peas (unless they are smashed), raw firm-fleshed vegetables (carrots, bell peppers) or fruit (apples, unripe pears, grapes), and chunks of meat or poultry.

Once the molars come in (the front teeth are for biting, and don't improve your child's ability to chew), somewhere around the end of the year for early teethers, foods that require real chewing can be added, such as raw apples (grated or cut into very small pieces) and other firm-fleshed raw fruits and vegetables, small slices of meat and poultry (cut across the grain), and seedless grapes (skinned and halved). But hold off until age 4 or 5 on common choking hazards such as raw carrots, popcorn, nuts, and whole hot dogs. Introduce them only when your child is chewing well.

What You May Be Wondering About

Loss of Interest in Nursing

"Whenever I sit down to breastfeed my son, he seems to want to do something else—play with the buttons on my shirt, pull up on my hair, look at the TV, anything but nurse."

Remember the early months when your newborn's whole world seemed to revolve around your breasts? When his adorable mouth would root and pucker as soon as he caught a whiff of mama's milk? When nothing spelled bliss like being at your breast, cuddled in your arms, contentedly lapsing in and out of a sweet, sticky, smiley milk stupor? Well, that was then and this is now. While there are plenty of babies who remain passionate about breastfeeding throughout the first year and significantly beyond, there are others who begin to get a little antsy at their once-favorite milk station starting somewhere around the ninth month. Some simply refuse the breast entirely, while others nurse seriously for a minute or two before pulling away—distracted by a passing shadow, the cat slinking by, a sudden urge to practice pulling up (maybe on mommy's hair)—or just the realization that time spent cooped up in mama's arms is time not spent banging blocks, yanking cushions off the sofa, or otherwise being busy.

Sometimes this baby breast boycott is just transient. Maybe your little one is going through a readjustment in his nutritional needs (especially if he's taking more solids), or perhaps he's put off by the funky taste of your breast milk brought on by hormonal changes during your period or from the garlic bread you toasted Friday night. Or maybe a virus or a bout of teething has him balking at breast business as usual.

More likely, it's busyness that's keeping him from getting busy at the breast—with a world of distractions, breastfeeding faces a lot of compelling competition for his attention. What's not likely to be the cause of your baby's breastfeeding ban? Readiness for weaning. Even if he may think he's ready to move on—or at least move on to other, more interesting activities, especially

---

Not Sitting Still for Bottles?

Got a bottle-baby who won't sit still for formula feeds? The same tips for nursing mamas apply to you, too: Minimize distractions by bottle-feeding in a quiet, dim room and when your little one seems most sleepy. Still not working? Consider switching to a cup during the day and bottles only in the morning (when baby's still revving up) and before bed (when sleepiness is setting in).

Or maybe more distractions are the ticket to better feeds. Try reading to your baby during feeds. Or hand over the bottle and let your baby hold it (or hold it with you), if you haven't already. A little control might win your little one over.

Finally, be sure you are using the right size nipple for your older baby. A flow that's too slow can be frustrating—and may lead to your baby giving up before he or she is done.

during the day—babies continue to do best on breast milk (supplemented with solids) until at least their first birthday, when whole cow's milk in a cup can start standing in. And even then, many toddlers (and their moms) continue to make time in their busy schedules for breastfeeding—if mainly for the pure pleasure of it.

So don't automatically wave the nursing scarf of surrender—instead, stay focused on riding out this late-stage nursing strike, striking back with these tips:

- Try some peace and quiet. An increasingly curious 8- or 9-month-old baby is easily distracted—by the TV (even on mute), the sound of a text coming in, a passing siren, a dog barking next door . . . and of course, by just about any bright, shiny object. To maximize baby's concentration on breast business, nurse in a dimly lit, quiet room. Power off anything that might divert him, your phone included. Stroke him and cuddle him gently as he nurses, to relax him.

- Nurse when he's sleepy. Breastfeed first thing in the morning, before all his busy-baby cylinders kick in. Breastfeed after a warm bath at night. Or after a relaxing massage. Or right before naptime. If he's tired enough, he might not mind braking for breast.

- Or nurse on the run. Some babies prefer to know that they're part of the action—that way they can be sure they're not missing something. If that's the case with your little bundle of energy, nurse while you're walking around the house. Securing baby in a sling will be easier on your arms.

Baby's still not taking breastfeeding lying down—or even sitting up? You can lead a baby to the breast, but you

Got Cow's Milk? Not Yet.

Your little one's growing and developing at an astonishing pace, but there's one milestone even the most advanced baby isn't ready to take on yet: the switch from breast milk or formula to cow's milk. That momentous transition should wait, advises the AAP, until a baby has turned 1 year old, at which point it's fine (with the pediatrician's go-ahead) for your little cupcake to chase down that birthday cupcake with a cup of whole milk. Most doctors will green-light whole-milk yogurt, cottage cheese, and hard cheese by 8 months or so (or even sooner), and some will even allow an occasional sip of whole milk before the first birthday or a splash mixed in baby's cereal (but ask first). When it does come time to move on to cow's milk, serve up whole milk until the second birthday, unless the doctor has suggested transitioning instead to reduced-fat milk (aka 2 percent).

can't always make him drink—especially if he's emotionally ready to move on. If you've exhausted the options for winning him back over to breast, consider pumping at least some of his daily quota of breast milk and serving it up in a bottle. More work for you, but more freedom of movement for him—and that might be especially appealing during those extra wriggly times of the day. Save breastfeeding sessions for when he's mellow or too sleepy to put up a fight. He's never taken a bottle? No point in starting now—after all, the AAP recommends weaning from the bottle at 12 months anyway. Use a cup for breast milk—just make sure he gets enough this way.

If you do end up weaning to formula, try to do so gradually. Gradual weaning will allow baby time to increase his intake of formula before he gives up breast milk entirely (you can mix them to start). And it will give your breasts the chance to put the brakes on production slowly, which will help you avoid painful engorgement. (See page 490 for tips on weaning. If your baby absolutely refuses to take any breastfeedings, see page 495 for making abrupt weaning easier.)

Fussy Eating Habits

"When I first introduced solids, my daughter seemed to lap up everything I gave her. But lately, it seems she won't eat anything but puffs, and if I'm lucky, a little banana."

So your baby's gone from "open wide" to "clamped shut"? That often happens once the novelty of spoon-fed solids (and sitting still for them) wears off. Happily, there's no need to worry about her suddenly picky ways—for three reassuring reasons. First, healthy little ones who are allowed to eat to appetite tend to eat as much as they need to grow and thrive. Second, those nibbles typically add up faster than parents usually realize. Third, your baby is still getting the bulk of her nutrients from breast milk or formula. While a variety of solids help round out her nutritional requirements—and new tastes and textures provide valuable eating experience—breast milk or formula can still pick up the slack.

As she passes the 9-month mark and begins to close in on her first birthday, your baby's requirement for breast milk or formula will ultimately decrease, and solids will ultimately become the mainstay of her daily diet—a nutritional must-have, instead of the nutritional gravy they are now. Even then, as long as she's getting the growing job done, you can leave stress about her solids intake (how much, which kind) off the menu. Instead, try these feeding strategies for pumping up your picky eater's nutritional intake . . . and maybe even have her opening wide to a wider range of foods:

Let 'em eat bread . . . or cereal, or bananas, or whatever food she favors. Many babies and toddlers seem to be on a food-of-the-week (or month) plan, refusing to eat anything but a single selection during that time. And it's fine to respect your little one's dietary preferences and aversions, even when taken to extremes: cereal for breakfast, lunch, and dinner, for example. Eventually, if given a chance to do so on her own—and if offered a wide variety of foods to choose from—your baby will expand her repertoire of tastes.

. . . but maybe not cake. Tiny tummies can handle only so much food—and let's face it, given a choice between filling up on cookies or steamed carrots, few babies will reach for the carrot (and really, would you?). Offer only healthy foods, and your baby (and later, toddler) will have no choice but to choose a healthy food every time . . . even if it's the same healthy food over and over again.

Add on when you can. While you shouldn't push food on your baby, there's nothing wrong with trying to sneak it by her. Serve her cereal and slip in a serving of fruit in the form of a diced banana, applesauce, or cooked, diced peaches. If it's bread your baby craves, spread it with mashed banana or ricotta, or melt a thin slice of swiss on it. Or turn it into French toast. Or try baking and buying breads that incorporate other nutritious ingredients, such as pumpkin, carrot, cheese, or fruit.

Offer what you're having. A side of cauliflower with that cereal? Sure, why not? Babies often clamor more for what their parents are eating, so offer—but never push—foods from your plate that she's developmentally ready for.

Move up from mush. Your little one's pickiness may simply be her way of telling you that she's had it with the baby stuff. Changing to chunky foods and finger foods that are soft enough for her to manage but intriguing enough in taste and texture to satisfy her maturing palate may turn her from fussy to epicure-ious. Variety may spice things up, too (see page 451).

Turn the tables. Perhaps it's just a newly emerging streak of stubborn independence that's keeping her mouth zipped at mealtime. Hand her the responsibility of feeding, and she may open her mouth eagerly to a wide range of food experiences she would never consider taking from the spoon you offer. (For appropriate choices for the self-feeding baby, see page 430.)

Don't drown her appetite. Many babies (and toddlers) eat very little because they're drinking too much juice, formula, or breast milk. At this point, your baby should have no more than 4 to 6 ounces of fruit juice (if any) and no more than 24 to 30 ounces of formula a day. If you're breastfeeding, you don't know exactly how much milk she's taking, but you can be pretty sure that nursing her more than 4 or 5 times a day will rain on her appetite for solids.

Attack snacks. Snacks play a big role when you're filling a little tummy, but they can also easily sabotage a baby's appetite for meals and suck parents into a snack cycle that's hard to break. Case in point: What do parents do when baby snubs breakfast? Ply her with snacks all morning, of course, which means she isn't likely to have any appetite for lunch. And what happens after lunch is turned down? Baby's hungry again in the afternoon, snacking continues, and there's no room for dinner. So try to limit snacks to one in midmorning and one in midafternoon (a bedtime snack can be added, too, as part of the nightly bedtime ritual, but it's not a must). Serve snacks seated for safety's sake—as well as to nix nonstop nibbling.

Leave pressure off the menu. Do you tend to pull out all the pushing, prodding, pleading, and coaxing stops when your baby fusses at mealtime? Time to shut down the "choo-choo train" service and let your baby choose when to open that tunnel wide and when to clamp it shut. For your little one to grow up with healthy feelings about food, she needs to eat because she's hungry (not because you want her to) and stop because she's full. In other words, let her appetite call the shots—even when it's calling it quits after just a few bites.

Self-Feeding

"Every time the spoon comes near my baby, he grabs for it. If his bowl is near enough, he dips his fingers in and makes a mess trying to feed himself. He's getting nothing to eat, and I'm getting frustrated."

Your little one is dipping his sticky fingers into the bowl of independence—and, unfortunately for your kitchen floor, the bowl of mashed squash, too. Let him. It's time to spoon up what he's hungry for: a chance to feed himself . . . or at least attempt to feed himself.

Stick with Some Cereal

Has your baby moved on from the strained and the bland to new and interesting tastes and textures? Good for your fledgling foodie! But in your excitement to encourage variety and adventure in the high chair, don't forget to include some iron-enriched cereal in your baby's daily diet. As ho-hum as it may be, it's the easiest way (unless your baby is formula-fed) of ensuring adequate iron intake—and it can be added to fruits, veggies, yogurt, and other cereals as well. Baby's not a cereal fan? No need to force the mush. Just make sure your baby is getting some iron-rich foods daily or a supplement (see page 449).

Start by spooning up another spoon, one to call his own. True, he probably won't be able to do much more with his spoon than wave it around, and if he does manage to actually fill it up with food, he's likely to haul it up to his face upside down (or to come in for a landing closer to his nose than his mouth). But that's not the point at this point in his development—being involved in his own mealtimes is, no matter how messy a proposition it becomes.

Hopefully, wielding his own spoon will make him less grabby about yours—and busily occupied enough with his own challenging project (fill spoon, bring to the vicinity of the open mouth) that he may make your project of feeding him less challenging.

Still missing the mark? Try offering him finger foods (or a mesh feeder he can safely munch soft fruits and veggies from) to self-feed while you spoon-feed him, too. Between a spoon to wave, a few finger foods to nibble on, a feeder to suck on, and a spouted cup to take swigs from, your little food freedom fighter should be a lot more amenable to being fed. If not, let him have it his way—let him self-feed full-time. Mealtimes will take longer and be messier, but just think of those splats and splatters as a learning experience (as in, you learn to spread a splat mat on the floor under baby's high chair before every meal). Remember, too, that for your baby, eating isn't just a matter of taste and nutrition, but of feeling food, smelling food, squishing food, and smearing food.

That said, when self-feeding dissolves into all play and no eating (some play is part of the feeding game), pick up the spoon and take over the meal. If your baby balks, it's time to wipe the carrots off his chin and the avocado from between his fingers and end the meal.

Strange Stools

"When I changed my baby's diaper today, I was really puzzled. Her BM seemed to be filled with grains of sand. But she never plays in a sandbox."

Just when you're getting bored with changing diapers, another surprise turns up in one. Sometimes it's easy to figure out what went into baby to produce the change in her poop. Halloween orange color? Probably the carrots. Frightening red? Maybe beets or beet juice. Black specks or strands? Bananas. Small, dark foreign objects? Usually mashed blueberries or chopped raisins. Light green pellets? Perhaps peas. Yellow ones? Corn. Seeds? Very likely tomatoes, cucumbers, or melon from which the seeds were not completely removed.

Because babies don't chew (they barely gum food before they swallow) and their digestive tracts are relatively short and not fully mature, what goes in often comes out largely unchanged in color and texture. Sandy stools, such as those in your baby's diaper, are fairly common, not because babies snack from the sandbox (though they will, given a chance) but because certain foods—particularly Cheerios and similar oat cereals, and pears—often appear sandy once they've passed through the digestive tract.

So before you panic at the sight of what's filling your baby's diaper, think about what's been filling her tummy. If you're still puzzled, take a picture to show (or email or text) the doctor.

Still Hairless

"Our daughter was born without hair and still barely has more than a light coating of peach fuzz. When will she get some hair?"

Hair today? Not always for babies this age—particularly those who are fair and destined (one day!) to have light locks. Hair tomorrow? Well . . . maybe day after tomorrow. Some cuties stay cue-ball bare throughout the first year and often well into the second. Happily, hairlessness (like toothlessness) isn't permanent, and doesn't predict a sparse hair supply later on in life. While you're waiting for your sprout to sprout some hair—at least enough to hold a barrette or two—look at the upside of slow-to-grow hair: easier shampoos, no tears over tangles.

Still Toothless

"Our baby is almost 9 months old and still doesn't have a single tooth. What could be holding up his teething?"

There are plenty of 9-month-olds who are all gums—and there are even a few who finish their first year without a single tooth to help them bite into their birthday cake. Though the average baby cuts a first tooth at 7 months, the range is from 2 months (occasionally earlier) to 12 (sometimes later). Late teething is usually hereditary and is no reflection on your baby's development—though you can probably expect the second round of teeth to come in later, too. Eventually, the tooth fairy comes to visit every baby, so enjoy these yummy gummy grins while you can.

By the way, being toothless doesn't interfere with a baby's ability to move on to chunkier foods. First teeth are for biting down on food, not for chewing. Until molars make their appearance midway through the second year, your little one will use his gums for mashing up food—and it's the same process for toothed and toothless babies.

And here's another bit of tooth trivia (and another example of the "every baby is different" rule). After the first pair (usually the bottom, but occasionally the top) poke through, other pearlies may pop up relatively quickly (within weeks), or there may be a lull in teething that lasts months. That's normal, too—and no reflection on your baby's development.

Teething Pain and Night Crying

"Our baby, who was sleeping through the night, has now started waking from teething pain. We don't want to let her cry, but we also don't want to encourage her waking. What should we do?"

It's true: Babies don't need a lot of encouragement to start (or restart) a night-waking habit. A few nights of

How to Care for Baby Hair

Whether it's a few silky strands or a thick tangle of curls, the long and short of baby hair is that it comes attached to babies—and babies (especially active older babies) aren't known for their love of hair care. Shampoos? No thanks—I'd rather squirm. Comb-outs? I think I'll pass. Brush and style? You're kidding, right?

Fortunately, less is more when it comes to baby hair care. Here's how to get maximum grooming with minimum struggle:

- **Shampoo only as needed.** Define "as needed"? About 2 or 3 times a week is plenty—though you can clearly add an extra shampoo on those days when baby decides to try using a full bowl of oatmeal as a hat. Many babies—especially those with African hair, or those with very dry hair—are best off with just a weekly shampoo. In between shampoo days, you can spray a little detangler on those smaller globs of stuck-on food and work them out with a wide-tooth comb.

- **Protect those peepers.** Even a "no tears" shampoo can produce tears if it gets into your little one's eyes. Protect baby's eyes by holding a washcloth across his or her forehead when shampooing and rinsing. Or—for an older baby—use a shampoo visor to keep those peepers dry. Remember, a handheld nozzle offers more control when rinsing. A plastic watering can or cup can also do the trick if your tub doesn't have a nozzle.

- **Don't tangle with tangles.** Is your baby's hair tangle prone? Untangle hair before beginning to shampoo, to prevent even worse tangles afterward. Post-shampoo, pat hair gently dry instead of rubbing. Always untangle from the ends up, keeping one hand firmly on the roots as you work, to minimize tugging.

- **Go easy on products.** Easy does it when you're trying to shampoo a squirming sweetie. So make the job as easy as possible by skipping the extra-step conditioner. Use a conditioning shampoo or, for a tough case of tangles, a spray-on detangler.

- **Choose the right tools.** Think gentle when you select combs and brushes. Baby's got thick hair? A wide-tooth comb may make wet hair comb-outs easier (and is a must-have for babies with extra-thick, frizzy, or African hair). Tight, curly hair? A brush with long, firm, and widely spaced bristles is a good choice. Little hair there? Stick with a fine-tooth comb to tame those few strands. A soft baby brush or one with plastic coated tips can also work for comb-outs on wet hair.

- **Style safely.** Let baby's hair air-dry—don't use a blow dryer on that sensitive scalp and those delicate tresses. Skip braids for now, and even if your baby girl is sporting a head full of hair, it's best to hold off on ponytails or pigtails—these styles can damage hair or even lead to patches of baldness. Clips or barrettes pose a choking risk if they're small enough (or have small enough parts), which rules out many hair accessories designed for babies. If you do use a band, clip, or barrette, always remove it before putting baby down for a nap or bedtime.

- **Make mirror magic happen.** Most babies can't get enough of that baby in the mirror (even though they have no clue who that baby is). Distract your little one from the grooming at hand by performing it in front of a mirror.

waking here, a few nights there—and bingo, sleeping through the night is just a distant dream. And that's what often happens when teething pain triggers night waking—the pain ends, the waking continues.

How to break the cycle before it gains momentum and you lose sleep? Offer comfort, by all means, but try to avoid starting a comfort habit that you'd prefer not to keep up indefinitely (say, feeding baby or bringing her into bed with you). Instead, keep comfort short, sweet, and not too addictive: a little patting, a soft lullaby, a teething ring, a quiet "It's okay, it's okay" until she begins to drift off again. Pretty soon, she'll relearn falling back to sleep on her own when she wakes during the night, and all of you will get a better night's sleep.

If she seems to be in a lot of teething-related pain at night, ask her doctor about giving her a dose of baby acetaminophen or ibuprofen before she goes to bed (also ask before applying numbing gel or giving homeopathic teething tablets; see page 322 for more teething tips). And check in with the doctor, too, if there seem to be any signs of illness—an ear infection, for example—that can get worse at night.

If your baby seems to be waking for reasons other than teething pain and you're wondering why she's suddenly regressing when it comes to sleep, see page 417.

Pulling Up

"Our baby just learned to pull up. He seems to love it for a few minutes but then starts screaming. Could standing be hurting him?"

Now that he's figured out how to pull up, your baby may have a leg up— make that two legs up—on two footed mobility. Exciting, until he realizes—as he does after just a few minutes—that he's all pulled up with no place to go, and with no way of getting down. In other words, he's standing stranded— and that's frustrating stuff. Like most babies who've just learned to stand, he's stuck standing until he falls, collapses, or is helped down (cue the screaming). And that's where you come in. As soon as you notice frustration setting in, gently help him down to a sitting position. Slowly does it—so that he can get the idea of how to do it himself, a skill he's likely to master within a few days to a few weeks. In the meantime, expect to spend a lot of time coming to the rescue of your stranded standing sweetie. Calls for help may come (inconveniently) during the middle of the night, too, since many babies are so pumped about pulling up that they start practicing standing while they're supposed to be sleeping (and sometimes even when they're half asleep), leaving them stranded standing in their cribs in the wee hours. As you would during the day, rescue your standing man, tenderly helping him lie back down. Hopefully he'll soon get the hang of plopping back down on his own.

One fun way to practice pulling up and sitting back down is in your lap— especially enjoyable if you turn the practice into a silly game.

"My baby is trying to pull up on everything in the house. She's excited about her accomplishment, but I'm a nervous wreck. How can I make sure that she's safe pulling up?"

First, your baby took in the world from the secure cocoon of your arms. Then, from a variety of other relatively safe venues—infant seat, swing, play yard. Then, on all fours. And finally, from two feet. Endlessly thrilling for her—and endlessly worrisome

Not Pulling Up

Baby's not pulling up or not reaching other milestones that the other babies you know are hitting? Don't worry, your little one is probably busy perfecting other skills right now. He or she will likely get to it soon enough. See the facing page for more.

for you. Pulling up and (coming soon!) cruising open up a whole new world for your little one, along with a whole lot of risks, from minor tumbles to major furniture toppling.

Her job as a curious almost-toddler is to explore this whole new world. Your job is to make sure she stays safe while she's at it. To help with that, see the tips beginning on page 391 for the lowdown on childproofing now that your baby's upwardly mobile. And don't forget that your baby's best defense is your vigilance—so make sure supervision is constant, and when it comes to judging her skills (or her lack of judgment), always overestimate.

To prevent slips and trips, be sure that papers, open books, and slippery magazines are not left lying around on the floor and that spills on smooth-surfaced floors are wiped up quickly. And to be sure her feet won't trip her up, keep her barefoot or in skidproof socks or slippers rather than in smooth-soled shoes or slippery socks.

Flat Feet

"My baby's arches look totally flat when he stands up. Could he have flat feet?"

In baby feet, flatness (like cuteness) is the rule, not the exception. And it's a rule that you're not likely to find an exception to. There are several reasons: First of all, since young babies don't do much walking, the muscles in their feet haven't been exercised enough to fully develop the arches. Second, a pad of fat fills the arch, making it difficult to discern, particularly in chubby babies. And when babies begin to walk, they stand with feet apart to achieve balance, putting more weight on the arch and giving the foot a flatter appearance.

Chances are that your baby's flat-footed look will slowly diminish over the years, and by the time he's finished growing, his feet will sport a well-formed arch. Around 20 to 30 percent of fully grown feet will end up flat, but that's not something that can be predicted now—or that would be considered a problem later.

Walking Too Early?

"Our baby wants to practice walking all the time, holding on to our hands. Will walking before she's ready to do it on her own hurt her legs?"

Your baby's next step on the road to walking—taking steps while holding on—may be a strain on your backs, but not on her legs. Babies have a knack for knowing when they're ready to take on a new skill—and when they're not ready, they'll let you know (say, by staging a sit-down). If she's happy practicing her steps, her legs are happy, too. Plus, assisted walking allows her legs to flex the same muscles she'll need to walk solo—and if she does it barefoot, she'll be strengthening her feet, as well. Another reassuring FYI: Despite what you might have heard, early walking (assisted or un-) won't cause bowing, a standard characteristic of baby and toddler legs no matter when those first steps are taken.

So as long as your backs hold out, let her walk to her legs' content. Or let her try out a push toy.

A baby who doesn't want to practice walking at this stage, of course, shouldn't be pushed into it. As with other aspects of development, just follow your half-pint-size leader.

Slow to Sit, Slow to Go?

"Our baby has begun only recently to sit well by himself, and he hasn't started trying to get around either. Does that mean he'll keep lagging developmentally?"

Maybe you've heard this one before, but maybe (like many parents) you need to hear it over and over again to help you shake those developmental doubts: Every baby is different, and every baby develops different skills at a different pace. Much of the timing for your one-of-a-kind cutie's development comes courtesy of his unique blend of genes, which are programmed with precision to determine when he'll master each skill. Chances are his development hasn't been (and won't be) uniform across the board—most babies are faster in some areas and slower in others. One, for instance, may be speedy with social and language skills (smiling, saying words) but lagging in large motor skills (like pulling up). Another might walk (again, a large motor skill) by 9 months but not finesse a pincer grasp (a fine-motor skill) until after his first birthday. What's more, the rate at which motor skills large or small develop isn't related in any way to intelligence. Some brainy babies sit early, some sit late.

While nature holds most of the developmental cards, nurture (and circumstances) can stand in the way of skills. That's definitely true of sitting: If your baby spent a lot of time on his back, buckled into an infant seat, or

When in Doubt, Check It Out

The doctor says your baby's development, while on the slow side, is still normal, but you still can't shake the nagging feeling that something's not quite right. Chances are, all's well within normal, and the best way to put those understandable fears to rest is to seek a referral to a developmental specialist. Occasionally a pediatrician, who sees babies only for brief evaluations, can miss signs of abnormally slow development that a parent sees or senses and that an expert doing a lengthier workup can pick up. A consultation with a specialist serves two purposes. First, if all checks out fine, worry can be checked. Second, if there does turn out to be a problem, early intervention can make a huge difference, often getting a slowly developing baby back on track. When in doubt, get it checked out.

snuggled in a sling, he may not have had much of a chance to figure out how to get himself into a sitting position, and that could have slowed him down. Weight can also weigh on certain skills—a roly-poly baby may find rolling over more challenging than a lightweight one, while a baby on solid stems may find stability on two feet sooner than one on spindly legs.

As long as development falls within the wide range considered normal and progresses from one step to the next, doing even most things later than other little ones is not usually a matter for concern. When a baby routinely reaches developmental milestones late, however, it's smart to check in with the doctor.

Fear of Strangers

"Our little girl used to be happy being held by anyone. Now she freaks out whenever someone new tries to be friendly—and she won't even let her grandparents come near her. What's going on?"

Has your once pliable infant suddenly started taking a pass on Pass the Baby? Being antisocial with strangers may seem strange behavior for someone who's always gone happily to the nearest lap, but this social snubbery isn't snobbery—it's a sign of maturity, and it's perfectly normal at this stage of development. When your little one was younger, she was a lot less picky about the peeps she hung out with. Now that she's a tad older and a wee bit wiser, she's clued in to the fact that mommy and daddy are the most important people in her life. Everyone else—even the grandparents she once adored—takes a backseat, and preferably, from her perspective, a seat as far away as possible.

The official term for this phenomenon is stranger anxiety, and it can begin at 6 months or even earlier, though it usually peaks around 9 months or so. This sudden shyness and newfound clinginess will pass, and in time your daughter will realize that she doesn't have to choose between you and others. But until then, don't push her to be Miss Congeniality. You'll have much better luck (and many fewer tears) if you let her socialize at her own pace, on her own terms.

In the meantime, give family members and friends a heads-up on what's going on in your little one's head, which will also help head off any hurt feelings. Tell them it's not personal—your baby is just going through an anxious phase and needs time to warm up. Coach them on how to woo your cutie.

For example, suggest that instead of trying to pick her up right away, they talk quietly and move closer at a snail's pace. You can also invite relatives and friends to play peekaboo with her or entice her with a toy while you hold your baby on your lap, the place she feels safest.

If that doesn't melt her resistance, be patient. Forcing her to come face-to-face with her anxiety—and those strangers—will only feed it. It'll be less stressful for everyone if you let your suddenly shrinking violet decide when and where to open up. And eventually she will.

Comfort Objects

"For the last couple of months, our baby has become more and more attached to his little monkey blanket. He even drags it around when he's crawling. Does needing a security object mean he's insecure?"

Your baby is a little insecure—but he has his reasons. With independent mobility (whether in the form of crawling, scooting, cruising, or—eventually—walking) comes the realization that he's not just an extension of you and your arms, not just a part of the mommy-and-daddy package. He's his own separate little person, who can separate (or be separated) from you at any time. Like many discoveries he's making right now, that epiphany is equal parts exhilarating and unsettling. How does he strike out on all fours without giving up the comforting security your two arms have always offered? Simple: by bringing along a friend. This comfort (or transitional, or security) object, aka "lovey," serves as a mommy or daddy substitute—a surrogate who can fill in as needed (say, when he's busy playing and you're busy working). Usually the object is

When Crib Slats Become Foot Traps

Baby arms, hands, feet, and legs are sweet as can be. Not so sweet is when those luscious limbs get stuck in between the crib slats. It happens to some babies more than others (usually it's the wriggly ones), and it happens more often as little ones get bigger, more active, and more curious. Often, babies are able to free their limbs on their own, and sometimes they'll cry to be freed (usually it just takes a little help from a grown-up friend). But once in a while, a knee, thigh, arm, or elbow gets wedged in so tightly that there's no easy way out. If that happens at your home, a little lotion or oil can help you and your baby out of a tight spot.

Thinking of putting up bumpers to keep the crib slats from trapping those baby parts? There are two good reasons not to. For one, bumpers won't always prevent baby's legs from getting caught (babies active enough to move around the crib are usually strong enough to kick bumpers off or get wedged between the slats above the bumper). For another, the AAP recommends keeping bumpers out of cribs altogether (even once baby's older). Bumpers, like soft bedding and pillows, have been shown to increase the risk for sleep-related deaths, including SIDS, entrapment, and suffocation.

So keep the bumpers out of the crib and keep this reassuring message in mind: While it's possible for a baby to get an arm or a leg stuck between crib slats, it's virtually impossible to break a limb by doing so. Which means that the experience will be (at worst) uncomfortable and upsetting, but certainly not life- (or limb-) threatening.

---

small and snuggly (an easy-to-clutch blanket or stuffed animal), though some babies latch on to something less obvious, like a cloth diaper, a washcloth, a t-shirt, or even a decidedly uncuddly toy. Some comfort objects come and go, others are clung to for years. Often, little ones give up their security blankets or toys by the time they're 2 to 5 years old, though a few children end up attached through the school years—and possibly even toting their tattered friend to college (discreetly, of course). Parting with a lovey—whether by choice or by necessity (as when it disintegrates into a pile of threads or puffs of cotton)—is often tough, but sometimes barely noticed.

For now, let your baby have the security he craves—no need to set limits on its use except for safety's sake (blankets and stuffed animals don't belong in cribs) and practicality (blankets and stuffed animals aren't so cuddly when they've been dunked in the tub). Also, for everyone's comfort, consider these comfort object policies:

Keep it clean. This is easier to do if you start from the early stages of your baby's devotion: Wash the object often, before he becomes just as attached to its smell as he is to its sight and feel. Can't pry his fingers off his monkey lovey during waking hours? Wash it while he's asleep.

Save a spare. Invest in a duplicate lovey (or two) to keep in reserve and swap it for the original whenever you need to wash one so that they wear evenly. Plus, now you have a backup in case the unthinkable happens (the lovey is inadvertently dropped at the mall, never to be seen again).

Heap on the love. Bring on the cuddles and snuggles as much as possible so your little one gets the comfort and attention he needs from you. But don't worry that his love of his lovey is a sign that he's not getting enough love from you—it's just that he needs a little something-something on the side.

Some babies never latch on to a comfort object of any kind—or even a comfort habit of any kind—and that's normal, too.

ALL ABOUT:
Games Babies Play

Babies love to play games, especially when someone else (you!) is in on the fun. But peekaboo and this little piggy do more than just bring squeals of delight and entertain. They also improve socialization skills and teach important concepts such as object permanence (peekaboo), coordination of words and actions (The Itsy-Bitsy Spider, pat-a-cake), counting skills (One, Two, Buckle My Shoe), and language skills (eyes-nose-mouth).

Chances are that even if you haven't heard a nursery game in decades, many of the ones your parents played with you will come back to you now that you're a parent yourself. If they don't, ask for a replay (a parent never forgets) or turn to Google or your message board buddies.

Here are a few that might ring a baby bell:

Peekaboo. The classic of all classics: Cover your face (with your hands, the corner of a blanket, a piece of clothing, a menu in a restaurant, or by hiding behind a curtain or the foot of the crib) and say, "Where's Daddy?" Then uncover your face and say, "Peekaboo, I see you!" An alternative version: Say "peekaboo" when you cover your face, "I see you" when you uncover it. Either way, be ready to repeat and repeat until you collapse . . . most babies have an insatiable appetite for this game.

Pat-a-cake (or other clapping games). There are plenty of variations on clapping games—and babies are fans of each and every one. How to play? Put your baby's hands in yours, and try bringing them together in a clapping motion. At first, your baby's hands will probably not open wide enough to clap (and for little fist-suckers, may end up in the mouth), but in time the ability to hold the hands flat will finally come, probably not until the end of the year. Until then, you can do the clapping—and the singing, of course. Clap to that time-honored favorite, pat-a-cake: "Pat-a-cake, pat-a-cake, baker's man, bake me a cake as fast as you can. Mix it, and pat it, and mark it with a B, and put it in the oven for baby and me!" (Or substitute baby's name, as in, "and mark it with a C and put it in the oven for Caitlin and me.") Or add a hiding game to the clapping by singing, "Clap your hands, one-two-three, play a clapping game with me. Now your hands have gone away, find your hands so we can play." Or you can try clapping baby's feet, for a change of pace. And don't forget a chorus of "yay!" at the end of each round.

The Itsy-Bitsy Spider. Use your fingers—the thumb of one hand to the pointer finger of the other—to simulate a spider climbing up an invisible web, and sing: "The itsy-bitsy spider went up the water spout." Then, use your fingers to imitate rain falling, and continue: "Down came the rain and washed the spider out." Throw your arms up and out for "Out came the sun and dried up all the rain." And then back to square one, the spider goes back up the web and you end with "And the itsy-bitsy spider went up the spout again." You can hold baby's hands while you play, too.

This Little Piggy. Take baby's thumb or big toe and start with "This little piggy went to market." Move on to the next finger or toe, "This little piggy stayed home." And the next, "This little piggy had roast beef" (or if you're a vegetarian, "pasta"), fourth finger, "This little piggy had none." As you sing the final line, "And this little piggy cried wee, wee, wee, all the way home," run your fingers up baby's arm or leg to under the arms or neck, gently tickling all the way. If your baby doesn't like tickling, just use a stroking motion instead. Expect endless squeals from your little piggy.

So Big. Ask, "How big is baby?" (or use child's name, the dog's name, or a sibling's name), help your baby spread his or her arms as wide as possible, and exclaim, "So big!"

Eyes-nose-mouth. Take both baby's hands in yours, touch one to each of your eyes, then both to your nose, then to your mouth (where you end with a kiss), naming each feature as you move along: "Eyes, nose, mouth, kiss." Nothing teaches these body parts faster.

Ring Around the Rosie, baby edition. Make this preschool favorite baby-friendly by adapting it for the lap. Hold your baby in a standing position on your lap and sing, "Ring around the rosie, a pocket full of posies, ashes, ashes, we all fall down!" at which point you help him or her plop down to sitting. A variation is to substitute "hopscotch, hopscotch" for "ashes, ashes" and to pop your lap (and baby) up at each one. You can also play a traditional Ring Around the Rosie while holding baby in your arms—standing and turning in a circle before plopping down on the floor together.

One, Two, Buckle My Shoe. When climbing stairs or counting fingers, sing, "One, two, buckle my shoe. Three, four, close the door. Five, six, pick up sticks. Seven, eight, close the gate. Nine, ten, start again."

Pop Goes the Weasel. You can turn slowly in a circle with baby if you're standing, or rock him or her back and forth if you're seated, as you sing, "All around the mulberry bush, the monkey chased the weasel. The monkey thought it was all in fun . . ." Then, "pop goes the weasel!" as you gently bounce baby with the pop. Once baby is familiar with the song, wait a moment or two before the bounce and the "punch line" to give him or her a chance to do the popping. Remember, a baby's reaction time is likely to be delayed a few beats to allow for processing.

CHAPTER 15

The Tenth Month

The only thing about baby that might be slowing slightly this month is appetite—at least, any appetite for sitting out long stints in the high chair. Most babies-on-the-go would much rather explore the living room (and the kitchen, and the hallway closet) than the high chair tray. Like any good explorer, baby's determined to reach previously uncharted territory—which often means doing some climbing. Unfortunately, the ability to climb up comes long before the ability to climb back down—often leaving baby stranded. Baby understands "no" but may just be starting to test your limits by defying it—or may already be a master at tuning the word out. Memory improves, and fears (which go hand in hand with increased cognitive skills, aka smarts) begin to multiply—for instance, of the vacuum cleaner, the lawn mower, or the blender (not so smooth if you're a fan of smoothies).

Feeding Your Baby: Eating Well for Beginners

During the first few months of life, your little one's nutritional needs were fully filled with mama's milk or formula. Then solids were added to the menu—though really any you were able to shovel into that sweet smiley mouth were just gravy (make that sweet potatoes), served up more for the experience of eating than for covering any nutritional bases (those were still conveniently covered by the liquids in baby's diet). Now, that's about to change. After all, once your baby's first birthday rolls

around, most nutritional requirements should be served up by sources other than the bottle, cup, or your breasts—even if you plan to continue breastfeeding into the second year and beyond.

Happily, feeding your little one well will still be pretty easy—a lot easier than it may be once he or she realizes you can get fries with that (and chips, and candy). It won't take much to spoon up the best for your baby in the months to come. Don't bother worrying about serving sizes or numbers of

Baby Basics at a Glance: Tenth Month

Sleeping. Your little snoozer will be sleeping an average of 10 to 12 hours per night and taking 2 naps during the day, each around 1½ to 2 hours long, for an average total of around 14 hours each day. The good news? Nearly 75 percent of babies are sleeping through the night by now. If yours is still part of the 25 percent, and you're ready to move on to sleep teaching, see page 349.

Eating. Breast milk or formula is still the most important part of baby's diet, but solids are beginning to take on more significance, so try to make them count nutritionally.

- Breast milk. Your baby will nurse around 4 times a day (some babies will breastfeed more often). Total intake will still tally up at somewhere between 24 and 30 ounces of breast milk a day, though as more solids are added, baby will drink less.

- Formula. Your baby will probably drink 3 to 4 bottles a day, filled with 7 to 8 ounces of formula, for a total of 24 to 30 ounces per day (some babies drink less formula more often). As more solids are added to the diet, baby will drink less—closer to the 24-ounce mark.

- Solids. Baby will probably lap up around ¼ to ½ cup each of grains, fruit, and veggies every day (or twice a day if your baby's a big eater), ¼ to ½ cup of dairy foods per day, ¼ to ½ cup of protein foods per day, and 3 to 4 ounces of juice per day (juice is always optional). Don't worry if your baby isn't following these measurements precisely. In fact, as long as baby is gaining weight and is happy and healthy, there's no need to get caught up in measurements at all.

Playing. Time to bring out the push toys (look for ones that are sturdy and won't tip over) and riding toys (wide, low-to-the-ground ones, such as a tot-size car or fire truck on wheels)—as well as any other playthings that encourage physical development (play tunnels to crawl through, large balls to roll, stacks of pillows that baby can climb over). Tap in to your baby's creative side by providing musical toys (toy keyboard, xylophone, drums, bells, and rhythm sticks) and maybe even an art supply or two (experiment with a large chunky crayon and a big sheet of paper to see what your pint-size Picasso can do). And now that baby's brain is getting more and more sophisticated, he or she will squeal with delight at toys that bring surprises (where did the ball roll to?). Blocks, activity cubes and tables, and stuffed animals are still favorites, also, and the way baby plays with them is becoming more sophisticated. Stacking toys and shape sorters, too—just don't expect your little one to finesse either yet without your help.

Bring Baby to the Table

Baby's feeding schedule and your own don't quite match up yet (early-bird special's not really your style)? Or you haven't managed to figure out how to spoon yogurt into your baby's mouth and salad into yours without mixing up the two? Until your little eater's an accomplished self-feeder, you may want to continue serving his or her main meals separately from yours. But that doesn't mean baby can't sit in on your meals—if only for a serving of sociability (and maybe, a pile of shredded cheese or a slice of avocado). So when you can pull it off, pull your baby's high chair tableside while you're eating. Provide a sippy or straw cup of water and an unbreakable bowl or plate (one that can't be upended) and spoon, and a few finger food selections. Include baby in the conversation—and maybe an occasional round of peekaboo with your napkin—but don't feel like you're obligated to perform dinner theater (it's your turn to eat). And for your romance's sake, reserve some tables for two—two parents, that is.

servings. Instead, provide a variety of healthy foods and a fun, relaxed mealtime atmosphere (one where pushing and prodding are never featured on the menu). Then sit back and watch healthy eating happen . . . and a future of healthy eating habits take shape.

Healthy Baby Eating

Babies are all over the appetite map at this stage of the game, when eating is still more for practice and pleasure than for filling nutritional requirements. Some babies eat a lot all the time, some eat very little most of the time, others eat like a mouse one day and a horse the next. Some are varied and adventurous eaters (maniacs for meat, voracious for veggies), others are particularly picky (cereal and bananas only, please—and don't even think about mixing them). But presented with a wide variety of wholesome foods and allowed to follow their appetites (whether it leads to a mostly empty bowl or a mostly full one), almost all healthy babies eat as much as they need to grow and thrive. No need to keep a running tab—or to cram a certain number of servings of each food group into your baby every day. Not only is that a sure way to drive yourself crazy, it's bound to set the stage for food squabbles in the high chair and, later, at the table. So as you introduce more and more foods into your baby's repertoire, resist the urge to push, measure, or count servings, and instead aim for a mix of good-for-baby foods from the following categories:

Protein. Baby's still getting most of the protein he or she needs from breast milk or formula. But since that picture will change once those first birthday candles are blown out, now's a good time for baby to start sampling other protein foods. As they're introduced, these can include eggs, meat, chicken, fish, and tofu. Calcium foods (especially whole milk cottage cheese and ricotta) and some grains (see below) can double as excellent protein sources.

Calcium foods. Again, baby's getting the lion cub's share of calcium from breast or bottle, but baby-friendly calcium foods, such as whole-milk cheese (cheddar, muenster, edam, havarti, baby swiss, colby, jack, for example) and whole-milk yogurt, ricotta, and cottage cheese are yummy, nutritious additions, and also add protein.

Whole grains and other complex carbohydrates. These high chair favorites will add essential vitamins and minerals, as well as some protein, to baby's daily intake. Good options, as they're introduced, include whole-grain bread, whole-grain cereal (baby cereal for spoon-feeding, bite-size cereal for self-feeding), whole-grain pasta (bite-size is typically a big hit), brown rice or quinoa (pronounced keen-wa), lentils, beans, peas, or edamame (soybeans, which are also high in protein).

Green leafy and yellow vegetables and yellow fruit. There are dozens of delicious vitamin A–rich fruits and vegetables under the green and yellow rainbow—experiment to see which ones your baby likes. Some to choose from: winter squash, sweet potatoes, carrots (look for yellow and purple ones, in addition to the standard orange), yellow peaches, apricots, cantaloupe, mango, broccoli, and kale.

Vitamin C foods. Citrus fruits and OJ are obvious sources of vitamin C, and most doctors green-light them after the eighth month. Baby can also get an A+ in C from mango, melon, kiwi, broccoli, cauliflower, sweet potato, and many other high chair favorites. Keep in mind, too, that most baby foods and juices are enriched with vitamin C— read labels to be sure.

Other fruits and vegetables. Still room in that cute little tummy? Fill it up with any of the following: unsweetened applesauce, banana, peas or green beans, and potatoes.

High-fat foods. Babies who get most of their calories from breast milk or formula get all the fat and cholesterol they need. As they switch to a more varied diet and spend less time at breast or bottle, it's important to make sure that fat and cholesterol intake doesn't dip too low. That's why most dairy products (cottage cheese, yogurt, hard cheese) you serve baby should be full-fat or made from whole milk. You can also add a healthy dose of fat by serving avocado, or cooking with canola or olive oil. Unhealthy fats (those found in fried and many processed foods) are another story, however. Loading baby up with those hard-to-digest fats can lead to an unbalanced diet, unneeded pounds, and tummy troubles. It can also set up unhealthy eating habits that'll be hard to break later on.

Iron-rich foods. Bottle-fed babies get their full share of iron from fortified formula, but after 4 months, breastfed babies need another source. Fortified baby cereal can fill the bill easily, and additional iron can come from iron-rich foods such as meat, egg yolks, wheat germ, whole-grain breads and cereals, and cooked dried peas and other legumes as they are introduced into the diet. Serving up iron-rich foods with a side of vitamin C (a sip of fortified juice or a little mango alongside baby's oatmeal, for instance) increases absorption of this important mineral.

Omega-3 fatty acids. Part of the family of essential fatty acids, omega-3s (including DHA) are vital for your infant's growth, vision, and optimal brain development—more than living up to their headline-making reputation as baby brain food. These fabulous fats are served up naturally in breast milk, but are also used to enrich some formulas and baby foods. Once baby's eating repertoire expands, you can add other foods high in omega-3 fatty acids, such as fish (like salmon), grass-fed meat, tofu, flaxseed and canola oil, and DHA-enriched yogurt, cereal, and eggs.

Fluids. During the first 5 to 6 months of life, virtually all of a baby's fluids come from bottle or breast—no supplementary water is usually needed. Now small amounts will start to come from other sources, such as juice and juicy fruits and vegetables—as well as, of course, from sips of water. As the quantity of formula or breast milk taken begins to decrease, it's important to be sure that the total fluid intake doesn't. In hot weather it should increase, so offer water and fruit juices diluted with water when temperatures soar.

Vitamin supplement. Many doctors recommend giving a vitamin supplement. If your baby's doctor does, or if you'll feel better giving it as nutritional insurance, make sure you choose a formulation that fits your baby's needs. See page 193 for more.

Getting a Head Start on Healthy Eating Habits

With just a couple of months of solids experience logged in, your baby's eating habits are still putty in your hands (and sweet squash squeezed between those curious fingers)—but they're already beginning to form. Tastes may continue to evolve as the months and years pass, but research consistently shows that much of what is learned in the high chair sticks for a lifetime. Which means that you now have the opportunity of a lifetime (your baby's lifetime, that is) to help your little one form a future of healthy eating habits—habits that can actually help shape a longer, healthier future.

To get your little one's eating habits off to the healthiest head start possible, start with these healthy feeding basics:

Keep white out of sight most of the time. You may already know that not all carbohydrates are created equal, nutritionally speaking. Complex carbs provide a wide range of naturally occurring nutrients, nutrients that are stripped away during the refining process (the process that makes whole grains white)—and nutrients that fuel your little one's growth and development. They're rich in naturally occurring fiber, too, and keep blood sugar steady. That's a compelling case for selecting 100 percent whole-grain pasta, bread, cereal, rice, and crackers at the supermarket, and when you're mixing up muffins or whisking up waffles at home, reaching for the whole-grain flour instead of the white. A whole-grain habit that's ingrained early is likely to go the distance, helping your little one make smart food choices later on in life (as in "I'll have mine on whole wheat, please").

Hold off on cutting that sweet tooth. Babies are certainly plenty sweet without added sugar. But that's not the only reason to skip the sugary sweets for now—and even to consider them (and the mostly empty calories they offer) off the menu entirely, or mostly, until baby's birthday or even beyond. While baby taste buds may have a natural affinity for sweet—after all, breast milk is naturally sweet—they're more open to other flavors (sharp, tangy, tart, even bitter) if they haven't been sweet-talked by sugar-added treats. No need to ban bananas, peaches, or other naturally sweet baby favorites—they're a yummy way to serve up nutrients. But as you're building baby's flavor foundation, avoid sweetening everything he or she eats with fruit. Your little one may surprise you by lapping up tangy plain Greek yogurt or gobbling up whole-grain cereal without applesauce. Were you raised to expect a sweet ending to every meal—and sweets to reward every accomplishment and celebrate every occasion? Consider breaking the dessert cycle, or at least limiting it—and thinking beyond the cookie jar when it comes to rewards and celebrations. Also remember that babies who haven't sampled their first cupcake don't care a lick about frosting yet. And, it could be argued . . . that's sweet.

Save the salt but not the spice. Babies don't need salt in their foods beyond what's found there naturally—and sparing the salt now will keep your little one from craving it later (a habit that's strongly associated with an increased risk of stroke and heart disease). So skip the salt when you're preparing baby food or table foods your little one may be sampling (the rest of the family can always add a sprinkle to taste). And when choosing prepared baby or toddler food, look for ones with no salt added. But while you're holding the salt, don't hold the flavor—challenge your little one's taste buds with cinnamon, nutmeg, ginger, garlic, basil, dill, oregano, chives, pepper, and curry powder.

Mix it up with variety. Who says baby food has to be bland and boring—and taste like, well, baby food? You'll both have more fun if you mix it up at mealtime. So be adventurous—think outside the baby food box, or jar, or pouch (within age-appropriate guidelines set by the pediatrician). Try dairy products in different forms: yogurt, cottage cheese, jack, cheddar, grated parmesan. Vary vegetables and fruits beyond carrots, peas, and bananas: avocado, soft steamed cauliflower and asparagus, sweet potato cubes, minced cooked eggplant, ripe cantaloupe, mango, papaya, watermelon, and kiwi, split fresh blueberries, grated pear, the gamut of grains. Add ground flax to baby's oatmeal, go wild with wild rice (as well as black, red, and brown rice), quinoa, barley, farro, whole-wheat couscous, and whole-grain polenta, pick

Is It Done Yet?

How do you make sure that the dinner you're serving your baby isn't half baked—and potentially harboring germs that could make him or her sick? By taking your dinner's temperature (a high enough temperature means you won't be serving bacteria along with that roast or that fish). The following foods can be considered safely cooked when they reach these temperatures:

Beef, veal, or lamb roasts, chops, or steaks: medium—160°F; well done—170°F

Ground beef, veal, lamb: 160°F

Pork: 145°F

Precooked ham: 140°F

Whole chicken or turkey: 180°F

Ground chicken or turkey: 165°F

Chicken breasts: 170°F

Stuffing: cooked in bird or alone— 165°F

Fish: 145°F

Egg dishes and casseroles: 160°F

Don't have a meat thermometer handy, or you're at the mercy of a restaurant kitchen? Meat can be considered safe to eat when it's gray or brown (though if the meat was previously frozen, as in a fast-food restaurant, the color test may not be an accurate gauge of doneness). Poultry should have no traces of pink, and juices should run clear. For fish, check to be sure that it flakes and is no longer translucent (salmon should turn pale pink).

pasta made with whole wheat, brown rice, buckwheat, spelt, kamut, and other whole grains. Take on tofu (most babies love it, straight out of the container), hummus and tahini, beans and legumes of all kinds, edamame. Spicing up your baby's menu with variety now doesn't mean you'll be spared a finicky eater later (most little ones play the picky card at some point)—but it will set the table for a more adventurous (and nutritious) eating future.

Be a model eater. Want to raise a broccoli buff—or a fast-food fanatic? A sweets snubber—or a devotee of donuts? The apple—or the candy bar—doesn't usually fall far from the tree. So watch what you eat and what you don't eat—your baby is watching, too, and is likely to model your eating habits, for better or worse.

What You May Be Wondering About

Messy Eating Habits

"Our baby doesn't eat anything until she's smushed it, smashed it, and rubbed it into her hair. Shouldn't we at least try to teach her some table manners?"

Mind your baby's manners . . . or, make that, her lack of manners? Not surprising. A little one's mealtime MO is more about playing with food than it is about eating it—with at least as much ending up on her (and her clothes, her high chair, and the floor) than in her. That's because mealtimes are no longer just for filling your baby's tummy and her nutritional requirements—at least not as far as she's concerned—but are also about filling her need to explore and discover. As in the sandbox and the bathtub, baby's finding out about cause and effect, about textures, about temperature differences. When she squeezes yogurt in her fist, mashes sweet potatoes into the table, slings a glob of oatmeal from her high chair tray, rubs banana into her t-shirt, blows bubbles in her cup of water, and combs crumbled crackers through her hair, it may be a mess for you, but it's a learning experience for her.

Is your older baby even remotely ready to mind her p's and q's (and really,

does it matter if her elbows are on the table, if those elbows are coated in cheese sauce anyway)? Probably not—she's at least a year away from having the developmental ability to self-feed neatly, to use a napkin for anything but peekaboo, or to gum her food with her mouth closed. Your best strategy at this point is to model the manners you'd like to one day (one fairly distant day) see her bring to the table, and occasionally point them out ("See, I put a napkin on my lap"). She'll master them eventually.

In the meantime, while you're waiting out the messy eating habits, your first impulse might be to take control—and take over feedings. While that strategy might result in neater mealtimes, it'll also result in a frustrated baby—one who doesn't get to flex her self-feeding muscles. Instead, there are plenty of ways you can minimize the mess at mealtime without squashing all the learning fun. Here's how:

Protect. An ounce of protection is worth a pound of paper towels, and it's a lot more planet friendly. Use all the protective measures available to you: Put a splat mat under and around the base of the high chair or table, to be wiped down after the meal. Outfit baby in a wipe-clean bib that covers her front and shoulders (a spill-catching pocket, which keeps the cereal and sweet pota toes from landing on her legs and the floor, is a plus). Roll baby's sleeves up past the elbow to keep them dry and relatively clean—or, room temperature permitting, dress baby only in a diaper and bib at feeding time.

Ration. Place just a few bites in front of your baby at a time. Not only will she be overwhelmed with a whole meal at once, she's also more likely to fling half of it while munching on the other half. Add more food once she finishes her first portion.

Be proactive. You don't want to inhibit your baby's experimentation, but you also don't want to make it too easy for her to play demolition dining room. So serve meals in a bowl, rather than a flat plate from which food can be pushed off easily—and preferably, use a bowl that attaches to the high chair tray with suction (she won't be able to fling her cereal across the kitchen like a Frisbee). Or serve up food directly on her high chair tray or the table. Use a sippy cup to minimize spills, and when using a lidless cup (something you should offer often so she becomes proficient in drinking from one) put just an ounce of liquid in it at a time.

Occupy. Seems like the definition of pointless, but put a spoon in your baby's hand. True, she's likely to use it only to bang on the table (while she con tinues to use her other hand for food transport). Eventually (though not for some months to come), she'll get the idea of actually using it to eat with— and until then it may distract her from overturning her applesauce. Offering her a feeder full of banana or avocado is another way to keep her hands busy while you spoon-feed her.

Stay neutral. Babies are natural-born performers. If you respond by laughing at high chair antics, you'll only encour age more of the same. Ditto for warn ings to "stop that now!" Not only won't that curb the behavior, it'll probably step it up. The best policy: Don't com ment on her lack of table manners, but do reward her with a round of applause when she takes a few neat bites.

Call a cease-fire. When your baby spends more time playing with her food than eating it, it's meal over.

Head Banging, Rocking, and Rolling

"My baby literally bangs his head repeat edly on the side of his crib every time we put him to sleep. It seems to calm him down, but it sounds painful to us!"

Remember when you used to rock your baby all night long (and often all day long, too)? That rhythmic rock ing movement was your little one's ticket to calm back then, and it sounds like it still is now. Except that he's picked up the beat where you've left off and put his own twist on it—adding rhythmic head banging to the mix. Head banging (like head rolling, rocking, and bounc ing, all of which are also common at this age—and more common among boys than girls) is a rhythmic ritual that may stress you out but actually relieves stress for your tiny rock-and-roller. Some babies bang only when they're falling asleep, while others bang when they're bored, overstimulated, in pain (from teething, for instance, or an ear infec tion), or when they are seeking atten tion (habits like head banging speak far louder than words at this point).

A little head banging is unlikely to hurt him—first, because his not yet fully fused skull is built to take it, and second, because babies usually will use only as much force as they comfortably can handle (they're not in the head-banging game to hurt themselves). As with other rhythmic comfort habits, head banging usually stops without any parental intervention (many tots will abandon banging in a few weeks or months as they discover other ways to self-soothe, though some will continue well into the toddler years). And while you can't force your baby to give up one of these habits before he's ready—and in fact, the more attention you pay to banging, the more banging you'll get—the following tips may make it easier for both you and your baby to live with it:

- Answer that call for attention. Extra cuddles, hugs, and rocking (especially at bedtime) can help fill your baby's comfort coffers, minimizing his need to self-comfort with banging. Remember, though, that head banging is not necessarily a sign that you aren't keeping up with your baby's comfort needs—even the most well-comforted babies sometimes just need to try a little DIY.

- Rock out together. Add a beat to your baby's day—and he may not feel as compelled to beat himself up at night. Explore more acceptable (at least to you) rhythmic activities: rocking him in a glider or letting him rock himself in a baby rocker (or when he's ready, in a toddler rocking chair), letting him bang on a play keyboard or drum (or the classic spoon-on-pot), pushing him on a swing, dancing to lively music or playing pat-a-cake or other finger or hand games, especially to music. A baby movement class can also help him find his rhythm without knocking his noggin.

- Tune into triggers. Does he bang when he's overtired? Make sure he's getting the naps and nighttime sleep he needs, preferably on a consistent schedule that meets those needs. Does he bang when he's frustrated or over-stimulated? Turn the beat around, diverting him to an activity that's less stressful, more chill. A change of venue may help distract him from banging during the day, especially if it's a transfer to a padded setting, say, to a play mat on the floor.

- Make time for wind-down. Brake gradually for naps and bedtime, giving your little ball of energy adequate opportunity to wind down, relax, and release stress before he hits the crib (and his head). Seek other routes to relaxation, such as a warm bath, soft lighting and music, quiet cuddles, massage with a lavender-scented lotion, hushed lullabies, and, of course, lots of gentle rocking in your arms.

- Head off any damage. If your baby rocks or bangs in his crib, minimize the risk to furniture and walls by setting the crib on a thick rug and removing the casters so the crib won't bounce across the floor. Place the crib as far from the wall or other furniture as possible. Remember to check the crib periodically for loose bolts, too, if your baby is a banger.

- Avoid haranguing about the banging. The less fuss you make over your baby's head banging or rocking or rolling, the less you'll see of these behaviors—and the sooner they'll stop for good. Intervene as needed, but hold the comments.

If your baby head bangs or body rocks a lot and it seems to be hurting him or interfering with daily activities, mention it to the doctor.

Hair Twirling or Pulling

"When my baby is sleepy or cranky, she pulls on her hair. What's that about?"

Hair stroking or pulling is another way little ones can put stress relief into their own hands, allowing them to release tension when they're overtired, stressed, or just plain fighting the fussies. It's pretty common (that is, among babies who have enough hair to grab on to), is often accompanied by thumb sucking, and typically isn't anything that needs your attention—in fact, as is true with most comfort habits, the more attention you pay to it, the more you'll likely see of it. If your baby seems to tug her hair hard enough to pull it out, or if she's always so busy hair twirling that she's not putting her hands to other, more productive uses (like playing with toys or mastering new motor skills), it may be time to try a little gentle intervention. Offer her something else to tug on, like a long-haired stuffed animal, or divert her hands in a game of pat-a-cake or The Itsy-Bitsy Spider, or just gather her up in a soothing cuddle. Also try the tips in the previous answer, all of which can help her find alternative routes to relaxation and comfort.

Biting

"My baby has started biting us playfully—on the shoulder, the cheek, any soft, vulnerable area. At first we thought it was cute. Now we're beginning to worry that he's developing a bad habit—and besides, it hurts!"

Feeling a little bit like a human teething ring? It's only natural for your baby to want to test-drive new chompers on every possible surface, you included. But it's also natural for you to balk at being bitten—and to want to nip that nibbling in the bud, before it becomes a habit, a habit that's not likely to win him friends in the sandbox or score you points with the other parents at the play gym or daycare.

When babies bite, it starts off as playful and experimental—no harm, no foul intended. In fact, baby bites are always served up without malice. It won't be until your little one develops full-fledged empathy (well into the toddler years) that he'll have the slightest idea that he's hurting the ones he bites. After all, he's bitten down on teething rings, chomped on stuffed toys, and chewed on his crib rail, all without a single complaint. But it doesn't take long for a nibbler to notice that human reactions to biting make for interesting cause and effect, typically encouraging more cause (biting) in the pursuit of more effect (reaction). He finds the expression on mommy's face when he bites down on her shoulder funny, the startled look and mock "ouch!" from daddy hilarious, and the "Isn't that cute—he's biting me" from grandma a definite two-thumbs-up. Even an angry "ouch!" can reinforce the biting habit, because baby either finds it amusing or sees it as a challenge to his emerging sense of independence, or both.

The best response to a little nipper? Swiftly, calmly, and matter-of-factly remove the biter from the part he's biting, with a firm, no-nonsense "no biting." You can add "biting hurts," but don't preach on. Then quickly divert baby's attention with a song, a toy, or another distraction. Do this each time he bites and he will eventually get the message.

Does your baby bite when he's tired or wired, frustrated, hungry for attention, or just plain hungry? Avoid those common triggers (preempt with a nap, a wind-down, a change of activity, some quiet cuddles and comfort, or a snack), and you'll likely avoid at least some of the nibbles.

Made with the Shades

Is the forecast for sunny skies? Though your little one will have it made in the shade, staying out of the sun isn't always practical. You're probably already protecting your baby's tender skin from the damaging effects of the sun with clothing and sunscreen—but don't forget to protect those baby blues (or greens, or browns), too. A wide-brimmed hat that keeps those peepers covered is a good place to start, but also consider adding a pair of sunglasses to your baby's outdoor outfit in sunny weather. Like hat wearing (and sunscreen), wearing sunglasses is a healthy habit that's best started early. When buying shades, be sure to choose ones with UV-blocking lenses, which block 99 percent of both UVA and UVB light. Unlabeled or novelty sunglasses may be cheap, but they're probably worse than no shades at all, since they can provide a false sense of protection. Keep sunglasses from sliding off (or from being pulled off—an even more likely scenario) by attaching them to a specially designed child glasses band that you can slip over baby's head.

Blinking

"For the last couple of weeks, my daughter has been blinking a lot. She doesn't seem to be in any discomfort, and she doesn't seem to have trouble seeing, but I can't help thinking that there's something wrong with her eyes."

It's probably more likely that there's something right with her curiosity. Your baby scientist knows what the world looks like through open eyes, but what if she closes her eyes partially, or opens and shuts them quickly? So she experiments, and often keeps up the blinking until the novelty wears off. Squinting is another temporary habit that some babies cultivate, also for the change of view. But if the blinking or squinting isn't accompanied by other eye symptoms (a wandering eye, for instance, a sensitivity to normal—not uncomfortably bright—daylight, or red or teary eyes), there's nothing to worry about. Let her get the blinking out of her system (without calling attention to it), and she'll move on to another curious new habit before you know it. And of course, if she's blinking outside, it may be because of the sunlight—and that's a good reminder that baby eyes, like grown-up eyes, should always wear protective shades in the sun, haze, and glare.

If you're still concerned about your baby's blinking (or if you have any concerns about your baby's eyes), mention it to the doctor at the next visit.

Breath Holding

"Recently my baby has started holding his breath when he's crying. Today he held it so long, he actually passed out. Could this be dangerous?"

With all those nights of checking on your baby's breathing behind you—you might have thought you'd be able to breathe easily now. And after you read this, you actually should be able to. In fact, even a baby who turns blue and passes out during a breath-holding session recovers quickly and completely.

Breath-holding spells that are triggered by crying—which, as you well know, can be triggered in babies by a variety of factors, from being mad, to being frustrated, to being in pain—are common and harmless. The crying,

For the Adoptive Parent: Telling Baby

Wondering when—and how—you should tell your little one that he or she was adopted? Experts agree that it's never too soon to start gradually introducing the concept, so that it becomes a natural and comfortable part of your baby's life and family story—as natural and comfortable as being born into a family would be. And you can begin right now, while your baby is tiny and still doesn't have the slightest clue of what you're saying. Just as birth parents occasionally talk about the day their baby was born, you can talk about the day you brought your baby home: "That was the best day of our lives!" Once in a while, when you're gurgling and cooing at your little one, you can say, "We made our family when we adopted you!" or "We're so happy that we were able to adopt you and make our family!" Though your baby won't be able to comprehend, even in the simplest terms, what adoption means until he or she is 3 or 4 years old, you'll have planted the seed of the concept, which will ultimately make the concept easier to make sense of later on. But

don't overdo the comments you make about the adoption—aim for natural and comfortable, not forced.

Another way to help your baby learn about his or her adoption is to create a scrapbook or photo book that commemorates it. You can include pictures and mementos from that first day, as well as some journal entries detailing how you felt when you first met and cuddled your adorable bundle and when you first came home together. If you traveled to a foreign country for the adoption, the book is the perfect place to document the journey—and to give your son or daughter a glimpse of his or her heritage. If the adoption was open, photos of the birth mother (especially if they were taken with you, while you were both waiting for your baby's arrival or just after) can also help make the concept of your baby's adoption more tangible. No matter what you include, looking at the book together is sure to become a favorite activity as your little one grows—a special record of your early days together as a family.

---

instead of letting up, becomes more and more hysterical, at which point baby begins to hyperventilate, then finally stops breathing. Sometimes, only the lips turn blue—scary enough, but considered mild by breath-holding standards. Less frequently (but even once is enough for a terrified parent who's standing by watching), a baby turns blue all over and then loses consciousness. While he's unconscious, his body may stiffen or even twitch. Fortunately, breathing resumes and consciousness returns in less than a minute as automatic respiratory mechanisms click into place and breathing resumes (the

respiratory system's version of autopilot)—long before any harm is done to baby (the same may not be said of your nerves). You may be able to stop a breath-holding episode sooner by blowing on your baby's face or sprinkling water on it—either may trigger auto-breathing.

About 1 in 5 babies holds his breath during a crying spell. Some have only occasional episodes, others may have one or two a day or more. Breath holding tends to run in families (so check with your parents to see if either of you had episodes when you were tots) and is most common between 6 months and

4 years, though it can occasionally begin earlier or continue later.

While you're waiting for it to run its developmental course (don't hold your breath), try to head off some of the crying spells that can result in breath-holding spells:

■ Avoid the triggers. You know the drill by now: A baby who is overtired or overstimulated is always more prone to major meltdowns (and less able to handle anger, frustration, and pain) than a well-rested one. Keep your little fellow mellow, and you'll avert some of the meltdowns that lead to breath holding.

■ Keep routines routine. Regular nap-times, regular mealtimes and snack times, and plenty of unwinding as needed will help prevent fits of temper.

■ Choose your battles. Too many no's can lead to too much frustration for baby. When you need to say no, try to offer an acceptable substitute.

■ Get your soothe on. Try to calm baby before hysteria sets in, using music, toys, or other diversions. Or just offer quiet comfort—a cuddle, some gentle rocking, a hushed "shh."

■ Stay as calm as you can. If you're worried about crying escalating to the point of breath holding, your first impulse when baby starts howling is (understandably) to panic. But the calmer you stay, the faster your little one is likely to regain his calm. Even if the breath holding has begun, being the calm in your baby's storm can help it pass more quickly—and return less often. After all, as your little one begins to use breath holding as a parent-button pusher (and he will), not playing into his mini-manipulations will pay off. (What's the point of making a scene if nobody seems to notice?)

■ Don't cave after a spell. On the subject of mommy-and-daddy manipulation, if your baby knows he can get what he wants by holding his breath, he will repeat, repeat, repeat.

Some research suggests that breath-holding spells can be a sign of iron deficiency, so check with the doctor to see if your little one's iron supplies could be low, especially if breath holding doesn't seem to be triggered by a tantrum or other fit of frustration. In fact, giving an iron supplement can sometimes help ease breath holding even when no deficiency is detected.

While passing out during a breath-holding episode triggered by crying isn't considered worrisome, check with the doctor if you need more reassurance (who wouldn't?). Certainly, any loss of consciousness that's not related to a crying spell definitely should be evaluated.

Fears

"My baby used to love to watch me turn on the vacuum cleaner, but now he's suddenly terrified of it—and anything else that makes a loud noise."

That's because he's wising up. When your baby was younger, loud noises didn't frighten him—even if they sometimes startled him—because he wasn't sophisticated enough to connect loud with potentially dangerous, and potentially dangerous with scary. As his understanding of the world grows—and with it his ability to sort out (in his still evolving baby brain) what's a legitimate threat and what isn't—his fears grow, too. In other words, while being afraid of a vacuum cleaner may seem the definition of irrational to you, it actually represents a thinking baby's thought process. Temperament may also play a role in fearful reactions—a little one who's "high sensitivity" may be especially bothered by loud noises, especially sudden ones.

There are any number of things in a baby's everyday life that, though harmlessly humdrum to you, can trigger terror in him: sounds (such as the roar of a vacuum cleaner, the whir of a blender, the barking of a dog, the whine of a siren, the ring of the doorbell, the flushing of a toilet, the gurgle of water draining from the bathtub), having a shirt pulled over his head, being lifted high in the air (especially if he's begun to climb, pull up, or otherwise develop depth perception), being plunked down in a bath, the motion of a wind-up or mechanical toy, and much more.

Probably all babies experience fears at some point, though some overcome them so quickly, their parents are never aware of them. Little ones who live in an especially busy, noisy environment that's always buzzing with activity (say, one where there are older siblings and multiple pets) may be less fear prone—or they may be more likely to experience fears earlier, as well as get rid of them earlier. Temperament also plays a role, of course, as it does in most behaviors.

Sooner or later, your little one will leave his baby fears behind (though an early fear of the vacuum cleaner may be sucked up by a somewhat more sophisticated fear—say, of monsters). Until then, you can help your baby cope with everyday fears in these ways:

Don't force facing fears. Making your baby come nose to nozzle with the vacuum cleaner won't help him overcome his fear, but it could dial up its intensity. A fear of household appliances you've turned on and off for years without incident may seem unreasonable to you, but with your baby's limited scope of experience, it's very legitimate to him. He needs to confront the noisy beast on his own terms and in his own time, when he feels it's safe.

Don't make fun. Yes, most everything your baby does is adorable—even his cowering at the sound of the vacuum cleaner's high-pitched hum. But try not to poke fun at his fears, laughing at them (again, as cute as they may be) or calling them silly. Remember, they're real—not silly—to him.

Do accept and sympathize. By accepting and respecting your baby's fears as real, and offering comfort for them as needed, you'll help him overcome them faster. If he wails when you switch on the vacuum cleaner (or flush the toilet, or turn on the blender), be quick to pick him up and give him a great big reassuring hug. But don't overdo the comfort and sympathy—otherwise you may reinforce the idea that there is something to fear.

Do build confidence and skills. While it's important for your baby's budding self-esteem to validate his fears, your ultimate goal is to help him conquer them. You can do that by giving him "safe" opportunities to become gradually familiar with the things he fears, to learn what they do and how they work, and to gain some sense of control over them (knowledge is, after all, power—even over a powerful vacuum cleaner). Let him touch or study the vacuum when it's turned off and unplugged—he's probably as fascinated with the machine as he is afraid of it.

Help him take baby steps toward vanquishing his vacuum fears. After he's become comfortable playing with the dust-sucking beast when it's off, try holding him securely in one arm while you vacuum with the other. (If that's out of his comfort zone, too, back off and try again another day.) Then show him how to turn the machine on himself, with a little help from you if the switch is tricky.

The Baby Social Scene

Of course you're still your baby's favorite playmate—but that doesn't mean you have to be the only one. And that might be a relief for you to hear right about now. After all, entertaining your baby as he or she starts hankering for some extra stimulation can become a growing challenge. Enter: the playgroup. While cooperatively playing in a group with other babies is more than a year away for the typical 9- to 10-month-old, there are lots of perks to these organized baby get-togethers—as many (or more) for you as for your little one. Advantages of a playgroup include:

Adult conversation for you. Your child's babbles may be the sweetest sounds to your ears, but if you're like most parents, especially stay-at-home ones, chances are you also long for a little adult dialogue. Meeting regularly with other parents will provide you with the opportunity to speak and be spoken to in full sentences.

Entertainment for baby. While it's still too early in your child's social career to expect anything close to cooperative play in a group situation, by the end of the first year most babies become more capable of some type of meaningful interaction with their peers—usually in the form of parallel play (playing side by side). There's also plenty of entertainment value for baby in just watching other babies at play—and if the playgroup is at someone else's house, trying out someone else's toys.

Friendships for you both. If the playgroup is a success, your baby may have a chance to pal around with the same bunch of children on a regular basis for years. And if the playgroup is a neighborhood one, many of the same children may end up in your baby's future classes—a familiarity that can breed comfort on that first day of preschool. As for you, the opportunity to create a whole new network of like-minded friends may be especially welcome, particularly if your old social network hasn't entered the baby phase of life yet.

Resources and referrals. Whether you're in the market for a new pediatrician or are wondering when and how to wean, chances are a fellow playgroup parent will have advice or a recommendation.

Support from those who know. Meeting regularly with other parents can remind you that you're not the only one who has (a) a baby who won't sleep, (b) no time for romance with your spouse, (c) career frustrations, (d) a breeding farm for mutant dust bunnies in your living room, or (e) all of the above.

There are many ways to find a playgroup for you and your baby to join. Ask around, check out online message boards (WhatToExpect .com links parents locally throughout the country) and Facebook, look for flyers promoting them in neighborhood stores, your local library, community center, house of worship, hospital, or doctor's office. Or check out the local parents' paper.

Can't find what you're looking for, or prefer to start fresh by starting your own playgroup? Sign up members by running listings in the above resources, or if you're lucky enough to have friends with babies close in age to yours, get them on board. And though flexibility is key to anything that involves babies (especially a group of babies), you may want to consider the following questions before you take the first meeting of your playgroup:

- What will the age range of children be? They don't all have to be exactly the same age, but this early on, a spread of a few months is better than a spread of a year or more. A relatively close age range will help ensure that junior members will be able to play with the same toys and relate on somewhat the same level.

- How often will the playgroup meet—twice a week, weekly, every other week?

- What time and day are most convenient for you and the other parents? Once you pick a schedule, try to hold to it as much as possible. Consistency is an important ingredient in a successful playgroup. Avoiding naptime and typically cranky times (such as late afternoon) is also wise.

- Where will the playgroup meet? In one parent's home or rotating from home to home? At a local park or community center? Rotating the location keeps things exciting for the baby group members while sharing the responsibilities that come with hosting the group equally. It also means that the children will have a chance to play with plenty of different toys.

- How many participants will there be? Will there be a limit on the number of parents and babies who can attend? Too many babies (say, 15) can make a playgroup chaotic and unwieldy, while too few (just 2 or 3) may provide too little stimulation. Keep in mind that not every member will show up at every playgroup meeting, thanks to colds, doctor's appointments, and other scheduling conflicts.

- Will there be refreshments? Who will provide the snacks? Will food allergies be respected? Will there be rules restricting junk food? What about snacks and drinks for the grown-ups?

- Will there be structured parent-child activities, or will it be a free time for children and social time for adults? Keep in mind that parents may have to spend lots of time serving as referees and peacekeepers until the kids are old enough (think at least 3 or 4) to play nicely on a consistent basis.

- Will the cleanup be a group effort, too? While the little ones may eventually have fun helping put away toys after a playdate, the parents will ultimately be responsible.

- Will there be guidelines about discipline and behavior expectations? You'll probably want to specify that parents are responsible for monitoring the behavior of their own offspring only.

- What will the sick-baby rules be? It's smart to set a sick-babies-stay-home statute, but remember that some tiny noses are always running and some tiny coughs can linger for weeks—even when nothing contagious is afoot. Also keep in mind that colds and other bugs happen when baby worlds collide, and that this inevitability is not necessarily such a bad thing (the more colds a little one has early on, the stronger his or her immune system will become and the fewer colds will be caught later). The most important rule you can set in a playgroup: Make sure that all babies and parents are up-to-date on their immunizations.

Does a playgroup sound too much like hard work for you or your baby? Socializing with other babies is by no means a requirement of the early years—especially not for those still under a year—so don't feel compelled to join or start a playgroup. And if you sign on only to find that you'd rather you hadn't, don't feel compelled to ride it out. Get your social fix and your baby's from impromptu playdates or at the playground instead of playing along with the playgroup concept.

If it's the toilet's flush he fears, have him throw a sheet or two of toilet paper into the toilet, then hold him while you flush it down together (happily waving bye-bye to the t.p. can make the process seem less menacing). If it's the draining tub, let him watch the water drain when he is safely out of it, wrapped securely in a towel and in your arms. If dogs are his demon, try petting one while your baby watches from a distance and from a safe spot—say, in a pair of friendly arms. When he's finally willing to approach a dog in your arms, encourage your baby (while you hold him) to "make nice doggie" to a dog you know is gentle and won't suddenly snap.

Starting Classes

"I hear so much about classes for babies, I'm wondering if enrolling my baby in one is important for her development."

Music, art, movement, sensory, swimming, and more—there's no shortage of classes available for little ones not yet able to stand on their own two feet. But there's no rush to enroll your pint-size pupil, especially when you consider that babies develop best and learn best by doing when they have the time and opportunity to explore the world their way, with just a little help (as needed) from the adults around them. In other words, babies develop and learn best through experience, not through instruction. In fact, being expected to learn a certain way, at a certain time, at a certain place, or at a certain pace can dampen a young child's natural curiosity and drive to discover.

While baby classes are definitely not a developmental must-do, however, they're certainly a can-do. There's no downside to opting out of them, but there can be plenty of benefits in signing up for one or more group baby activities. After all, it's nice—if not necessary—for your baby to have the chance to play alongside other babies her age, and for you to have a chance to spend time (and share insights and tips) with other parents. Just choose the classes wisely—opt for those that are just for fun, where your baby can do her own thing (whether it's bop to a beat or tumble around on a play mat) or watch her classmates do theirs. Avoid any class that has a formal agenda or curriculum, and look for a very loose, flexible, no-pressure format. It's always a good idea to check out a sample class before you sign up. To find out what's available where you live, check online, local parents' magazines, community centers, your pediatrician's office—or ask around at the playground.

A more ambitious approach: Bring the class to you. Some teachers will hold classes in homes, so if you have the space, the inclination, and a group of parents and babies to sign up, that's another way to go.

ALL ABOUT:
The Beginning of Discipline

You applauded wildly your baby's first successful attempt at pulling up, and cheered proudly from the sidelines as creeping finally became crawling. Now you're starting to wonder: What was all the celebration about? Along with that impressive inventory of new skills has come an astonishing talent for getting into trouble. If your baby's not adroitly deleting apps on your iPad, he's clicking "place your order now" on an order you didn't place. If she's not performing tablecloth tricks in the dining room, she's gleefully unraveling whole rolls of toilet paper, or industriously emptying the contents of drawers, cabinets, and bookshelves onto the floor. Before, all you had to do to keep both baby and home from harm was to plop him or her down in a safe spot—now, no such spot exists.

Perhaps all this late-breaking mayhem has got you wondering: Is it time to start thinking about discipline? Saying no, meaning no—and following through with discipline when your baby doesn't take no for an answer? The answer: a resounding yes. Discipline means "teaching" (not "punishment," as you might have assumed), and the timing's just right for beginning to teach your little one some basic differences between what's right and what's wrong (or really, at this early stage in your baby's evolution as a human being, what's okay to do and what's not okay to do). While even a month or two ago, your choruses of "no!" "hot!" "don't touch!" "stop now!" went in one adorable ear and out the other, your baby's memory is now improving, as is his or her comprehension. Your little one is starting to make sense out of your words, actions, and tone of voice and to recall them from one day to the next. That's not to say that he or she is ready to live by the rules, or even to understand what the rules are yet—it will take years of baby steps before you'll be able to count on your child approximating anything consistent in terms of compliance, impulse control, a moral compass, or good citizenry. But helping your baby take those first steps now can make all the difference later.

Here's how to get started:

Begin with love. What's the foundation for all effective discipline? Unconditional love—that unbreakable bond between a parent and child that comes with no strings attached to behavior expectations. The kind of love that's on tap every moment of every day—whether baby happens to be acting like an adorable angel or a raging mini-monster. And while it's admittedly easier to show the love when your little one is cuddling contentedly in your arms than it is when he's beaning the cat with a block or she's just tossed her sippy cup into a mud puddle, it's that love that provides your baby with the rock solid foundation good behavior is always built on.

Individualize. Every child is different, every family is different, every circumstance is different. Although there are universal rules of behavior that apply to everyone, every time (no hitting, no biting), there's no one-size-fits-all discipline approach. In figuring out what discipline fits for your little one, you'll have to factor in temperament (yours and your child's), circumstance (discipline in the supermarket may be different from discipline at home, discipline when your baby's down with a bad cold may be different from when he or she is feeling frisky), and what feels right for your family (just as rules will vary from home to home, how those rules will be enforced will vary, too).

Set limits. Yes, they fight limits. They test limits. And yet, believe it or not, little ones crave limits, too. Knowing what to expect and what's expected of them (as long as those expectations are fair, consistent, and age-appropriate) makes children feel grounded, secure, and loved—which, in turn, inevitably makes them better behaved. That said, limits have their limits when it comes to babies, so limit yours to those that matter most. Draw the line in the sand, for instance, when your little one throws sand, or when toy cars are used as projectiles, or when a tug-of-war over a doll stroller escalates to hair pulling, or when Junior keeps reaching for your hot cup of joe.

Be consistently consistent. Just as important as setting those few key limits is consistently enforcing them. If you didn't allow baby to play with your phone yesterday, but you're looking the other way today, or if magazine shredding was a no-no last week, but this week it's been mostly ignored, the only lesson your child will learn is that the world is confusing and rules are meaningless (so what's the point of trying to follow them?). There goes your discipline credibility, there goes your parental authority, there goes your baby's compliance. Hitting is unacceptable on Monday? Then it has to be unacceptable on Tuesday and Wednesday and Thursday—and it has to be unacceptable whether mommy's in charge, daddy's in charge, or the babysitter's in charge (and yes, even if grandpa is in charge). If your rules are all over the place, behavior's bound to be, too. Doesn't mean you can't sometimes bend nonessential rules or even break them once in a while—just that a consistently inconsistent approach to discipline can be predicted to fail.

Avoid the "no!" game. A constant chorus of "no, no, no!" strips that all-important word of its power, fast—not to mention sets the stage for toddler negativity (which is just around the corner). So choose your battles, with first choice always going to matters of safety and well-being (of people and things), but avoid making everything a battle. You can limit your use of "no's" by creating a childproof environment in your home, with plenty of opportunities for exploration under safe conditions.

Turn "don'ts" into "do's," when you can, too: "This is how we pet a cat" instead of "Don't pull Fluffy's tail!" Along with each no, try to offer a yes in the form of an alternative: "No, you can't play with Daddy's book, but you can look at this one," or "You can't empty the cereal shelf, but you can empty the plastic container cabinet." Instead of "No, don't touch those papers in Mommy's desk," try, "Those papers go in Mommy's drawer. Let's see if we can put the papers back and close the drawer." This win-win approach gets the message across and teaches a lesson—without going negative.

Keep age in mind. The same standards of behavior don't stand for a 5-year-old (who's developmentally capable of impulse control and reason) and an under-1-year-old (who clearly isn't), and neither should the same discipline approach. Time-outs, for instance, aren't effective for babies or young toddlers who don't yet have the attention span, memory, or cognitive ability to "sit there and think about what you've done." Rules should factor in the limitations of age, too. You can expect that 5-year-old not to interrupt you when you're on the phone (at least most of the time) or to put away toys before bed (with a reminder), but expecting either of a 1-year-old isn't realistic. Set limits that are age-appropriate, and you're more likely to get the compliance you're looking for. Expect more than your little one can deliver, and you can ultimately expect discipline to fail.

Repeat and repeat. Babies have limited memories, minimal attention spans, and nominal impulse control. Disciplining your little one will be a process—a very long and very repetitive process. You told him not to touch the remote? Be

Spanking: Don't Do It

Let's face it—being a parent isn't easy, and there are some days when it's really, really hard: the days when you're beat, you're drained, when your little one is testing every reserve of self-control you have, and you're edging closer and closer to the breaking point. You feel like you might snap . . . and maybe, you have that impulse to spank. The impulse is a normal one, only natural when you consider that you're only human (as is your baby). And it's especially natural if spanking was used for discipline by your parents when you were growing up (didn't you grow up just fine?). Spanking is, after all, a time-honored disciplinary tradition, passed from generation to generation in many families.

But nearly all experts agree: It's time to retire spanking for good. Hitting a child (spanking, slapping, or otherwise lashing out physically) is, research shows, an ineffective way to discipline. For one thing, it sets an example of aggression most parents wouldn't want their little ones to follow. Numerous studies show that children who are spanked are more likely to use physical force against peers, and later against their own children. Another strike against spanking: It represents the abuse of power by a very large, strong party (or bully) against a very small, comparatively weak one—definitely behavior you don't want modeled on the playground later on. Finally, spanking may discourage a child from repeating a misdeed, but compliance comes from fear of another spanking, not from the development of self-discipline—which after all, is the ultimate goal. Unless you plan to follow your little one around for life, he or she will have to learn the difference between "right" behavior and "wrong" behavior, not just the difference between behaviors that result in spanking and those that don't.

The most important reason not to spank or otherwise strike: It can hurt your baby. Physically, it's just too easy to cross the line from a swat or a slap to something more harmful. Emotionally, spanking can take a toll, too, shaking a little one's sense of security and sometimes eroding the bond between a parent and child. Can a child grow up happy, healthy, and well adjusted despite a few spankings? Absolutely—but with such a compelling case against spanking, why go there at all?

The best policy: Make no-spanking the policy in your home—even on those especially hard days (and there will be many more ahead to test you). For best results, use other, more effective, and less risky discipline strategies.

And the same goes, even more emphatically, for shaking a baby. Many parents who would never consider hitting don't think twice about shaking, especially in the heat of the moment. But shaking a baby is extremely dangerous and could cause serious injury to eyes and/or brain, or even death. So never, ever shake a baby.

prepared to tell him 100 times—and to take it away from him each time he goes for it. You told her biting is for food, not for people? That doesn't mean you won't be removing her mouth from your shoulder many times to come.

Be patient, persistent, and prepared to repeat the same message ("Don't eat the dog food") every day for weeks, or even months, before it finally sinks in. Even once it does, that itchy trigger finger may not be able to exercise restraint when faced with temptation. Don't give up, don't give in—but do give it time.

Be the calm in the storm. Yes, you're only human, and you're the parent of a baby who's only human, so you're bound to lose your temper some of the time. But try your hardest to temper that loss of temper, because anger doesn't work with wee ones. When you're over-the-top angry, you lose patience and perspective (two things you need lots of when you're disciplining a small child). You model a behavior you're always trying to curb in your baby (loss of control) instead of one you're always trying to encourage (practicing self-control). You may even scare your child, and if you're angry a lot, bruise that just-emerging sense of self.

And here's another important reason why uncontrolled anger is ineffective: It teaches nothing about right from wrong. Screaming or hitting in the heat of the moment may give you a quick release—and may even temporarily stun your little one into submission—but it doesn't further your long-term goal of promoting good behavior. In fact, it promotes just the opposite (screamers and hitters tend to raise screamers and hitters—check out any playground and you'll see).

So be the calm in the storm, as much as you can. When your baby has done something that makes you angry, take a few moments to cool down before you attempt discipline. Then respond calmly. Simply explain what was wrong about what your baby did and what the consequences will be. ("You threw the truck. Trucks are not for throwing. I am taking the truck away.") A good example modeled, a teaching moment seized, an action connected with consequence—and best of all, effective discipline doled out. Plus, you behaved like the adult you are.

But since you're only human, there'll be times when you can't slam on the temper brakes. As long as the meltdowns don't come too often or last too long—and are aimed at your child's behavior, not your child—they won't interfere with effective parenting, or even with your overall discipline strategy. When you do lose it, however, be sure to apologize for it: "I'm sorry I yelled at you, but I was very angry." Adding a comforting cuddle and a reassuring "I love you" will let your little one know that sometimes we get angry at people we love and that's okay—it's part of being human.

Discipline That Works

Can't imagine where to start when it comes to choosing discipline strategies for a baby who's not even old enough to understand the rules, never mind follow them? Keep it direct, simple, and easy to follow through on:

Catch your child doing good. By calling attention to good behavior, you'll be asking for more. So comment about the nice way your baby turned the pages in a book (instead of trying to tear them), say thank you when your baby hands you a toy to put back on the shelf, offer praise when he plays quietly with a stacking toy while you sort the laundry, applaud all efforts to put shredded cheese into her mouth instead of strewing it on the floor.

Make the discipline fit. When your baby pulls all the books off the bookshelves, have him or her hand you each one to help you put them back. If your baby throws blocks around, take them away for now. If your baby bites your arm, put him or her down promptly, firmly saying, "No biting. Daddy can't hold you when you bite."

Divert attention. For most babies, especially young ones, what's out of sight is quickly out of mind—making distraction an especially smart discipline strategy now. She's throwing a fit on the way to the park? Divert her (fortunately limited) attention to two squirrels playing on a tree. He's banging a block against your painted pine dining set? Pull out a toy that won't chip the chairs, like a stuffed dog. With distraction, everyone wins.

Use your serious voice. When you're telling your baby no, tone matters. Mean what you say, without being mean. Bring down your usually high-pitched, singsong, playful, baby-friendly voice an octave or two to get your little one's attention and to let him or her know that you're all business—and the adult in the room. Be firm but matter-of-fact—screaming can scare your baby, and too much screaming can eventually be tuned out.

Laugh it off . . . sometimes. Humor can actually work wonders under certain circumstances—and it's a discipline strategy that can be used to defuse countless potentially explosive scenarios. Use it liberally in situations that would otherwise lead you to exasperation, for instance, when baby refuses to allow you to put a snowsuit on. Instead of doing battle over screeches of protest, head off the struggle with some unexpected silliness. Suggest, say, that you put the snowsuit on the dog (or on yourself), and then pretend to do so. The incongruity of what you're proposing will probably take your baby's mind off objections long enough for you to get him or her suited up. That sticky face needs a cleanup, but just spying the washcloth is a nonstarter? Win baby

---

Losing Control

Sometimes, anger can get the best of even the most loving parent. But if you feel you can't control your anger and that losing control leads to hitting or shaking, if one slap leads to another, if the slap is hard enough to leave a mark on your child or aims for the face, ears, or head, or if you strike out under the influence of alcohol or drugs, you should talk about your feelings and actions with your child's doctor, a family therapist, or another helping professional, or talk to someone at Childhelp National Child Abuse Hotline (1-800-4-A-CHILD) as soon as possible. Though you may not have seriously hurt your child yet, the potential for physical or emotional damage is there. Now is the time to get some professional help, before an angry outburst leads to something more serious—even if that something serious isn't physical but verbal abuse.

If your spouse shows issues with anger and aggression, or if you feel he or she has the potential to do harm to your baby, physically or emotionally, he or she also needs help from a professional. Call for that help now.

---

over with funny songs ("This is the way we wash the face, wash the face . . .") or outlandish play-by-play commentary ("Here comes the cleanup monster" as the washcloth swoops down and "gobbles" the jelly-smeared cheeks) or make goofy faces in the mirror to distract from the dastardly deed. Just make sure you don't laugh when the situation demands a serious approach.

CHAPTER 16

The Eleventh Month

You may have a Baby Houdini on your hands this month, whose major preoccupations are getting into things he or she shouldn't be getting into and getting out of things he or she shouldn't be getting out of. There's no shelf too high and no cabinet handle too unwieldy to deter a 10-month-old baby on a mission of seek and (what seems like) destroy. Accomplished as an escape artist, baby may now try to wriggle out of diaper changes, strollers, high chairs—in other words, any confining (read: safe) situation. Along with great physical advances, which may even include first steps for a few babies in the eleventh month, come remarkable verbal strides. Not in the number of words spoken (a couple, max, if any) but in the number of words understood (as many as 20 to 50). Looking at books becomes a much more interesting and enriching experience as baby begins to recognize and possibly even point to familiar pictures. In fact, pointing (or gesturing with a few fingers, or even the whole hand) will soon become a favorite activity no matter what baby's doing—just one way he or she is able to communicate quite capably without words.

Feeding Your Baby: Weaning from the Bottle

Ask most pediatricians when a baby should be weaned from the bottle, and the majority will say by the first birthday—and definitely no later than 18 months. Ask most parents when they actually weaned their baby off

Baby Basics at a Glance: Eleventh Month

Sleeping. Like last month, your sweet dreamer should be clocking an average of 10 to 12 hours per night and taking two naps during the day, each around 1½ to 2 hours long, for an average total of around 14 hours each day. A few babies may start to fight their morning nap this month (probably not in their best interest). If yours does, be sure he or she is getting enough overall sleep.

Eating. Your cutie will be taking in less breast milk and formula now that solids are figuring more prominently into his or her diet. As the first year comes to a close, baby will likely breast- or bottle-feed no more than 3 to 4 times a day, taking about 24 ounces total. More than that in fluids, and baby's appetite for solids may be drowned. Baby's breastfeeding more than 4 times a day? That's fine as long as there's also room for solids.

Baby will probably gobble up around ¼ to ½ cup each of grains, fruit, and veggies every day (or even more if your baby's a big eater), ¼ to ½ cup (or more) of dairy foods per day, ¼ to ½ cup (or more) of protein food per day, and 3 to 4 ounces of juice per day (optional). Don't worry if your baby is eating more or less than that. As long as he or she is gaining weight and is happy and healthy, there's no need to get caught up in measurements.

Playing. Blocks, stacking toys, puzzles, peg boards, bead mazes, activity cubes, and other toys that encourage eye-hand coordination are perfect for your 10-month-old. Toys like baby basketball hoops and balls will do double duty in the eye-hand coordination and physical development departments (even if your cutie hasn't quite mastered the slam dunk yet). And speaking of physical development, keep the push toys and riding toys within reach to encourage your little one's get-up-and-go. Role-play toys—especially ones that mimic mom's and dad's toys (like a play phone or keys)—will be especially fun for your little one this month. So will musical toys: a toy keyboard, a xylophone, drums, tambourines, bells, and rhythm sticks. And don't forget to provide your budding artist with lots of crayons, washable markers, and chunky chalk for scribbling, though make sure they're non-toxic, since they're likely to end up in baby's mouth, not just on paper.

the bottle, and many will say . . . much later than that. There are lots of reasons why parents (and little ones) hang on to the bottle for longer than doctors (and dentists) recommend—reasons ranging from convenience for mom and dad, to comfort for Junior, to less mess for everyone involved. Babies who are used to falling asleep with a bottle, or to nipping from one during the night or early in the morning, and parents who are used to buying themselves a good night's sleep or a later wake-up call, don't tend to be in a hurry to drop the bottle either. Add in the dreaded withdrawal process (rare is the tot who gives up the bottle without a fight . . . make that, many fights), and it's no wonder there are plenty of 2- and 3-year-olds who still haven't kicked the bottle habit.

But here's the message about bottles most experts would like parents to pay attention to: Weaning at 12 months—or as soon as possible after the first birthday—is best for your baby. And there's no shortage of reasons why. First of all, as with many other attachment objects of babyhood (such as a pacifier, being rocked to sleep, and so on), old habits die hard. And the older the habits (and the baby) are, the harder they are to break. Weaning a fairly flexible 1-year-old is like taking candy from a baby compared to tussling with a strong-willed 2-year-old over the beloved bottle—especially at naptime and bedtime.

Second, when an older baby uses a bottle, he or she runs the risk of developing tooth decay from bottle-feeding, and not only because there are now teeth to decay. While an infant is usually fed in a parent's arms—and the bottle removed when the feeding ends—a mobile toddler often totes the bottle wherever he or she goes. This drinking-on-the-go and nipping-all-day-long allows the milk or juice to bathe teeth in sugar, with cavities the potential result. So does falling asleep with a bottle, nipping during the night, or falling back to sleep in the early morning hours with a bottle in hand. Another health risk tots over 12 months run when they take a bottle to bed (or otherwise drink one lying down): a greater susceptibility to ear infections.

Third, toddlers who are bottle drinkers often end up drinking more juice or milk than they should, filling up on too many liquids and taking in too few solids. Not only are these toddlers more likely to become fussy eaters (not surprising, since their tummies are always full of juice and milk), but they may miss out on important nutrients. If their bottles are filled with juice—particularly apple juice—they can also wind up with chronic diarrhea.

And if you're still not persuaded to switch to a cup in the next month or two, consider these potential developmental drawbacks of continued bottle use: A toddler who's constantly toting and nipping from a bottle has only one hand free for playing and exploring—and a mouth too full to speak out of.

If your baby hasn't started on a cup yet, it's time to make the introduction—see page 412 for tips on how to begin. While introducing the cup is relatively easy at this age, getting your baby to give up the bottle entirely and take all of his or her liquid from a cup is a little more challenging. Following these suggestions can make the switch from all bottle to all cup a little smoother:

Time it right. While you shouldn't expect your baby to be completely bottle-weaned until closer to a year, there's no reason not to start the process now. But be smart about timing. It's best not to start weaning your baby from the bottle if he or she is sick, teething, or otherwise out of sorts. And wait until baby has settled down again after a big move, new child care, or any other stressful time before pulling the bottle plug. Also hold off on weaning if your little one hasn't yet mastered the cup. Get the cup up and running before you retire the bottle—otherwise baby won't have anything to drink from.

Go slow. Unless you're planning a cold turkey approach to kicking the bottle habit—a technique probably better suited for an older toddler whose help can actually be enlisted in the plan—the best way to transition from a bottle to a cup is by gradually phasing out the bottles while phasing in the cup. There are a number of ways to do this:

- Drop one bottle-feeding session at a time and replace it with a cup. Allow a few days or a week before replacing the next one with a cup. Middle-of-the-day bottles will be easier to cut out first. The early morning and bedtime ones are usually harder to give up—as well as any bottle baby takes before naptimes, especially if it's been used as a fall-asleep habit (in other words, it has become a sleep association).

- Put less formula or milk (formula for babies under a year, whole milk for those over a year) in each bottle than your baby normally takes and top off each bottle-feeding with a cup. Slowly decrease the amount of formula or milk in the bottle while you increase the amount of formula or milk in the cup.

- Swap out the formula or milk in bottles with water, starting with one feeding at a time (serve that feeding in a cup). Pretty soon, your baby may decide that bottles aren't worth it just for water alone—and even if he or she does cling to water bottles, at least no harm will come to baby's teeth. Juice, if it's on the menu at all, should be served up only in a cup. Just make sure, as you transition to cup, that your little one gets enough total formula or milk, or enough in the way of other calcium foods (say, cheese and yogurt).

Banish the bottles. Out of sight, out of mind—hopefully. To make the transition a little easier, start stashing the bottles behind closed cabinet doors, where your baby can't see them. When you're ready to call it quits on the bottles altogether,

box them up, give them away, or recycle them promptly. At the same time, make sure your baby spies cups around the house often—in the refrigerator, on the kitchen counter, on the dining room table, in the diaper bag.

Go cup crazy. Choose cups with features designed to charm your little sipper. Cups with bright colors and cute designs, or see-through cups that allow baby to watch the liquid swish around. Valve-free sippy cups with straws, cups with handles, cups without handles, bottom-weighted cups that don't tip over (but can roll around . . . how fun!). Cups indented in the middle or shaped like an hourglass for easy gripping . . . or ones made out of rubber for even easier gripping. Cups that are tiny enough to fit completely in baby's small hands, or cups that baby can wear as a bracelet (they're shaped like donuts). Cups with silicone spouts (they feel more nipplelike), ones with slanted interiors that keep drinks angled toward baby as he or she drinks, or open cups with inserts that control the flow of liquid anywhere along the cup's rim (in other words, without a cover and spout). The options are endless, so experiment with a few (or a lot) to see what your baby likes best.

Put the cup in baby's hands. It may take longer for your little one to finish a cup of formula than it did a bottle, but with practice, that should turn around fast. Try to avoid interfering with baby's practice (maneuvering the cup into his or her mouth yourself, for instance, or constantly correcting technique), even if it's messier or less efficient than you'd like. Remember, the bottle was in baby's control, so the cup needs to be, too.

Expect less. Less milk, that is. Expect your baby to take fewer ounces of formula during the weaning process. Once he or she adjusts to taking all daily liquid from a cup, you'll see the number of ounces tick up again. Keep in mind that older babies approaching their first birthday need fewer total ounces of formula (only 16 to 24 ounces) than younger babies do, making the end of that 12-month mark a perfect time to wean.

Teach by example. Babies at this age love imitating adults (particularly adults they love). Take advantage of this urge to mimic and drink from a sippy or straw cup along with your baby.

Be positive. Every time your baby uses a cup, serve up positive reinforcement—clap, praise, make up a cup song to keep up your little one's motivation. Try toasting, too. Show your tot how to clink his or her sippy cup with your cup, along with a chorus of "Cheers!" or "Bottoms up!" It will quickly become a beloved ritual for your baby at meal and snack times. On the flip side, avoid criticizing your baby for slow progress with the cup or belittling your little one for clinging to the bottle (that will only make him or her cling more tightly).

Be patient. Habits of a year or longer generally don't get kicked overnight. You can expect Mission Bottle Wean to take several weeks, even a month or two, to be completely accomplished. Hang in there, and help your baby hang in there, too. Be consistent (and don't cave—once you've dropped a bottle from the schedule, keep it dropped) and you'll be rewarded, eventually. If it takes more time than you'd anticipated, that's fine (even if you don't end up fully weaning until months after the first birthday deadline)—as long as you're gradually making progress.

Fill baby up with love. For most babies, the bottle provides not only nourishment but also comfort. As you limit the amount of time your baby has the bottle, be prepared to fill in the comfort gap with extra hugs, extra play sessions, an extra bedtime story on your lap to help your baby feel secure in the face of change. A new comfort object—a blanket or a stuffed animal—can also help ease the transition.

What You May Be Wondering About

Bowed Legs

"My baby just started taking steps, and she seems to be bowlegged."

Bowed until 2, knock-kneed at 4, a typical tot's legs certainly won't give a supermodel a run for her money. But even the legs that grace fashion's top catwalks were likely bowed when they took their first steps. Almost all children are bowlegged (their knees don't touch when their feet are together) during the first 2 years of life, and the bowing

becomes easier to notice once they start to stand. Then, as they spend more time walking, they typically become knock-kneed (their knees meet, but their ankles don't). Not until the preteen to teen years do the knees and ankles align and the legs appear to be shaped standardly straight. In the meantime, enjoy those adorable baby bows while you can.

If you have concerns about your little one's bowing, check with the pediatrician for reassurance.

Falls

"I feel like I'm living on the edge since my baby started to take his first steps. He trips over his own feet, bangs his head on table corners, topples off chairs. He's fearless, I'm not."

Being a brand new walker can definitely trip a baby up. And slip him up, bump him up, and bruise him up . . . not to mention walk him into a whole lot of trouble fast. For baby, that means countless close calls and falls—for you, it means frazzled nerves and skipped heartbeats. But steel yourself, because misadventures on two feet will not deter your intrepid adventurer—and it's a good thing, too, or he'd never learn to get around on his own (or, in fact, learn much of anything at all). Mastering walking (and the climbing and running and kicking a ball and throwing and hopping and jumping to come) takes plenty of practice, along with lots of ups and downs (at this point, he may be down more than he's up). So don't bother running interference while he perfects his stride. Your role, other than that of proud but nervous spectator, is not to stand in the way—but to do everything possible to ensure that when your baby falls, he falls safely. While taking a tumble on the living room rug can bruise his ego, tumbling down the stairs can bruise a lot more. Bumping into the rounded edge of the sofa may draw some tears, but colliding with the sharp corner of a glass table may draw blood. To decrease the chance of serious injuries, be sure that your house is safe for your baby (see page 391). And even if you have removed the most obvious hazards from your baby's path, remember that the most important safety feature in your home is close and constant adult supervision.

Remember, too, that how you react to your baby's slip-ups shapes his response. Panic with each fall, and so will he. Worry endlessly about every bump, and he'll believe there's reason to worry. Shrieks of "Are you okay? Are you okay?" or dramatic gasps and shudders are sure to cue the crying—even if the fall didn't hurt. The idea is to protect him without becoming overprotective (which may make him overcautious). Respond instead with a calm "Oops, you fell down! You're all right. Up you go," and you'll help your little trooper take minor tumbles in stride, getting right back on his feet without missing a beat.

Shoes for Walking

"Our baby has just taken her first steps. What kind of shoes does she need now?"

The best shoes for a new walker are . . . no shoes at all. Since walking barefoot actually helps build arches and strengthen ankles, those tiny feet will develop best when they're bare, not covered and confined. But barefoot won't always cut it—as when your baby is outside and her feet need protection from broken glass, dog poop, or from being stepped on by other people's shoes. So it's time for a trip to the shoe store to look for shoes that are as close to bare feet as possible. Look for:

Just-right fit. Your baby's shoes should fit her just right. Too big, and your baby may slip, slide, and even trip in them. Too small, and they'll pinch and restrict. Check the width by pinching the side of the shoe at its widest point. If you can grasp a tiny bit of it between your fingers, the width is just right. Check the length by pressing your thumb just beyond the tip of the big toe. If there's a thumb's width (about half an inch) of room, the length is right. Check the heel fit by trying to slide your pinky between baby's heel and the back of the shoe. It should fit, but snugly. Reddened areas on baby's toes or feet when shoes are removed mean the fit is too tight.

Lightweight. New walkers have a hard enough time putting one bare foot in front of another. The weight of a heavy shoe can make this tricky new skill even more challenging. So think lightweight: soft leather, canvas, or cloth.

Flexible nonslip soles. Feet are flexible, and shoes should be, too. You should be able to bend the toe of the shoe up (about 40 degrees) easily. And look for a shoe that has good traction to help keep your baby on her feet. Nonskid leather or rubber soles, especially those equipped with grooves or bumps for when baby becomes a more proficient walker, will keep your baby from slipping as she walks and won't be so ground-gripping that it'll be hard for her to lift her feet. Even dress shoes should have good traction on the soles.

Padding. The shoes should offer firm support but should be padded on the heel backs and around the ankles to minimize rubbing and on the bottom inside for comfort.

Secure closures. Whether the shoes are secured with velcro, snaps, or laces, be sure that they are easy for you to secure onto baby's feet, but not so easy they can come loose by themselves (or be undone by baby's agile fingers). Slip-on shoes might be easy-on, but keep in mind that they're also easy-off (and can fall off easily, too).

Reasonable price. Shoes should be built to take it, but they don't have to be built to last forever. After all, your baby will be growing out of them every 3 months or so.

Remember, too, that a good shoe is only as good as the sock in it. Socks, like shoes, should fit well and be of a material (such as cotton) that allows feet to breathe. Make sure they fit without restricting the foot, and that they don't bunch up or wrinkle. When socks start leaving marks on the feet, it's time to move up to the next sock size.

Not Pulling Up Yet

"Although she's been trying for some time, my baby hasn't yet pulled up to stand. Shouldn't she be able to by now?"

For babies, life's a never-ending series of physical challenges. The skills that grown-ups take for granted—rolling over, sitting up, standing—are for them major hurdles to be confronted and conquered. And no sooner is one new skill mastered than another looms ahead. For your baby, next up is pulling up—and it's no small feat on those two little feet.

As with all skills, there's a wide range of normal when it comes to pulling up. A few scrappy babies will pull themselves up by 6 months, others won't pull off pulling up until well after the first birthday, though the majority will fall (make that, stand) somewhere in between: The average age for pulling up is 9 months. A baby's weight may have an impact on when she first pulls up—a chunkier baby has more bulk to take with her than a lighter one does, and so the effort needed may be greater. On the other hand, some lightweights may lack the muscle power needed to pull to a stand, especially if their legs are on the scrawny side. The baby who's cooped up in a stroller, baby carrier, or bouncer much of the day won't be able to practice her pull-ups. True, too, of a baby who has no steady furniture around her to pull up on. Slippery shoes or socks can also slip up pull-up efforts, making a bare foot the best foot to stand on.

As is true with almost every developmental milestone, pushing pulling up is only likely to delay it—babies need to know that their own pace is the right pace (and it is!) You can encourage your baby to try to pull up by putting a favorite toy in a place where she has to stand to get to it, and by giving her frequent opportunities to pull up to standing in your lap (she'll build her leg muscles and her confidence). Otherwise, all you need to do is sit back and wait for her to stand—in her own good time.

Baby Tooth Injuries

"My son fell and chipped one of his front teeth. Should I take him to the dentist?"

Since those cute little pearly whites will fall out someday anyway to make room for permanent teeth, a small chip in a baby tooth is usually nothing to worry about—and pretty common, considering the number of tumbles the typical fledgling toddler takes in the course of a day. Still, it's a good idea to make sure you're not dealing with anything that's more than cosmetic. First, do a quick check of the tooth. If there seem to be any sharp edges, give the doctor or dentist a call when you have a chance. The dentist may want to smooth out the edge. If your baby seems to be in any pain (even days later), if the tooth appears to have shifted positions or become infected (swollen gums can tip you off to this), or if you see a pink spot in the center of the chipped tooth, let the doctor or dentist know right away. An injury to the nerve, if left untreated, can damage the permanent tooth that is already forming in your baby's mouth. Either way, try to smile—chances are there will be plenty more bumps for your baby on the road to walking.

Boo-Boos Happen

Even in the most carefully baby-proofed of homes, even with the most vigilant supervision, boo-boos (those bumps to the noggin, those scraped knees, those fat lips) happen. Most are the kiss-and-make-better variety, but some need a little first aid, and occasionally, medical attention. See Chapter 20, starting on page 574, for all the details on injuries and treatments.

Growth Swings

"The pediatrician just told me that my son has dropped from the 90th to the 50th percentile in height. She said not to worry, but it seems like such a big drop."

There's much more to a baby's growth than percentages on a chart—and that's why pediatricians look beyond the numbers when assessing a little one's progress. Are both height and weight curves keeping pace fairly closely? Is baby passing developmental mileposts (sitting, pulling up, for example) at about the right time? Is he active and alert? Eating and sleeping normally (for him)? Does he appear happy? Does he seem to interact well with his parents? Are his hair and skin healthy looking? It sounds like the doctor is completely satisfied with the way your baby's growth and development are adding up, even with the apparent dip he's taken on the chart.

Most of the time what appears to be a sudden growth shift is just the result of a miscalculation—one made at this last visit or at a previous one. Babies are usually measured while they're lying down, and wriggling can easily mess with the results. When a child graduates to upright measurement, he may actually appear to lose an inch or so in height because his bones settle a little when he stands (plus, getting a toddler to stand up straight and stand still for a precise reading isn't easy).

Another common reason for such a growth shift at this time is that a baby who was born on the large side or who grew quickly at first is just slowing down as he moves closer to his genetically predestined size. If neither parent is tall, you shouldn't expect your son to stay in the 90th percentile—chances are that's not nature's plan for him. Height, however, isn't inherited through a single gene. So a child with a 6-foot father and a 5-foot mother may reach adulthood at the same height as one or the other (or taller or shorter than either), but he's more likely to end up somewhere in between. On average, however, each generation is a bit taller than the previous one.

Unless you have some reason (other than this drop in height) to believe that something's amiss with your son's growth and development, take your cues from the doctor. If you do have a nagging concern, ask for more reassurance.

Snacking

"My baby seems to want to eat all the time. How much snacking is good for him?"

The snacks are attacking? That's okay. Snacks in moderation play an important supporting role to those three daily squares. Here's why:

Snacks are a learning experience. How does baby eat at mealtimes? Often, spoon-fed from a bowl. How does he munch away at snack time? By picking up a piece of banana or cracker or a puff with his pudgy fingers and maneuvering it to and into his mouth all by himself—no small feat, considering how tiny his mouth is and how primitive his coordination.

Snacks fill a void. Babies have small stomachs that fill quickly and empty quickly, which means they can't go long stretches between feeds. Enter, snacks—which keep that tiny tank filled and blood sugar level, and, as solids become the mainstay of your baby's diet, nutritional gaps covered.

Snacks give baby a break. Play is a baby's work, and just as adults do, babies need breaks during their workday. A snack provides a breather—a chance to chill with some cheese and crackers before going back on the job.

Snacks make for better sleep. Blood sugar can dip during a (hopefully) long night's sleep—and that can actually prevent a baby from sleeping as long as he should. The right snack, built into the bedtime routine, can help a little one settle down faster and stay settled longer. The right snack before a nap can do the same—while helping your little one wake up feeling more energetic and less cranky.

Snacks provide oral gratification. Babies are very orally oriented—everything they pick up goes right to the mouth, and that's only natural. Snacking gives them a welcome chance to put things in their mouths without having them fished right out by a disapproving parent.

Snacks smooth the way for weaning . . . eventually. Thinking ahead to weaning—whether from a bottle at a year, or sometime after that from the breast? Getting in the snack habit now will help your little one make that large developmental leap later, with fewer hitches (a bedtime snack can supplement a bedtime feed now, supplant it later).

Snacking Smarts

Long associated with lumpy couch potatoes and mindlessly consumed calories (and don't even get Mom started on how they'll spoil your dinner), snacks have definitely gotten a bad rap, and sometimes for good reason . . . that is, if there's ever a good reason to plunge headfirst into a jumbo bag of Doritos. But the right snacks at the right time can be smart, especially for your sweetie. Just remember to:

Schedule smart. Mom was right about this: Snacks that come too close to mealtime can interfere with a baby's appetite for meals. Schedule snacks midway between meals to avoid this appetite-sabotaging snafu.

Nip nonstop snacking. Snacking that goes on all day—aka grazing—is fine for a little lamb, but not so fine for your little human. Wondering why? Nonstop nibbling can:

- Trigger tooth troubles. A mouth that's always full of food is a mouth that's ripe for decay-causing bacteria, which love to feast on sugars even healthy snacks (like whole-wheat crackers or yogurt melts) leave behind on tender teeth.

- Weigh your baby down. Certainly your baby won't have a waistline for years to come (and that's a good thing—rounded tummies are standard issue for tots). But a baby who's always eating doesn't learn appetite regulation (eat when you're hungry, stop when you're full, eat when you're hungry again). Always having something in his or her mouth now can lead to waistline struggles later.

- Slow talking. Ever try talking with your mouth full? It isn't polite or pretty—plus, it makes it really hard for others to understand what you have to say. For a baby who's experimenting with new sounds nearly every waking hour of every day, a forever-full mouth can limit valuable verbal practice.

- Cramp a baby's play style. Always having a cracker in hand (like always wielding a sippy cup or a bottle) limits play and exploration . . . especially if your baby tends to be a two-fisted snacker. Crawling or cruising with a cracker? Definitely not easy.

Snack for the right reasons. There are good reasons to snack and not-so-good reasons. Avoid offering snacks if baby's bored (distract with a toy instead of puffs), hurt (soothe with a hug and a song instead of a sippy cup), or has accomplished something that's worthy of highlighting (try a fist pump instead of a fistful of cookies).

Snack safely. Snacking should be treated pretty much as seriously as mealtime eating. Snacks should be given while baby is sitting, preferably in the high chair. Why? It's safer (a baby eating lying on his or her back, crawling around, or walking can choke too easily), it teaches table manners (always best learned at the table), and it's easier on you (you'll appreciate not finding crumbs on the sofa and spills on the carpet). Of course, if you're out and baby is in the stroller or car seat at snack time, you can serve it up there. But don't give your munching munchkin the idea that a snack is compensation for serving time in these confining quarters—being strapped into a stroller or car seat should not be a signal to bring on the crackers and the sippy cup.

Aim for one snack in the morning, one in the afternoon, and (if you think baby needs it—not all do) one before bed. You can build that last snack of the day right into the bedtime routine as long as it's scheduled before tooth-brushing time.

Increased Separation Anxiety

"We've left our baby with a sitter before, and it never seemed to bother her. But now she makes a terrible fuss every time we start walking out the door."

Separation anxiety affects most babies and toddlers, some more than others, and many . . . a lot. Which means that when it comes to being separated from their parents, absence doesn't just make the heart grow fonder, it makes the wails grow louder.

Though it may seem like your little one's regressing—after all, your coming and going never bothered her much before—separation anxiety is, in fact, a sign that she's maturing. First, she's becoming more independent, but with strings attached . . . to you. As she ventures off to explore the world on two feet (or on her hands and knees), she takes comfort in knowing that you're just a toddle away should she need you. When she separates from you (as when she leaves your side to explore the other side of the playroom, or the playground), it's on her own terms. When you separate from her (as when you leave her with a babysitter for a movie and dinner), it's not. You're the one who's leaving, she's the one who's being left—and that opens the door to separation anxiety.

Second, she's now able to comprehend the complex (for a baby) concept of object permanence—that when

someone or something isn't visible, it still exists. When she was younger and you left, she didn't miss you—out of her sight meant you were off her mind. Now when you're out of sight, you're still very much on her mind—which means she can miss you. And because she hasn't yet grasped the even more complicated concept of time, she has no idea when, or even if, you're coming back. Enter more anxiety.

Improved memory—another sign of growing maturity—also plays a role. Your baby recalls what it means when you put on your coat and say "Bye-bye" to her. She's now able to anticipate that you will be gone for some indefinite length of time when you walk out the door. A baby who hasn't been left often with a babysitter (and seen her parents return often) may also wonder whether you'll ever return. Enter still more anxiety.

While some babies can show signs of separation anxiety as early as 7 months, it usually peaks between 11 and 18 months for most. But, as with everything in child development, the timing of separation anxiety varies from tot to tot. Some little ones never experience it at all, while some start sweating separations much later, around 3 or 4 years of age. For some it lasts just a few months—for others it continues for years, sometimes continuously, sometimes on and off. Certain life stresses, such as moving, a new sibling, a new babysitter, or even tension at home can trigger a first episode of separation anxiety or a brand new bout of it . . . or just step it up.

Separation anxiety most commonly strikes when you leave your child in someone else's hands—when you're heading off to work, going out for the evening, or dropping your baby off at daycare. But it can also happen at night when you put your baby to bed (see next question). No matter what the trigger, the symptoms are the same: She'll cling to you for dear life (with superhuman baby strength that makes those arms and sticky fingers particularly difficult to pry off), cry and scream inconsolably, and resist all attempts by anyone to calm her down. In short, she'll try every trick in the baby book to keep you from walking out the door. All of which will leave you feeling guilty and stressed out over leaving her—and maybe even have you thinking twice about leaving again.

But as unsettling as it is for you (and as it appears to be for her), separation anxiety is a normal part of your baby's development—as normal (if not quite as inevitable) as learning to walk and talk. Helping her weather separations well now will help her handle them better later on (especially when the separations become ever more challenging . . . say, being left for the first time at preschool).

To minimize baby's anxiety and yours, follow these steps before stepping out:

- Choose a sitter who can take it. Make sure you're leaving your baby with a babysitter who isn't only qualified, reliable, and experienced, but can be counted on to respond with patience and understanding, no matter how hysterical your little one becomes once the door closes behind you. Gauge your baby's comfort level with a new sitter by leaving them alone together for just short periods at first—say, an hour or so—before staying out longer.

- Meet and greet before you make your retreat. Have the sitter arrive at least 15 minutes before you're planning to leave, so that she and your little one can get involved in an activity (playing with the shape sorter, stacking blocks,

putting teddy to bed). Keep in mind, however, that your baby may refuse to have anything to do with the sitter (even if she's a familiar one . . . even if she's grandma herself) while you're still home. After all, consenting to playing with the sitter might mean she's consenting to being left with her. Don't worry—once you're out the door, she'll almost certainly agree to join in the fun.

- Tame those triggers. As you've probaby noticed, even the mellowest baby can melt down in a flash when she's tired or hungry. So try to time separations for when she's recently napped and been fed. Being down with a cold or fussy from teething can also make separations more painful for all involved—just add an extra dose of comfort before you leave and when you return, and ask the sitter to offer plenty while you're away.

- Don't sneak out the back, Jack. Sure, it's easier to leave after your baby's sound asleep for the night, or before she's woken from her nap, or just when she's not looking—but that's a strategy that's bound to backfire at some point soon. She'll probably panic when she notices you're gone (or wakes up to find you're not home)—and that could result in a whole lot of crying in the short term and trust issues in the long term. You may avoid a scene this time—only to have twice the scene next time. Plus, fear that you can leave without warning at any time can increase clinginess even when you're right by her side. Unless you have to leave when she's sleeping, be up front about stepping out.

- Take your baby's anxiety seriously, but not too seriously. Separation anxiety is normal and age-appropriate, and to your baby, it's real. So don't laugh it off or ignore it, and definitely don't lose your temper over it. Validate her feelings—let her know that you understand she's upset—and then reassure her calmly and lovingly that you will come back soon. Just make sure you don't go overboard with the validation—meeting her tears with your tears or matching her anxiety with your own. After all, you don't want to give her the sense that there really is something to worry about when you leave.

■ Let her know when you'll be back. Your baby is by no means a clock watcher yet (the passing of time is meaningless to her), but it's still a good idea to start plugging in concepts of time that she will eventually be able to relate to: "I'll be back after your nap" or "I'll be home when you're eating dinner" or "I'll see you when you wake up."

■ Start a happy bye-bye tradition. "See you later, alligator . . . in a while, crocodile" is a time-honored phrase that your little one can begin associating with your leaving and returning. Say it with a smile, a quick hug, and a kiss. Other rituals you can add: blowing a kiss (baby will soon be blowing back one of her own), a special wave, or, if there's a window, having the sitter hold her there so you can wave from outside.

■ Once you leave, leave. Make the parting short and sweet—and final. Repeated appearances at the door (definitely check and double-check to make sure you have your wallet and car keys so you don't have to return for them) will make leaving harder for everyone—especially your baby, who won't be able to settle down until she knows you've really left the building.

Remember that separation anxiety doesn't last forever—though it may be a year or more before your little one's human cling wrap days are behind her. All too quickly, your child will learn to separate easily and painlessly from you. Possibly, for you, a little too easily and painlessly. One day, when your teenager heads off to school with a mumbled "bye" and (if you ask really nicely) a halfhearted hug, you'll look back fondly on the days when you couldn't pry those little fingers and arms off your leg.

Bedtime Separation Anxiety

"Our baby used to fall asleep easily and sleep through the night. But suddenly he's clinging to us and crying when we put him down—and also waking up crying during the night."

Separation anxiety, the familiar gremlin of the daylight hours, can also come out at night—and for some babies, it can produce even more anxiety in the evening. That's not really surprising, given that separating at night (if baby's sleeping in his own crib and in his own room) means being not only left, but left alone . . . often in the dark (hello, gremlins). Like daytime separation anxiety, the nighttime variety is normal and age-appropriate, and while it doesn't accompany every baby to bed, at some point, it does bed down with most. It also has the same triggers: your baby's improved memory, his increased independence and mobility, his maturing sense of himself and others (he's wised up considerably since his infant days), and at the same time, his lack of maturity (he's still sorting out the world around him and his place in it).

Playing on Team Blue, Team Pink . . . or Team Neutral?

You've stocked your baby's shelves with all kinds of toys, from baby dolls to tractors and everything in between—in other words, the gender neutral way. So why is it that your little girl always reaches for the baby doll, or your little boy for the tractor?

It's unsettling to parents understandably eager to shatter dated gender stereotypes, but sometimes it seems as plain as the pink or blue beanies babies get matched with in the hospital nursery. Though there's definitely plenty of individual variation from child to child, and lots of overlap, too, some little ones seem born to play on either Team Blue or Team Pink. As a whole, boys and girls tend to exhibit developmental differences even in infancy, thanks to the different hormones they're exposed to in utero. Right from birth, girls (on average) show more interest in people and faces than boys do, which may be one reason why little girls are ultimately more likely to play with dolls.

On the other hand, boys are born with more muscle mass, which might be why they're (on average) more physically active and may advance physically faster than girls. As they grow, they're also typically better at—and tend to gravitate toward—activities that take advantage of their mechanical and spatial skills, such as playing with blocks, flipping switches, and pushing buttons. Though boys can be as eager to work their smiles as girls, they tend to be somewhat less focused on faces and more focused on objects.

While nature definitely plays a role in how girls and boys play and play differently, nurture is believed to make a considerable contribution as well—those societal "norms" have a way of sticking around long after society tries to shed them. Even with best intentions and conscious efforts to remain gender neutral in the care of their babies, parents may inadvertently choose sides based on long-passé pink or blue perceptions—in nursery color schemes and beyond. Both moms and dads tend to talk to baby girls more than they do baby boys, reinforcing any biological predisposition girls have for focusing on their social development. They may offer comfort more freely to a little girl, nurturing the nurturer in her more than they might in a boy. Boys might get the short end of the comfort stick but get more in the way of roughhousing fun.

Which absolutely isn't to say that your little one is locked from birth into gender stereotypes, destined to play actively on Team Blue, or socially on Team Pink. Many babies buck gender trends right from the start—and clearly, they should be encouraged to color their world any way they'd like (pink, blue, or some unique blend of both). Nor does it mean that you should give up trying to break those outmoded pink and blue molds. Filling your baby's toy box with dolls and trucks, balls and strollers, blocks and crayons is a great place to start—and so is filling your baby boy's need for verbal and emotional attention, and your baby girl's need to get physical.

If you co-sleep with your cutie, no separation means no separation anxiety . . . and no problem (that is, unless you expect your baby to fall asleep without you earlier in the evening before joining him later). But if you're determined to keep (or make) your bed your own, you'll want to find ways to ease the anxiety that sometimes comes out at night and that can prevent everyone from getting the restful evening they need. Here are some strategies for nipping bedtime anxiety in the bud:

- Have a peaceful prelude to bedtime. Keep the hour or two leading up to bedtime as calm, reassuring, and nurturing as possible, especially if you've been at work all day, but even if you've just been busy around the house. Try to give your baby as much attention as you can, putting everything else (such as making and eating your dinner or catching up on work) on hold until he's asleep. This will help keep his stress level low before bedtime while storing up some reserves of mommy and daddy comfort he can tap into later, when he needs it most.

- Rely on routines. A bedtime ritual isn't just sleep-inducing—it's comforting at a time in your little one's life when comfort comes from consistency. Each night it reassures your baby (and soon, your toddler) that the same predictable events will take place in the same predictable sequence—no surprises means fewer anxieties. A bedtime routine can also become the start of a nighttime cycle that your little one will come to anticipate with good feelings—instead of fear. See page 355 for more on bedtime rituals.

- Bridge the gap with a lovey. A transitional (or comfort) object often helps make the tricky transition from awake to sleep easier for your cutie. It could be a favorite small stuffed animal or a tiny blanket for clutching (big blankets for covering are still not recommended at this age). Not all tots get their comfort fix from a blanket or other type of lovey— but many do. If yours does, bring it on. Think your baby is unsettled by being left alone in the dark? A nightlight can help bring the comfort he needs.

- Be reassuring. Give your baby a hug and kiss before you put him down in his crib, then say your good-night. Consistency is valuable here, too— it's best if you keep the good-nights as routine as the rest of the bedtime ritual (something like, "Nighty-night, sleep tight, see you in the morning light"). A loving but light tone in your voice will help, as well. Just as by day, if your baby senses that you're anxious about separating at bedtime, he will likely be, too.

  If your baby cries, continue to calmly and quietly reassure him— gently putting him back down if he's pulled up. Use this strategy, too, if your baby wakes up again during the night. Be consistent in your approach to comfort—using the same techniques, the same words—but also try to do progressively less each night (offering the comfort first from cribside, then from a few feet away, then from the doorway). Saying something like, "Mommy (or Daddy) is right here. Go back to sleep. I'll see you in the morning" will reinforce the message that night will end predictably with day. Or just repeat your chosen good-night phrase.

- Be consistent. This deserves repeating. And repeating. Without consistency, life is confusing and unnecessarily stressful for little ones. And without consistency, even the best tricks in the parenting book won't work. So even if your new strategy for separations doesn't seem to ease anxiety at first, keep at it. With a consistent approach, your baby will learn to handle nighttime separations—and stop fighting bedtime and sleep.

■ Check the guilt at the door. Just as co-sleeping is a valid option, so is deciding you'd like to keep sleeping arrangements separate. Once you've made that decision, feel free to feel good about it, instead of guilty. Staying with your little one all night won't help him overcome nighttime separation anxiety (any more than avoiding leaving him with a babysitter would help him overcome separation anxiety during waking hours), but a consistent routine, lovingly applied, will . . . eventually.

Giving Up on a Nap

"Suddenly my son doesn't want to nap in the morning. Is one nap a day enough for him?"

Although your little guy's single nap a day may not be enough for you, that's all some babies need as they approach 1 year of age. Most often it's the morning nap that gets dropped, but occasionally it's the after-lunch siesta. A very few babies even try to give up both naps at this time (yikes!). Babies of other lucky parents continue to nap twice a day well into the second year, and that's perfectly normal, too, as long as it doesn't seem to be interfering with a good night's sleep.

But here's something to keep in mind while you're lamenting the loss of your baby's morning nap: How many times a day your baby sleeps matters less than how well he functions on the sleep he's getting (how well you function on the sleep he's getting is another matter entirely). If nap skipping doesn't bring out the crankies and if he's not too overtired to settle down for a good afternoon nap and a full night's sleep, then you may have to kiss those two-nap days good-bye.

If your baby fights his morning nap but is consistently overtired later in the day, it may be that he's resisting the extra rest because it cuts into his busy schedule. Time wasted sleeping, he figures, could be better spent pulling books off the shelf or trying to eat your cell phone. Not clocking in necessary naptime, however, makes for a less-happy baby by day—and often one who's too overcharged to settle down at night.

To help your baby get the sleep he needs, try a naptime routine that's an abridged version of his bedtime one. Feed and change him, create a relaxing environment (darken the room and sing a lullaby, for example), and then put him down. Don't give up if he doesn't fall asleep right away, since some babies need more time to settle down during the day. If he still refuses, you can try a sleep training method (see page 349), but not for as long as you would at night (more than 20 minutes of crying, and there goes his naptime).

He's definitely not down for the morning nap, but he's rubbing his eyes long before his usual afternoon nap? Consider having him take that single nap earlier in the afternoon to keep the crankies (his—and yours) at bay. If necessary you can move his bedtime up a bit to accommodate the earlier nap.

For Parents: Thinking About the Next Baby

Mother Nature's whims (and birth control malfunctions) notwithstanding, the decision of how many months or years to wait before getting pregnant again is a couple's alone to make, and different couples feel very differently about the subject. Some feel very strongly that they'd like to cluster their children together. Others feel just as strongly that they'd like several years—or more—of breathing (and sleeping) room between deliveries. And the way couples feel about child spacing before they actually become parents ("Wouldn't it be great to have them just a year apart?") isn't necessarily the way they feel once the reality of endless diaper changes and sleepless nights sinks in ("Maybe we need a break before we try this again").

There aren't very many firm facts to help parents make their decision. Most experts agree that postponing conception for at least a year after baby number one allows a woman's body to recover from pregnancy and childbirth before beginning the reproductive cycle all over again. But that health issue aside, there's little evidence of an ideal spacing period between children. Researchers haven't found that spacing affects intelligence or emotional development, or sibling relationships (which have more to do with their personalities than their age difference).

The bottom line: It's all your call. The best time for you to add to your family is when you feel your family is ready.

Still don't have a clue? Ask yourselves these questions:

Will we be able to handle two babies at one time? Children under 2 (or even 3) are high maintenance—requiring constant attention and care. If your second baby arrives before your oldest is 2, you'll be doing double diaper duty, enduring endless sleepless nights, and, if they're really close in age, dealing with the more difficult aspects of toddler behavior (such as tantrums and negativity) in two toddlers at once. On the flip side, although caring for closely spaced children will probably leave you exhausted at first, once the first few years have passed, you'll have put those challenges behind you (unless you decide to start all over again with number three). Spacing kids more closely together will also mean that you won't have to dig as deep to remember baby-care basics (though recommendations can change surprisingly quickly). Another perk for parents: Sibs close in age are likely to enjoy the same toys, movies, activities, and vacations.

Do we want to start all over again? Once you're in baby mode, it's sometimes easier to just stay that way, consolidating the years spent on baby care into a shorter (if more intense) time frame. The crib is set up, the diaper wipes are in place, the stroller isn't yet collecting dust in the attic, the safety gates are still up, and you don't remember what sleep or a sex life is, so you won't miss them when they're once again gone. Spacing children far apart requires you to reorient yourself to the demands of having a baby again, just when your oldest is independently off at school and you're getting your lives back in order. Of course, having a new baby a few years after the first allows you ample time to shower attention on one child before the arrival of the next. And since the oldest most likely won't be at home all the time, you'll get that same opportunity to provide individual attention to your younger child.

Am I physically ready to go through a new pregnancy? This is a question only a mom can answer. Maybe you just don't feel ready to roll through pregnancy again so soon, especially if your first was a rough ride. Maybe you're not super pumped about the prospect of chasing a 1-year-old while you're headed to the bathroom with morning sickness. Or toting a toddler along when you have a watermelon-size belly (talk about heavy lifting!). Maybe you'd just like a baby-free-body break before resuming reproduction and breastfeeding.

On the other hand, if you've had nothing but joy producing and nursing your first bundle of joy—maybe you don't feel there's any reason to postpone additional bundles of joy. Or maybe the sound of a ticking biological clock, or the feeling that you'd like to finish up your baby-making days by the time you're a certain age, has you resolute about resuming reproduction sooner than later.

What gap will make the kids closer? There's certainly no consensus on this issue, and results can vary widely, depending on the children's temperament, the way sibling conflicts are resolved, the atmosphere around the home, and many more factors. For instance, if there is a very large gap in ages between siblings, they might grow up not feeling like siblings at all—or they might have a very special affection for each other. Siblings spaced far apart may experience less rivalry than those closer in age, since the oldest sibling already has a life outside the home (school, sports, friends), may actually appreciate the new addition more, and may even help out with the baby. Plus, when sibs aren't playing on a level developmental field, there's no need to compete. Or an older sib may resent the responsibilities of having a baby around the house—or the social life adjustments.

Though your little ones won't necessarily be close if they're close in age, their developmental similarities are more likely to make them natural playmates for each other. Of course, it's those similarities that will also make them more prone to sibling squabbles. The fact that they'll probably enjoy the same toys might be both a convenience (fewer toys to buy) and a hassle (more tug-of-war over the toys). Having children close in age may minimize the adjustment of a very young older child to a new sibling—after all, there's less to miss about being the only child if you've been one for only a short time. On the other hand, a very young older sibling may resent the sudden shortage of much needed lap space.

What about us? Also factor in your twosome when contemplating when to expand your family of three to a family of four (or more). Clearly, you'll want to make this decision as a united team, considering work and child care, time together as a couple, romance . . . and yes, your sex life.

How close in age are my siblings to me? If you had a great experience growing up with a much younger or much older sibling, you might hope the same for your children. If you found yourself always fighting with your close-in-age sister or feeling distant from your already-grown brother, you may choose to space your own kids farther apart.

Thinking about expanding the family again? There are plenty of preconception steps you and your spouse can take to improve your chances of fertility success, as well as the odds of having a safe pregnancy and a healthy baby. For more, check out *What to Expect Before You're Expecting*.

Content with your one and not looking for more in the near future—or even ever? One-and-happily-done can be the perfect decision, too.

"Forgetting" a Skill

"Last month my daughter was waving bye-bye all the time, but now she seems to have forgotten how. I thought she was supposed to move forward developmentally, not backward."

She is moving forward developmentally . . . it's probably just forward to other skills. It's very common for a baby to practice perfecting a skill almost continuously for a while—to her delight and everyone else's—and then, once she's mastered it, to put it aside while she takes on a new developmental challenge. There's also the possibility that she's getting tired of taking "bye-bye" requests. Your baby is way cuter than any monkey, but she may be feeling like a performing chimp if you're forever asking for repeat performances. Though your baby has tired of her old trick of waving bye-bye, she's more than likely excited by a new one she's rehearsing now, perhaps barking every time she sees a four-legged animal or playing peekaboo and pat-a-cake. All of which she will eventually temporarily retire, too, once they become ho-hum. Instead of worrying about what your baby seems to have forgotten (or prodding her to pull an old trick out again), tune in to and encourage her in whatever new skills she's busy developing. You need to be concerned only if your baby suddenly seems unable to do many things she did before and if she doesn't seem to be learning anything new. If that's the case, check with the doctor.

ALL ABOUT:
Baby Talk for the Older Baby

You've come a long way, baby, since you breathed in your first gulp of air and let out your first cry, heralding your own arrival ("Look out, world—here I come!"): from a newborn whose only form of communication was crying and who understood nothing but his or her own primal needs . . . to a smiling, cooing 3-month-old . . . to a 6-month-old who started finding a voice (and collecting a repertoire of sounds, from babble to bubbles), making sense out of words, and expressing a wide range of emotions . . . to an 8-month-old who began conveying meaningful messages through primitive sounds and gestures . . . and now, to a 10-month-old who has spoken (or will soon speak) those first real words. And yet with all the communication accomplishments already behind your baby, still more astounding verbal achievements are just around the bend. In the months to come, your little one's comprehension will increase at a remarkable rate—and though it will lag at first behind receptive language (words understood), your baby's expressive vocabulary (words spoken) will expand exponentially in the next year.

Here's how you can help your baby's language development:

Label, label, label. Everything in your baby's world has a name. And there's no better way to teach those names than by saying them—often. Label objects around the house (bathtub, sink, stove, crib, lights, chair, couch) and food that you and baby eat or that you're dropping into the shopping cart at the store.

Play eyes-nose-mouth (take baby's hand and touch your eyes, your nose, and your mouth, kissing that sweet hand at the last stop). Point out arms, legs, hands, and feet as well as shirt, pants, skirt, shoes, boots, coat. Identify birds, dogs, trees, leaves, flowers, cars, trucks, and fire engines wherever you see them. Don't leave out people—point out mommies, daddies, babies, women, men, girls, boys. And don't forget about baby's name, too. Using it often will help your little one develop a sense of self ("Wait a second . . . that's me!").

Listen, listen, listen. While keeping up a steady stream of speech helps your baby beef up his or her vocabulary, everyone needs a chance to express themselves—especially baby talkers. When your baby starts jabbering on (about what, you're not sure), pause, look him or her in the face, and really listen as if you understood every attempt at words. Even if you haven't identified any real words yet, listen to the babble and respond, the best you can: "Really? That's awesome!" Baby's not buying it—the communication gap is so massive that you can't figure out what baby's trying to say or asking for, and frustration's building fast? Point to possible candidates ("Do you want the ball? The bottle? The puzzle?"), giving baby a moment to let you know whether you've guessed right (maybe not through words, but through body language). You won't always bridge the communication gap or ease frustration, but your sweet talker will take note that you're paying close attention—which will encourage more verbal efforts.

Question, question, question. Ask lots of questions. ("Should we walk to the park or the play gym?" "Do you think Grandma would like this birthday card with flowers on it, or this one with the birds?") Then follow up with an answer.

("Yes, I think Grandma would like these pretty birds.") Yup, you're talking to yourself, technically, but you're also modeling the give-and-take of conversation.

Give a play-by-play. Stumped for a topic of conversation? Just tell your baby what you're doing. "Mama is zipping up Jayden's jacket—zzzip! That will keep you nice and warm. Now let's put on some mittens—one, two—and a hat. How about this one with the blue dots?" Hear something? Point it out to your baby: "Listen, a doggie is barking!" or "I hear a car going zoom, zoom down the street." And be sure to explain what's going on around your little one, too: "It's sunny today." "The apple is in the fridge." "Daddy uses a little brush to brush your teeth and a big brush for your hair." "The ball goes up, the ball comes down." "Soap makes my hands clean." And so on.

Concentrate on concepts. Language learning isn't just about words—it's about concepts, too. So take the time to teach your baby as you go about your day:

- Hot and cold: Let baby touch the outside of your warm (not hot) coffee cup, then an ice cube. Cold water, then warm water. Warm oatmeal, then cold milk. Point out that the yogurt you took out of the fridge is cold, the peas you took out of the freezer are very cold . . . brrrrr.

- Up and down: Gently lift baby up in the air, then lower to the ground. Place a toy up on the dresser, then put it down on the floor. Go up the stairs (or escalator, or elevator) together, then down.

- In and out: Put blocks in a container, dump them out. Pour water in a cup, then pour it out. Fill the shopping cart, with groceries then take them out at the checkout.

■ Empty and full: Show baby a container filled with bathwater, then one that's empty. A pail filled with sand, then an empty one.

■ Stand and sit: Hold baby's hands, stand together, then sit down together (use Ring Around the Rosie to help with this concept). If baby's not yet standing, hold him or her while you stand and sit.

■ Wet and dry: Compare a wet washcloth and a dry towel. Baby's just-shampooed hair with your dry hair. Wet laundry with dry laundry. Dry cereal with cereal that's moistened with milk.

■ Big and little: Set a big ball beside a little one or sit a big teddy next to a little one. Show baby that "Daddy is big and baby is little" in the mirror.

Become color conscious. Colors are everywhere, so start identifying them whenever you can: "Look at that red balloon. It's red, just like your shirt," or "That truck is green, and your stroller is green, too," or "Look at those pretty yellow flowers." Keep in mind, however, that most little ones don't "learn" their colors (they may notice different colors but can't typically identify them) until sometime around age 3.

Use doublespeak. Use adult phrases, then translate them into baby shorthand: "Did you hurt yourself when you fell? Did Connor get a boo-boo?" "Oh, you've finished your snack. Kylie made all gone." Talking twice as much will help baby understand twice as much.

Don't talk like a baby. Baby talk is precious—especially when you're imitating your baby. But opting for simplified grown-up talk, rather than baby talk,

will help your baby learn to speak your language faster: "Abby wants a bottle?" instead of "Baby wanna baba?" Forms like doggie or dolly, however, are always fine to use with babies—they're naturally more appealing.

Introduce pronouns. Baby won't know a "he" from a "him" or an "I" from a "me" for at least a year to come, but that's no reason to pass by those pronouns now. Help develop familiarity with pronouns by using them along with names. "Daddy is going to get Liam breakfast—I'm going to get you breakfast." "This book is Mommy's—it's mine. That book is Ella's—it's yours."

Encourage talking back. Use any ploy you can think of to get your baby to respond—and it doesn't matter if the response comes in the form of words or gestures. Ask your little chatterbox-to-be questions: "Do you want bread or crackers?" or "Do you want to wear your Elmo pajamas or the ones with Thomas on them?" or "Are you sleepy?" and then give baby a chance to answer. Any answer counts—it could be a shake of the head, a pointing finger or hand, a gesture, a grunt, or another creative preverbal response. Get baby to help you locate things (even if they aren't really lost): "Can you find the ball?" Give baby plenty of time to turn up the item, and reinforce with cheers. Even looking in the right direction should count: "That's right, there's the ball!" And remember: Never withhold something because your little one doesn't have the word power to ask for it by name or, later, when pronunciation is less than perfect, and later still, when grammar's not quite up to speed.

Keep directions simple. Sometime around the first birthday (often before), most little ones can begin following simple commands, but only if they're issued one step at a time. Instead of "Please pick up the spoon and give it to me," try, "Please pick up the spoon," and when that's been done, add, "Now, please give the spoon to Daddy."

Correct carefully. Don't count on your baby saying those new words perfectly for a while, or even understandably. Many consonants will be beyond your baby's reach for the next several years, and even basic words may be abbreviated ("mo mi" may mean "more milk" and "dow" signal "go down"). When your baby (age appropriately) mispronounces a word, use a subtle approach to correct—teaching without preaching—so you don't discourage next efforts. When baby looks up at the sky and says, "Moo, tar," respond with "That's right. There's the moon and the stars." Though baby mispronunciations are adorable, resist the temptation to repeat them, which will be confusing (baby's supposed to be learning how they should sound).

Expand your reading repertoire. Books are a super source of new words for a baby—so call for storytime often. Baby's attention span's still too short for a cover-to-cover sitting? Keep it interesting by making reading interactive. Stop to discuss the pictures ("Look, that cat is wearing a hat!"), ask your child to point to familiar objects (naming them will come later), and name those he or she hasn't seen before or doesn't remember. Simplify language where necessary to boost comprehension, and find the rhythm in rhymes.

Pretty soon your little listener will be able to fill in words that have become familiar.

Think numerically. Counting may be a long way off for baby, but that doesn't mean numbers—and the concept of one or many—don't count now. Comments like "Here, you can have one cookie," or "Look, see how many birds are in that tree," or "You have two kitty cats" add basic mathematical concepts. Count, or recite, "One, two, buckle my shoe" as you climb the stairs with your baby, particularly once he or she can walk up while you hold both hands. Sing number rhymes, such as "Baa, baa, black sheep" (when you get to the "three bags full," hold up three fingers, then bend down one finger at a time as you pretend to distribute the bags) or "This old man, he played one, he played knick-knack on my thumb." Integrate counting into your baby's life: Count out your crunches, the cups of flour you're adding to the muffin batter, the banana slices you're topping baby's cereal with.

Sign up. Using signs and hand motions for words reduces frustration for both of you by allowing your baby to communicate before he or she is able to say real words (those pudgy little fingers can speak volumes). And signing doesn't interfere with your little one's spoken language development—in fact, most experts say the reverse is true. As you teach signs, you also use your words—and talking to your baby is the best way to get him or her talking. For more on using baby signs, see page 415.

CHAPTER 17

The Twelfth Month

....

Life's a game to baby these days, or actually, due to a still relatively short attention span, many different games played in rapid succession. One game that will soon become particularly engaging: dropping things (baby's finally figured out how to let go of objects), seeing them fall, watching mommy or daddy pick them up, and then repeating the sequence over and over—preferably until parental backs are aching and patience is worn thin. Push toys may become another obsession, since they help little ones who are just starting out on two feet stay steady as they go . . . and go . . . and go. If the push toy has a place to hold stuff—say, a favorite stuffed animal, a collection of blocks, mommy's wallet, daddy's keys, or anything else picked up along the way—all the better. This month you may also notice signs that your baby—small and cute though he or she still is—won't be a baby much longer. As independent mobility progresses, you'll slowly but surely begin to glimpse behaviors (the dawn of negativity, primitive temper tantrums, a mini my-way-or-the-highway mind-set) that foreshadow the theme of the year that lies ahead: I Am Toddler, Hear Me Roar.

Feeding Your Baby: Weaning from the Breast

Weaning from the breast may be just around the corner, or months (or even years) down the line. Either way, it's a big step on that long road to independence—a step that means your little one will never again be quite so dependent on you for a meal. It's also a step that's almost as big for you as it is

Baby Basics at a Glance: Twelfth Month

Sleeping. As the first birthday approaches, expect your nearly-tot to sleep around 10 to 12 hours per night, plus take two daytime naps (they might get shorter) or one longer nap—for a total of anywhere between 12 and 14 hours.

Eating. Breast milk or formula intake tops out at about 24 ounces (or less) per day and should edge closer to 16 ounces per day by the first birthday, with solid food becoming the more important part of baby's diet. Some babies are big eaters, some are smaller eaters—which means intake will vary a lot. So what's the average? Around ¼ to ½ cup each of grains, fruit, and veggies twice a day, ¼ to ½ cup (or more) of dairy foods per day, ¼ to ½ cup (or more) of protein foods per day, and 3 to 4 ounces of juice per day (as always, juice is optional). Keep in mind that some babies will eat less as they enter the second year and as their rate of growth slows down.

Playing. Baby's walking (or almost walking)? Pull and push toys will top the list of favorites now. So bring out the baby doll stroller, the toy shopping cart, or the activity center on wheels that baby can push around the house. Ride-on toys that push your little one toward independent mobility will also appeal to your almost-toddler. But don't neglect the old-time favorites: blocks and other stacking toys, puzzles and shape sorters, puppets, activity cubes, musical toys, crayons and markers, and, of course, books and lots of them. Role-play toys will start to play a role, too, as baby becomes more imaginative and a master mimic (think dolls, a playhouse, a play kitchen, pretend food and tableware, a toy phone, a workbench, a doctor kit).

for your baby, and one you'll want to be prepared for physically and emotionally. For support and strategies dealing with this major milestone, whenever it comes, read on.

When to Wean

Those early days of breastfeeding—when you fumbled through every feeding session, when you spent as much time nursing sore nipples as you did nursing your baby, when let-down often let you down—are now just a blur. These days, breastfeeding is second nature for both you and baby—something you can both do in your sleep (and probably occasionally do). You feel as if you've been breastfeeding forever—and in a way, you wish that you could breastfeed forever. At the same time, maybe you're wondering whether it's almost time to call it quits.

When to wean? While there are plenty of facts and feelings to consider, ultimately, Mom, it's up to you. Meanwhile, think on:

The facts. You've heard this one before (over and over again): Though any amount of breastfeeding is better than none, the AAP recommends that breastfeeding continue—ideally—for at least a full year, and then for as long as both mom and baby want to keep it up. Waiting until the first birthday to wean means that the baby who has never taken formula can move directly from breast milk to cups of milk, with no formula stopgap in between—and that's definitely a plus.

Not in any hurry to wean your baby, and your baby's in no hurry to be weaned? There are no facts standing in the way of continued breastfeeding—into the second year, the third year, or even beyond. Just remember that since busy toddlers need more protein, vitamins, and other nutrients than breast milk alone can provide, they'll need to do their share of eating (and cow's milk drinking), too.

Does your breastfeeding teammate co-sleep and do a lot of all-night nipping? Just one caveat to consider: While as a group, breastfed children develop fewer cavities than those who bottle-feed, according to the American Academy of Pediatric Dentistry, throughout-the-night breastfeeds (which aren't necessary for an older baby anyway) can lead to dental decay—especially once carbs have been introduced into baby's diet. While the risk is far lower than it is for all-night bottle-feeders, it makes sense to avoid this potential pitfall by nursing at bedtime but not throughout the night.

Your feelings. Are you still enjoying breastfeeding as much as ever? Are you in absolutely no rush to give up this special part of your relationship with baby? Then continue as long as you and baby like.

Or are you starting to grow weary of hauling your breasts in and out of your nursing bra (and weary of wearing nursing bras)? Are you beginning to yearn for some of the freedom and flexibility that seem but a pipe dream as long as you're piping in your baby's milk supply? Is the idea of breastfeeding a toddler just not within your comfort zone? If that sounds like your profile, you may want to consider weaning soon after baby's first birthday.

Your baby's feelings. Is your little one restless at the breast? Indifferent when you unhook your nursing bra? Nursing for only a minute before wriggling to get down? Your baby might be telling you something. Not in so many words, but in so many actions—actions that show your little nurser may be ready to move on to the future, a future where liquid nourishment comes from a different source. Self-weaning is most likely to happen somewhere between 9 and 12 months, so if your baby seems to want to bid the breast bye-bye, it may be time to let go. Just remember, taking those first steps to self-weaning doesn't mean your baby is rejecting you—only the milk delivery service you've been providing.

Of course, it's very possible to misinterpret a baby's signals. At 5 months, lack of interest in nursing may only be a sign of your little one's growing interest in the world around him or her. (Who has time to nurse when there are so many bright, shiny objects vying for baby's attention?) At 7 months, it may suggest a craving for getting-up-and-going that outweighs any craving for hunkering-down-and-eating. At 9 months or later, it may be the first sign of an emerging independent streak—and a preference for sipping fluids from a cup. And at any age, it could be a response to distractions (nursing in a dark, quiet room can minimize those), a stuffy nose (it's hard to breathe when your nose is stuffed and your mouth is stuffed with a nipple), or teething (ouch!).

Your baby is as attached to the breast as ever—maybe more so? It's possible that he or she will never be the one to take the initiative in weaning, which means weaning will be your call when the time comes. That's just as common, and just as normal.

Your situation. Recommendations aside, sometimes the logistics of juggling breast, baby, and life (including work or school) get in the way of continued breastfeeding. Penciling nursing into a busy schedule starts to get tricky, especially if the logistics must include a breast pump as well as transporting and storing milk. For some moms, it's just a matter of the physical toll continued breastfeeding can take—it can be a drain, literally, particularly for pumpers. If breastfeeding just isn't fitting in with your life or your lifestyle anymore, consider weaning—either fully or partially.

Your baby's situation. The best time to wean a baby is when all's quiet on the home front. Baby's sick? Teething? Are you moving? Going on vacation? Returning to work? Have you changed babysitters? Has daddy just been deployed on a long mission or gone on an extended business trip? It's probably best to hold off on weaning until there's less uncertainty and stress in your little one's life.

Your baby's bottle and cup skills. If your baby is a pro at bottles because you've been supplementing or pumping, weaning from breast to bottle will be a breeze. Likewise, if your baby has picked up cup drinking already, weaning directly to a cup—and bypassing

the bottle completely—will be a cinch. If, however, your baby resists taking milk from any source but your breast, weaning will have to wait until either the bottle or the cup (a better option as baby approaches the first birthday) is mastered.

Whenever and however it comes for you, weaning is bound to be a time of mixed emotions. On the one hand, you may be somewhat relieved to be relieved of your breastfeeding responsibilities—positively giddy at the prospect of more freedom (a late night out on the town, a weekend out of town), of leaving for work without a breast pump, of ditching your nursing bras. But, at the same time, you'll probably be more than a little misty at the end of this chapter in your mommy-baby relationship.

Whether early or late, weaning is an inevitable milestone in a child's development—as they say, nobody goes off to college still breastfeeding. Your little one probably won't end up missing breastfeeding for more than a brief time, and will likely move on more quickly than you'd really like. And you, too, will survive this monumental mommyhood moment—though realistically, you'll always have a special place in your heart reserved for the months (and maybe years) spent breastfeeding your baby.

How to Wean from the Breast

Have you decided to call it quits on the breast? With weaning right around the corner, it's probably looming large. So it might be comforting to know that the process is already in progress: You actually started to wean the first time you offered your baby a sip from the cup, a nip from the bottle, or a nibble from a spoon. And whether you realized it or not, you've been taking baby steps ever since.

Weaning is basically a two-phase process, one of which is likely well under way or even fully accomplished:

Phase One: Getting baby used to other sources of food beyond your breasts. Chances are, you've already begun baby on solids, but what about the cup? Ultimately, the cup will be an important conveyer of nutritive fluids every growing child needs, probably in the form of cow's milk. But since it takes lots of practice to become a cup pro, it's ideal to get that practice started as soon as possible, while your baby is still somewhat open to change (fast-forward a few months, and you'll definitely hit a cooperation speed bump). Getting the cup established now is smart no matter when you'll be weaning, but it's especially key if you'll be moving on to Phase Two of weaning soon. Keep in mind that weaning to a bottle doesn't make sense at this late date—after all, doctors recommend weaning from a bottle at the first birthday.

Is your almost-toddler resisting the cup already—refusing to sip from anything but the best (breast)? Break down resistance by:

- Serving up a cup when baby's hungry. Hunger can (sometimes) wear a baby down—so try offering the cup instead of a scheduled breastfeed. Baby just becomes cranky, not pliable, when hungry? Then offer the cup after a feed. Or serve it with meals and snacks.

- Staying out of the picture. As when you were introducing the bottle (if you did), baby's more likely to be up for the cup when mom's not the one offering it. After all, breasts can be distracting to a breastfeeding baby.

- Switching it up. Some babies are more likely to consider the cup if it's filled with familiar breast milk. Others are more open to the cup if it doesn't remind them of the breast. In that case, substitute formula (before age 1). You can also offer water or watered-down juice for practice. After a year (and the doctor's go-ahead), you can switch directly to whole cow's milk.

- Varying the cups. If you've been trying a sippy cup, try a straw cup—or a cup that allows baby to drink from the rim, just like you do (these are available in covered, spillproof form or with special inserts that slow the flow of liquid).

- Being relaxed. Of course you're eager for baby to start taking the cup, especially if you're eager to get weaning. But don't let your baby know that. Put on an indifferent front (as if you couldn't care less whether baby took the cup or not), practice patience, and give it time.

Phase Two: Cutting back on breast-feedings. Are you considering a cold-turkey approach to weaning (say, leaving your breastfed baby for an overnight or a weekend, and taking your breasts with you)? Usually, that's not the best game plan for either member of the breastfeeding team. For your little one, it may be too unsettling. For you, sudden weaning can make a mom an emotional mess (especially once hormonal havoc has been unleashed) and a physical one, too (leaking, painful engorgement, clogged ducts, and infection are all more likely if nursing stops suddenly). So unless illness, a sudden need for travel without baby, or some other event in your lives makes cold-turkey weaning necessary, take it slowly. Wean gradually, beginning at least several weeks—and up to many

For Parents: Making the Breast Adjustment

For your little one, moving on after weaning probably won't take long—a little extra comfort, a few distracting activities, and he or she will be ready to toddle off to face a future that doesn't include breastfeeding. For you and your breasts, weaning may be a . . . heavier lift. Though taking it slowly will lessen that load—literally, since you'll gradually be making less milk, meaning your breasts will become gradually lighter—it won't guarantee a perfectly smooth adjustment. Some discomfort is a given, and if you wean more suddenly, you can experience engorgement—though thankfully, the fullness shouldn't be nearly as bad as it was when your milk first came in. You can find relief in warm showers, warm compresses, a dose of pain reliever as needed, and perhaps expressing just enough milk to relieve the pressure but not enough to stimulate production.

Several weeks after weaning, your breasts may seem totally empty of milk. But don't be surprised if you're still able to express small amounts of milk months, even a year or more, later. This is perfectly normal. It's also normal for breasts to take time to return to their former size, or close to it, and they often end up somewhat larger or smaller, and very often lopsided. A possible unexpected side effect of weaning: You may start shedding the hair that you accumulated during pregnancy. Sometimes this normal postpartum hair loss is delayed until after breastfeeding wraps up.

Weaning can also take an emotional toll on you. Your hormones will have to adjust to the new reality of retirement—an adjustment that isn't made overnight (there is no "off" switch for milk production). You may become irritable, have mood swings, feel down, even a little depressed. Add to that the sense of loss and sadness you may have about giving up this special part of your relationship with your little one, and you may feel a familiar sense of baby blues. That's not only completely understandable, it's completely normal (though if you feel more than a little depressed, check in with the doctor—sometimes postpartum depression can surface for the first time after weaning).

months—before your targeted weaning completion date. (Once you're down to a single feed, you can consider taking yourself and your breasts out of the picture entirely for a day or two, leaving baby with daddy, grandparents, or another favorite non-lactating care provider. This kind of mommy break can sometimes ease the final adjustment to the world of weaned.)

There are two common approaches to gradual weaning:

- Dropping feedings. This is usually the easier way to go: Begin dropping one feeding at a time, waiting at least a few days, but preferably a week, until your breasts and your baby have adjusted to that loss before dropping another. First to go should be the feedings your baby is least attached to—most likely those midday ones. Over a couple of weeks, cut back to just two favorite feedings a day (typically those that offer the most comfort for both of you: first-in-the-morning and bedtime), then one. Bedtime's usually the last to go—you might want to continue the bedtime nursing for weeks or even months, even if your baby's otherwise weaned. Be sure to add formula (or milk, once it's been approved) and a snack or meal to replace any feedings you drop. And don't forget to supplement, too, with generous amounts of affection and attention.

- Cutting down on each feeding. Instead of cutting out feedings, you can cut down on each one: To start, take the edge off of your little one's appetite before feeds by offering a snack, along with a cup of formula (or whole cow's milk if your baby has already turned 1). Then offer the breast. Gradually, over the course of several weeks, he or she will be taking more from the cup or bottle and less from your breast. Eventually, your baby will wean completely.

How will your baby handle weaning from the breast? Since every baby's different, reactions will vary—but all will be normal. Some little ones will turn to alternative sources of comfort, such as the thumb or a blanket, during weaning. Some will become extra clingy (pawing or sniffing at your breasts or trying to lift up or open your shirt are all definite possibilities). But even the most committed breastfeeding fans don't seem to miss nursing for very long. Some, in fact, move on so quickly that it takes their misty-eyed moms aback. As you adjust to the new feeding norm— and the fact that it no longer includes the special bond of breastfeeding—it may help to remember that nursing is only one part of your relationship with your baby. Giving it up won't weaken the bond or lessen the love between you—that's already cemented for life. In fact, you may find that closing up shop on breastfeeding means that you'll open up even more dimensions in your relationship with your baby.

What You May Be Wondering About

Not Yet Walking

"My son will turn 1 next week, and he hasn't even tried taking his first step. Shouldn't he be walking by now?"

It may seem fitting for a baby to take his first steps by his first birthday (after all, isn't that when he officially becomes a toddler?), but many opt to crawl their way into their second year instead. Though some little ones start walking weeks, or even months, earlier, others won't totter toward the momentous milestone until much later. The majority of tots, in fact, don't begin their adventures on two feet until after their first birthday (though the vast majority will be stepping out on their own by 18 months). And when it comes to walking, age doesn't matter, either—whether a little one takes those first steps at 9 months, 15 months, or even later is no reflection on his future abilities, not even athletic ones.

When your little one starts walking may be determined by genetics—early (or late) walking runs in families. Or by his weight and build—a wiry, muscular baby is more likely to walk earlier than a placid, plump one. Or by personality— a tot who's a born risk-taker is more likely to rise to the challenge of walking sooner than one who's naturally cautious. It may also be related to when and how well he learns to crawl. A little one who's an ineffective crawler or who doesn't crawl at all sometimes walks before the baby who is perfectly content racing about on all fours.

A negative experience—perhaps a bad fall the first time a tentative 1-year-old let go of a parent's hand—can also delay those first steps. If that happened to your fledgling toddler, he may decide it's not worth chancing steps again until he's very steady, at which point he may take off like a pro. Feeling under the weather—energy and exuberance zapped by teething, a cold, an ear infection, for instance—can also put walking on hold.

Some babies don't give toddling a try because they're too often corralled in a play yard, strapped in a stroller, enclosed in an ExerSaucer, or otherwise given little chance to develop their leg muscles and their confidence through standing and cruising. Give your baby plenty of time and space to practice pulling up, cruising, standing, and stepping. He'll do best if he's barefoot, since babies use their toes for gripping when they take their first steps—socks can be slippery, and (some) shoes can be stiff. And bring on the encouragement, too, since a baby who's quite content sitting it out may need a little coaxing to join the action. Playfully challenge him to come walking after you ("Try to catch me!").

Remember, your little one will start performing great feats on two feet when he's ready. Until then, don't stress the finish line—enjoy the journey (yes, the one with all the bumps and falls, false starts, and baby steps), and that victory lap will come soon enough.

Shyness

"My wife and I are very outgoing, so we're sort of surprised to see how shy our son is. Whenever anyone tries to talk to him, he'll hide his face."

It's way too soon to assume your son hasn't inherited the genial gene from you, or that he won't follow in your

Handle with Care

Now that your toddler is on two feet, or almost so, you may be tempted to try out that childhood classic "One-two-three... wheee!," with you and another adult swinging your little one through the air as he or she walks between you, holding your hands. But because of a young child's still rather loose ligaments and not fully formed bones, swinging or lifting him or her by the hands, or suddenly twisting or tugging an arm to get a tot moving faster can result in a partially dislocated elbow, aka "nursemaid's elbow." The injury, while very easy to repair (a doctor can pop the dislocation right back into place), is extremely painful. It's also very simple to avoid: Always lift from the armpits, and avoid tugging on your little one's arms.

friendly footsteps. After all, he's still very short on social experiences and limited in the interactions he's had (with others besides you, at least). So what seems shy to you is actually developmentally appropriate social tentativeness. Hiding his face (in the stroller seat, your shoulder, your leg) is a normal, common, and very reasonable reaction to having people in his face, particularly people who are (as most people he encounters are) big and unfamiliar. While being the life of the party may well be in his future, right now he may be dealing with:

- Stranger anxiety. Some babies start showing this hesitation around anyone but mommy and daddy as early as 7 months, but many don't start shying away from "strangers" (keeping in mind that this category can lump

The First Birthday Party

What do 1-year-old babies know about parties? Not much, actually. Which is why you might want to resist the urge to throw a huge birthday bash for your baby of honor—who might end up cracking under the pressure (of too many guests, too much excitement, too much entertainment) and spending much of the celebration in tears. So think small (like your little one) when thinking about the first birthday party and follow this strategy so it's a party to remember instead of one you'd rather forget:

Keep the invites light. A room too crowded even with familiar faces may overwhelm your birthday baby. Unless you're sure your little one can handle a big crowd, consider keeping it on the intimate side—maybe just a few family members and close friends. If your baby spends time with other babies, you may want to invite a few, along with their parents (you probably won't want to be responsible for supervising any baby but yours). If not, a first birthday party probably isn't the best time to launch your little one's social career.

Ditto the decor. A room decorated with all that your local party store has to offer and then some may be your dream—but maybe not your baby's. Too many balloons, streamers, banners, masks, noisemakers, and hats, like too many people, may prove too much for a 1-year-old to process. So decorate with a light hand. If balloons will round out your party picture, remember to dispose of them post party—tiny tots can choke on the rubber scraps left after balloons go pop. Or choose Mylar balloons—though remember that any string tied to a balloon also presents a safety risk. Simple, safe favors such as brightly colored large rubber balls, board books, or bath toys are a fun extra and can be handed to young guests just before the gifts are opened.

Serve up safety. Many favorite party nibbles pose a choking risk, from M&Ms, Skittles, and jelly beans to olives, popcorn, nuts, and cocktail franks. So choose the party menu accordingly.

Time it right. Scheduling is everything when it comes to a baby's party. Try to orchestrate the big day's activities so that baby is well rested, recently fed (don't hold off on lunch, figuring he or she will eat at the party), and on a normal schedule. Don't plan a morning party if baby usually naps in the morning, or an early afternoon party if he or she usually conks out after lunch.

together strangers as well as people baby knows, or even knows well) until closer to the first year (see page 442).

- Separation anxiety. Situations that require socializing often require separating from mommy and daddy. Clinging at a playgroup or when a family friend tries to pick up your son isn't a sign that he's shy—just that he's unsure about venturing off or even socializing without you (see page 478).

- "Unfamiliar" anxiety. For a newly mobile baby, the world is an exciting place to explore, but it can also be a scary one. In the face of so much change, older babies often shrink away from the unfamiliar, deriving comfort from continuity and consistency (all mommy and daddy, all the time). If they're going to explore the unfamiliar, you better believe it will be on their terms (say, trying to slip away into a crowd at the mall—a

Inviting a tired baby to participate in the festivities is inviting disaster. Keep the party brief—1½ to 2 hours at the most—so your baby won't be a wreck when the party's over or, worse, in the middle of it all.

Don't send in the clowns. Or magicians, or any other entertainment that might frighten your baby or any other young guests—1-year-olds can be sensitive and unpredictable. What delights them one minute may terrify them the next. Also don't try to organize the pre-toddler set into formal party games—they're not ready for that yet. If there are several young guests, however, put out a selection of toys for nonstructured play, with enough of the same items to avoid competition, and maybe a few age-appropriate craft activities that little ones and their parents can work on together (or just a pile of paper and washable markers or crayons).

Have the budget to rent out a party space, like a play gym? That can be a fun option (and an easier option for you if it comes with staff to set up, clean up, and help out with the little ones)—just make sure the facilities are 1-year-old appropriate.

Don't command a performance. It would be nice, of course, if baby would smile for the camera, take a few steps for the company, open each present with interest, and coo appreciatively over it—but don't count on it. He or she might learn to blow out the candles if you give it enough practice during the month before the party, but don't expect complete cooperation, and don't apply pressure. Instead, let your baby be your baby, whether that means squirming out of your arms during that party pose, refusing even to stand on his or her own two feet during the step-taking exhibition, or opting to play with an empty box instead of the expensive gift that came in it.

Take the cake, and make it a smash. What first birthday party is complete without a smash cake (or cupcake) for baby to dive into headfirst? Whether it features layers of frosting or something a little healthier, it makes sense to undress your baby to a diaper before serving it up—and for safety's sake, to make sure that any candles or any chokeable decorations (including candy) are removed first.

Record it, of course. The party will be over much too quickly, so you'll want plenty of pictures and video taken (preferably by someone else, so you can enjoy the event in real time). And speaking of enjoying it—make sure you do. Another perk of a smaller, more casual party: You're less likely to stress, more likely to have fun—which, in turn, will mean more fun all around.

---

good reason why you shouldn't count on "unfamiliar" anxiety to keep your little one safely by your side).

■ **Social anxiety.** This is, again, a matter of social experience—or rather, lack of social experience. You've been talking your way around town for years—your little one can't even talk. You've worked more rooms than you can recall—your baby may not even have worked a playroom. Factor in his size—far smaller than the adults who try to interact with him—and it's not surprising he's stressed in social situations.

Of course, some children (like some adults) turn out to be more socially reserved by nature, and some are, by temperament, especially slow to warm up. Still others are naturally more outgoing. Not only is it too soon to call where your little one will eventually fall on the social spectrum, but labeling him now can actually prevent him from reaching his social potential (any label can stick—from "shy" to "troublemaker"—which is why it's best to avoid applying them at any age). Instead, gently support and encourage your baby in social situations, but never force him to face his fears—or show his face to a stranger when he'd rather bury it in the security of your armpit. Sit down with him on the floor so he'll feel more comfortable playing at a birthday party, but don't push him to smile, say hi, or sit in someone else's lap. Let him respond to people on his own terms and at his own pace—while letting him know that you're always there for him if he needs a leg to cling to or a shoulder to hide his head in—and the social butterfly within your little caterpillar will eventually open up.

Social Skills

"We've been involved in a playgroup for the last few weeks, and I've noticed that my baby doesn't play with the others. How can I get her to be more sociable?"

Sit back and relax—this could take a while. Though a baby is a social being from birth, she isn't capable of being truly sociable until at least the age of 18 months—as you'll see if you peek in at any group of babies and young toddlers "at play." Tots at a playgroup may interact (often just long enough to grab another child's shovel or shove a peer away from a push toy that's caught their eye), but most of their play is done in the parallel mode—they'll play side by side but not together. They definitely get a kick out of watching peers at play, but they won't necessarily join in with them. Naturally and normally me-centric, babies and young toddlers aren't yet able to recognize that other children might make worthy playmates.

In fact, they still see them largely as objects—moving, interesting objects, but objects nonetheless.

All of which is completely age-appropriate. While 1-year-olds who have had plenty of group-play practice (for instance, at daycare) may progress faster in the sociability department, every child will progress eventually. Pushing your daughter to play with other children in her group when she'd rather play by herself (or cling to your leg, also common) won't advance her social skills faster, and it might trigger more tentativeness. For best results, continue to offer your cutie opportunities to socialize, and then let her socialize at her own pace—whatever that pace turns out to be.

Of course, more opportunities for socializing also allow for more opportunities for hitting, toy grabbing, and having trouble with sharing and taking turns—all normal behavior for kids this age. To learn more about these and other toddler behaviors, check out *What to Expect the Second Year* (you may want to check it out soon—many of these behaviors get their start before the first birthday).

Putting the Weaned Baby to Bed

"I've never put my daughter to bed awake—she's always been nursed to sleep. How am I going to get her to sleep at night once she's weaned to a cup?"

How easy it's always been for your baby to suckle her way blissfully into dreamland. And how easy for you to nurse your way hassle-free to a peaceful evening. From now on, however, if you're serious about weaning your baby from her nightcap, bedding her down is going to take a little more effort on both sides of the crib rail. To make this goal a reality, follow this plan, starting well before you plan to wean (and actually, even if you're planning to continue bedtime feeds indefinitely, since learning how to fall asleep without the breast is a skill your baby will eventually need):

Keep the old rituals. A bedtime routine, with each step played out in the same order each evening, can work its sleepy magic on anyone, babies included. If you haven't made evening (and naptime) routines routine at your home, start now. And get a game plan together for getting your little one sleepy without her favorite nightcap. See page 355 for tips.

Add a new twist. Before you retire that bedtime feed, add a bedtime snack to your baby's ritual (if it's not already on the schedule)—a slot after bath and PJs usually works well. Keep it light but satisfying—a whole-grain mini-muffin and a half cup of milk (once milk has been cleared), perhaps, or a piece of cheese and some crackers or banana slices. Not only will the mini-meal eventually come to take the place of the nursing she'll be giving up, but the milk will have a sleep-inducing effect. Of course, if you've been brushing baby's teeth earlier in the evening, you will now have to move this part of the routine to after her snack. If she's thirsty once her teeth are brushed, offer her water.

Break the old habit, but try not to replace it with a new one. Sure, it might be easier just to reroute baby's nightly trip to dreamland via the rocking express or the lullaby local once you discontinue bedtime breastfeeding service. But if you'd like her to develop sleep self-sufficiency (she'll need to at some point), you'll have to let her figure out how to fall asleep on her own. Do plenty of cuddling during the bedtime routine, then put her down, happy (hopefully), snug, and drowsy—but awake. If you'd like to stay a while, patting and reassuring her, go for it. See page 349 for more tips on helping a baby fall asleep on her own.

Expect a fuss. Chances are your baby will resist this bold new approach to bedtime—loudly. Few babies will accept the switch willingly, though some may accept it much more readily if mom (and her breasts, constant reminders of what was) isn't the one doing the bedding down. But expect, too, that baby will adjust fairly quickly to a bedtime without nursing, as she will to all aspects of weaning. Heap on other forms of comfort in the meantime.

Switching to a Bed

"We're expecting a second baby in 6 months. Should we switch our son from his crib to a bed?"

The best place for your little one is in his crib—even if he's soon to become a big brother. Experts recommend that toddlers transition from crib to bed at about age 2½ to 3, or when they're taller than 35 inches (though if they reach this height at a younger age but still aren't climbing out, it's better to hold off on crib graduation until they're closer to age 3). Until then, your son is safer in the confines of his crib—especially if he hasn't started trying to climb out of it yet (most 1-year-olds don't attempt escape). After all, having the ability to hop out of bed and roam your home during the night presents plenty of risks. Even a new baby isn't reason to push your pre-toddler out of his digs. You're better off buying or borrowing a second crib for your second baby, or switching your big boy to a crib that can convert into a junior bed when he's ready, or keeping the new arrival in a bassinet and then a portable crib until your older child is truly ready to move out of the crib and into a bed.

Using a Pillow and a Blanket

"I haven't given my baby a pillow or a blanket in her crib because of the risk of SIDS. But now that she's almost 1, I'm wondering if it's safe to let her sleep with them."

For you, a bed might not be a bed without a pillow (or two or three) to rest your head on and a fluffy comforter to cuddle beneath. But for a baby who has slept flat and uncovered on the mattress since birth, pillows and blankets aren't an issue—what she doesn't know can't bother her or keep her up at night. And that's just as well. While the time of greatest risk for suffocation and SIDS has passed, most experts agree there's no compelling reason to put a pillow in your little one's crib. Besides, since she probably does a lot of tossing, turning, and shifting during sleep, chances are, her head wouldn't stay on a pillow anyway. So wait until she moves to a bed to pony up a pillow.

As for the blanket, the same advice holds true—later is better than sooner. Though some parents start tucking in their babies with a blanket closer to 12 months, most experts advise holding off until at least midway through the second year. The risk of using a blanket, especially with an active baby, is less of suffocation and more that she might get tangled up in the blanket when she stands up in the crib, leading to falls, bruises, and frustration. Many parents opt instead for the one-piece footed pajamas on top of lightweight cotton ones to keep their babies warm on cold nights.

When you do decide to throw in the pillow and blanket, don't let your preference for fluffy bed accessories guide your selection. Choose a "toddler" pillow that's smaller and very flat and a blanket that is lightweight.

Wondering about your baby's little lovey? That small comfort blanket that never leaves your baby's hands is fine to bed down with from a safety perspective. From a cleanliness perspective (if it never leaves your tot's hands) . . . well, that's a whole other story. Check out page 442 for more on comfort objects.

A Drop in Appetite

"My baby used to eat like there was no tomorrow. Suddenly, he seems to have zero interest in eating—he only picks at his food and can't wait to get out of the high chair. Could he be sick?"

More likely, the ever-sensible Mother Nature has curbed his appetite—and for very good reason. If he continued packing on the pounds at the rate he's been going so far, your baby would swell to the size of a third-grader by his second birthday. Most babies triple their birthweight in the first year, but in the second year they add only about a third of their weight. So a decline in appetite now is your baby's body's way of ensuring this normal decline in his weight gain rate.

But that's not the only reason your 1-year-old is clamping shut instead of opening wide. During most of his first year of life, mealtimes—whether spent in your arms or in a high chair—were among his favorite times. Now they represent an unwelcome interruption in his busy day. He'd much rather be on the go than sitting still for a bowl of cereal (so many things to do, so many places to see, so much stuff to get into—so little time!).

Don't Have a Cow

Your 1-year-old is ready to graduate from formula to milk. Only problem is, he or she is allergic to cow's milk, and your pediatrician has suggested that you use a milk alternative. But you worry that your toddler won't get enough fat in his or her diet, since most milk alternatives (see below) have only about half the fat of whole milk. Not to worry. While it's true that nondairy milk alone wouldn't provide all the fat a child under the age of 2 needs for optimum brain development, whole milk definitely isn't the sole source of fat. Ask the doctor about how your toddler can best meet those important fat requirements—chances are he or she can get plenty from a balanced diet that includes avocado, nut butters (if your little one's not allergic), meat, poultry, and fish, as well as oils used for cooking. After the second birthday, your toddler's fat requirements will be trimmed, anyway, to about the same as an adult's. What about calcium and other nutrients naturally found in cow's milk? Some milk alternatives stack up better than others, so make sure you talk over the options with your pediatrician, who can help you figure out which of these will work best for your 1-year-old (opt for the unsweetened variety of any you choose):

- Soy milk. The amount of protein in soy milk is comparable to that in cow's milk, as is the amount of calcium (if you choose the fortified kind, which you should). It also has roughly the same fat content as 2 percent milk.

- Almond milk has some fat in it (the good monounsaturated kind), and it's high in vitamin E and calcium. Choose one that's calcium and vitamin D fortified (most are). Downside: It's low in protein—and it won't work if your little one also has a nut allergy.

- Coconut milk is high in fat but low in protein and calcium (some varieties are fortified with calcium and vitamin D).

- Rice milk is low in fat and protein, though higher in calories than other milk alternatives—but it's also the least allergenic of all the milk alternatives. Some brands are fortified with calcium and vitamin D.

- Hemp milk is high in omega-3 and omega-6 fatty acids with a moderate amount of protein, but most brands have thickeners in them and taste funky.

Growing independence is another reason he's shunning the spoon. He'd rather assert his autonomy than allow you to run the show—even (or perhaps especially) when it comes to eating. If you haven't already, you may want to retire your spoon and graduate him to all finger foods (and a spoon of his own for practice). Maybe you're just serving too much food for his very tiny tummy—toddler portions of food are surprisingly small (think tablespoons, not cups). Scale down portions, and he may be less daunted in the face of food (you can always offer seconds). Maybe he's downing too many liquids and drowning his appetite (cut back on bottles and sippy cups, especially those containing juice).

Or maybe your baby's on a feeding strike because he dislikes being exiled to the high chair and would rather join the party at your table—a booster chair could erase the isolation and get him back in the eating game. Or maybe he can't sit still as long as the rest of the family can (and there's no reason why he should be expected to at this stage). Maybe he's lost his appetite temporarily because he's teething. Or maybe he's coming down with a cold.

Bottom line: Respect the appetite. As long as your baby is growing well and isn't showing signs of serious illness, there's nothing you need to do about food intake that's slacking. What's more, pushing, cajoling, or urging plate cleaning or one more bite will only trigger more mealtime resistance. In fact, healthy babies and healthy toddlers who are allowed to eat to appetite can be counted on to eat as much (no more, no less) as they need to so they can grow and thrive. Your job: to offer him nutritious foods. His job: to eat as much or as little of them as he wants.

Increase in Appetite

"I thought a 1-year-old was supposed to experience a drop in appetite. My daughter's has seemed to grow and grow. She's not fat, but I can't help worrying that she will be if she keeps eating at this rate."

Maybe your baby's pit is bottomless because she's drinking less. Babies who are either just, or just about, weaned from the breast or bottle to the cup are likely to be getting less of their total calorie intake from milk and other liquids, and they may compensate by stepping up their intake of solids. Though it may seem as if your little one is taking in more calories, she probably is taking in the same number or fewer, only in a different form.

Or, it could be that she's eating more because she's going through a growth spurt or because she's become more active—possibly because she's walking a lot—and her body needs the extra calories.

Healthy babies, when allowed to eat to their appetites—hearty or skimpy—without any prodding by parents, will grow at a normal rate. If your little one's weight and height are still following a familiar curve, there's no need to worry that she's overeating. Instead, pay more attention to the quality, rather than the quantity, of what she's gobbling up (if she's hungry for two bowls of fruit, that's fine—if she's hungry for two bowls of ice cream, not so fine).

Also keep in mind that young children, like adults, can pretty easily fall into the habit of eating for the wrong reasons—that is, for any reason besides hunger. If you've been unwittingly feeding such a habit—giving her a snack to keep her content while you're shopping, or when she's really just craving cuddles, or to make boredom disappear, or to make a boo-boo get better, now's the time for a switch to a more sensible strategy: feeding her when she's hungry.

Refusing to Self-Feed

"I know my son is perfectly capable of feeding himself—he's done it several times. But now he refuses to hold his bottle or even pick up a cup. If I don't feed him, he won't eat."

Growing up is hard to do. Even as your almost-toddler tackles more and more skills that bring him closer and closer to the independence he seems to crave, his inner baby may balk at taking on too much self-sufficiency too soon. So he tries to find a happy yet secure balance between big boy and baby: Maybe he'll let go of your hands to stand on his own two feet, but not to feed himself. For now, he's content to let

Going Nuts?

When it comes to peanut butter, most children—and their parents—are big fans. Kids love it for its taste (what's a PB&J without the PB?). Parents love it because it's an inexpensive and versatile source of protein, fiber, vitamin E, and minerals that even the pickiest eater will gobble up.

But food allergies in general and peanut allergies in particular are on the rise among children, forcing this lunch-box favorite to take some heat. Precisely when to introduce peanuts is still up for debate, though research seems to indicate that early introduction can prevent peanut allergy, so it's likely your pediatrician will give you the go-ahead on smooth peanut butter once baby has reached the first birthday, maybe even sooner (to minimize the choking risk, spread very thinly, never allow eating by the finger or the spoonful, and wait until age 4 before bringing on the chunky variety).

These guidelines generally are also applied to tree nuts (almonds, walnuts, cashews) and nut butters, though some doctors will green-light nut butters even earlier. When nuts are cleared for your cutie, serve them only finely chopped or ground (as in baked goods). Whole nuts (like whole peanuts) pose a choking risk and should not be given until a child is 4 or 5.

---

you do the heavy lifting of bottles and spoons while he sits back and enjoys those last cushy comforts of babyhood.

Eventually, inevitably, the big boy will triumph over the baby. In the meantime, when he wants to be fed like the baby he still very much is, feed him—without a fuss. Make the bottle, the cup, and even a spoon available to him without insisting he use them. Offer him finger foods often, at meals as well as snack times—his early ventures into self-feeding will be more successful and satisfying if he uses the five-pronged utensils that are conveniently attached to his wrists (besides, it's still too early to expect him to use a spoon). Also make sure that you don't unwittingly sabotage self-feeding by getting exasperated over the mess it makes (neat eating won't be on the table for at least a year to come).

When he opts to feed himself, applaud his initiative and his efforts—and stick around to offer him lots of reassuring attention. He needs to know that giving up being fed by mommy or daddy doesn't have to mean giving up mommy or daddy.

Growing Independence

"My baby can't seem to make up her mind about what she wants. One minute she's crawling after me wherever I go, hanging on my legs while I'm trying to get work done. The next, she's trying to get away from me when I sit down to hug her."

Is your baby ready to declare her independence? Well, that . . . depends. It depends on the day she's been having (a triumphant one of toddles . . . or a trying one of tumbles?), on how she's feeling (napped and recently fed . . . or hungry, overtired, and wired?), even on how those around her are feeling (stress in the house? She'll feel it, too—and cling accordingly). But most of all it depends on the terms of her independence. She spies something shiny, bright, and deserving of a closer look?

She'll leave your side in a heartbeat to check it out—without a moment's hesitation about separating from you. Independence declared. You get up from playing with her to check your text messages? That's independence on your terms, not on hers—and in her mind, that's not cool. Independence rejected, dependence declared.

Like most older babies and younger toddlers, your little one is conflicted—split between a craving for independence and a fear of paying too high a price for that independence. When you're busy with something other than her, especially when you're moving about faster than she can follow, she worries that she's losing her hold on you and the love, comfort, and safety that you represent, so she tightens her human velcro grip. You're all hers? Then she feels confident letting go and putting her independence to the test.

As she becomes more comfortable with her independence and more secure in the fact that you'll be her mommy and daddy no matter how grown-up she becomes, she'll feel less conflicted. But expect this inner struggle between dependence and independence to continue on and off throughout her childhood—definitely through her teen years, and even into her adult life. (Don't you ever look back longingly on the days when you could always count on being taken care of?)

In the meantime, you can help her strike out on her own by making her feel safe and reassured when she does. If you're in the kitchen making a salad and she's across the divider in the family room, chat with her, stop periodically and visit with her, or invite her to help you, stationing her high chair next to you at the sink, for example, and giving her some zucchini and a soft vegetable scrub brush to work with. Support and applaud your baby's steps toward independence, but be patient, understanding, and welcoming when she stumbles and rushes back to the security and comfort of your arms. And most of all, be realistic in your expectations of her—there are just so many minutes (and you can probably count them on one hand) she'll agree to play or otherwise keep herself busy independently.

But also be realistic in terms of the amount of time you can humanly supply in response to her demand. There will be moments when you'll have to let her hang on your legs crying while you get the groceries unpacked and moments when you will be able to provide only intermittent bursts of attention while you work on the taxes. As much as it's important for her to know that you'll always love her and meet her needs, it's important for her to know that other people—you included—have needs, too.

Negativity

"Ever since my son learned to shake his head and say no, he's been responding negatively to everything—even to things I'm sure he wants."

Congratulations—your baby is becoming a toddler. And with this transition comes the beginning of a behavior pattern you're going to see a lot more of, with increasing intensity, in the next year or so: negativity.

As hard as it is to be on the receiving end of it, negativity is a normal and healthy part of a little one's developmental transition from dependent baby to more independent child. For the first time in his very young life, he's no longer just part of the parent package, an extension of your arms—he's his own little person, on (or soon to be on) his own two little feet. He's determined to determine his destiny, define his individuality, assert his autonomy, test his limits—and of course, test your limits. It may not yet be his-way-or-the-highway (that's coming, probably somewhere later in the second year), but he's definitely figuring out that he has a way, and that if he pushes hard enough, he might actually get his way. He has opinions, and he's not afraid to express them, and though his options for self-expression are still pretty limited, he's realized that "no" can say it all. Even if he can still say it only with a shake of his head, it has an impact.

Fortunately, at this stage of negativity, your child isn't likely to mean "no" as fiercely as he expresses it (again, that's coming). In fact, sometimes it's likely that he doesn't mean it at all—as when he says no to the banana he was just clamoring for, or shakes his head when you offer the ride on the swing that you know he really wants. Like pulling up or taking steps, learning how to say no and how to shake his head are skills—and he needs to practice them, even when they're not appropriate. That babies invariably shake their heads no long before they nod their heads yes has less to do with negativity than with the fact that it's a less complex, more easily executed movement that requires less coordination.

True negativity can sometimes be avoided with a little clever verbal manipulation on your part. If you don't want to hear a no, don't ask a question that can be answered with one. Instead of "Do you want an apple?" try "Would you like an apple or a banana?," offering one in each hand for your baby to gesture at. Instead of "Do you want to go on the slide?" ask "Would you like to go on the slide or the swing?" Be aware, however, that some tots will

The Second Year . . . Continued

Think you've seen negativity? Believe you've glimpsed willfulness—or even a first tantrum or two? That's just a preview of the toddler years—when these toddler-centric behaviors and more will enchant and exasperate, delight and dumbfound, fascinate and frustrate, and test both your resourcefulness and your patience as a parent. From food fetishes to ritualism, toddlers have a unique way of approaching life that keeps their parents guessing—and looking for advice on the best way to handle their quirky and fiercely independent offspring. Since many toddler behaviors begin appearing late in the first year, you'll be able to glean some tips for tackling toddlerhood in this chapter. But for much more help on many more typically toddler topics (including lots on those sleep and feeding challenges), read *What to Expect the Second Year*.

answer even multiple-choice questions with a no.

The no's will probably have it in your household for at least another year or two, and they'll probably intensify before they taper off. The best strategy for negativity is to stay positive. Instead of fussing over the no's (you'll only hear more of them if you do), try to pay as little attention to negativity as possible—while reinforcing positive behaviors of all kinds. Keeping your little naysayer's negativity in perspective while keeping your sense of humor handy may not help check the no's, but it can help you cope with them more positively.

Watching TV

"Is it so terrible if I turn on the TV for my 1-year-old to keep her out of my hair while I make dinner? It's the only thing that keeps her occupied for long enough to allow me to get anything done."

W ho can say no to a babysitter who's always on call, reliable, eager to please, and essentially free of charge? When it comes to TV, experts say you probably should say no—at least most of the time. Though there's plenty of television programming aimed at the baby and toddler set, the AAP and most others who take the study of child development seriously recommend that children under age 2 tune out entirely. And they have their reasons. According to the AAP, children aged 12 months and younger don't follow sequential screen shots or a program's dialogue, making TV watching during the first year pointless—and screen time during the first 2 years potentially damaging to development. That's because research shows that the more TV tots watch, the fewer spoken words they're exposed to—even when the programming is touted as brain boosting. In sharp contrast to the kind of human-to-human interaction that stimulates a young, fast-growing brain, screen time is a sensory blur. Babies aren't able to process fast-paced bright, flashing images they see on the television screen. The barrage of stimuli from television shows overloads their circuits, overwhelms their senses, but doesn't benefit their brains the way simple verbal interactions with another person do. The result can be a lag in language development.

Delayed language isn't the only potential downside to screen time. Too much time spent in front of the TV means too little time being active,

playing with others, using imagination, being curious and creative, and, not surprisingly, looking at (and later reading) books. It also is linked to an increased risk of obesity, and an increase in attention problems and aggressive behavior.

Is there an upside to screen time? For many parents, there's an obvious one: the babysitting it buys, the sanity-saving break from providing round-the-clock entertainment, the few peaceful moments needed to catch up on laundry or start dinner, the chance to regroup after a long day at work, and the next best thing to a baby "pause" button. Sound familiar? Then you're in plenty of company. Ninety percent of tots under the age of 2 watch some sort of media (TV, tablets, apps)—which means most parents share the same reality you do, a reality where, despite the research, the studies, and the recommendations, TV happens. And it happens regularly.

What's the bottom line on plopping your baby's bottom in front of a screen? It's better not to. Still, if you do—and odds are, you will, at least sometimes—there are steps you can take to make sure your little one get the most benefit from her screen time with the least downside:

- Time it. It's too easy for those "just 5 minutes while I empty the dishwasher" to lapse into 20, then a half hour, then an hour, and then . . . you get the picture. So limit TV watching to no more than 10 to 15 minutes per day. Set a timer if you must, but stick to these limits. Choose programming that comes in short bites instead of in longer blocks.

- Watch together. Experts agree that if a young child does watch television, she's much better off watching it with a parent, who can make the experience more educational and interactive by asking questions, pointing out images, discussing themes—something that's not possible when you're using TV as a babysitter. This doesn't mean you have to sit next to her in front of the TV (there goes your time off), but it does mean that you should leave your dinner prep every 2 minutes or so to comment on the screen action: "Look how nicely the boy is sharing his toy!" or to sing along with the theme song.

- Choose carefully. Even if you're limiting screen time, make it count. Select programming designed for the very young, with simple language and short segments. Anything your little one watches should be slow moving, have music and singing to keep a tot engaged, encourage interaction, and have some educational value (counting, for instance, or comparing shapes). Preview shows before letting your baby see them to make sure they have an educational component, to see that they promote healthy values, and to be certain they don't have violent undertones (cartoons can be surprisingly violent). Also a good idea: Choose programs that are free from commercials and product placements—like most shows on public television.

Your not-quite-toddler is already clamoring for the remote? TV watching habits can form earlier than you'd think—but the truth is that avoiding or limiting screen time will never again be easier than it is right now. Distract your baby with more enriching activities now (while you can) and you'll spare yourself more struggle over screen time later.

Technology for Tots

"My baby's always grabbing my phone or my iPad, and seems fascinated by manipulating the screen. Should I start downloading apps for him?"

Should your cutie be clicking and swiping and tapping away already? While there's no doubt that there's technology in your baby's future, it's not so clear if it should play a significant role in his life this early on. In fact, most experts agree that screen time—whether the screen is on a television, a computer or laptop, an iPad or smartphone—should be limited in kids under age 2, and that babies and young toddlers are better off left unwired (at least electronically) in general.

The downside to feeding your child a diet of computer chips this early in life? For one thing, unlike other kinds of play, computer or app play doesn't challenge baby's brainpower all that much. When he's putting together a puzzle on the living room floor, he has to visualize how the piece will fit, then turn the piece in his hand to reflect that image, and then manipulate it into the board. When he's putting together a puzzle on the computer, he can do it by randomly hitting keys on the keyboard or by swiping his finger aimlessly across the screen. Creativity isn't nurtured, either. While the scope of your child's vision on a screen is limited to what the software or website provides, his imagination is limitless when he role-plays with a family of teddy bears or a kid-size garage full of cars. What's more (or, really, less): Too much screen time limits the opportunities babies and toddlers have to learn valuable real-life social skills that can't come from cyber-experiences, such as self-control, sharing, and getting along with others. Human interface? There's no app for that.

Babies and toddlers learn best by exploring their environment, not by swiping a screen. That's why most of your little one's time should be spent the old-fashioned way—playing with tangible toys, like blocks, dolls, trucks, and shape sorters, looking at books, watching birds fly from tree to tree at the park, learning how to pack sand into a pail, smelling a flower, scribbling with crayons, rocking a teddy bear to sleep, splashing in water.

Which isn't to say that it's necessary to keep your baby completely unplugged—or even realistic (especially if your phone is always within reach, your baby's going to reach for it)—but that there is a compelling case for keeping your little one low on the tech for now. Research shows overdoing computer games, apps, and other appealing electronics can lead to stifled creativity and social skills, lagging language skills, eyestrain, overstimulation, and of course, less physical activity (tapping on a screen isn't quite the workout a baby needs). Besides, at this early age, the world around him (from the nice lady at the supermarket to the squirrel in the driveway to the fire engine screeching by to the little girl riding a bike) is by far the best portal for your baby—that's where life and learning intersect, making the biggest impact on growing brains.

How can you introduce technology to your baby without overloading his circuits? Keep these guidelines in mind:

- Don't "byte" off more than baby can chew. Limit usage to 10 to 15 minutes per day. Too much time spent on the computer or iPad can result in too little time spent working on social, emotional, physical, and intellectual skills. It prevents baby from learning by doing. And it could lead to overstimulation. Tots who become too dependent on all that stimulation may have trouble later focusing on quieter pastimes (like reading or drawing) and paying attention to less high-tech educational mediums (say, a classroom teacher).

- Use IT for the right reasons. Apps and games (even learning games) are entertaining, somewhat stimulating, possibly educational. They're sure to divert a baby who's threatening to melt down during a long wait at a restaurant or the doctor's office. They might turn him into a techno tot, but they won't raise your baby's IQ or give him a lasting edge in school. Rely on electronic distractions too often for quick fixes in challenging (aka boring) situations, and your little one will come to rely on them to keep himself occupied—instead of on his own imagination and resourcefulness.

- Swipe and tap together. Instead of plunking your baby in front of the computer or handing him a tablet, interact while he plays, just as you would if you were reading a book to him. Ask questions about the screen images ("Where's the kitty?"), and point out things he may not know. ("Look at that flower. That flower is red. It's called a rose. It's a red rose.")

- Choose right. Look for games with simple pictures and simple songs. Read reviews of apps or software online, or visit websites that rate them. And check them out yourself before letting your little one log on. Things to watch for during your solo surfing session: Make sure any toddler computer content is truly little-kid-friendly (no violence, scary images, or too-loud noises) and the content jibes with what you want him to learn—and how.

- Keep it age-appropriate. No matter how compelling some older kids' games and apps look (or how precocious your precious one is), they may be overwhelming and overstimulating for a baby who's still getting the hang of reality (never mind the virtual kind). So avoid aging up—take the rating on the app store listing or software box seriously and stick to games, activities, and apps intended for very young children.

- Don't force it. If you decide to opt out of the tot-technology craze and reserve your lap time for sessions with *Goodnight Moon* and rounds of The Itsy-Bitsy Spider, don't worry that you're shortchanging your baby on the preparation he'll need to succeed in a wired world. There's plenty of time to hook your little cookie up.

ALL ABOUT:
Stimulating Your 1-Year-Old

First words . . . first steps . . . first friends . . . maybe even, first tantrum. The developmentally packed first year finishes up with your baby closing in on (or passing) some pretty amazing milestones—ones you probably couldn't even imagine at the start. Now, as your little one cruises (or even toddles) into the second year, more exciting achievements are right around the corner. Your baby is growing by leaps and bounds—as is the world he or she is busy conquering. Help your just-about-toddler learn all about it—tackling new challenges, honing new skills, and mastering new firsts—by offering the following:

A safe environment for taking risks. Always afraid your almost-toddler will walk (or climb, or cruise) into trouble? That's a good reason to be extra-vigilant, but not to be overly protective. To really tackle toddlerhood, your little one needs to have opportunities to take risks—carefully supervised risks, but risks nonetheless. To stop and smell a flower, to peek behind a tree, to see where a path leads or what's under a rock. To clamber up a play structure, to scale a pile of couch cushions, to climb up stairs and down again. Of course you'll want to set limits (climbing off the bed is fine, but jumping on the bed is not), of course you'll need to be ever alert (and always overestimating your little one's ability to find trouble), of course you'll have to pull out all the childproofing stops (including installing gates at both the top and bottom of stairways). But keeping your tiny explorer fenced in (whether in a play yard, a stroller, or a backpack) will stand in the way of him or her making important discoveries—about the world, and about him- or herself.

A world of difference. The baby who sees nothing but home or daycare, the car, and the supermarket gets a very limited worldview—and that's too bad. There's a world of difference outside the door, and even if it's all pretty standard stuff to you by now, it's all new to baby. So get out—even when the weather's not great, the opportunities for learning are. Take your baby places—area playgrounds, parks, art museums, a

The Eyes Have It . . . Already

All parents hope that their children will look to them for direction. Well, according to some interesting research, children do look to their parents (and other adults) for direction—and a lot earlier than previously believed. Scientists found that 12-month-old babies are more likely to look in the direction of an object if an adult looks at it first. According to the researchers, this shows that babies this young understand the significance of eyes—and begin to look to them for social cues.

children's, science, or natural history museum, toy stores (before the gimmes take hold, you can call them "toy museums"), the fire station, restaurants, the farmers market, pet shops, shopping malls, or other busy business areas with lots of store windows to peer into and lots of people to see.

Plenty to play with. The world is sometimes toy enough to enjoy, but to give your baby the widest variety of experiences and the greatest opportunities to flex muscles of all kinds (including those creative, imaginative, intellectual, and social ones), provide:

- Pull-and-push toys. Toys that need to be pushed or pulled provide practice for those who've just begun to walk, and confidence (and physical support) for those just tottering on the brink—plus, if they can be used to "shop" for toy groceries or to transport a "baby," they nurture imagination, too. Riding toys babies can sit on and propel with their feet may

also be a fun step toward independent mobility—and toward trike rides to come.

- Art supplies. There's a mini Monet inside every near-toddler—all you have to do is release the creative genius within. Offer crayons, washable markers, and chunky chalk to scribble with, along with a variety of approved surfaces—paper taped to the floor or coffee table (so it doesn't slide around), a large pad, a tiny easel (once your baby can stand comfortably), a wipe-off board, a chalkboard, or the sidewalk for chalk masterpieces. Afraid of your baby making his or her mark on the walls? Supervise art projects carefully, and confiscate crayons and markers when they're used where they shouldn't be, or when they end up in baby's mouth (or nose, or ear). Pens and pencils are risky business, since they're pointy, so supervise their use super-carefully or don't allow them in baby's hands at all. Finger painting can be fun for some tykes, while others are uncomfortable with the messy fingers that come with this art form (clearly, don't push it if that's the case with your tot).

- Music makers. Let your baby bang on a toy keyboard (or on a real one, if you're lucky enough to have access to one), xylophone, or drum, or shake a tambourine or rhythm stick. Also encourage (headaches notwithstanding) musical improvisation—banging two pot lids together, or a spoon in a pot. And of course, make music the easy way—by turning on songs that your little one can move to.

- Putting-and-taking toys. Babies love to put things in and take them out, although the latter skill develops before the former. You can buy putting-in-and-taking-out toys, or just use safe objects around the house such as empty boxes, baskets, wooden spoons, measuring cups, paper cups and plates, napkins, and scraps of fabric. Practice putting in and taking out at cleanup time, too (baby will be way better at taking out than putting in, but that's where the practice comes in). Sand, or if you're in the house, raw rice or water, allow for putting in and taking out in the form of pouring (you can limit its indoor use to the tub and baby's high chair), and most toddlers love those materials (just add constant supervision).

- Shape sorters. Usually long before toddlers can say circle, square, or triangle, they learn to recognize these shapes and fit them in the proper openings in a shape-sorter toy for endless fun. That is, once they get the hang of it (what looks simple to you requires a high level of manual dexterity and spatial awareness for your little one). Be prepared to sit by and offer help as needed if frustration starts to set in.

- Dexterity toys. Toys that require turning, twisting, pushing, pressing, and pulling encourage children to use their hands in a variety of ways. It'll take a while before your little one's dexterity is well honed, but provide opportunities to fine-tune small motor skills with peg boards, play dough (if baby can be trusted to play without eating), large bead mazes (beads that move on preformed twisted metal loops or a wooden abacus), puppets, and activity cubes.

- Bath toys for water play. Ah . . . the joy of water play. Besides the fun that comes with splish splashing away, baby can use cups to fill and pour to his or her heart's content.

Different-size cups can teach the concepts of big and small, while cups with holes in the bottom can help teach about empty and full (baby fills the cup with water, the water streams out, the cup is empty). Bath toys in the shape of animals (that rubber ducky, for instance, or a rubber elephant that sprays water out of its trunk) teach about different animals (a floating zoo!). Foam letters that stick to the wall when wet are a good introduction to the ABCs. The tub is also a good place for blowing bubbles, but you'll probably have to do the blowing yourself—let your baby do the tracking and popping for now.

- Books. You can't have a live horse, elephant, and lion in your living room—but they can all visit your home in a book. Look at and read picture books with your baby several times during the day, and always leave a stack within his or her reach. An age-appropriate fleeting attention span may mean storytime will be brief (maybe just a few minutes), but it will build the foundation that future readers need.

- Pretend playthings. Toy dishes, a playhouse or kitchen, pretend food, a toy phone or doctor's kit or broom, trucks and cars, dolls and a stroller, stuffed animals, hats, grown-up shoes, paper shopping bags, empty handbags, sofa cushions—almost anything can be magically transformed in an imaginative toddler's world of make-believe. This kind of play not only nurtures imagination and creativity, but offers an opportunity to practice social skills as well as small motor coordination (putting on and taking off clothing, "scrambling" eggs or "cooking" soup or serving "tea").

Keep Your Toddler Safe from . . . Your Toddler

Your little one is getting smarter and more coordinated all the time—but it will be a long while before judgment catches up with intelligence and motor skills. Since baby is now capable of thinking up and acting on new ways of getting into trouble, it's those smarts and skills that put him or her at even more risk than before.

So as baby enters the second year of life, be sure to continue your constant vigilance as well as all the safety precautions you have already put into effect. But also do a second safety inventory, taking into account the fact that your toddler is now, or will soon be, a proficient climber. This means that virtually nothing in your home that is not behind lock and key or safety latch is safe from tiny hands. In your survey, look not only to things that your 1-year-old can reach from the floor, but also anything he or she could conceivably get to by climbing. Removing or safeguarding all items that might be hazardous to baby (or vice versa) would be a wise move. Consider, too, that toddlers can be quite resourceful in obtaining what they want—piling up books to reach a shelf, pulling over a chair to reach a window, standing on a toy to reach the kitchen counter. Also be sure that anything your tiny exlorer might climb on—chairs, tables, shelves—is sturdy enough to hold his or her weight. Continue setting limits ("No, you can't climb on that!"), but don't, just yet, depend on your still-very-young child to remember today's rules tomorrow. For more on keeping your toddler safe, see *What to Expect the Second Year*.

Encouragement, appreciation, and patience. It may go without saying, but here goes anyway: Cheer your baby on as new skills are mastered. Achievement is satisfying to an almost-toddler's fledgling sense of self, but it's extra-sweet when you give it the nod (and a round of applause). Be wary of cheering too much or too often, though, since the idea is to motivate your baby to accomplish more, not to make him or her dependent on the applause. (If there's a standing ovation for every step taken, what does baby do for an encore?)

And speaking of attention, are you wondering when your baby will pay more than a few fleeting moments of it to any activity? Though your little one's skills have advanced by leaps and bounds as he or she totters on the brink of toddlerhood, that attention span definitely hasn't kept pace—especially when it comes to activities that require sitting still (say, storytime or working on a block tower). Be understanding of these very normal limitations, don't push your 1-year-old beyond them, and definitely don't worry—as little ones grow, so do their attention spans.

CHAPTER 18

Traveling with Your Baby

In the days before parenthood, any season was the season for a trip. Summer fun at a friend's lake house, winter getaways on the beach, last-minute ski weekends, a slow roll through wine country, or a fall tour of changing leaves and B & Bs. All you had to do was pack a bag, maybe score a deal on airfare and hotel . . . and go.

That was then, and this is now. And now, considering the effort involved in packing up and taking your baby across town to do grocery shopping, the logistics of a 2-week resort holiday (or even a 2-day trip to grandma's) might seem too overwhelming to even contemplate. And far too much like hard work to qualify as a vacation.

Happily, you can have baby . . . and still travel. Though vacations with your little one aren't likely to be as carefree or restful as they were prebaby, they can, in fact, be both feasible and fun.

On the Go with Your Baby

Remember those spur-of-the-moment weekend getaways, when a sense of adventure, a few bathing suits, and a pair of flip-flops flung into an overnight bag took you where you wanted to go? Well, those were so last year. With baby's arrival, you can expect to spend more time planning a trip than taking one. Here's how to prep:

Underschedule yourself. Forget itineraries that will take you through six cities in 5 whirlwind days. Instead, set a slow pace with plenty of unscheduled time—for an extra day on the road should you end up needing it (4 hours in the car were 3 hours too much for your smallest passenger), an extra afternoon at the beach or a morning by the pool should you end up wanting it (4 museums were 3 too many for everyone involved). In other words, be flexible.

Don't pass on a passport. You won't be able to take your baby out of the country (including to Canada or Mexico) on your passport. Every traveler, no matter what age, needs his or her own—and you'll need to give yourself enough time to secure one. If you're traveling out of the country with your baby but without your baby's other parent, you may need special documentation showing proof that you have permission from the other parent, or that you are your child's sole legal guardian. For information on obtaining a passport for your baby and other travel information, go to travel .state.gov.

Check with the doctor. Before heading away from home, make sure your baby is in good health and that you have an ample supply of any OTC or prescription meds he or she may need on the road, especially those that might not be readily available locally. Plan for unexpected illnesses by bringing along a children's pain reliever (ask the doctor what else you should pack in case baby gets sick).

Also, check with the doctor to be sure baby's immunizations are up-to-date, especially if you'll be traveling internationally. Some foreign destinations require special immunizations or other precautions. Health information on travel with children is available from your baby's doctor and online at both cdc.gov/travel and healthychildren.org.

Make sleeping arrangements. Whether you'll be staying at a hotel or at grandma's, make sure your baby will have a safe place to sleep each night. Most hotels, motels, and resorts can supply a crib, sometimes for a fee. Call ahead to reserve one and check to make sure

it's safe (run through the guidelines on choosing a safe crib, page 43). You can also drag along a portable crib. But the most convenient option on some trips (especially if you're trying to travel light) may be to rent all the baby gear you'll need, including that crib (as well as a stroller), from a well-reviewed, reputable online or local rental service that caters to tourists. It'll be delivered, assembled if necessary, and taken away when your stay is over (all at a price, of course).

If your baby is a crawler or walker, consider bringing along outlet covers, a toilet lock, or anything else you think you may need to babyproof the place where you'll be staying (some hotels may offer a babyproofing kit, but don't count on it—or count on it being adequate). When you get to your destination, be sure open windows, blind or drape cords, electrical cords, the minibar, and so on aren't accessible to your baby.

Scout for sitting services. Most hotels and resorts offer some type of babysitting. But what they offer can vary—a lot. It might be a hotel housekeeper looking to make some extra cash, it might be a list of phone numbers of babysitting agencies in the area (you're on your own to call and hire), or it might be an on-site childcare program (most common with big resorts that cater to families). Call ahead to find out your options if you're hoping to spend some adults-only time on your trip. Once there, check out any babysitter on the road as carefully as you would on your home turf: Interview the sitter (or at least the service), if possible, and make sure anyone you hire is screened, licensed, insured, and bonded, and preferably certified in CPR and up-to-date on vaccinations and boosters. Meet the sitter at the concierge or front desk so you'll be sure you've got the right person.

Equip yourself. Getting around, especially if you're traveling without another adult or with more than one child, will be easier if you have the right equipment:

- A baby carrier or sling. It will free your hands to juggle luggage—important when you're boarding and disembarking. But don't forget to bend at the knees when picking up that collection of bags, so baby doesn't fall out.

- A lightweight and very compact umbrella stroller, for an older baby.

- A portable baby seat—a cloth one adds almost no weight to your luggage.

- A car seat.

- Toys to entertain. A soft-sided play mirror, a rattle or two, and a small stuffed animal can help hold a younger baby's attention. For an older baby, tote a small activity board and a few board books, as well as a toy or two that's fun to manipulate, like a small bead maze, play keys on a ring, or an activity cube. Leave home toys with a lot of pieces that can get lost or those that are too bulky for easy packing and use in tight spaces—as well as toys that make annoying noise (and headaches). For a teether, be sure to take a couple of items to gnaw on.

- A waterproof pad for diaper changes on the fly and at your destination.

Don't rock the boat before you set sail. To avoid unnecessary problems on your trip, avoid unnecessary changes just before it. Don't try weaning your baby from the breast, for instance, just before departure—the unfamiliar surroundings and changes in routine will be hard enough to deal with, without adding other stresses. Besides, no other way of feeding baby on the road is as easy for you or as comforting for baby as breastfeeding. Don't introduce solids close to departure, either. Beginning to spoon-feed is enough of a challenge (for both of you) at home. If your baby is ready for finger foods, however, consider introducing them pretrip. Portable nibbles are great for keeping babies occupied and happy en route, and usually make for neater eating than spooned foods do.

If your baby isn't sleeping through the night, now is not the time to start sleep teaching. There's likely to be some regression into night waking during a trip (and after you return), and letting baby cry it out in a hotel room or at grandma's will wear you out—and your welcome.

Traveling by Car

When traveling long distances on the open roads (or the jammed highways), keep these tips in mind:

Never start without the car seat. It's essential any time you're getting into a car, no matter how long or short the road ahead—and no matter whose car you're getting into (and yes, that goes for car services, Uber, taxis, and vans, too). If you're a big traveler—or take taxis often—you'll have to know how to install your car seat without the base, using the seat belt. (Practice your technique at home—before the taxi meter's running). If you're renting the car, ask the rental company to supply you with a safe, up-to-date car seat (for a fee), though check with them ahead of time to find out what car seats they are able to supply. Or far better still, bring your own.

Screen out the sun. Here comes the sun—right into baby's eyes? You're going to hear about it. So if you don't already have sunshades on the back-seat windows of your car, make sure you've added them before you leave on a road trip.

Take your show on the road. Remember, if baby's not happy in the car—nobody's going to be happy in the car. If you don't already have one, install a car mirror for baby's entertainment, and add links to the car seat with a bunch of safe toys. Download plenty of baby-friendly music and refresh your own playlist of nursery rhymes to recite and songs to sing.

Break it up. Remember, with a baby on board, getting there probably won't be half the fun (and might not be any fun at all) . . . and it'll likely take twice as long. The best drive time will be during naptime, of course. When baby's awake, break up stints in the car with breaks for fresh air, diaper changes, feeds, snacks, stretching, and, for your walker, circulation-stimulating breaks.

Schedule right. Try leaving really early in the morning or late at night, so your baby will sleep through part of the journey—depending on your baby's sleep schedule. Big caveat: Make sure the driver stays awake—start out well rested, take turns at the wheel, and pull over as soon as the designated driver becomes drowsy.

Don't forget cleanup supplies. Travel with a baby is rarely neat. Make sure you bring loads of wipes, hand sanitizer, disposable bags for dirty diapers (and potential carsickness), paper towels for spills, and an extra set of clothes for baby and those near baby (kept in a reachable spot).

For safety's sake. For a safe car trip:

- Make sure everyone is buckled up.

- Don't drive to the point of fatigue (accidents are more likely to occur when the driver is tired).

- Never drive if you've been drinking.

- Don't talk on the cell phone while driving—in many states it's against the law. Even hands-free is too distracting to be completely safe.

- Never text, post, or email (or read them) while driving

- Store heavy luggage or potential flying objects in the trunk or secured by a cover.

- Ban smoking in the car, of course.

Traveling by Plane

Taking flight with your baby? Keep these plane pointers in mind:

Book early. If you can, get your tickets well in advance. On many (but not all) airlines, this allows you to choose the seats you want. If you can, print out your boarding passes at home before leaving for the airport, or at a kiosk when you get there. Or take advantage of mobile boarding passes. It could save stressful waits at the airport.

Travel at off-peak times. The less crowded the terminal, the shorter the security lines will be. The less crowded the flight, the more comfortable you will be, the better the service will be, and the fewer passengers your baby will be able to potentially annoy. So check flight loads before you book. Try, too, to choose flights at times when your baby ordinarily sleeps (night flights are great for long trips, nap times for short trips). Maybe, just maybe, your pint-size passenger will cooperate by snoozing in flight. Just keep in mind that flight delays can foil even the best-booked plans.

Consider a nonstop. In most cases, the faster you get from here to there, the better for all. That said, sometimes a very long daytime nonstop may be too much for anyone to handle (your baby, you, the passengers sitting near you). If you think a coast-to-coast flight might put your baby over the top, consider breaking up the trip into two shorter ones (you may get a less expensive fare while you're at it). You'll want a layover to be long enough so you can get to the next gate without huffing and puffing, and have time to get a bite to eat, wash up, take care of diapering (it's a lot easier to change a squirmy baby in an airport bathroom than in a tiny airplane one), let your baby expend some crawling energy, watch a few planes take off and land, and—if there is one—visit the airport play center. But too much time in the terminal can be . . . interminable.

Consider an extra seat. Though on most airlines kids under 2 can travel for free (if you keep them on your lap), you may want to consider purchasing a seat for baby anyway. Paying full fare for a baby who can fly for free may seem like an extravagance, but it will make sitting, playing, and eating less of a hassle for both of you. Plus, it's a lot safer—babies buckled into an FAA-approved car seat secured in a separate seat are less likely to be injured in severe turbulence than those restrained only by a parent's arms.

If you're traveling with another adult and your flight isn't crowded, you may be able to book an aisle and a window seat with an empty seat in between them. If you specify that you have a lap child, some airlines won't sell that seat unless absolutely necessary. As long as the seat stays unbooked, you've got a free seat for your baby. If it doesn't, you can be pretty sure the middleman (or woman) will be willing to trade seats with one of you rather than having a baby passed back and forth over his or her lap during the entire flight.

Favor the aisle. Opt for the aisle seat—otherwise you're going to end up trying the patience of those you'll have to keep scrambling over to take your restless baby for a diaper change or for a walk (but keep in mind if you bring along a car seat that the flight attendants won't let you place your baby in an aisle seat for safety reasons). Parents often favor bulkhead seats because they provide extra room in front of the seats for a baby to play and some planes have space there for a baby bassinet. There are some downsides: Trays usually unfold over your lap, leaving no room for your child, the armrest usually can't be raised (which means your baby can't spread out across two seats to nap), you're right on top of the movie screen, if there is one, and worst of all, there's no underseat storage (everything, including your diaper bag, must be stored overhead during takeoff and landing . . . as well as during delays on the runway).

Check bags curbside. To avoid having to lug your luggage through a sprawling airport, check everything but valuables and the essentials (your diaper bag and carry-on bag) through at the curb. To avoid having to lug your baby, use a lightweight stroller and check it at the gate (protect it, if possible, by packing it in a stroller bag).

Plan ahead for the security line. Preferably, way ahead. To make your whole security experience easier on many flights, consider signing up online for TSA PreCheck (go to tsa.gov/tsaprecheck/application-program). With PreCheck, there are faster-moving lines and fewer hassles (no taking off shoes or coats, no separating laptops or liquids).

Any child under the age of 12, if accompanied by a PreCheck-qualified adult, can go through these expedited lines, too—making this program a big help for families on the go.

If your baby's old enough for one, a light umbrella stroller can be your best friend when going through security, whatever line you're in. It'll be easy to fold up at the last second and plop on the x-ray's conveyer belt. (You'll probably be allowed to take it right down the jetway and leave it at the plane's door before you board—it will be waiting for you at the door after landing.) Slip-on shoes are your second-best friends at the security checkpoint (that way, if you don't have PreCheck and/or you're asked to take them off, it won't be a last-minute struggle—but do wear socks so you don't have to walk barefoot on that icky floor). You'll be able to hold your baby in your arms (though not in a carrier or sling) to go through the screening, but you'll both have to be hand screened if the security officer singles you out for a pat down—which you probably will be since you won't be able to have one of those full body scans while holding your little one. Again, measures are likely to be less strict with PreCheck.

You'll likely be able to bring through security enough formula, breast milk, baby food, or juice boxes to last the flight, but be sure to check out tsa.gov for the latest information, since regulations often change.

Think twice about that early boarding. If the airline you're flying does preboards for families, think twice before you take advantage. Yes, boarding first allows you to snag much-needed overhead-bin space and gives you some extra time to negotiate those tight aisles with baby and baby gear. But early board can equal early bored, since it means about an extra half hour on the plane—probably not something you want to endure voluntarily with a squirmy baby who needs constant entertainment.

Find a friendly flight attendant. If you're alone, don't be shy (but do be nice) about asking the flight crew for help. After all, it can be nearly impossible to lift a bag and put it in the overhead bin while holding a baby. So ask a flight attendant (or fellow passenger) for a hand.

Don't expect to be fed. Food on domestic flights has just about disappeared in coach (you may still find it on international flights)—the best you can expect is usually a snack for purchase, if that. Call ahead to find out exactly what will be served and if baby meals are available for purchase (or for free on international flights). Sometimes a snack means nothing more than a beverage and a bag of snack mix, which, as a choking hazard, is off-limits for babies. And no matter what food's been promised, don't ever board without your own supply of baby-appropriate (and approved) snacks. Takeoff delays can result in mealtime delays, food service carts can move at a maddeningly slow rate down the aisles, and special meals sometimes don't show up at all (plus, let's face it—they're not all that special).

Bring extra supplies. Bring as many toys as you can fit into your carry-on luggage and twice as many diapers as you could possibly need, endless wipes and hand sanitizer, at least one change of clothing for your baby, and an extra t-shirt for you (forgetting the last item guarantees you'll be spit up on, thrown up on, spilled on . . . or all of the above). Don't forget an extra layer of clothes for your baby—it can get cold on a plane. Toss in a small blanket, too, since blankets on planes (if you can find one) are often used by many passengers between washings.

Put safety first. If your child is occupying a seat, plan to bring aboard a car seat that's FAA-approved (not all are), and know how to install it without the base. Babies should ride in a rear-facing position. Even if you didn't buy a separate seat for baby, bring the approved car seat with you to the gate, just in case there's an extra seat next to you on board. If there isn't, the flight attendants will gate check it for you. This should limit the amount of handling—and tossing around—the car seat might encounter during regular baggage checking (you can also purchase a bag for some car seats as extra protection). If your baby is on your lap, do not belt him or her in with you—serious injury could result from even a mild impact. But do secure your belt around yourself and then hold your baby around the waist with your hands, grasping your wrists during takeoffs and landings. Don't allow your baby to crawl around alone in the aisles or to sleep or play on the floor in front of you because of the risk of injury if the plane should suddenly hit an area of turbulence.

Also carefully review the information on oxygen masks and find out where there are extras in case your baby doesn't have a seat (and therefore a mask) of his or her own. There's usually an extra mask provided in every row or section of seats. Remember, just like they say in the preflight safety video, you should put on your own mask first and then attend to your child's. If you try to do it the other way around in a low-oxygen emergency, you could lose consciousness before you manage to get either mask on.

Clean up before you take off. Use sanitizing wipes to clean around areas that baby might touch or mouth (and that many passengers have handled before)—the seat back, armrests, tray table, and window shade.

Mind those ears. Changes in altitude and air pressure are tough on little ears. Drinking during takeoff and landing can help by encouraging swallowing, which helps release the pressure that builds up in the ears (start as the plane starts speeding down the runway and again when the pilot announces the initial descent). Let your baby drink from a bottle, a sippy cup, or a cup with a built-in straw. Nothing to drink? A paci or feeder bag could do the trick if your baby sucks on it enough to require saliva swallowing—and as a last resort, you could try squirting water into baby's mouth with a medicine syringe. Though always comforting, breastfeeding during takeoff and landing isn't recommended for safety's sake.

If all else fails and your baby screams all the way up and all the way down, ignore the dirty looks from other passengers (you're likely to see a lot of sympathetic faces, too). At least the screaming will help reduce the pressure on your baby's eardrums and ease the pain.

Have a baby with a stuffy nose, and a ticket to fly? It's a good idea to visit the doctor first for clearance, since congestion can block Eustachian tubes and make in-flight ear pain much worse. You can also try relieving some of the congestion by placing saline drops in baby's nose before takeoff and landing.

Traveling by Train

Not in a rush? Take your time and take a train. You'll save yourself the wear and tear of driving—and the drag of airport hassles. Plus, baby will have more freedom of movement, plenty of distractions (with nobody driving, everyone can be in entertainment mode), and an always-changing view. Your family train trip will be easier if you remember to:

Book in advance. Ordering train tickets in advance (online or over the phone) allows you to arrive at the train station with tickets in hand, so you won't have to wait in a long ticket line. If it's possible to make seat or compartment reservations, do this in advance, too. Remember, however, that for most U.S. train reservations in coach, you are guaranteed a seat for each ticket, but not that those seats are together.

Be timely. Peak travel times can be very crowded, especially during holiday seasons, so avoid them if you can. A late-evening train may be a good option if your baby is likely to sleep during the trip.

Pack appropriately. For overnight train travel, your carry-on bag should also be an overnight bag, packed with extra clothes, diapers, and all those baby-care basics. This should make digging into your neatly packed suitcases unnecessary. Better still, it may make it possible to check your heavy baggage through, giving you less to lug and more room in your compartment or at your seat.

Arrive early. Check ahead to find out what time the train ordinarily arrives at your station. If there is a 10- or 15-minute gap between arrival and departure, try to get there before the train arrives rather than just as it's about to leave. The goal: a better chance of seating the family together. If there are two adults, send one ahead, as soon as the platform number is announced, to save seats for all while the other struggles down the platform at a snail's pace with baby. If you can, grab a window seat (plus the aisle one) so your little one can watch the scenery go by.

Don't pass on the redcap. If uniformed redcap service is available, take it. For a minimal tip, a redcap will take your bags and escort you down to and onto the train so you don't have to lug anything but your little one. Redcaps also have the inside track on which platform a train will be arriving on before it's announced, which means you'll be on your way there before the crowds descend.

Derail boredom. Your baby will enjoy watching the scenery for only so long. So tote those toys, books, and crayons—and lots of them.

Take advantage of longer stops. Even a 15-minute stop gives you and your baby a chance to get off the train for a stretch, and possibly even wander down to see the engine that's been pulling the train (just be sure someone is watching your luggage and that you reboard in time).

Bring your own. Even if there's a dining or snack car on board, there's no guarantee your baby will be willing or able to eat what they're serving. So, just as you would when traveling by car or plane, bring your own snacks and drinks.

CHAPTER 19

Keeping Your Baby Healthy

I f there's anything sadder-looking than a sick baby—it's a sick baby's parents. Even a little bout of sniffles in their little one can hit mommy and daddy hard, especially if it's the first sniffles in a first baby. Add an elevated temperature—even if it's only a slight rise—and parental anxiety can soar. Questions multiply with every passing minute, with every symptom (was that a cough?): Should we call the doctor? Should we wait for the office to open in the morning or on Monday (babies always seem to get sick in the middle of the night or on weekends), or call right away? Should we give baby medicine to bring down that fever while we're waiting for the doctor to call back? Will the doctor ever call back (it's been only 5 minutes, but it already feels like forever!)?

Fortunately, infant illnesses are usually mild—a few extra cuddles, and it's back to baby business as usual. Still, it makes sense to prevent as many as possible—to keep your baby healthy through healthy eating, healthy habits, and on-time delivery of scheduled well-baby visits and childhood immunizations. Of course, even the best prevention isn't always a match for determined germs, which is why it's important to learn what to do when your baby is sick: how to evaluate symptoms, how to take and interpret a baby's temperature, what to feed a sick child, what the most common childhood illnesses are, and how to treat them.

What You Can Expect at Checkups

If you're like most parents, you'll look forward to well-baby checkups—a lot. Not only to see how much your baby's grown, but also to get answers to the dozens of questions that have come up since the last doctor's visit (at least, the ones that you managed not to frantically call about already—there will be plenty of those, too). Make sure you keep a list of these questions and bring them along to appointments . . . and don't forget to ask them.

Baby will usually have his or her very first doctor's visit within several days of being released from the hospital. The schedule for the rest of the year will vary from office to office and baby to baby (depending on individual health needs and concerns), but most doctors recommend well-baby visits at 1, 2, 4, 6, 9, and 12 months of age.

First Test Results

During baby's first well-baby visit you'll probably get the results of neonatal screening tests (for PKU, hypothyroidism, and other inborn errors of metabolism), if they weren't given previously. If the doctor doesn't mention the tests, the results were very likely normal, but do ask for them for your own records. If your baby was released from the hospital before these tests were performed, they will probably be performed at that first visit. Some states have specific protocols about when testing should be done. Ask your pediatrician whether any of your newborn's metabolic screens will have to be repeated after discharge, based on your state's protocol.

Though every well-baby visit will be a little different, the doctor will be looking at your little one's growth, overall health, and development. You can expect most of the following at each visit, but keep in mind that you may not notice some of the physical checks, since the doctor will move through them quickly:

- A chance to ask all the baby-related questions you've collected since the last visit

- Questions from the doctor about how you and baby are doing, and about baby's feeding, sleeping, and development

- Measurement of baby's weight, length, and head circumference (which will be plotted on a growth chart to see baby's progress)

- Vision and hearing assessments

- A physical exam that will include all or most of the following:

  - A check of your baby's heartbeat and breathing with a stethoscope

  - A check of baby's belly by gently pressing on it to feel for anything out of the ordinary

  - A check of baby's hips to make sure there's no dislocation (the doctor will rotate your little one's legs)

  - A check of baby's arms, legs, back, and spine to make sure they're growing and developing normally

  - A check of the eyes (with an ophthalmoscope and/or a penlight) for normal reflexes and focusing, and for tear duct functioning

  - An ear check (with an otoscope)

For Parents:
The Pediatrician's Role in Postpartum Depression

Sure, the pediatrician is your baby's doctor, but a mom's well-being affects her baby's in so many ways. Postpartum depression (PPD) can keep a new mom from nurturing her little one, which can lead to slower development (babies of depressed moms are less vocal, less active, make fewer facial expressions, and are more anxious, passive, and withdrawn). And since pediatricians have many more opportunities to interact with new moms than do ob practitioners (PPD sometimes doesn't start until after that 6-week postpartum visit and sometimes begins well before it), they're considered the first line of defense in fighting PPD. That's why the AAP recommends that pediatricians screen for PPD at babies' 1-, 2-, and 4-month visits by asking new moms to complete a short checklist called the Edinburgh Postnatal Depression Scale—basically 10 questions designed to reveal whether a new mother is struggling with PPD. If you think you or your partner might have symptoms of PPD, ask the pediatrician for a screening if it's not offered (and don't wait for the next appointment if the symptoms are serious enough to interfere with functioning—call for help right away). A prompt diagnosis and the right treatment can make all the difference in helping a new mom enjoy her new life with her new baby.

- A peek in the nose (also with an otoscope) to make sure the mucus membranes are healthy

- A quick look into the mouth and throat (using a tongue depressor) to check for color, sores, and bumps

- Feeling the neck and underarms to check on the lymph glands

- A check of the fontanels (the soft spots on the head)

- A check of the genitals for hernias or undescended testicles (and while the doctor's at it, he or she will also check the femoral pulse in the groin, for a strong, steady beat)

- A peek at the anus to check for cracks or fissures

- A check of umbilical cord and circumcision healing (when applicable)

- An overall assessment of baby's skin color and tone, and a check for any rashes or birthmarks

- A quick look at reflexes specific to baby's age

- As baby grows, an assessment of his or her overall movement and behavior and ability to relate to others

- Advice on feeding, sleeping, development, and infant safety

- Immunizations, if they're scheduled and there's no medical reason to postpone them (see page 526). These are typically scheduled for last so that baby's crying won't interfere with the exam.

When you get home, record everything (baby's weight, length, head circumference, blood type, test results, birthmarks) in a permanent file, a baby book, or an app.

Making the Most of Those Monthly Checkups

Even healthy babies spend a lot of time at the doctor's office. Well-baby checkups, which are scheduled throughout the first year, allow the doctor to keep track of your baby's growth and development, ensuring that everything's on target. But they're also the perfect time for you to ask the long list of questions you've accumulated since your last visit, and to walk away with a whole lot of advice on how to keep your well baby well.

To make sure you make the most of every well-baby visit:

Time it right. When scheduling appointments, try to steer clear of naptimes—and any time your baby's typically fussy. Also good to avoid: those peak hours at the doctor's office, when waiting rooms are packed and waits are long. Mornings are usually quieter because older children are in school—so in general, a pre-lunch appointment will beat the 4 o'clock rush. And if you feel you'll need extra time (you have even more questions and concerns than usual), ask whether it's possible

to schedule it into the visit so you won't feel so hurried.

Follow office etiquette. Arrive for appointments on time or, if the office perpetually runs late, call half an hour or so before a scheduled appointment and ask how much later you can safely arrive. If you must cancel, be sure to give at least 24 hours' notice.

Fill 'er up. A hungry patient is a cranky and uncooperative patient. So show up for your well-baby visits with a well-fed baby, or plan to feed while you wait (once finger foods have been started, you can also bring a snack for the waiting room). Keep in mind, however, that overfilling a young baby's tank with breast milk or formula just before the appointment may mean baby is ripe for spitting up once the exam begins (and all of you may smell ripe afterward).

Dress for undressing success. When choosing baby's wardrobe for the visit, think easy-on, easy-off. Skip outfits with lots of snaps that take forever to do and undo, and snug clothes that

Immunizations

Maybe you've heard about childhood diseases like measles, mumps, and polio—but it's likely you have only the vaguest idea of what they actually are, and even more likely that you've never known anyone who's come down with any of them. The reason? Immunizations—one of the most important and successful public health interventions in history. Because of immunization, widespread epidemics of smallpox, polio, diphtheria, measles,

rubella, and mumps—devastating childhood diseases that were once serious threats to children in this country—are mostly a thing of the past.

Mostly . . . but not entirely. There are still outbreaks of childhood diseases around the world, even in the United States, usually among children who haven't been fully immunized or haven't been immunized at all. For vaccines to protect all children, all children have to be vaccinated. And while no parent likes are difficult to pull over baby's head. And don't be too quick to undress your baby if he or she isn't a fan of being naked—wait until the exam is about to begin before stripping down.

Make baby comfortable. Few babies enjoy the poking and prodding of a doctor's exam—but many enjoy it even less when it takes place on the wide-open spaces of the exam table. If that's the case with your baby, ask if at least part of the exam can be done with baby on your lap. Keep in mind, though, that some older babies find the exam table paper fun to crinkle—and that can provide a welcome diversion.

Keep track. Remember those 200 questions you wanted to ask the doctor? You won't, once you've spent 20 minutes in the waiting room and another 20 in the exam room trying to keep your baby (and yourself) busy and calm. So instead of relying on your memory, bring a list (on paper, on your phone) you can read off. Be sure, too, to jot down the answers to those questions, plus any other advice and instructions the doctor dispenses as well as baby's height, weight, immunizations received that visit, and so on.

Trust your instincts. Your doctor sees your baby only once a month—you see your baby every day. Which means that you may notice subtle things the doctor doesn't. If you feel something isn't right with your baby—even if you're not sure what it is—bring it up. Remember, you're a valuable partner in your baby's health care, and your instincts may be among the most perceptive diagnostic tools.

End a relationship that's not right. Not feeling the love for your baby's doctor anymore? Even in the best of partnerships, there's bound to be some disagreement, but if you're starting to suspect that Dr. Right is really all wrong for you and your baby, it might be time to cut bait and switch doctors. To be sure you don't leave your baby's health care in the lurch, keep up the relationship while shopping around for a replacement. Once you have a new pediatrician on board, be sure to have your little one's medical records transferred.

to see a needle headed toward baby's tender skin, keeping up with the schedule of recommended immunizations is by far one of the best strategies to help keep your little one (and all the rest of the little ones in your community) healthy. Read on to find out more.

The ABCs of DTaPs ... and MMRs ... and IPVs ...

It helps to know what the needle that's headed your baby's way is loaded with. The following is a guide to the vaccines your little one will probably receive in the first year and beyond:

Diphtheria, Tetanus, acellular Pertussis vaccine (DTaP). Your child needs five DTaP shots (though they are often given in combination with other vaccines to reduce the number of needle sticks your baby gets), and they're recommended at 2, 4, and 6 months, 15 to 18 months, and between 4 and 6 years. This combo vaccine protects against three serious diseases: diphtheria, tetanus, and pertussis.

Diphtheria is spread through coughing and sneezing. It begins with a

For the Adoptive Parent: Adoption Medicine

Are you adopting your baby from a country where health care practices aren't up to U.S. standards? Though your initiation into parenthood will be no different from that of parents who adopt or give birth in this country (a baby is a baby no matter where he or she is born), there may be some issues or questions unique to foreign adoption—and your regular pediatrician may not always have the answers to those questions. That's why you might want to seek out a pediatrician who specializes in foreign adoption medicine, one with extensive experience in the medical, emotional, developmental, and behavioral issues of children born abroad (especially in developing countries) and adopted by parents in the United States. Such a doctor can offer preadoption counseling (including an assessment of potential health risks) based on existing medical records, and since those records are often incomplete or nonexistent, can also offer postadoption care, which routinely screens for problems specific to the child's country of origin.

While most adoptive parents don't need a consultation with an adoption medicine specialist, you might find it useful—particularly if you have reason to be concerned about your new baby's health. You can search for adoption doctors online or by asking your local pediatrician. Can't find one in your neighborhood? Ask your pediatrician if he or she can consult with one to get responses to your specific concerns.

---

sore throat, fever, and chills, and then a thick covering forms over the back of the throat, blocking airways and making breathing difficult. If it isn't properly treated, the infection causes a toxin to spread in the body that can then lead to heart failure or paralysis. About 1 in 10 of those affected will die.

Tetanus is not a contagious disease, but it is an extremely serious one. A person typically becomes infected if tetanus bacteria found in soil or dirt enters the body through a wound or cut. Symptoms include headache, irritability, and painful muscle spasms. In some cases, tetanus is fatal.

Pertussis (aka whooping cough) is a very contagious airborne bacterial infection that causes violent, rapid coughing and a loud "whooping" sound with inhalation. One in 10 children who get pertussis develop pneumonia, too.

Pertussis can also lead to convulsions, brain damage, and even death.

Up to one-third of children who receive DTaP shots have very mild local reactions where the shot was given, such as tenderness, swelling, or redness, usually within 2 days of getting the shot. Some children are fussy or lose their appetite for a few hours or perhaps a day or two. A low fever may also develop. These reactions are more likely to occur after the fourth and fifth doses than after the earlier doses. Occasionally, a child will have a fever of over 104°F.

Polio vaccine (IPV). Children should receive four injections of inactivated polio vaccine (IPV)—at 2 months, at 4 months, at 6 to 18 months, and at 4 to 6 years (though the schedule may be stepped up if you're traveling to a country where polio is still common).

Vaccine Smarts

Vaccines are extremely safe, and they're even safer when both parents and doctors take the right precautions:

- Be sure your child receives a checkup before an immunization. If your baby has been sick, let the doctor know. A common cold or other mild illness isn't considered a reason to postpone a scheduled vaccine, but a fever might be. If the doctor suggests postponing immunization, make sure it's rescheduled as soon as your baby is feeling better.

- Ask about reactions. Reactions to vaccines are almost always very mild (a little fussiness, maybe some soreness at the injection site) and nothing to be concerned about. Still, it's a good idea to ask the doctor for a list of possible reactions and to watch your little one for any during the 3 days after immunization (or in the case of the MMR vaccine, in the week or two afterward). As a precaution, call the doctor if your baby experiences any of the following symptoms (these reactions usually are not serious). Keep in mind that any symptoms that seem related to a recent vaccination might actually be triggered by an unrelated illness—another good reason to call the doctor:

  - A fever over 104°F

  - Seizures/convulsions (jerking or staring with a lack of awareness and responsiveness for a brief time, like 20 seconds, is usually febrile (caused by fever) and is not serious)

  - Major alterations in consciousness within 7 days of the shot

  - Listlessness, unresponsiveness, excessive sleepiness

  - An allergic reaction (swelling of mouth, face, or throat; breathing difficulties; immediate rash). Slight swelling and warmth at the injection site are common and nothing to be concerned about (a cool compress should bring relief)

  Make a note of any reactions in your child's immunization or health record.

- Make sure that the vaccine manufacturer's name and the vaccine lot/batch number is noted in your child's chart, along with any reactions you report. Bring along your child's immunization record to every checkup so that it can be updated.

- Severe reactions should be reported to the Vaccine Adverse Event Reporting System (VAERS) by your doctor or by you (see vaers.hhs.gov/index). If you believe your child may have been harmed by any vaccine, contact the Vaccine Injury Compensation Program (800-338-2382) or hrsa.gov/vaccinecompensation for information. This government program protects both those who produce the vaccine and those who receive it.

Polio (aka infantile paralysis), once a dreaded disease that left thousands of children physically disabled each year, has virtually been eliminated in the United States through immunization.

Polio is caused by a virus that is spread through contact with the feces of an infected person (such as when changing diapers) or via throat secretions. It can cause severe muscle pain and paralysis

For Parents:
Vaccines—They're Not Just for Kids

Think your days of routine vaccinations, booster shots, and lines like "This will just pinch a bit" are over, mom and dad (or grandma and grandpa . . . or uncle and auntie)? Think again. Adults need vaccines, too—not just because you want to be in good shape to take care of your children, but also because you want to do everything you can to lessen their risk of contracting serious illnesses. If you're vaccinated against preventable diseases, you're less likely to get these diseases and, in turn, pass them on to the little ones you love—it's as simple as that.

The Centers for Disease Control and Prevention (CDC) recommends you (and any adults caring for your baby, including babysitters) receive the following vaccinations, depending on your medical history and other circumstances:

Influenza (aka the flu) vaccine. If you have had any vaccine as an adult, it's probably this one. That's because the flu shot (or the nasal-spray flu vaccine) is recommended each year in the fall (ideally) or winter. The flu shot helps prevent some strains of the flu, which can be very unpleasant for adults and much more serious (even deadly) to babies, small children, the elderly, and anyone with a chronic medical condition or compromised immune system (including pregnant women). So you should be vaccinated if you're caring for a small child (or if you're pregnant), and make sure your little ones over 6 months old get vaccinated, too. Remember that you (and all other adults and children regularly in your baby's life) will need an annual flu vaccine each fall: The protection doesn't last, as it does for other vaccines, in part because flu strains vary from year to year.

within weeks, though some children with the disease experience only mild cold-like symptoms or no symptoms at all.

The IPV doesn't cause side effects except for a little soreness or redness at the site of the injection and the rare allergic reaction. A child who had a *severe* allergic reaction to the first dose generally won't be given subsequent doses.

Measles, mumps, rubella (MMR). Children get two doses of MMR, the first between 12 and 15 months, and the second between ages 4 and 6 (though it can be administered any time as long as it is 28 days after the first one). It's recommended that the

MMR be given early (between 6 and 12 months) if a baby will be traveling internationally—though baby will still need two more MMR shots after that. The vaccine prevents (not surprisingly) measles, mumps, and rubella.

Measles is a serious disease with sometimes severe, potentially fatal, complications. Rubella, also known as German measles, is often so mild that its symptoms are missed. But because it can cause birth defects in the fetus of an infected pregnant woman, immunization in early childhood is recommended—both to protect the future fetuses of girl babies and to reduce the risk of infected children exposing pregnant women. Mumps rarely

Tetanus, Diphtheria, and Pertussis (Tdap) vaccine. Tdap is the DTaP formulation for teens and adults. If you haven't had a booster for these serious diseases in the past 10 years (or weren't immunized as a child), you need one now, not only to protect yourself, but to protect your baby. Pertussis (whooping cough), for instance, is most often passed on to babies by their unvaccinated or not-fully-vaccinated parents. Choose the Tdap vaccine over the Td, which doesn't protect against pertussis. Expectant moms should receive a booster during every pregnancy, regardless of whether they have received one previously—it's recommended by the CDC during the third trimester (between 27 and 36 weeks).

Measles, Mumps, Rubella (MMR) vaccine. While it's likely you're already immunized against these highly contagious diseases, sometimes immunity wears off—and that could be dangerous for you (especially if you plan to get pregnant again) and your unprotected baby. That's because these diseases are still present in other parts of the world and the prevalence of international travel means these serious illnesses can and do cross borders often. In fact, there have been numerous outbreaks of measles and mumps in this country in recent years.

Varicella vaccine. If you didn't have chicken pox as a child—or were not vaccinated—and you catch it as an adult, it could end up being a very serious case (it's much worse in adults than in children). What's more, contracting chicken pox when you're expecting or when you have a newborn can be very dangerous for your baby.

Also recommended for adults with particular risk factors are the hepatitis A vaccine (if you might be exposed to hepatitis A through your work or travel, if you live in a high incidence area, or if you take blood products to help your blood clot) and the hepatitis B vaccine (if you're a health care worker, dialysis patient, or someone who travels to countries where the disease is prevalent).

---

presents a serious problem in childhood, but because it can have severe consequences (sterility or deafness) when contracted in adulthood, early immunization is recommended.

Reactions to the MMR vaccine are usually very mild and don't usually occur until a week or two after the shot. Some children may get a mild fever or rash (which is not contagious). Studies have definitively shown there is absolutely no link between the MMR vaccine and autism or other developmental disorders.

If babies too young to be vaccinated are exposed to measles, they can get the MMR shot (if over 6 months and within 72 hours of exposure) or an IG (immunoglobulin) shot.

Varicella vaccine (Var). A dose of varicella vaccine is recommended between 12 and 18 months and another at age 4 to 6. A child who already had chicken pox (aka varicella) doesn't need to be immunized against it (you usually can't catch it again). The vaccine appears to prevent chicken pox in 70 to 90 percent of those who are vaccinated once, and the second dose pushes the protection rate close to 100 percent. The small percentage who do get chicken pox after receiving a single dose of the vaccine usually get a much milder case than if they hadn't been immunized.

Varicella was until recently one of the most common childhood diseases. Highly contagious through coughing,

Staying Up-to-Date

For the most up-to-date facts on vaccine safety, as well as the latest immunization recommendations for your child, visit the CDC website at cdc.gov/vaccines or go to WhatToExpect.com. You can also download the VIS (Vaccine Information Statement) on each vaccine, available at the CDC website. The doctor or clinic, by law, will provide the appropriate VIS whenever a shot is given, but checking it out ahead of time will allow you to read up on vaccine benefits, risks, side effects, and contraindications.

sneezing, and breathing, chicken pox causes fever, drowsiness, and an itchy blisterlike rash all over the body. Though usually mild, it occasionally causes more serious problems such as encephalitis (brain inflammation), pneumonia, secondary bacterial infections, and in rare instances, even death. Those who contract the disease when they are older are much more likely to develop serious complications. And the disease can be fatal to high-risk children, such as those with leukemia or immune deficiencies, those who take medications that suppress the immune system (such as steroids), and newborns born to unvaccinated mothers.

The varicella vaccine is very safe. Rarely, there may be redness or soreness at the site of the injection. Some children also get a mild rash (just a handful of spots) a few weeks after being immunized.

Haemophilus Influenzae type b vaccine (Hib). Your child should get the Hib vaccine at 2, 4, and 6 months, with a fourth dose at 12 to 15 months. (One brand of the vaccine calls for only three doses, at 2 and 4 months and between 12 and 15 months of age.)

The vaccine is aimed at preventing the deadly Hib bacteria (which has no relation to influenza, or "flu"), the cause of a wide range of very serious infections in infants and young children. The disease is spread through the air by coughing, sneezing, even breathing—and before the introduction of the vaccine, thousands of children contracted serious infections of the blood, the lungs, the joints, and the covering of the brain (meningitis). Hib meningitis frequently led to permanent brain damage and killed hundreds of young children every year.

The Hib vaccine appears to have few, if any, side effects. A very small percentage of children may have fever, redness, and/or tenderness at the site of the shot.

Hepatitis B (hep B). Your child needs three doses of this vaccine. It's recommended that the first be given shortly after birth, the second at 1 to 2 months, and the third at 6 to 18 months. If the hepatitis B vaccine is administered in combination with other vaccines, doses are given at 2, 4, and 6 months instead, in addition to the newborn dose (receiving one "extra" dose of the hepatitis B vaccine is not harmful in any way). If prenatal testing showed that you are a carrier of hepatitis B, your baby will receive a shot of immunoglobulin right after birth, in addition to the newborn dose of hep B vaccine, to prevent him or her from becoming infected by you.

Hepatitis B, a chronic liver disease, is spread through contact with the blood or other body fluids of an infected person. Those who become infected with the disease can have serious problems such as cirrhosis (scarring of the liver) or liver cancer. Nearly 5,000 people die from complications of chronic hepatitis B each year in the U.S. Thanks to the hep B vaccine, your child will probably never have to worry about catching this devastating disease.

Side effects of the hep B vaccine—slight soreness and fussiness—are not common and pass quickly.

Hepatitis A (hep A). Two doses of the vaccine for hepatitis A are recommended for children between 12 months and 2 years living in high-risk states, mostly in the western U.S., or in high-risk countries (check with your doctor to see if you are living in a high-risk area). The first dose is given when a child is 12 months of age, and a booster dose is given at 24 months of age or at least 6 months after the first. The vaccine can also be given to older children in high-risk areas if they didn't receive it earlier.

Hepatitis A is a liver disease that affects 125,000 to 200,000 people a year in the U.S., about 30 percent of them children under age 15. The virus is spread through personal contact or by eating or drinking contaminated food or water. Symptoms of the illness in children over 6 years include fever, loss of appetite, stomach pain, vomiting, and jaundice (yellow skin or eyes). Although hep A infection rarely has the lifelong implications hep B infection often has, it's still a significant contagious illness that can be easily and safely prevented with immunization in early childhood.

Side effects, such as tenderness at the injection site or a low-grade fever, occasionally occur and are not harmful.

Pneumococcal conjugate vaccine (PCV). Children should get the PCV vaccine at 2, 4, and 6 months, with a booster given at 12 to 15 months.

Vaccines for an Adopted Baby

If you've adopted an older baby, you'll need to pay extra attention when it comes to vaccinations. Because some adoption agencies don't have accurate records, it's hard to know which vaccinations, if any, your little one has already received. If you are adopting your baby from a foreign country, he or she may not have been immunized on a schedule recommended in the U.S. Even if there is a vaccination record for your overseas baby, it's no guarantee of adequate protection, since in many developing countries, vaccines may not be uniformly stored or administered properly.

To determine the level of immunity your baby has against a vaccine-preventable disease, the pediatrician can do a blood test to measure antibodies. If the test shows a lack of antibodies for any disease, your baby will be vaccinated. Don't worry about the potential of your baby being vaccinated for the same disease twice. Any adverse reactions to the shots (which are usually minor and quite rare) are still safer than contracting a disease.

Internationally adopted older babies will also need to be screened for a variety of infectious diseases they are at higher risk of having been exposed to, such as TB and hepatitis B.

The PCV vaccine protects against the pneumococcus bacterium, a major cause of serious or invasive illness among children. It is spread through person-to-person contact (touch) and is most common during the winter and early spring.

The Reality About Immunization Myths

The vast majority of concerns parents have about immunization—though perfectly understandable—are unfounded. Don't let the following myths keep you from immunizing your baby:

Myth: *Giving so many vaccines all at once—either during the same visit or in a combo shot—isn't safe.*

Reality: Current vaccines are just as safe and effective when given together as when given separately. More and more combos are being introduced—for instance, one combines the DTaP, hep B, and IPV vaccines, and another combines the MMR vaccine with the varicella (chicken pox) vaccine. The best part about these combo vaccines is that they mean fewer total shots for your baby—something you'll both likely appreciate. Getting different shots at the same visit doesn't present a safety or effectiveness issue either.

Myth: *If everyone else's children are immunized, mine can't get sick.*

Reality: Some parents believe that they don't have to immunize their own children if everyone else's children are immunized—because there won't be any diseases around to catch. That so-called "herd" theory doesn't hold up. First of all, there's the risk that other parents are subscribing to the same myth as you, which means their children won't be immunized either, creating the potential for an outbreak of a preventable disease. Second, unvaccinated children put vaccinated (as well as unvaccinated and not-fully-vaccinated) children at risk for the disease. Since vaccines are about 90 percent effective, the high percentage of immunized individuals limits the spread of the disease but does not eliminate it completely. So not only might you be putting your own child at risk, but other children as well. Something

else to keep in mind: Some diseases, like tetanus, aren't transmitted person to person. An unvaccinated child can contract tetanus after being cut by a rusty object or having contaminated soil seep through a scratch—so even universal immunization of the "herd" won't be protective.

Myth: *Vaccines have wiped out childhood diseases, so my child won't get sick.*

Reality: Wondering why you should bother having your child immunized against diseases that seem to be a thing of the past? The truth is that many of these diseases are still around, and can harm unvaccinated children. In fact, between 1989 and 1991, lapsing rates of MMR vaccinations among preschoolers in the United States led to a sharp jump in the number of measles cases—with 55,000 people becoming sick and 120 dying. In 2006, an outbreak of mumps occurred in a few Midwest states, affecting more than 4,000 people. Experts believe that outbreak—the first in 20 years—started with an infected traveler to the United States from England (where vaccination rates are lower), but was able to spread in the U.S. due to incomplete vaccinations. A mumps outbreak in 2010 in the New York area affected more than 2,000 children and teenagers, a number of whom suffered serious complications as a result. Pertussis is definitely still around, causing severe disease and many deaths yearly, sometimes at epidemic proportions. And experts say 2014 saw the most measles cases since 1996—mostly striking unvaccinated children and adults.

Myth: *One vaccine in a series gives a child enough protection.*

Reality: Skipping vaccines puts your child at increased risk for contracting the diseases, especially measles and pertussis. So if the recommendations are for a series of four shots, for example, make sure your child receives all so he or she is not left unprotected.

Myth: *Multiple vaccines for such young children put them at increased risk for other diseases.*

Reality: There is no evidence that multiple immunizations increase the risk for diabetes, infectious disease, or any other illnesses. Neither is there any evidence of a connection between multiple vaccines and allergic diseases.

Myth: *Shots are very painful for a baby.*

Reality: The pain of a vaccination is only momentary and not significant, compared with the pain of the serious diseases the immunization is protecting against. And there are ways of minimizing the pain your baby feels. Studies show that babies who get shots while they are being held and distracted by their parents cry less, and those who are breastfed immediately before or during the immunization experience less pain. You can also ask your baby's doctor about giving a sugar solution just before the shot (to reduce the pain) or applying a numbing cream an hour earlier.

Myth: *There's mercury in vaccines.*

Reality: Most of the recommended childhood vaccines (MMR, IPV, varicella, and PCV, for instance) never contained mercury (thimerosal) at all. And, since 2001, all routinely recommended vaccines have either been mercury-free or (in the case of the flu vaccine, for instance) have contained only extremely small amounts of mercury. How small? Around 12.5 micrograms per dose—and to put that number into perspective, 6 ounces of canned chunk white tuna contains 52.7 micrograms of mercury. Most important, many studies have proved that this extremely low level of thimerosal doesn't cause harm and the type of mercury used in the flu vaccine is expelled from a child's body faster than the mercury found in fish, leaving little chance for a buildup. Thimerosal-free flu vaccines are available, too, so ask the baby's doctor if you're still concerned.

Myth: *Vaccines cause autism or other developmental disorders.*

Reality: Despite numerous large scale studies that have thoroughly discredited a link between autism and vaccines (including one from the Institute of Medicine based on years of data), it's a controversy that just doesn't go away—at least as long as internet legends and celebrity-driven misinformation keep getting passed around. Even a federal court ruled that routine childhood immunizations (including the MMR vaccine that gets all the press) are not (repeat, not) linked to autism and there is no evidence to back up the claims that suggest otherwise. The entire vaccine-autism scare began in 1998 when a British doctor published one study (involving only 12 children) that suggested a possible link between the MMR vaccine and autism. The journal that published the study (*The Lancet*) retracted it in 2004, and in 2010 it was found that the doctor responsible for that faulty study actually fudged the data, manipulated the outcomes, and misreported results in his research (his medical license was subsequently revoked). In 2011, the *British Medical Journal* called the flawed study "an elaborate fraud." In other words, there was never any credibility to the theory that vaccines cause autism. They don't and they never did.

Recommended Immunization Schedule

This is the schedule for childhood immunizations set by the CDC and recommended by the AAP. Keep in mind that different brands of the same vaccine may require a slightly different dosing schedule, and that some vaccines may be given as combos (a good thing for your baby, since it means fewer needle pricks). A pediatrician may also adjust the schedule if a child gets behind on immunizations and needs to catch up.

Age	DTaP	IPV	MMR	Hib	Hep A	Hep B	Var	PCV	Rotavirus	Influenza
Birth						×				
2 months	×	×		×				×	×	
1 to 2 months						×				
4 months	×	×		×				×	×	
6 months	×			×				×	×	
6 to 18 months		×				×				
6 months on										×
12 to 15 months			×	×			×	×		
12 to 18 months										
12 to 24 months					×					
15 to 18 months	×									
18 to 42 months					×					
4 to 6 years	×	×	×				×			

Large studies and clinical trials have shown that the PCV vaccine is extremely effective in preventing the occurrence of certain types of meningitis, pneumonia, blood infections, and other related, sometimes life-threatening infections. Though the vaccine wasn't intended to prevent ear infections, it's somewhat effective in preventing those caused by these same bacteria.

Side effects, such as low-grade fever or redness and tenderness at the injection site, occasionally occur and are not harmful.

Influenza (flu). One dose of the flu vaccine, given at the start of flu season (usually October or November), is recommended for children 6 months of age and older. Children younger than 9 years of age receiving the vaccine for the first time need two doses at least 4 weeks apart. Once your child is over the age of 2, he or she can receive the yearly FluMist, an influenza vaccine that is delivered as a nasal mist instead of a shot. If your baby is under 6 months during flu season, it's especially important that everyone around him or her receive a vaccine.

Influenza, or flu, is a seasonal illness spread through droplets that are made when an infected person coughs, sneezes, or even talks, and then land in the nose or mouth or on a surface that's later touched (or mouthed by a baby). The influenza virus (there are many different strains) causes fever, sore throat, coughs, headache, chills, and muscle aches. Complications can range from ear and sinus infections to pneumonia and even death. Influenza is different from most other diseases in that the viruses are always changing, meaning that immunity acquired one year may not protect against future influenza viruses. That's why a yearly vaccine is recommended, and it can reduce the chances of getting the flu by up to 80 percent during the season. See page 559 for more on the flu.

Rotavirus (Rota). This oral vaccine (given as drops) prevents rotavirus—an intestinal virus that causes vomiting, watery diarrhea, and often dehydration. It's extremely contagious, spreading easily through contact with contaminated hands or objects and through the air, and before the vaccine was made available, infecting nearly all children by the age of 5. The vaccine is given at either 2, 4, and 6 months or at 2 and 4 months, depending on the brand. Studies show that the vaccine prevents 75 percent of cases of rotavirus and 98 percent of severe cases of the disease.

Calling the Doctor

Most pediatricians want to hear from you if you think your baby is really sick—no matter what the time of day or night. But how will you know what calls for a call? How high does baby's fever have to be? Does a runny nose deserve a call? What about a cough?

Here's what you need to know about calling the doctor.

WHEN TO CALL THE DOCTOR

Deciding which symptoms say "Call immediately," which say "Call sometime today," and which say "Wait and see" isn't always easy—especially for a new parent. That's why you should ask your child's doctor, nurse-practitioner, or physician's assistant for specific when-to-call recommendations for your baby . . . preferably before those first symptoms strike. Have a pediatrician who answers questions from parents via email or text? Ask what the protocol is for those forms of communication, too. (Is a call a better bet than an email when a situation is time sensitive—say, when your baby is running a high fever or has taken a fall? Or is a text better than either?)

No matter what instructions you've been given, call immediately (or go to the emergency room if the doctor can't be reached) if you feel that there is something very wrong with your baby—even if you can't confirm it with the help of this list and even if you can't quite put your finger on what it is. Parents—yes, even brand new parents—often know best.

If your baby develops any of the following symptoms, call as noted. If a symptom that warrants a call during regular office hours appears on the weekend, you can wait until Monday to contact the doctor. If a symptom that requires a call within 24 hours appears on the weekend, call within that time frame, even if you have to call the doctor's answering service.

Fever (unless otherwise specified, temperatures given here are for rectal readings)

- In a baby under 2 months with fever 100.4°F or greater—call immediately

- In a baby over 2 months with fever over 104°F or greater—call immediately, particularly if he or she is acting ill

- In a baby 2 to 6 months with fever over 101°F—call within 24 hours

- In a baby older than 6 months with fever over 103°F—call within 24 hours

- In a baby older than 6 months with fever 100.4°F or greater, with mild cold or flu symptoms, that lasts for more than 3 days—call during regular office hours

- That isn't brought down at all by a fever-reducing medication within an hour—call within 24 hours

- Of 100.4°F or greater that returns after being gone for a couple of days, or that suddenly develops in a baby who has been sick with a cold

or flu (this may indicate a secondary infection, such as an ear infection)—call within 24 hours, unless the baby appears sicker or if breathing becomes fast and labored, in which case, call right away

- That appears following a period of exposure to an external heat source, such as the sun on a hot day or the closed interior of a car in hot weather—immediate emergency medical attention is required (see heat illness, page 587)

- That suddenly increases when a child with a moderate fever has been overdressed or bundled in blankets. This should be treated as heat illness—call right away

Fever accompanied by

- Limpness or unresponsiveness—call right away

- Convulsions (the body stiffens, eyes roll, limbs flail)—call immediately the first time it happens. If your baby has had convulsions in the past, call within 24 hours, unless the doctor has advised you to do otherwise (see page 547)

- Convulsions that last longer than 5 minutes—call 911 immediately for emergency assistance

- Inconsolable, out of the ordinary crying (i.e., not colic) that lasts 2 or 3 hours—call right away

- Crying, as if in pain, when your child is touched or moved—call immediately

- Purple spots appear anywhere on the skin—call immediately

- Difficulty breathing—call immediately

- Excessive drooling and a refusal to swallow liquids—call immediately

- Neck stiffness (baby resists having his

or her head moved forward toward the chest)—call immediately

- A mild rash (not dark or purple)—call during regular office hours

- Repeated vomiting (baby's not able to keep anything down)—call within 6 to 12 hours. Repeated and forceful vomiting—call right away

- Mild dehydration (see page 565 for typical signs)—call within 12 hours

- Any dehydration that seems to be more than "mild" (see page 565 for signs)—call immediately

- Uncharacteristic behavior—excessive crankiness or crying, excessive sleepiness, lethargy, sleeplessness, sensitivity to light, total loss of appetite, more than usual ear pulling or clutching—call within 24 hours

A cough

- That is mild (not barking or whooping) and lasts more than 2 weeks—call during regular office hours

- That disturbs sleep at night—call during regular office hours

- That brings up blood-tinged phlegm—call immediately

- That sounds very barky or chesty—call during regular office hours, unless it's accompanied by breathing problems, in which case you should call sooner (see below)

A cough accompanied by

- Difficulty breathing (it seems like it's hard for baby to breathe)—call immediately

- Wheezing (a whistling sound on breathing out)—call during regular office hours, unless breathing seems labored, then call immediately

- Retractions (the skin between the ribs appears to be sucked in with each breath)—call immediately

- Rapid breathing (see page 540)—call during regular office hours. If persistent or accompanied by fever—call the same day

Bleeding

Report any of the following symptoms to the doctor immediately:

- Blood in the urine

- Blood in the stool, except for small streaks of blood, which you can wait to report until regular office hours

- Blood in coughed-up mucus

- Blood leaking from the ears

General behavior

Call immediately if your baby displays any of the following symptoms:

- Noticeable lethargy, with or without fever; a semi-awake state from which he or she can't fully be roused; lack of responsiveness

- Crying or moaning (as if in pain), when moved or touched

Parent's Intuition

Sometimes you can't put your finger on any specific symptom—or the symptoms you've noticed don't seem serious according to the checklists in this chapter—but your baby just doesn't seem "right" to you. Put a call in to the doctor. Most likely you'll be reassured, but it's also possible that your parent's intuition will have picked up something subtle that needs attention.

- Continuous crying for more than 3 hours not related to colic, high-pitched crying, faint whimpering or moaning
- Refusal to eat or drink anything at all for a few hours beyond a normal feed time

Other

- Swollen glands that become red, hot, and tender—call within 24 hours
- Severe pain anywhere in the body (a nonverbal baby might clutch, tug, or swat at the affected body part)—call immediately
- Yellowing of the whites of the eyes or of the skin—call during regular office hours

BEFORE YOU CALL THE DOCTOR

Once you've decided that a call to the doctor is necessary (or you think it might be—when in doubt, go with your gut), make the most of the call by being as specific as possible when describing your baby's symptoms and by having the answers to questions the doctor may ask.

Information on your baby's symptoms. Often, just looking at your baby will tell you something isn't right. But the doctor or nurse needs more information to figure out what's going on. So before you call to report an illness, check your baby for any of the following symptoms that might be related:

- **Temperature.** If your baby's forehead feels cool to the touch (with the back of your hand or your lips), you can assume there's no significant fever. If it feels warm, get a more accurate

reading with a thermometer (see page 543).

- **Breathing.** Newborns normally take about 40 to 60 breaths per minute, older babies around 25 to 40. Breathing is more rapid during activity (including crying) than during sleep, and may speed up during illness. If your baby is coughing or seems to be breathing rapidly or irregularly, check respiration (rate of breathing). If your baby's respiration is faster or slower than usual or is outside the normal range, or if his or her chest doesn't seem to rise and fall with each breath or breathing appears labored or raspy (unrelated to a stuffy nose), report this to the doctor.

- **Respiratory symptoms.** Is your baby's nose runny or stuffy? Is the discharge watery or thick? Clear, white, yellow, or green? If there's a cough, is it dry, hacking, heavy, crowing, or barking? Has your child vomited mucus during a forceful cough?

- **Behavior.** Is it behavior as usual, or is there any change from the norm in your baby's behavior? Would you describe your baby as sleepy and lethargic, cranky and irritable, inconsolable or unresponsive? Can you elicit a smile (for babies over 2 months)?

- **Sleeping.** Is your baby sleeping much more than usual, or is he or she unusually drowsy or difficult to wake? Or is he or she having more trouble sleeping than usual?

- **Crying.** Is your baby crying more than usual? Does the cry have a different sound or unusual intensity—is it high pitched, for instance, or low pitched?

- **Appetite.** Has there been a sudden change in appetite? Is your baby refusing fluids and/or usual solids? Or eating and drinking as per usual?

- **Skin.** Does your baby's skin appear or feel different in any way? Is it red and flushed? White and pale? Bluish or gray? Does it feel moist and warm (sweaty) or moist and cool (clammy)? Or is it unusually dry or wrinkly? Are lips, nostrils, or cheeks excessively dry or cracking? Are there spots anywhere on your baby's skin—under the arms, behind the ears, on the extremities or trunk, or elsewhere? How would you describe their color, shape, size, and texture? Is your baby scratching or rubbing them?

- **Mouth.** Are there any red or white spots or patches visible on the gums, inside the cheeks, or on the palate or tongue? Any bleeding?

- **Fontanel.** Is the soft spot on top of your baby's head sunken or bulging?

- **Eyes.** Do your baby's eyes look different from usual? Do they seem glazed, glassy, vacant, sunken, dull, watery, or reddened? Is there yellowing of the whites? Do they have dark circles under them, or seem partially closed? If there's discharge, how would you describe its color, consistency, and quantity? Do you notice any "pimples" on the eyelids? Is your child squinting or unwilling to open his or her eyes in the light?

- **Ears.** Is your baby pulling or poking at one or both ears? Is there a discharge from either ear? If there is, what does it look like?

- **Upper digestive system.** Has your baby been vomiting (forceful throwing up of stomach contents through the mouth as opposed to just the usual spitting up)? How often? Is there a lot of material being vomited,

or are your baby's heaves mostly dry? How would you describe the vomit—like curdled milk, mucus streaked, greenish (bile stained), pinkish, bloody, like coffee grounds? Is the vomiting forceful? Does it seem to project a long distance? Does anything specific seem to trigger the vomiting—eating or drinking, for example, or coughing? Do you know, or suspect, that your baby has ingested a toxic substance? Is there an increase or decrease in saliva? Excessive drooling? Or any apparent difficulty swallowing?

- **Lower digestive system.** Has there been any change in bowel movements? Does your baby have diarrhea, with loose, watery, mucousy, or bloody stools? Are color and smell different from usual? Are movements more frequent (how many in the last 24 hours?), sudden, explosive? Or does your baby seem constipated?

- **Urinary tract.** Does your baby seem to be urinating more or less frequently? Have diapers been dryer than usual? Is the urine different in color—dark yellow, for example, or pinkish—or have an unusual odor?

- **Abdomen.** Is your baby's tummy flatter, rounder, more bulging, or firmer than usual? When you press on it gently, or when you bend either knee to the abdomen, does baby seem to be in pain? Where does the pain seem to be—right side or left, upper or lower abdomen, or all over?

- **Motor symptoms.** Has your baby been experiencing neck stiffness (can he or she bend chin to chest without difficulty?), chills, shakes, stiffness, or convulsions? Does he or she seem to have difficulty moving any other part of the body?

- **Other unusual signs.** Do you note any unusual smell coming from your child's mouth, nose, ears, vagina, or rectum? Is there bleeding from any of these?

The progress of the illness so far. No matter what the illness, symptoms won't tell the whole story. You should also be ready to report:

- When did the symptoms first appear?

- What, if anything, triggered the symptoms?

- Are symptoms affected by the time of day? (Are they worse at night?)

- Which over-the-counter or home remedies, if any, have you already tried?

- Has your baby recently been exposed to a virus or infection—a sibling's stomach bug, the flu at daycare, or pinkeye at playgroup?

- Has your baby recently been involved in an accident (like a fall), in which an unnoticed injury could have occurred?

- Has your baby recently had a new or unusual food or drink or one that might have been spoiled?

- Have you traveled with baby out of the country lately?

Your baby's health history. If the doctor doesn't have your baby's chart at hand (sometimes the case when you're calling, especially between office hours), you'll have to refresh his or her memory about certain relevant details. This information is especially important if the doctor has to prescribe medication:

- Your baby's age and approximate weight

- If your baby has a chronic medical condition and/or is currently taking medication

- If there is a family history of drug reactions or allergies

- If your child has had any previous reactions to medications or known allergies

- The telephone number, fax number, and/or email address of your pharmacy (if a prescription is to be called, faxed, or emailed in)

Your questions. In addition to details of your baby's symptoms, it will also help to have ready any questions you have (about recommended dietary changes, calling back if the symptoms continue, and so on) and to have a place to write down answers. Keeping an illness journal (in your child's health history record) will come in handy in the future when you're trying to remember which medicines your baby won't tolerate and how many ear infections baby's had.

Figuring Out Fever

It's hard to relax when your little bundle spikes a fever. But while fevers in babies can unnerve even the most seasoned parent (especially in newborns, when a fever needs immediate attention)—not all fevers are panic-worthy. In fact, fever is actually one of the immune system's most effective tools. It's the body's way of letting you know an infection has settled in, and that your baby's immune system is fighting it with all it's got. Still, fever always needs to be evaluated, and here's how to do it.

TAKING YOUR BABY'S TEMPERATURE

The fastest and easiest way to tell whether your baby has a fever is to touch your lips or the back of your hand to the center of his or her forehead, the nape of the neck, or the torso. With a little practice, you'll quickly learn to figure out the difference between normal and feverish, low fever and higher (though the system may be thrown off if your little one has just woken up or has recently been outside in the cold or the heat, or in a warm bath, or if you recently sipped a hot or cold drink). But your touch can't read a temperature precisely—for that you'll need to use a thermometer.

What kind of thermometer should you reach for? Definitely not a glass one (even those that are mercury-free are unsafe, since they can break during use). While there are safe plastic thermometers available that are nondigital and nonmercury, most parents opt for the digital versions because they're readily available, relatively inexpensive, and easy to use, registering temperature quickly (within 20 to 60 seconds), which is an advantage when

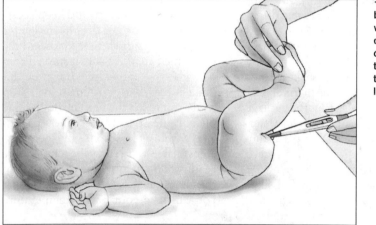

◄ Positioning baby as you would for a diaper change can make taking a rectal temperature a lot easier.

► Placing your little one belly-down on your lap can keep a squirmy baby stable while you take a rectal reading.

dealing with a squirmy baby. There are a number of ways to take a temperature (some of which require a specialized thermometer):

Rectal. When it comes to taking your little one's temperature, most experts agree that the bum is best. A rectal temperature is the most accurate of all methods because it indicates core body temperature, and that's why it's considered the standard for young children—especially babies in their first year, when every degree counts. Start by cleaning the end of the thermometer with rubbing alcohol or soap and water, and rinse with cool water. Turn the thermometer on and make sure you've erased any old readings from its memory. (Since every digital thermometer is different, be sure to read the instructions *before* you have a half-naked baby on your lap.) If you're using a non-digital thermometer, shake it down before using it. Prepare the thermometer by lubricating the sensor tip (the package instructions will tell you whether a water-soluble lubricant, like K-Y, or petroleum jelly, like Vaseline, is preferred). Sit down and place your baby belly-down in your lap with a pillow for comfort (see illustration on page 543). Keep your hand on the lower back to keep your squirmy baby stable. If that's uncomfortable, lay him or her tummy-down on a flat surface, or tummy-up with his or her legs bent in toward the chest, positioned as for diaper changes (see illustration on page 543). To ease anxiety in an older baby, be gentle, talk reassuringly, and try distraction (with a couple of favorite songs, a toy).

Spread the buttocks with one hand, so you can see the rectal opening. Then slip the thermometer in until about a half inch to one inch of the bulb is in the rectum (don't push if you feel resistance). A thermometer with a flexible tip may provide extra comfort, but it's not a must. Hold the thermometer in place until it beeps or visually signals that the reading is done (usually 20 to 60 seconds). Don't worry if baby poops immediately after a temperature reading—that sometimes happens because the thermometer stimulates the muscles that help elimination.

Temporal artery. This easy-to-use, non-invasive thermometer reads your baby's temperature by measuring the heat coming from the temporal artery, which runs across your little one's forehead. To use, place the sensor of the specialized temporal artery thermometer on the center of your baby's forehead (midway between the eyebrow and the hairline), hold down the button, and keep pressing it while sliding the thermometer straight across the forehead toward the top of the ear. Make sure it stays in contact with the skin (which might be difficult if baby is squirming a lot). Stop when you reach the hairline on the side of baby's head, and release the scan button. Within a few seconds the thermometer will beep and show the temperature reading on the display. A big plus of the temporal artery thermometer is that you can take your baby's temperature

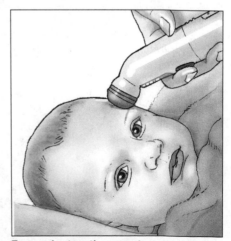

Temporal artery thermometer

when he or she is sleeping. Studies have shown that temporal artery thermometers are more accurate than underarm and in-ear thermometers, but they're still not as precise as rectal readings.

Axillary (underarm). Use this somewhat less precise method of temperature taking when your baby won't lie still for a rectal or has diarrhea, which would make the rectal route messy and uncomfortable, and if you don't have a temporal artery thermometer. Clean the thermometer with rubbing alcohol or soap and water, and rinse with cool water. Place the tip of the thermometer well up into your baby's armpit (the thermometer should touch only his or her skin, not any clothing) and hold his or her arm down over it by gently pressing the elbow against his or her side (see illustration). Hold the thermometer in place until it beeps or visually signals that the reading is done.

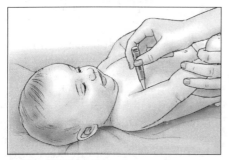

Axillary thermometer

Oral. Using a standard oral thermometer is not appropriate for babies, obviously, but pacifier thermometers have some advantages—they're inexpensive and relatively easy to use. But there are enough disadvantages that might make you think twice before using one. First, they're not as accurate as a rectal, temporal artery, or underarm reading. Second, the pacifier has to stay in your baby's mouth for at least 90 seconds to get an accurate reading. If baby won't keep the thermometer in for that long, it won't work. Finally, some babies gag on the pacifier since the nipple is longer than it is on a regular pacifier. If you do try a pacifier thermometer, be sure the pacifier portion stays in your baby's mouth for about 2 to 3 minutes.

Tympanic (ear). Ear thermometers aren't recommended for babies under 6 months because an infant's narrow ear canals make it hard to insert the sensor properly. And though ear thermometers are safe and can provide a reading in just seconds, they can be difficult to position in babies over 6 months as well—if you don't insert the ear thermometer exactly right, it can be hard to get an accurate, consistent reading. Wax in the ear can also interfere with the temperature reading. In general, a reading in the ear is less reliable than an underarm one, and neither is as accurate as a rectal reading—still considered the gold standard. If you want to try the ear method of taking temperature, make sure you have the correct specialized tympanic thermometer, and ask the doctor or a nurse to show you how to use it (or follow the package directions), practicing until you get a consistent result.

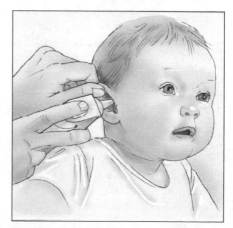

Tympanic thermometer

After reading and recording your baby's temperature, wash the thermometer with cool, soapy water or clean it with rubbing alcohol. Be careful not to wet the digital display, on/off button, or battery cover. And be sure to follow the manufacturer's instructions for proper storage.

EVALUATING THE TEMPERATURE

What's in the numbers? It depends where the reading's coming from. When the doctor asks what your little one's temperature is, it's a given that he or she is referring to a rectal reading, so if you've taken another kind of reading, let the doctor know:

- Rectal. Normal rectal temperature averages 98.6°F, but it can range from 98°F to 100°F. Anything over 100.4°F is considered a fever.

- Temporal artery is nearly as accurate as a rectal reading. Anything over 100.4°F is considered a fever (though if your baby is under 3 months, follow up with a rectal temperature to confirm).

- Axillary (underarm). Normal axillary temperature may average around 97.6°F, but it can range from 96°F to 99°F (about 1 to 2 degrees lower than a rectal reading). Anything over 99°F is considered a fever (though if your baby is under 3 months, follow up with a rectal temperature to confirm).

- Oral. Pacifier thermometers yield results that are a bit low, so add half a degree to the reading you get. Anything over 100°F is considered a fever (though if your baby is under 3 months, follow up with a rectal temperature to confirm).

- A tympanic thermometer can be adjusted to give a reading that is comparable to a rectal reading, but it's not recommended for babies under 6 months. Anything over 100.4°F is considered a fever.

TREATING A FEVER

Different fevers need different treatment—and some don't need any treatment at all. A fever that's triggered by a viral infection (upward of 90 percent of all fevers in young children are) will come and go with the virus—running its course whether it's treated or not. While the doctor may recommend dosing with acetaminophen (after age 2 months) or ibuprofen (after age 6 months) to make a feverish child more comfortable (especially if fever's affecting sleep or appetite), fever relief won't make your baby better faster.

A fever that's triggered by bacteria will usually—though not always—be treated with antibiotics, which lowers temperature indirectly (usually within 24 hours or so) by wiping out the infection. Depending on the type of infection, the antibiotic being given, the child's level of comfort, and how high the fever is, antibiotics and fever reducers may or may not be prescribed together.

A fever that always needs immediate treatment is one that's caused by environmental heat-related illness (brought on by a too-warm environment or overbundling); see page 587.

In general, take these steps when your baby has a fever (unless the doctor has recommended otherwise):

Keep your baby cool. Dress your feverish baby lightly to allow body heat to escape, and maintain a comfortable room temperature. When necessary, use an air conditioner or fan to keep

Febrile Convulsions

It's estimated that 2 to 5 of every 100 young children between the ages of 6 months and 5 years experience convulsions (their eyes roll back, the body stiffens, arms and legs twitch and jerk involuntarily) caused simply by a high fever, usually at its onset. Though febrile convulsions are frightening for parents, studies show they are not usually harmful and don't cause neurological damage. Though these convulsions tend to run in families, in most cases febrile convulsions are due to a young baby's immature brain. When the brain matures, febrile seizures stop happening.

If your baby has a febrile convulsion, stay calm (remember, these kinds of seizures aren't dangerous) and take the following steps:

- Check the clock, so that you can time the seizure.

- Hold your child gently in your arms or place him or her beside you on a bed or another soft surface, lying on one side, with his or her head lower than the rest of the body, if possible.

- Don't try to forcefully restrain your child in any way.

- Loosen any tight clothing.

- Don't put anything in your baby's mouth, including food, a drink, or a pacifier. Remove anything that you see in baby's mouth, like a bit of food, a pacifier, or another object. To do this, use a sweep of one finger, rather than a two-finger pincer grasp, which might force the food or object farther into his or her mouth.

A child may briefly lose consciousness during a seizure, but will usually revive quickly without help. The seizure will probably last only a minute or two (though it'll feel like a lifetime to you).

Call the doctor when the febrile seizure has ended (unless this is a repeat and the doctor has told you it isn't necessary to call). If you don't reach the doctor immediately, you can give acetaminophen to try to lower the temperature while you're waiting. But don't put your child in the tub to try to reduce the fever, because if another seizure occurred, your baby could inhale bathwater.

If your child isn't breathing normally after the seizure, or if the seizure lasts 5 minutes or more, get immediate emergency help by dialing 911 or your local emergency number. A trip to the emergency room will probably be necessary to determine the cause of this kind of complex seizure.

---

baby's environment comfortably cool, but keep your little one out of the path of the airflow or draft. If your baby has chills or goose bumps, the environment is too cool. When that happens, heat is retained, causing your baby's temperature to stay elevated.

Up the fluid intake. Because fever increases the loss of water through the skin, it's important to be sure a feverish baby gets an adequate intake of fluids. Give young infants frequent feedings of breast milk or formula. Older babies can also have water or diluted juice. Encourage fluids, but don't force them—and if your little one refuses to take any fluids for several hours beyond his or her normal mealtimes, tell the doctor.

Dose the fever. Acetaminophen can be given without the doctor's advice once your baby is 2 months old. Ibuprofen can be given once your baby is 6 months old. Younger than that, you'll need to ask the doctor for specific recommendations for a fever. Read dosing instructions carefully each time you give fever-reducing medication, and be careful not to exceed the recommended dose. Do not give any medication (other than acetaminophen or ibuprofen), except under a doctor's directions. Do not give any medication (including acetaminophen) when you suspect heat illness.

Encourage a slow-down. Fever or no fever, a little one who's really feeling yucky will naturally slow down and get the rest his or her body needs. Your baby's running a fever and still running (or crawling) circles around you? That's common, too. Take cues on activity mostly from your baby—allow moderate activity if your little one's raring to go, but put the brakes on babies-gone-wild behavior, since strenuous activity can raise body temperature. Divert to a calmer activity.

Feed the fever. The work of running a fever raises the body's caloric requirements, which means that babies who are sick actually need more calories, not fewer. Don't force food, though.

ALL ABOUT:
Medication

Sometimes, all you'll need to make a sick baby all better is cuddles, comfort, and rest. Other times, you'll need to add medication to the mix. But before you dole out any drug— prescription or over-the-counter—to your little one, you'll want to make sure you're using the right one the right way. Here's what you need to know about medication safety for babies.

GETTING MEDICATION INFORMATION

Whether the doctor has suggested an over-the-counter pain reliever or a prescription antibiotic, you'll need to do more than pick it up at the pharmacy. You'll also need to become familiar with what the medication is, what it does, what dose should be given, how to give it, how to store it, what side effects might be expected, and more. Hopefully, the prescribing doctor will give you most of the information (and if not, hopefully you'll have remembered to ask for it). But you should also do some homework at the pharmacy before you bring the medication home. When it comes to medications and your baby, of course, it pays to be extra careful.

Pharmacists provide an information sheet along with prescription drugs that usually answers most (if not all) of these questions. Prescription drugs—and some over-the-counters—will also come with a manufacturer's package insert or detailed labeling. Check out the information when you pick up the prescription, and if you still have questions or need clarification, ask the pharmacist or the prescribing doctor. Here are some of the questions you may need answers to before you give your baby a medication (some questions may not apply):

- Does this medication have a generic (less expensive) equivalent? Is it as effective as the brand-name equivalent?

- What is the drug supposed to do?

- How should it be stored?

- Does it have a baby-friendly taste, or can the pharmacist add a more pleasant flavoring? Keep in mind that some babies lap up all medications, no matter what flavor, and others clamp shut for most or all of them—but it helps to try different flavorings if you're facing resistance.

- What is the dose?

- How often should the medication be given? Should I wake my baby in the middle of the night for a dose? (This is rarely necessary, fortunately.)

- Should it be given before, with, or after meals?

- Can it be given with formula, juice, or other liquids? Does it interact negatively with any foods?

- If the prescribed medication is to be given 3 or more times a day, is there an equally effective alternative that can be given just once or twice a day?

- If the dose is spit out or vomited up, should I give another dose?

- What if a dose is missed? Should I give an extra, or double, dose? What if an extra dose is inadvertently given?

- How soon can I expect to see an improvement? When should I contact the doctor if there is no improvement?

- When can the medication be discontinued? Does my baby have to finish the full prescription?

- What common side effects may be expected?

- What adverse reactions could occur? Which should be reported to the doctor?

- Could the medication have a negative effect on any chronic medical condition my baby has?

- If my baby is taking any other medication (prescription or over-the-counter), could there be an adverse interaction?

- Is the prescription refillable?

- What is the shelf life of the medication? If any is left, can it be used again at a later date if the doctor advises use of the same medication?

GIVING MEDICINE SAFELY

To be sure that your child gains the maximum benefit from medication, with the least amount of risk, always observe these rules:

- Do not give a baby under 2 months of age any medication (not even an over-the-counter one) not recommended or prescribed for him or her by a doctor.

- Do not give your baby medication of any kind (over-the-counter, his or her own leftover prescription, or anyone else's prescription) without a specific go-ahead from the doctor. In most cases, this will mean getting an okay to medicate each time your baby is sick, except when the doctor has given standing instructions. (For example, your doctor may tell you that whenever your baby runs a temperature over 102°F, give acetaminophen; or when wheezing begins, use the asthma medicine.)

Acetaminophen or Ibuprofen?

There are many kinds of pain relievers and fever reducers on the market, but only two that should be considered for young children: acetaminophen (such as Tylenol, Tempra, and Panadol) for babies 2 months and older, and ibuprofen (such as Motrin and Advil) for babies 6 months and older. Never give your baby under 2 months medication, even over-the-counter pain and fever reducers, without consulting with the doctor first.

Both acetaminophen and ibuprofen are generally recommended interchangeably by pediatricians to relieve pain or fever, though they work differently in the body and have different side effects. Acetaminophen is a pain and fever reliever only—it doesn't reduce inflammation that might be triggering pain. It's considered safe when used as recommended (dosing is every 4 to 6 hours)—a good thing, since you'll likely pull it off the shelf multiple times in your baby's first year—but shouldn't be given regularly for more than a week at a time, since long-term use can cause liver damage. A large overdose of acetaminophen (about 15 times the recommended dose) can cause fatal liver damage, yet another reason why all medicines should be stored out of your baby's reach. Your baby won't swallow liquid meds? Ask the doctor about giving acetaminophen in suppository form (Feverall) after age 6 months.

In addition to relieving fever and pain, ibuprofen has an anti-inflammatory effect, making it more effective when there's inflammation at the root of the pain, as there is with teething. It's also slightly more powerful and longer lasting (dosing is every 6 to 8 hours). Ibuprofen is generally safe, with the biggest drawback being the potential for stomach upset. To avoid, don't give it on an empty stomach, and don't use it to treat stomach pain.

Never give your baby a pain reliever formulated for older children or adults (even in a reduced dose). Make sure you use the infant formulations.

- Unless the doctor specifically instructs you otherwise, give a medication only for the indications listed on the label or information insert.

- Do not give your baby more than one medication at a time, unless you've checked with the doctor or pharmacist to be sure the combination is safe.

- Check the expiration date. Drugs that have expired aren't only less potent, but may also have undergone chemical changes that in some cases can make them harmful (this applies to prescription meds you may have hanging around from a baby's previous illness, too). Always check the expiration or discard-by date before you buy a drug or pick up a prescription. Recheck expiration dates periodically—otherwise you may end up making a pharmacy run in the wee hours.

- Store medication according to instructions on the label or package insert. If a medication must be kept cold, store it in the refrigerator at home and in an insulated bag with an ice pack when you'll need to give it while away from home.

- Administer medications only according to the directions your child's doctor (or the pharmacist) has given you, or according to label directions on over-the-counter products. If directions on the label—or on the printed pharmacy materials that come with the drug—conflict with the doctor's instructions (or aren't specified for your baby's age), call the doctor or pharmacist to resolve the conflict before giving the medication. Follow suggested dosing information about timing, shaking, and giving with or without food.

- Reread the label before each dose, both to be sure you have the right medication and to remind yourself about dosing, timing, and other pertinent information. If you're giving it at night, check the label first to make sure you haven't grabbed the wrong bottle.

- Measure medications meticulously. Once you've nailed down the correct dose, make sure you dispense that dose precisely. Dispense the medication in a calibrated medicine spoon, dropper, syringe, cup, or medicine pacifier (if your baby will suck on it—not all will). Never increase or decrease a dosage unless the doctor has directed you to.

- If your baby spits out or vomits up part of a dose of pain relievers or vitamins, it's usually smart to play it safe and not give extra—underdosing is less risky than overdosing. If you're giving antibiotics, however, check with the doctor about what to do if your baby spits out or vomits up part of one or more doses.

- To prevent choking, don't squeeze your baby's cheeks, hold his or her nose, or force his or her head back when giving medicine. If your baby is old enough to sit, dispense it with him or her in an upright position. If your baby doesn't sit yet, aim the dropper

Don't Give These to Your Baby

Some of the medications you may be used to reaching for can be unsafe for babies. These include:

Cough and cold remedies. Studies have shown that children's over-the-counter cough and cold remedies don't stop the sniffles or silence the hacking in little ones, and they may even cause young kids to develop serious side effects, such as a rapid heart rate and convulsions. That's why the FDA advises that these drugs not be given to children under age 2, and why cough and cold remedy labels recommend against using these meds to treat children 4 years old and younger.

Aspirin (and anything containing salicylates). Doctors have been warning parents for years against giving their kids aspirin, but it's a message that bears repeating: Don't give aspirin (even children's aspirin), or a medication containing aspirin, to children younger than 18 years, unless it has been specifically prescribed by the doctor. Aspirin has been linked to the onset of Reye's syndrome, a potentially fatal disease in children. Although research comes down hardest on aspirin, the National Reye's Syndrome Foundation advises against giving children any medication that contains any form of salicylate, so read ingredient lists on drug labels carefully.

toward the inside of baby's cheek while you prop baby up slightly. This will prevent choking. Don't point the dropper toward the back of the mouth, since that could trigger gagging.

Herbal Remedies

They've been used for centuries to relieve the symptoms of hundreds of ailments. They're available without a prescription. They're natural. But are herbal remedies really effective and safe, especially when it comes to your little one?

No one knows for sure. What is known is that some herbs have a medicinal effect (some very powerful prescription drugs are actually derived from herbs), and that any substance that has a medicinal effect should be categorized as a drug. That means the same precautions need to be taken with herbs as with other drugs.

But there are additional concerns with herbal remedies: Herbs are not regulated by the federal government for either effectiveness or safety. So when you pick up an herbal remedy, you may not get what you think you're getting, and you may get ingredients or contaminants that you didn't expect and that you certainly don't want. So just as you wouldn't give your baby a medicine without the doctor's approval, you shouldn't give an herbal remedy without a medical okay either (and no, the guy in the supplement department of the health food market doesn't count). That includes homeopathic treatments for colic, gas, teething, and so on. Check with the doctor before dosing your baby with any of them.

- Don't put medicine in a bottle or sippy cup of breast milk, formula, or juice unless your doctor recommends it. Your child may not drink the whole bottle or cup and won't get the entire medication dose. Once baby is taking solids, ask the doctor if it's okay to mix the medicine with food (say, pureed fruit)—though only if you're sure baby will eat all the medicine-spiked food.

- Keep a record of the time each dose is given, so you'll always know when you gave the last one (it's easy to forget). This will minimize the chance of missing a dose or accidentally doubling up. But don't stress if you're a little late with a scheduled medication. Just get back on schedule with the next dose.

- Always complete a course of antibiotics, as prescribed, even if your baby seems completely recovered, unless the doctor has specifically told you not to.

- Don't continue giving a medication longer than prescribed.

- If your baby seems to be having an adverse reaction to a medication, stop it temporarily and check with the doctor right away before resuming use.

- If another caregiver, at home or at daycare, is responsible for giving your child medication during the day, be sure that he or she is familiar with the drug-dispensing protocol.

- Never pretend medicine is a treat. Sure, that trick might get the dose down without a fuss, but that kind of association could lead to overdosing if your baby somehow finds and manages to open the medication (or any medication) later and is tempted to sample more of the "treat."

HELPING THE MEDICINE GO DOWN

If you're lucky, your baby is one of those who actually looks forward to (or at least doesn't strongly object to) medicine taking, who savors (or tolerates) the taste of those sweet, syrupy liquids, and who opens up wide at the sight of a medicine dropper. If you're not so lucky, your little one possesses a sixth sense that says, "Clamp mouth shut" when medicine is anywhere in the vicinity. To break the seal on your baby's tight lips, consider:

Timing. Unless you're instructed to give the medication with or after meals, plan on serving it up just before feeding or snacking. First, because your baby's more likely to accept it when hungry, and second, because if medication is vomited up, less food will be lost.

Delivery. If your baby turns up that button nose at the medicine dropper, use a plastic syringe that squirts out liquid meds, or a medicine spoon (never use a regular spoon). Or try a bottle nipple or medicine pacifier so baby can suck the medicine out (if baby will suck long enough to get all the medication out). Follow this with breast milk or formula (or water for an older baby) from the same nipple so any medication remaining in the nipple can be rinsed out in the baby's mouth. If you meet resistance, try switching up the delivery system—a little variety may distract enough to get a dose in. If any liquid leaks out of your baby's mouth, use your finger to push it back in—chances are, your baby will latch right on to your finger and suck the rest off.

Location. Taste buds are concentrated on the front and center of the tongue,

Dose Right

Once a baby is old enough to be given an over-the-counter medication (such as acetaminophen or ibuprofen), the appropriate dose is based on weight, not age. Which is why you'll need to get the proper dosing from the doctor or pharmacist before you medicate your little one.

so bypass those finicky taste zones by placing the medicine between the rear gum and the inside of the cheek, where it will easily glide down the throat with minimal contact with taste buds.

Temperature. Ask the pharmacist whether chilling the medication will affect potency. If it won't, offer the medicine to your baby cold—the taste will be less pronounced. If the medicine can't be chilled, offer your baby a cold bottle first (or a mesh feeding bag with crushed ice or frozen fruit in it for an older baby) so his or her tongue gets slightly chilled.

A trick. Gently blow on your baby's face when giving the medicine. It will trigger the swallowing reflex in young babies. Or give your little one a pacifier to suck on immediately after dropping or squirting the medicine into that sweet mouth. The sucking action will help the medicine get where it needs to go.

Flavor. Ask your pharmacy whether a better-tasting flavoring can be added to a yucky-tasting liquid. FDA-approved medication flavorings, such as FLAVORx, come in every flavor from bubble gum to tangerine and are designed to combat the bad taste and smell of liquid medicines.

The Most Common Infant Illnesses

Happily, babies in their first year of life are generally healthy. Even when they do get sick, the bugs they catch don't usually bug them for very long. What's more, these common illnesses are typically easy to treat. Here's what you need to know:

COMMON COLD

The common cold is even more common among the very young. That's because babies and small children haven't yet had the chance to build up immunities against the many different cold viruses in circulation. So be prepared to have at least a few run-ins with a runny nose during the first couple of years, probably more if your child attends daycare or has older siblings.

Symptoms. Happily, most cold symptoms are mild. They include:

- Runny nose (discharge is watery at first, then thickens and becomes opaque and sometimes yellowish or even greenish)

- Nasal congestion or stuffiness

- Sneezing

- Sometimes, mild fever

- Sometimes, sore or scratchy throat (not easy to spot in a baby)

- Dry cough (which may get worse at night and toward the end of a cold)

- Fatigue, crankiness

- Loss of appetite

Cause. Contrary to popular belief, colds aren't caused by being cold, going bare-headed in the winter, getting feet wet, exposure to drafts, and so on (though being chilled can lower a baby's immunity). Colds (also known as upper-respiratory infections, or URIs) are caused by viruses. These viruses are spread via hand-to-hand contact (a child with a cold wipes her snotty nose with her hand and then holds hands with another child, and the infection is passed on), via droplet transmission from sneezes or coughs, and via contact with an object that's been contaminated—such as a toy that's mouthed first by a sick child and then by a healthy child. There are more than 200 viruses known to cause colds, which explains why colds are so "common."

The incubation period for a cold is usually 1 to 4 days. A cold is typically most contagious a day or two before symptoms even appear, but can also be passed along when the cold is already under way. Once the really runny nose dries up, a cold is less contagious.

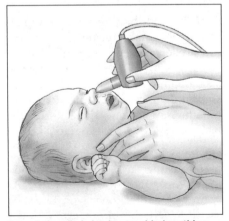

For a baby who's having trouble breathing through a stuffy nose, saline drops to soften the mucus and aspiration to suction it out will bring welcome relief.

Duration. The common cold usually lasts 7 to 10 days (day 3 is usually the worst). A residual dry nighttime cough, which may not appear until the end of the cold, may linger longer.

Treatment. There is no known cure for the common cold, but symptoms can be treated, as necessary, with:

- Saline nose drops to soften dried mucus that may be clogging your baby's nostrils. Suctioning of mucus with a nasal aspirator (see illustration on facing page) may be necessary to help baby breathe through the nose.

- Moist air to help clear nasal passages. Run a cool-mist humidifier (which is safer than a warm-mist humidifier, but do keep it clean) in baby's bedroom at night.

- Moisturizing ointment, spread lightly on the rims of the nostrils and under the nose to help prevent chapping and soreness.

- Elevation of the head of the crib (by placing pillows *under* the mattress) to make breathing easier.

- Acetaminophen (for babies over 2 months) or ibuprofen (for babies over 6 months) for fever reduction if needed (it usually isn't with a cold). Check with your doctor for guidelines.

- Plenty of fluids, particularly warm ones (chicken broth, once the ingredients have been introduced, really is effective—and it can be served strained and slightly warm in a sippy cup), and a nutritious diet. If baby isn't taking solids yet, be sure to keep up breastfeeding or formula bottles. For babies on solids, try to offer vitamin C–rich foods each day. Frequent small meals may be more appealing than three squares.

The Frequent Cold Program

Does it seem as if your baby has enrolled in the Frequent Cold Program—catching every cold or other virus the older siblings come down with, or bringing one home from daycare every other week? There's an upside, believe it or not: Frequent colds (and bouts with other bugs) boost your baby's immune system, making it stronger in the long run and helping your little one better fend off the next bug making the rounds. For more on common contagious illnesses, go to WhatToExpect.com.

Prevention. The number one way to prevent a cold is to wash your baby's hands regularly. Can't get to a sink? Hand-sanitizing gels or wipes will do in a pinch, though they're not as effective as soap and water in washing away those germs. Keep your baby away from anyone with a cold, when possible. Use a disinfectant solution to clean surfaces that may be contaminated with cold germs, and follow other tips for preventing the spread of illness (see page 562). Breastfeeding can reduce susceptibility to colds, but not entirely. Remember that there's no way to entirely protect your little one from cold viruses. The average child has 6 to 8 colds a year, and that's not usually a concern as long as growth and development are normal.

When to call the doctor. Usually, there's no need to contact the doctor for a simple cold, but if it's your baby's first cold or if baby is under 3 months, a call to the pediatrician is a good idea, if only to put your mind at ease.

Allergies This Year?

The good news is that allergies to inhaled substances (pollen, pet dander, dust mites, and mold) are rare among infants in their first year. For more on those kinds of allergies see *What to Expect the Second Year*. More common in the first year are allergies to foods (see page 326) and eczema (see page 325)—two allergic reactions more common in babies with a family history of allergies, asthma, hay fever, or eczema.

Also call if your baby shows any of the following:

- Extreme lethargy

- Refusal to eat or drink

- Difficulty sleeping, is very restless during the night, or has pain that causes night waking (will be difficult to detect in a small baby)

- Foul-smelling, greenish or yellowish nasal discharge from nose or from coughing

- Wheezing

- Breathing significantly more rapidly than usual

- A cough that's getting worse or continues during the day after other symptoms are gone

- Swollen glands in the neck

- Pulling on ears day or night

- Running a fever over 102°F or has a low-grade fever for more than 4 days

- Symptoms last longer than 10 days

If your baby seems to have a continuous cold, a chronically runny nose, or very long-lasting or frequent colds (especially when accompanied by under-eye circles), talk to the doctor about the possibility that allergies might be responsible (though it's rare for this to be the case in babies).

EAR INFECTION

Symptoms. Also known as acute otitis media, an ear infection is when the middle ear (between the outer part of the ear and the innermost part of the ear) gets plugged with fluid and becomes infected and inflamed. When examined by the doctor (you won't be able to see this from the outside), the eardrum appears pink early in the illness, then red and bulging. Symptoms include:

- Pain, often worse at night because lying down changes pressure in the ear. Your baby may complain, or tug, rub, or clutch at an affected ear—crying when sucking on breast or bottle may indicate ear pain that has radiated to the jaw

- Fever

- Fatigue

- Crankiness and irritability

If the infection persists or worsens, the eardrum could perforate (develop a small hole, which usually heals in less than a week). If this happens, pus, often tinged with blood, may spill into (and be seen in) the ear canal. The perforation will relieve the pressure and thus the pain, but treatment of the infection will help prevent further damage—so it's crucial that you tell the doctor if you suspect a rupture (crust in and around the ear is a telltale sign).

Often, even after treatment, fluid remains in the middle ear, a condition called otitis media with effusion. Symptoms include mild hearing loss (your baby may fail to respond consistently to sounds, such as your voice). While typically temporary (usually lasting about 4 to 6 weeks), the hearing loss can become permanent if the condition continues untreated for many months, especially if there are also frequent bouts of infection.

Cause. Ear infections are often secondary infections brought on by a cold or other upper-respiratory infection (or, rarely in babies, allergies), which causes the lining of the Eustachian tube (the tube that connects the middle ear to the nose and the back of the throat) to swell, become congested, and accumulate fluid. The fluid becomes a breeding ground for infection-causing germs. Behind the inflamed eardrum, the buildup of pus and mucus produced by the body in an attempt to respond to the infection causes the pain of earache. Young children are more likely than older children and adults to get ear infections because their Eustachian tubes are short (allowing germs to travel up them more quickly and making it easy for them to become blocked) and horizontal rather than slanted (making drainage poor), and because they get more colds and other respiratory illnesses in general than older kids and adults do.

Duration. Although pain, fever, and other symptoms usually diminish or disappear shortly after treatment is begun, it can take 10 days or more of treatment with antibiotics to resolve an acute ear infection. Fluid may remain in the middle ear for much longer.

Treatment. If you suspect an ear infection, call the doctor so that you can get your child's ears checked. If there's infection, the doctor will probably prescribe a course of antibiotics for your infant (the wait-and-see approach is usually reserved for children over age 2 or 3). You might be asked to come back into the office for a recheck, but this is usually not needed—especially if baby seems to be feeling better.

Your doctor will likely recommend acetaminophen (for babies over 2 months) or ibuprofen (for babies over 6 months) for pain and fever relief. Heat (applied with a heating pad set on low, warm compresses, or a covered hot-water bottle filled with warm water) or cold (applied with an ice pack wrapped in a wet washcloth) can also be used to relieve pain. Elevating your little one's head (with pillows *under* the crib mattress) during sleep may also be helpful.

Prevention. Here's what you can do to minimize your child's risk:

- Breastfeed for at least 6 months, preferably the entire first year, or longer.

- Reduce exposure to germs as much as possible, since even common colds can lead to ear infections. That means steering clear of sick kids and washing your hands and your child's hands frequently.

- Stay up-to-date on your child's immunizations. The pneumococcal vaccine, which is given to prevent serious infections such as pneumonia and meningitis, may also reduce the risk of ear infections. Since ear infections are a common complication of flu, make sure your baby receives a yearly flu vaccine after age 6 months.

- Be sure to feed baby in a more upright feeding position, especially when he or she has a respiratory infection.

- Limit pacifier use to sleep time only.

Some Probiotics with Those Antibiotics?

No matter how many times you wash your baby's hands or how much sanitizer you use, sooner or later your little one is going to come down with an infection—let's say an ear infection—that requires antibiotics. While antibiotics are wonderful for wiping out bacterial infections, broad-spectrum antibiotics aren't all that discerning—they aren't able to differentiate between the infection-causing bacteria and other benign bacteria in the body. Which means that along with the bad bacteria that gets wiped out, some good and very important bacteria—especially those found in the digestive tract—are also destroyed. And that can come with a very unpleasant drawback: diarrhea.

One way to manage antibiotic-related diarrhea (besides investing in extra-absorbent diapers) is to give your baby probiotics. Probiotics (live active cultures, like Lactobacillus or Bifidobacterium) are beneficial (or "pro") bacteria that help counterbalance the negative effects of antibiotics. Research shows that giving probiotics to children can reduce antibiotic-related diarrhea by 75 percent. For this reason, pediatricians often recommend that kids take probiotics whenever they're on antibiotics. Another reason: Probiotics help prevent the overgrowth of yeast (the culprit in candida diaper rash) that can be triggered by antibiotic use.

But that's not the only thing probiotics can do. They also may combat regular diarrhea and constipation, sinus and respiratory infections, urinary tract infections, and possibly even asthma and eczema. What's more, probiotics are believed to boost the immune system in general, making it even less likely that your baby will come down with those illnesses in the first place. Think of probiotics as the reserve corps—the reinforcements sent in to bulk up the numbers of helpful bacteria and crowd out the illness-causing bacteria. These good little soldiers also help strengthen the intestinal lining so that bad bugs can't cross into the bloodstream. Probiotics can change the intestinal environment, too, making it more acidic and therefore less desirable for bad bacteria.

So how can you get probiotics into your baby? Some formulas have probiotics added in. Once your baby is on solids, the most obvious source is in yogurt (once it's introduced into baby's diet). Be sure to choose ones with active cultures—it'll say so on the label. Or ask the pediatrician to recommend a probiotic supplement (there are many available over-the-counter, and they come in powder form or drops for babies). Ask, too, about how frequently that supplement should be given, how to space out doses (probiotics shouldn't be given at the same time as antibiotics), and how it should be stored (sometimes in the refrigerator).

- Wean off the bottle at 12 months.

- Prevent exposure to secondhand smoke, which makes children more vulnerable to ear infections.

When to call the doctor. Call during regular office hours if you suspect an ear infection (it's not an emergency). Call again if your child isn't feeling better after 3 days (with or without antibiotics) or if the infection seems to get better and then returns (it could be a sign of a chronic ear infection). Call, too, if you notice any hearing loss.

FLU

Symptoms. The flu (short for "influenza") is a contagious viral infection that usually rears its very infectious head between the months of October and April (aka flu season). Its symptoms include:

- Fever

- Dry cough

- Sore throat (your baby may reject food and drink, or seem in pain when swallowing)

- Runny or stuffy nose

- Muscle aches and pains

- Headache

- Extreme fatigue, lethargy

- Chills

- Loss of appetite

- Sometimes in young children, vomiting and diarrhea

Cause. The flu is caused by the influenza virus—and different strains (or, rarely, new strains like the H1N1 virus) circulate each year. Your little one can catch the flu by coming into contact with an infected person (especially if that sick someone sneezes or coughs on your baby) or by touching or mouthing something (a toy, a cell phone, a shopping cart handle, a sippy cup) that an infected person has touched. The incubation period for the flu is usually 2 to 5 days. If your little one comes down with the flu, symptoms usually last about a week, though some can linger for up to 2 weeks.

Treatment. Treatment includes fluids and rest. To relieve flu symptoms, humidify the air in your baby's room, and give acetaminophen or ibuprofen only as needed for pain or high fever (do not give aspirin or any medication containing aspirin or salicylates). An antiviral drug may be prescribed for those children (even newborns) with severe symptoms or at high risk of complications, but it needs to be administered in the first 48 hours to be effective.

Prevention. Since complications from the flu are more serious in children under age 5, you should do everything you can to protect your little one from the flu, including getting your older baby the flu shot (see page 537), making sure the whole family and all childcare providers are also vaccinated, and steering clear of sick people.

When to call the doctor. If you suspect your child has come down with the flu (just check the symptom list above if you're not sure), call your doctor.

RESPIRATORY SYNCYTIAL VIRUS (RSV)

Symptoms. In most infants, the virus causes symptoms resembling those of the common cold, including:

- Runny nose

- Low-grade fever

- Decreased appetite

- Irritability

In some infants, the infection can progress to include some or all of these lower-respiratory symptoms (bronchiolitis):

- Rapid breathing

- Hacking cough

- Wheezing sound when breathing

- Grunting

For Parents: Keeping Your Germs to Yourself

Mom's got a cold? Dad's got the flu? Germs have a way of making the rounds through the family, and later on, when your little one is in school, he or she will be bringing plenty your way. For now, chances are much better that you or other family members will pass germs on to him or her.

To minimize the possibility that your baby will catch your cold—or any other infection you or another family member comes down with—wash your hands thoroughly before touching him or her or anything that goes into his or her mouth (including hands, bottle, pacifier, and your nipples), and avoid drinking from the same cup. Keep baby from touching any cold sore or other contagious rash, and steer clear of kissing while you have symptoms of infection. And make sure your immunizations are up-to-date (see box, page 530). Anyone who lives with or cares for your baby should make sure to follow the same rules. By the way, it's fine to continue nursing your baby while you're sick. In fact, breastfeeding strengthens your baby's immune system.

All that said, you'll also have to resign yourself to the fact that few babies escape their first year cold-free. Even with all the above precautions, your little one is likely to succumb to the sniffles at some point—and because you spend so much close time together and share susceptibility (he or she receives only immunities from you that you already have), baby is actually more liable to catch a cold from you than from a passing sneezer on the street.

- Retractions (the skin between the ribs is visibly sucked in with each breath)

- Lethargy, sleepiness, dehydration

- Noticeable bluish color in the skin around the mouth

Cause. RSV is such a common virus that nearly all adults and children are affected by it sooner or later. A normal cold virus or mild RSV infection affects just the nose and upper part of the lungs. But these symptoms can worsen rapidly in some babies as the virus infects the lungs, inflaming the lower part of the respiratory tract and the smallest inner branches of the airways, making it difficult to breathe (such an infection is called bronchiolitis). For most babies, the illness is mild. But babies at risk (such as premature babies, because their lungs are underdeveloped and they haven't yet received enough antibodies from their mothers to help them fight off RSV disease once they've been exposed to it) are more likely to get severe bronchiolitis and end up in the hospital.

Method of transmission. RSV is highly contagious and is transmitted by direct hand contact from infected individuals. The infection can also be spread through the air, by coughing and sneezing. The period of greatest contagiousness is in the first 2 to 4 days of the infection. RSV infections are most common during the winter and early spring.

Duration. Mild RSV lasts 3 to 5 days. It can last much longer in premature babies or if there are complications.

Treatment. For mild RSV, treat as you would for a cold (see page 554). For those whose RSV has caused more severe bronchiolitis:

- Nebulizer, which may help open up the airways

- In severe cases, hospitalization, oxygen administration, and IV fluids

Prevention. To help prevent RSV:

- Breastfeed, if possible.

- Make hand washing a priority around the house.

- Keep older siblings away from the baby as much as possible if they have a runny nose, cold, or fever.

- Do not take a high-risk baby out to crowded areas such as shopping centers during RSV season.

- Do not smoke or let anyone smoke around your baby.

- An intramuscular shot (of the antibody palivizumab) that helps prevent the illness is given once a month during the cold winter months to certain high-risk babies.

When to call the doctor. Call the doctor if:

- Your baby has breathing difficulties or changes in breathing pattern (rapid breathing, wheezing, or the skin between the ribs is sucked in with each breath).

- A fever persists for more than 4 or 5 days and/or remains elevated despite giving acetaminophen or ibuprofen.

CROUP

Symptoms. Croup (laryngotracheobronchiolitis) is an infection—usually seen in late fall and winter—that causes the voice box and windpipe to become inflamed, and the airways just below the vocal cords to swell and get very narrow. Symptoms include:

- Labored or noisy breathing—you may hear a high-pitched breathing sound when your child inhales (called stridor)

- A harsh, barking cough that sounds like a seal's call and usually comes on at night

- Retractions (the skin between the ribs is visibly sucked in with each breath)

- Sometimes, fever

- Hoarseness

- Stuffy nose (coldlike symptoms may appear first)

- Difficulty swallowing

- Irritability

Cause. Croup, most common in early childhood, is usually caused by the parainfluenza virus (a respiratory virus that isn't related to the flu), though it can also be caused by other respiratory viruses, including the influenza virus. It's spread the same way other contagious germs are spread: Your child can become exposed by coming into contact with another child (like an older sib or daycare peer) who has croup (especially through a cough or sneeze), or by coming into contact with something an infected child has touched (the germs can survive on surfaces, like toys).

Duration. Croup can last several days to a week and may recur.

Treatment. Though the cough may sound scary, these simple measures will usually relieve discomfort in your croupy baby:

- Steam inhalation. Take your baby into the bathroom with you, run hot water

Containing Germs

Germs have a way of getting around, especially around a family with young children. Here's how you can help to contain those germs before they make your whole family sick:

- Wash those hands. Hand washing is probably the single most effective way to stop the spread of illness, so make it a house rule—whether family members are healthy or sick. Wash your hands before touching your mouth, nose, or eyes; before eating and handling food; and after nose blowing or coughing, using the toilet, or contact with someone who's sick. No sink around? Keep antibacterial wipes or gels handy when you can't manage frequent washing or when you're out of the house.

- Separate the sick. As much as possible (and it won't always be), try to isolate sick family members, at least for the first few days of a contagious illness.

- Put tissues in their place. Do sick family members tend to leave a trail of dirty tissues behind (or beside) them? Then they're leaving a trail of germs, too. Make sure tissues are disposed of immediately after use, flushed or deposited in a covered trash container. Ditto for wipes you've cleaned up baby boogers with.

- Cover those coughs. If they can't do their coughing or sneezing into a tissue, train your crew (mom, dad, babysitter, older sibs) to do it into the inside of their elbows, not their hands. Just make sure your baby doesn't end up mouthing or snuggling in the area coughed or sneezed on.

- Don't pass the cup. To each their own in the bathroom (their own cup, or disposable ones, their own toothbrush, their own towel) and at the table (no sharing from the same cup, spoon, fork, bowl, or plate).

- Mind your surfaces. Wash or spray possibly contaminated "hot spot" surfaces (such as bathroom faucets, phones, remotes, toys, keyboards, doorknobs, and so on) with a disinfectant.

---

in the shower, and close the bathroom door. Stay in there, if you can, until the barking noise settles down.

- Cool moist air. On a cool night, take your baby out into the fresh air for 15 minutes. Or open the freezer and have your little one breathe in that cold air for several minutes.

- Humidification. Run a cool mist humidifier in the room your baby sleeps in.

- Upright position. Try to keep your child in an upright position for a while, since this can make it easier to breathe. You can place pillows *under* the mattress to prop your baby up safely at night (no pillows in the crib).

- Comfort and cuddles. Do your best to minimize your baby's crying since it can make the symptoms worse.

When to call the doctor. If you suspect your baby has croup, call the doctor, especially if this is your baby's first attack. If it's a repeat, follow instructions the doctor has given you previously. Also call if:

- The steam or cold air doesn't stop the barky cough.

- Your child lacks good color (if there's a bluish or grayish hue around your child's mouth, nose, or fingernails).

- Your child has difficulty catching his or her breath (especially during the day), or you can see retractions (when the skin between the ribs pulls in with each breath).

- You hear stridor (a high-pitched, musical sound made when breathing) during the day, or nighttime stridor that isn't promptly relieved by exposure to steam or cold.

Often, the pediatrician will prescribe a dose of steroids for a case of croup to relieve the swelling in the airways and make breathing easier.

CONSTIPATION

Constipation is rarely a problem for exclusively breastfed babies (though a breastfed newborn who isn't having frequent soft poops may not be getting enough to eat; see page 182). But constipation can sometimes occur in formula-fed babies and in some breastfed babies once solids are added to the diet.

Symptoms. Timing isn't everything when it comes to bowel movements—in fact, when it comes to diagnosing constipation, it's a matter of quality, not frequency. An older baby who goes a few days without pooping isn't necessarily clogged up (just as a baby who goes 4 times a day doesn't necessarily have diarrhea). If the stool comes out easily and looks normal (soft when on a pure liquid diet, formed but soft once solids are introduced), everything's moving along just fine—if at a somewhat slower pace. On the other hand, if

your formula-fed newborn is producing firm stools less than once a day or your older baby is producing small, round, hard stool that seems difficult to pass, the diagnosis is most likely constipation.

Cause. Some children (like some adults) are more prone to constipation than others. But often constipation is linked to not eating enough high-fiber foods, not drinking enough fluids, and not getting enough physical activity. The result is dry, hard stool that builds up in the lower bowels. Constipation can also develop during or after an illness (because a child's not eating, drinking, or moving much), and can be a side effect of certain medications.

Treatment. To help get your older baby back on track (or prevent constipation in the first place), include plenty of:

- Fiber. Serve high-fiber foods as they're introduced, such as fresh fruits (ripe pears and kiwi are particularly effective), soft-cooked, minced dried fruits (especially raisins, prunes, apricots, and figs), vegetables, and whole grains. Avoid serving any refined grains (including baby cereal that doesn't specify "whole grain" or "brown rice"), which can clog up the works.

- Probiotics. These beneficial bacteria can help get things moving again— and keep them moving. Feed your older baby whole milk yogurt that contains active cultures, and ask the doctor about whether a probiotic supplement might be a good idea, too.

- Fluids. Make sure your baby is getting enough fluids (at least a quart of fluids a day)—especially if he or she was recently weaned off the bottle or breast (many babies drink much less after graduating to a cup). Certain fruit juices (such as prune juice or pear juice) are particularly productive, but water works, too.

■ Exercise. While there's no need to sign your baby up at the local gym, do make sure his or her whole day isn't spent cooped up in an infant seat or carrier. Moving gets your child's digestive system moving. Baby isn't mobile yet? Try bicycling his or her legs to get things moving down below.

■ Lubrication. Daubing a bit of petroleum jelly at the anal opening may help the movement slip out more easily. For an extra-stubborn case, consider slipping in a lubricated rectal thermometer to help stimulate the muscles that get movements going.

Don't give any medication or laxatives for constipation unless it's been recommended or prescribed by the doctor.

When to call the doctor. Call the doctor when:

■ Your formula-fed newborn baby has firm stool less than once a day or your older baby has not had a bowel movement for 4 or 5 days or is producing small, round, difficult-to-pass stool.

■ Constipation is accompanied by abdominal pain or vomiting.

■ There is blood in or around the stool.

■ Constipation is chronic and the treatments described above have been ineffective.

Chronic constipation can be very painful and can affect your child's appetite and sleep. Some kids suffering from constipation also develop anal fissures (cracks or tears in the skin near the anus) that bleed and cause stool to have streaks of blood. The fissure should heal once the constipation clears up.

DIARRHEA

This problem, too, is unusual in breastfed babies, since breast milk protects against diarrhea.

Symptoms. When your baby's poop flows a little too freely (very loose, watery poops—not seedy like a breastfed baby's stool—that make an appearance several times a day), you're dealing with diarrhea. Other symptoms of diarrhea include poop color and/or odor that may vary from the usual, mucus in the stool, and/or redness and irritation around the rectum. When diarrhea continues for several days to a week, dehydration and weight loss can occur. Keep in mind that some children are naturally on a more-frequent pattern of elimination, but as long as that stool—even if it comes frequently—is normal in appearance, that's not considered diarrhea.

Cause. Diarrhea occurs most often when your child has a virus, has eaten something irritating to the digestive system, or has gone a little overboard in the fruit department (apple juice is a common culprit). An allergy or food intolerance (to milk, for instance) can also cause diarrhea, as can certain medications (such as antibiotics). Diarrhea that lasts longer than 6 weeks (after all the above mentioned culprits are discontinued) is called intractable and may be linked to an overactive thyroid gland, cystic fibrosis, celiac disease, enzyme deficiencies, or other disorders.

Method of transmission. Diarrhea that's caused by microorganisms can be transmitted via the feces-to-hand-to-mouth route or by contaminated foods. Diarrhea can also be triggered by excesses of, intolerances of, or allergies to, certain foods or drinks.

Signs of Dehydration

Babies who are losing fluids through diarrhea and/or vomiting may become dehydrated. Call the doctor if you note the following in a baby who is vomiting, has diarrhea or a fever, or has otherwise been ill:

- Dry mucous membranes (you might notice cracked lips)

- Tearless crying

- Decreased urination. Fewer than six wet diapers in 24 hours or diapers that stay dry for 2 or 3 hours should alert you to the possibility that urinary output is abnormally scant. Also look out for urine that appears darker yellow and more concentrated.

- A sunken fontanel—the "soft spot" on the top of the head appears depressed instead of flat

- Listlessness

Additional signs appear as dehydration progresses. These require immediate medical treatment. Do not delay in calling the doctor or getting your child to an emergency room if you note any of the following symptoms:

- Unusual coolness and mottling of the skin of the hands and feet

- Very dry mucous membranes (dry mouth, cracked lips, dry eyes)

- No urinary output (diapers are dry) for 6 or more hours

- Extreme fussiness or unusual sleepiness

Duration. An occasional looser-than-normal stool (lasting anywhere from a few hours to several days) is not a cause for concern. Some intractable cases can last indefinitely, unless the underlying cause is found and corrected. A very sick baby may need hospitalization to stabilize body fluids.

Treatment. To treat diarrhea:

- Continue breast or formula feedings. Since a baby with persistent diarrhea may develop temporary lactose intolerance, a switch to a lactose-free formula may be recommended if the diarrhea doesn't improve on baby's regular formula.

- Give fluids. Make sure your baby is breastfeeding or taking a bottle often (at least as often as usual, if not more). For older babies, water or diluted white grape juice (a better choice than apple juice—which you should probably stop altogether until the diarrhea clears) may be sufficient in mild cases. If there is substantial fluid loss, and particularly if there's also vomiting, ask the doctor about giving your older baby an oral electrolyte solution (such as Pedialyte) to replace sodium and potassium lost in the diarrhea and to help prevent dehydration.

- Feed right. Is your little one on solids already? Mild diarrhea tends to improve more quickly when solids are continued. Severe diarrhea (with or without vomiting) usually calls for oral electrolyte solution (if the doctor recommends it) the first day, followed by a slow resumption of the normal diet over the next couple of days.

■ Become a pro. Some research suggests that probiotics can help prevent or treat diarrhea in babies. If your baby is formula-fed, choosing a formula with probiotics could help. For older babies on solids, yogurts containing active cultures or a probiotic supplement (in drops or powder form) can help prevent or help treat a case of diarrhea—particularly during antibiotic therapy.

Prevention. Prevent diarrhea by:

■ Giving probiotics regularly if the pediatrician recommends it

■ Following food safety guidelines (see page 451)

■ Thoroughly washing hands after bathroom use or after changing diapers.

When to call the doctor. Call the doctor if your baby:

■ Shows signs of dehydration (see box, page 565)

■ Has loose, watery stools for 24 hours (but not seedy breastfed stools, which are often watery)

■ Is vomiting for longer than 24 hours

■ Refuses fluids

■ Has stools that are bloody, or vomit that is greenish, bloody, or looks like coffee grounds

■ Has a bloated or swollen abdomen or if there seems to be anything more than mild abdominal discomfort

URINARY TRACT INFECTION (UTI)

Symptoms. The symptoms of UTI (some of which are hard to recognize in young babies) include frequent and painful urination, blood in the urine, pain in the lower abdomen, lethargy, unusual-smelling urine, and/or fever.

Cause. UTIs occur because bacteria enter the urethra (the tube that carries urine from the bladder for excretion), causing infection. Because the urethra is shorter in girls and bacteria can travel up it more easily, girls have UTIs more often than boys (and when boys do get a UTI, it's more likely the result of a urinary tract abnormality). Not getting enough fluids can encourage the development of a UTI.

A Better Juice for Your Sick Baby?

A sick tummy got your older baby down? It may be time for a change of juice. Researchers have found that children recover more quickly from diarrhea when they drink white grape juice than when they stick to those high chair standards, apple and pear. They're also less likely to experience a recurrence on the white grape. Apparently, the sugar and carbohydrate composition of white grape juice is better for the digestive system (and a lot less challenging in the laundry department than its purple cousin). Apple and pear juices naturally contain sorbitol (an indigestible carbohydrate that can cause gas, bloating, and discomfort) and a higher amount of fructose than glucose, while white grape juice is sorbitol-free, and has an even balance of fructose and glucose. Remember to always dilute the juice, no matter which kind, with water. Or skip the juice altogether and stick with water, formula, and breast milk.

Treatment. The treatment of choice is antibiotics. Also important: making sure baby gets enough fluids.

Prevention. To prevent UTIs, take extra care when diapering your baby: Wipe front to back, and wash your hands before and after diapering. Again, make sure your baby gets enough fluids and diaper changes, and avoid using potentially irritating bubble baths and soaps.

When to call the doctor. As soon as you notice symptoms of a possible UTI, call the doctor.

The Most Common Chronic Conditions

ASTHMA

What is it? Asthma is a condition in which the small breathing tubes (called bronchial airways) occasionally become inflamed, swollen, and filled with mucus, often in response to an irritation to the airways, such as a cold (or an allergen, although this is less common in a baby or toddler than in an older child). Asthma flareups can cause shortness of breath, tightness in the chest, coughing, and/or wheezing—and when it happens to your baby, it can be downright frightening for both of you. In young children, sometimes the only symptom may be a recurrent croupy, "barky" cough that is worse with activity or at night and may sometimes lead to vomiting. But there may also be rapid and/or noisy breathing, retractions (the skin between the ribs appears to be sucked in with each breath), and chest congestion.

Asthma is the most common chronic disease in children, and 70 percent of all cases of childhood asthma develop before a child turns 3. Certain hereditary and environmental risk factors can predispose a child to developing asthma, including a family history of asthma or allergies, having eczema or other allergic conditions, living with a smoker, exposure to smoke in the womb, living in an urban, polluted area, low birthweight, and overweight.

It's often not easy to diagnose asthma in babies, because it's hard to distinguish between a viral respiratory tract infection (like RSV) and asthma that results from a virus, since the symptoms are so similar. That means the doctor will rely heavily on what you reveal about your child's symptoms. So take careful notes about what your baby's symptoms are, how often they happen, and under what conditions— and bring these notes with you to your appointment. The doctor will also ask you about your family's medical history (does baby's mom or dad have asthma

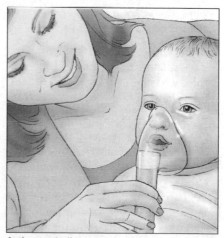

Asthma nebulizer

Asthma . . . or RAD?

Your baby has a cold and then starts to wheeze. And the wheezing happens each time your little one gets sick. You're bracing yourself for a diagnosis of asthma, but the doctor tells you it's actually reactive airway disease (RAD) instead. What's the difference? Actually, not much. Both conditions manifest themselves (and are often treated) in the same way: Following a cold (and often continuing for many weeks after the runny nose goes away), residual viral inflammation and excess mucus in your baby's tiny airways result in coughing and wheezing. But because of the uncertainty of asthma diagnosis in a small child, doctors often call the episodes RAD, and officially call the condition asthma only if the wheezing doesn't go away, if it keeps recurring, if coughing is frequent, or if there's a family history of asthma or allergies. In fact, while 50 percent of babies may have episodes of RAD before age 3, only one-third of those children will go on to develop true asthma by age 6.

or other allergic conditions?) to try to determine if your baby is genetically predisposed to developing asthma.

Management. Depending on the nature of your child's asthma, the doctor might prescribe one or both of these types of medications:

- A quick-relief (short-acting) "rescue" medication called a bronchodilator that quickly opens up your child's airways when they are swelling during an asthma attack

- A preventive (long-acting) medication, like an anti-inflammatory corticosteroid, which your baby would need to take daily to keep the airways from getting inflamed in the first place

Unlike other medications that come in a liquid form that's swallowed, most asthma medications need to be inhaled so they get delivered directly into your baby's airways. The doctor will prescribe a metered-dose inhaler with an attachable plastic tube (or holding chamber) spacer device, which makes the inhaler easier to use and more effective (the medicine gets farther down the airway). You place the mask that is attached to the spacer device over your baby's mouth and nose, activate the inhaler by pressing down on the canister so the correct dose goes into the spacer device, and then your child breathes normally for a few breaths and the medication makes its way into the airways.

Another option is a nebulizer machine, which creates a mist from the liquid medicine and delivers it to your baby via a mask (see illustration page 567). The nebulizer is powered by a small air pump that you plug in.

Whether or not your baby is prescribed medication, it's also crucial that you do your best to prevent your little one from catching colds, flu, and other infections that can step up symptoms (the flu shot is a must for little ones over 6 months with asthma). Probiotics may show promise, also, in helping to manage asthma while boosting the immune system in general.

Prognosis. While many children with asthma exhibit prolonged remission as they approach the teen years, airway hypersensitivity is lifelong. Symptoms often return in adulthood, though sometimes only mildly and intermittently. But even when asthma continues into adulthood, most asthmatics can keep the condition under control with the right medicines, medical care, and self-care.

CELIAC DISEASE

What is it? Also called celiac sprue or gluten-sensitive enteropathy, celiac disease is an autoimmune digestive disorder in which there is a sensitivity to gluten (found in wheat, rye, and barley) When the gluten comes in contact with the small bowel during digestion, it damages the small intestines and interferes with the absorption of nutrients from food. Celiac disease can begin anytime after foods containing gluten are introduced into a baby's diet, or anytime in childhood or adulthood.

There is a wide range of symptoms (and sometimes there aren't symptoms), but most infants and toddlers with celiac disease have stomach pain, diarrhea-like stools (or less commonly, constipation) for more than a few weeks, a distended abdomen, and they fail to thrive. Occasionally, the only symptom is failure to thrive.

Some experts estimate that as many as 1 in 200 people have celiac disease, but many cases go undiagnosed. Since celiac disease is inherited, the odds are increased if either parent or any other siblings have the condition.

If you suspect your baby may be showing signs of celiac disease, ask the doctor about testing. A blood test can determine if your baby has increased levels of certain antibodies related to celiac disease. If the blood test is positive for the antibodies (or inconclusive), the doctor will likely want to take a biopsy of the small intestines via an endoscope through the mouth and stomach to check for damage to the villi, tiny fingerlike projections that line the wall of the intestines.

Management. Once the diagnosis is confirmed, you'll have to keep your baby on a strict gluten-free diet. Foods with gluten include most grains, pasta, and cereal, and many processed foods. But baked goods and pasta made with rice, corn, soy, potato, or other gluten-free flours can easily replace the traditional grains. And happily, most supermarkets carry gluten-free products (check the label, and look for ones that are gluten-free but also whole grain). Plus, there are plenty of "regular" foods that easily fit into a gluten-free diet—like fruits and veggies, dairy, eggs, fish, meat, and poultry. There is some preliminary research that suggests probiotics could be beneficial in managing celiac disease.

You can get more information from the Children's Digestive Health and Nutrition Foundation (cdhnf.org), the Celiac Sprue Association (csaceliacs .org), and the Celiac Disease Foundation (celiac.org).

Prognosis. The good news is that a gluten-free diet will keep your child symptom-free for life.

GASTROESOPHAGEAL REFLUX DISEASE (GERD)

What is it? First, here is what GERD isn't: GER. GER (gastroesophageal reflux) is just a fancy term for spitting up, something the majority of babies do

Projectile Vomiting

Newborns spit up—and many spit up a lot. Usually, that's new-baby digestion as usual (GER), less often it's GERD, and either way, most of the time, it's something a little one will outgrow. But if your baby throws up frequently and so forcefully that the vomit projects clear across the room, there's likely another cause—and that could be pyloric stenosis, a condition in which thickening or overgrowth of the muscle at the exit of the stomach causes a blockage, leading to increasingly severe and more forceful projectile vomiting (spewing a foot or more). Pyloric stenosis is more common in boys (it affects 1 in 200 boys and 1 in 1,000 girls), with symptoms usually appearing somewhere around 2 or 3 weeks of age.

Call the doctor if your baby vomits forcefully. If a diagnosis of pyloric stenosis is made (the doctor may be able to feel a lump or notice muscle spasms that indicate this, or an ultrasound will help diagnose it), surgery will probably be scheduled to correct the condition. Happily, the procedure is very safe and almost always completely effective, which means your little one's digestive system will be up and running normally—usually within a week's time.

during the first year. Most babies have some form of GER, and as long as it isn't associated with poor weight gain, pain, or other symptoms of GERD (see below), it's nothing to be concerned about.

GERD, on the other hand, is not normal, and it isn't nearly as common, though it's seen more often in premature infants. It is similar to heartburn (acid reflux) in adults. Normally during swallowing, the esophagus propels food or liquid down to the stomach by a series of squeezes. Once food has entered the stomach, it is mixed with acid to start digestion. When this mixing occurs, the circular band of muscles at the lower end of the esophagus becomes tight, keeping the food from backing up. In premature and some term infants, the junction between the stomach and esophagus is underdeveloped and sometimes relaxes when it should be tightening. This relaxation of the muscles allows the liquid and food to come back up. When the acid in the stomach backs up into the esophagus or even up to the back of the throat, it causes symptoms of GERD, which may include some or all of the following:

- Frequent spitting up or vomiting (sometimes forceful vomiting) and irritation of the esophagus

- Excessive drooling

- A gurgling, congested, or wheezing sound during feedings

- Sudden or inconsolable crying (usually due to severe pain) or more than usual fussiness

- Arching of the back during feeding (again, because of the pain)

- Erratic feeding patterns (baby refuses food, for instance, or eats or drinks constantly)

- Slow weight gain

GERD usually begins between 2 and 4 weeks of age and in some cases can last until age 1 or 2. Symptoms peak around 4 months and begin to subside around 7 months when the baby begins to sit upright and take more solid foods. GERD is usually much

The Special-Needs Baby

After 9 months of hoping for a perfectly healthy baby, it can be heartbreaking to discover that your baby has been born with a birth defect or special needs. And if the condition wasn't detected prenatally, shock can compound feelings of pain and disappointment. But thanks to medical advances, tremendous strides have been made toward improving the prognosis for many special-needs babies. In many cases, a birth disorder—even one that seems frightening at first—is relatively easily corrected with surgery, medication, physical therapy, or other treatment. In other cases, the condition—and the outlook for the baby—can be greatly improved. And while it may be hard to imagine at first, you'll find that raising your special-needs baby adds another dimension to your lives—initially challenging, certainly, but ultimately enriching. Though caring for your special-needs baby can be double the effort, it can also bring double the rewards. And as time passes, you'll likely discover that your child, in addition to teaching you something about challenges, teaches you a lot about love. For information, coping tips, and helpful resources about your baby's specific condition, see WhatToExpect.com.

less severe in breastfed babies because breast milk is more easily and more quickly digested than formula.

Management. Treatment is aimed not at curing the condition but at helping baby feel better until it's outgrown:

- Offer smaller amounts of breast milk, formula, or solid food more frequently, instead of feeding large amounts less often.

- If your baby is on formula, ask the doctor if a switch in formula might help.

- Give your little one probiotics. There are drops available, or mix powder into a bottle of breast milk, or if you're formula feeding, choose one with probiotics and/or mix probiotics in.

- Burp your baby frequently.

- If you can, prop your baby upright during feeding and for 1 to 2 hours after feedings. If your baby falls asleep after a feeding, be sure to prop up the crib mattress (put a pillow or two *under* the head of the mattress) so he or she can lie at an incline. Do not use any specially designed sleep positioners or wedges (even those designed for babies with GERD), since they are considered unsafe and a SIDS hazard.

- Avoid bouncing baby immediately after feedings.

- Try offering a pacifier after feedings since sucking often eases reflux.

Ask the doctor about medications that reduce stomach acid, that neutralize stomach acids, or that make digestion more efficient (such as Prevacid or Zantac). For cases that aren't helped with standard management, these meds are safe and are often helpful. Just keep in mind that because they may occasionally cause some side effects, they should be used only in diagnosed cases of GERD, not for ordinary spitting up (GER).

Prognosis. The good news is that almost all babies with GERD will outgrow it. And once they do, it usually doesn't recur. Occasionally, reflux can continue into adulthood.

HEARING LOSS OR IMPAIRMENT

What is it? There are many degrees of hearing impairment or hearing loss, and not all children with hearing loss are considered deaf. The child who is deaf has a profound hearing loss and cannot understand speech through hearing alone, even with the use of a hearing aid.

There are two main types of congenital hearing loss in young children:

- Conductive hearing loss. With this type of hearing loss, there may be an abnormality in the structure of the ear canal or there may be fluid in the middle ear (the space just beyond the eardrum). As a consequence, sound is not conducted efficiently through the ear canal and/or middle ear, making sound extremely low or inaudible.

- Sensorineural hearing loss. With this type of hearing loss, there is damage to the inner ear or to the nerve pathways from the inner ear to the brain. Usually present at birth, this type of hearing impairment is most often an inherited condition. It can also be caused by maternal infection before birth, or by certain medications taken by a mom-to-be.

Two to four out of 1,000 babies are born with some hearing loss each year. Some will have hearing loss in only one ear, some in both. Most newborns are given hearing tests in the hospital soon after birth. If your baby did not receive a hearing test as a newborn or if you suspect hearing loss now (even a child who "passed" the hearing test as an infant can develop hearing loss), speak to the pediatrician about getting a hearing test (see box, page 124). Since hearing deficits are more common among graduates of the neonatal intensive care unit (NICU), babies who were preemies should be screened more carefully.

Management. It is important to diagnose a hearing loss early and to determine the level of impairment, which can range from mild to profound. Treatment of hearing loss, beginning as soon as a diagnosis is made, is very important to maximize your little one's future hearing and language development.

Treatment depends on the cause and may include:

- Hearing aids. If a hearing loss is due to a malformation of the middle or inner ear, hearing aids (which amplify sounds) may be able to restore hearing to normal (or almost normal) levels. Hearing aids can also help with some types of sensorineural hearing loss. There are many types of devices, and the type used will depend on your little one's age and the type of hearing loss.

- Surgery. Cochlear implants (electronic devices that are surgically placed in the bone behind the ear), possibly in conjunction with amplifying hearing aids, can make a huge difference by restoring hearing and vastly improving the ability of totally deaf children to learn spoken language. The earlier a child receives the cochlear implants (preferably between age 1 and age 3), the better.

- Education. An education program should be begun as soon as hearing loss is diagnosed, and may include teaching your little one to use devices that assist in learning to hear and/or to speak; cued speech, in which a system of manual cues is used to supplement speech (or lip) reading; and a total communication program, which uses a combination of speech reading, signing, and finger spelling and may also emphasize listening skills and speech production. Speech and language therapy (as well as counseling and training for parents) will also be part of the education process. The pediatrician and hearing specialist can work together with you to help you find the program that best meets your child's needs. The doctor can also point you to state-administered Early Intervention programs that provide services free of charge.

Prognosis. With proper proactive treatment, children with hearing impairments are likely to have completely fulfilling lives. Some may eventually hear and speak, while others (such as those with more profound impairment) will learn to communicate through signing. Whether a child with a hearing impairment is mainstreamed (that is, attends regular classes with hearing

---

Hearing Loss Due to Fluid in Ears

Temporary hearing loss that's not congenital may sometimes occur due to persistent fluid in the ears. First-line treatment for this type of hearing loss is careful observation over time, and occasionally a trial of antibiotics. If the fluid persists into the toddler years, the doctor may recommend inserting tubes. Happily, the tubes will clear up any temporary hearing loss and resulting language delays. For more on tubes, see *What to Expect the Second Year.*

---

children) depends on the individual child, the programs that local schools offer, and the availability of special classes in speech and language development in the mainstream schools in your area.

CHAPTER 20

Treating Injuries

B oo-boos happen. Even when you're conscientious, careful, and vigilant—even when you've taken all the precautions and then some—you can't prevent every injury. But, you can prepare for them—and that preparation can make all the difference. Hopefully, most of the boo-boos that happen in your baby's life will be small (the kiss-and-make-better variety). Still, you'll need to know how to respond in the event of a bigger mishap, and how to care for injuries (such as cuts, bruises, burns, and breaks) that need more treatment than a cuddle—and that's what this chapter is for. It'll also give you guidelines on lifesaving CPR and what to do if your child is choking.

Preparing for Emergencies

B ecause quick action after an injury is often critical, don't wait until your baby dunks a hand in your hot coffee or takes a swig of laundry detergent to look up what to do in an emergency. Before an accident happens is the best time to get as familiar as possible with the procedures for dealing with and treating common injuries. Review the protocol for handling less common injuries (snakebites, for instance) when you're more likely to encounter them (say, you're about to go on a camping trip).

But don't stop there. It's one thing to read about injury treatment—it's another thing to apply your skills when an emergency strikes. So reinforce what you learn in this chapter by taking a course in baby safety, cardiopulmonary resuscitation (CPR), and basic first aid. Courses are available at many community centers and hospitals, and through fire departments, ambulance corps, the American Red Cross, and the American Heart Association—check online or with your child's doctor for options. Some certified instructors will even bring the course to you (that way, anyone who might be caring for your baby, including grandparents, aunts, uncles, and babysitters, can attend with you in your home). Keep your skills current and ready to use with periodic refresher courses (or a video course approved by th AAP or Red Cross)—and be sure that anyone else who cares for your baby is also fully trained and prepared to deal with emergencies, from minor to major.

To further prepare yourself for emergencies:

- Discuss with your baby's doctor what the best course of action would be in case of a non-life-threatening injury as well as in a serious emergency: when to call the doctor's office, when to go to the emergency room (and when to do both), when to call 911, and when to follow some other protocol. For minor injuries, the ER—with its long waits, abundance of germs, and priority given to life-threatening conditions—may not be the best place to go.

- Keep your first-aid supplies in a child-proof, easily manageable all-inclusive kit or box that can be moved where it's needed. Always keep a charged phone easily accessible so that it can be used at the site of an injury, wherever it happens.

- Always keep handy (and accessible to anyone who cares for your child):

  - Emergency phone numbers. The pediatrician, the Poison Control Center (800-222-1222), the hospital emergency room of your choice, your pharmacy, the Emergency Medical Service (EMS, which can be accessed by dialing 911 in most areas), and your places of work, as well as the number of a close relative, friend, or neighbor who can be called on in an emergency. A regular care provider should have these numbers programmed into her own phone for instant access.

  - Personal information (updated regularly). Your child's age, approximate weight, immunization record, medications, allergies, and/or chronic illnesses, if any. In an emergency, these should be supplied to the EMS and/or taken to the hospital or ER.

  - Location information. Home address (include cross streets and landmarks, if necessary), apartment number, telephone number—for use by babysitters or other caregivers calling for emergency help.

  - A pad and pen. For taking instructions from the doctor or 911 dispatcher, or Poison Control.

- Be sure there's a clearly distinguishable number on your house and a light that makes the number visible after dark.

- Know the quickest route to the ER or other emergency medical facility your child's doctor recommends.

- If you live in a city, keep some cash reserved in a safe place and the car seat handy in case you need to call a taxi to get to the ER or doctor's office in an emergency. (If you're very anxious, or you're busy caring for your injured child, it's best if you don't drive.) Let any babysitter who stays with your little one know where that

---

ED or ER

Have you been told to head to the ED . . . but you're not sure what an ED is? ED is short for Emergency Department, and it's preferred by medical professionals over the term ER, or Emergency Room. Same place (where emergencies are handled in the hospital), different name.

emergency money is, too. An easier option in cities where it's available: an app for a taxi or car service (like Uber) that pinpoints your location instantly, picks you up usually within minutes, and charges your account for the ride.

- If you tend to overreact in stressful or emergency situations, try to learn how to respond calmly to your little one's illnesses and injuries. Practice with everyday bumps and bruises, so that if a serious injury ever occurs, you'll be better equipped to keep your cool. Taking a few deep breaths will help you relax and focus no matter what you're facing. Try to remember that your expression, tone of voice, and general demeanor will affect how your baby responds to an injury. If you panic, your baby is more likely to panic—and less likely to be able to cooperate. And an uncooperative baby is more difficult to treat.

- To help you both stay calm when there's been an injury, big or small, divert your baby's attention from the injury by engaging at least three senses. Stand where your baby can see you, speak calmly so he or she can hear you, and touch a part of the body that doesn't seem to be injured.

First Aid in the First Year

Following are the most common injuries, what you should know about them, how to treat (and not treat) them, and when to seek medical care for them. Types of injuries are listed alphabetically, with individual injuries numbered for easy cross-reference.

ABDOMINAL INJURIES

1. Internal bleeding. A severe blow to your baby's abdomen could result in internal injury. The signs of such injury would include bruising or other discoloration of the abdomen, vomited or coughed-up blood that is dark or bright red and has the consistency of coffee grounds (this could also be a sign that a caustic substance has been swallowed), blood (it may be dark or bright red) in the stool or urine, and shock (cold, clammy, pale skin; weak, rapid pulse; chills; confusion; and possibly nausea, vomiting, and/or shallow breathing). Seek emergency medical assistance (call 911). If baby appears to be in shock (#48), treat immediately. Do not give food or drink.

2. Cuts or lacerations of the abdomen. Treat as for other cuts (#51, #52). With a major laceration, intestines may protrude. Do not try to put them back into the abdomen. Instead, cover them with a clean, moistened washcloth or diaper and get emergency medical assistance immediately (call 911).

BITES

3. Animal bites. Try to avoid moving the affected part. Call the doctor immediately. Then wash the wound gently with soap and water. Do not apply antiseptic or anything else. Control bleeding (#51, #52, #53) as needed with pressure, and apply a bandage.

Bats, skunks, coyotes, foxes, and raccoons that bite may be rabid, especially if they attacked unprovoked. The same is true for dogs and cats. Although most household pets are vaccinated against rabies, you can't be sure unless you see proof of vaccination. You'll need to consult with the pediatrician to determine if your baby needs post-exposure rabies protection. Keep in mind that while rabies in humans is extremely rare, it is almost always fatal if not treated.

If a dog or cat bite breaks the skin, call the doctor for advice, even if the animal is known not to have rabies. Antibiotics may be prescribed to prevent infection. Call the doctor immediately if redness, swelling, and tenderness develop at the site of the bite—these are signs of infection, which must be treated with antibiotics. Infection is more common with a cat bite than a dog bite.

4. Human bites. If your baby is bitten by another child, don't worry unless the skin is broken. If it is, wash the bite area thoroughly with mild soap and cool water. Don't rub the wound or apply any spray or ointment (antibiotic or otherwise). Simply cover the bite with a sterile dressing and call the doctor. Use pressure to stem the bleeding (#52), if necessary. Antibiotics will likely be prescribed to prevent infection.

5. Insect stings or bites. Treat insect stings or bites as follows:

- Apply calamine lotion or another anti-itching medication to itchy bites, such as those caused by mosquitoes.

- Remove ticks promptly, using blunt tweezers or your fingertips protected by a tissue, paper towel, or rubber glove. Grasp the bug as close to the child's skin as possible and pull upward, steadily and evenly. Don't twist, jerk, squeeze, crush, or puncture the tick. If you're not sure whether it's a deer tick, you can save

it and compare it with a picture of a deer tick (or take a photo of it and email or show the doctor later). But there's no need to save it for any other reason—the doctor won't need it for testing.

- If your baby is stung by a honeybee, remove the stinger by scraping it horizontally, using the edge of a blunt butter knife, your fingernail, or a credit card, or gently remove it with tweezers or your fingers. Try not to pinch the stinger, because doing so could inject more venom into the wound. Then treat as below.

- Wash the site of a minor bee, wasp, ant, spider, or tick bite with soap and water. Then apply cold compresses or ice wrapped in a towel if there appears to be swelling or pain.

- If there seems to be extreme pain after a spider bite, apply cold compresses and call Poison Control for emergency advice. If possible, describe the spider's appearance to help determine if it is poisonous. If you know the spider is poisonous—a black widow or brown recluse spider, a tarantula, or a scorpion, for example—get emergency treatment (call 911) immediately, even before symptoms appear.

- Watch for signs of hypersensitivity, such as severe pain or swelling or any degree of shortness of breath after a bee, wasp, or hornet sting. About 90 percent of children react to an insect sting with brief (less than 24 hours) redness, swelling, and pain in a 2-inch area at the site of the sting. But the other 10 percent have a much more severe local reaction, with extensive swelling and tenderness covering an area 4 inches or more in diameter that doesn't peak until 3 to 7 days after the sting. Those who experience such symptoms with a first sting usually develop hypersensitivities (or allergies) to the venom, in which case a subsequent sting could be fatal without immediate emergency treatment. Life-threatening anaphylactic reactions (which are uncommon) usually begin within 5 to 10 minutes of the sting. They may include swelling of the face and/or tongue; signs of swelling of the throat, such as tickling, gagging, difficulty swallowing, or voice change; bronchospasm (chest tightening, coughing, wheezing, or difficulty breathing); a drop in blood pressure causing dizziness or fainting; and/or cardiovascular collapse. Fatal outcomes in children are extremely rare, but do seek medical help immediately if you notice any systemic reaction (affecting body parts and/or systems other than the site of the sting). Should your child have a life-threatening systemic reaction, call 911 immediately.

After any systemic reaction, a skin test, and possibly other testing, will be performed to determine sensitivity to insect venom. If it is determined that your child is at risk of a life-threatening episode from an insect sting, it'll probably be recommended that an epinephrine auto injector (EpiPen or other brand) be taken along on all outings during bee season.

6. Snakebites. Babies are rarely bitten by poisonous snakes, but such a bite is very dangerous. The four major types in the United States are rattlesnakes, copperheads, coral snakes, and cottonmouths or water moccasins. All have fangs, which usually leave identifying marks when they bite. Because of a baby's size, even a tiny amount of venom can be fatal. After a poisonous snakebite, it is important to keep the baby and the affected part as still as possible. If the bite is on a limb, immobilize the limb with a splint and keep it below the level of the heart. Use a cool compress if available to relieve pain, but do not apply ice or give any medication without medical advice. Get prompt emergency medical help, and be ready to identify the variety of snake, if possible. If you won't be able to get medical help within an hour, apply a loose constricting band (a belt, tie, or scrunchie loose enough for you to slip a finger under) 2 inches above the bite to slow circulation. (Do not tie such a tourniquet around a finger or toe, or around the neck, head, or trunk.) Check the pulse beneath the tourniquet frequently to be sure circulation is not cut off, and loosen it if the limb begins to swell. Make a note of the time the tourniquet was tied. Sucking out the venom by mouth (and spitting it out) may be helpful if done immediately. But do not make an incision of any kind, unless you are 4 to 5 hours from help and severe symptoms occur. If baby is not breathing and/or the heart has stopped, begin rescue techniques (page 598). Treat for shock (#48), if necessary.

Treat nonpoisonous snakebites as puncture wounds (#54), and notify the doctor.

7. Marine animal stings. The stings of marine animals are usually not serious, but occasionally a child can have a severe reaction. Medical treatment should be sought immediately after any marine sting. First-aid treatment varies with the type of marine animal involved, but in general, any clinging fragments of the stinger should be carefully brushed away with a diaper, a credit card, or a piece of clothing (to protect your own fingers). Heavy bleeding (#52), shock (#48), or cessation of breathing (see page 598), should be treated immediately, and if necessary, call 911. Don't worry about light bleeding, since it may help purge toxins. If possible, the site of the sting of a stingray, lionfish, catfish, stonefish, or sea urchin should be soaked in warm water (to break down the toxins) for 30 minutes, or until medical help arrives. The toxins from the sting of a jellyfish or Portuguese man-of-war can be counteracted by applying regular white vinegar or rubbing alcohol on the sting (pack a couple of alcohol pads in your beach bag, just in case). Unseasoned meat tenderizer, baking soda, ammonia, and lemon or lime juice can also help prevent pain.

BLEEDING

see #51, #52, #53

BLEEDING, INTERNAL

see #1

BROKEN BONES OR FRACTURES

8. Possible broken arms, legs, or fingers. It's hard to tell when a bone is broken in a baby. Most "broken" bones in babies are usually just bent or buckled, not snapped, making a break harder to detect visually. Signs of a break can include inability to move or put weight on the part, severe pain (persistent crying could be a clue, or an extreme reaction of pain when the area is tapped), numbness or tingling (neither of which a baby would be able to communicate), swelling, discoloration, and/or deformity (though this could also indicate a dislocation, #17). If a fracture is suspected, don't try to straighten it out. Try to immobilize the injured part by splinting it in the position it's in with a ruler, a magazine, a book, a roll of newspaper, or another firm object, padded with a soft cloth to protect the skin. Or use a small, firm pillow as a splint. Fasten the splint securely with bandages, strips of cloth, scarves, or neckties, but not so tightly that circulation is restricted. If no potential splint is handy, try to immobilize the injured limb against your arm. Check regularly to be sure the splint or its wrapping isn't cutting off circulation. Apply an ice pack to reduce swelling. Take your child to the doctor or ER even if you only suspect a break.

9. Compound fractures. If bone protrudes through the skin, don't touch it. Cover the injury, if possible, with gauze or with a clean diaper, control bleeding with pressure (#52), and get emergency medical assistance (call 911).

10. Possible neck or back injury. If a neck or back injury is suspected, don't move baby at all. Call 911 for emergency medical assistance. (If you must move baby away from a life-threatening situation, such as a fire or road traffic, splint the back, neck, and head with a board, a chair cushion, or your arm. Move him or her without bending or twisting the head, neck, or back.) Cover and keep baby comfortable while waiting for help, and if possible, put some heavy objects, such as books, around the child's head to help immobilize it. Don't give food or drink. Treat severe bleeding (#53), shock (#48), or absence of breathing and/or pulse (see page 598) immediately.

BRUISES, SKIN

see #49

BURNS

IMPORTANT: If a child's clothing is on fire, use a coat, blanket, rug, bedspread, or even your own body to smother the flames.

11. Limited burns from heat (first degree). Immerse burned fingers, hands, feet, toes, arms, or legs in cool—not cold—water (50°F to 60°F). If baby is cooperative, hold the burned part under running cool water. Apply cool compresses to burns on the face or trunk. Continue until baby doesn't seem to be in pain anymore, usually 15 to 30 minutes. Don't apply ice, butter, or burn ointments (all of which could compound skin damage), and don't break any blisters that form. After soaking the burned area, gently pat it dry with a soft towel and cover it with a gauze pad, a cloth bandage, or another nonadhesive bandage. If redness and pain persist for more than a few hours, call the doctor.

Call the doctor immediately for burns that look raw, that blister (second-degree burns), or are white or charred looking (third-degree burns), any burns on the face, hands, feet, or genitals, or burns that are the size of your child's hand or larger.

12. Extensive burns from heat. Call 911 for emergency medical assistance. Keep baby lying flat. Remove any clothing from the burn area that does not adhere to the wound (cut it away as necessary but do not pull). Apply cool, wet compresses (you can use a washcloth) to the injured area (but not to more than 25 percent of the body at one time). Keep baby comfortably warm, with burned extremities higher than the heart. Do not apply pressure, ointments, butter or other fats, powder, or boric-acid soaks to burned areas. If baby is conscious and doesn't have severe mouth burns, nurse or offer sips of fluid to prevent dehydration.

13. Chemical burns. Caustic substances (such as lye, drain cleaner, and other acids) can cause serious burns. Using a clean, soft cloth, gently brush off dry chemical matter from the skin (wear rubber gloves to protect your hands) and remove any contaminated clothing. Immediately flush the skin with large amounts of water. Call a physician, Poison Control (800-222-1222), or the doctor for further advice. Get immediate medical assistance (call 911) if there is difficult or painful breathing, which could indicate lung injury from inhalation of caustic fumes. (If a chemical has been swallowed, see #44.)

14. Electrical burns. Immediately disconnect the power source, if possible, or separate baby from the source using a dry, nonmetallic object such as a wooden broom, wooden ladder, rope, cushion, chair, or even a large book—but not your bare hands. If baby isn't breathing and/or has no pulse, initiate rescue techniques (page 598) and call 911. Even a minor electrical burn should be evaluated by a physician, so call your baby's doctor as soon as possible.

15. Sunburn. If your baby gets a sunburn, treat it by applying cool compresses for 10 to 15 minutes, 3 or 4 times a day, until the redness subsides—the evaporating water helps to cool the skin. In between these treatments, apply a baby-safe sunburn relief spray or a mild moisturizing cream. Don't use Vaseline or baby oil on a burn, because it seals in heat and seals out air, which is needed for healing. Acetaminophen may reduce pain of sunburn, but if there's swelling and the baby is over 6 months, ibuprofen (which is anti-inflammatory) is a better choice. Antihistamines shouldn't be given unless they are prescribed by the doctor. When sunburn is severe—there is blistering, pain, nausea, or chills—call the doctor immediately.

CHEMICAL BURNS

see #13

CHOKING

see page 594

COLD INJURIES

see Frostbite and Frostnip, #31, Hypothermia, #35

CONVULSIONS

16. Symptoms of a seizure or convulsion include collapse, eyes rolling upward, foaming at the mouth, stiffening of the body followed by uncontrolled jerking movements, and in the most serious cases, breathing difficulty. Brief convulsions are not uncommon with high fevers (see page 547 for how to deal with febrile seizures). For nonfebrile seizures: Clear the immediate area around baby or move baby to the middle of a bed or carpeted area to prevent injury. Loosen clothing around the neck and middle, and lay baby on one side with head lower than hips (elevate the hips with a pillow). Don't put anything in the mouth, including food or drink, breast or bottle. Call the doctor.

If baby isn't breathing or has no pulse, begin rescue techniques (see page 598) immediately. If someone else is with you, have them call 911. If you're alone, wait until breathing has started again to call, or call if breathing hasn't resumed within a few minutes. Also call 911 if the seizure lasts more than 2 to 3 minutes, seems very severe, or is followed by one or more repeat seizures.

Seizures may be caused by the ingestion of prescription medicines or toxic substances, so check the immediate vicinity for any sign that your baby may have gotten into any. If it's clear that he or she has swallowed something hazardous, see #44.

CUTS

see #51, #52

DISLOCATION

17. Elbow dislocations (also known as nursemaid's elbow) are not as common among babies as they are among toddlers, who get them mostly because they are often tugged along by the arm by adults in a hurry (or "flown" through the air by their arms). Inability or unwillingness to move the arms, usually combined with persistent crying because of pain, is typical with a dislocation. A trip to the doctor's office or the ER, where an experienced professional can easily reposition the dislocated part, will provide virtually instant relief. If pain seems severe, apply an ice pack and splint before leaving.

DOG BITES

see #3

DROWNING (SUBMERSION INJURY)

18. Even a child who quickly revives after being taken from the water unconscious should get a medical evaluation. For one who remains unconscious, have someone else call 911 for emergency medical assistance, if possible, while you begin rescue techniques (see page 598). If no one is available to phone for help, call later. Don't stop CPR until the child revives or help arrives, no matter how long that takes. If there is vomiting, turn baby to one side to avoid choking. If you suspect a back or neck injury, immobilize these parts (#10). Keep the baby warm and dry.

EAR INJURIES

19. Foreign object in the ear. Try to dislodge the object with these techniques:

- For a live insect, use a flashlight to try to lure it out.

- For a metal object, hold a strong magnet at the ear canal to draw the object out (but don't insert the magnet into the ear).

- For a plastic or wooden object that can easily be seen and is not deeply embedded in the ear, dab a drop of quick-drying glue on a straightened paper clip and touch it to the object (don't touch the ear). Don't probe into the ear where you can't see. Wait for the glue to dry, then pull the clip out, ideally with the object attached. Don't attempt this if there's no one around to help hold baby still.

If you're not comfortable attempting the above techniques, you don't have the necessary equipment to try them, or you try them and they fail, don't try to dig out the object with your fingers or with an instrument. Instead, take baby to the doctor's office or the ER.

20. Injury to the ear. If a pointed object has been pushed into the ear or if your baby shows signs of ear injury (bleeding from the ear canal, sudden difficulty hearing, a swollen earlobe), call the doctor.

ELECTRIC SHOCK

21. Break contact with the electrical source by turning off the power, if possible, or separate baby from the current by using a dry nonmetallic object such as a wooden broom, wooden ladder, robe, cushion, chair, rubber boot, or even a large book. If baby is in contact with water, do not touch the water yourself. Once baby has been separated from the power source, call 911. If he or she isn't breathing and/or has no pulse, begin rescue techniques immediately (see page 598). For electrical burns, see #14.

EYE INJURY

IMPORTANT: Don't apply pressure to an injured eye, touch the eye with your fingers, or administer medications without a physician's advice. Keep baby from rubbing the eye by holding a small cup or glass over it or, if necessary, by restraining his or her hands.

22. Foreign object in the eye. If you can see the object (an eyelash or grain of sand, for example), wash your hands and use a moist cotton ball to gently attempt to remove it from baby's eye while someone else holds baby still (attempt this only in the corner of the eye, beneath the lower lid, or on the white of the eye—stay away from the pupil). Or try pulling the upper lid down over the lower one for a few seconds. If those techniques don't work, and if baby is very uncomfortable, try to wash out the object by pouring a stream of tepid (body temperature) water into the eye while someone holds baby still. Don't worry about your little one crying—tears may help wash out the object.

If after these attempts you can still see the object in the eye or if baby still

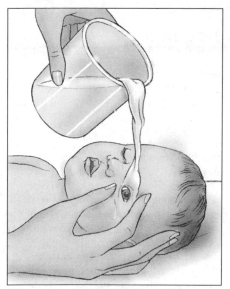

Baby won't enjoy an eye bath, but it's necessary to wash away a corrosive substance.

seems uncomfortable, the object may have become embedded or may have scratched the eye. Don't try to remove an embedded object yourself—proceed to the doctor's office or ER. Cover the eye with a small cup, a gauze pad taped loosely in place, or with a few clean tissues or a clean cloth to alleviate some of the discomfort en route. Do not apply pressure.

23. Corrosive substance in the eye. Flush baby's eye immediately and thoroughly with lukewarm water for 15 minutes, holding the eye open with your fingers (see illustration). If one eye is involved, keep the chemical runoff out of the other eye by turning baby's head so that the unaffected eye is higher than the affected one. Don't use drops or ointments, and keep baby from rubbing the eye or eyes. Call Poison Control (800-222-1222) for further instructions. Depending on the substance, Poison Control may recommend a follow-up with an eye doctor to be safe.

24. Injury to the eye with a pointed or sharp object. Keep baby in a semi-reclining position while you seek help. If the object is still in the eye, do not try to remove it. If it isn't, cover the eye lightly with a small cup, gauze pad, clean washcloth, or tissue, but do not apply pressure. In either case, get emergency medical assistance (call 911) immediately. Though such injuries often look worse than they are, check with the doctor any time the eye is scratched or punctured, even slightly.

25. Injury to the eye with a blunt object. Keep baby lying face up. Cover the injured eye with an ice pack or cold compress for about 15 minutes. Repeat every hour as needed to reduce pain and swelling. Consult the doctor if there is bleeding in the eye, if the eye blackens, if baby seems to be having difficulty seeing or keeps rubbing the eye a lot, if the object hit the eye at high speed, or if there seems to be continued eye pain.

FAINTING/LOSS OF CONSCIOUSNESS

26. Check for breathing and pulse. If they are absent, begin CPR immediately (see page 598). If you detect breathing, keep baby lying flat, head slightly lower than the rest of the body, lightly covered for warmth if necessary. Loosen clothing around the neck. Turn baby's head to one side and clear the mouth of any food or objects. Call 911 immediately.

FINGER AND TOE INJURIES

27. Bruises. Babies, ever curious, are particularly prone to painful bruises from catching fingers in drawers and doors. For such a bruise, soak the finger

Making a Boo-Boo Better

Babies, by nature, don't make very cooperative patients. No matter how much pain or discomfort they're in from an illness or an injury, they're likely to consider any treatment worse. Plus, it won't help to tell them that applying pressure to a cut will make it stop bleeding faster or that the ice pack will keep a bruised finger from swelling—not only won't they understand, but they also don't care. For better results, try distraction.

Entertainment (begun before the treatment, and hopefully, before baby realizes what's about to happen) in the form of favorite music, a toy dog that yaps and wags its tail, a choo-choo train that can travel across the coffee table, or a parent or sibling who can dance, jump up and down, or sing silly songs can help make the difference between a successful treatment session and one that isn't.

How much you have to push the treatment agenda will depend on how bad the injury is. A slight bruise may not be worth upsetting a baby who's rejecting the ice pack. A severe burn, however, will certainly require the cold soaks, even if baby screams and thrashes during the entire treatment. In most cases, try to treat injuries at least briefly—even a few minutes of a cold pack on a bumped head will reduce the bleeding under the skin. But chuck the treatment if it's clearly not worth the struggle and the injury is minor.

---

in cold water (add a couple of ice cubes to keep it cool). As much as an hour of soaking is recommended, with breaks every 10 minutes (long enough for the finger to rewarm) to avoid frostbite. Though few babies will sit still for this long, you may be able to treat your little one's injury for a few minutes by using distraction or holding him or her tightly.

A stubbed toe will also benefit from soaking, but again, it often isn't easy to do with a baby. Bruised fingers and toes will swell less if they are kept elevated.

If the injured finger or toe becomes very swollen very quickly, is misshapen, or can't be voluntarily straightened by the baby, call the doctor. It may be broken (#8). Call the doctor immediately if the bruise is from a wringer-type injury or from catching a hand or foot in the spokes of a moving wheel. In these kinds of "crush" injuries, there may be more damage than is visible or apparent.

28. Bleeding under the nail. When a finger or toe is badly bruised, a blood clot may form under the nail, causing painful pressure. If blood oozes out from under the nail, press on it to encourage the flow, which will help to relieve the pressure. Soak the injury in cold water if baby will cooperate. If the pain continues, the doctor may have to make a hole in the nail to relieve the pressure.

29. A torn nail. For a small tear, secure with a piece of adhesive tape or a bandaid until the nail grows to a point where it can be trimmed. For a tear that is almost complete, carefully trim away along the tear line with scissors or baby nail clippers, and keep covered with a bandaid until the nail is long enough to protect the finger or toe tip.

30. Detached nail. If your baby injures a fingernail to the point that it detaches or almost detaches, don't try to pull it off—just let it fall off by itself in time. Soaking the finger or toe is not recommended, since moisture can increase the risk of fungal infections. Do make sure, however, to keep the area clean. An antibiotic ointment can be applied but isn't always necessary (ask the pediatrician). Keep the nail bed covered with a fresh bandaid until the nail starts growing back in (after that, you can leave it uncovered). It usually takes 4 to 6 months for a nail to grow all the way back. If at any point you notice redness, heat, and swelling, it could mean the area is infected, and you should call the doctor.

FOREIGN OBJECTS

in the ear, see #19; in the eye, see #22; in the mouth or throat, see #40; in the nose, see #42

FRACTURES

see #8, #9, #10

FROSTBITE AND FROSTNIP

31. Babies are extremely susceptible to frostbite, particularly on fingers and toes, ears, nose, and cheeks. In frostbite, the affected part becomes very cold and turns white or yellowish gray. In severe frostbite, the skin is cold, waxy, pale, and hard. If you notice any signs of frostbite in your baby, immediately try to warm the frosty parts against your body—open your coat and shirt and tuck baby inside next to your skin. You can also breathe warm air on baby's skin. As soon as possible,

get to a doctor or an ER. If that isn't feasible immediately, get baby indoors and begin a gradual rewarming process. Don't massage the damaged parts or put them right next to a radiator, stove, open fire, or heat lamp—the damaged skin may burn. Don't try to "quick-thaw" in hot water, either, since this can further damage the skin. Instead, soak affected fingers and toes directly in tepid water (about 102°F—just a little warmer than normal body temperature and just slightly warm to the touch). For parts that can't be soaked, such as nose, ears, and cheeks, very gently apply warm compresses (wet washcloths or towels soaked in water slightly warm to the touch). Continue the soaks until color returns to the skin, usually in 30 to 60 minutes (add warm water to the soaks as needed to maintain tepid temperature). Nurse baby or give warm (not hot) fluids by bottle or cup. As frostbitten skin rewarms, it becomes red and slightly swollen, and it may blister. Gently pat the skin dry. If baby's injury hasn't yet been seen by a doctor, it is important to get medical attention now.

Once the injured parts have been warmed, and you have to go out again to take baby to the doctor (or anywhere else), be especially careful to keep the affected areas warm (wrapped in a blanket) en route, since refreezing of thawed tissues can cause additional damage.

Much more common than frostbite—and fortunately, much less serious—is frostnip. In frostnip, the affected body part is cold and pale, but rewarming (as for frostbite) takes less time and causes less pain and swelling. As with frostbite, avoid dry heat and avoid refreezing. Though an office or ER visit isn't necessary, a call to the doctor makes sense.

After prolonged exposure to cold, a baby's body temperature may drop below normal levels. This is a medical emergency known as hypothermia (see #35). Don't waste any time getting a baby who seems unusually cold to the touch to the nearest ER. Keep baby warm next to your body en route.

HEAD INJURIES

IMPORTANT: Head injuries are usually more serious if a child falls onto a hard surface from a height equal to or greater than his or her own height, or is hit with a heavy object. Blows to the side of the head may do more damage than those to the front or back of the head.

32. Cuts and bruises to the scalp. Because of the profusion of blood vessels in the scalp, heavy bleeding is common with cuts to the head, and bruises there tend to swell to egg size very quickly. Treat as you would any cut (#51, #52) or bruise (#49). Check with the doctor for all but very minor scalp wounds.

33. Possibly serious head trauma. Most babies experience several minor bumps on the head during the first year. Usually these require no more than a few make-it-better cuddles and kisses. However, after a bad blow to the head, it's wise to keep a close eye on your baby for the first 6 hours. Symptoms may occur immediately or not show up for several days—so continue to watch a child who has had a serious head injury even if he or she initially seems fine. Call the doctor or 911 immediately if your baby shows any of these signs after a head injury:

- Loss of consciousness (though a brief period of drowsiness—no more than 2 to 3 hours—is common and nothing to worry about)

- Difficulty being woken. Check every

hour or two during daytime naps, and two or three times during the night for the first day after the injury, to be sure baby is responsive. If you can't wake a sleeping baby, immediately check for breathing (see page 600).

- Vomiting

- Black-and-blue areas appearing around the eyes or behind the ears

- A depression or indentation in the skull

- A large swelling at the site of the injury, through which you would be unable to detect a depression or indentation

- Oozing of blood or watery fluid (not mucus) from the ears or nose

- Inability to move an arm or leg

- Unusual lack of balance that persists beyond 1 hour after the injury (a sign of dizziness)

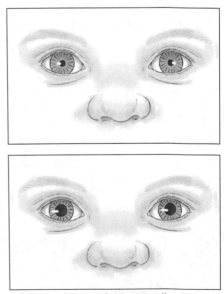

Pupils should constrict (get smaller, top) in response to a light, and dilate (expand, bottom) when the light is removed.

- Unequal pupil size, or pupils that don't respond to the light of a penlight by shrinking or to the removal of the light by growing larger (see illustration)

- Unusual paleness that persists for more than a few minutes immediately after the injury

- Convulsions (see #16)

- Your baby just isn't acting like him- or herself—seems dazed, confused, doesn't recognize you, is unusually clumsy or unable to coordinate movements as usual, or any other behavior that is unusual, unexpected, or worrisome.

While waiting for help, keep your baby lying quietly with his or her head turned to one side. Do not move your baby if you suspect a neck injury, unless not doing so would be dangerous. Treat for shock (#48), if necessary. Begin rescue techniques (see page 598) if baby stops breathing or doesn't have a pulse. Don't offer any food or drink until you talk to the doctor.

HEAT INJURIES

34. Heat exhaustion, or mild hyperthermia (high body temperature), is the most common form of heat injury. Signs may include profuse sweating, thirst, headache, muscle cramps, dizziness or light-headedness, and/or nausea (a baby may be cranky, refuse food, or vomit). Body temperature may rise to 101°F to 105°F. Treat heat exhaustion by bringing your baby into a cool environment (air-conditioned, if possible) and giving cold fluids to drink. Cool compresses applied to the body and a fan may also help. If baby doesn't quickly return to normal, vomits after drinking, or has a high fever, call the doctor.

Heatstroke, or severe hyperthermia, is less common and more serious. It typically comes on suddenly after overheating, as when a baby has been enclosed in a car in warm weather. Signs to watch for include hot and dry (or occasionally, moist) skin, very high fever (sometimes over 106°F), diarrhea, agitation or lethargy, confusion, convulsions, and loss of consciousness. If you suspect heatstroke, wrap baby in a large towel that has been soaked in cold tap water and summon immediate emergency medical help (call 911), or rush baby to the nearest ER. If the towel becomes warm, repeat with a freshly chilled one.

HYPERTHERMIA

see #34

HYPOTHERMIA

35. After prolonged exposure to cold, when heat loss exceeds heat production, a child's body temperature may drop below normal levels. A child with hypothermia may seem unusually cold, shiver, be lethargic, or move stiffly. In severe hypothermia, shivering stops and there is a loss of muscle control and a decline in consciousness. Hypothermia is a medical emergency. Don't waste any time in getting a child who appears to have hypothermia to the nearest ER (call 911 if you don't have quick transportation). Remove any wet clothing, wrap your baby in blankets, and turn on the car heater en route to the hospital. If you are waiting for emergency medical help at home, tuck your baby under an electric blanket (if you have one), in a very warm bath (not hot enough to burn, of course), or against your body skin-to-skin and covered with blankets.

INSECT STINGS OR BITES

see #5

LIP, SPLIT OR CUT

see #36, #37

MOUTH INJURIES

36. Split lip. Few babies escape the first year without at least one cut on the lip. Fortunately, these cuts usually look a lot worse than they are and heal a lot more quickly than you'd think. To ease pain and control bleeding, apply an ice pack, or let an older baby suck on a feeder bag filled with ice. If the cut gapes open, or if bleeding doesn't stop in 10 or 15 minutes, call the doctor. Also call if you suspect a lip injury may have been caused by chewing on a plugged-in electrical cord.

37. Cuts inside the lip or mouth. Such injuries are also common in young children. To relieve pain and control bleeding inside the lip or cheek, give an older baby a feeder bag filled with ice to suck on. To stop bleeding of the tongue, if it doesn't stop spontaneously, apply pressure to the cut with a piece of gauze, a washcloth, or a cloth diaper. Call the doctor if the injury is in the back of the throat or on the soft palate (the rear of the upper mouth), if there is a puncture wound from a sharp object (such as a pencil or a stick), or if bleeding doesn't stop within 10 to 15 minutes.

38. Knocked-out tooth. If one of your baby's teeth has been knocked out, there's no need to try to preserve it, since there's little chance that the dentist will attempt to reimplant it (such implantations rarely hold). But the dentist or doctor will want to see the tooth to be sure it's whole, as fragments left in the gum could be expelled and then inhaled or choked on, or the area could become infected. So take the tooth along to the dentist or to the doctor (before you tuck it into a memento box, that is).

39. Broken tooth. Clean dirt or debris carefully from the mouth with warm water and gauze or a clean cloth. Be sure the broken parts of the tooth are not still in baby's mouth, since they could cause choking. Place cold compresses on the face in the area of the injured tooth to minimize swelling. Call the dentist or doctor as soon as you can for further instructions.

40. Foreign object in the mouth or throat. Removing a foreign object from the mouth that can't be grasped easily is tricky. Unless done carefully, the effort can push the object in even farther. To remove a soft object (such as a piece of tissue paper or bread), pinch baby's cheeks to open the mouth, and use tweezers to take the object out. For anything else, try a finger swipe: Curl your finger (index or pinky) and swipe quickly at the object with a sideways motion. Do not attempt a finger swipe, however, if you can't see the object. If a foreign object is lodged in the throat, see choking rescue procedures, beginning on page 594.

NOSE INJURIES

41. Nosebleeds. Keeping baby in an upright position or leaning slightly forward (not back), pinch both nostrils gently between your thumb and index finger for 10 minutes. (Baby will automatically switch to mouth breathing.) Try to calm baby, because crying will increase the blood flow. If bleeding persists, pinch for 10 minutes more and/or apply cold compresses or ice (or an ice pack) wrapped in a dampened washcloth to the nose to constrict the blood vessels. If this doesn't work and bleeding continues, call the doctor, keeping baby upright—to reduce swallowing of blood and the risk of choking on it—while you do. Frequent nosebleeds, even if easily stopped, should be reported to baby's doctor. Sometimes, adding humidity to the air in your house with a humidifier will reduce the frequency of nosebleeds.

42. Foreign object in the nose. Difficulty breathing through the nose and/or a foul-smelling, possibly bloody nasal discharge may be a sign that something has been pushed up the nose. Keep baby calm and encourage mouth breathing. Remove the object with your fingers if you can reach it easily, but don't probe or use tweezers or anything else that could injure the nose if baby moves unexpectedly or that could push the object farther into the nasal canal. If this fails, take baby to the doctor or ER.

43. A blow to the nose. If there is bleeding, keep baby upright and leaning forward to reduce the swallowing of blood and the risk of choking on it. Use an ice pack or cold compresses to reduce swelling. If swelling persists, or if there is a noticeable deformity, see the doctor.

POISONING

44. Swallowed poisons. Any nonfood substance is a potential poison. The more common symptoms of poisoning include lethargy, agitation, or other behavior that deviates from the norm; racing, irregular pulse and/or rapid

breathing; difficulty breathing; diarrhea or vomiting; excessive watering of the eyes, sweating, or drooling; hot, dry skin and mouth; dilated (wide open) or constricted (pinpoint) pupils; flickering, sideways eye movements; and tremors or convulsions.

If your baby has some of these symptoms and there's no other obvious explanation for them, or if you have evidence that your baby definitely has swallowed a questionable substance (you saw it happen) or possibly has (you found your child with an open bottle of pills or hazardous liquid, found spilled liquid on clothing or loose pills on the floor, smelled chemicals on his or her breath), immediately call (or have someone else call) Poison Control (800-222-1222) or the ER for instructions. Call promptly for suspected poisoning even if there are no symptoms—they may not appear for hours. When calling, be ready to provide the name of the product ingested, along with the ingredients and package information, if available (if part of a plant was ingested, supply the name, or at least a description, of the plant); the time the poisoning was believed to have occurred; how much of it you know or believe baby ingested (give an estimate if you don't know for sure); any symptoms that have appeared; and any treatment already tried. Have a pad and pen handy to write down exact instructions.

If your child has excessive drooling, breathing difficulty, convulsions, or excessive drowsiness after the ingestion (or suspected ingestion) of a dangerous substance, call 911 for emergency medical assistance. Begin emergency treatment immediately if your baby is unconscious (see page 598).

Do not try to treat poisoning on your own without expert advice, and don't rely on the directions on the product label. Get explicit medical advice before giving anything by mouth (including food or drink, or anything to induce vomiting). The wrong treatment can do harm.

45. Noxious fumes or gases. Fumes from gasoline, auto exhaust, and some poisonous chemicals, and dense smoke from fires, can all be harmful. Symptoms of carbon monoxide poisoning include headache, dizziness, coughing, nausea, drowsiness, irregular breathing, and unconsciousness. Promptly take a baby who has been exposed to hazardous fumes into fresh air (open windows or go outside with baby). If baby is not breathing and/or doesn't have a pulse, begin rescue techniques (see page 598) immediately. If possible, have someone else call 911. If no one else is around, call 911 yourself after 2 minutes of resuscitation efforts—and then return immediately to CPR, and continue until a pulse and breathing are established or until help arrives. Unless an emergency vehicle is on its way, transport baby to a medical facility promptly. Have someone else drive if you must continue CPR or if you were also exposed to the fumes and your judgment and reflexes may be impaired. Even if you are able to successfully reestablish breathing, immediate medical attention will be necessary.

POISON IVY, POISON OAK, POISON SUMAC

46. Most children who come in contact with poison ivy, poison oak, or poison sumac will have an allergic reaction (usually a red, itchy rash, with possible swelling, blistering, and oozing) that develops within 12 to 48 hours and can last from 10 days to 4 weeks. If you know your baby has had contact with one of these plants, protect your hands from the sap (which contains urushiol, the resin that triggers the reaction) with gloves, paper towels, or a clean diaper and remove his or her clothes. To prevent resin from "fixing" to skin, immediately wash it with soap and cool water for at least 10 minutes and rinse thoroughly. In a pinch, use a wipe. The rash itself is not contagious and won't spread from person to person or from one part of the body to another once the sap has been washed away. Also wash anything else that may have come in contact with the plants (including clothes, pets, stroller, and so on), since urushiol can remain active on them for up to a year. Shoes can be thoroughly wiped down if they aren't washable.

If a reaction occurs, calamine lotion, or better yet, an anti-itch lotion that contains pramoxine (such as Caladryl), will help relieve the itching, but avoid lotions that contain antihistamines (such as Benadryl). Topical hydrocortisone cream can be applied to decrease inflammation. Cool compresses, and/or a colloidal oatmeal bath may also offer relief. Make sure your baby's nails are cut short to minimize scratching. Contact the doctor if the rash is severe or is causing a great deal of discomfort because of its location (around the eyes, on the genitals).

PUNCTURE WOUNDS

see #54

SCALDS

see #11, #12, #13

SCRAPES

see #50

SEIZURES

see #16

SEVERED LIMB OR DIGIT

47. Such serious injuries are rare, but knowing what to do when one occurs can mean the difference between saving and losing an arm, leg, finger, or toe. Take these steps as needed immediately:

- Control bleeding. Apply heavy pressure to the wound with several gauze pads, a maxi pad, or a clean diaper or washcloth. If bleeding continues, increase pressure. Don't worry about pressing too hard. Do not apply a tourniquet.

- Treat shock if it is present (#48).

- Check for breathing and a pulse, and begin rescue techniques (see page 598) as needed.

- Preserve the severed limb or digit. As soon as possible, wrap it in a wet clean cloth or sponge, and place it in a plastic bag. Tie the bag shut and place it in another bag filled with ice (do not use dry ice). Do not place the severed part directly on ice, and don't immerse it in water or antiseptics.

- Get help. Call or have someone else call 911 for immediate emergency medical assistance, or rush to the ER, calling ahead so they can prepare for your arrival. Be sure to take along the ice-packed limb, finger, or toe, since surgeons may attempt to reattach it. During transport, keep pressure on the wound and continue other basic life support procedures, if necessary.

SHOCK

48. Shock can develop in severe injuries or illnesses. It occurs when an inadequate amount of oxygen-containing blood is getting to the brain and body tissues to meet their needs. Signs include cold, clammy, pale skin; rapid, weak pulse; chills; convulsions; nausea or vomiting; excessive thirst; and/or shallow breathing. Call 911 immediately for emergency medical assistance. Until help arrives, position baby on his or her back. Loosen any restrictive clothing; elevate hips and legs on a pillow, folded blanket, or folded piece of clothing to help direct blood to the brain, and cover baby lightly to prevent chilling or loss of body heat. If breathing seems labored, raise baby's head and shoulders very slightly. Do not give food or water.

SKIN WOUNDS

IMPORTANT: Exposure to tetanus is a possibility whenever the skin is broken. If your child gets an open skin wound, check to be sure his or her tetanus immunization (part of the DTaP vaccine) is up-to-date. Also be alert for signs of possible infection (swelling, warmth, tenderness, reddening of surrounding area, oozing of pus from the wound), and call the doctor if they develop.

49. Bruises or black-and-blue marks. If the injury is painful, apply cold compresses, an ice pack, or cloth-wrapped ice (do not apply ice directly to the skin) to reduce bruising and swelling. Half an hour of soaking is ideal, but unlikely to be accomplished with a baby, and isn't necessary for a minor bump. If the skin is broken, treat the bruise as you would an abrasion (#50) or cut (#51, #52). Call the doctor immediately if the bruise is from a wringer-type injury (for instance, from catching a hand or foot in the spokes of a moving wheel), no matter how minor it looks. Bruises that seem to appear out of nowhere or that coincide with a fever should also be seen by a doctor.

50. Scrapes or abrasions. In such injuries (most common on knees and elbows) the top layer (or layers) of skin is scraped off, leaving the underlying area raw and tender. There is usually slight bleeding from the more deeply abraded areas. Using gauze, cotton, or a clean washcloth, gently sponge the wound with soap and water to remove dirt and other foreign matter. If baby resists this treatment, try soaking the wound in the bathtub. Apply pressure if the bleeding doesn't stop on its own. Apply a spray or cream antiseptic, if your baby's doctor generally recommends one, and then cover with a bandaid that is loose enough to allow air to reach the wound. If there is no bleeding, no bandage is necessary. Most scrapes heal quickly.

51. Small cuts. Wash the area with clean water and soap, then hold the cut under running water to flush out dirt and foreign matter. Some doctors recommend applying an antiseptic spray before applying a bandaid. A butterfly bandage will keep a small cut closed while it heals. Remove the bandaid after 24 hours and expose the cut to air; rebandage only as necessary to keep the wound clean and dry. Check with the doctor about any cuts that show signs of infection (redness, swelling, warmth, and/or oozing of pus or a white fluid).

52. Large cuts. With a gauze pad, a fresh diaper, a maxi pad, a clean washcloth—or, if you have nothing else available, your bare finger—apply pressure to try to stop the bleeding. At the same time, elevate the injured part above the level of the heart, if possible. If bleeding persists after 15 minutes of pressure, add more gauze pads or cloth and increase the pressure. (Don't worry about doing damage with too much pressure.) If the wound gapes open, appears deep, or is jagged; if blood is spurting or flowing profusely; or if bleeding doesn't stop within 30 minutes, call the doctor for instructions or take baby to the ER. If there are other injuries, try to tie or bandage the pressure pack in place so that your hands can be free to attend to them. Apply a nonstick bandage to the wound when the bleeding stops, loose enough so that it doesn't interfere with circulation. Do not put anything else on the wound, not even antiseptic, without medical advice. If the cut is deep or large, or on the face or the palm, stitches may be needed. In some cases the doctor may be able to use Dermabond (skin glue) instead of stitches. If the cut is on the face, consider having a plastic surgeon take a look at it.

53. Massive bleeding. Get immediate emergency medical attention by calling 911 or rushing to the nearest ER if a limb is severed (#47) and/or blood is gushing or pumping out of a wound. In the meantime, apply pressure to the wound with gauze pads, a fresh diaper or maxi pad, or a clean washcloth or towel. Increase the packing and pressure if bleeding doesn't stop. Do not use a tourniquet without medical advice, as it can sometimes do more harm than good. Maintain pressure until help arrives.

54. Puncture wounds. Soak a small puncture wound (one caused by a thumbtack, needle, pen, pencil, or nail) in comfortably warm, soapy water for 15 minutes. Then consult the doctor about what to do next. For deeper, larger punctures—from a knife or a stick, for example—take your baby to the doctor or the ER immediately. (If there is extensive bleeding, see #53.) If the object still protrudes from the wound, do not remove it, as this could lead to increased bleeding or other damage. Pad or otherwise stabilize the object, if necessary, to keep it from moving around while on route to medical care. Keep baby as calm and still as possible to prevent thrashing that might make the injury worse.

55. Splinters or slivers. Wash the area with clean water and soap, then numb it with an ice pack or ice cube. If the sliver is completely embedded, try to work it loose with a sewing needle that has been sterilized with alcohol or the flame of a match. If one end of the sliver is clearly visible, try to remove it with tweezers (also sterilized by alcohol or flame). Don't try to remove it with your fingernails or your teeth. Wash the site again after you have removed the splinter. If the splinter is not easily removed, and if baby will cooperate, try soaking the area in warm, soapy water for 15 minutes, 3 times a day for a couple of days, which may help it work its way out or make it easier to remove. Consult the doctor if the splinter remains embedded or if the area becomes infected (indicated by redness, heat, swelling). Also call the doctor if the splinter is deeply embedded or very large and your baby's tetanus shots (part of the DTaP vaccine) are not up-to-date, or if the splinter is metal or glass. Some wood splinters that are embedded just end up being absorbed into the skin, and that's fine. In that case, trying to remove the splinter can do more harm than good.

SNAKEBITES

see #6

SPIDER BITES

see #5

SPLINTERS

see #55

SUNBURN

see #15

SWALLOWED FOREIGN OBJECTS

56. Coins, marbles, and other small objects. If a baby has swallowed such an object and doesn't seem to be in any discomfort, check with the doctor for advice. If, however, your baby has difficulty swallowing, or if wheezing, drooling, gagging, vomiting, or difficulty swallowing develop immediately or later, the object may have lodged in the esophagus. Immediately call the doctor or take your child to the ER. If baby is coughing or seems to have difficulty breathing, the object may have been inhaled rather than swallowed. Treat this as a choking incident (see page 594).

57. Button batteries. If your child swallows a button battery of any kind, call the doctor and head to the ER immediately. The danger: The battery can become lodged in the digestive tract—anywhere from the esophagus to the intestines—and once there can start to burn through the organs, leading to serious injury and even death. Prompt medical attention (within hours) is necessary.

58. Sharp objects. Get prompt medical attention if a swallowed object is sharp (a pin or needle, a fish bone, a toy with sharp edges). It may have to be removed in the ER.

TEETH, INJURY TO

see #38, #39

TICK BITES

see #5

TOE INJURIES

see #27, #28, #29, #30

TONGUE, INJURY TO

see #37

Choking and Breathing Emergencies for Babies

The instructions that follow should serve only to reinforce what you learn in a baby first-aid and CPR course. (The training you receive may vary somewhat from the protocol described here, and should be the basis for your actions.) Participating in a formal course is the best way to ensure you'll be able to carry out these life support procedures correctly. Periodically review the guidelines below and/or the materials you receive from course instructors.

When Baby Is Choking

Coughing is nature's way of trying to clear the airways or dislodge an obstruction. A baby (or anyone else) who is choking on food or some foreign object and who can breathe, cry, and cough forcefully should be encouraged to keep coughing. But if the baby who is choking continues to cough for more than 2 to 3 minutes, call 911 for emergency medical assistance. If the cough becomes ineffective (baby tries to cough, but no sound comes out) or baby is struggling for breath, making high-pitched crowing sounds, unable to cry, and/or starting to turn blue (usually starting around the lips and fingernails), begin the following rescue procedures:

IMPORTANT. An airway obstruction may also occur when a baby has croup or epiglottitis (an inflammation of the epiglottis, the tissue that covers the windpipe). A baby who is struggling to breathe and seems ill—has fever and possibly congestion, hoarseness, drooling, lethargy, or limpness—needs immediate medical attention at an ER. Do not waste time trying to treat your baby by yourself—that could be dangerous. Call 911.

1. Get help. Have someone call emergency medical assistance (911) immediately. If you're alone, call 911 yourself, even if you're familiar with rescue procedures (though do provide about 2 minutes of care before calling, if you can). This will ensure that help will be on the way in case the situation worsens. If you're unfamiliar with rescue procedures—or if you panic and forget them—bring a phone to your baby's side (or take baby with you to a phone if there is no cordless or cell phone available) and the 911 operators can help walk you through rescue procedures

CPR: The Most Important Skill You'll Hopefully Never Need

Chances are, you'll never need to apply a single lesson learned in a first aid class—but there's no more compelling case for "just in case." More than any safety information you could read in a baby-care book, or pick up online, or even hear from your baby's doctor, a first aid course will arm you with the skills you would need to save your little one's life should the improbable—and unthinkable—actually happen.

A baby CPR class will provide you with invaluable hands-on instruction from a certified teacher, showing you exactly what steps you'd need to take in an emergency. And since the best way to learn is through doing, you'll get to practice the skills you're learning on a baby-size mannequin: where to place your hands for compressions, how hard and where to strike a baby's back when trying to dislodge something stuck in the windpipe, how to tilt a baby's head back to give rescue breaths, and much more.

Some classes focus only on infant (from birth to age 1) rescue techniques, other classes teach child (ages 1 through 12) techniques, and many classes teach both—a curriculum you might want to consider, especially since your little one will be out of the infant category before you know it (and toddlers are even more vulnerable to life-threatening injury than babies are).

The cost for a first aid class is usually minimal, depending on where you live, where you take the course, and which organization is giving the class (free classes are available in some areas). You can go to redcross.org to find classes in your area, or contact your local hospital or community center to see if classes are offered there.

If you can't get to a class because of either location or time constraints, the American Heart Association and the AAP offer a self-directed CPR learning kit called Family & Friends CPR Anytime. The kit (which costs around $35) comes with an inflatable infant mannequin, an instructional DVD that walks you through the training steps, and an instruction booklet. You can get more information and order the kit online through the American Heart Association website (heart.org—put the words "CPR kit" in the search box).

Another option is hiring an instructor to come to your home to train you and anyone else who will be spending time alone with your baby. It's pricier than group classes, but if you have several people (grandparents or other relatives, a babysitter or nanny) in need of training, a private class might be convenient and cost-effective.

---

as you wait for emergency medical assistance to arrive (put your phone on speaker or hands-free mode if possible).

If baby is unconscious, skip to Step 5 below. If baby is conscious:

2. Position baby. Position baby faceup on your forearm, with baby's head on your hand. Place your other hand on top of baby, using your thumb and fingers to hold baby's jaw while sandwiching him or her between your arms. Turn baby over so that he or she is facedown on your forearm. Lower your arm onto your thigh so that baby's head is lower than his or her chest (see illustration, page 596, left). If baby is too big for you to comfortably support on your

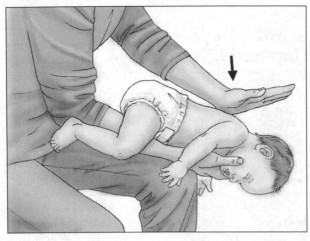

BACK BLOWS. With your arm resting on your thigh and baby's head lower than the chest, give 5 forceful back blows to help dislodge what baby is choking on.

CHEST THRUSTS. With baby in a faceup position, head lower than the chest, give 5 chest thrusts with the pads of your fingers.

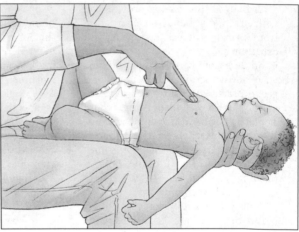

forearm, sit in a chair or on your knees on the floor and place baby facedown across your lap in the same head-lower-than-body position. You can give back blows effectively whether you stand or sit, as long as the baby is supported on your thigh.

3. Administer back blows. Give 5 consecutive forceful slaps between baby's shoulder blades with the heel of your free hand while keeping the arm that is holding the baby supported on your thigh (see illustration above, top). Deliver each slap with enough force to attempt to dislodge the foreign body. After 5 back blows, continue to Step 4.

4. Administer chest thrusts. Turn baby from a facedown position to a faceup position by sandwiching him or her between your two hands and forearms, supporting baby's head between your thumb and fingers from the front while you cradle the back of the head with your other hand (see illustration above, bottom). Lower the arm that is supporting baby's back onto your opposite thigh. The baby's head should be lower than his or her chest, which will assist in dislodging the object. (A baby who is too large to hold in this position can be placed faceup on your lap or on a firm surface.)

Locate the correct place to give chest thrusts by imagining a line

For Older Babies

The rescue procedures described in this chapter are for babies under a year old. Since there are different techniques to use on toddlers over a year and older children, it's important you learn those as well. See *What to Expect the Second Year* for more on first aid for toddlers.

running across baby's chest between the nipples. Place the pads of 2 or 3 fingers in the center of baby's chest. Use the pads of these fingers to compress the breastbone to a depth of 1½ inches (about one-third of the depth of the chest) and then let the chest return to its normal position. Keep your fingers in contact with baby's breastbone and give a total of 5 chest thrusts.

If baby is conscious, keep repeating the back blows and chest thrusts until the airway is cleared and the baby can cough forcefully, cry, or breathe—or the baby becomes unconscious. If baby becomes unconscious, call 911 if this has not already been done, and continue below.

5. Do a foreign-body check. Look in the mouth for a foreign object. If you can see the object and can easily remove it, do so with a finger sweep (see description and illustration, right).

6. Give two rescue breaths. Open baby's airway by gently tilting baby's head back slightly while lifting the chin (see description, page 599; illustration, page 598, left). Give two rescue breaths with your mouth sealed over baby's nose and mouth (see illustration, page 598, right). If baby's chest does not rise and fall with each breath, reposition baby's airway by re-tilting the head and

try to give rescue breaths again. If the breaths still do not make baby's chest rise, locate the correct hand position for chest compressions (imagine a line between the nipples and place two fingers just below that line in the center of the chest). Give 30 chest compressions in about 18 seconds (a rate of 100 per minute). Each compression should be about 1½ inches deep, or one-third the depth of the chest (see illustration, page 599).

7. Repeat sequence. If the breaths do not go in, repeat the cycle of chest compressions, rescue breaths, and foreign-object check until the airway is clear and the baby is conscious and breathing normally, or until emergency medical assistance arrives.

IMPORTANT: Even if your child recovers quickly from a choking incident, medical attention will be required. Call the doctor or go to the ER immediately.

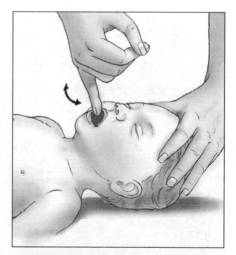

FINGER SWEEP. If you can see an easily removable object in your baby's mouth, hook your finger to sweep it out. Do not do a blind finger sweep (aka if you don't see anything in the mouth) because doing so risks pushing an unseen object further into the airway, causing more choking.

Breathing and Cardiopulmonary Emergencies

Begin the protocol below only on a baby who has stopped breathing, or on one who is struggling to breathe and is turning blue (check around the lips and fingertips).

How will you know if you need to start resuscitation techniques? Assess your baby's condition with the Check, Call, Care method recommended by the American Red Cross.

STEP 1. CHECK THE SCENE, THEN THE BABY

Check to make sure the location is safe to stay in. Then check baby for consciousness. Try to rouse a baby who appears to be unconscious by tapping the soles of her feet and shouting her name: "Ava, Ava, are you okay?"

STEP 2. CALL

If you get no response, have anyone else present call 911 for emergency medical assistance while you continue to Step 3 without delay. If you are alone,

provide about 2 minutes of care, then call 911. If you can, periodically call out to try to attract help from neighbors or passersby. If, however, you are unfamiliar with CPR or feel overwhelmed by panic, bring a phone to baby's side immediately (or, if there are no cordless or cell phones nearby and if there are no signs of head, neck, or back injury, go to the nearest phone with your baby), and call 911. The dispatcher will be able to guide you in the best course of action (put your phone on speaker or hands-free mode if possible).

IMPORTANT: The person calling for emergency medical assistance should stay on the phone as long as necessary to give complete information to the dispatcher. This should include the name, age, and approximate weight of the baby; any allergies, chronic illnesses, or medications taken; and present location (address, cross streets, apartment number, best route if there is more than one). Also tell the

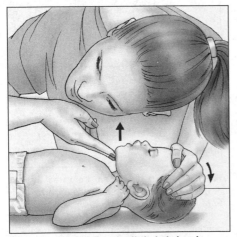

Open the airway: Gently tilt baby's head back slightly while lifting the chin.

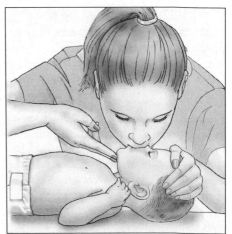

Begin rescue breathing: Form a tight seal with your mouth over baby's nose and mouth.

emergency dispatcher baby's condition (Is baby conscious? Breathing? Bleeding? In shock? Is there a pulse?), cause of condition (fall, poison, drowning), and the telephone number where you can be reached. Tell the person calling for help not to hang up until the EMS dispatcher has concluded questioning and to report back to you after completing the call.

STEP 3. CARE

Move baby, if necessary, to a firm, flat surface, carefully supporting the head, neck, and back as you do. Quickly position baby faceup, head level with heart, and proceed with the C-A-B survey below.

If there is a possibility of a head, neck, or back injury—as there may be after a bad fall or car accident—go to Step B (Breathing) to look, listen, and feel for breathing before moving baby. If baby is breathing, don't move him or her unless there is immediate danger (from traffic, fire, an imminent explosion). If breathing is absent and rescue breathing cannot be accomplished in the baby's present position, roll the baby as a unit to a faceup position, so that head, neck, and body are moved as one, without twisting, rolling, or tilting the head.

C-A-B

C: CHEST COMPRESSIONS

1. Position your hands. Position the three middle fingers of your free hand on baby's chest. Imagine a horizontal line from nipple to nipple. Place the pad of the index finger just under the intersection of this line with the breastbone, or sternum (the flat bone running midline down baby's chest between the ribs). The area to compress is one finger's width below this point of intersection (see illustration, above).

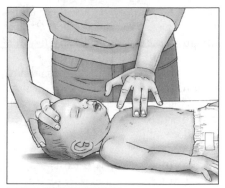

CHEST COMPRESSIONS

2. Begin compressions. Using two or three fingers, compress the sternum straight down to a depth of 1½ inches (your elbow should be bent) for 30 compressions. At the end of each compression, release the pressure without removing your fingers from the sternum and allow it to return to its normal position. Each compression should take less than a second.

A. OPEN THE AIRWAY

Tilt baby's head back slightly by gently pushing down on baby's forehead with one hand while pulling up on the bony part of the jaw with two or three fingers of your other hand to lift the chin (see illustration, page 598, left). If there is a possibility of a head, neck, or back injury, try to minimize movement of the head and neck when opening the airway.

IMPORTANT: The airway of an unconscious baby may be blocked by a relaxed tongue or by a foreign object. It must be cleared before the baby can resume breathing (finger sweep, see description and illustration, page 597).

B: BREATHING

Maintaining your baby's head in the same position, airway opened (A), take a breath in through your mouth and place your mouth over baby's mouth and nose, forming a tight seal (see illustration, page 598, right). Blow 2 slow breaths (lasting 1 second each) into the baby's mouth. Pause between rescue breaths (so you can lift your head and breathe in again, and to let the air flow out of baby's mouth). Observe with each breath whether the baby's chest rises. If it does, allow it to fall again before beginning another breath. After two successfully delivered breaths (as evident from the rising chest), repeat the C-A-B cycle of 30 compressions and 2 breaths.

NOTE: If the chest doesn't rise and fall with each breath, your breaths may have been too weak or the baby's airway may be blocked. Try to open the airway again by readjusting baby's head (tilt the chin upward a bit more) and give 2 more breaths. If the chest still does not rise with each breath, it is possible the airway is obstructed by food or by a foreign object— in which case, move quickly to dislodge it, using the procedure described in When Baby Is Choking on page 594.

ACTIVATE EMERGENCY MEDICAL SYSTEM NOW

If you're alone, provide care for about 2 minutes before calling 911. If a phone is close by, bring it to your baby's side. If not, and there is no evidence of head or neck injury, carry baby to the phone, supporting the head, neck, and torso. Continue rescue breathing as you go. Quickly and clearly report to the EMS dispatcher, "My baby isn't breathing," and give all pertinent information the dispatcher requests. Don't hang up until the dispatcher does. If

When Breathing Returns

If, after performing CPR, normal breathing has resumed, maintain an open airway as you continue to look for other life-threatening conditions. You can now call 911 for emergency medical assistance if no one has yet called for help.

If the baby regains consciousness and has no injuries that make moving inadvisable, turn him or her on one side. Coughing when the baby starts to breathe independently may be an attempt to expel an obstruction. Do not attempt to interfere with the coughing.

If vomiting should occur at any point, turn the baby on one side and clear the mouth of vomit with a finger sweep (hook your finger to sweep it out; see illustration, page 597). Reposition the baby to maintain an open airway and resume rescue procedures. If there is a possibility of neck or back injury, be very careful to turn the baby as a unit, carefully supporting the head, neck, and back as you do. Do not allow the head to roll, twist, or tilt.

possible, continue compressions while the dispatcher is speaking. If it's not possible, return to CPR immediately on hanging up.

IMPORTANT: Continue CPR until an automated external defibrillator (AED) becomes available or emergency medical assistance arrives.

The Low-Birthweight Baby

Most parents-to-be expect their babies to arrive right around their due date, give or take a couple of days or weeks. And the majority of babies do arrive pretty much on schedule, allowing them plenty of time to prepare for life outside the womb and their parents plenty of time to prepare for life with a baby.

But in about 12 percent of births in the United States, that vital preparation time is cut unexpectedly—and sometimes dangerously—short when baby is born prematurely and/or too small. Some of these babies weigh in at just a few ounces under the low-birthweight (5-pound, 8-ounce) cutoff, and are able to quickly and easily catch up with their full-term peers. But others, deprived of many weeks of vital uterine development, arrive so small that they can fit in the palm of a hand. It can take months of intensive medical care to help them do the growing they were supposed to have done in the cozy, nurturing confines of the womb.

Though the low-birthweight baby (whether born early or born small for gestational age) is still at higher risk than larger babies, rapid advances in medical care for tiny infants have made it possible for the great majority of them to grow into normal, healthy children. But before they are carried proudly home from the hospital—and sometimes even after they're home—a long road often lies ahead for these babies and their parents.

If your baby has arrived too soon and/or too small, you'll find the information and support you'll need to navigate that road in the pages that follow.

Feeding Your Baby: Nutrition for the Preterm or Low-Birthweight Infant

Learning to eat outside the womb isn't easy at first, even for a full-term baby who must master the basics of nursing from a breast or a bottle. For preterm or low-birthweight babies, the challenges may multiply. Those who are born just 3 or 4 weeks early are usually able to breastfeed or take the bottle right after birth—again, after mastering the basics. Ditto for babies who were born close to term but at a low birthweight. But babies born before 34 to 36 weeks usually (but not always) have special nutritional needs that traditional feeding can't satisfy—not only because they're born smaller, but because they grow at a faster rate than full-term babies do, may not be able to suck effectively, and/or may have digestive systems that are less mature. These littlest babies also need a diet that mirrors the nutrition they would be receiving if they were still growing in utero and that helps them gain weight quickly. And those vital nutrients need to be served up in the most concentrated form possible, because preemies and low-birthweight babies can take only tiny amounts of food at a time—partly because their stomachs are so small, and partly because their immature digestive systems are sluggish, making the passage of food a very slow process. And since they can't always suck well or even suck at all, they can't take their meals from a bottle or a breast—at least not right away. Luckily, breast milk, fortified breast milk, or specially designed formulas can usually provide all the nutrients preemies and low-birthweight babies need to grow and thrive.

Feeding in the Hospital

As a parent of a premature or very-low-birthweight infant, you will find that feeding and monitoring weight gain become two of the most consuming aspects of caring for your baby in the hospital—in terms of both time and emotion. The neonatologists and nurses will do everything they can to ensure that your preemie receives the nutrition needed to gain weight. Just how your baby receives that nutrition depends on how early he or she was born:

IV feeding. When a very small newborn is rushed to the intensive care nursery, an intravenous solution of water, sugar, and certain electrolytes is often given to prevent dehydration and electrolyte depletion. Very sick or small babies (usually those who arrive before 28 weeks gestation) continue to receive nutrition through their IV. Called total parenteral nutrition (TPN) or parenteral hyperalimentation, this balanced blend of protein, fat, sugar, vitamins, minerals, and IV fluids is given until the baby can tolerate milk feedings. Once your baby is able to begin milk feedings by gavage, TPN will decrease.

Gavage feeding. Babies who arrive between 28 and 34 weeks gestation and who don't need IV nutrition (or babies who started out on TPN but have progressed to the point where they can tolerate milk feedings) are fed by gavage—a method not dependent on sucking, since babies this young usually have not yet developed this reflex. A small flexible tube (gavage tube; see illustration, facing page) is placed into the baby's mouth or nose and passed down to the stomach. Prescribed amounts of pumped breast milk, fortified breast milk, or formula are fed through the tube every few hours. Gavage tubes are either left in place between feedings or removed and reinserted for each feeding. (The tube won't bother your preemie because the gag reflex doesn't develop until about 35 weeks.)

It may be a relatively long time before you'll be able to feed your baby as you'd always imagined you would, through breast or bottle. Until then, you can still take part in feedings by holding the tube and measuring how much your baby takes, cuddling skin-to-skin during tube feedings, or giving your baby your finger to practice sucking on while he or she is being fed (this helps strengthen the sucking reflex and may also help your baby associate sucking with getting a full tummy).

Nipple feeding. One of the most momentous milestones of your preemie's stay in the hospital will be the switch from gavage feeding to nipple feeding. When it comes to readiness for this milestone, there can be some big differences among little babies. Some are ready to tackle the breast or bottle as early as 30 to 32 weeks gestational age.

Others won't be ready to take on the nipple until 34 weeks, still others, not until 36 weeks gestational age.

The neonatologist will consider several factors before giving you the green light to begin breastfeeding or bottle-feeding: Is your baby's condition stable? Can he or she handle being fed in your arms? Have all the other physical requirements of readiness been met—for instance, can baby suck rhythmically on a pacifier or feeding tube and coordinate breathing and sucking? Is baby awake for longer periods? Are there active bowel sounds and no sign of abdominal distension or infection, and has meconium stool been passed?

Since nipple feedings are tiring for a small baby, they'll be started slowly one or two a day, alternated with tube feedings. Infants with respiratory problems may have an even harder time, requiring extra oxygen while feeding or experiencing short episodes of apnea (breathing cessation) while sucking (they might concentrate too hard on sucking and forget to breathe). For babies who have trouble mastering the suck, a specially designed pacifier may be used to help them practice and perfect their technique before graduating to breast or bottle.

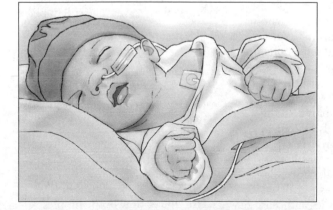

Babies who can't yet feed from a nipple are fed through a small, flexible gavage that is placed through the baby's mouth or nose into the stomach.

Early Weight Loss

As parents of a premature or low-birthweight baby, you'll be particularly anxious to start seeing the numbers on the scale creeping up. But don't be discouraged if instead your baby seems to be losing weight at first. It's normal for a premature infant (as it is for a full-term baby) to drop quite a few ounces—typically between 5 and 15 percent of his or her birthweight—before beginning to gain. As with a full-term baby, much of that weight loss will be water. Premature babies don't usually regain their birthweight before they are 2 or more weeks old, at which point they can begin surpassing it.

What are preemies and low-birthweight babies nourished with? Whether fed through gavage or nipple, your tiny baby will get either breast milk, fortified breast milk, or formula:

■ Breast milk. Breast is best not only when it comes to full-term infants, but also (or especially) when it comes to preemies, and for a number of reasons: First, it's custom designed for a preemie's special nutritional needs. Milk from moms who deliver early is different from milk from those who deliver at term. It contains more protein, sodium, calcium, and other nutrients than full-term breast milk does. This preemie-perfect balance prevents tiny babies from losing too much fluid, which helps them maintain a stable body temperature. It's also easier to digest and helps babies grow faster.

Second, breast milk has important substances not found in formula. Colostrum (early breast milk) is extremely rich in antibodies and cells that help fight infection. This is especially important when babies are sick or premature and may have a higher chance of developing an infection.

Third, research has shown that breastfed preemies have a lower risk of developing necrotizing enterocolitis, an intestinal infection unique to preemies (see page 628). They also tolerate feedings better, have a lower risk of allergies, and receive all the benefits that a full-term baby gets from breast milk (see page 3). Even if you don't plan to breastfeed long-term or full-time, providing breast milk for your baby while he or she is in the hospital—either by nursing or pumping or both—gives your baby the best possible start at a time when that start has begun too soon. Moms who can't produce milk (or enough milk) can feed their preemies the best, too, since donated milk is often available through the hospital or a recognized and licensed milk bank.

To ensure your baby is still getting enough nutrition in the early stages of breastfeeding (when baby's suck may still be weak or your breasts are not producing sufficient amounts of milk), talk to the doctor about the following supplemental feeding methods that don't interfere with nursing.

If you're nursing, you can:

◆ Nurse with the gavage still in place

◆ Use a supplemental nutrition system (see page 184)

If you're pumping you can:

◆ Bottle-feed with the gavage still in place

◆ Use a feeding system taped to your finger (finger feeding)

◆ Feed the milk through a syringe

◆ Use slower-flow bottle nipples

Expressing Milk for a Premature Baby

The decision to breastfeed a preterm baby is not always an easy one, even if you always had your heart set on nursing your newborn. After all, the major bonus of breastfeeding, that close mom-baby contact, is usually missing, at least at first. Instead, an impersonal pump stands in the way of that intimate experience until nipple feeding can begin. But though almost all women find pumping milk for their preemie exhausting and time-consuming, most who commit to it find it well worth the effort, knowing that this is one way—and one of the best ways— they can contribute to the health and well-being of their tiny baby.

Here's how you can make the most out of pumping for your preterm baby:

- Figure out the logistics. Most hospitals have a special room (with comfortable chairs and an electric double breast pump) set aside for moms of preemies to use throughout their baby's stay in the neonatal intensive care unit (NICU—pronounced nik-u). But first things first—make sure you're familiar with the mechanics of pumping (see page 171). Rent a hospital-grade pump or buy a high-quality double pump so you can pump at home, too, and bring milk to the NICU. Read more about safely storing and transporting breast milk on page 178.

- Begin expressing milk as soon after delivery as possible, even if your baby isn't ready to take it. Pump every 2 to 3 hours (about as often as a newborn nurses) if your baby is going to use the milk immediately, every 4 hours or so if the milk is going to be frozen for later use. You may find getting up to pump once in the middle of the night helps build up your milk supply. On the other hand, you may value a full night's sleep more. Whatever works for you is best.

- It's likely you will eventually be able to express more milk than your tiny baby can use. Don't cut back, however, figuring you're wasting too much. Regular pumping now will help to establish a plentiful milk supply for the time when your baby takes over where the machine leaves off—so it's never a waste. In the meantime, the excess milk can be dated and frozen for later use.

- Don't be discouraged by day-to-day or hour-to-hour variations in supply. That's completely normal—and something you wouldn't be aware of if you were nursing your little one directly. It's also normal to have a drop in milk production after several weeks. Baby will ultimately be a much more efficient stimulator of your milk supply than even the most efficient pump. When actual suckling begins, your supply is almost certain to increase quickly.

- When baby is ready for feeding by mouth, try offering the breast first, instead of a bottle of pumped milk (even if you're planning to do both). Studies show that low-birthweight babies take to the breast more easily than to the bottle. But don't worry if yours does better on the bottle—use it while your baby gets the hang of breastfeeding, or use a supplemental nursing system (see page 184). And remember, how you ultimately end up feeding your baby is less important than the side of nurturing attention you serve nourishment up with.

For more on breastfeeding your premature baby, see page 618.

- **Fortified breast milk.** Sometimes, even the milk of a preemie's mother isn't enough for a preemie. Since some babies, particularly very tiny ones, need even more concentrated nutrition—including more fat, proteins, sugars, calcium, and phosphorus, and possibly, more of such other nutrients as zinc, magnesium, copper, and vitamin B_6—the breast milk being fed through a tube or a bottle may be fortified with human milk fortifier (HMF) as needed. HMF comes in a powdered form that can be blended with breast milk, or in a liquid form for use when adequate amounts of breast milk are not available.

- **Formula.** Babies can do well, too, when they're fed formula specially designed for preemies. Even if you are breastfeeding, your baby may get additional feedings with a bottle or supplemental nursing system. Preemies are fed using small plastic bottles marked in cubic centimeters (cc) or milliliters (ml). The nipples are specially designed and require less sucking strength from your baby. Ask a nurse to show you the correct position for bottle-feeding your preemie—it may differ slightly from that for a full-term infant.

Feeding Challenges

Feeding a newborn often comes with challenges. Feeding a preemie or low-birthweight baby multiplies those challenges:

Sleepiness. Many preemies get tired easily—and sometimes sleeping can win out over eating. But frequent feeds are needed so a small baby can start catching up on growth—and it's up to you to make sure your extra-little one doesn't sleep through the feeds he or she needs. For tips on how to wake a sleepy baby, see page 139.

Breath holding. Some preemies, especially those who were born without good sucking-breathing coordination, will forget to breathe when feeding. This can be tiring for baby and anxiety producing for you. If you notice your baby hasn't taken a breath after a number of sucks or looks pale while feeding, remove the nipple from baby's mouth and let him or her take a breath. If your baby seems to be holding his or her breath all the time during feedings, regularly remove the nipple after every three to four sucks.

Oral aversion. Babies who have spent a lot of time in the NICU may come to associate their mouths with feeding tubes, ventilator tubes, suctioning, and other unpleasant sensations and experiences. As a result, some preemies develop a strong aversion to having anything in or around their mouths. To combat this, try to replace the unpleasant oral associations with more pleasant ones. Gently stroke your baby around the mouth, give your baby a pacifier or your finger to suck, or encourage your baby to touch his or her own mouth or suck on his or her thumb or fist.

Reflux. Many preemies are prone to gastroesophageal reflux disease (GERD) because of their immature digestive systems. For tips on coping with spitting up and GERD, see pages 197 and 569.

Feeding at Home

If by the time you get home together you're breastfeeding your preemie exclusively, you'll be all set—your breast milk supply will continue to grow with your baby. If you're formula feeding (or doing a combo), you may or may not need to continue using formula specifically designed for preemies once you're home with your little one. It'll depend on your baby's progress, and your doctor will be able to steer you to the right formula. You might decide to continue to use the same small bottles that were used in the hospital, especially because preemies need to be fed smaller amounts and need to be fed more often than full-termers. But keep in mind that what worked in the hospital might not work as well once you're home and your baby continues to grow in both size and maturity.

Wondering about when to start solids? Like full-term babies, preemies should start receiving solids at about 6 months. But for preemies, that date is based on adjusted age rather than chronological age (which means a preemie who was born 2 months early might not be ready for solids until 8 chronological months). Because some preemies experience delays in development, solid feedings should not be started until there are signs of readiness (see page 319), even if the corrected age says it's time to bring on solids. Some preemies have a more difficult adjustment to solids—especially once they graduate to chunkier foods—often because of negative oral associations picked up earlier. Working with a speech or occupational therapist can help a baby overcome oral aversions and move on to a lifetime of healthy eating.

What You May Be Wondering About

Bonding

"How will I ever bond with my preemie if she's spending the first few months of her life in the NICU?"

Your baby was whisked away moments after birth and before you even got a good look at her, she's too fragile to breastfeed, and she spends more time being poked and prodded by the hospital staff than snuggling in your arms. It's no wonder you're feeling as if bonding with your new baby—something that may seem so easy and natural to parents of full-termers—is an impossible goal to reach. But here's the real truth about bonding: The love and attachment between mom, dad, and baby develop over many months and years, blossoming over a lifetime rather than bursting into full bloom during the first few moments of life.

So if you didn't get the chance to bond with your preemie newborn the way you had dreamed of, all is not lost—in fact, nothing at all is lost. Plus, there are plenty of ways to start the lifelong process now—even while your baby is still in the hospital. Here's how:

Ask for a picture, along with a thousand words. Baby's not with you? Sometimes preemies have to be moved to another hospital for upgraded intensive care while mom's still stuck in the hospital postdelivery. If that's the case with you and your new bundle, have your spouse (or the hospital staff) email or text you some pictures and videos of your baby so you can enjoy looking at them until you're able to look at the real thing. Even if more tubing and gadgets are visible than baby, what you see will likely be less frightening and more reassuring than what you might

Kangaroo Care

It turns out kangaroos are more than just cute—when it comes to caring for their new babies, research shows they're smart, too. Snuggling a baby (particularly a preemie) skin-to-skin is a marsupial-inspired parenting practice that comes with many substantial benefits, right from the start and continuing throughout the NICU stay and beyond. For your baby, and for you.

You can start skin-to-skin contact, known as kangaroo care, as soon as the neonatologist determines that your baby is stable enough—even if she is very sick or very small, and hooked up to machines. Not only can't the snuggling hurt your baby, it can help in so many ways. Your baby will be comforted by your heartbeat, your scent, and the rhythm of your voice and your breathing. Kangaroo care will help maintain your baby's body warmth, regulate his or her heart and breathing rates, and speed weight gain and development. It'll also encourage deeper sleep, and help your baby spend more of his or her awake time quiet and alert instead of stressed and crying—all of which help boost development.

The benefits of kangaroo care extend to you, too. Being close to your baby (even when you're not feeding) can help improve a mom's milk supply and your chances of breastfeeding success. It'll also, not surprisingly, help nurture bonding between you and your baby while building your confidence as a new parent. (It will be something you can do for your baby, in a NICU where most of baby's care is provided by strangers.)

What's more, both you and your baby will collect on the benefits of skin-to-skin contact even if it's only for short periods of time each day. Have the time, and protocol and treatment permit? The more kangaroo care—ideally at least an hour at a time—the better.

Moms and dads can both offer kangaroo care—there's no special equipment required (and dad's hairy chest definitely doesn't disqualify him). Simply hold your diapered baby upright on your bare chest (between your breasts if you're the mom), positioned tummy to tummy with a blanket or your clothes draped over your baby's back. Then breathe in your baby's scent, close your eyes, and relax. You're doing a world of good for your tiny bundle of joy, and for yourself.

have imagined. As helpful as a picture may be, you'll still want those thousand words—from your spouse, and later the medical staff—describing every detail of what your baby is like and how she's doing.

Be hands-on. You may be afraid to touch your tiny, fragile baby—and you may even feel that he or she is better off not being touched—but studies have shown that premature infants who are stroked and lightly massaged while they are in intensive care grow better and are more alert, active, and behaviorally mature than babies who are handled very little. So, assuming the neonatologist gives the okay (some very early preemies can't tolerate touch and find any kind of handling stressful), let your hands do the bonding. Start by gently touching those arms and legs, since they are less sensitive at first than the trunk. Try to work up to at least 20 minutes of stroking a day.

Care like the kangaroos do. Skin-to-skin contact can not only help you get close to your baby, it can help with her growth and development. In fact, studies have shown that babies who receive so-called kangaroo care are likely to leave the NICU sooner. To cuddle your baby marsupial-style, place her on your chest under your shirt so that she's resting directly on your skin (she'll probably be wearing only a diaper and a hat, which prevents heat loss via the head). Loosely place your shirt over her to keep her even warmer, or cover her with a blanket. See box, facing page, for more.

Carry on a conversation. Sure, it'll be a one-way conversation at first—your baby won't be doing any talking, or even much crying, while she's in the NICU. She may not even appear to be listening. Still, she'll recognize your voice, and that will not only comfort her but help the hearing center of her brain develop. Can't be with your baby as often as you'd like? Leave a recording of yourself talking or singing (and if possible of your heartbeat, which also aids brain development) that the nurses can play for your baby when you're not around. Just keep the volume down whenever you're near your little one, since her ears are still very sound sensitive. In fact, for some very small preemies, any extra sounds can be extremely disturbing, so

check with your baby's doctor about how much sound is just right for her and how much is too much.

See eye-to-eye. If your baby's eyes are shielded because she's getting phototherapy for the treatment of jaundice, ask to have the bili lights turned off and her eyes uncovered for at least a few minutes during your visit so that you can make eye-to-eye contact while you're doing your kangaroo cuddling or through the isolette walls.

Take over for the nurses. As soon as your baby's out of immediate danger, the NICU nurse will show you how to diaper, feed, and bathe her. You may even be able to perform some simple medical procedures for her. Caring for your tiny baby will help make you more comfortable in your new parent skin, offer a sense of normalcy, and give you some valuable experience for the months that lie ahead (particularly those first few weeks at home). If staff doesn't offer to show you these basics or give you the opportunity to get some hands-on experience, ask.

Look at the NICU

"My baby is in the NICU, and it's scary seeing all that medical equipment he's hooked up to . . . all those tubes and wires."

A first look at a NICU can be frightening, especially if your baby is one of the tiny patients in it. Knowing what you're looking at can keep your fears from overwhelming you. Here's what you can expect in most NICUs:

A main nursery area comprising a large room or a series of rooms. There may also be a couple of isolation rooms in an area separate from the main nursery. Adjoining may be several small family

NICU Words to Know

You'll hear many probably unfamiliar words and terms in the NICU. The faster you learn the lingo of prematurity, the more comfortable you'll be hearing it used when referencing your baby and his or her care. The following is a glossary of some of the most common NICU terms. Ask the NICU staff if they have more information or pamphlets that might list the common terms used in their hospital (which may be more comprehensive than this list).

A's and B's. An abbreviation referring to episodes of apnea (breathing lapses) and bradycardia (too-slow heartbeat).

Asphyxia. A condition in which not enough oxygen is getting to the organs of the body. The brain and the kidneys are the organs most sensitive to a lack of oxygen. This may have been a problem just before birth in some preemies, making their delivery at that time an urgent matter to prevent or minimize organ damage.

Aspiration. The breathing of liquid (such as formula, stomach fluids, meconium) into the lungs. Aspiration could lead to pneumonia and other lung problems.

Bagging. Breathing for the baby—filling the lungs with air by squeezing a bag that is connected to an endotracheal tube (see facing page) or attached to a mask fitted over the face.

Bili lights. Blue fluorescent lights used to treat jaundice (aka phototherapy).

Blood gas. A blood test to check levels of oxygen and carbon dioxide in the blood. Blood gases need to be in proper balance for baby to grow properly. Blood gases are checked regularly for preemies on breathing machines.

Broviac. See Central catheter.

CBC or complete blood count. A blood test to count the red cells (that carry oxygen), white blood cells (that fight infection), and platelets (that prevent bleeding) in the blood.

Central catheter or central line. A small, thin plastic tube through which fluids are given or removed from the body. Broviac catheters are usually placed in the upper chest to reach the vena cava (the large blood vessel in the center of the body). PICC lines (percutaneously inserted central catheters) are usually threaded through a vein in the arm. Umbilical catheters can also be inserted into the vein or artery of the umbilical stump after birth.

Chest tube. A small plastic tube placed through the chest wall into the space between the lung and chest wall to remove air or fluid from this space. (See Pneumothorax on the facing page.)

---

rooms where moms can express milk (breast pumps are usually provided), and where families can spend cuddling time with their babies as they get stronger.

An often busy atmosphere. Depending on the size and occupancy of the NICU, there may be many nurses and doctors bustling about, treating and monitoring babies. Other parents may also be caring for or feeding their own infants.

Relative quiet. Though it's one of the busiest places in the hospital, it's

Cyanosis. A description of color changes to the skin when there's not enough oxygen in the blood. When a baby is cyanotic, the skin will turn blue.

Echocardiogram. An ultrasound of the heart.

Endotracheal tube (ET tube). A plastic tube that goes through baby's nose or mouth into the windpipe and is then connected to a ventilator (breathing machine) to help baby breathe.

Extubation. Removal of the ET tube (see above).

Hematocrit (Crit). A blood test to see how many red blood cells there are.

Intravenous (IV). A small plastic tube placed into one of the baby's veins as a means to deliver fluids, nutrition, and medication.

Intubation. The insertion of an endotracheal tube (see above).

Lumbar puncture (spinal tap). A test in which spinal fluid is drawn through a small needle placed in the lower back. The spinal fluid is then tested to check for problems (bacteria, infection, and so on).

Meconium aspiration. The inhalation of meconium (baby's first poop) into the lungs, which can lead to problems.

Nasal cannula. Soft plastic tubing that goes around a baby's head and under the nose, where there are openings (prongs) to deliver oxygen.

Neonatologist. A pediatrician who has special training in newborn intensive care.

Oxyhood. A clear plastic hood placed over the baby's head that supplies oxygen.

PICC line. See Central catheter.

Pneumothorax. When air from baby's lungs leaks out into the space between the lungs and chest wall. This could lead to a lung collapse. Treated with a chest tube; see the facing page.

RDS. See page 625.

Sepsis. An infection of the blood. Such an infection can begin as an infection elsewhere in the body and then spread to the blood. Likewise, blood infection can spread to virtually any organ in the body.

Surfactant. A substance that keeps small air sacs in the lungs from collapsing. Natural surfactant is lacking in preemies, which is why artificial surfactant is often given to preemies in the NICU.

Transfusion. Donated blood that is given to the baby when baby is anemic (has too few red blood cells) or has lost too much blood.

Umbilical catheter. A thin tube that is inserted into a blood vessel in the belly button to draw blood or give fluids, medication, or nutrients.

Ventilator. Mechanical breathing machine.

typically also one of the quietest. That's because very loud noises can be stressful for tiny babies or even harmful to their ears. To help keep the sound level down, you should talk quietly, close doors and isolette portholes gently, and take care not to drop things or place items loudly on the tops of incubators. (One sound that is important for your preemie, however, is the sound of your voice and heartbeat; see page 609.)

Dim lights. Since still-sensitive eyes need protection, too (after all, they'd

Being Part of Your Baby's Team

Remember that you are one of the most important partners in your baby's care. Educate yourself as much as possible about the NICU's equipment and procedures, and familiarize yourself with your baby's condition and progress. Ask for explanations of how ventilators, machines, and monitors are helping your baby. Request written information that explains the medical jargon you'll be hearing (and check out the box on page 610). Learn as much as you can about the routine: visiting hours and visitor restrictions, when nurses change shifts, when doctors make rounds. Find out who will give you updates on your baby's progress and when you'll get them. Give the staff your cell phone numbers, so they can always reach you.

be exposed to no light at all if they were still in the womb), NICU staff usually tries to control the brightness in the nursery. While bright lights are often necessary so that the doctors and nurses can do what they need to do (and see what they're doing) to keep your baby healthy and thriving, most NICUs do their best to keep the lights down to simulate life in the womb. Putting a blanket over your baby's isolette when the lights are bright may help somewhat as well—though ask the staff first, because it's also important that your baby not be kept in the dark all the time. Research shows that constant dim light can disturb body rhythms and slow the development of normal sleep-wake cycles. In fact, preemies who are exposed to natural cycles of light and dark that mimic day-night rhythms gain weight faster than those kept around-the-clock in either bright light or low light.

Strict hygiene standards. Keeping germs that can spread infection (and make sick babies sicker) out of the nursery is a major priority in the NICU. Each time you visit, you'll need to wash your hands with antibacterial soap or sanitizer (there's usually a sink or dispenser for this purpose right outside the nursery doors). You may be asked to put on a hospital gown, too. If your baby is in isolation, you may also need to wear gloves and a mask.

Tiny babies. Some will be in clear incubators or isolettes (bassinets that are totally closed except for four porthole-like doors that allow you and the staff to reach in and care for your baby) or in open bassinets. Some may be on warming tables under overhead heat lamps. Some very small babies may be wrapped in a plastic (polyethylene) skin wrap to minimize the loss of fluids and body heat through the skin, particularly in the few hours right after birth. This helps preemies keep warm—particularly those less than 4 pounds, who lack the fat necessary to regulate body temperature, even when they're swaddled in blankets.

An array of apparatus. You'll notice an abundance of technology near each bed. Monitors that record vital signs (and will warn, by setting off an alarm, of any changes that need prompt attention) are hooked up to babies via leads that are either held on the skin with gel or inserted by needle just under the skin. In addition to a monitor, your baby may be linked to a feeding tube, an IV (via arm, leg, hand, foot, or head), a catheter in his umbilical stump, temperature probes (attached to the skin with a patch), and a pulse oximeter that measures the oxygen level in his blood using

Portrait of a Preemie

The parents of full-term newborns may be surprised when they first see their babies. The parents of preterm infants are often shocked. The average preemie weighs between 1,600 grams (about 3½ pounds) and 1,900 grams (about 4 pounds, 3 ounces) at birth, and some weigh considerably less. The smallest can fit in the palm of an adult hand and have wrists and hands so tiny that a wedding band could be slipped over them. The preemie's skin is translucent, leaving veins and arteries visible. It seems to fit loosely because it lacks a fat layer beneath it (making it impossible for baby's temperature to self-regulate), and often it is covered with a fine layer of prenatal body hair, or lanugo, that has usually been shed by full-term infants. Because of an immature circulatory system, you may notice some skin coloring changes when you touch or feed your baby. Your little one's ears may be flat, folded, or floppy because the cartilage that will give them shape has yet to develop. Preemies often lie with arms and legs straight rather than classic newborn style—curled or tucked in—not only because their muscles still lack strength, but because they never had to fold to fit in a cramped uterus as full-term babies do.

Sexual characteristics are usually not fully developed—testicles may be undescended, the foreskin in boys and the inner folds of the labia in girls may be immature, and there may be no areola around the nipples. Because muscular and nerve development are not complete, many reflexes (such as grasping, sucking, startle, rooting) may be absent. Unlike term babies, a preemie may cry little or not at all. He or she may also be subject to periods of breathing cessation, known as apnea of prematurity.

But the physical characteristics of preemies that make up this portrait are only temporary. Once preterm newborns reach 40 weeks of gestation, the time when, according to the calendar, they should have been born, they very much resemble the typical newborn in size and development.

a small light attached to the hand or foot. A mechanical ventilator (breathing machine) may be used to help your baby breathe normally if he is less than 30 to 33 weeks gestation. Otherwise, your baby may receive oxygen through a mask or delivered into his nose through soft plastic prongs attached to tubing. There will also be suction setups that are used periodically for removing excess respiratory secretions, as well as lights for phototherapy (bili lights), used to treat babies with excess jaundice. (Babies undergoing this treatment will be naked except for eye patches, which protect their eyes from the bili lights.)

A place for parents to cuddle (and kangaroo) their babies. In the midst of all this high-tech equipment, there will likely be rocking chairs or gliders where you can feed or hold your baby.

A large team of highly trained medical specialists. The staff caring for your baby in the NICU might include a neonatologist (a pediatrician who has had special training in newborn intensive care), pediatric residents and neonatal fellows (doctors undergoing training), a physician assistant or nurse practitioner, a clinical nurse specialist, a primary nurse (who will be your baby's primary caregiver as well as your primary go-to), a nutritionist, a respiratory therapist, other physician specialists (depending on your baby's particular needs), social workers, physical and occupational therapists, x-ray and lab technicians, and lactation specialists.

Handling a Long NICU Stay

"The doctors say my preemie will have to spend many weeks in the hospital. How long is it likely to be—and how will I be able to handle her long stay?"

Chances are, you'll be able to bring your baby home from the hospital at about the same time you would have if she had arrived at term—about 37 to 40 weeks gestational age—though if your preemie faces other medical challenges besides being small, the stay may be extended. But no matter how long your baby's hospitalization ends up being, it will likely feel even longer. To make the most of that time and to even help it pass somewhat faster, try:

Striking up a partnership. Parents of a preemie often begin to feel that their baby belongs less to them and more to the doctors and nurses, who seem so competent and do so much for him. But instead of worrying that you can't measure up to the staff, try teaming up with them. Get to know the nurses (easier if your baby has a primary nurse in charge of care at each shift, which is likely), the neonatologist, and the residents. Let them know you'd like to do as much of the baby care as possible—diapering, swaddling, bathing—which can save them time, help you pass yours, and help you feel less like a bystander and more like an involved participant in your little one's care.

Getting a medical education. Learn the jargon and terminology used in the NICU. Ask the in-charge nurse to show you how to read your baby's chart. Ask the neonatologist for details about your baby's condition and for clarification when you don't understand. Parents of preemies often become experts in neonatal medicine very quickly, throwing around terms like RDS and intubation as easily as a neonatologist. See the box on page 610 for some frequently used terms.

Being a fixture at your baby's side. Some hospitals may let you move in, but even if you can't, you should spend as much time as possible with your baby, alternating shifts with your spouse as needed. This way you will get to know not only your baby's condition but your baby as well. (If you have other children at home, however, they'll also need you now. See page 621 for more on siblings).

Making your baby feel at home. Even though the isolette's only a temporary stop for your baby, try to make it as much like home as possible. Ask permission to put friendly-looking stuffed animals around your baby and tape pictures (perhaps including stimulating black-and-white enlargements of snapshots of mommy and daddy) to the sides of the isolette for her viewing pleasure. Ask if you can pipe in a recording of your voice for when you're not there, or soft music. Remember, however, that anything you put in the baby's isolette will have to be sterilized and obviously can't interfere with life-sustaining equipment.

Readying your milk supply. Your milk is the perfect food for your premature baby. Until she's able to nurse, pump milk for indirect feedings and to keep up your supply. Pumping will also give you a welcome feeling that you're "doing something."

Hitting the shops. Since your baby arrived ahead of schedule, you may not have had time to order furniture, layette items, and other necessities. If so, now's the time to get online and get that shopping done. If you feel superstitious about filling your home with baby things before she is discharged from the hospital, fill up the cart but don't complete the order until you're closer to the homecoming (especially because you won't know what size to buy those diapers or baby clothes in just yet). You'll not only have taken care of some necessary chores, but will also

have filled some of the long hours of baby's hospitalization and made a statement (at least to yourself) that you're confident you'll be bringing your new bundle home soon.

The Emotional Roller Coaster

"I'm trying to be strong for my son while he's in the NICU, but I'm scared, overwhelmed, and feeling out of control."

Most parents whose babies are in the NICU experience a wide spectrum of ever-changing emotions, which can range from shock to anger to frustration, stress to fear to numbness, disappointment to confusion, intense sadness to equally intense hope—all of which are valid, understandable, and normal. You may feel overwhelmed by all the medical equipment attached to your baby and the constant activity of nurses and doctors. You may be frightened of the procedures your baby is undergoing or frustrated by feelings of helplessness. You may feel disappointed that your little one isn't the dimpled, adorable full-term baby you'd been expecting (and envisioning) throughout your pregnancy, frustrated that you can't take him home to begin your life together, and guilty about both sets of emotions. You may also feel guilty for not feeling happy about your baby's birth or guilty about not being able to keep the pregnancy going longer (even if there was absolutely nothing you could have done to prevent your baby's prematurity, which most often, there isn't). You may feel unsettled at the uncertainty of your baby's future, particularly if he is very small or sick. You may even unconsciously distance yourself from your preemie for fear of becoming too attached or because you

Preemies by Category

Your preemie's care, length of stay in the NICU, and chances of complications will depend on the category of preemie he or she is. In general, the earlier your baby was born, the longer and more complicated a stay in the NICU:

Near-term or late preterm preemie (born at about 33 to 37 weeks gestation). Babies born near term are less likely to have severe breathing problems (thanks to some development of lung maturing surfactant in utero), but may still have blood sugar problems as well as a slightly elevated risk of infection. They are more likely than full-term babies to have elevated jaundice levels requiring at least brief phototherapy. These preterm babies may also have some difficulty feeding, but the vast majority of near-term preemies have a short stay in the NICU (if at all) with few complications.

Moderate preemie (born at about 28 to 32 weeks gestation). Many babies born before 31 weeks will have breathing difficulties and will likely need to be placed on a respirator for a while. And since babies born this early didn't get the immunity protection boost from mom during the last trimester, they are more prone to infections in general as well as hypoglycemia (low blood sugar) and hypothermia (they have a hard time staying warm). Moderate preemies usually won't be able to start with breastfeeding or bottle-feedings right away, and they may also encounter feeding problems when they are ready for nipple feedings.

Extreme preemies (born before 28 weeks gestation). These tiniest of babies are at highest risk of breathing difficulties because their lungs are so immature and not yet ready to function independently. Extreme preemies are also at highest risk of complications of prematurity, infections, hypoglycemia, and hypothermia (see page 625 for more).

Premature babies aren't categorized only by gestational age. A preterm baby's health and course of treatment in the NICU also has a lot to do with size at birth—usually the smaller the baby, the greater the chances for a longer hospital stay, and possibly for complications:

- **Very low birthweight** are those babies born weighing less than 3 pounds, 5 ounces.
- **Extremely low birthweight** are those babies born weighing less than 2 pounds, 3 ounces.
- **Micro preemies** are the smallest and youngest preemie babies—born weighing less than 1 pound, 12 ounces (800 grams) or before 26 weeks gestation.

Happily, advances in medical care have improved the outcomes of preterm babies and micro preemies, and even the smallest of babies have a much greater chance of survival. According to some studies, more than 50 percent of babies born at 23 weeks survive, more than three-quarters of babies born at 25 weeks survive, and more than 90 percent of babies born at 26 weeks survive.

find bonding difficult to accomplish through the portholes of an isolette. Or, you may feel unexpectedly strong feelings of love and attachment—deepened, instead of challenged, by the ordeal you're both enduring. You may be angry at yourself for your reactions, at your partner for not reacting the same way you are, at your family and friends for not understanding what you're going through or for acting as if nothing has happened, at your ob for not preventing this. Confusing these emotions further may be the fact that they may often conflict or fluctuate wildly—for instance, leaving you feeling hopeful one minute, hopeless the next, deeply in love with your baby one day, afraid to love him the next. Compounding them may be the physical exhaustion that comes from keeping a round-the-clock vigil at your baby's bedside, which may be more debilitating still if you haven't yourself recovered from delivery or are suffering from nipples painfully cracked from pumping.

Coping with these emotions may be extremely difficult, but keeping the following in mind may help:

- What you're feeling, saying, and doing is perfectly normal. Such extreme and sometimes contradictory emotions are experienced by nearly every parent of a premature baby at some time or another (though you may often believe that no one else has ever felt the way you do).

- There is no one right way to feel. Your emotions may differ from those of your partner, the parents of the baby in the next isolette, or from other parents of preemies you've talked to. Everyone will react to it a little differently—and that's normal, too. Remember, too, as you speak to other parents of preemies (and you should) that they may be feeling all of the same unsettling emotions on the inside, but those feelings may not show on the outside. Deep emotions often stay deep inside.

- Emotions need expressing. Keeping your feelings inside will only compound them—and make you feel more isolated. Let the NICU staff know what your feelings and fears are. Not only will they understand what you're

going through (since helping parents is almost as important a part of their job as helping babies), but they may offer insights that can help you cope.

- You and your partner need each other. You can each gain strength by leaning on the other—and can be more effective as a team than individually. Open communication can also help keep the stress inherent in parenting a preemie (or having a sick baby) from hurting your relationship.

- Support best comes from those who know. Try talking with other parents in the NICU. You'll find that they also feel alone, unsure, and scared. Friendships are easily formed in the NICU because other parents need you as much as you need them. Many hospitals make support available through groups run by the NICU social worker, or can hook you up with support families whose babies have left the NICU—especially through online groups. No one can relate better to what you're experiencing—and share more wisdom and empathy—than parents who've experienced it themselves. Also be sure to tap into the message boards at WhatToExpect.com to look for support from those who know. A mobile source of support will be especially invaluable during those long days and nights of waiting at the NICU.

- It will take time. You probably won't be on an even emotional keel at least until your baby's on an even physical one. Until then, you'll have good days and bad days (usually corresponding to your baby's ups and downs). If you're a brand new mom of a preemie, your physical recovery and normal hormonal fluctuations can intensify feelings of all kinds. Reminding yourself that your feelings are normal—that all parents of preemies ride an

Give Yourself a Break

Of course you want to spend every moment you can at your baby's side in the NICU, cuddling kangaroo-style, helping with feeds, whispering lullabies, holding those tiny hands through the isolette portholes—and if you're a mom, pumping breast milk to nourish your precious preemie.

But every parent needs a break—and no one needs it (or deserves it) as much as a parent of a preemie. So take one, and don't feel guilty about it. Whether you break for a movie with your partner, dinner with friends, a jog around the lake, or a few hours to browse for baby's layette, you'll return feeling less stressed, refreshed, and better equipped to handle the days ahead. Plus, you'll have learned an important lesson about being a parent: Taking the best care of your baby means taking time for yourself, too.

emotional roller coaster at least until their babies are safely home and completely well (and sometimes even longer than that)—won't make the feelings go away, but it will help give you the perspective you need to cope with them. Of course, if you (or your partner) are feeling sadness, hopelessness, anxiety, or an inability to function that's too significant to attribute to the very normal stresses of being the parent of a preemie, it could be that you're also dealing with postpartum depression. See page 525 and *What to Expect When You're Expecting* for more on recognizing the symptoms of PPD, and be sure to seek the help you need to get better fast. Remember:

To take the best care possible of your little baby, you'll also need to take the best care possible of yourself.

Breastfeeding

"I've always been determined to breast-feed my baby, and since she was born at 28 weeks, I've been pumping milk to be fed to her through a tube. Will she have trouble switching to nursing later?"

So far, so good. From birth your baby has been provided with the best possible food for a premature newborn—her mommy's milk—in the only way such a tiny baby is able to take nourishment, through a tube. Naturally, you're concerned that she be able to continue to get this perfect food once she graduates to suckling. But you have little to worry about. Research finds that premature infants weighing as little as 1,300 grams, or nearly 3 pounds, and as young as 30 gestational weeks may be able to suckle at the breast and are more successful at it than they are with the bottle.

Once you do put your baby to the breast, you'll want to make conditions as conducive to success as possible. Here's how:

- Read all about breastfeeding, beginning on page 60, before getting started. Also enlist the help of a lactation consultant (hopefully there will be one on staff to help you out).

- Be patient if the neonatologist or nurse wants your baby monitored for temperature and/or oxygen changes during breastfeeding. This won't interfere with the breastfeeding process itself, and it will protect your baby by sounding an alarm in case she is not responding well to the feeding.

- Be sure you're relaxed and that your baby is awake and alert.

- Ask the staff if there is a special nursing area for preemie moms, a private corner with an armchair or glider for you and your baby, or a privacy screen that can be put up to shield you—especially because it's best if you cuddle and nurse your baby skin-to-skin.

- Get comfortable, propping your baby on pillows, supporting her head. Many new moms find a football hold (see page 66) comfortable as well as easy on the nipples.

- If your baby doesn't yet have a rooting reflex (she probably doesn't), help her get started by placing your nipple, with the areola, into her mouth. Compress your breast lightly with your fingers to make it easier for her to latch on (see page 67), and keep trying until she succeeds.

- Watch to be sure your baby is getting milk. Your breasts are used to mechanical pumping and will take a while to adjust to the different motions generated by your baby's mouth. At first, your baby's suckling will be rapid—an attempt to stimulate let-down. Then, as the milk is let down, your baby will slow down her suck and switch to a suckle-swallow pattern.

- If your baby doesn't seem interested in your breast, try expressing a few drops of milk into her mouth to give her a taste of what's in store.

- Nurse your baby for as long as she's willing to stay at the breast. Keep her on your breast until she's stopped active suckling for at least 2 minutes. Small preemies may nurse for close to an hour before being satisfied.

- Don't be discouraged if the first session or first several sessions seem unproductive. Many full-term babies take a while to catch on, and preemies deserve at least the same chance. Still having trouble? Ask for help.

- Ask that any feedings at which you can't nurse be given by gavage (through the nose) rather than by bottle. If human milk fortifier or other fortification is given to your baby to supplement the breast milk, ask that it, too, be given by gavage or by the supplementary nutrition system (see page 184).

You'll be able to tell how well your baby is doing on the breast by following her daily weigh-in. If she continues gaining about 1 to 2 percent of her body weight daily, or about 3½ to 7½ ounces a week, she'll be doing fine. By the time she reaches her original due date, she should be approaching the weight of a full-termer—somewhere around 6 to 8 pounds. Do keep in mind that breastfed preemies (as with term infants) will gain a little more slowly than formula-fed ones.

Handling a Tiny Baby

"So far I've handled our baby only through the portholes of his isolette. But I'm worried about how well I'll be able to handle him when he finally comes home. He's so tiny and fragile."

When your baby finally makes that long-anticipated trip home, he'll probably seem pudgy and sturdy to you, rather than tiny and fragile. After all, depending on how small he was when he arrived, he may have doubled his birthweight when he hits 4 or 5 pounds—the average weight at discharge for preemies. And chances are, you won't have any more trouble caring for him than most new parents have caring for their full-term babies. In fact, if you have a chance to do some baby care at the hospital (something you should be encouraged to do, especially when it comes to his specialized care) in the

Sending Baby Home

After spending many weeks there, the NICU may begin to feel like a second home—and the staff like a second family. Still, you're probably more than ready for discharge day—and that momentous homecoming you've eagerly been waiting for. Chances are, it will come at approximately the same time it would have if baby had arrived full term, at 40 weeks, though occasionally a baby may be discharged as early as 2 to 4 weeks before his or her due date or might need to stay longer than the 40-week mark. Most hospitals don't have a specific weight requirement for discharge. Instead, babies are usually sent home once they:

- Are able to maintain normal body temperature in an open crib

- Have graduated to feeding by breast or bottle only

- Are gaining weight on breast or bottle

- Are breathing on their own

- Show no sign of apnea (pauses while breathing)

weeks before your baby's homecoming, you'll actually be ahead of the new parent curve. Which is not to say it will be easy—it rarely is for new parents, whether the bundle they're bringing home is preemie or full term.

If you're wondering how well you and your baby will do without a nurse or neonatologist looking over your shoulder, be assured that hospitals don't send home babies who are still in need of full-time professional care. Any care that you'll need to provide at home

(beyond the baby basics), the staff will prepare you for—and if they don't give you the instructions and preparation you need, ask for them. Also ask about getting infant CPR training before you take baby home, an important skill for any new parent, but especially one of a preemie (see page 598). To help parents feel more confident before discharge, most NICUs offer parents the opportunity to spend a night with their baby in a family room close to the nursery but without any nursery staff supervision—on their own, but with backup a call light away.

If you're still feeling overwhelmed at the thought of going it alone by the time your baby's getting ready for discharge (especially if he's being sent home with an assortment of medical apparatus, such as breathing monitors and oxygen hoods), consider hiring a baby nurse who has experience with preemies and their care to help out for the first week or two, finances permitting.

Permanent Problems

"Though the doctor says our baby is doing well, I'm still afraid that she'll come through this with some kind of permanent problems."

One of the greatest miracles of modern medicine is the rapidly increasing survival rate for premature infants. At one time, a baby weighing in at 1,000 grams (about 2 pounds, 3 ounces) had no chance of making it. Now, thanks to the advances in neonatology, many babies who are born even smaller than that can be expected to survive (see box, page 616). Which means the odds of your baby coming home well from her hospital stay are very much in her favor.

Overall, better than two out of three babies born prematurely will turn out to be perfectly normal, and most of

For Siblings: The Littlest Sib

Wondering what—if anything— you should tell your older child about your new premature baby? Your first impulse might be to try to protect a big sib (especially one who's still pretty young) by not saying much at all about the baby's condition. But even very young children pick up more than the adults around them usually give them credit for—and without comforting context, stress signals can be especially unsettling and scary. Why is everyone distracted? Why are routines being disrupted? Why are mommy and daddy so stressed out? And where is the baby if it's not still in mommy's belly? The imagined can actually be more frightening for a young child than the reality—and what he or she doesn't know can hurt more than it has to.

Instead, give your older child some very basic facts about what's going on with the new baby. Explain that the baby came out of mommy too soon, before growing enough, and has to stay in a special crib in the hospital until he or she is big enough to come home. With the hospital's okay, take your older child for an initial visit, and if it goes well and he or she seems eager, visit together regularly. Big sibs who are still little are just as likely to be fascinated by the wires and tubes as they are to be scared, particularly if adults set the right tone—confident and cheerful rather than nervous and somber. Having the new older sib bring a present to place in the isolette will help him or her feel a part of the team caring for the new baby. If your older child would like to, and if you have the staff's permission, let him or her scrub up and then touch the baby through the portholes. Encourage the brand new big brother or sister to sing, talk to, and make eye contact with his or her brand new sibling. This early bonding, even through isolette walls, can help your older child feel closer to the baby when that homecoming finally takes place. Big sib seems to want nothing to do with this extra tiny, extra needy new member of the family? That's fine, too. As always, follow your child's lead.

In the meantime, keep routines as close to "normal" as possible, and make sure that anyone who is caring for your older child is familiar with favorite foods, books, music, toys, games, and of course, bedtime as usual. During times of change and stress—which your preemie's stay in the NICU will inevitably be—the same-old, same-old will be particularly comforting to a young older sibling.

the others will have only mild to moderate disabilities. Most often the baby's IQ will be normal, though preterm infants do have an increased risk of learning challenges. The risks of permanent development issues are much greater for those who are born at 23 to 25 weeks and/or weigh less than 25 ounces. Still, of the 40 percent of these infants who survive, more than half do well.

As your baby grows, it will be important to keep in mind that she will have some catching up to do before her development reaches the normal range for her birth age. Her progress is likely to follow more closely that of babies of her adjusted age (see next question). If she was very small, or had serious complications during the neonatal period, she is very likely to lag behind her corrected age mates, too, particularly in motor development.

It may also be slower going in the neuromuscular department. Some

Home Care for Preterm Babies

Even once they've reached the age of full-term babies, preemies continue to need some special care. As you prepare to take your baby home, keep these tips in mind:

- Read the month-by-month chapters in this book. They apply to your preterm baby as well as to full-termers. But remember to adjust for your baby's corrected age.

- Keep your home warmer than usual (but not overheated), at least 72°F or so, for the first few weeks that your baby is at home. The temperature regulating mechanism is usually functioning in premature infants by the time they go home, but because of their small size and greater skin surface in relation to fat, they may have difficulty keeping comfortable without a little help. In addition, having to expend a great many calories to keep warm could interfere with weight gain. If your baby seems unusually fussy, check the room temperature to see if it's warm enough. Feel baby's arms, legs, or the nape of the neck to be sure it isn't too cool in the room. But don't go overboard by overbundling your little baby. It's dangerous for a baby to be dressed too warmly while sleeping. Again, feel baby's arms, legs, or the nape of the neck to be sure he or she is at the right temperature—not too cool and not too warm.

- Buy diapers made for preemies. You can also buy baby clothes in preemie sizes. Just don't buy too many—before you know it, they'll be outgrown.

- Ask the doctor if you should sterilize bottles, if you're giving them, between feedings by boiling them or running them through a hot dishwasher. Though sterilizing after each feeding may be an unnecessary precaution for a term baby, the doctor might recommend it for your preemie, who is more susceptible to infection. Continue for a few months, or until baby's doctor tells you it's no longer necessary. Sterilizing between uses might also be a must-do with breast pump parts,

preemies may not lose those telltale newborn reflexes such as the Moro, tonic neck, or grasp reflexes (see page 146) as early as term infants do, even taking adjusted age into account. Or their muscle tone may be weak, in some cases causing the head to be floppy, in other cases causing the legs to be stiffer than normal and the toes to point. Though such signs may signal something's wrong in full-term babies, they're usually nothing to worry about in pretermers (but do have them evaluated by the doctor).

Slow developmental progress is definitely to be expected in a preemie, and is not usually a cause for concern. If, however, your baby seems not to be making any progress week to week, month to month, or if she seems unresponsive (when she's not ill), speak to her doctor. If a problem is discovered, the early diagnosis could lead to early treatment, which may make a tremendous difference in the long term.

Catching Up

"Our son, who was born nearly 2 months early, seems very far behind compared with other 4-month-olds. Will he ever catch up?"

so ask the doctor about that as well. Microwave bags designed for sterilizing baby feeding equipment can make the job easier.

- Feed frequently . . . and patiently. The smaller the baby, the tinier the tummy—which means that preemies may need a refill as often as every 2 hours (timed from the beginning of one feed to the start of the next). Feeding can be slowgoing, too, especially with breastfed preemies—who may not be able to suckle as efficiently as full-termers. They may take longer—as long as an hour—to drink their fill at each feed. Let your extra-little one take all the time he or she needs to feed.

- Feed extra . . . if your doctor tells you to. Some preemies need a little extra boost in the calorie department, so the doctor might suggest you add a small amount of extra formula powder to fortify bottles, or to include a small amount of cereal in the bottle after a certain age. Reminder: Don't do this unless specifically recommended by the doctor for your bottle-fed baby.

- Ask the doctor about a multivitamin and iron supplement. Preemies can be at greater risk of becoming vitamin deficient than full-termers and may need this extra insurance.

- Don't start solids until your doctor gives the go-ahead. Generally, solids are introduced to a preterm infant when his or her weight reaches 13 to 15 pounds, when more than 32 ounces of formula is consumed daily for at least a week, and/or when adjusted age is 6 months. Occasionally, when a baby is not satisfied with just formula or breast milk, solids may be started as early as 4 months adjusted age—assuming your baby is developmentally ready.

- Relax. Without a doubt, your baby has been through a lot—and so have you. But once your little bundle is home, try to put the experience behind both of you. As great as the impulse may be to hover or overprotect, aim instead to treat your preemie like the normal, healthy baby he or she is now.

Your little guy's probably not "behind" at all. In fact, he's probably just where a baby conceived when he was should be. Traditionally, a baby's age is calculated from the day he was born. But this system is misleading when assessing the growth and development of premature infants, since it fails to take into account that at birth they have not yet reached term. Your baby, for example, was just a little more than minus 2 months old at birth. At 2 months of age he was, in terms of gestational age (calculated according to his original due date), equivalent to a newborn. At 4 months, he's more like a 2-month-old. Keep this in mind when you compare him with other children his age or with averages on development charts. For example, though the average baby may sit well at 7 months, your child may not do so until he's 9 months old, when he reaches his seventh-month corrected age. If he was very small or very ill in the newborn period, he's likely to sit even later. In general, you can expect motor development to lag more than the development of the senses (vision and hearing, for example).

Experts use the gestational age, usually called adjusted or corrected

Preemie Vaccines

For most of your premature baby's first 2 years, his or her adjusted age will be the one that counts most, except in one area: immunizations. Most of a baby's vaccine schedule isn't delayed because of prematurity, so instead of receiving vaccines according to gestational age, he or she will receive them according to birth age. In other words, if your baby was born 2 months early, he or she will still get those first shots at age 2 months—not age 4 months. Even the hepatitis B vaccine, which is normally given at birth, isn't delayed for a preemie. The AAP recommends all babies—even premature ones—get vaccinated at birth or before the baby is discharged from the hospital to return home.

Don't worry about your tiny baby's immune system not being mature enough or able to produce antibodies to the vaccines. Researchers have found that at 7 years, even children who were born extremely small have antibody levels similar to other children the same age.

age, in evaluating a premature child's developmental progress until he's 2 to 2½ years old. After that point, the 2 months or so differential tends to lose its significance—there isn't, after all, much developmental difference between a child who is 4 years old and one who is 2 months shy of 4. As your baby gets older, the gap between his adjusted age and his birth age will likely diminish and finally disappear, as will any developmental differences between him and his peers (though occasionally, extra nurturing may be needed to bring a preemie to that point). In the meantime, if you feel more comfortable using his adjusted age with strangers, go ahead (they'll never know the difference). Certainly do so when looking at your baby's developmental progress.

You can encourage motor development by placing your baby on his tummy, facing outward toward the room rather than toward the wall, as often and for as long as he'll put up with it (but only when he is carefully supervised). Since preemies and low-birthweight babies spend most of their early weeks, sometimes months, on their backs in isolettes, they often resist this "tummy-to-play" position, but it's a necessary one for building arm and neck strength. Tummy time on your tummy or chest may be more fun for both of you . . . plus you'll both reap the benefits that come from such kangaroo care if you do it skin-to-skin.

Car Seats

"My baby seems way too small for the infant car seat. Wouldn't she be safer in my arms?"

It's not only unsafe but illegal for a baby (premature or full-term) to ride in somebody's arms rather than in a car seat. Every baby, no matter how tiny, must be buckled up safely, securely, and snugly each and every time she's in a moving vehicle. But parents of low-birthweight babies often find that their especially little babies seem lost in a standard rear-facing infant car seat. The AAP recommends the following when choosing and using a car seat for your preemie:

- Select a car seat that will fit your baby. Choose an infant car seat, not a convertible seat, and look for one that has less than 5½ inches from the crotch strap to the seat back. This will help keep your baby from slouching. Also, look for one that measures less than 10 inches from the lowest harness strap position to the seat bottom so that the harness won't cross over your baby's ears.

- Make it fit even better. Use the newborn insert that comes with the car seat (most infant seats include one) to cocoon your baby. If baby still seems too small to fit, roll a towel or small blanket and arrange it so that it pads the seat at the sides of her head. And if there's still a big gap between your baby's body and the harness, use a folded towel or blanket to fill it in (but don't place one under baby).

Also consider having a certified car seat installation technician check how your preemie fits into her car seat—to make sure she's getting the support she needs and is seated safely, as well as to show you how to make any necessary adjustments. (Search on nhtsa.gov/apps/cps/index.htm for a location near you.)

Some premature babies have trouble breathing in the semipropped position the seat requires. One study has shown that these infants may show a decreased oxygen supply while riding in a car seat, and that this deficit may last for as long as 30 minutes or more afterward. Some may also experience short periods of apnea (breathing cessation) in car seats. Make sure your baby is observed and monitored in the car seat by the hospital staff before going home. If she does experience breathing problems in a car seat, it's best to limit the amount of auto travel you do with her for the first month or two at home (or use an approved car bed), especially if she has had spells of apnea previously. Ask her doctor about monitoring her breathing when she's in an ordinary car seat, at least for a while, to see if she is experiencing any problems.

The same breathing problems may occur in young premature babies in infant seats and baby swings, so don't use either without the doctor's approval.

ALL ABOUT:

Health Problems Common in Low-Birthweight Babies

Prematurity is risky business. Tiny bodies are not fully mature, many systems (heat regulatory, respiratory, and digestive, for example) aren't yet fully operative, and not surprisingly, the risk of neonatal illness is increased. As the technology for keeping such babies alive improves, more attention is being given to these common preemie conditions, and completely successful treatment is becoming more and more the norm for many of them. (New treatments are being developed almost daily and so

may not be detailed here, so be sure to ask your neonatologist or pediatrician about recent advances.) The medical problems that most frequently complicate the lives of preterm infants include:

Respiratory distress syndrome (RDS). Because of immaturity, the premature lung often lacks pulmonary surfactant, a liquid that coats the inside of the lungs and helps keep the air sacs (alveoli) in the lungs from collapsing. Without surfactant the tiny air sacs collapse like deflating balloons each time baby breathes out, forcing him or her to work harder and harder to breathe. This is called RDS. Interestingly, babies who have undergone severe stress before birth, usually during labor and delivery, are more likely to have surfactant, since the stress appears to speed lung maturation.

RDS, the most common lung disease of premature infants, was once frequently fatal, but more than 80 percent of babies who develop RDS today survive, thanks to an increased understanding of the syndrome and new ways of treatment. Extra oxygen is given via a plastic oxygen hood, or via continuous positive airway pressure (CPAP), which is administered through tubes that fit into the nose or mouth. The continuous pressure keeps the lungs from collapsing until the body begins producing sufficient surfactant, usually in 3 to 5 days. With severe RDS, a breathing tube is placed in the mouth and the baby is put on a respirator. Artificial surfactant is then administered directly to the baby's lungs via the breathing tube. Sometimes, when lung immaturity is detected in utero, RDS can be prevented entirely by the prenatal administration of a hormone to the mother, to speed lung maturation and production of surfactant.

A mild case of RDS usually lasts for the first week of life, though if the baby must be placed on a respirator, the recovery may be much slower. Babies with severe cases of RDS may be at an increased risk of colds or respiratory illnesses during their first 2 years of life, and may be more likely to experience childhood wheezing or asthma-like illnesses and be hospitalized in their first 2 years.

Bronchopulmonary dysplasia (BPD). In some babies, particularly those born very small, long-term oxygen administration and mechanical ventilation used to help treat RDS appear to combine with lung immaturity to cause BPD, or chronic lung disease. The condition, which results from lung injury, is usually diagnosed when a newborn still requires increased oxygen after reaching 36 weeks gestation and lung changes (such as scarring) are seen on x-rays. Babies with BPD have to work harder than other babies to breathe, and breastfeeding or bottle-feeding makes them work especially hard. Because they end up using so many calories when they exert themselves to breathe, and because they have a harder time eating, babies with BPD often have nutritional challenges such as poor weight gain.

BPD is a chronic condition, and the only cure is giving it time, since over time, new healthy lung tissue will grow and the symptoms will ease. That's why treatment is only to lessen the symptoms of the condition while the lungs grow and mature. Treatment can include extra oxygen, continued mechanical ventilation, medications such as bronchodilators (to help open the airways) or steroids (to reduce inflammation), and medication to prevent RSV (respiratory syncytial virus; see page 559) prevention medication. Some babies will require oxygen at home, and all require a high caloric intake to improve growth. Happily, most babies with BPD outgrow their symptoms and lead healthy lives.

Apnea of prematurity. Though apnea (periods when breathing stops) can occur in any newborn, the problem is much more common among premature infants. Apnea of prematurity occurs when immature respiratory and nervous systems cause preterm babies to stop breathing for short periods. It is diagnosed when a baby has such periods that last more than 20 seconds or shorter ones that are associated with bradycardia, a slowing of the heart rate. It is also considered apnea if the cessation of breathing is associated with the baby's color changing to pale, purplish, or blue. Almost all babies born at 30 weeks or less will experience apnea.

Apnea is treated by stimulating the infant to start rebreathing by rubbing or patting the baby's skin, administering medication (such as caffeine or theophylline), or using continuous positive airway pressure (CPAP), in which oxygen is delivered under pressure through little tubes into the baby's nose. Apnea of prematurity is not associated with SIDS (Sudden Infant Death Syndrome), and many babies will outgrow it by the time they reach 36 weeks gestation. If a baby has breathing pauses after apnea has been outgrown, it is not considered apnea of prematurity and is more likely caused by some other problem.

Patent ductus arteriosus. While baby is still in the uterus, a duct called the ductus arteriosus connects the aorta (the artery through which blood from the heart is sent to the rest of the body) and the main pulmonary artery (the one leading to the lungs). This duct shunts blood away from the nonfunctioning lungs and is kept open during pregnancy by high levels of prostaglandin E (one of a group of fatty acids produced by the body) in the blood. Normally, levels of prostaglandin E fall at delivery, and the duct begins to close within a few hours. But in about half of very small premature babies (those weighing less than 3 pounds, 5 ounces), and in some larger babies, levels of prostaglandin E don't drop, and the duct remains open or "patent." In many cases there are no symptoms, except a heart murmur and a little shortness of breath on exertion and/or blueness of the lips, and the duct closes by itself soon after birth. Occasionally, however, severe complications occur. Treatment with an antiprostaglandin drug (indomethacin) is often successful in closing the duct. When it isn't, surgery will do the job.

Retinopathy of prematurity (ROP). The blood vessels in the eyes are not fully developed until about 34 weeks gestation. When babies are born too early, the immature blood vessels in the retinas sometimes begin to grow too quickly, damaging the retina. Retinopathy of prematurity (ROP) is the name for the improper growth of the blood vessels on the retina and the damage caused by that growth. In most preemies, the growth of the retinal blood vessels will slow down on its own, and vision will develop normally. The incidence of ROP increases as birthweight decreases. More than half of babies born weighing less than 2 pounds, 12 ounces (1,250 grams) will develop ROP, most often mild. Severe retinopathy of prematurity is largely a problem of those babies born before 28 weeks.

Most cases of ROP will get better on their own, requiring no treatment, and the babies will recover with no lasting visual problems. But since ROP can sometimes lead to scarring and distortion of the retina, increased risk of nearsightedness, wandering eye, involuntary rhythmic movements of the eye, and even blindness, a newborn with ROP will be seen by a pediatric ophthalmologist. Infants with severe ROP may require treatment (laser therapy, cryotherapy, or surgery) to stop the progression of the abnormal vessels.

Intraventricular hemorrhage (IVH). IVH, or bleeding in the brain, is extremely common among premature infants because the vessels in their developing brains are very fragile and can bleed easily. Intraventricular hemorrhage most often affects preemies weighing less than 3 pounds, 5 ounces,

CPR Training: Don't Go Home Without It

Didn't have a chance to take infant CPR classes before your baby arrived, because your baby arrived too soon? Now's the time—before you bring your very little bundle home. It's a skill no parent hopes to use—but one that every parent should know, particularly every parent of a preemie. Even if it's not required for discharge at your baby's NICU (it sometimes is), make sure you ask for it.

usually within the first 72 hours of life. The most severe hemorrhages (which affect only 5 to 10 percent of extremely premature babies) require close observation to correct any further problems that develop—for example, hydrocephalus (blockage of spinal fluid). Regular follow-up ultrasounds are usually ordered for such hemorrhages until they are resolved. Unfortunately, there is no way to stop an intraventricular hemorrhage once it has begun. In mild cases (and most cases are), the blood is absorbed by the body. In a less mild case, the treatment targets symptoms of the bleed instead of the bleed itself. The good news is that in most mild cases the follow-up ultrasound of the head is normal and the baby's development is normal for a preterm baby.

Necrotizing enterocolitis (NEC). NEC is a condition where the intestines become infected and can begin to die. If the disease is not treated promptly, a hole can form through the bowel wall, spilling the bowel's contents into the abdominal cavity. No one knows for sure what causes NEC, but because the more premature a baby is, the greater the risk of NEC, doctors speculate that the intestines of very premature babies are not developed enough to completely handle digestion. Delaying feedings doesn't seem to prevent the condition, but babies fed breast milk usually are at less risk of NEC (breast milk has protective factors that encourage good intestinal development and reduce the amount of harmful bacteria in the intestines). The symptoms of this serious bowel disease include abdominal distension, vomiting, apnea, and blood in the stool. A baby with necrotizing enterocolitis is usually put on intravenous feedings (to let the bowels rest) and antibiotics (to treat the infection). If there is serious deterioration of the intestine, surgery is usually performed to remove the damaged portion. Unfortunately, preemies who are medically or surgically treated for NEC may have growth delays, trouble absorbing nutrients, and trouble with their livers and gall bladders. NEC also seems to increase the risk of developmental delays.

Anemia. Many premature infants develop anemia (too few red blood cells) because their red blood cells (like those of all babies) have a shorter life than red blood cells of adults, they make few new red blood cells in the first few weeks of life (like all infants), and the frequent blood samples that must be taken from the baby to do necessary laboratory tests make it difficult for red blood cells to replenish. Anemia is also more common in preemies because they missed out on the transfer of iron from their moms that happens during the last weeks of pregnancy and because the bone marrow process that makes new red blood cells is immature in preemies.

Mild anemia may not need treatment if the number of red blood cells is enough to carry oxygen to meet the baby's needs. More serious anemia is usually treated by blood transfusions, iron supplementation, and limiting the amount of blood drawn to only what is necessary. Since preemies, whether they're anemic or not, are born with low levels of iron, they are usually given iron supplements to help build up the reserves necessary to produce red blood cells.

Infection. Premature infants are most vulnerable to a variety of infections because they are born before the transfer of disease-fighting antibodies from the mother that normally occurs toward the end of pregnancy. Preemies also have an immature immune system, making it more difficult to fight germs, including those that are inadvertently introduced via feeding tubes, IV lines, and blood tests. Among the infections preemies are more likely to come down with are pneumonia, urinary tract infections, sepsis (infection of the body or bloodstream), and meningitis. Babies whose blood, urine, or spinal fluid cultures come back positive for signs of infection are treated with a full course of IV antibiotics, which usually helps resolve the infection and puts baby on the right track back to health again.

Jaundice. Premature babies are much more likely to develop jaundice than are full-term infants. Also, their bilirubin levels (the measure of jaundice) are likely to be higher and the jaundice longer lasting. Read about the condition on page 152.

Hypoglycemia. Premature and low-birthweight babies often have low blood sugar or hypoglycemia. But since the brain depends on blood glucose

Rehospitalization

Happily, most premature babies who go home from the hospital stay home. But sometimes, a preemie ends up back in the hospital during the first year, usually for the treatment of a respiratory illness or dehydration. When this happens, it's particularly tough on the parents, who have been struggling to put the time spent in the NICU behind them and begin a normal life with their babies. Memories and all-too-familiar emotions may come flooding back if your baby is rehospitalized, from feelings of guilt ("What did I do wrong?") to feelings of fear and panic ("What happens if my baby gets sicker?"). After finally having your baby home and under your care, you may also feel as though you've lost control again.

Keep in mind that a hospital readmission is absolutely no reflection on the care you've been giving your baby at home, or on your parenting skills. Preemies in general are more vulnerable healthwise than full-termers, which means even little problems may require the extra medical attention and extra precautions that only a hospital setting can offer.

Try to remember, too, that rehospitalizations usually don't last long, and that, like your very little one's stay in the NICU as a newborn, the stay in the hospital (more likely to be in the PICU, or pediatric intensive care unit) will also come to an end—at which point you'll be able to bring your (healthier) baby home once again, this time, hopefully, for good.

as its main source of fuel, it's crucial that a baby's blood sugar gets regulated as soon as possible so that it doesn't lead to serious (and rare) complications such as brain damage. Problem is, hypoglycemia may not be obvious in newborn babies because the symptoms are hard to pinpoint. Luckily a simple blood test for blood glucose levels can diagnose hypoglycemia, and treatment is straightforward and works well. Treatment includes a rapid-acting source of glucose, which may be as simple as giving baby a glucose/water mixture intravenously or early feedings of formula or breast milk, if baby is well enough to feed. Breast milk is considered as beneficial as formula in treating hypoglycemia. Blood glucose levels are closely monitored after treatment to see if the hypoglycemia occurs again, and if it does, treatment will resolve the issue once again with no long-lasting negative results.

First Year Moments & Milestones

Birth:

Month 1:

Month 2:

Month 3:

Month 4:

Month 5:

Month 6:

Month 7:

Month 8:

Month 9:

Month 10:

Month 11:

Month 12:

Index

M